Real Econometrics

The Right Tools to Answer Important Questions

Michael A. Bailey

New York   Oxford
OXFORD UNIVERSITY PRESS

Oxford University Press is a department of the University of Oxford.
It furthers the University's objective of excellence in research,
scholarship, and education by publishing worldwide.

Oxford   New York
Auckland   Cape Town   Dar es Salaam   Hong Kong   Karachi
Kuala Lumpur   Madrid   Melbourne   Mexico City   Nairobi
New Delhi   Shanghai   Taipei   Toronto

With offices in
Argentina   Austria   Brazil   Chile   Czech Republic   France   Greece
Guatemala   Hungary   Italy   Japan   Poland   Portugal   Singapore
South Korea   Switzerland   Thailand   Turkey   Ukraine   Vietnam

For titles covered by Section 112 of the US Higher Education Opportunity
Act, please visit www.oup.com/us/he for the latest information about
pricing and alternate formats.

Published by Oxford University Press.
198 Madison Avenue, New York, NY 10016
http://www.oup.com

Library of Congress Cataloging-in-Publication Data
Names: Bailey, Michael A., 1969- author.
Title: Real econometrics : the right tools to answer important questions /
    Michael Bailey.
Description: First Edition. | New York : Oxford University Press, 2016. |
    2017 | Includes bibliographical references and index.
Identifiers: LCCN 2015047786 | ISBN 9780190296827 (paperback)
Subjects: LCSH: Econometrics–Textbooks. | Economics–Study and teaching. |
    BISAC: BUSINESS & ECONOMICS / Economics / General. | BUSINESS & ECONOMICS
    / Econometrics.
Classification: LCC HB139 .B344 2016 | DDC 330.01/5195–dc23 LC record available at
http://lccn.loc.gov/2015047786

Printing number: 9 8 7 6 5 4 3 2 1

Printed in the United States of America
on acid-free paper

CONTENTS

1   The Quest for Causality   1

2   Stats in the Wild: Good Data Practices   24

I   THE OLS FRAMEWORK   43

3   Bivariate OLS: The Foundation of Econometric Analysis   45

4 Hypothesis Testing and Interval Estimation: Answering Research Questions   91

5 Multivariate OLS: Where the Action Is   128

6 Dummy Variables: Smarter Than You Think   167

7   Transforming Variables, Comparing Variables   207

II   THE CONTEMPORARY ECONOMETRIC TOOLKIT   245

8   Using Fixed Effects Models to Fight Endogeneity in Panel Data and Difference-in-Difference Models   247

9   Instrumental Variables: Using Exogenous Variation to Fight Endogeneity   287

10 Experiments: Dealing with Real-World Challenges   325

11 Regression Discontinuity: Looking for Jumps in Data   365

III   LIMITED DEPENDENT VARIABLES   399

12   Dummy Dependent Variables   401

IV   ADVANCED MATERIAL   447

13   Time Series: Dealing with Stickiness over Time   449

14   Advanced OLS   481

APPENDICES

LIST OF FIGURES

LIST OF TABLES

USEFUL COMMANDS FOR STATA

Task	Command	Example	Chapter
Help	help	help summarize	2
Comment line	*	* This is a comment line	2
Comment on command line	/* */	use "C:\Data.dta" /* This is a comment */	
Continue line	/* */	reg y X1 X2 X3 /* */ X4 X5	
Load Stata data file	use	use "C:\Data.dta"	2
Load text data file	insheet	insheet using "C:\Data.txt"	2
Display variables in memory	list	list /* Lists all observations for all variables */	2
		list Y X /* Lists all observations for Y and X */	2
		list X in 1/10 /* Lists first 10 observations for X */	2
Descriptive statistics	summarize	summarize X1 X2 Y	2
Frequency table	tabulate	tabulate X1	2
Scatter plot	scatter	scatter Y X	2
		scatter Y X, mlabel(name) /* Adds labels */	2
Limit data	if	summarize X1 if X2 == 1	2
Not equal	!=	summarize X1 if X2!=0	3
Equal (as used in if statement, for example)	==	summarize X1 if X2 == 1	2
Missing data in Stata	.	Stata treats missing data as having infinite value, so list X1 if X2 > 0 will include values of X1 for which X2 is missing	
Regression	reg	reg Y X1 X2	3
Heteroscedasticity robust regression	, robust	reg Y X1 X2, robust	3
Generate predicted values	predict	predict FittedY /* Run this after reg command */	3
Add regression line to scatter plot	twoway, lfit	twoway (scatter Y X) (lfit Y X)	3
Critical value for t distribution, two-sided	invttail	display invttail(120, .05/2) /* For model with 120 degrees of freedom and alpha = 0.05; note that we divide alpha by 2 */	4
Critical value for t distribution, one-sided	invttail	display invttail(120, .05) /* For model with 120 degrees of freedom and alpha = 0.05 */	4
Critical value for normal distribution, two-sided	invnormal	display invnormal(.975) /* For alpha = 0.05, note that we divide alpha by 2 */	4
Critical value for normal distribution, one-sided	invnormal	display invnormal(.05)	4
Two sided p values		[Reported in reg output]	4
One sided p values	ttail	display 2*ttail(120, 1.69) /* For model with 120 degrees of freedom and a t statistic of 1.69 */	4
Confidence intervals		[Reported in reg output]	4
Difference of means test	reg	reg Y Dum /* Where Dum is a dummy variable */	6
Create an interaction variable	gen	gen DumX = Dum * X	6

Task	Command	Example	Chapter
Create a squared variable	gen	gen X_sq = X^2	7
Create a logged variable	gen	gen X_log =log(X)	7
Delete a variable	drop	drop X7	7
Produce standardized regression coefficients	, beta	reg Y X1 X2, beta	7
Produce standardized variable	egen	egen X_std = std(X) /* Creates variable called X_std */	7
F-test	test	test X1 = X2 = 0 /* Run this after regression with X1 and X2 in model */	7
Critical value for F test	invF	display invF(2, 120, 0.95) /* Degrees of freedom equal 2 and 120 (order matters!) and alpha = 0.05 */	7
Generate dummy variables for each unit	tabulate and generate	tabulate City, generate(City_dum)	8
LSDV model for panel data	reg	reg Y X1 X2 City_dum2 - City_dum80	8
De-meaned model for panel data	xtreg	xtreg Y X1 X2, fe i(City)	8
Two-way fixed-effects	xtreg	xtreg Y X1 X2 i.year Yr2- Yr10, fe i(City)	8
2SLS model	ivregress	ivregress 2sls Y X2 X3 (X1 = Z), first	9
Probit	probit	probit Y X1 X2 X3	12
Logit	logit	logit Y X1 X2 X3	12
Critical value for chi-square test	invchi2	display invchi2(1, 0.95) /* Degrees of freedom = 1 and 0.95 confidence level */	12
Account for autocorrelation in time series data	prais	tsset Year prais Y X1 X2, corc twostep	13
Include lagged dependent variable	L.Y	reg Y L.Y X1 X2 /* Run tsset command first */	13
Augmented Dickey-Fuller test	dfuller	dfuller Y, trend lags(1) regress	13
Generate draws from standard normal distribution	rnormal	gen Noise = rnormal(0,1) /* Length will be same as length of variables in memory */	14
Indicate to Stata unit and time variables	tsset	tsset ID time	15
Panel model with autocorrelation	xtregar	xtregar Y X1 X2, fe rhotype(regress) twostep	15
Include lagged dependent variable	L.Y	xtreg Y L.Y X1 X2, fe i(ID)	15
Random effects panel model	, re	xtreg Y X1 X2, re	15

USEFUL COMMANDS FOR R

Task	Command	Example	Chapter
Help	?	?mean	2
Comment line	#	# This is a comment	2
Load R data file		Data = "C:\Data.RData"	2
Load text data file	read.table	Data = read.table("C:\Data.txt", header = TRUE)	2
Display names of variables in memory	objects	objects() # Will list names of all variables in memory	2
Display variables in memory	[enter variable name]	X1 # Display all values of this variable; enter directly in console or highlight in editor and press ctrl-r	2
		X1[1:10] # Display first 10 values of X1	2
Missing data in R	NA		
Mean	mean	mean(X1)	2
		mean(X1, na.rm=TRUE) # Necessary if there are missing values	
Variance	var	var(X1)	2
		var(X1, na.rm=TRUE) # Necessary if there are missing values	
		sqrt(var(X1)) # This is the standard deviation of X1	
Minimum	min	min(X1, na.rm=TRUE)	2
Maximum	max	max(X1, na.rm=TRUE)	2
Number of observations	sum and is.finite	sum(is.finite(X1))	2
Frequency table	table	table(X1)	2
Scatter plot	plot	plot(X, Y)	2
		text(X, Y, name) # Adds labels from variable called "name"	2
Limit data (similar to an if statement)	[]	plot(Y[X3<10], X1[X3<10])	2
Equal (as used in if statement, for example)	==	mean(X1[X2==1]) # Mean of X1 for cases where X2 equals 1	
Not equal	!=	mean(X1[X1!=0]) # Mean of X1 for observations where X1 is not equal to 0	
Regression	lm	lm(Y ~X1 + X2) # lm stands for "linear model"	3
		Results = lm(Y~X) # Creates an object called "Results" that stores coefficients, standard errors, fitted values and other information about this regression	3
Display results	summary	summary(Results) # Do this after creating "Results"	3
Install a package	install.packages	install.packages("AER") # Only do this once for each computer	3
Load a package	library	library(AER) # Include in every R session in which we use package specified in command	3
Heteroscedasticity robust regression	coeftest	coeftest(Results, vcov = vcovHC(Results, type = "HC1")) # Need to install and load AER package for this command. Do this after creating OLS regression object called "Results"	3
Generate predicted values	$fitted.values	Results$fitted.values # Run after creating OLS regression object called "Results"	3
Add regression line to scatter plot	abline	abline(Results) # Run after plot command and after creating "Results" object based on a bivariate regression	3

Task	Command	Example	Chapter
Critical value for t distribution, two-sided	qt	qt(0.975, 120) # For alpha = 0.05 and 120 degrees of freedom; divide alpha by 2	4
Critical value for t distribution, one-sided	qt	qt(0.95, 120) # For alpha = 0.05 and 120 degrees of freedom	4
Critical value for normal distribution, two-sided	qnorm	qnorm(0.975) # For alpha = 0.05; divide alpha by 2	4
Critical value for normal distribution, one-sided	qnorm	qnorm(0.95) # For alpha = 0.05	4
Two sided p values		[Reported in summary(Results) output]	
One sided p values	pt	2*(1-pt(abs(1.69), 120) # For model with 120 degrees of freedom and a t statistic of 1.69	4
Confidence intervals	confint	confint(Results, level = 0.95) # Do after creating OLS object called "Results"	4
Difference of means test	lm	lm(Y~Dum) # Where Dum is a dummy variable	6
Create an interaction variable		DumX = Dum * X # Or use <- in place of =	
Create a squared variable		X_sq = X^2	7
Create a logged variable		X_log =log(X)	7
Produce standardized regression coefficients	scale	Res.std = lm(scale(Y) ~scale(X1) + scale(X2))	7
Display R squared	$r.squared	summary(Results)$r.squared	7
Critical value for F test	qf	qf(.95, df1 = 2, df2 = 120) # Degrees of freedom equal 2 and 120 (order matters!) and alpha = 0.05	7
LSDV model for panel data	factor	Results = lm(Y ~ X1 + factor(country)) # Factor adds a dummy variable for every value of variable called country	8
One-way fixed-effects model (de-meaned)	plm	library(plm) Results = plm(Y ~X1+ X2+ X3, data = dta, index=c("country"), model="within")	8
Two-way fixed-effects model (de-meaned)	plm	library(plm) Results = plm(Y ~X1+ X2+ X3 data = dta, index=c("country", "year"), model="within", effect = "twoways")	8
2SLS model	ivreg	library(AER) ivreg(Y ~X1 + X2 + X3 |Z1 + Z2 + X2 + X3)	9
Generate draws from standard normal distribution	rnorm	Noise = rnorm(500) # 500 draws from standard normal distribution	14
Panel model with autocorrelation		[See Computing Corner in Chapter 15]	15
Include lagged dependent variable	plm with lag(Y)	Results = plm(Y ~lag(Y) + X1 + X2, data = dta, index = c("ID", "time"), effect = "twoways")	15
Random effects panel model	plm with "random"	Results = plm(Y ~X1 + X2, data = dta, model = "random")	15

PREFACE FOR STUDENTS: HOW THIS BOOK CAN HELP YOU LEARN ECONOMETRICS

"Less dull than traditional texts."—Student A.H.

"It would have been immensely helpful for me to have a textbook like this in my classes throughout my college and graduate experience. It feels more like an interactive learning experience than simply reading equations and facts out of a book and being expected to absorb them."—Student S.A.

"I wish I had had this book when I was first exposed to the material—it would have saved a lot of time and hair-pulling. . . ."—Student J.H.

"Material is easy to understand, hard to forget."—Student M.H.

This book introduces the econometric tools necessary to answer important questions. Do antipoverty programs work? Does unemployment affect inflation? Does campaign spending affect election outcomes? These and many more questions not only are interesting but also are important to answer correctly if we want to support policies that are good for people, countries, and the world.

When using econometrics to answer such questions, we need always to remember a single big idea: correlation is not causation. Just because variable Y rises when variable X rises does not mean that variable X *causes* variable Y to rise. The essential goal is to figure out when we can say that changes in variable X will lead to changes in variable Y.

This book helps us learn how to identify causal relationships with three features seldom found in other econometrics textbooks. First, it focuses on the tools that economic researchers use most. These are the *real* econometric techniques that help us make reasonable claims about whether X causes Y, and by using these tools, we can produce analyses that others can respect. We'll get the most out of our data while recognizing the limits in what we can say or how confident we can be.

Our emphasis on *real econometrics* means that we skip obscure econometric tools that *could* come up under certain conditions: they are not discussed here. Econometrics is too often complicated by books and teachers trying to do too much. This book shows that we can have a sophisticated understanding of statistical inference without having to catalog every method that our instructor had to learn as a student.

Second, this book works with a single unifying framework. We don't start over with each new concept; instead, we build around a core model. That means there is a single equation and a unifying set of assumptions that we poke, probe, and expand throughout the book. This approach reduces the learning costs of moving through the material and allows us to go back and revisit material. As with any skill, we probably won't fully understand any given technique the first time we see it. We have to work at it, we have to work *with* it. We'll get comfortable, we'll see connections. Then it will click. Whether the skill is jumping rope, typing, throwing a baseball, or analyzing data, we have to do things many times to get good at it. By sticking to a unifying framework, we have more chances to revisit what we have already learned. You'll also notice that I'm not afraid to repeat myself on the important stuff. Really, I'm not afraid to repeat myself.

Third, this book uses many examples from the policy, political, and economic worlds. So even if you do not care about "two-stage least squares" or "maximum likelihood" in and of themselves, you will see how understanding these techniques will affect what you think about education policy, trade policy, election outcomes, and many other interesting issues. The examples and case studies make it clear that the tools developed in this book are being used by contemporary applied economists who are actually making a difference with their empirical work.

Real Econometrics is meant to serve as the primary course textbook in an introductory econometrics course or as a supplemental text providing more intuition and context in a more advanced econometric methods course. As more and more public policy and corporate decisions are based on statistical and econometric analysis, this book can also be used outside of course work. Econometrics has infiltrated into every area of our lives—from entertainment to sports (I no longer spit out my coffee when I come across an article on regression analysis of National Hockey League players)—and a working knowledge of basic econometric techniques can help anyone make better sense of the world around them.

What's In This Book?

The preparation necessary to use this book successfully is modest. We use basic algebra a fair bit, being careful to explain every step. You do not need calculus. We refer to calculus when useful, and the book certainly could be used by a course that works through some of the concepts using calculus, but you can understand everything without knowing calculus.

We start with two introductory chapters. Chapter 1 lays out the central challenge in econometrics. This is the challenge of making probabilistic yet accurate claims about causal relations between variables. We present experiments as an ideal way to conduct research, but we also show how experiments in the real world are tricky and can't answer every question we care about. This chapter provides the "big picture" context for econometric analysis that is every bit as important as the specifics that follow.

Chapter 2 provides a practical foundation related to good econometric practices. In every econometric analysis, data meets software, and if we're not careful, we lose control. This chapter therefore seeks to teach good habits about documenting analysis and understanding data.

The five chapters of Part I constitute the heart of the book. They introduce ordinary least squares (OLS), also known as regression analysis. Chapter 3 introduces the most basic regression model, the bivariate OLS model. Chapter 4 shows how to use OLS to test hypotheses. Chapters 5 through 7 introduce the multivariate OLS model and applications. By the end of Part I, you will understand regression and be able to control for anything you can measure. You'll also be able to fit curves to data and assess whether the effects of some variables differ across groups, among other skills that will impress your friends.

Part II introduces techniques that constitute the modern econometric toolkit. These are the techniques people use when they want to get published—or paid. These techniques build on multivariate OLS to give us a better chance of identifying causal relations between two variables. Chapter 8 covers a simple yet powerful way to control for many factors we can't measure directly. Chapter 9 covers instrumental variable techniques, which work if we can find a variable that affects our independent variable but not our dependent variable. Instrumental variable techniques are a bit funky, but they can be very useful for isolating causal effects. Chapter 10 covers randomized experiments. Although ideal in theory, in practice such experiments often raise a number of challenges we need to address. Chapter 11 covers regression discontinuity tools that can be used when we're studying the effect of variables that were allocated based on a fixed rule. For example, Medicare is available to people in the United States only when they turn 65; admission to certain private schools depends on a test score exceeding some threshold. Focusing on policies that depend on such thresholds turns out to be a great context for conducting credible econometric analysis.

Part III covers dichotomous dependent variable models. These are simply models in which the outcome we care about takes on two possible values. Examples and case studies cover include high school graduation (someone graduates or doesn't), unemployment (someone has a job or doesn't), and alliances (two countries sign an alliance treaty or don't). We show how to apply OLS to such models and then provide more elaborate models that address the deficiencies of OLS in this context.

Part IV supplements the book with additional useful material. Chapter 13 covers time series data. The first part is a variation on OLS; the second part introduces dynamic models that differ from OLS models in important ways. Chapter 14 derives important OLS results and extends discussion on specific topics. Chapter 15 goes into greater detail on the vast literature on panel data, showing how the various strands fit together.

Chapter 16 concludes the book with tips on adopting the mind-set of an econometric realist. In fact, if you are looking for an overall understanding of the power and limits of statistics, you might want to read this chapter first—then read it again once you've learned all the statistical concepts covered in the other chapters.

How to Use This Book

Real Econometrics is designed to help you master the material. Each section ends with a "Remember This" box that highlights the key points of that section. If you remember what's in each of these boxes, you'll have a great foundation in statistics. Key Terms are boldfaced where they are first introduced in the text, defined briefly in the margins, and defined again in the glossary at the end of the book.

Review Questions and Discussion Questions appear at the end of selected sections. I recommend using these. Answering questions helps us be realistic about whether we're truly on track. What we're fighting is something cognitive psychologists call the "illusion of explanatory depth." That's a fancy way of saying we don't always know as much as we think we do. By answering the Review Questions and Discussion Questions, we can see where we are. The Review Questions are more concrete and have specific answers, which are found at the end of the book. The Discussion Questions are more open-ended and encourage us to explore how the concepts apply to issues we care about. Once invested in this way, we're no longer doing econometrics for the sake of doing econometrics; instead, we're doing econometrics to help us learn about issues we care about.

And remember, learning is not only about answering questions: coming up with your own questions for your instructor or classmates or the dude next to you on the bus is a great way to learn. Doing so will help you formulate exactly what is unclear and will open the door to an exchange of ideas. Heck, maybe you'll make friends with the bus guy or, worst case, you'll see an empty seat open up next to you . . .

Finally, you may have noticed that this book is opinionated and a bit chatty. This is not the usual tone of econometrics books, but being chatty is not the same as being dumb. You'll see real material, with real equations and real research—sometimes accompanied by smart-ass asides that you may not see in other books. This approach makes the material more accessible and also reinforces the right mind-set: Econometrics is not simply a set of mathematical equations. Instead, econometrics provides a set of practical tools that curious people use to learn from the world. But don't let the tone fool you. This book is not *Econometrics for Dummies*; it's *Real Econometrics*. Learn the material and you will be well on your way to using econometrics to answer important questions.

PREFACE FOR INSTRUCTORS: HOW TO HELP YOUR STUDENTS LEARN ECONOMETRICS

We econometrics teachers have high hopes for our students. We want them to understand how econometrics can shed light on important economic and policy questions. Sometimes they humor us with incredible insight. The heavens part, angels sing. We want that to happen daily. Sadly, a more common experience is seeing a furrowed brow of confusion and frustration. It's cloudy and rainy in that place.

It doesn't have to be this way. If we distill the material to the most critical concepts, we can inspire more insight and less brow-furrowing. Unfortunately, conventional statistics and econometrics books all too often manage to be too simple and too confusing at the same time. Many are too simple in that they provide a semester's worth of material that hardly gets past rudimentary ordinary least squares (OLS). Some are too confusing in that they get to OLS by way of going deep into the weeds of probability theory without showing students how econometrics can be useful and interesting.

Real Econometrics is predicated on the belief that we are most effective when we teach the tools we use. What we use are regression-based tools with an increasing focus on experiments and causal inference. If students can understand these fundamental concepts, they can legitimately participate in analytically sound conversations. They can produce analysis that is interesting—and believable! They can understand experiments and the sometimes subtle analysis required when experimental methods meet social scientific reality. They can appreciate that causal effects are hard to tease out with observational data and that standard errors estimated on crap coefficients, however complex, do no one any good. They can sniff out when others are being naive or cynical. It is only when we muck around too long in the weeds of less useful material that statistics becomes the quagmire students fear.

Hence this book seeks to be analytically sophisticated in a simple and relevant way. It focuses on tools actually used by real analysts. Nothing useless. No clutter. To do so, the book is guided by three principles: relevance, opportunity costs, and pedagogical efficiency.

Relevance

Relevance is a crucial first principle for successfully teaching econometrics in the social sciences. Every experienced instructor knows that most students care more about the real world than math. How do we get such students to engage with econometrics? One option is to cajole them to care more and work harder. We all know how well that works. A better option is to show them how a sophisticated understanding of statistical concepts helps them learn more about the topics they are in class to learn about. Think of a mother trying to get a child to commit to the training necessary to play competitive sports. She *could* start with a semester of theory.... No, that would be cruel. And counterproductive. Much better to let the child play and experience the joy of the sport. Then there will be time (and motivation!) to understand nuances. Thus every chapter is built around examples and case studies on topics students might actually care about — topics like violent crime in the United States (Chapter 2), global warming (Chapter 7), and the relationship between alcohol consumption and grades (Chapter 11).

Learning econometrics is not that different from learning anything else. We need to care to truly learn. Therefore this book takes advantage of a careful selection of material to spend more time on the real examples that students care about.

Opportunity Costs

Opportunity costs are, as we all tell our students, what we have to give up to do something. So, while some topic might be a perfectly respectable part of an econometric toolkit, we should include it only if it does not knock out something more important. The important stuff all too often gets shunted aside as we fill up the early part of students' analytical training with statistical knick-knacks, material "some people still use" or that students "might see."

Therefore this book goes quickly through descriptive statistics and doesn't cover χ^2 tests for two-way tables, weighted least squares, and other denizens of conventional statistics books. These concepts—and many, many more—are all perfectly legitimate. Some are covered elsewhere (descriptive statistics are covered in elementary schools these days). Others are valuable enough to rate inclusion here in an "advanced material" section for students and instructors who want to pursue these topics further. And others simply don't make the cut. Only by focusing the material can we get to the tools used by researchers today, tools such as panel data analysis, instrumental variables, and regression discontinuity. The core ideas behind these tools are not particularly difficult, but we need to *make* time to cover them.

Pedagogical Efficiency

Pedagogical efficiency refers to streamlining the learning process by using a single unified framework. Everything in this book builds from the standard regression model. Hypothesis testing, difference of means, and experiments can be, and often are, taught independently of regression. Causal inference is sometimes taught with potential outcomes notation. There is nothing intellectually wrong with these approaches. But is using them pedagogically efficient? If we teach these concepts as stand-alone concepts we have to take time and, more important, student brain space, to set up each separate approach. For students, this is really hard. Remember the furrowed brows? Students work incredibly hard to get their heads around difference of means and where to put degrees of freedom corrections and how to know if the means come from correlated groups or independent groups and what the equation is for each of these cases. Then BAM! Suddenly the professor is talking about residuals and squared deviations. The transition is old hat for us, but it can overwhelm students first learning the material. It is more efficient to teach the OLS framework and use that to cover difference of means, experiments, and the contemporary canon of econometric analysis, including panel data, instrumental variables, and regression discontinuity. Each tool builds from the same regression model. Students start from a comfortable place and can see the continuity that exists.

An important benefit of working with a single framework is that it allows students to revisit the core model repeatedly throughout the term. Despite the brilliance of our teaching, students rarely can put it all together with one pass through the material. I know I didn't when I was beginning. Students need to see the material a few times, work with it a bit, and then it will finally click. Imagine if sports were coached the way we do econometrics. A tennis coach who said, "This week we'll cover forehands (and only forehands), next week backhands (and only backhands), and the week after that serves (and only serves)" would not be a tennis coach for long. Instead, coaches introduce material, practice, and then keep working on the fundamentals. Working with a common framework throughout makes it easier to build in mini-drills about fundamentals as new material is introduced.

Course Adoption

Real Econometrics is organized to work well in three different kinds of courses. First, it can be used in an introductory econometrics course that follows a semester of probability and statistics. In such a course, students should probably be able to move quickly through the early material and then pick up where they left off, typically with multivariate OLS.

Second, this book can be used with students who have not previously (or recently) studied statistics, either in a one-semester course covering Part I or a year-long course covering the whole book. Using this book as a first course avoids the "warehouse problem," which occurs when we treat students' statistical education as a warehouse, filling it up with tools first and accessing them only later. One challenge is that things rot in a warehouse. Another challenge is that instructors tend to hoard a bit, putting things in the warehouse "just in case" and creating clutter. And students find warehouse work achingly dull. Using this book in a first-semester course avoids the warehouse problem by going directly to interesting and useful material, providing students with a more just-in-time approach. For example, they see statistical distributions, but in the context of trying to solve a specific problem, rather than as an abstract concept that will become useful later.

Finally, *Real Econometrics* can be used as a supplement in a more advanced econometric course, providing intuition and context that sometimes gets lost in the more technical courses.

Real Econometrics is also designed to encourage two particularly useful pedagogical techniques. One is interweaving, the process of weaving in material from previous lessons into later lessons. Numbered sections end with a "Remember This" box that summarizes key points. Connecting back to these points in later lessons is remarkably effective at getting the material into the active part of students' brains. The more we ask students about omitted variable bias or multicollinearity or properties of instruments (and in sometimes surprising contexts), the more they become able to actively apply the material on their own.

The second teaching technique is to use frequent low-stakes quizzes to convert students to active learners with less stress than the exams they will also be taking. These quizzes need not be hard. They just need to give students a chance to independently access and apply the material. Students can test themselves with the Review Questions at the end of many sections, as the answers to these questions are at the back of the book. It can also be useful for students to discuss or at least reflect on the Discussion Questions at the ends of many sections, as these enable students to connect the material to real world examples. Brown, Roediger, and McDaniel (2014) provide an excellent discussion of these and other teaching techniques.

Overview

The first two chapters of the book serve as introductory material and introduce the science of statistics. Chapter 1 lays out the theme of how important—and hard—it is to generate unbiased estimates. This is a good time to let students offer hypotheses about questions they care about, because these questions can help bring to life the subsequent material. Chapter 2, which introduces computer programs and good practices, is a confidence builder that gets students who are not already acclimated to statistical computing over the hurdle of using statistical software.

Part I covers core OLS material. Chapter 3 introduces bivariate OLS. Chapter 4 covers hypothesis testing, and Chapter 5 moves to multivariate OLS. Chapters 6 and 7 proceed to practical tasks such as use of dummy variables, logged variables, interactions, and F tests.

Part II covers essential elements of the contemporary econometric toolkit, including panel data, instrumental variables, analysis of experiments, and regression discontinuity. Chapter 10, on experiments, uses instrumental variables, but Chapters 8, 9, and 11 can be covered in any order, so instructors can pick and choose among these chapters as needed.

Part III contains a single chapter (Chapter 12) on dichotomous dependent variables. It develops the linear probability model in the context of OLS and uses the probit and logit models to introduce students to maximum likelihood.

Instructors can cover this chapter any time after Part I if dichotomous dependent variables play a major role in the course.

Part IV introduces some advanced material. Chapter 13 discusses time series models, introducing techniques to account for autocorrelation and to estimate dynamic time series models; this chapter can also be covered at any time following Part I. Chapter 14 offers derivations of the OLS model and additional material on omitted variable bias. Instructors seeking to expose students to derivations and extensions of the core OLS material can use this chapter as an auxiliary to Chapters 3 through 5. Chapter 15 introduces more advanced topics in panel data. This chapter builds on material from Chapters 8 and 13. Chapter 16 concludes the book by discussing ways to maximize the chances that we use econometrics properly to answer important questions about the world.

Every chapter ends with a series of learning tools. Each conclusion summarizes the learning objectives by section and provides a list of key terms introduced in the chapter (along with the page where first introduced). Each Further Reading section guides students to additional resources on the material covered in the chapter. The Computing Corners provide a guide to the syntax needed to implement the analysis discussed in the chapters. We provide this syntax for both Stata and R computing languages. Finally, the Exercises provide a variety of opportunities for students to analyze real data sets from important papers on interesting topics.

Several appendices provide supporting material. An appendix on math and probability covers background ranging from mathematical functions to important concepts in probability. The appendix on citations and additional notes is linked to the text by page numbers and elaborates on some finer points. A separate appendix provides answers to Review Questions.

Teaching econometrics is difficult. When the going gets tough it is tempting to blame students, to say they are unwilling to do the work. Before we go that route, we should recognize that many students find the material quite foreign and (unfortunately) irrelevant. If we can streamline what we teach and connect it to things students care about, we can improve our chances of getting students to understand the material, material that not only is intrinsically interesting but also forms the foundation for all empirical work. When students understand, teaching becomes easier. And better. The goal of this book is to help get us there.

Supplements Accompanying *Real Econometrics*

A broad array of instructor and student resources for *Real Econometrics* are available online at www.oup.com/us/bailey.

Data

Much of the supplementary material for *Real Econometrics* focuses on data—through online access to the data sets referenced in the chapters, their documentation, and additional data sets. These include:

- Downloadable data sets (and their documentation) for the examples and exercises found in the text

- Links to other data sets (both experimental and nonexperimental) for creating new assignments.

Instructor's Manual

Each chapter in the Instructor's Manual provides an overview of the chapter goals and section-by-section teaching tips along with suggested responses to the in-chapter Discussion Questions. The Instructor's Manual also contains sample data sets for the Computing Corner activities and solutions to the Exercises found at the end of each chapter.

PowerPoint Presentations

Presentation slides offer bullet-point summaries as well as all the tables and graphs from the book. A separate set of slides containing only the text tables and graphs is also available.

Test Bank and Computerized Test Bank

A test bank with True/False, Multiple Choice, and Short Answer questions for each chapter may be downloaded for use with Wimba Diploma 6.

Learning Management Systems Support

For instructors using an online learning management system (e.g., Moodle, Sakai, Blackboard, or others), Oxford University Press can provide all the electronic components of the package in a format suitable for easy upload. Adopting instructors should contact their local Oxford University Press sales representative or OUP's Customer Service (800-445-9714) for more information.

Companion Website (www.oup.com/us/bailey)

The Companion Website offers the following resources to help students review, practice, and explore additional topics:

- Chapter Quizzes. These allow students to test their basic understanding of the chapter and review where they have gaps.

- Web links. The author has gathered together a collection of resources and data for further exploration and course projects.

ACKNOWLEDGMENTS

This book has benefited from close reading and probing questions from a large number of people, including students at the McCourt School of Public Policy at Georgetown University and my current and former colleagues and students at Georgetown, including Shirley Adelstein, Rachel Blum, David Buckley, Ian Gale, Ariya Hagh, Carolyn Hill, Mark Hines, Dan Hopkins, Jeremy Horowitz, Huade Huo, Wes Joe, Karin Kitchens, Jon Ladd, Jens Ludwig, Jean Mitchell, Paul Musgrave, Sheeva Nesva, Hans Noel, Irfan Nooruddin, Ji Yeon Park, Parina Patel, Betsy Pearl, Lindsay Pettingill, Carlo Prato, Barbara Schone, George Shambaugh, Dennis Quinn, Chris Schorr, Frank Vella, and Erik Voeten.

Credit (and/or blame) for the *Simpsons* figure goes to Paul Musgrave.

Participants at a seminar on the book at the University of Maryland, especially Antoine Banks, Brandon Bartels, Kanisha Bond, Ernesto Calvo, Sarah Croco, Michael Hanmer, Danny Hayes, Eric Lawrence, Irwin Morris, and John Sides, gave excellent early feedback.

In addition, colleagues across the country have been incredibly helpful, especially Allison Carnegie, Chris Way, Craig Volden, Sarah Croco, and Wendy Tam-Cho. Reviewers for Oxford University Press provided supportive yet probing reviews that were very useful. These reviewers included:

Steve Balla, *George Washington University;* Yong Bao, *Purdue University;* Renato Corbetta, *University of Alabama at Birmingham*; Sarah Croco, *University of Maryland*; David E. Cunningham, *University of Maryland;* José M. Fernández, *University of Louisville;* Luca Flabbi, *Georgetown University*; Mark A. Gebert, *University of Kentucky;* Seyhan Erden, *Columbia University;* Kaj Gittings, *Texas Tech University;* Brad Graham, *Grinnell College;* Jonathan Hanson, *University of Michigan;* David Harris, *Benedictine College*; Daniel Henderson, *University of Alabama*; Matthew J. Holian, *San Jose State University*; Todd Idson, *Boston University*; Changkuk Jung, *SUNY Geneseo*; Manfred Keil, *Claremont McKenna College*; Subal C Kumbhakar, *State University of New York at Binghamton*; Latika Lagalo, *Michigan Technological University*; Matthew Lang, *Xavier University*; Jing Li, *Miami University*; Quan Li, *Texas A&M University*; Drew A. Linzer, *Emory University*; Steven Livingston, *Middle Tennessee State University*; Aprajit Mahajan, *Stanford University*; Brian McCall, *University of Michigan*; David Peterson, *Iowa State University*; Leanne C. Powner, *Christopher Newport University*; Zhongjun Qu, *Boston University*; Sam Schulhofer-Wohl, *Federal Reserve Bank of Minneapolis*; Christina Suthammanont, *Texas A&M University, San Antonio*; Christopher Way, *Cornell University*; Phanindra V. Wunnava, *Middlebury College*; Jie Jennifer Zhang, *University of Texas at Arlington*.

I also appreciate the generosity of colleagues who shared data, including Bill Clark, Anna Harvey, Dan Hopkins, and Hans Noel.

The editing team at Oxford has done wonders for this book. Valerie Ashton brought energy and wisdom to the early life of the book. Ann West has been supportive and insightful throughout, going to great lengths to make this book the best it can be. Thom Holmes and Maegan Sherlock provided expert development oversight. Micheline Frederick has been a very capable editor; without her help this book would have a lot more mistakes . . . and a bit more cussing. Steve Rigolosi, Brenda Griffing, and Eric Wesley Morrison performed the unenviable work of copy and proof reading my writing with verve. Emily Mathis helped with the photo choices, and Clare Castro has been enthusiastically conveying the message of this book to the marketplace.

I am grateful for the support of my family, Mari, Jack, Emi, and Ken. After years of working on *Real Econometrics*, now we can work on a *real vacation*.

The Quest for Causality

How do we know what we know? Or, at least, why do we think what we think? The modern answer is evidence. In order to convince others—in order to convince *ourselves*—we need to provide information that others can verify. Something that is a hunch or something that we simply "know" may be important, but it is not the kind of evidence that drives the modern scientific process.

What is the basis of our evidence? In some cases, we can see cause and effect. We see a burning candle tip over and start a fire. Now we know what caused the fire. This is perfectly good knowledge. Sometimes in politics and policy we trace back a chain of causality in a similar way. This process can get complicated, though. Why did Barack Obama win the presidential election in 2008? Why did some economies handle the most recent recession better than others? Why did crime go down in the United States in the 1990s? For these types of questions, we are not looking only at a single candle; there are lightning strikes, faulty wires, arsonists, and who knows what else to worry about. Clearly, it will be much harder to trace cause and effect.

When there is no way of directly observing cause and effect, we naturally turn to data. And data holds great promise. A building collapses during an earthquake. What about the building led it—and not others in the same city—to collapse? Was it the building material? The height? The design? Age? Location near a fault? While we might not be able to see the cause directly, we can gather information on buildings that did and did not collapse. If the older buildings were more likely to collapse,

correlation ≠ causation

FIGURE 1.1: Rule #1

we might reasonably suspect that building age mattered. If buildings built without steel reinforcement collapsed no matter what their age, we might reasonably suspect that buildings with certain designs were more likely to collapse.

And yet, we should not get overconfident. Even if old buildings were more likely to collapse, we do not know for certain that age of the building is the main explanation for building collapse. It could be that more buildings from a certain era were designed a certain way; it could be that there were more old buildings in a neighborhood where the seismic activity was most severe. Or the collapse of many buildings that happened to be old could represent a massive coincidence. The econometrics we learn in this book will help to identify causes and make claims about what really mattered—and what didn't.

As Figure 1.1 makes clear, correlation is not causation. This statement is old news. Our task is to go to the next step: Well, then, what *does* imply causation? It will take the whole book to fully flesh out the answer, but here's the short version: *If we can find exogenous variation*, then correlation is probably causation. Our task then will be to figure out what exogenous variation means and how to distinguish randomness from causality as best we can.

In this chapter we introduce three concepts at the heart of the book. Section 1.1 explains the core model we use throughout. Section 1.2 introduces two things that make econometrics difficult. Neither is math (really!). One is randomness: sometimes the luck of the draw will lead us to observe relationships that aren't real or fail to observe relationships that are real. The second is endogeneity, a phenomenon that can cause us to wrongly think a variable causes some effect when it doesn't. Section 1.3 presents randomized experiments as the ideal way to overcome endogeneity. Usually, these experiments aren't possible and even when they are, things can go wrong. Hence, the rest of the book is about developing a toolkit that helps us meet (or approximate) the idealized standard of randomized experiments.

1.1 | The Core Model

When we talk about cause and effect we'll refer to the outcome of interest as the **dependent variable**. We refer to a possible cause as an **independent variable**.

▶ dependent variable
The outcome of interest, usually denoted as Y.

The dependent variable, usually denoted as Y, is called that because its value *depends* on the independent variable. The independent variable, usually denoted by X, is called that because it does whatever the hell it wants. It is the presumed cause of some change in the dependent variable.

▶ independent variable A variable that possibly influences the value of the dependent variable.

At root, social scientific theories posit that a change in one thing (the independent variable) will lead to a change in another (the dependent variable). We'll formalize this relationship in a bit, but let's start with an example. Suppose we're interested in the U.S. obesity epidemic and want to analyze the influence of snack food on health. We may wonder, for example, if donuts cause health problems. Our model is that eating donuts (variable X, our independent variable) causes some change in weight (variable Y, our dependent variable). If we can find data on how many donuts people ate and how much they weighed, we might be on the verge of a scientific breakthrough.

Let's conjure up a small midwestern town and do a little research. Figure 1.2 plots donuts eaten and weights for 13 individuals from a randomly chosen town, Springfield, U.S.A. Our raw data is displayed in Table 1.1. Each person has a line in the table. Homer is observation 1. Since he ate 14 donuts per week, $Donuts_1 = 14$. We'll often refer to X_i or Y_i, which are the values of X and Y for person i in the data set. The weight of the seventh person in the data set, Smithers, is 160, meaning $Weight_7 = 160$, and so forth.

▶ scatterplot A plot of data in which each observation is located at the coordinates defined by the independent and dependent variables.

Figure 1.2 is a **scatterplot** of data, with each observation located at the coordinates defined by the independent and dependent variable. The value of donuts per week is on the X-axis and weights are on the Y-axis. Just by looking at this plot, we sense there is a positive relationship between donuts and weight because the more donuts eaten, the higher the weight tends to be.

TABLE 1.1 Donut Consumption and Weight

Observation number	Name	Donuts per week	Weight (pounds)
1	Homer	14	275
2	Marge	0	141
3	Lisa	0	70
4	Bart	5	75
5	Comic Book Guy	20	310
6	Mr. Burns	0.75	80
7	Smithers	0.25	160
8	Chief Wiggum	16	263
9	Principal Skinner	3	205
10	Rev. Lovejoy	2	185
11	Ned Flanders	0.8	170
12	Patty	5	155
13	Selma	4	145

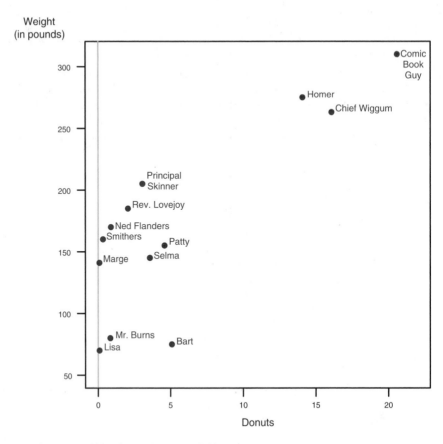

FIGURE 1.2: Weight and Donuts in Springfield

We use a simple equation to characterize the relationship between the two variables:

$$Weight_i = \beta_0 + \beta_1 Donuts_i + \epsilon_i \tag{1.1}$$

- The dependent variable is $Weight_i$ which is the weight of person i.

- The independent variable, $Donuts_i$, is how many donuts person i eats per week.

▶ **slope coefficient**
The coefficient on an independent variable. It reflects how much the dependent variable increases when the independent variable increases by one.

- β_1 is the **slope coefficient** on donuts, indicating how much more[1] a person weighs for each donut eaten. (For those whose Greek is a bit rusty, β is the Greek letter beta.)

▶ **constant** The parameter β_0 in a regression model. It is the point at which a regression line cross the Y-axis. Also referred to as the *intercept*.

- β_0 is the **constant** or **intercept**, indicating the expected weight of people who eat zero donuts.

_____
[1] Or less—be optimistic!

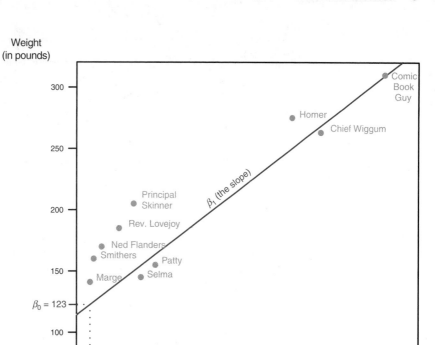

FIGURE 1.3: Regression Line for Weight and Donuts in Springfield

▶ **error term** The term associated with unmeasured factors in a regression model, typically denoted as ϵ.

- ϵ_i is the **error term** that captures anything else that affects weight. (ϵ is the Greek letter epsilon)

This equation will help us estimate the two parameters necessary to characterize a line. Remember $Y = mX + b$ from junior high? This is the equation for a line where Y is the value of the line on the vertical axis, X is the value on the horizontal axis, m is the slope and b is the intercept, the value of Y when X is zero. Equation 1.1 is essentially the same, only we refer to the "b" term as β_0 and we call the "m" term β_1.

Figure 1.3 shows an example of an estimated line from this model for our Springfield data. The intercept (β_0) is the value of weight when donut consumption is zero ($X = 0$). The slope (β_1) is the amount that weight increases for each donut eaten. In this case, the intercept is about 122, which means that the average weight for those who eat zero donuts is around 122 pounds. The slope is around 9.1, which means that for each donut eaten per week, weight is about 9.1 pounds higher.

More generally, our core model can be written as

$$Y_i = \beta_0 + \beta_1 X_i + \epsilon_i \tag{1.2}$$

where β_0 is the intercept that indicates the value of Y when $X = 0$ and β_1 is the slope that indicates how much change in Y is expected if X increases by one unit. We almost always care a lot about β_1, which characterizes the relationship between X and Y. We usually don't care a whole lot about β_0. It plays an important role in helping us get the line in the right place, but determining the value of Y when X is zero is seldom our core research interest.

We see that the actual observations do not fall neatly on the line that we're using to characterize the relationship between donuts and weight. The implication is that our model does not perfectly explain the data. Of course it doesn't! Springfield residents are much too complicated for donuts to explain them completely (except, apparently, Comic Book Guy).

The error term, ϵ_i, comes to the rescue by giving us some wiggle room. It is what is left over after the variables have done their work in explaining variation in the dependent variable. In doing this service, the error term plays an incredibly important role for the entire econometric enterprise. As this book proceeds, we will keep coming back to the importance of getting to know our error term.

The error term, ϵ, is not simply a Greek letter. It is something real. What it covers depends on the model. In our simple model—in which weight is a function only of how many donuts a person eats—oodles of factors are contained in the error term. Basically, anything else that affects weight will be in the error term: sex, height, other eating habits, exercise patterns, genetics, and on and on. The error term includes everything we haven't measured in our model.

We'll often see ϵ referred to as *random error*, but be careful about that one. Yes, for the purposes of the model we are treating the error term as something random, but it is not simply random in the sense of a roll of the dice. It is random more in the sense that we don't know what it will be for any individual. But every error term reflects, at least in part, some relationship to real things that we have not measured or included in the model. We come back to this point often.

REMEMBER THIS

Our core statistical model is

$$Y_i = \beta_0 + \beta_1 X_i + \epsilon_i$$

1. β_1, the slope, indicates how much change in Y (the dependent variable) is expected if X (the independent variable) increases by one unit.

2. β_0, the intercept, indicates where the regression line crosses the Y-axis. It is the value of Y when X is zero.

3. β_1 is almost always more interesting than β_0.

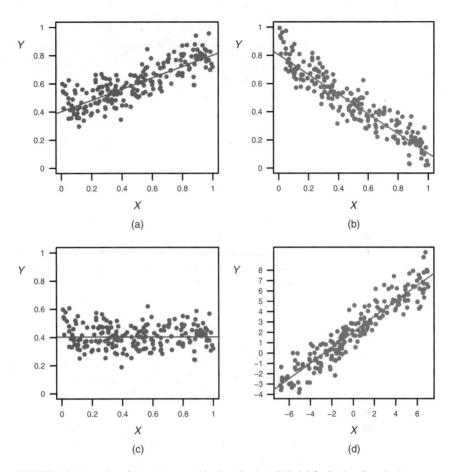

FIGURE 1.4: Examples of Lines Generated by Core Statistical Model (for Review Question)

Review Question

For each of the panels in Figure 1.4, determine whether β_0 and β_1 are greater than, equal to, or less than zero. [Be careful with β_0 in panel (d)!]

1.2 Two Challenges: Randomness and Endogeneity

Understanding that there are real factors in the error term helps us be smart about making causal claims. Our data seems to suggest that the more donuts people ate, the more they packed on the pounds. It's not crazy to think that donuts cause weight gain.

But can we be certain that donuts, and not some other factor, cause weight gain? Two fundamental challenges in econometric analysis should make us cautious. The first challenge is randomness. Any time we observe a relationship in data, we need to keep in mind that some coincidence could explain it. Perhaps we happened to pick some unusual people for our data set. Or perhaps we picked perfectly representative people, but they had happened to have unusual measurements on the day we measured them.

In the donut example, the possibility of such randomness should worry us, at least a little. Perhaps the people in Figure 1.3 are a bit odd. Perhaps if we had more people, we might get more heavy folks who don't eat donuts and skinny people who scarf them down. Adding those folks to the figure would change the figure and our conclusions. Or perhaps even with the set of folks we observe, we might have gotten some of them on a bad (or good) day, whereas if we had looked at them another day, we might have observed a different relationship.

Therefore every legitimate econometric analysis will account for randomness in an effort to distinguish results that could happen by chance from those that would be unlikely to happen by chance. The bad news is that we will never escape the possibility that the results we observe are due to randomness rather than a causal effect. The good news, though, is that we can often do a pretty good job characterizing our confidence that the results are not simply due to randomness.

The other major challenge arises from the possibility that an observed relationship between X and Y is actually due to an other variable, which causes Y and is associated with X. In the donuts example, worry about scenarios in which we wrongly attribute to our key independent variable (in this case, donut consumption) changes in weight that were caused by other factors. What if tall people eat more donuts? Height is in the error term as a contributing factor to weight, and if tall people eat more donuts we may wrongly attribute to donuts the effect of height.

There are loads of other possibilities. What if men eat more donuts? What if exercise addicts don't eat donuts? What if people who eat donuts are also more likely to down a tub of Ben and Jerry's ice cream every night? What if thin people can't get donuts down their throats? Being male, exercising, bingeing on ice cream having itty-bitty throats—all these things are probably in the error term (meaning they affect weight), and all could be correlated with donut eating.

Speaking econometrically, we highlight this major statistical challenge by saying that the donut variable is **endogenous**. An independent variable is endogenous if changes in it are related to factors in the error term. The prefix "endo" refers to something internal, and endogenous variables are "in the model" in the sense that they are related to other things that also determine Y.

In the donuts example, donut consumption is likely endogenous because how many donuts a person eats is not independent of other factors that influence weight gain. Factors that cause weight gain (such as eating Ben and Jerry's ice cream) might be associated with donut eating; in other words, factors that influence the dependent variable Y might also be associated with the independent variable X, muddying the connection between correlation and causation. If we can't be sure that our variation in X is not associated with factors that influence Y, we worry

endogenous An independent variable is endogenous if changes in it are related to other factors that influence the dependent variable.

about wrongly attributing to X the causal effect of some other variable. We might wrongly conclude that donuts cause weight gain when really donut eaters are more likely to eat tubs of Ben and Jerry's, which is the real culprit.

In all these examples, something in the error term that really causes weight gain is related to donut consumption. When this connection exists, we risk spuriously attributing to donut consumption the causal effect of some other factor. Remember, anything not measured in the model is in the error term and here, at least, we have a wildly simple model in which only donut consumption is measured. So Ben and Jerry's, genetics, and everything else are in the error term.

Endogeneity is everywhere; it's endemic. Suppose we want to know if raising teacher salaries increases test scores. It's an important and timely question. Answering it may seem easy enough: we could simply see if test scores (a dependent variable) are higher in places where teacher salaries (an independent variable) are higher. It's not that easy, though, is it? Endogeneity lurks. Test scores might be determined by unmeasured factors that also affect teacher salaries. Maybe school districts with lots of really poor families don't have very good test scores and don't have enough money to pay teachers high salaries. Or perhaps the relationship is the opposite—poor school districts get extra federal funds to pay teachers more. Either way, teacher salaries are endogenous because their levels depend in part on factors in the error term (like family income) that affect educational outcomes. Simply looking at test scores' relationship to teacher salaries risks confusing the effect of family income and teacher salaries.[2]

exogenous An independent variable is exogenous if changes in it are unrelated to factors in the error term.

The opposite of endogeneity is exogeneity. An independent variable is **exogenous** if changes in it are *not* related to factors in the error term. The prefix "exo" refers to something external, and exogenous variables are "outside the model" in the sense that their values are unrelated to other things that also determine Y. For example, if we use an experiment to randomly set the value of X, then changes in X are not associated with factors that also determine Y. This gives us a clean view of the relationship between X and Y, unmuddied by associations between X and other factors that affect Y.

Our central challenge is to avoid endogeneity and thereby achieve exogeneity. If we succeed, we can be more confident that we have moved beyond correlation and closer to understanding if X causes Y—our fundamental goal. This process is not automatic or easy. Often we won't be able to find purely exogenous variation, so we'll have to think through how close we can get. Nonetheless, the bottom line is this: if we can find exogenous variation in X, we can use data to make a reasonable inference about what will happen to variable Y if we change variable X.

correlation Measures the extent to which two variables are linearly related to each other.

To formalize these ideas we'll use the concept of **correlation**, which most people know, at least informally. Two variables are correlated ("co-related") if they move together. A *positive correlation* means that high values of one variable are associated with high values of the other; a *negative correlation* indicates that high values of one variable are associated with low values of the other.

---

[2] A good idea is to measure these things and put them in the model so that they are no longer in the error term. That's what we do in Chapter 5.

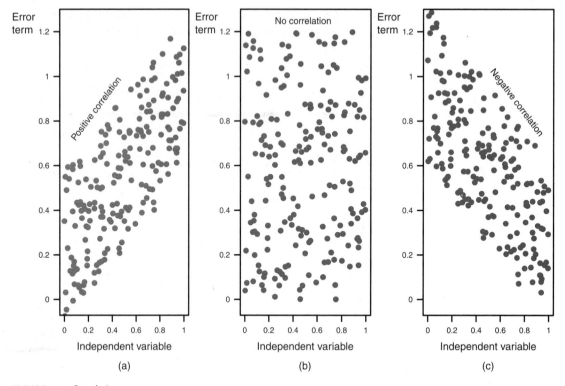

FIGURE 1.5: Correlation

Figure 1.5 shows examples of variables that have positive correlation [panel (a)], no correlation [panel (b)], and negative correlation [panel (c)]. Correlations range from 1 to −1. A correlation of 1 means that the variables move perfectly together.

Correlations close to zero indicate weak relationships between variables. When the correlation is zero, there is no linear relationship between two variables.[3]

We use correlation in our definitions of endogeneity and exogeneity. If our independent variable has a relationship to the error term like the one in panel (a) (which shows positive correlation) or panel (c) (which shows negative correlation), then we have endogeneity. In other words, we have endogeneity when the unmeasured stuff that constitutes the error term is correlated with our independent variable, and endogeneity will make it difficult to tell whether changes in the dependent variable are caused by our variable or the error term.

---

[3] In the appendix (page 524) we provide an equation for correlation and discuss how it relates to our ordinary least squares estimates from Chapter 3. Correlation measures linear relationships between variables; we'll discuss non-linear relationships in OLS on page 208.

On the other hand, if our independent variable has no relationship to the error term as in panel (b), we have exogeneity. In this case, if we observe Y rising with X, we can feel confident that X is causing Y.

The challenge is that the true error term is not observable. Hence much of what we do in econometrics attempts to get around the possibility that something unobserved in the error term may be correlated with the independent variable. This quest makes econometrics challenging and interesting.

As a practical matter, we should begin every analysis by assessing endogeneity. First, look away from the model for a moment and list all the things that could determine the dependent variable. Second, ask if anything on the list correlates with the independent variable in the model and explain why it might. That's it. Do that and we are on our way to identifying endogeneity.

REMEMBER THIS

1. There are two fundamental challenges in econometrics: randomness and endogeneity.

2. Randomness can produce data that suggests the existence of a relationship between X and Y even when there is none, or it may suggest that there is no relationship even when there is one.

3. An independent variable is endogenous if it is correlated with the error term in the model.

   (a) An independent variable is exogenous if it is not correlated with the error term in the model.

   (b) The error term is not observable, making it a challenge to know whether an independent variable is endogenous or exogenous.

   (c) It is difficult to assess causality for endogenous independent variables.

Discussion Questions

1. Each panel of Figure 1.6 on page 12 shows relationships among three variables: X is an observed independent variable, ϵ is a variable reflecting some unobserved characteristic, and Y is the dependent variable. (In our donut example, X corresponds to the number of donuts eaten, ϵ corresponds to an unobserved characteristic such as exercise, and Y corresponds to the outcome of interest, which is weight.) If an arrow connects X and Y, then X has a causal effect on Y. If an arrow connects ϵ and Y, then the unobserved characteristic has a causal effect on Y. If a double arrow connects X and ϵ, then these two variables are correlated (and we won't worry about which causes which).

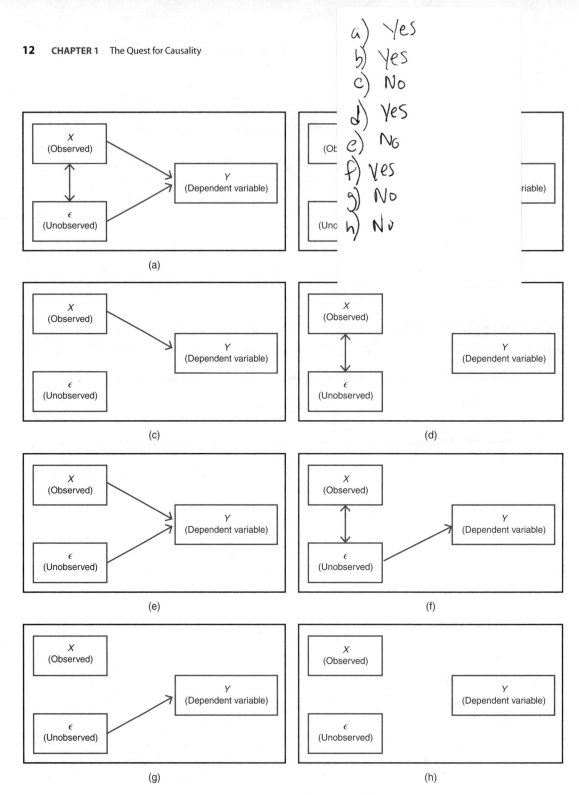

FIGURE 1.6: Possible Relationships Between X, ϵ, and Y (for Discussion Questions)

For each panel, explain whether endogeneity will cause problems for an analysis of the relationship between X and Y. For concreteness, assume X is grades in college, ϵ is IQ, and Y is salary at age 26.

2. Come up with your own independent variable, unmeasured error variable, and dependent variable. Decide which of the panels in Figure 1.6 you think best characterizes the relationship of the variables you chose and discuss the implications for econometric analysis.

CASE STUDY   ## Flu Shots

A great way to appreciate the challenges raised by endogeneity is to look at real examples. Here is one we all can relate to: Do flu shots work? No one likes the flu. It kills about 36,000 people in the United States each year, mostly among the elderly. At the same time, no one enjoys schlepping down to some hospital basement or drugstore lobby, rolling up a shirt sleeve, and getting a flu shot. Nonetheless, every year 100,000,000 Americans dutifully go through this ritual.

The evidence that flu shots prevent people from dying from the flu must be overwhelming. Right? Suppose we start by considering a study using data on whether people died (the dependent variable) and whether they got a flu shot (the independent variable).

$$Death_i = \beta_0 + \beta_1 Flu\ shot_i + \epsilon_i \qquad (1.3)$$

where $Death_i$ is a (creepy) variable that is 1 if person i died in the time frame of the study and 0 if he or she did not. $Flu\ shot_i$ is 1 if the person i got a flu shot and 0 if not.[4]

A number of studies have done essentially this analysis and have found that people who get flu shots are less likely to die. According to some estimates, those who receive flu shots are as much as 50 percent less likely to die. This effect is enormous. Going home with a Band-Aid with the little bloodstain is worth it after all.

But are we convinced? Is there any chance of endogeneity? If there exists some factor in the error term that affected whether someone died and whether he or she got a flu shot, we would worry about endogeneity.

What is in the error term? Goodness, lots of things affect the probability of dying: age, health status, wealth, cautiousness—the list is immense. All these factors and more are in the error term.

---

[4] We discuss dependent variables that equal only zero or one in Chapter 12 and independent variables that equal zero or one in Chapter 6.

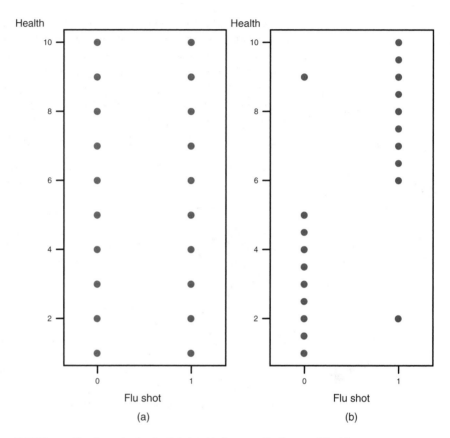

FIGURE 1.7: Two Scenarios for the Relationship between Flu Shots and Health

How could these factors cause endogeneity? Let's focus on overall health. Clearly, healthier people die at a lower rate than unhealthy people. If healthy people are also more likely to get flu shots, we might erroneously attribute life-saving power to flu shots when perhaps all that is going on is that people who are healthy in the first place tend to get flu shots.

It's hard, of course, to get measures of health for people, so let's suppose we don't have them. We can, however, speculate on the relationship between health and flu shots. Figure 1.7 shows two possible states of the world. In each figure we plot flu-shot status on the X-axis. A person who did not get a flu shot is in the 0 group; someone who got a flu shot is in the 1 group. On the Y-axis we plot health related to everything but flu (supposing we could get an index that factors in age, heart health, absence of disease, etc.). In panel (a), of Figure 1.7, health and flu shots don't seem to go together; in other words the correlation is zero. If panel (a) represents the state of the world, then our results that flu shots are associated with lower death rates is looking pretty good because flu shots are not reflecting overall health. In panel (b), health and flu shots do seem to go together, with the flu shot population being healthier. In this case, we have correlation of our main variable (flu shots) and something in the error term (health).

Brownlee and Lenzer (2009) discuss some indirect evidence suggesting that flu shots and health are actually correlated. A clever approach to assessing this matter is to look at death rates of people in the summer. The flu rarely kills people in the summer, which means that if people who get flu shots also die at lower rates in the summer, it is because they are healthier overall; if people who get flu shots die at the same rates as others during the summer, it would be reasonable to suggest that the flu-shot and non-flu-shot populations have similar health. It turns out that people who get flu shots have an approximately 60 percent lower probability of dying outside the flu season.

Other evidence backs up the idea that healthier people get flu shots. As it happened, vaccine production faltered in 2004 and 40 percent fewer people got vaccinated. What happened? Flu deaths did not increase. And in some years, the flu vaccine was designed to attack a set of viruses that turned out to be different from the viruses that actually spread in those years; again, there was no clear change in mortality. This data suggests that people who get flu shots may live longer because getting flu shots is associated with other healthy behavior, such as seeking medical care and eating better.

The point is not to put us off flu shots. We've discussed only mortality—whether people die from the flu—not whether they're more likely to contract the virus or stay home from work because they are sick.[5] The point is to highlight how hard it is to really know if something (in this case, a vaccine) works. If something as widespread and seemingly straightforward as flu shots is hard to assess definitively, think about the care we must take when trying to analyze policies that affect fewer people and have more complicated effects.

CASE STUDY   ## Country Music and Suicide

Does music affect our behavior? Are we more serious when we listen to classical music? Does bubblegum pop make us bounce through the halls? Both ideas seem plausible, but how can we know for sure?

Stack and Gundlach (1992) decided to look to data to assess one particular question: does country music depress us? They argued that country music, with all its lyrics about broken relationships and bad choices, may be so depressing that it increases suicide rates.[6] We can test this claim with the following statistical model:

$$Suicide\ rates_i = \beta_0 + \beta_1 Country\ music_i + \epsilon_i \qquad (1.4)$$

---

[5] See, for example, DiazGranados, Denis, and Plotkin (2012) and Osterholm, Kelley, Sommer, and Belongia (2012) for evidence on the flu vaccine based on randomized experiments.

[6] Really, this is an actual published paper.

where *Suicide rates$_i$* is the suicide rate in metropolitan area *i* and *Country music$_i$* is the proportion of radio airtime devoted to country music in metropolitan area *i*.[7]

It turns out that suicides are indeed higher in metro areas where radio stations play more country music. Do we believe this is a *causal* relationship? (In other words, is country music exogenous?) If radio stations play more country music, should we expect more suicides?

Let's work through this example.

What does β_0 mean? What does β_1 mean?   In this model, β_0 is the expected level of suicide in metropolitan areas that play no country music. β_1 is the amount by which suicide rates change for each one-unit increase in the proportion of country music played in a metropolitan area. We don't know what β_1 is; it could be positive (suicides go up), zero (no relation to suicides), or negative (suicides decrease). For the record, we don't know what β_0 is either, but since this variable does not directly characterize the relationship between music and suicides the way β_1 does, we are less interested in it.

What is in the error term?   The error term contains factors that are associated with higher suicide rates, such as alcohol and drug use, availability of guns, divorce and poverty rates, lack of sunshine, lack of access to mental health care, and probably many more.

What are the conditions for *X* to be endogenous?   An independent variable is endogenous if it is correlated with factors in the error term. Therefore, we need to ask whether the amount of country music played on radio stations in metropolitan areas is correlated with drinking, drug use, and all the other stuff in the error term.

Is the independent variable likely to be endogenous?   Are booze, divorce, and guns likely to be correlated to the amount of country music someone has listened to? Have you listened to any country music? Drinking and divorce come up now and again. Could this music appeal more in areas where people drink too much and get divorced more frequently? (To complicate matters, country music lyrics also feature more about family and religion than most other types of music.) Or, could it simply be that people in rural areas who like country music also have a lot of guns? And all of these factors—alcohol, divorce, and guns—are plausible influences on suicide rates. To the extent that country music is correlated with any of them, the country music variable would be endogenous.

Explain how endogeneity could lead to incorrect inferences.   Suppose for a moment that country music has no effect whatsoever on suicide rates, but that regions with lots of guns and drinking also have more suicides and that people in these regions also listen to more country music. If we look only at the relationship between country music and suicide rates, we will see a positive relationship: places with lots of country music will have higher suicide rates and places with little

---

[7] Their analysis is based on a more complicated model, but this is the general idea.

country music will have lower suicide rates. The explanation could be that the country music areas have lots of drinking and guns and the areas with little country music have less drinking and fewer guns. Therefore while it may be correct to say that in places where there is more country music, there are more suicides, it would be incorrect to conclude that country music *causes* suicides. Or, to put it in another way, it would be incorrect to conclude that we would save lives by banning country music.

As it turns out, Snipes and Maguire (1995) account for the amount of guns and divorce in metropolitan areas and find no relationship between country music and metropolitan suicide rates. So there's no reason to turn off the radio and put away those cowboy boots.

Discussion Questions

1. Labor economists often study the returns on investment in education (see, e.g., Card 1999). Suppose we have data on salaries of a set of people, some of whom went to college and some who did not. A simple model linking education to salary is

$$Salary_i = \beta_0 + \beta_1 College\ graduate_i + \epsilon_i$$

where the value of $Salary_i$ is the salary of person i and the value of $College\ graduate_i$ is 1 if person i graduated from college and is 0 if person i did not.

   (a) What does β_0 mean? What does β_1 mean?

   (b) What is in the error term?

   (c) What are the conditions for the independent variable X to be endogenous?

   (d) Is the independent variable likely to be endogenous? Why or why not?

   (e) Explain how endogeneity could lead to incorrect inferences.

2. Donuts aren't the only food that people worry about. Consider the following model based on Solnick and Hemenway (2011):

$$Violence_i = \beta_0 + \beta_1 Soft\ drinks_i + \epsilon_i$$

where $Violence_i$ is the number of physical confrontations student i was in during a school year and $Soft\ drinks_i$ is the average number of cans of soda student i drinks per week.

   (a) What does β_0 mean? What does β_1 mean?

   (b) What is in the error term?

   (c) What are the conditions for the independent variable X to be endogenous?

   (d) Is the independent variable likely to be endogenous? Why or why not?

   (e) Explain how endogeneity could lead to incorrect inferences.

3. We know U.S. political candidates spend an awful lot of time raising money. And we know they use the money to inflict mind-numbing ads on us. Do we know if the money and the ads it buys actually work? That is, does campaign spending increase vote share? Jacobson (1978), Erikson and Palfrey (2000), and others grapple at length with this issue. Consider the following model:

$$Vote\ share_s = \beta_0 + \beta_1 Campaign\ spending_s + \epsilon_s$$

where *Vote share_s* is the vote share of a candidate in state *s* and *Campaign spending_s* is the spending by candidate *s*.

   (a) What does β_0 mean? What does β_1 mean?

   (b) What is in the error term?

   (c) What are the conditions for the independent variable X to be endogenous?

   (d) Is the independent variable likely to be endogenous? Why or why not?

   (e) Explain how endogeneity could lead to incorrect inferences.

4. Researchers identified every outdoor advertisement in 228 census tracts in Los Angeles and New Orleans and then interviewed 2,881 residents of the cities about weight. Their results suggested that a 10 percent increase in outdoor food ads in a neighborhood was associated with a 5 percent increase in obesity.

   (a) Do you think there could be endogeneity?

   (b) How would you test for a relationship between food ads and obesity?

   (c) Read the article "Does the Ad Make Me Fat?" by Christopher Chabris and Daniel Simmons in the March 10, 2013, *New York Times* and see how your answers compare to theirs.

1.3   Randomized Experiments as the Gold Standard

The best way to fight endogeneity is to have exogenous variation. A good way to have exogenous variation is to *create* it. If we do so, we know that our independent variable is unrelated to the other variables that affect the dependent variable.

In theory, it is easy to create exogenous variation with a randomized experiment. In our donut example, we could randomly pick people and force them to eat donuts while forbidding everyone else to eat donuts. If we can pull this experiment off, the amount of donuts a person eats will be unrelated to other unmeasured variables that affect weight. The only thing that would determine donut eating would be the luck of the draw. The donut-eating group would have some ice cream bingers, some health food nuts, some runners, some round-the-clock video gamers, and so on. So, too, would the non-donut-eating group. There wouldn't be systematic differences in these unmeasured factors across groups. Both treated and untreated groups would be virtually identical and would resemble the composition of the population.

In an experiment like this, the variation in our independent variable X is exogenous. We have won. If we observe that donut eaters weigh more or have other health differences from non-donut-eaters, we can reasonably attribute these effects to donut consumption.

Simply put, the goal of such a randomized experiment is to make sure the independent variable, which we also call the *treatment*, is exogenous. The key element of such experiments is **randomization**, a process whereby the value of the independent variable is determined by a random process. The value of the independent variable will depend on nothing but chance, meaning that the independent variable will be uncorrelated with *everything*, including any factor in the error term affecting the dependent variable. In other words, a randomized independent variable is exogenous; analyzing the relationship between an exogenous independent variable and the dependent variable allows us to make inferences about a causal relationship between the two variables.

This is one of those key moments—a concept that may not be very complicated turns out to have enormous implications. By randomly picking some people to get a certain treatment, we rule out the possibility that there is some other way for the independent variable to be associated with the dependent variable. If the randomization is successful, the treated subjects are not systematically taller, more athletic, or more food conscious—or more left-handed or stinkier, for that matter.

The basic structure of a randomized experiment is simple. Based on our research question, we identify a relevant population that we randomly split into two groups: a **treatment group**, which receives the policy intervention, and a **control group**, which does not. After the treatment, we compare the behavior of the treatment and control groups on the outcome we care about. If the treatment group differs substantially from the control group, we believe the treatment had an effect; if not, then we're inclined to think the treatment had no effect.[8]

For example, suppose we want to know if an ad campaign increases enrollment in ObamaCare. We would identify a sample of uninsured people and split them into a treatment group that is exposed to the ad and a control group that is not. After the treatment, we compare the enrollment in ObamaCare of the treatment and control groups. If the treated group enrolled at a substantially higher rate, that outcome would suggest the ad works.

Because they build exogeneity into the research, randomized experiments are often referred to as the gold standard for causal inference. The phrase "gold standard" usually means the best of the best. But experiments also merit the gold

▶ **randomization** The process of determining the experimental value of the key independent variable based on a random process.

▶ **treatment group** In an experiment, the group that receives the treatment of interest.

▶ **control group** In an experiment, the group that does not receive the treatment of interest.

---

[8] We provide standards for making such judgments in Chapter 3 and beyond.

standard moniker in another sense. No country in the world is actually on a gold standard. The gold standard doesn't work well in practice and, for many research questions, neither do experiments. Simply put, experiments are great, but they can be tricky when applied to real people going about their business.

The human element of social scientific experiments makes them very different from experiments in the physical sciences. My third grader's science fair project compared cucumber seeds planted in peanut butter and in dirt. She did not have to worry that the cucumber seeds would get up and say, "There is NO way you are planting me in that." In the social sciences, though, people can object, not only to being planted in peanut butter, but also to things like watching TV commercials or attending a charter school or changing health care plans or pretty much anything else we might want to study with an experiment.

Therefore an appreciation of the virtues of experiments should come also with recognition of their limits. We devote Chapter 10 to discussing the analytical challenges that accompany experiments. No experiment should be designed without thinking through these issues, and every experiment should be judged by how well it deals with them.

Social scientific experiments can't answer all social scientific research questions for other reasons as well. The first is that experiments aren't always feasible. The financial costs of many experiments are beyond what most major research organizations can fund, let alone what a student doing a term paper can afford. And for many important questions, it's not a matter of money. Do we want to know if corruption promotes civil unrest? Good luck with our proposal to randomly end corruption in some countries and not others. Do we want to know if birthrates affect crime? Are we really going to randomly assign some regions to have more babies? While the randomizing process could get interesting, we're unlikely to pull it off. Or do we want to know something historical? Forget about an experiment.

And even if an experiment is feasible, it might not be ethical. We see this dilemma most clearly in medicine: if we believe a given treatment is better but are not sure, how ethical is it to randomly subject some people to a procedure that might not work? The medical community has developed standards relating to level of risk and informed consent by patients, but such questions will never be easy to answer.

Consider flu shots. We may think that assessing the efficacy of this public health measure is a situation made for a randomized experiment. It would be expensive but conceptually simple. Get a bunch of people who want a flu shot, tell them they are participating in a random experiment, and randomly give some a flu shot and the others a placebo shot. Wait and see how the two groups do.

But would such a randomized trial of flu vaccine be ethical? When we say "Wait and see how the two groups do," we actually mean "Wait and see who dies." That changes the stakes a bit, doesn't it? The public health community strongly believes in the efficacy of the flu vaccine and, given that belief, considers it unethical to deny people the treatment. Brownlee and Lenzer (2009) recount in *Atlantic Monthly* how one doctor first told interviewers that a randomized-experiment trial might be acceptable, then got cold feet and called back to say that such an experiment would be unethical.[9]

generalizable A statistical result is generalizable if it applies to populations beyond the sample in the analysis.

Finally, experimental results may not be **generalizable**. That is, a specific experiment may provide great insight into the effect of a given policy intervention at a given time and place, but how sure can we be that the same policy intervention will work somewhere else? Jim Manzi, the author of *Uncontrolled* (2012), argues that the most honest way to describe experimental results is that treatment X was effective in a certain time and place in which the subjects had the characteristics they did and the policy was implemented by people with the characteristics they had. Perhaps people in different communities respond to treatments differently. Or perhaps the scale of an experiment could matter: a treatment that worked when implemented on a small scale might fail if implemented more broadly.

internal validity A research finding is internally valid when it is based on a process that is free from systematic error.

external validity A research finding is externally valid when it applies beyond the context in which the analysis was conducted.

Econometricians make this point by distinguishing between internal validity and external validity. **Internal validity** refers to whether the inference is biased; **external validity** refers to whether an inference applies more generally. A well-executed experiment will be internally valid, meaning that the results will on average lead us to make the correct inferences about the treatment and its outcome in the context of the experiment. In other words, with internal validity, we can say confidently that variable X is what causes the change in variable Y. Even with internal validity, however, an experiment may not be externally valid: the causal relationship between the treatment and outcome could differ in other contexts. That is, even if we have internally valid evidence from an experiment that aardvarks in Alabama procreate more if they listen to Mozart, we can't really be sure aardvarks in Alaska will respond in the same way.

observational study Use data generated in an environment not controlled by a researcher. They are distinguished from experimental studies and are sometimes referred to as *non-experimental studies*.

Hence, even as experiments offer a conceptually clear approach to defeating endogeneity, they cannot always offer the final word for economic, policy, and political research. Hence most scholars in most fields need to grapple with non-experimental data. **Observational studies** use data that has been generated by non-experimental processes. In contrast to randomized experiments in which a researcher controls at least one of the variables, in observational studies the data is what it is and we do the best we can to analyze it in a sensible way. Endogeneity will be a chronic problem, but we are not totally defenseless in the fight against it. Even if we have only observational data, the techniques explained in this book can help us achieve, or at least approximate, the exogeneity promised by randomized experiments.

---

[9] Another flu researcher came to the opposite conclusion, saying, "What do you do when you have uncertainty? You test. . .We have built huge, population-based policies on the flimsiest of scientific evidence. The most unethical thing to do is to carry on business as usual."

REMEMBER THIS

1. Experiments create exogeneity via randomization.

2. Social science experiments are complicated by practical challenges associated with the difficulty of achieving randomization and full participation.

3. Experiments are not always feasible, ethical, or generalizable.

4. Observational studies use non-experimental data. They are necessary to answer many questions.

Discussion Questions

1. Is it possible to have a non-random exogenous independent variable?

2. Think of a policy question of interest. Discuss how an experiment might work to address the question.

3. Does foreign aid work? How should we create an experiment to assess whether aid to very poor communities works? What might some of the challenges be?

4. Do political campaigns matter? How should we create an experiment to assess whether phone calls, mailings, and visits by campaign workers matter? What might some of the challenges be?

5. How are health and medical spending affected when people have to pay each time they see a doctor? How should we create an experiment to assess whether the amount of co-payments (payments tendered at every visit to a doctor) affects health costs and quality? What might some of the challenges be?

Conclusion

The point of econometric research is almost always to learn if X (the independent variable) causes Y (the dependent variable). If we see high values of Y when X is high and low values of Y when X is low, we might be tempted to think X causes Y. We need always to be aware that the observed relationship could have arisen by chance. Or, if X is endogenous, we need to remember that interpreting the relationship between X and Y as causal could be wrong, possibly completely wrong. When another factor both causes Y and is correlated with X, any relationship we see between X and Y may be due to the effect of that other factor.

We spend the rest of this book accounting for uncertainty and battling endogeneity. Some approaches, like randomized experiments, seek to create exogenous change. Other econometric approaches, like multivariate regression, winnow down the number of other factors lurking in the background that can cause endogeneity. These and other approaches have strengths, weaknesses, tricks, and pitfalls. However, they all are united by a fundamental concern with counteracting endogeneity. Therefore if we understand the concepts in this chapter, we understand the essential challenges of using econometrics to better understand policy, economics, and politics.

Based on this chapter, we are on the right track if we can do the following:

- Section 1.1: Explain the terms in our core statistical model: $Y_i = \beta_0 + \beta_1 X_i + \epsilon_i$.

- Section 1.2: Explain two major econometric challenges. Define endogeneity. Explain how endogeneity can undermine causal inference. Define exogeneity. Explain how exogeneity can enable causal inference.

- Section 1.3: Explain how experiments achieve exogeneity. Explain challenges and limitations of experiments.

Key Terms

Constant (4)
Control group (19)
Correlation (9)
Dependent variable (2)
Endogenous (8)
Error term (5)

Exogenous (9)
External validity (21)
Generalizable (21)
Independent variable (2)
Intercept (4)
Internal validity (21)

Observational study (21)
Randomization (19)
Scatterplot (3)
Slope coefficient (4)
Treatment group (19)

2 Stats in the Wild: Good Data Practices

Endogeneity makes it difficult to use data to learn about the world. Ideally, we overcome endogeneity by conducting experiments in clean rooms staffed by stainless steel robots. That's not really how the world works, though. Social science experiments, if they can be conducted at all, can produce some pretty messy data. Observational data is even messier.

One example of data messiness occurred in 2009. Prominent economists Carmen Reinhart and Ken Rogoff (2010) analyzed more than 3,700 annual observations of economic growth from a large sample of countries. Panel (a) of Figure 2.1 depicts one of their key results, grouping average national GDP growth into four categories depending on the national ratio of public debt to GDP. The shocking finding was that average economic growth dropped off a cliff for countries with government debt above 90 percent of GDP. The implication was obvious: governments should be very cautious about using deficit spending to fight unemployment.

There was one problem with the economists' story. The data didn't quite say what they said it did. Herndon, Ash, and Pollin (2014) did some digging and found that some observations had been dropped, others were typos, and, most ignominiously, some calculations in Reinhart and Rogoff's original Excel spreadsheet were wrong. With the data corrected, the graph changed to panel (b) of Figure 2.1. Not quite the same story. Economic growth didn't plummet once government debt passed 90 percent of GDP. While people can debate whether the slope in the panel (b) is a bunny hill or an intermediate hill, it clearly is nothing like the cliff in the data originally reported.[1]

---

[1] A deeper question is whether we should treat this observational data as having any causal force. Government debt levels are likely to be related to other factors that affect economic growth, like wars and the quality of a country's institutions. In other words, government debt is likely to be

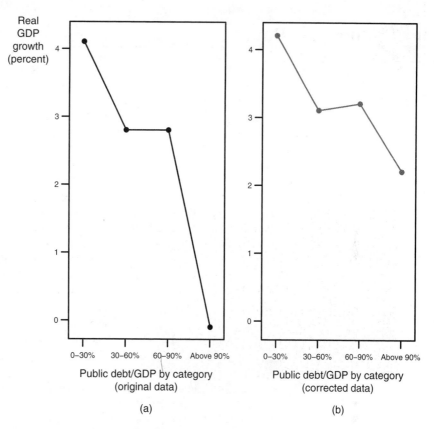

FIGURE 2.1: Two Versions of Debt and Growth Data

Reinhart and Rogoff's discomfort can be our gain when we realize that even top scholars can make data mistakes. Hence we need to create habits that help us to minimize mistakes and maximize the chance that others can find them if we do.

Therefore this chapter focuses on the crucial first steps for any econometric analysis. First, we need to understand our data. Section 2.1 introduces tools for describing data and sniffing out possible errors or anomalies. Second, we need to be prepared to convince others. If others can't recreate our results, people shouldn't believe them. Therefore Section 2.2 helps us establish good habits so that our code is understandable to ourselves and others. Finally, we sure as heck aren't going to do all this work by hand. Therefore, Section 2.3 introduces two major statistical software programs, Stata and R.

---

endogenous, meaning that we probably can't draw any conclusions about the effects of debt on growth without implementing techniques we cover later in this book.

Know Our Data

Experienced researchers know that data is seldom pristine. Something, somewhere is often off, even in data sets that are well traveled in academic circles. This is especially true for data from real-world sources.[2]

Therefore the first rule of data analysis is to know our data. This rule sounds obvious and simple but not everyone follows it, sometimes to their embarrassment. For each variable we should know the number of observations, the mean and standard deviation, and the minimum and maximum values. Knowing this information gives us a feel for data, helping us know if we have missing data and what the scales and ranges of the variables are. Table 2.1 shows an example for the donut and weight data we discussed on page 3. The number of observations, frequently referred to as "N" (for number), is the same for all variables in this example, but it varies across variables in many data sets. We all know the *mean* (also known as average). The **standard deviation** measures how widely dispersed the values of the observation are.[3] The *minimum* and *maximum*, which tell us the range of the data, often point to screwy values of a variable when the minimum or maximum doesn't make sense.

It is also helpful to look at the distribution of variables that take on only a few possible values. Table 2.2 is a frequency table for the male variable, a variable

▶ **standard deviation**

The standard deviation describes the spread of the data.

TABLE 2.1 **Descriptive Statistics for Donut and Weight Data**

Variable	Observations (N)	Mean	Standard deviation	Minimum	Maximum
Weight	13	171.85	76.16	70	310
Donuts	13	5.41	6.85	0	20.5

TABLE 2.2 **Frequency Table for Male Variable in Donut Data Set**

Value	Observations
0	4
1	9

[2] Chris Achen (1982, 53) memorably notes "If the information has been coded by nonprofessionals and not cleaned at all, as often happens in policy analysis projects, it is probably filthy."

[3] The appendix contains more details (page 522). Here's a quick refresher. The standard deviation of X is a measure of the dispersion of X. The larger the standard deviation, the more spread out the values. Standard deviation is calculated as $\sqrt{\frac{1}{N}\sum(X_i - \overline{X})^2}$, where $\overline{X}$ is the mean of X. We record how far each observation is from the mean. We then square each value because for the purposes of calculating dispersion we don't distinguish whether a value is below the mean or above it; when squared, all these values become positive numbers. We record the average of these squared values. Finally, since they're squared values, taking the square root of the average brings the final value back to the scale of the original variable.

TABLE 2.3 Frequency Table for Male
Variable in Second Donut
Data Set

Value	Observations
0	4
1	8
100	1

that equals 1 for men and 0 for women. The table indicates that the donut data set consists, of nine men and four women. Fair enough. Suppose that our frequency table looked like Table 2.3 instead. Either we have a very manly man in the sample or (more likely) we have a mistake in our data. The econometric tools we use later in this book will not necessarily flag such issues, so we need to be alert.

Graphing data is useful because it allows us to see relationships and to notice unusual observations. The tools we develop later quantify these relationships, but seeing them for ourselves is an excellent and necessary first step. For example,

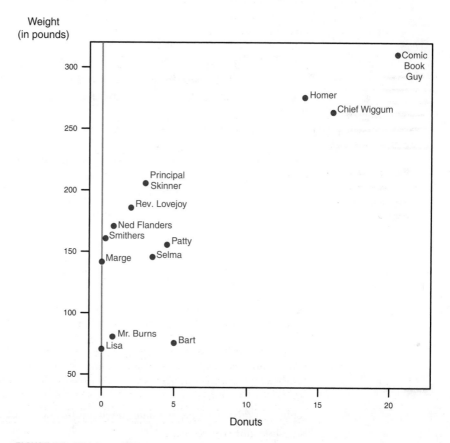

FIGURE 2.2: Weight and Donuts in Springfield

Figure 2.2 shows the scatterplot we saw earlier of the weight and donut data. We can see that there does seem to be a relationship between the two variables.

We also see some relationships that we might have missed without graphing. Lisa and Bart are children and their weight is much lower; we'll probably want to account for that in our analysis. Women also seem to weigh less.

Effective figures are clean, clear, and attractive. We point to some resources for effective visualization in the Further Reading section at the end of the chapter, but here's the bottom line: get rid of clutter. Don't overdo axis labels. Avoid abbreviations and jargon. Pick colors that go together well. And 3D? Don't. Ever.

REMEMBER THIS

1. A useful first step toward understanding data is to review sample size, mean, standard deviation, and minimum and maximum for each variable.

2. Plotting data is useful for identifying patterns and anomalies in data.

2.2 Replication

▶ **replication** Research that meets a replication standard can be duplicated based on the information provided at the time of publication.

▶ **replication files** Files that document how exactly data is gathered and organized. When properly compiled, these files allow others to reproduce our results exactly.

▶ **codebook** A file that describes sources for variables and any adjustments made.

At the heart of scientific knowledge is the **replication** standard. Research that meets a replication standard can be duplicated based on the information provided at the time of publication. In other words, an outsider who used that information would produce identical results.

We need **replication files** to satisfy this standard. Replication files document exactly how data is gathered and organized. Properly constructed, these files allow others to check our work by following our steps and seeing if they get identical results.

Replication files also enable others to probe our analysis. Sometimes—often, in fact—statistical results hinge on seemingly small decisions about what data to include, how to deal with missing data, and so forth. People who really care about getting the answer right will want to see what we've done to our data and, realistically, will be wary until they determine for themselves that other reasonable ways of doing the analysis produce similar results. If a certain coding or statistical choice substantially changes results, we need to pay a lot of attention to that choice.

Committing to a replication standard keeps our work honest. We need to make sure that we base our choices on the statistical merits, not on whether they produce the answer we want. If we give others the means to check our work, we're less likely to fall to the temptation of reporting only the results we like.

Therefore every statistical or econometric project, whether a homework assignment, a thesis, or a multi-million-dollar consulting project, should start with replication files. One file is a data **codebook** that documents the data. Sometimes this file simply notes the website and when the data was downloaded. Often,

TABLE 2.4 Codebook for Height and Wage Data

Variable name	Description
wage96	Adult hourly wages (dollars) reported in 1996 (salary and wages divided by hours worked in past calendar year)
height85	Adult height (inches), self-reported in 1985
height81	Adolescent height (inches), self-reported in 1981
athletics	Participation in high-school athletics (1 = yes, 0 = no)
clubnum	Number of club memberships in high school, excluding athletics, academic/honor society clubs, and vocational clubs
male	Male (1 = yes, 0 = no)

though, the codebook will include information about variables that come from multiple sources. The codebook should note the source of the data, the type of data, who collected it, and any adjustments the researcher made. For example, is the data measured in nominal or real dollars? If it is in real dollars, which inflation deflator has been used? Is the data measured in fiscal year or calendar year? Losing track of this information can lead to frustrating and unproductive backtracking later.

Table 2.4 contains a sample of a codebook for a data set on height and wages.[4] The data set, which was used to assess whether tall people get paid more, is pretty straightforward. It covers how much money people earned, how tall they were, and their activities in high school. We see, though, that details matter. The wages are stated in dollars per hour, which itself is calculated based on information from an entire year of work. We could imagine data on wages in other data sets being expressed in terms of dollars per month or year or in terms of wages at the time the question was asked. There are two height variables, one measured in 1981 and the other measured in 1985. The athletics variable indicates whether the person did or did not participate in athletics. Given the coding, a person who played multiple sports will have the same value for this variable as a person who played one sport. Such details are important in the analysis, and we must be careful to document them thoroughly.

A second replication file should document the analysis, usually by providing the exact code used to generate the results. Which commands were used to produce the analysis? Sometimes the file contains a few simple lines of software code. Often, however, we need to explain the complicated steps in merging or cleaning the data. Or we need to detail how we conducted customized analysis. These steps are seldom obvious from the description of data and methods that makes its way into the final paper or report. It is a great idea to include commentary in the replication material explaining the code and the reasons behind decisions. Sometimes statistical code will be pretty impenetrable (even to the person who wrote it!) and detailed commentary helps keeps things clear for everyone. We show examples of well-documented code in the Computing Corner beginning on page 34.

---

[4] We analyze this data on page 73.

Having well-documented data and analysis is a huge blessing. Even a modestly complex project can produce a head-spinning number of variables and choices. And because the work often extends over days, weeks, or months, we learn quickly that what seems obvious when fresh can fade into oblivion when we need it later. How exactly did we create our wonderful new variable at 3 am, three weeks ago? An analysis we can't recreate from scratch is useless. We might as well have gone to bed. If we have a good replication file, on the other hand, we can simply run the code again and be up to full speed in minutes.

A replication file is also crucial in analyzing the robustness of our results. A result is **robust** if it does not change when we change the model. For example, if we believe that a certain observation was mismeasured, we might exclude it from the data we analyze. A reader might be nervous about this exclusion. It will therefore be useful to conduct an robustness check in which we estimate the model including the contested observation. If the statistical significance and magnitude of the coefficient of interest are essentially the same as before, then we can assure others that the results are robust to inclusion of that observation. If the results change, the coefficient of interest changes; then the results are not robust, and we have some explaining to do. Knowing that many results are not robust, experienced researchers demand extensive robustness checks.

> **robust** Statistical results are robust if they do not change when the model changes.

▶ REMEMBER THIS

1. Analysis that cannot be replicated cannot be trusted.

2. Replication files document data sources and methods that someone could use to exactly recreate the analysis in question from scratch.

3. Replication files also allow others to explore the robustness of results by enabling them to assess alternative approaches to the analysis.

CASE STUDY ## Violent Crime in the United States

Violent crime is one of our worst fears. The more we can understand its causes, the more we can design public policies to address it. Many wonder if crime is a result of the breakdown of the family, poverty, or dense urban living.

For a preliminary picture of how violent crime and such demographic features are related, consider some data drawn from census records from 2009 for the 50 states and Washington, DC. We can see in Table 2.5 that no data is missing (because each variable has 51 observations). We also see that the violent crime rate has a broad range, from 119.9 per 100,000 population all the

TABLE 2.5 **Descriptive Statistics for State Crime Data**

Variable	Observations (N)	Mean	Standard deviation	Minimum	Maximum
Violent crime rate (per 100,000 people)	51	406.53	205.61	119.90	1,348.90
Percent single parents	51	0.33	0.07	0.18	0.61
Percent urban	51	73.92	14.92	38.83	100.00
Percent poverty	51	13.85	3.11	8.50	21.92

way to 1,348.9 per 100,000 people. The single-parent percent variable is on a 0-to-1 scale, also with considerable range, from 0.18 to 0.61. The percent urban (which is the percent of people in the state living in a metropolitan area) is measured on a 0-to-100 scale. These scales mean that 50 percent is indicated as 0.5 in the single-parent variable and as 50 in the urban variable. Getting the scales mixed up could screw up the way we interpret results about the relationships among these variables.

Scatterplots provide excellent additional information about our data. Figure 2.3 shows scatterplots of state-level violent crime rate and percent urban, percent of children with a single parent, and percent in poverty. Suddenly, the

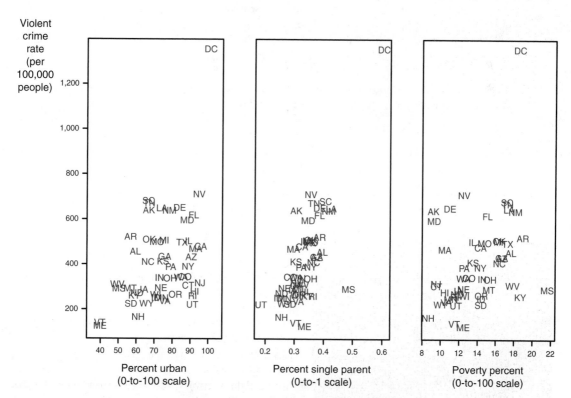

FIGURE 2.3: Scatterplots of Violent Crime against Percent Urban, Single Parent, and Poverty

character of the data is revealed. Washington, DC, is a clear outlier, being very much higher than the 50 states in level of violent scrime. Perhaps it should be dropped.[5]

We can also use scatterplots to appreciate nonobvious things about our data. We may think of highly urbanized states as being the densely populated states in the Northeast like Massachusetts and New Jersey. Actually, though, the scatterplot helps us see that Nevada, Utah, and Florida are among the most urbanized according to the Census Bureau measure. Understanding the reality of the urbanization variable helps us better appreciate what the data is telling us.

Being aware of the data can help us detect possible endogeneity. Many of the states showing high single-parent populations and high poverty are in the South. If this leads us to suspect that southern states are distinctive in other social and political characteristics, we should be on high alert for potential endogeneity in any analysis that uses the poverty or single-parenthood variable. These variables capture not only poverty and single parenthood, but also "southernness."

2.3   Statistical Software

We need software to do statistics. We have many choices, and it's worthwhile to learn at least two different software packages. Because different packages are good at different things, many researchers use one program for some tasks and another program for other tasks. Also, knowing multiple programs reinforces clear statistical thinking because it helps us think in terms of statistical concepts rather than in terms of the software commands.

We refer to two major statistical packages throughout this book, as these are the two most commonly used languages for applied econometrics. Stata and R. (Yes, R is a statistical package referred to by a single letter; the folks behind it are a bit minimalist.) Stata provides simple commands to do many complex econometric analyses; the cost of this simplicity is that we sometimes need to do a lot of digging to figure out what exactly Stata is up to. And it is expensive. R can be a bit harder to get the hang of, but the coding is often more direct, and less is hidden to the user. Oh yes, it's also free, at http://www.r-project.org/. Free does not mean cheap or basic, though. In fact, R is so powerful that it is the program of choice for many sophisticated econometricians.

In this book we learn by doing, showing specific examples of code in the chapter Computing Corners. The best way to learn code is to get working; after a while the command names become second nature. Replication files are also a great learning tool. Even if we forget a specific command, it's not so hard to remember "I want to do something like I did for the homework on about education and wages." All we have to do, then, is track down the replication file and build from that.[6]

---

[5] Despite the fact that more people live in Washington, DC, than in Vermont or Wyoming! Or, so says the resident of Washington, DC . . .

[6] In the Further Reading section at the end of chapter, we indicate some good sources for learning Stata and R and mention some other statistical packages in use.

> ## REMEMBER THIS

1. Stata is a powerful statistical software program. It is relatively user friendly, but it can be expensive.

2. R is another powerful statistical software program. It is less user friendly, but it is free.

Conclusion

This chapter prepares us for analyzing real data. We begin by understanding our data. This vital first step makes sure that we know what we're dealing with. We should use descriptive statistics to get an initial feel for how much data we have and the scales of the variables. Then we should graph our data. It's a great way to appreciate what we're dealing with and spot interesting patterns or anomalies.

The second step of working with data is documenting our data and analysis. Social science depends crucially on replication. Analyses that cannot be replicated cannot be trusted. Therefore all statistical projects should document data and methods, ensuring that anyone (including the author!) can recreate all results.

We are on track with the key concepts in this chapter when we can do the following.

- Section 2.1: Explain descriptive statistics and what to look for.

- Section 2.2: Explain the importance of replication and the two elements of a replication file.

- Section 2.3 (and Computing Corner below): Do basic data description in Stata and R.

Further Reading

King (1995) provides an excellent discussion of the replication standard.

Data visualization is a growing field, with good reason as analysts increasingly communicate primarily via figures. Tufte (2001) is a landmark book. Schwabish (2004) and Yau (2011) are nice guides to graphics.

Chen, Ender, Mitchell, and Wells (2003) is an excellent online resource for learning Stata. Gaubatz (2015) is an accessible and comprehensive introduction to R. Other resources include Verzani (2004) and online tools such as Swirl (2014).

Venables and Ripley (2002) is a classic reference book on S, the language that preceded R. Virtually all of it applies to R.

Other programs are widely used, as well. EViews is a powerful program often chosen by those doing forecasting models (see eviews.com). Some people use Excel for basic statistical analysis. It's definitely useful to have good Excel skills, but to do serious analysis, most people will need a more specialized program.

Key Terms

Codebook (28)

Replication (28)

Replication files (28)

Robust (30)

Standard Deviation (26)

Computing Corner

Stata

- The first thing to know is what to do when we get stuck (*when*, not *if*). In Stata, type `help commandname` if you have questions about a certain command. For example, to learn about the `summarize` command, we can type `help summarize` to get a description of the command. Probably the most useful information comes in the form of the examples at the end of these files. Often the best approach is to find an example that seems closest to what we're trying to do and apply that example to the problem. Googling usually helps, too.

- A comment line is a line in the code that provides notes for the user. A comment line does not actually tell Stata to do anything, but it can be incredibly useful to clarify what is going on in the code. Comment lines in Stata begin with an asterisk (*). Using ** makes it easier to visually identify these crucial lines.

- To open a "syntax file" to document an analysis, click on Window – Do file editor – new Do-file editor. It's helpful to resize this window to be able to see both the commands and the results. Save the syntax file as "SomethingSomething.do"; the more informative the name, the better. Including the date in the file name aids version control. To run any command in the syntax file, highlight the whole line and then press ctrl-d. The results of the command will be displayed in the Stata results window.

- One of the hardest parts of learning new statistical software is loading data into a program. While some data sets are prepackaged and easy, many are not, especially those we create ourselves. Be prepared for the process of loading data to take longer than expected. And because data sets can sometimes misbehave (columns shifting in odd ways, for example) it is very important to use the descriptive statistics diagnostics described in this chapter to make sure the data is exactly what we think it is.

– To load Stata data files (which have .dta at the end of the file name), there are two options.

1. Use syntax
   ```
   ** For data located on the web
   use "http://www9.georgetown.edu//faculty//baileyma
   //RealStats/DonutData.dta"
   ** For data located on a computer
   use "C:\Users\SallyDoe\Documents\DonutData.dta"
   ```
   The "path" tells the computer where to find the file. In this example, the path is C:\Users\SallyDoe\Documents. The exact path depends on a computer's file structure.

2. Point-and-click: Go to the File – Open menu option in Stata and browse to the file. Stata will then produce and display the command for opening that particular file. It is a good idea to save this command in the syntax file so that you document exactly the data being used.

– Loading non-Stata data files (files that are in tab-delimited, comma-delimited, or other such format) depends on the exact format of the data. For example, use the following to read in data that has tabs between variables on each line:

1. Use syntax
   ```
   ** For data located on the web
   insheet using "http://www9.georgetown.edu//faculty
   //baileyma//RealStats/DonutData.raw"
   ** For data located on a computer
   insheet using "C:\Users\SallyDoe\Documents\
   DonutsData.raw"
   ```

2. Point-and-click: Go to File – Import and then select the file where the data is stored. Stata will then produce and display the command for opening that particular file. It is a good idea to save this command in the syntax file so that you document exactly the data being used. Often it is easiest to use point-and-click the first time and syntax after that.

• To see a list of variables loaded into Stata, look at the variable window that lists all variables. We can also click on Data – Data editor to see variables.

- To make sure the data loaded correctly, display it with the `list` command. To display the first 10 observations of all variables, type `list in 1/10`. To display the first 8 observations of only the weight variable, type `list weight in 1/8`. We can also look at the data in Stata's "Data Browser" by going to Data/Data editor in the toolbar.

- To see descriptive statistics on the weight and donut data as in Table 2.1, use `summarize weight donuts`.

- To produce a frequency table such as Table 2.2, type `tabulate male`. Use this command only for variables that take on a limited number of possible values.

- To plot the weight and donut data as in Figure 2.2, type `scatter weight donuts`. There are many options for creating figures. For example, to plot the weight and donut data for males only with labels from a variable called "name," type `scatter weight donuts if male==1, mlabel(name)`.

R

- To get help in R, type `?commandname` for questions about a certain command. For questions about the `mean` command type `?mean` to get a description of the command, options, and most importantly, examples. Often the best approach is to find an example that seems closest to what we're trying to do and apply that example to the problem. Googling usually helps, too.

- Comment lines in R begin with a pound sign (#). Using ## makes it easier to visually identify these crucial lines.

- To open a syntax file where we document our analysis, click on File – New script. It's helpful to resize this window to be able to see both the commands and the results. Save the syntax file as "SomethingSomething.R"; the more informative the name, the better. Including the date in the file name aids version control. To run any command in the syntax file, highlight the whole line and then press ctrl-r. The results of the command will be displayed in the R console window.

- To load R data files (which have .RData at the end of the file name), there are two options.

  1. Use syntax. The most reliable way to work with data from the web is to download it and then access it as a file on the computer. To do so, use the `download` command, which needs to know the location of the data (which we name URL in this example) and where on the

computer to put the data (which we name Dest in this example). Then use the `load` command. The following four commands load the donut data into R's memory:

```
URL = "http://www9.georgetown.edu//faculty//
baileyma//RealStats//DonutData.RData"
Dest = "C:\\Users\\SallyDoe\\Documents\\
DonutData.RData"
download.file(URL, Dest)
load("C:\\Users\\SallyDoe\\Documents\\
DonutData.RData")
       ## We need the double backslashes in file name.
       ## Yes, they're different than double forward
       ## slashes in the URL.
```

2. Point-and-click. Click on the R console (where we see results) and go to the File – Load Workspace menu option and browse to the file. This method is easier, but it does not leave a record in the .R file of exactly which data set is being used.

- Loading non-R data files (files that are in .txt or other such format) requires more care. For example, to read in data that has commas between variables on each line, use `read.table`:
```
RawData = read.table("C:\\Users\\SallyDoe\\Documents\\
DonutData.raw", header=TRUE)
```
This command saves variables as Data$VariableName (or for example RawData$weight, RawData$donuts). It is also possible to install special commands that load in various types of data. For example, search the web for "read.dta" to see more information on how to install a special command that reads Stata files directly into R.

- It is also possible to manually load data into R. Here's a sample set:
```
weight = c(275, 141, 70, 75, 310, 80, 160, 263, 205,
185, 170, 155, 145)
donuts = c(14, 0, 0, 5, 20.5, 0.75, 0.25, 16, 3, 2,
0.8, 4.5, 3.5)
name = c("Homer", "Marge", "Lisa", "Bart", "Comic
Book Guy", "Mr. Burns", "Smithers", "Chief Wiggum",
"Principal Skinner", "Rev. Lovejoy", "Ned Flanders",
"Patty", "Selma").
```

- To make sure the data loaded correctly, use the following tools to display the data in R:

1. Use the `objects()` command to show the variables and objects loaded into R.

2. For a single variable, enter the variable's name in the R console or highlight it in the syntax file and press ctrl-r.[7]

3. To display only some observations for a single variable, use brackets. For example, to see the first 10 observations of the donuts variable use `donuts[1:10]`.

- To see the average of the weight variable, type `mean(weight)`. One tricky thing R does is choke on variables that having missing data; this is undesirable because if a single observation is missing, the simple version of the mean command will produce a result of "NA." Therefore we need to tell R what to do with missing data by modifying the command to `mean(weight, na.rm=TRUE)`. R refers to missing observations with an "NA." The ".rm" is shorthand for remove. A way to interpret the command, then, is to tell R, "Yes, it is true that we will remove missing data from our calculations." This syntax works for other descriptive statistics commands as well. Working with the na.rm command is a bit of an acquired taste, but it becomes second nature soon enough.

  To see the standard deviation of the weight variable, type `sqrt(var((weight)))`, where the `sqrt` part refers to the square root function. The minimum and maximum of the weight variable are displayed with `min(weight)` and `max(weight)`. To see the number of observations for a variable, use `sum(is.finite(weight))`. This command is a bit clumsy: the `is.finite` function creates a variable that equals 1 for each non-missing observation and the sum function sums this variable, creating a count of non-missing observations.

- To produce a frequency table such as Table 2.2 on page 26, type `table(male)`. Use this command only for variables that take on a limited number of possible values.

- To plot the weight and donut data as in Figure 2.2, type `plot(donuts, weight)`. There are many options for creating figures. For example, to plot the weight and donut data for males only with labels from a variable called "name," type

```
plot(donuts[male == 1], weight[male == 1])
text(donuts[male == 1], weight[male == 1], name[male == 1]).
```

---

[7] R can load variables directly such that each variable has its own variable name. Or, it can load variables as part of data frames such that the variables are loaded together. For example, our commands to load the .RData file loaded each variable separately, while our commands to load data from a text file created an object called "RawData" that contains all the variables. To display a variable in the "RawData" object called "donuts," type `RawData$donuts` in the .R file, highlight it, and press ctrl-r. This process may take some getting used to, but experiment freely with any data set you load in and it should become second nature.

The syntax donuts[male == 1] tells R to use only values of donuts for which male equals 1.[8]

Exercises

1. The data set DonutDataX.dta contains data from our donuts example on page 26. There is one catch: each of the variables has an error. Use the tools discussed in this chapter to identify the errors.

2. What determines success at the Winter Olympics? Does population matter? Income? Or is it simply a matter of being in a cold place with lots of mountains? Table 2.6 describes variables in olympics_HW.dta related to the Winter Olympic Games from 1980 to 2014.

   (a) Summarize the medals, athletes, and GDP data.

   (b) List the first five observations for the country, year, medals, athletes, and GDP data.

   (c) How many observations are there for each year?

   (d) Produce a scatterplot of medals and the number of athletes. Describe the relationship depicted.

TABLE 2.6	Variables for Winter Olympics Questions
Variable name	**Description**
ID	Unique number for each country in the data set
country	Name of country
year	Year
medals	Total number of combined medals won
athletes	Number of athletes in Olympic delegation
GDP	Gross domestic product (GDP) of country (per capita GDP in $10,000 U.S. dollars)
temp	Average high temperature (in Fahrenheit) in January if country is in Northern Hemisphere or July if Southern Hemisphere (for largest city)
population	Population of country (in 100,000)
host	Equals 1 if host nation and 0 otherwise

---

[8] R plots are very customizable. To get a flavor, use text(donuts[male == 1], weight[male == 1], name[male == 1], cex=0.6, pos=4) as the second line of the plot sequence of code. The "cex" command controls the size of the label and the "pos=4" puts the labels to the right of the plotted point. Refer to the help menus in R, or Google around for more ideas.

(e) Explain any suspicion you might have that other factors might explain the observed relationship between the number of athletes and medals.

(f) Create a scatterplot of medals and GDP. Briefly describe any clear patterns.

(g) Create a scatterplot of medals and population. Briefly describe any clear patterns.

(h) Create a scatterplot of medals and temperature. Briefly describe any clear patterns.

3. Persico, Postlewaite, and Silverman (2004) analyzed data from the National Longitudinal Survey of Youth (NLSY) 1979 cohort to assess the relationship between height and wages for white men who were between 14 and 22 years old in 1979. This data set consists of answers from individuals who were asked questions in various years between 1979 and 1996. Here we explore the relationship between height and wages for the full sample that includes men and women and all races. Table 2.7 describes the variables we use for this question.

(a) Summarize the wage, height (both *height*85 and *height*81), and sibling variables. Discuss briefly.

(b) Create a scatterplot of wages and adult height (*height*85). Discuss any distinctive observations.

(c) Create a scatterplot of wages and adult height that excludes the observations with wages above $500 per hour.

(d) Create a scatterplot of adult height against adolescent height. Identify the set of observations where people's adolescent height is less than their adult height. Do you think we should use these observations in any future analysis we conduct with this data? Why or why not?

TABLE 2.7 Variables for Height and Wages Data in the United States

Variable name	Description
wage96	Hourly wages (in dollars) in 1996
height85	Adult height: height (in inches) measured in 1985
height81	Adolescent height: height (in inches) measured in 1981
siblings	Number of siblings

4. Anscombe (1973) created four data sets that had interesting properties. Let's use tools from this chapter to describe and understand these data sets. The data is in a Stata data file called AnscombesQuartet.dta. There are four possible independent variables ($X1$–$X4$) and four possible dependent variables ($Y1$–$Y4$). Create a replication file that reads in the data and implements the analysis necessary to answer the following questions. Include comment lines that explain the code.

(a) Briefly note the mean and variance for each of the four X variables. Briefly note the mean and variance for each of the four Y variables. Based on these, would you characterize the four sets of variables as similar or different?

(b) Create four scatterplots: one with $X1$ and $Y1$, one with $X2$ and $Y2$, one with $X3$ and $Y3$, and one with $X4$ and $Y4$.

(c) Briefly explain any differences and similarities across the four graphs.

PART I

The OLS Framework

Bivariate OLS: The Foundation of Econometric Analysis   **3**

Every four years Americans elect a president. Each campaign has drama: controversies, gaffes, over-the-top commercials. And yet, the results are actually quite predictable based on how the economy grew the previous four years. Panel (a) of Figure 3.1 is a scatterplot of the vote share of the incumbent U.S. president's party and changes in income for each election between 1948 and 2012. The relationship jumps right out at us: higher income growth is indeed associated with larger presidential vote shares.[1]

This chapter introduces the foundational statistical model for analyzing such data. The model allows us to quantify the relationship between two variables and to assess whether the relationship occurred by chance or resulted from some real cause. We build on these methods in the rest of the book in ways that help us differentiate, as best we can, true causes from simple associations.

Basically we take data like the data found in panel (a) of Figure 3.1 and estimate a line that best characterizes the relationship between the two variables. We include this line in panel (b) of Figure 3.1. Look for the year 2012. It's almost right on the line. That's a bit lucky (other years aren't so close to the line), but the figure shows that we can get a remarkably good start on understanding presidential elections with a data set that's not particularly big and the tools we develop in this chapter.

The specific tool we introduce in this chapter is OLS, which stands for *ordinary least squares*; we'll explain why later. It's not the best name. Regression

---

[1] The figure is based on Noel (2010). The figure plots vote share as a percent of the total votes given to Democrats and Republicans only. We use these data to avoid the complication that in some years third-party candidates such as Ross Perot (in 1992 and 1996) or George Wallace (in 1968) garnered nontrivial vote share.

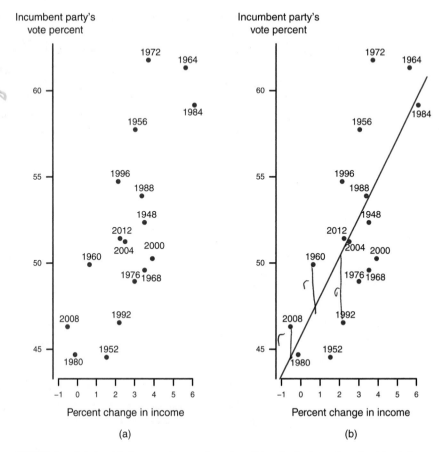

FIGURE 3.1: Relationship between Income Growth and Vote for the Incumbent President's Party, 1948–2012

and linear regression are other commonly used names for the method—also lame names.[2]

The goal of this chapter is to introduce OLS. In Section 3.1 we show how to estimate coefficients that use OLS to produce a fitted line. The following sections then show that these coefficient estimates have many useful properties. Section 3.2 demonstrates that the OLS coefficient estimates are themselves random variables. Section 3.3 explains one of the most important concepts in statistics: the OLS estimates of $\hat{\beta}_1$ will not be biased if X is exogenous. That is, the estimates won't be systematically higher or lower than the true values as long as the independent variable is not correlated with the error term.

---

[2] In the late nineteenth century Francis Galton used the term "regression" to refer to the phenomenon that children of very tall parents tended to be less tall than their parents. He called this phenomenon "regression to the mean" in heights of children because children of tall parents tend to "regress" (move back) to average heights. Somehow the term "regression" bled over to cover statistical methods to analyze relationships between dependent and independent variables. Go figure.

Section 3.4 shows how to characterize the precision of the OLS estimates. Section 3.5 shows how the distribution of the OLS estimates converge to a point as the same size gets very, very large. Section 3.6 discusses issues that complicate the calculation of the precision of our estimates. These issues have intimidating names like *heteroscedasticity* and *autocorrelation*. Their bark is worse than their bite, however, and most statistical software can easily address them. Finally, Sections 3.7 and 3.8 discuss tools for assessing how well the model fits the data and whether any crazy observations could distort our conclusions.

3.1 Bivariate Regression Model

*Bi*variate OLS is a technique we use to estimate a model with two variables—a dependent variable and an independent variable. In this section, we explain the model, estimate it, and try it out on our presidential election example. We extend the model in later chapters when we discuss *multi*variate OLS, a technique we use to estimate models with multiple independent variables.

The bivariate model

Bivariate OLS allows us to quantify the degree to which X and Y move together. We work with the core statistical model we introduced on page 5:

$$Y_i = \beta_0 + \beta_1 X_i + \epsilon_i \tag{3.1}$$

where Y_i is the dependent variable and X is the independent variable. The parameter β_0 is the intercept (or constant). It indicates the expected value of Y when X_i is zero. The parameter β_1 is the slope. It indicates how much Y changes as X changes. The random error term ϵ_i captures everything else other than X that affects Y.

Adapting the generic bivariate equation to the presidential election example produces

$$Incumbent\ party\ vote\ share_i = \beta_0 + \beta_1 Income\ change_i + \epsilon_i \tag{3.2}$$

where *Incumbent party vote share$_i$* is the dependent variable and *Income change$_i$* is the independent variable. The parameter β_0 indicates the expected vote percentage for the incumbent when income change equals zero. The parameter β_1 indicates how much more we expect vote share to rise as income change increases by one unit.

This model is an incredibly simplified version of the world. The data will not fall on a completely straight line because elections are affected by many other factors, ranging from wars to scandals to social issues and so forth. These factors comprise our error term, ϵ_i.

For any given data set, OLS produces estimates of the β parameters that best explain the data. We indicate estimates as $\hat{\beta}_0$ and $\hat{\beta}_1$, where the "hats" indicate that these are our estimates. Estimates are different from the true values, β_0 and β_1, which don't get hats in our notation.[3]

How can these parameters best explain the data? The $\hat{\beta}$'s define a line with an intercept ($\hat{\beta}_0$) and a slope ($\hat{\beta}_1$). The task boils down to picking a $\hat{\beta}_0$ and $\hat{\beta}_1$ that define the line that minimizes the aggregate distance of the observations from the line. To do so we use two concepts: the fitted value and the residual.

The **fitted value** is the value of Y predicted by our estimated equation. The fitted value $\hat{Y}$ (which we call "Y hat") from our bivariate OLS model is

$$\hat{Y}_i = \hat{\beta}_0 + \hat{\beta}_1 X_i \tag{3.3}$$

▶ **fitted value** A fitted value, $\hat{Y}_i$, is the value of Y predicted by our estimated equation. For a bivariate OLS model it is $\hat{Y}_i = \hat{\beta}_0 + \hat{\beta}_1 X_i$. Also called *predicted value*.

Note the differences from Equation 3.1—there are lots of hats and no ϵ_i. This is the equation for the **regression line** defined by the estimated $\hat{\beta}_0$ and $\hat{\beta}_1$ parameters and X_i.

▶ **regression line** The fitted line from a regression.

A fitted value tells us what we would expect the value of Y to be, given the value of the X variable for that observation. To calculate a fitted value for any value of X, use Equation 3.3. Or, if we plot the line, we can simply look for the value of the regression line at that value of X. All observations with the same value of X_i will have the same $\hat{Y}_i$, which is the fitted value of Y for observation i. Fitted values are also called predicted values.

A **residual** measures the distance between the fitted value and an actual observation. In the true model, the error, ϵ_i, is that part of Y_i not explained by $\beta_0 + \beta_1 X_i$. The residual is the estimated counterpart to the error. It is the portion of Y_i not explained by $\hat{\beta}_0 + \hat{\beta}_1 X_i$ (notice the hats). If our coefficient estimates exactly equaled the true values, then the residual would be the error; in reality, of course, our estimates $\hat{\beta}_0$ and $\hat{\beta}_1$ will not equal the true values β_0 and β_1, meaning that our residuals will differ from the error in the true model.

▶ **residual** The difference between the fitted value and the observed value.

The residual for observation i is $\hat{\epsilon}_i = Y_i - \hat{Y}_i$. Equivalently, we can say a residual is $\hat{\epsilon}_i = Y_i - \hat{\beta}_0 - \hat{\beta}_1 X_i$. We indicate residuals with $\hat{\epsilon}$ ("epsilon-hat"). As with the β's, a Greek letter with a hat is an *estimate* of the true value. The residual $\hat{\epsilon}_i$ is distinct from ϵ_i, which is how we denote the true, but not directly observed, error.

Estimation

The OLS estimation strategy is to identify values of $\hat{\beta}_0$ and $\hat{\beta}_1$ that define a line that minimizes the sum of the squared residuals. We square the residuals because

---

[3] Another common notation is to refer to estimates with regular letters rather than Greek letters (e.g., b_0 and b_1). That's perfectly fine, too, of course, but we stick with the hat notation for consistency throughout this book.

we want to treat a residual of +7 (as when an observed Y_i is 7 units above the fitted line) as equally undesirable as a residual of −7 (as when an observed Y_i is 7 units below the fitted line). Squaring the residuals converts all residuals to positive numbers. Our +7 residual and −7 residual observations will both register as +49 in the sum of squared residuals.

Specifically, the expression for the sum of squared residuals for any given estimates of $\hat{\beta}_0$ and $\hat{\beta}_1$ is

$$\sum_{i=1}^{N} \hat{\epsilon}_i^2 = \sum_{i=1}^{N} (Y_i - \hat{\beta}_0 - \hat{\beta}_1 X_i)^2$$

The OLS process finds the $\hat{\beta}_1$ and $\hat{\beta}_0$ that minimize the sum of squared residuals. The "squares" in "ordinary least squares" comes from the fact that we're squaring the residuals. The "least" bit is from minimizing the sum of squares. The "ordinary" indicates that we haven't progressed to anything fancy yet.

As a practical matter, we don't need to carry out the minimization ourselves—we can leave that to the software. The steps are not that hard, though, and we step through a simplified version of the minimization task in Chapter 14 (page 482). This process produces specific equations for the OLS estimates of $\hat{\beta}_0$ and $\hat{\beta}_1$. These equations provide estimates of the slope ($\hat{\beta}_1$) and intercept ($\hat{\beta}_0$) combination that characterizes the line that best fits the data.

The OLS estimate of $\hat{\beta}_1$ is

$$\hat{\beta}_1 = \frac{\sum_{i=1}^{N} (X_i - \overline{X})(Y_i - \overline{Y})}{\sum_{i=1}^{N} (X_i - \overline{X})^2} \tag{3.4}$$

where $\overline{X}$ (read as "X bar") is the average value of X and $\overline{Y}$ is the average value of Y.

Equation 3.4 shows that $\hat{\beta}_1$ captures how much X and Y move together. The numerator has $\sum(X_i - \overline{X})(Y_i - \overline{Y})$. The first bit inside the sum is the difference of X from its mean for the ith observation; the second bit is the difference of Y from its mean for the ith observation. The product of these bits is summed over observations. So if Y tends to be *above* its mean [meaning $(Y_i - \overline{Y})$ is positive] when X is above its mean [meaning $(X_i - \overline{X})$ is positive], there will be a bunch of positive elements in the sum in the numerator. If Y tends to be *below* its mean [meaning $(Y_i - \overline{Y})$ is negative] when X is below its mean [meaning $(X_i - \overline{X})$ is negative], we'll also get positive elements in the sum because a negative number times a negative number is positive. Such observations will also push $\hat{\beta}_1$ to be positive.

On the other hand, $\hat{\beta}_1$ will be negative when the signs of the $X_i - \overline{X}$ and $Y_i - \overline{Y}$ are mostly opposite signs. For example, if X is above its mean [meaning $(X_i - \overline{X})$

is positive] when Y is below its mean [meaning $(Y_i - \overline{Y})$ is negative], we'll get negative elements in the sum and $\hat{\beta}_1$ will tend to be negative.[4]

The OLS equation for $\hat{\beta}_0$ is easy once we have $\hat{\beta}_1$. It is

$$\hat{\beta}_0 = \overline{Y} - \hat{\beta}_1 \overline{X} \tag{3.5}$$

We focus on the equation for $\hat{\beta}_1$ because this is the parameter that defines the relationship between X and Y, which is what we usually care most about.

Bivariate OLS and presidential elections

For the election and income data plotted in Figure 3.2, the equations for $\hat{\beta}_0$ and $\hat{\beta}_1$ produce the following estimates:

$$\textit{Incumbent } \widehat{\textit{party vote share}}_i = \hat{\beta}_0 + \hat{\beta}_1 \textit{Income change}_i$$
$$= 45.9 + 2.3 \times \textit{Income change}_i$$

Figure 3.2 shows what these coefficient estimates mean. The $\hat{\beta}_1$ estimate implies that the incumbent party's vote percentage went up by 2.3 percentage points for each one-percent increase in income. The $\hat{\beta}_0$ estimate implies that the expected election vote share for the incumbent president's party for a year with zero income growth was 45.9 percent.

Table 3.1 and Figure 3.3 show predicted values and residuals for specific presidential elections. In 1960, income growth was rather low (at 0.58 percent). The vote percentage for the Republicans (who controlled the presidency at the time of the election) was 49.9 (Republican Richard Nixon lost a squeaker to Democrat John F. Kennedy). The fitted value, denoted by a triangle in Figure 3.3, is $45.9 + 2.3 \times 0.58 = 47.2$. The residual, which is the difference between the actual and fitted, is $49.9 - 47.2 = 2.7$ percent. In other words, in 1960 the incumbent president's party did 2.7 percentage points better than would be expected based on the regression line.

In 1964, income growth was high (at 5.58 percent). The Democrats controlled the presidency at the time of the election, and they received 61.3 percent of the vote (Democrat Lyndon Johnson trounced Republican Barry Goldwater). The fitted value based on the regression line was $45.90 + 2.30 \times 5.58 = 58.7$. The residual, which is the difference between the actual and the fitted, is $61.3 - 58.7 = 2.6$ percent. In other words, in 1964 the incumbent president's party did

---

[4] There is a close affinity between the regression coefficient in bivariate OLS and covariance and correlation. By using the equations for variance and covariance from the appendix (pages 522 and 523) we see that Equation 3.4 can be rewritten as $\frac{\text{cov}(X,Y)}{\text{var}(X)}$. The relationship between covariance and correlation can be used to show that Equation 3.4 can equivalently be written as $\text{corr}(X,Y)\frac{\sigma_Y}{\sigma_X}$, which indicates that the bivariate regression coefficient is simply a rescaled correlation coefficient. The correlation coefficient indicates the strength of the association, while the bivariate regression coefficient indicates the effect of a one-unit increase in X on Y. It's a good lesson to remember. We all know "correlation does not imply causation"; this little nugget tells us that bivariate regression (also!) does not imply causation. The appendix provides additional details (page 524).

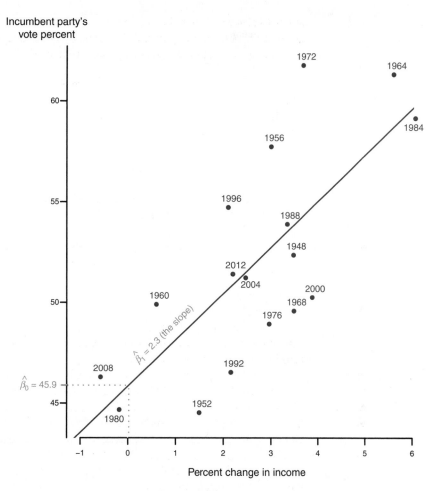

FIGURE 3.2: Elections and Income Growth with Model Parameters Indicated

2.6 percentage points better than would be expected based on the regression line. In 2000, the residual was negative, meaning that the incumbent president's party (the Democrats at that time) did 4.5 percentage points worse than would be expected based on the regression line.

TABLE 3.1 Selected Observations from Election and Income Data

Year	Income change (X)	Incumbent party vote share (Y)	Fitted value ($\hat{Y}$)	Residual ($\hat{\epsilon}$)
1960	0.58	49.9	47.2	2.7
1964	5.58	61.3	58.7	2.6
2000	3.85	50.2	54.7	−4.5

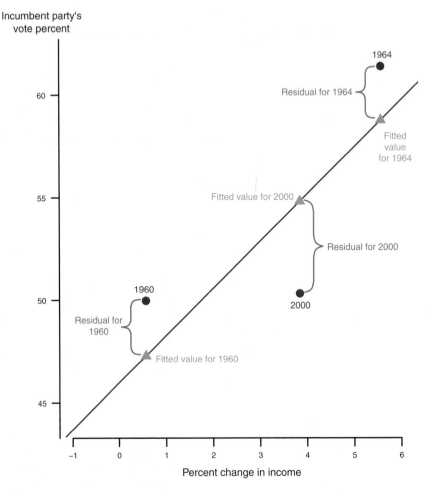

FIGURE 3.3: Fitted Values and Residuals for Observations in Table 3.1

REMEMBER THIS

1. The bivariate regression model is

$$Y_i = \beta_0 + \beta_1 X_i + \epsilon_i$$

- The slope parameter is β_1. It indicates the change in Y associated with an increase of X by one unit.

- The intercept parameter is β_0. It indicates the expected value of Y when X is zero.

- β_1 is almost always more interesting than β_0.

2. OLS estimates $\hat{\beta}_1$ and $\hat{\beta}_0$ by minimizing the sum of squared residuals:

$$\sum_{i=1}^{N} \hat{\epsilon}_i^2 = \sum_{i=1}^{N} (Y_i - \hat{\beta}_0 - \hat{\beta}_1 X_i)^2$$

- A fitted value for observation i is $\hat{Y}_i = \hat{\beta}_0 + \hat{\beta}_1 X_i$.

- The residual for observation i is the difference between the actual and fitted value for person i: $\hat{\epsilon}_i = Y_i - \hat{Y}_i$

3.2 Random Variation in Coefficient Estimates

The goal of bivariate OLS is to get the most accurate idea of β_0 and β_1 that the data can provide. The challenge is that we don't observe the values of the β's. All we can do is *estimate* the true values based on the data we observe. And because the data we observe is random, at least in the sense of containing a random error term, our estimates will have a random element, too.

In this section we explain where the randomness of our coefficient estimates comes from, introduce the concept of probability distributions, and show that our coefficient estimates come from a normal probability distribution.

$\hat{\beta}$ estimates are random

There are two different ways to think about the source of randomness in our coefficient estimates. First, our estimates may have **sampling randomness**. This variation exists because we may be observing only a subset of an entire population. Think of some population, say the population of ferrets in Florida. Suppose we want to know whether old ferrets sleep more. There is some relationship between ferret age and sleep in the overall population, but we are able to get a random sample of only 1,000 ferrets. We estimate the following bivariate OLS model:

$$Sleep_i = \beta_0 + \beta_1 Age_i + \epsilon_i \tag{3.6}$$

Based on the sample we have selected, we generate a coefficient $\hat{\beta}_1$. We're sensible enough to know that if we had selected a different 1,000 ferrets in our random sample we would have gotten a different value of $\hat{\beta}_1$ because the specific values of sleep and age for the selected ferrets would differ. Every time we select a different 1,000 ferrets, we get a different estimate $\hat{\beta}_1$ even though the underlying population relationship is fixed at the true value, β_1. Such variation is called random variation in $\hat{\beta}_1$ due to sampling. Opinion surveys typically involve a random sample of people and are often considered through the sampling variation perspective.

sampling randomness Variation in estimates that is seen in a subset of an entire population. If a given sample had a different selection of people, we would observe a different estimated coefficient.

▌modeled randomness Variation attributable to inherent variation in the data-generation process. This source of randomness exists even when we observe data for an entire population.

Second, our estimates will have **modeled randomness**. Think again of the population of ferrets. Even if we were to get data on every last one of them, our model has random elements. The ferret sleep patterns (the dependent variable) are subject to randomness that goes into the error term. Maybe one ferret had a little too much celery, another got stuck in a drawer, and yet another broke up with his girlferret. Unmeasured factors denoted by ϵ affect ferret sleep, and having data on every single ferret would not change that fact.

In other words, there is inherent randomness in the data-generation process even when data is measured for an entire population. So even if we observe a complete population at any given time, thus eliminating any sampling variation, we will have randomness due to the data-generation process. In other words, virtually every model has some unmeasured component that explains some of the variation in our dependent variable, and the modeled-randomness perspective highlights this.

▌random variable Takes on values in a range and with the probabilities defined by a distribution.

An OLS estimate of $\hat{\beta}_1$ inherits randomness whether from sampling or modeled randomness. The estimate $\hat{\beta}_1$ is therefore a **random variable**, that is, a variable that takes on a set of possible different values, each with some probability. An easy way to see why $\hat{\beta}_1$ is random is to note that it depends on the values of the Y_i's, which in turn depend on the ϵ_i values, which themselves are random.

Distributions of $\hat{\beta}$ estimates

▌distribution The range of possible values for a random variable and the associated relative probabilities for each value.

To understand these random $\hat{\beta}_1$'s, it is best to think of the **distribution** of $\hat{\beta}_1$. That is, we want to think about the various values we expect $\hat{\beta}_1$ to take and the relative likelihood of these values.

Let's start with random variables more generally. A random variable with discrete outcomes can take on one of a finite set of specific outcomes. The flip of a coin or roll of a die yields a random variable with discrete outcomes. These random variables have **probability distributions**. A probability distribution is a graph or formula that identifies the probability for each possible value of a random variable.

▌probability distribution A graph or formula that gives the probability for each possible value of a random variable.

Many probability distributions of random variables are intuitive. We all know the distribution of a coin toss: heads with 50 percent probability and tails with 50 percent probability. Panel (a) of Figure 3.4 plots this data, with the outcome on the horizontal axis and the probability on the vertical axis. We also know the distribution of the roll of a six-sided die. There is a $\frac{1}{6}$ probability of seeing each of the six numbers on it, as panel (b) of Figure 3.4 shows. These are examples of random variables with a specific number of possible outcomes: two (as with a coin toss) or six (as with a roll of a die).

▌continuous variable A variable that takes on any possible value over some range.

This logic of distributions extends to **continuous variables**, which are variables that can take on any value in some range. Weight in our donut example from Chapter 1 is essentially a continuous variable. Because weight can be measured to a very fine degree of precision, we can't simply say there is some specific number of possible outcomes. We don't identify a probability for each

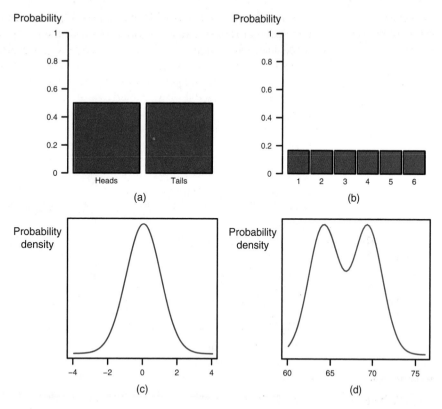

FIGURE 3.4: Four Distributions

possible outcome for continuous variables because there is an unlimited number of possible outcomes. Instead we identify a **probability density**, which is a graph or formula that describes the relative probability that a random variable is near a specified value for the range of possible outcomes for the random variable.

Probability densities run the gamut from familiar to weird. On the familiar end of things is a **normal distribution**, which is the classic bell curve in panel (c) of Figure 3.4. This plot indicates the probability of observing realizations of the random variable in any given range. For example, since half of the area of the density is less than 0, we know that there is a 50 percent chance that this particular normally distributed random variable will be less than zero. Because the probability density is high in the middle and low on the ends, we can say, for example, that the normal random variable plotted in panel (c) is more likely to take on values around zero than values around −4. The odds of observing values around +1 or −1 are still reasonably high, but the odds of observing values near +3 or −3 are small.

Probability densities for random variables can have odd shapes, as in panel (d) of Figure 3.4, which shows a probability density for a random variable that

▶ probability density
A graph or formula that describes the relative probability that a random variable is near a specified value.

▶ normal distribution
A bell-shaped probability density that characterizes the probability of observing outcomes for normally distributed random variables.

has its most likely outcomes near 64 and 69.[5] The point of panel (d) is to make it clear that not all continuous random variables follow the bell-shaped distribution. We could draw a squiggly line and, if it satisfied a few conditions, it too would be a valid probability distribution. We discuss probability densities in more detail in the appendix starting on page 524.

$\hat{\beta}$ estimates are normally distributed

The cool thing about OLS is that for large samples the $\hat{\beta}$'s will be normally distributed random variables. While we can't know exactly what the value of $\hat{\beta}_1$ will be for any given true β_1, we know that the distribution of $\hat{\beta}_1$ will follow a normal bell curve. We'll discuss how to calculate the width of the bell curve in Section 3.4, but knowing the shape of the probability density for $\hat{\beta}_1$ is a huge advantage. The normal distribution has well-known properties and is relatively easy to deal with, making our lives much easier in what is to come.

The normality of our OLS coefficient estimates is amazing. If we have enough data, the distribution $\hat{\beta}_1$ will follow a bell-shaped distribution even if the errors follows a weird distribution like the one in panel (d) of Figure 3.4. In other words, just pour ϵ_i values from any crazy random distribution into our OLS machine, and as long as our sample is large enough, it will spit out $\hat{\beta}_1$ estimates that are normally distributed.[6]

Why is $\hat{\beta}_1$ normally distributed for large samples? The reason is a theorem at the heart of all statistics: the **central limit theorem**. This theorem states that the average of *any* random variable follows a normal distribution.[7] In other words, get a sample of data from some distribution and calculate the average. For example, roll a six-sided die 50 times and calculate the average across the 50 rolls. Then roll the die another 50 times and take the average again. Go through this routine again and again and again and plot a histogram of the averages. If we've produced a large number of averages, the histogram will look like a normal distribution. The most common averages will be around the true average of 3.5 (the average of the six numbers on a die). In some of our sets of 50 rolls we'll see more sixes than usual and those averages will tend to be closer to 4. In other sets of 50 rolls we'll see more ones than usual, and those averages will tend to be closer to 3. Crucially, the shape of the distribution will look more and more like a normal distribution the larger our sample of averages gets.

▶ **central limit theorem** The mean of a sufficiently large number of independent draws from any distribution will be normally distributed.

---

[5] The distribution of adult heights measured in inches looks something like this. What explains the two bumps in the distribution?

[6] If the errors in the model (the ϵ's) are normally distributed, then the $\hat{\beta}_1$ will be normally distributed *no matter what the sample size is*. Therefore in small samples, if we could make ourselves believe the errors are normally distributed, that belief would be a basis for treating the $\hat{\beta}_1$ as coming from a normal distribution. Unfortunately, many people doubt that errors are normally distributed in most empirical models. Some statisticians therefore pour a great deal of energy into assessing whether errors are normally distributed (just Google "normality of errors"). But we don't need to worry about this debate as long as we have a large sample.

[7] Some technical assumptions are necessary. For example, the "distribution" of the values of the error term cannot consist solely of a single number.

Even though the central limit theorem is about averages, it is relevant for OLS. Econometricians deriving the distribution of $\hat{\beta}_1$ invoke the central limit theorem to prove that $\hat{\beta}_1$ will be normally distributed for a sufficiently large sample size.[8]

What sample size is big enough for the central limit theorem and, therefore, normality to kick in? There is no hard-and-fast rule, but the general expectation is that around 100 observations is enough. If we have data with some really extreme outliers or other pathological cases, we may need a larger sample size. Happily, though, the normality of the $\hat{\beta}_1$ distribution generally applies even for data with as few as 100 observations.

REMEMBER THIS

1. Randomness in coefficient estimates can be the result of

- Sampling variation, which arises due to variation in the observations selected into the sample. Each time a different random sample is analyzed, a different estimate of $\hat{\beta}_1$ will be produced even though the population (or "true") relationship is fixed.

- Modeled variation, which arises because of inherent uncertainty in outcomes. Virtually any data set has unmeasured randomness, whether the data set covers all observations in a population or some subsample (random or not).

2. The central limit theorem implies the $\hat{\beta}_0$ and $\hat{\beta}_1$ coefficients will be normally distributed random variables if the sample size is sufficiently large.

3.3 Exogeneity and Unbiasedness

We know that $\hat{\beta}_1$ is not simply the true value β_1; it is an estimate, after all. But how does $\hat{\beta}_1$ relate to β_1? In this section we introduce the concept of unbiasedness, explain the condition under which our estimates are unbiased, and characterize the nature of the bias when this condition is not satisfied.

---

[8] One way to see why is to think of the OLS equation for $\hat{\beta}_1$ as a weighted average of the dependent variable. That's not super obvious, but if we squint our eyes and look at Equation 3.4, we see that we could rewrite it as $\hat{\beta}_1 = \sum_{i=1}^{N} w_i(Y_i - \overline{Y})$, where $w_i = \frac{(X_i - \overline{X})}{\sum_{i=1}^{N}(X_i - \overline{X})^2}$. (We have to squint really hard!) In other words, we can think of the $\hat{\beta}_1$'s as a weighted sum of the Y_i's, where w_i is the weight (and we happen to subtract the mean of Y from each Y_i). It's not to hard to get from a weighted sum to an average [rewrite the denominator of w_i as $N \text{var}(X)$]. Doing so opens the door for the central limit theorem (which is, after all, about averages) to work its magic and establish that $\hat{\beta}_1$ will be normally distributed for large samples.

Conditions for unbiased estimates

▶ **unbiased estimator**
An unbiased coefficient estimate will on average equal the true value of the parameter.

▶ **bias** A biased coefficient estimate will systematically be higher or lower than the true value.

Perhaps the central concept of this whole book is that $\hat{\beta}_1$ is an **unbiased estimator** of the true value β_1 when X is uncorrelated with ϵ. This concept is important; go slowly if it is new to you.

In ordinary conversation we say a source of information is biased if it slants things against the truth. The statistical concept of **bias** is rather close. For example, our estimate $\hat{\beta}_1$ would be biased if the $\hat{\beta}_1$'s we observe are usually around -12 but the true value of β_1 is 16. In other words, if our system of generating a $\hat{\beta}_1$ estimate was likely to produce a negative value when the true value was 16, we'd say the estimating procedure was biased. As we discuss here, such bias happens a lot (and the villain is almost always endogeneity).

Our estimate $\hat{\beta}_1$ is unbiased if the average value of the distribution of the $\hat{\beta}_1$ is equal to the true value. An unbiased distribution will look like Figure 3.5, which shows a distribution of $\hat{\beta}_1$'s centered around the true value of β_1. The good news about an unbiased estimator is that on average, our $\hat{\beta}_1$ should be pretty good. The bad news is that any given $\hat{\beta}_1$ could be far from true value, depending on how wide the distribution is and on luck—by chance alone we could get a value at the low or high end of the distribution.

In other words, unbiased does not mean perfect. It just means that, in general, there is no systematic tendency to be too high or too low. If the distribution of $\hat{\beta}_1$

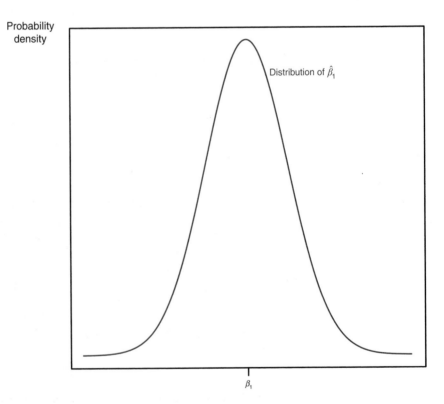

FIGURE 3.5: Distribution of $\hat{\beta}_1$

happens to be quite wide, even though the average is the true value, we might still observe values of $\hat{\beta}_1$ that are far from the true value, β_1.

Think of the figure skating judges at the Olympics. Some are biased—perhaps blinded by nationalism or wads of cash—and they systematically give certain skaters higher or lower scores than the skaters deserve. Other judges (most?) are not biased. These judges do not get the right answer every time.[9] Sometimes an unbiased judge will give a score that is higher than it should be, sometimes lower. Similarly, an OLS regression coefficient $\hat{\beta}_1$ that qualifies as an unbiased estimate of β_1 can be too high or too low in a given application.

Here are two thought experiments that shed light on unbiasedness. First, let's approach the issue from the sampling-randomness framework from Section 3.2. Suppose we select a sample of people, measure some dependent variable Y_i and independent variable X_i for each, and use those to estimate the OLS $\hat{\beta}_1$. We write that down and then select another sample of people, get the data, estimate the OLS model again, and write down the new estimate of $\hat{\beta}_1$. The new estimate will be different because we'll have different people in our data set. Repeat the process again and again and write down all the different $\hat{\beta}_1$'s and then calculate the average of the estimated $\hat{\beta}_1$'s. While any given realization of $\hat{\beta}_1$ could be far from the true value, we will call the estimates unbiased if the average of the $\hat{\beta}_1$'s is the true value, β_1.

We can also approach the issue from the modeled-randomness framework from Section 3.2. Suppose we generate our data. We set the true β_1 and β_0 values as some specific values. We also fix the value of X_i for each observation. Then we draw the ϵ_i for each observation from some random distribution. These values will come together in our standard equation to produce values of Y that we then use in the OLS equation for $\hat{\beta}_1$. Then we repeat the process of generating random error terms (while keeping the true β and X values the same). Doing so produces another set of Y_i values and a different OLS estimate for $\hat{\beta}_1$. We keep running this process a bunch of times, writing down the $\hat{\beta}_1$ estimates from each run. If the average of the $\hat{\beta}_1$'s we have recorded is equal to the true value β_1, then we say that $\hat{\beta}_1$ is an unbiased estimator of β_1.

OLS does not automatically produce unbiased coefficient estimates. A crucial condition must be satisfied for OLS estimates to be unbiased: the error term cannot be correlated with the independent variable. The exogeneity condition, which we discussed in Chapter 1, is at the heart of everything. If this condition is violated, then something in the error term is correlated with our independent variable, and there is a chance that it will contaminate the observed relationship between X and Y. In other words, while observing large values of Y associated with large values of X naturally inclines us to think X pushes Y higher, we worry that something in the error term that is big when X is big is actually what is causing Y to be high. In that case, the relationship between X and Y is spurious and the real causal influence is that unidentified factor in the error term.

---

[9] We'll set aside for now the debate about whether a right answer even exists. Let's imagine there is a score that judges would on average give to a performance if the skater's identity were unknown.

Bias in crime and ice cream example

Almost every interesting relationship between two variables in the policy and economic worlds has some potential for correlation between X and the error term. Let's start with a classic example. Suppose we wonder whether ice cream makes people violent.[10] We estimate the following bivariate OLS model

$$Violent\ crime_t = \beta_0 + \beta_1 Ice\ cream\ sales_t + \epsilon_t \tag{3.7}$$

where violent crime in period t is the dependent variable and ice cream sales in period t is the independent variable. We'd find that $\hat{\beta}_1$ is greater than zero, suggesting crime is indeed higher when ice cream sales go up.

Does this relationship mean that ice cream is causing crime? Maybe. Probably not. OK, no, it doesn't. What's going on? There are a lot of factors in the error term, and one of them is probably truly associated with crime and correlated with ice cream sales. Any guesses? Heat. Heat makes people want ice cream and, it turns out, makes them cranky (or gets them out of doors) such that crime goes up. Hence a bivariate OLS model with just ice cream sales will show a relationship, but because of endogeneity, this relationship is really just correlation, not causation.

Characterizing bias

As a general matter, we can say that as the sample size gets large, the estimated coefficient will on average be off by some function of the correlation between the included variable and the error term. We show in Chapter 14 (page 483) that the expected value of our bivariate OLS estimate is

$$E[\hat{\beta}_1] = \beta_1 + \text{corr}(X,\epsilon)\frac{\sigma_\epsilon}{\sigma_X} \tag{3.8}$$

where $E[\hat{\beta}_1]$ is short for the expectation of $\hat{\beta}_1$, $\text{corr}(X,\epsilon)$ is the correlation of X and ϵ, σ_ϵ (the lowercase Greek letter sigma) is the standard deviation of ϵ, and σ_X is the standard deviation of X. The fraction at the end of the equation is more a normalizing factor, so we don't need to worry too much about it.[11]

The key thing is the correlation of X and ϵ. The bigger this correlation, the further the expected value of $\hat{\beta}_1$ will be from the true value. Or, in other words, the more the independent variable and the error are correlated, the more biased OLS will be.

The rest of this book mostly revolves around what to do if the correlation of X and ϵ is not zero. The ideal solution is to use randomized experiments for which $\text{corr}(X_1,\epsilon)$ is zero by design. But in the real world, experiments often fall prey to challenges discussed in Chapter 10. For observational studies, which are more

---

[10] Why would we ever wonder that? Work with me here. . . .

[11] If we use $\text{corr}(X,\epsilon) = \frac{\text{covariance}(X,\epsilon)}{\sigma_\epsilon \sigma_X}$, we can write Equation 3.8 as $E[\hat{\beta}_1] = \beta_1 + \frac{\text{cov}(X,\epsilon)}{\sigma_X^2}$, where cov is short for *covariance*.

common than experiments, we'll discuss lots of tricks in the rest of this book that help us generate unbiased estimates even when $\text{corr}(X_1, \epsilon)$ is non-zero.

REMEMBER THIS

1. The distribution of an unbiased estimator is centered at the true value, β_1.

2. The OLS estimator $\hat{\beta}_1$ is an unbiased estimator of β_1 if X and ϵ are not correlated.

3. If X and ϵ are correlated, the expected value of $\hat{\beta}_1$ is $\beta_1 + \text{corr}(X, \epsilon)\dfrac{\sigma_\epsilon}{\sigma_X}$.

3.4 Precision of Estimates

There are two ways to get a $\hat{\beta}_1$ estimate that is not close to the true value. One is bias, as discussed earlier. The other is random chance. Our OLS estimates are random, and with the luck of the draw we might get an estimate that's not very good. Therefore, characterizing the variance of our random $\hat{\beta}_1$ estimates will help us appreciate when we should expect estimates near the true value and when we shouldn't. In this section we explain what we mean by "precision of estimates" and provide an equation for the variance of our coefficient estimates.

Estimating coefficients is a bit like trick-or-treating. We show up at a house and reach into a bowl of candy. We're not quite sure what we're going to get. We might get a Snickers (yum!), a Milky Way (not bad), a Mounds bar (trade-bait), or a severed human pinkie (run away!). When we estimate OLS coefficients, it's like we're reaching into a bowl of possible $\hat{\beta}_1$'s and pulling out an estimate. When we reach into the unknown, we never quite know what we'll get.

But we do know certain properties of the $\hat{\beta}_1$'s that went in to the bowl. If the exogeneity condition holds, the average of the $\hat{\beta}_1$'s in the bowl is β_1. It also turns out that we can say a lot about the range of $\hat{\beta}_1$'s in the bowl. We do this by characterizing the width of the $\hat{\beta}_1$ distribution.

To give you a sense of what's at stake, Figure 3.6 shows two distributions for a hypothetical $\hat{\beta}_1$. The lighter, higher curve is much wider than the darker, lower curve. The darker curve is more precise because more of the distribution is near the true value.

▶ **variance** A measure of how much a random variable varies.

The primary measure of precision is the **variance** of $\hat{\beta}_1$. The variance is—you guessed it—a measure of how much something varies. The wider the distribution, the larger its variance. The square root of the variance is the **standard error** (**se**) of $\hat{\beta}_1$. The standard error is a measure of how much $\hat{\beta}_1$ will vary. A large standard error indicates that the distribution of $\hat{\beta}_1$ is very wide; if the standard error is small, the distribution of $\hat{\beta}_1$ is narrower.

▶ **standard error** Refers to the accuracy of a parameter estimate, which is determined by the width of the distribution of the parameter estimate.

We prefer $\hat{\beta}_1$ to have a smaller variance. With smaller variance, values close to the true value are more likely, meaning we're less likely to be far off when we

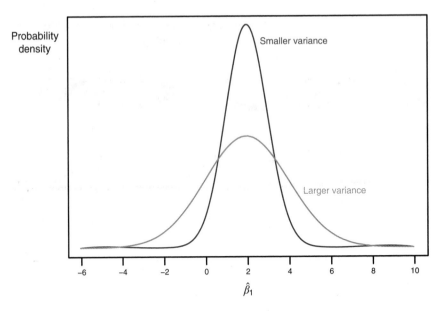

FIGURE 3.6: Two Distributions with Different Variances of $\hat{\beta}_1$

generate the $\hat{\beta}_1$. In other words, our bowl of estimates will be less likely to have wacky stuff in it.

Under the right conditions, we can characterize the variance (and, by extension, the standard error) of $\hat{\beta}_1$ with a simple equation. We discuss the conditions on page 67. If they are satisfied, the estimated variance of $\hat{\beta}_1$ for a bivariate regression is

$$\text{var}(\hat{\beta}_1) = \frac{\hat{\sigma}^2}{N \times \text{var}(X)} \tag{3.9}$$

This equation tells us how wide our distribution of $\hat{\beta}_1$ is.[12] We don't need to calculate the variance of $\hat{\beta}_1$ by hand. That is, after all, why we have computers. We can, however, understand what causes precise or imprecise $\hat{\beta}_1$ estimates by looking at each part of this equation.

First, note that the variance of $\hat{\beta}_1$ depends directly on the **variance of the regression**, $\hat{\sigma}^2$. The variance of the regression measures how well the model explains variation in Y. (And, just to be clear, the variance of the regression is different from the variance of $\hat{\beta}_1$.) That is, do the actual observations cluster fairly closely to the line implied by $\hat{\beta}_0$ and $\hat{\beta}_1$? If so, the fit is pretty good and $\hat{\sigma}^2$ will be low. If the observations are not particularly close to the line implied by the $\hat{\beta}$'s, the fit is pretty poor and $\hat{\sigma}^2$ will be high.

▶ **variance of the regression.** The variance of the regression measures how well the model explains variation in the dependent variable. For large samples, it is estimated as $\hat{\sigma}^2 = \frac{\sum_{i=1}^{N}(Y_i - \hat{Y}_i)^2}{N}$.

[12] We derive a simplified version of the equation on page 487 in the advanced OLS chapter.

We calculate $\hat{\sigma}^2$ based on how far the fitted values are fr
observed values. The equation is

$$\hat{\sigma}^2 = \frac{\sum_{i=1}^{N}(Y_i - \hat{Y}_i)^2}{N - k}$$

$$= \frac{\sum_{i=1}^{N}\hat{\epsilon}_i^2}{N - k} \tag{3.10}$$

which is (essentially) the average squared deviation of fitted values of Y from the actual values. It's not quite an average because the denominator is $N - k$ rather than N. The $N - k$ in the denominator is the **degrees of freedom**, where k is the number of variables (including the constant) in the model.[13]

The more individual observations deviate from their fitted values, the higher $\hat{\sigma}^2$ will be. This is also an estimate of the variance of ϵ in our core model, Equation 3.1.[14]

Next, look at the denominator of the variance of $\hat{\beta}_1$ (Equation 3.9). It is $N \times$ var(X). Yawn. There are, however, two important *substantive* facts in there. First, the bigger the sample size (all else equal), the smaller the variance of $\hat{\beta}_1$. In other words, more data means lower variance. More data is a good thing.

Second, we see that variance of X reduces the variance of $\hat{\beta}_1$. The variance of X is calculated as $\frac{\sum_{i=1}^{N}(X_i - \bar{X})^2}{N}$. In other words, the more our X variable varies, the more precisely we will be able to learn about β_1.[15]

degrees of freedom
The sample size minus the number of parameters. It refers to the amount of information we have available to use in the estimation process.

Review Questions

1. Will the variance of $\hat{\beta}_1$ be smaller in panel (a) or panel (b) of Figure 3.7 on page 64? Why?

2. Will the variance of $\hat{\beta}_1$ be smaller in panel (c) or panel (d) of Figure 3.7 on page 64? Why?

---

[13] For bivariate regression, $k = 2$ because we estimate two parameters ($\hat{\beta}_0$ and $\hat{\beta}_1$). We can think of the degrees of freedom correction as a penalty for each parameter we estimate; it's as if we use up some information in the data with each parameter we estimate and cannot, for example, estimate more parameters than the number of observations we have. If N is large enough, the k in the denominator will have only a small effect on the estimate of $\hat{\sigma}^2$. For small samples, the degrees of freedom issue can matter more. Every statistical package will get this right, and the core intuition is that $\hat{\sigma}^2$ measures the average squared distance between actual and fitted values.

[14] Recall that the variance of $\hat{\epsilon}$ will be $\frac{\sum(\hat{\epsilon}_i - \bar{\hat{\epsilon}})^2}{N}$. The OLS minimization process automatically creates residuals with a average of zero (meaning $\bar{\hat{\epsilon}} = 0$). Hence, the variance of the residuals reduces to Equation 3.10.

[15] Here, we're assuming a large sample. If we had a small sample, we would calculate the variance of X with a degrees of freedom correction such that it would be $\frac{\sum_{i=1}^{N}(X_i - \bar{X})^2}{N-1}$. Doing so would mean we would have $N - 1$ instead of N in the denominator of Equation 3.10, but it would not change the intuition that more data lowers the variance for coefficient estimates.

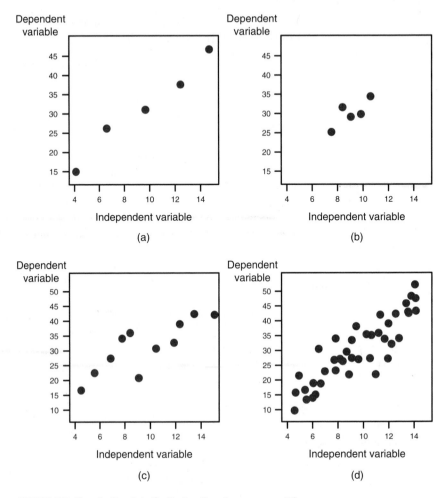

FIGURE 3.7: Four Scatterplots (for Review Questions on page 63)

REMEMBER THIS

1. The variance of $\hat{\beta}_1$ measures the width of the $\hat{\beta}_1$ distribution. If the conditions discussed in Section 3.6, are satisfied, then the estimated variance of $\hat{\beta}_1$ is

$$\text{var}(\hat{\beta}_1) = \frac{\hat{\sigma}^2}{N \times \text{var}(X)}$$

2. Three factors influence the estimated variance of $\hat{\beta}_1$:

    (a) Model fit. The variance of the regression, $\hat{\sigma}^2$, is a measure of how well the model explains variation in Y. It is calculated as

$$\hat{\sigma}^2 = \frac{\sum_{i=1}^{N}(Y_i - \hat{Y}_i)^2}{N - k}$$

    The lower $\hat{\sigma}^2$, the lower will be var$(\hat{\beta}_1)$.

    (b) Sample size. The more observations, the lower var$(\hat{\beta}_1)$.

    (c) Variation in X. The more the X variable varies, the lower will be var$(\hat{\beta}_1)$.

3.5 Probability Limits and Consistency

▶ probability limit
The value to which a distribution converges as the sample size gets very large.

The variance of $\hat{\beta}_1$ shrinks as the sample size increases. This section discusses the implications of this fact by introducing the statistical concepts of probability limit and consistency, two concepts that are crucial to econometric analysis.

    The **probability limit** of an estimator is the value to which the estimator converges as the sample size gets very large. Figure 3.8 illustrates the intuition behind probability limit by showing the probability density of $\hat{\beta}_1$ for hypothetical experiments in which the true value of β_1 is zero. The flatter dark curve is the probability density for $\hat{\beta}_1$ for an experiment with $N = 10$ people. The most likely value of $\hat{\beta}_1$ is 0 because this is the place where the density is highest, but there's still a pretty good chance of observing a $\hat{\beta}_1$ near 1.0 and even a reasonable chance of observing a $\hat{\beta}_1$ near 4. For a sample size of 100, the variance shrinks, which means we're less likely to see $\hat{\beta}_1$ values near 4 than we were when the sample size was 10. For a sample size of 1,000, the variance shrinks even more, producing the tall thin distribution. Under this distribution, we're not only unlikely to see $\hat{\beta}_1$ near 4, we're also very unlikely to see $\hat{\beta}_1$ near 2.

    If we were to keep plotting distributions for larger sample sizes, we would see them getting taller and thinner. Eventually the distribution would converge to a vertical line at the true value. If we had an infinite number of observations, we would get the right answer every time. That may be cold comfort if we're stuck with a sad little data set of 37 observations, but it's awesome when we have 100,000 observations.

▶ consistency A consistent estimator is one for which the distribution of the estimate gets closer and closer to the true value as the sample size increases. The OLS estimate $\hat{\beta}_1$ consistently estimates β_1 if X is uncorrelated with ϵ.

    Consistency is an important property of OLS estimates. An estimator, such as OLS, is a consistent estimator if the distribution of $\hat{\beta}_1$ estimates shrinks to be closer and closer to the true value β_1 as we get more data. If the exogeneity condition is true, then $\hat{\beta}_1$ is a consistent estimator of β_1.[16] Formally,

---

[16] There are some more technical conditions necessary for OLS to be consistent. For example, the values of the independent variable have to be meaningful enough to ensure that the variance will

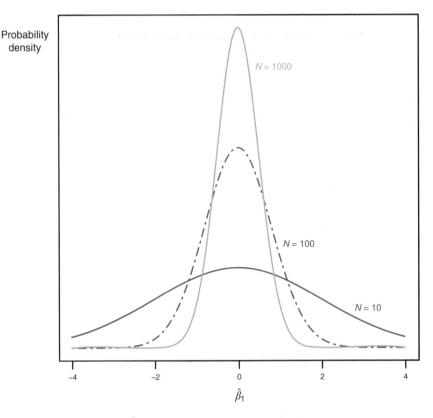

FIGURE 3.8: Distributions of $\hat{\beta}_1$ for Different Sample Sizes

we say

$$\text{plim } \hat{\beta}_1 = \beta_1 \tag{3.11}$$

▶ plim A widely used abbreviation for probability limit, the value to which an estimator converges as the sample size gets very, very large.

where **plim** is short for "probability limit."

Consistency is quite intuitive. If we have only a couple of people in our sample, it is unreasonable to expect OLS to provide a precise sense of the true value of β_1. If we have a bajillion observations in our sample, our $\hat{\beta}_1$ estimate should be very close to the true value. Suppose, for example, that we wanted to assess the relationship between height and wages in a given classroom. If we base our estimate on information from only one student, we're not very likely to get an accurate estimate. If we ask 10 students, our answer is likely to be closer to the true relationship in the the classroom, and if we ask 20 students, we're even more likely to be closer to the true relationship.

Under some circumstances an OLS or other estimator will be inconsistent, meaning it will converge to a value other than the true value. Even though the

_____

actually get smaller as the sample increases. If we simply add X values that always equal 0, this condition might not be satisfied.

details can get pretty technical, the probability limit of an estimator is often easier to work with than the expectation. This is why statisticians routinely characterize problems in terms of probability limits that deviate from the true value. We see an example of probability limits that go awry when we assess the influence of measurement error in Section 5.3.[17]

REMEMBER THIS

1. The probability limit of an estimator is the value to which the estimator converges as the sample size gets very, very large.

2. When the error term and X are uncorrelated, OLS estimates of β are consistent, meaning that plim $\hat{\beta} = \beta$.

3.6 Solvable Problems: Heteroscedasticity and Correlated Errors

Equation 3.9 on page 62 accurately characterizes the variance of $\hat{\beta}_1$ when certain conditions about the error term are true. In this section, we explain those conditions. If these conditions do not hold, the calculation of the variance of $\hat{\beta}_1$ will be more involved, but the intuition we have introduced about $\hat{\sigma}^2$, sample size, and variation in X will carry through. We discuss the calculation of $\text{var}(\hat{\beta}_1)$ under these circumstances in this section and in Chapter 13.

Homoscedasticity

The first condition for Equation 3.9 to be appropriate is that the variance of ϵ_i must be the same for every observation. That is, once we have taken into account the effect of our measured variable (X), the expected degree of uncertainty in the model must be the same for all observations. If this condition holds, the variance of the error term is the same for low values of X as for high values of X. This condition gets a fancy name, *homoscedasticity*. "Homo" means same. "Scedastic" (yes, that's a word) means variance. Hence, errors are **homoscedastic** when they all have the same variance.

homoscedastic
Describing a random variable having the same variance for all observations.

When errors violate this condition, they are **heteroscedastic**, meaning that the variance of ϵ_i is different for at least some observations. That is, some

heteroscedastic A random variable is heteroscedastic if the variance differs for some observations.

---

[17] The two best things you can say about an estimator is that it is unbiased and consistent. OLS estimators are both unbiased and consistent when the error is uncorrelated with the independent variable. These properties seem pretty similar, but they can be rather different. These differences are typically only relevant in advanced statistical work. For reference, though, we discuss in the appendix on page 539 examples of estimators that are unbiased but not consistent, and vice versa.

observations are on average closer to the predicted value than others. Imagine, for example, that we have data on how much people weigh from two sources: some people weighed themselves with a state-of-the-art scale and others had a guy at a state fair guess their weight. Definite heteroscedasticity there, as the weight estimates on the scale would be very close to the truth (small errors) and the weight estimates from the fair dude will be farther from the truth (large errors).

Violating the homoscedasticity condition doesn't cause OLS $\hat{\beta}_1$ estimates to be biased. It simply means we shouldn't use Equation 3.9 to calculate the variance of $\hat{\beta}_1$. Happily for us, the intuitions we have discussed so far about what causes var($\hat{\beta}_1$) to be big or small are not nullified, and there are relatively simple ways to implement procedures for this case. We show how to generate these **heteroscedasticity-consistent standard errors** in Stata and R in the Computing Corner of this chapter (pages 82 and 85). This approach to accounting for heteroscedasticity does not affect the values of the $\hat{\beta}$ estimates.[18]

> **heteroscedasticity-consistent standard errors** Standard errors for the coefficients in OLS that are appropriate even when errors are heteroscedastic.

Errors uncorrelated with each other

The second condition for Equation 3.9 to provide an appropriate estimate of the variance of $\hat{\beta}_1$ is that the errors must not be correlated with each other. If errors are correlated with each other, knowing the value of the error for one observation provides information about the value of the error for another observation.

There are two fairly common situations in which errors are correlated. The first involves clustered errors. Suppose, for example, we're looking at test scores of all eighth graders in California. It is possible that the unmeasured factors in the error term cluster by school. Maybe one school attracts science nerds and another attracts jocks. If such patterns exist, then knowing the error term for a kid in a school gives some information about error terms of other kids in the same school, which means errors are correlated. In this case, the school is the "cluster" and errors are correlated within the cluster. It's inappropriate to use Equation 3.9 when errors are correlated.

This sounds worrisome. It is, but not terribly so. As with heteroscedasticity, violating the condition that errors must not be correlated doesn't cause an OLS $\hat{\beta}_1$ estimate to be biased. It only renders Equation 3.9 inappropriate. So what should we do if errors are correlated? Get a better equation for the variance of $\hat{\beta}_1$! It's a bit more complicated than that, but the upshot is that it is possible to derive

---

[18] The equation for heteroscedasticity-consistent standard errors is ugly. If you must know, it is

$$\text{var}(\hat{\beta}_1) = \left(\frac{1}{\sum (X_i - \overline{X})^2} \right)^2 \sum (X_i - \overline{X})^2 \hat{\epsilon}_i^2 \tag{3.12}$$

This is less intuitive than in Equation 3.9, so we do not emphasize it. As it turns out, we derive heteroscedasticity-consistent standard errors in the course of deriving the standard errors that assume homoscedasticity (see page 488). Heteroscedasticity-consistent standard errors are also referred to as *robust standard errors* (because they are robust to heteroscedasticity) or as *Huber-White standard errors*. Another approach to dealing with heteroscedasticity is to use "weighted least squares." This approach is more statistically efficient, meaning that the variance of the estimate will theoretically be lower. The technique produces $\hat{\beta}_1$ estimates that differ from the OLS $\hat{\beta}_1$ estimates. We point out references with more details on weighted least squares in the Further Reading section at the end of this chapter.

variance of $\hat{\beta}_1$ when errors are correlated within cluster. We simply note the issue here and use the computational procedures discussed in the Computing Corner to deal with clustered standard errors.

▶**time series data**
Consists of observations for a single unit over time. Time series data is typically contrasted to cross-sectional and panel data.

Correlated errors are also common in **time series data**—that is, data on a specific unit over time. Examples include U.S. growth rates since 1945 or data on annual attendance at New York Yankee games since 1913. Errors in time series data are frequently correlated in a pattern we call **autocorrelation**. Autocorrelation occurs when the error in one time period is correlated with the error in the previous time period.

▶**autocorrelation**
Errors are autocorrelated if the error in one time period is correlated with the error in the previous time period. Autocorrelation is common in time series data.

Correlated errors can occur in time series when an unmeasured variable in the error term is sticky, such that a high value in one year implies a high value in the next year. Suppose, for example, we are modeling annual U.S. economic growth since 1945 and we lack a variable for technological innovation (which is very hard to measure). If technological innovation was in the error term boosting the economy in one year, it probably did some boosting to the error term the next year. Similar autocorrelation is likely in many time series data sets, ranging from average temperature in Tampa over time to monthly Frisbee sales in Frankfurt.

As with the other issues raised in this section, *autocorrelation does not cause bias*. Autocorrelation only renders Equation 3.9 inappropriate. Chapter 13 discusses how to generate appropriate estimates of the variance of $\hat{\beta}_1$ when there is autocorrelation.

It is important to keep these conditions in perspective. Unlike the exogeneity condition (that X and the errors are uncorrelated), we do not need the homoscedasticity and uncorrelated-errors conditions for unbiased estimates. When these conditions fail, we simply do some additional steps to get back to a correct equation for the variance of $\hat{\beta}_1$. Violations of these conditions may seem to be especially important because they have fancy labels like "heteroscedasticity" and "autocorrelation." They are not. The exogeneity condition matters much more.

REMEMBER THIS

1. The standard equation for the variance of $\hat{\beta}_1$ (Equation 3.9) requires errors to be homoscedastic and uncorrelated with each other.

   - Errors are homoscedastic if their variance is constant. When errors are heteroscedastic, the variance of errors is different across observations.

   - Correlated errors commonly occur in clustered data in which the error for one observation is correlated with the error of another observation from the same cluster (such as a school).

   - Correlated errors are also common in time series data where errors are autocorrelated, meaning the error in one period is correlated with the error in the previous period.

2. Violating the homoscedasticity or uncorrelated-error conditions does *not* bias OLS coefficients.

Discussion Questions

Come up with an example of an interesting relationship you would like to test.

1. Write down a bivariate OLS model for this relationship.

2. Discuss what is in the error term and whether you suspect endogeneity.

3. Approximate how many observations you would expect to have (speculate if necessary). What are the implications for the econometric analysis? Focus on the effect of sample size on unbiasedness and precision.

4. Do you suspect heteroscedasticity or correlated errors? Why or why not? Explain the implications of your answer for your OLS model.

3.7 Goodness of Fit

▶ **goodness of fit** How well a model fits the data.

Goodness of fit is a statistical concept that refers to how well a model fits the data. If a model fits well, knowing X gives us a pretty good idea of what Y will be. If the model fits poorly, knowing X doesn't give as good an idea of what Y will be. In this section we present three ways to characterize the goodness of fit. We should not worry too much about goodness of fit, however, as we can have useful, interesting results from models with poor fit and biased, useless results from models with great fit.

Standard error of the regression ($\hat{\sigma}$)

▶ **standard error of the regression** A measure of how well the model fits the data. It is the square root of the variance of the regression.

We've already seen one goodness of fit measure, the variance of the regression (denoted as $\hat{\sigma}^2$). One limitation with this measure is that the scale is not intuitive. For example, if our dependent variable is salary, the variance of the regression will be measured in dollars squared (which is odd).

Therefore the **standard error of the regression** is commonly used as a measure of goodness of fit. It is simply the square root of the variance of the regression and is denoted as $\hat{\sigma}$. It corresponds, roughly, to the average distance of observations from fitted values. The scale of this measure will be the same units as the dependent variable, making it much easier to relate to.

The trickiest thing about the standard error of the regression may be that it goes by so many different names. Stata refers to $\hat{\sigma}$ as the *root mean squared error* (or *root MSE* for short); *root* refers to the square root and *MSE* refers to mean squared error, which is how we calculate $\hat{\sigma}^2$, or the mean of the squared residuals. R refers to $\hat{\sigma}^2$ as the *residual standard error* because it is the estimated standard error for the errors in the model based on the residuals.

Plot of the data

Another way to assess goodness of fit is to plot the data
close the observations are to the fitted line. Plotting al
or other surprises in the data. Assessing goodness of fit based o.
is pretty subjective, though, and hard to communicate to others.

R^2

Finally, a very common measure of goodness of fit is R^2, so named because it
is a measure of the squared correlation of the fitted values and actual values.[19]
Correlation is often indicated with an "r," so R^2 is simply the square of this value.
(Why one is lowercase and the other is uppercase is one of life's little mysteries.)

If the model explains the data well, the fitted values will be highly correlated
with the actual values and R^2 will be high. If the model does not explain the data
well, the fitted values will not correlate very highly with the actual values and R^2
will be near zero. Possible values of R^2 range from 0 to 1.[20]

R^2 values often help us understand how well our model predicts the
dependent variable, but the measure may be less useful than it seems. A high R^2
is neither necessary nor sufficient for an analysis to be useful. A high R^2 means
the predicted values are close to the actual values. It says nothing more. We can
have a model loaded with endogeneity that generates a high R^2. The high R^2 in
this case means nothing; the model is junk, the high R^2 notwithstanding. And to
make matters worse, some people have the intuition that a good fit is necessary
for believing regression results. This intuition isn't correct, either. There is no
minimum value we need for a good regression. In fact, it is very common for
experiments (the gold standard of statistical analyses) to have low R^2 values.
There can be all kinds of reasons for low R^2—the world could be messy, such that
σ^2 is high, for example—but the model could nonetheless yield valuable insight.

Figure 3.9 shows various goodness of fit measures for OLS estimates of
two different hypothetical data sets of salary at age 30 (measured in thousands
of dollars) and years of education. In panel (a), the observations are pretty
closely clustered around the regression line. That's a good fit. The variance of
the regression is 91.62; it's not really clear what to make of that, however, until
we look at its square root, $\hat{\sigma}$ (also known as the standard error of the regression,
among other terms) which is 9.57. Roughly speaking, this value of the standard
error of the regression means that the observations are on average within 9.57
units of their fitted values.[21] From this definition, therefore, on average the fitted
values are within \$9,570 of actual salary. The R^2 is 0.89. That's pretty high. Is
that value high enough? We can't answer that question because it is not a sensible
question for R^2 values.

---

[19] This interpretation works only if an intercept is included in the model, which it usually is.

[20] The value of R^2 also represents the ratio of the variance of the fitted values to the actual variance of
Y. It is therefore also referred to as a measure of the proportion of the variance explained.

[21] We say "roughly speaking" because this value is actually the square root of the average of the
squared residuals. The intuition for that value is the same, but it's quite a mouthful.

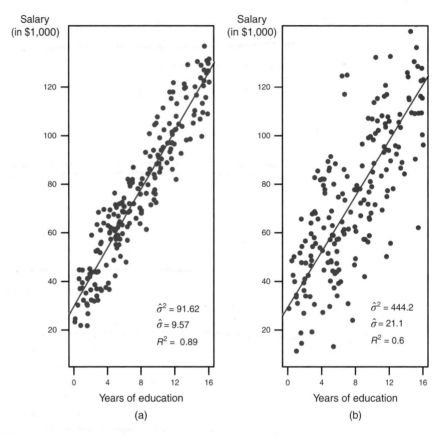

FIGURE 3.9: Plots with Different Goodness of Fit

In panel (b) of Figure 3.9, the observations are more widely dispersed. Not as good a fit. The variance of the regression is 444.2. As with panel (a), it's not really clear what to make of that variance until we look at its square root, $\hat{\sigma}$, which is 21.1. This value means that the observations are on average within \$21,100 of actual salary. The R^2 is 0.6. Is that good enough? Silly question.

REMEMBER THIS

There are four ways to assess goodness of fit.

1. The variance of the regression ($\hat{\sigma}^2$). This value is used in the equation for $\text{var}(\hat{\beta}_1)$. It is hard to interpret directly.

2. The standard error of the regression ($\hat{\sigma}$). It is measured on the same scale as the dependent variable and roughly corresponds to the average distance between fitted values and actual values.

3. Scatterplots can be quite informative, not only about goodness of fit but also about possible anomalies and outliers.

4. R^2 is a widely used measure of goodness of fit.

   - It is the square of the correlation between the fitted and observed values of the dependent variable.

   - R^2 ranges from 0 to 1.

   - A high R^2 is neither necessary nor sufficient for an analysis to be useful.

CASE STUDY   ## Height and Wages

You may have heard that tall people get paid more—and not just in the NBA. If true, that makes us worry about what exactly our economy and society are rewarding.

Persico, Postlewaite, and Silverman (2004) tested this idea by analyzing data on height and wages from a nationally representative sample. Much of their analysis used the multivariate techniques we'll discuss in Chapter 5, but let's use bivariate OLS to start thinking about the issue. The researchers limited their data set to white males to avoid potentially important (and unfair) influences of race and gender on wages. (We look at other groups in the homework for Chapter 5.)

Figure 3.10 shows the data. On the X-axis is the adult height of each guy and on the Y-axis is his wage in 1996. The relationship is messy, but that's not unusual. Data is at least as messy as life.[22]

The figure includes a fitted regression line based on the following regression model:

$$Wage_i = \beta_0 + \beta_1 Adult\ height_i + \epsilon_i$$

The results reported in Table 3.2 look pretty much like the results any statistical software will burp out. The estimated coefficient on adult height $(\hat{\beta}_1)$ is 0.412. The standard error estimate will vary depending on whether

---

[22] The data is adjusted in two ways for the figure. First, we jitter the data to deal with the problem that many observations overlap perfectly because they have the same values of X and Y. Jittering adds a small random number to the height, causing each observation to be at a slightly different point. If there are only two observations with the same specific combination of X and Y values, the jittered data will show two circles, probably overlapping a bit. If there are many observations with some specific combination of X and Y values, the jittered data will show many circles, overlapping a bit, but creating a cloud of data that indicates lots of data near that point. We don't use jittered data in the statistical analysis; we use jittered data only for plotting data. Second, six outliers who made a ton of money ($750 per hour for one of them!) are excluded. If they were included, the scatterplot would be so tall that most observations would get scrunched up at the bottom.

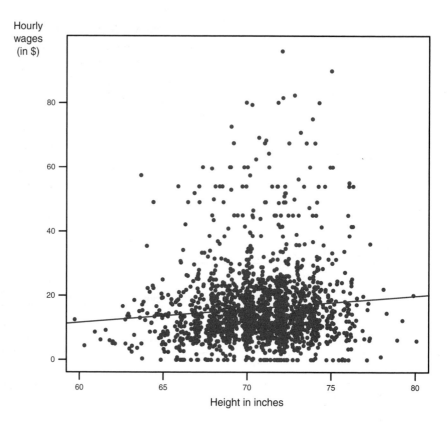

FIGURE 3.10: Height and Wages

we assume errors are or are not homoscedastic. The column on the left shows that if we assume homoscedasticity (and therefore use Equation 3.9), the estimated standard error of $\hat{\beta}_1$ is 0.0976. The column on the right shows that if we allow for heteroscedasticity, the estimated standard error for $\hat{\beta}_1$ is 0.0953. This isn't much of a difference, but the two approaches to estimating standard errors can differ more substantially for other examples. The estimated constant ($\hat{\beta}_0$) is −13.093 with estimated standard error estimates of 6.897 and 6.691, depending on whether or not we use heteroscedasticity-consistent standard errors.

Notice that the $\hat{\beta}_0$ and $\hat{\beta}_1$ coefficients are identical across the columns, as the heteroscedasticity consistent standard error estimate has no effect on the coefficient.

What, exactly, do these numbers mean? First, let's interpret the slope coefficient, $\hat{\beta}_1$. A coefficient of 0.41 on height implies that a one-inch increase in height is associated with an increase in wages of 41 cents per hour. That's a lot![23]

---

[23] To put that estimate in perspective, we can calculate how much being an inch taller is worth per year for someone who works 40 hours a week for 50 weeks per year: it is $0.41 \times 1 \times 40 \times 50 = \$820$

TABLE 3.2 Effect of Height on Wages		
Variable	Assuming homoscedasticity	Allowing heteroscedasticity
Adult height	0.412	0.412
	(0.0976)	(0.0953)
Constant	−13.093	−13.093
	(6.897)	(6.691)
N	1,910	1,910
$\hat{\sigma}^2$	142.4	142.4
$\hat{\sigma}$	11.93	11.93
R^2	0.009	0.009

Standard errors in parentheses.

The interpretation of the constant, $\hat{\beta}_0$, is that someone who is zero inches tall would get negative $13.09 dollars an hour. Hmmm. Not the most helpful piece of information. What's going on is that most observations of height (the X variable) are far from zero (they are mostly between 60 and 75 inches). For the regression line to go through this data, it must cross the Y-axis at −13.09 for people who are zero inches tall. This example explains why we don't spend a lot of time on $\hat{\beta}_0$. It's hard to imagine what kind of sicko would want to know—or believe—the extrapolation of our results to such little tiny people.

If we don't care about $\hat{\beta}_0$ why do we have it in the model? It plays a very important role. Remember that we're fitting a line, and the value of $\hat{\beta}_0$ pins down where the line starts when X is zero. Failing to estimate the parameter is the same as setting $\hat{\beta}_0$ to be zero (because the fitted value would be $\hat{Y}_i = \hat{\beta}_1 X_i$, which is zero when $X_i = 0$). Forcing $\hat{\beta}_0$ to be zero will typically lead to a much worse model fit than letting the data tell us where the line should cross the Y-axis when X is zero.

The results are not only about the estimated coefficients. They also include standard errors, which are quite important as they give us a sense of how accurate our estimates are. The standard error estimates come from the data and tell us how wide the distribution of $\hat{\beta}_1$ is. If the standard error of $\hat{\beta}_1$ is huge, then we should not have much confidence that our $\hat{\beta}_1$ is necessarily close to the true value. If the standard error of $\hat{\beta}_1$ is small, then we should have more confidence that our $\hat{\beta}_1$ is close to the true value.

Are these results the final word on the relationship between height and wages? (*Hint*: NO!) As for most observational data, a bivariate analysis may not be sufficient. We should worry about endogeneity. In other words, there could be elements in the error term (factors that influence wages but have not been

---

per year. Being 3 inches taller is associated with earning $0.41 \times 3 \times 40 \times 50 = \$2,460$ more per year. Being tall has its costs, though: tall people live shorter lives (Palmer 2013).

included in the model) that could be correlated with adult height and, if so, then the result that height causes wages to go up may be incorrect. Can you think of anything in the error term that is correlated with height? We come back to this question in Chapter 5 (page 132), where we revisit this data set.

Table 3.2 also shows several goodness of fit measures. The $\hat{\sigma}^2$ is 142.4; this number is pretty hard to get our heads around. Much more useful is the standard error of the regression, $\hat{\sigma}$, which is 11.93, meaning roughly that the average distance between fitted and actual heights is almost $12 per hour. In other words, the fitted values really aren't particularly accurate. The R^2 is close to 0.01. This value is low, but as we said earlier, there is no set standard for R^2.

One reasonable concern might be that we should be wary of the OLS results because the model fit seems pretty poor. That's not how it works. The coefficients provide the best estimates, given the data. The standard errors of the coefficients incorporate the poor fit (via the $\hat{\sigma}^2$). So, yes, the poor fit matters, but it's incorporated into the OLS estimation process.

3.8 Outliers

▶ outlier An observation that is extremely different from those in the rest of sample.

One practical concern we have in statistics is dealing with **outliers**, observations that are extremely different from the rest of sample. The concern is that a single goofy observation can skew the analysis.

We saw on page 31 that Washington, DC, is quite an outlier in a plot of crime data for the U.S. Figure 3.11 shows a scatterplot of violent crime and percent urban. Imagine drawing an OLS line by hand when the nation's capital is included. Then imagine drawing an OLS line by hand when it's excluded. The line with Washington, DC, will be steeper, as will be necessary to get close to the observation for Washington, DC; the other line will be flatter because it can stay in the mass of the data without worrying about Washington, DC. Hence a reasonable person may worry that the DC data point could substantially influence the estimate. On the other hand, if we were to remove an observation in the middle of the mass of the data, such as Oklahoma, the estimated line would move little.

We can see the effect of including and excluding DC in Table 3.3, which shows bivariate OLS results in which violent crime rate is the dependent variable. In the first column, percent urban is the independent variable and all states plus DC are included (therefore the N is 51). The coefficient is 5.61 with a standard error of 1.8. The results in the second column are based on data without Washington, DC (dropping the N to 50). The coefficient is quite a bit smaller, coming in at 3.58, which is consistent with our intuition from our imaginary line drawing.

The table also shows bivariate OLS coefficients for a model with single-parent percent as the independent variable. The coefficient when we include DC is 23.17. When we exclude DC, the estimated relationship weakens to 16.91. We see a similar pattern with crime and poverty percent in the last two columns.

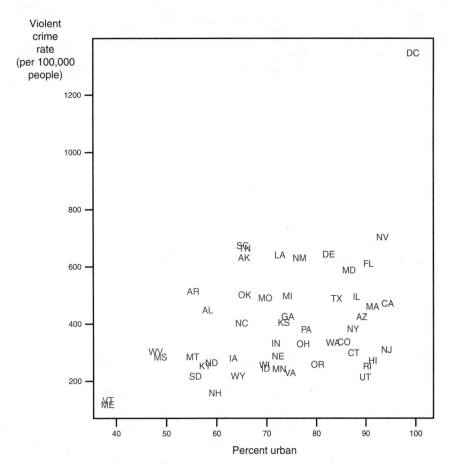

FIGURE 3.11: Scatterplot of Violent Crime and Percent Urban

TABLE 3.3 OLS Models of Crime in U.S. States

	With DC	Without DC	With DC	Without DC	With DC	Without DC
Urban	5.61	3.58				
	(1.80)	(1.47)				
Single parent			23.17	16.91		
			(3.03)	(3.55)		
Poverty					23.13	14.73
					(8.85)	(7.06)
Constant	−8.37	124.67	−362.74	−164.57	86.12	184.94
	(135.57)	(109.56)	(102.58)	(117.59)	(125.55)	(99.55)
N	51	50	51	50	51	50
R^2	0.17	0.11	0.54	0.32	0.12	0.08

Standard errors in parentheses.

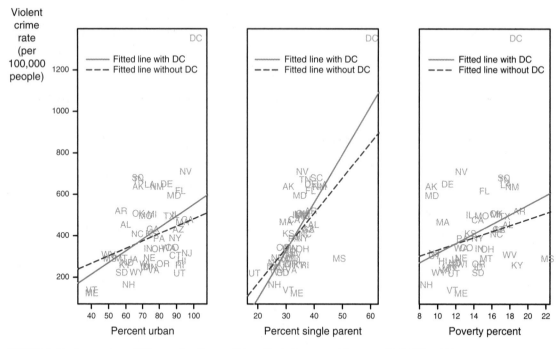

FIGURE 3.12: Scatterplots of Crime against Percent Urban, Single Parent, and Poverty with OLS Fitted Lines

Figure 3.12 shows scatterplots of the data with the fitted lines included. The fitted lines based on all data are the solid lines and the fitted lines when DC is excluded are the dashed lines. In every case, the fitted lines including DC are steeper than the fitted lines when DC is excluded.

So what are we to conclude here? Which results are correct? There may be no clear answer. The important thing is to appreciate that the results in these cases depend on a single observation. In such cases, we need to let the world know. We should show results with and without the excluded observation and justify substantively why an observation might merit exclusion. In the case of the crime data, for example, we could exclude DC on the grounds that it is not (yet!) a state.

Outlier observations are more likely to influence OLS results when the number of observations is small. Given that OLS will minimize the sum of squared residuals from the fitted line, a single observation is more likely to play a big role when only a few residuals must be summed. When data sets are very large, a single observation is less likely to move the fitted line substantially.

An excellent way to identify potentially influential observations is to plot the data and look for unusual observations. If an observation looks out of whack, it's a good idea to run the analysis without it to see if the results change. If they do, explain the situation to readers and justify including or excluding the outlier.[24]

---

[24] Most statistical packages provide tools to assess the influence of each observation. For a sample size N, these commands essentially run N separate OLS models, each one excluding a different

> # REMEMBER THIS
>
> Outliers are observations that are very different from other observations.
>
> 1. When sample sizes are small, a single outlier can exert considerable influence on OLS coefficient estimates.
> 2. Scatterplots are useful in identifying outliers.
> 3. When a single observation substantially influences coefficient estimates, we should
>   - Inform readers of the issue.
>   - Report results with and without the influential observation.
>   - Justify including or excluding that observation.

Conclusion

Ordinary least squares is an odd name that refers to the way in which the $\hat{\beta}$ estimates are produced. That's fine to know, but the real key to understanding OLS is appreciating the properties of the estimates produced.

The most important property of OLS estimates is that they are unbiased if X is uncorrelated with the error. We've all heard "correlation does not imply causation." "Regression does not imply causation" is every bit as true. If there is endogeneity, we may observe a big regression coefficient even in the absence of causation.

---

observation. For each of these N regressions, the command stores a value indicating how much the coefficient changes when that particular observation is excluded. The resulting output reflects how much the coefficients change with the deletion of each observation. In Stata, the command is `dfbeta`, where the "df" refers to difference and "beta" refers to $\hat{\beta}$. In other words, the command will tell us for each observation the difference in estimated $\hat{\beta}$'s when that observation is deleted. In R, the command is also called `dfbeta`. Google these command names to find more information on how to use them.

OLS estimates have many other useful properties. With a large sample size, $\hat{\beta}_1$ is a normally distributed random variable. The variance of $\hat{\beta}_1$ reflects the width of the $\hat{\beta}_1$ distribution and is determined by the fit of the model (the better the fit, the thinner), the sample size (the more data, the thinner), and the variance of X (the more variance, the thinner). If the errors satisfy the homoscedasticity and no-correlation conditions, the variance of $\hat{\beta}_1$ is defined by Equation 3.9. If the errors are heteroscedastic or correlated with each other, OLS still produces unbiased coefficients but we will need other tools, covered here and in Chapter 13, to get appropriate standard errors for our $\hat{\beta}_1$ estimates.

We'll have mastered bivariate OLS when we can accomplish the following:

- Section 3.1: Write out the bivariate regression equation and explain all its elements (dependent variable, independent variable, slope, intercept, error term). Draw a hypothetical scatterplot with a small number of observations and show how bivariate OLS is estimated, identifying residuals, fitted values, and what it means to be a best-fit line. Sketch an appropriate best-fit line and identify $\hat{\beta}_0$ and $\hat{\beta}_1$ on the sketch. Write out the equation for $\hat{\beta}_1$ and explain the intuition in it.

- Section 3.2: Explain why $\hat{\beta}_1$ is a random variable and sketch its distribution. Explain two ways to think about randomness in coefficient estimates.

- Section 3.3: Explain what it means for the OLS estimate $\hat{\beta}_1$ to be an unbiased estimator. Explain the exogeneity condition and why it is so important.

- Section 3.4: Write out the standard equation for the variance of $\hat{\beta}_1$ in bivariate OLS and explain three factors that affect this variance.

- Section 3.5: Define probability limit and consistency.

- Section 3.6: Identify the conditions required for the standard variance equation of $\hat{\beta}_1$ to be accurate. Explain why these two conditions are less important than the exogeneity condition.

- Section 3.7: Explain four ways to assess goodness of fit. Explain why R^2 alone does not measure whether or not a regression was successful.

- Section 3.8: Explain what outliers are, how they can affect results, and what to do about them.

Further Reading

Beck (2010) provides an excellent discussion of what to report from a regression analysis.

Weighted least squares is a type of generalized least squares that can be used when dealing with heteroscedastic data. Chapter 8 of Kennedy (2008) discusses weighted least squares and other issues associated with errors that are heteroscedastic or correlated with each other. These issues are often referred to as violations of a "spherical errors" condition. *Spherical errors* is pretentious statistical jargon meaning that errors are both homoscedastic and not correlated with each other.

Murray (2006b, 500) provides a good discussion of probability limits and consistency for OLS estimates.

We discuss what to do with autocorrelated errors in Chapter 13. The Further Reading section at the end of that chapter provides links to the very large literature on time series data analysis.

Key Terms

Autocorrelation (69)
Bias (58)
Central limit theorem (56)
Consistency (65)
Continuous variable (54)
Degrees of freedom (63)
Distribution (54)
Fitted value (48)
Goodness of Fit (70)
Heteroscedastic (67)

Heteroscedasticity-consistent
   standard errors (68)
Homoscedastic (67)
Modeled randomness (54)
Normal distribution (55)
Outlier (76)
Plim (66)
Probability density (55)
Probability distribution (54)
Probability limit (65)
Random variable (54)

Regression line (48)
Residual (48)
Sampling randomness (53)
Standard error (61)
Standard error of the
   regression (70)
Time series data (69)
Unbiased estimator (58)
Variance (61)
Variance of the regression
   (62)

Computing Corner

Stata

1. Use the donut and weight data described in Chapter 1 on page 34 to estimate a bivariate OLS regression by typing `reg weight donuts`. The command "reg" stands for "regression." The general format is `reg Y X` for a dependent variable Y and independent variable X.

Stata's regression output looks like this:

Source	SS	df	MS					
					Number of obs =			13
					F(1, 11) =			22.48
Model	46731.7593	1	46731.7593		Prob > F	=		0.0006
Residual	22863.933	11	2078.53936		R-squared	=		0.6715
					Adj R-squared =			0.6416
Total	69595.6923	12	5799.64103		Root MSE	=		45.591

weight	Coef.	Std. Err.	t	P>|t|	[95% Conf. Interval]	
donuts	9.103799	1.919976	4.74	0.001	4.877961	13.32964
_cons	122.6156	16.36114	7.49	0.000	86.60499	158.6262

STATA CHART

There is a lot of information here, not all of which is useful. The vital information is in the bottom table that shows that $\hat{\beta}_1$ is 9.10 with a standard error of 1.92 and $\hat{\beta}_0$ is 122.62 with a standard error of 16.36. We cover t, P>|t|, and 95% confidence intervals in Chapter 4.

The column on the upper right has some useful information too, indicating the number of observations, R^2, and Root MSE. (As we noted in the chapter, Stata refers to the standard error of the regression, $\hat{\sigma}$, as *root MSE*, which is Stata's shorthand for the square root of the mean squared error.) We discuss the adjusted R^2 later (page 151). The F and Prob > F to the right of the output relate information that we cover later (page 227); it's generally not particularly useful.

The table in the upper left is pretty useless. Contemporary researchers seldom use the information in the Source, SS, df, and MS columns.

2. In Stata, commands often have subcommands that are invoked after a comma. To estimate the model with heteroscedasticity-consistent standard errors (as discussed on page 68), simply add the , robust subcommand to Stata's regression command: reg weight donuts, robust.

3. To generate predicted values, type predict YourNameHere after running an OLS model. This command will create a new variable named "YourNameHere." In our example, we name the variable Fitted: predict Fitted. A variable containing the residuals is created by adding a , residuals subcommand to the predict command: predict Residuals, residuals.

We can display the actual values, fitted values, and residuals with the list command: list weight Fitted Residuals.

```
        | weight    Fitted      Residua |
        |-------------------------------|
  1. |     275   250.0688      24.93121 |
  2. |     141   122.6156      18.38439 |
  3. |      70   122.6156     -52.61561 |
        . . .
```

4. In Chapter 2 we plotted simple scatterplots. To produce more elaborate plots, work with Stata's `twoway` command (yes, it's an odd command name). For example, to add a regression line to a scatterplot, use `twoway (scatter weight donuts) (lfit weight donuts)`. The `lfit` command name stands for linear fit.[25]

5. To exclude an observation from a regression, use the `if` subcommand. The syntax "!=" means "not equal." For example, to run a regression on data that excludes observations for which name is not Homer, run `reg weight donuts if name !="Homer"`. In this example, we use quotes because the name variable is a string variable, meaning it is not a number. To include only observations where weight is greater than 100, we can type `reg weight donuts if weight > 100`.

R

1. The following commands use the donut data from Chapter 1 (page 36). Since R is an object-oriented language, our regression commands create objects containing information, which we ask R to display as needed. To estimate an OLS regression, we create an object called OLSResults (we could choose a different name) by typing `OLSResults = lm(weight ~ donuts)`. This command stores information about the regression results in an object called OLSResults. The `lm` command stands for "linear model" and is the R command for OLS. The general format is `lm(Y ~ X)` for a dependent variable Y and independent variable X. To display these regression results, type `summary(OLSResults)`, which produces

```
lm(formula = weight ~ donuts)
Residuals:
      Min      1Q   Median       3Q      Max
  -93.135  -9.479    0.757   35.108   55.073
```

---

[25] We jittered the data in Figure 3.10 to make it a bit easier to see more data points. Stata's `jitter` subcommand jitters data [e.g., `scatter weight donuts, jitter(3)`]. The bigger the number in parentheses, the more the data will be jittered.

```
Coefficients:
             Estimate Std. Error t value  Pr(>|t|)
(Intercept)   122.616      16.361   7.494 0.0000121
donuts          9.104       1.920   4.742 0.000608
Residual standard error: 45.59 on 11 degrees of freedom
Multiple R-squared:  0.6715,     Adjusted R-squared:  0.6416
F-statistic: 22.48 on 1 and 11 DF,  p-value: 0.0006078
```

The vital information is in the bottom table that shows that $\hat{\beta}_1$ is 9.104 with a standard error of 1.920 and $\hat{\beta}_0$ is 122.616 with a standard error of 16.361. We cover t value and Pr(>|t|) in Chapter 4.

R refers to the standard error of the regression ($\hat{\sigma}$) as the *residual standard error* and lists it below the regression results. Next to that is the degrees of freedom. To calculate the number of observations in the data set analyzed, recall that degrees of freedom equals $N - k$. Since we know k (the number of estimated coefficients) is 2 for this model, we can infer the sample size is 13. (Yes, this is probably more work than it should be to display sample size.)

The multiple R^2 (which is just the R^2) is below the residual standard error. We discuss the adjusted R^2 later (page 151). The F statistic at the bottom refers to a test we cover on page 227. It's usually not a center of attention.

The information on residuals at the top is pretty useless. Contemporary researchers seldom use that information.

2. The regression object created by R contains lots of other information as well. The information can be listed by typing the object name, a dollar sign, and the appropriate syntax. For example, the fitted values for a regression model are stored in the format of Object$fitted.values. In our case, they are OLSResults$fitted.values. For more details, type help(lm) in R and look for the list of components associated with "objects of class lm," which is R's way of referring to the regression results like those we just created. To see the fitted values, type OLSResults$fitted.values, which produces

1	2	3	4	5	6	
250.0688	122.6156	122.6156	168.1346	309.2435	129.4435	...

To see the residuals, type OLSResults$residuals, which produces

1	2	3	4	5	6	
24.9312	18.3843	−52.6156	−93.1346	0.7565	−49.4434	...

3. To create a scatterplot with a regression line included, we can type[26]
   ```
   plot(donuts, weight)
   abline(OLSResults)
   ```

---

[26] Figure 3.10 jittered the data to make it a bit easier to see more data points. To jitter data in an R plot, type plot(jitter(donuts), jitter(weight)).

4. One way to exclude an observation from a regression is to use brackets to limit the variable to observations for which the condition in the brackets is true; to indicate a "not equal" condition use "!=". In other words, `weight[name != "Homer"]` refers to values of the weight variable for which the name variable is not equal to "Homer." To run a regression on data that excludes observations for which name is Homer, run `OLSResultsNoHomer = lm(weight[name != "Homer"] ~ donuts[name != "Homer"])`. Here we use quotes because the name variable is a string variable, meaning it is not a number.[27] To include only observations where weight is greater than 100, we can type `OLSResultsNoLow = lm(weight[weight>100] ~ donuts[weight>100])`.

5. There are a number of ways to estimate the model with heteroscedasticity-consistent standard errors (as discussed on page 68). The easiest may be to use an *R package*, which is a set of R commands that we install for specific tasks. For heteroscedasticity-consistent standard errors, the useful AER package must be installed once and loaded at each use, as follows.

- To install the package, type `install.packages("AER")`. R will ask us to pick a location—this is the source from which the package. It doesn't matter what location we pick. We can also install a package manually from the packages command in the toolbar. Once installed on a computer, the package will be saved and available for use by R.

- Tell R to load the package every time we open R and want to use the commands in the AER (or other) package. We do this with the `library` command. We have to use the library command in every session we use a package.

Assuming the AER package has been installed, we can run OLS with heteroscedasticity-consistent standard errors via the following code:
```
library(AER)
OLSResults = lm(weight ~ donuts)
coeftest(OLSResults, vcov = vcovHC(OLSResults,
type = "HC1"))
```
The last line is elaborate. The command `coeftest` is asking for information on the variance of the estimates (among other things) and the `vcov=vcovHC` part of the command is asking for heteroscedasticity-consistent standard errors. There are multiple ways to

---

[27] There are more efficient ways to exclude data when we are using data frames. For example, if the variables are all included in a data frame called *dta*, we could type `OLSResultsNoHomer = lm(weight ~ donuts, data = dta[name != "Homer", ])`.

estimate such standard errors, and the HC1 asks for the most commonly used form of these standard errors.[28]

Exercises

1. Use the data in PresVote.dta to answer the following questions about the relationship between changes in real disposable income and presidential election results. Table 3.4 describes the variables.

   (a) Create a scatterplot like Figure 3.1.

   (b) Estimate an OLS regression in which the vote share of the incumbent party is regressed on change in real disposable income. Report the estimated regression equation and interpret the coefficients.

   (c) What is the fitted value for 1996? For 1972?

   (d) What is the residual for 1996? For 1972?

   (e) Estimate an OLS regression only on years in which the variable *Reelection* equals 1: that is, years in which an incumbent president is running for reelection. Interpret the coefficients.

   (f) Estimate an OLS regression only on years in which the variable *Reelection* equals 0: that is, years in which an incumbent president is not running for reelection. Interpret the coefficients and discuss the substantive implications of differences from the model with incumbents only.

TABLE 3.4 Variables for Questions on Presidential Elections and the Economy

Variable name	Description
year	Year of election
rdi4	Change in real disposable income since previous election
vote	Percent of two-party vote received by the incumbent president's party
demcand	Name of the Democratic candidate
repcand	Name of the Republican candidate
reelection	Equals 1 if incumbent is running for reelection and 0 if not

---

[28] The vcov terminology is short for *variance-covariance*, and "vcovHC" is short for *heteroscedasticity-consistent standard errors.*

2. Suppose we are interested in the effect of education on salary as expressed in the following model:

$$Salary_i = \beta_0 + \beta_1 Education_i + \epsilon_i$$

For this problem, we are going to assume that the true model is

$$Salary_i = 10{,}000 + 1{,}000 Education_i + \epsilon_i$$

The model indicates that the salary for each person is $10,000 plus $1,000 times the number of years of education plus the error term for the individual. Our goal is to explore how much our estimate of $\hat{\beta}_1$ varies.

Enter the following code into a Stata .do file. It will simulate a data set with 100 observations (as determined with the set obs command). Values of education for each observation are between 0 and 16 years. The error term will be a normally distributed error term with a standard deviation of 10,000 (as determined with the scalar SD command).

```
program OLS_Sim
  clear
  set obs 100          /* Set sample size */
  gen Ed = 16*runiform()   /* Generate education (ind. variable) */
  scalar SD = 10000        /* Set value of standard deviation of error term */
  gen Salary = 10000 + 1000* Ed + SD*rnormal()  /* Generate salary (dep. variable) */
  regress Salary Ed        /* Run regression */
end
simulate _b _se, reps(50): OLS_Sim   /* Run simulation 50 times */
```

The simulate line runs the code 50 times (as determined in the reps(50) command) and will save the $\hat{\beta}$ coefficients and standard errors for each simulation. The values of $\hat{\beta}_{Education}$ for each simulation are listed in a variable called _b_Ed; the values of $\hat{\beta}_0$ for each simulation are listed in a variable called _b_cons. The values of $se(\hat{\beta}_{Education})$ for each simulation are listed in a variable called _se_Ed; the values of $se(\hat{\beta}_0)$ for each simulation are listed in a variable called _se_cons.

We can look at the estimated coefficients (via the list command) and summarize them (via the summarize command):

```
list _b_* _se* /* Coefficient estimates & std. errors for each simulation */
summarize _b* /* Summarize coefficient estimates for each simulation */
```

(a) Explain why the means of the estimated coefficients across the multiple simulations are what they are.

(b) What are the minimum and maximum values of the estimated coefficients on education? Explain whether these values are inconsistent with our statement in the chapter that OLS estimates are unbiased.

(c) Rerun the simulation with a larger sample size in each simulation. Specifically, set the sample size to 1,000 in each simulation. (Do this by changing the set obs line of the code.) Compare the mean, minimum, and maximum of the estimated coefficients on education to the original results above.

(d) Rerun the simulation with a smaller sample size in each simulation. Specifically, set the sample size to 20 in each simulation. Compare the mean, minimum, and maximum of the estimated coefficients on education to the original results above.

(e) Reset the sample size to 100 for each simulation and rerun the simulation with a smaller standard deviation for each simulation. Specifically, set StdDev to 500 for each simulation. (Do this by changing the scalar StdDev line of the code.) Compare the mean, minimum, and maximum of the estimated coefficients on education to the original results above.

(f) Keeping the sample size at 100 for each simulation, rerun the simulation with a larger standard deviation for each simulation. Specifically, set StdDev to 50,000 for each simulation. Compare the mean, minimum, and maximum of the estimated coefficients on education to the original results above.

(g) Revert to original model (sample size at 100 and SD at 10,000). Now run 500 simulations. [Do this by changing the simulate _b _se, reps(50) line of the code so that it has reps(500).] Summarize the distribution of the $\hat{\beta}_{Education}$ estimates as you've done so far, but now also plot the distribution of these coefficients using

```
kdensity _b_Ed /* Density plot of beta estimates */
```

Describe the density plot in your own words.

3. In the chapter we discussed the relationship between height and wages in the United States. Does this pattern occur elsewhere? The data set heightwage_british_males.dta contains data on males in Britain from Persico, Postlewaite, and Silverman (2004). This data is from the British National Child Development Survey (NCDS), which began as a study of children born in Britain during the week of March 3, 1985. Information was gathered when these subjects were 7, 11, 16, 23, and 33 years old. For this question, we use just the information about respondents at age 33. Table 3.5 shows the variables we use.

TABLE 3.5 Variables for Height and Wage Data in Britain

Variable name	Description
gwage33	Hourly wages (in British pounds) at age 33
height33	Height (in inches) measured at age 33

(a) Estimate a model where height at age 33 explains income at age 33. Explain $\hat{\beta}_1$ and $\hat{\beta}_0$.

(b) Create a scatterplot of height and income at age 33. Identify outliers.

(c) Create a scatterplot of height and income at age 33 but exclude observations with wages per hour more than 400 British pounds and height less than 40 inches. Describe the difference from the earlier plot. Which plot seems the more reasonable basis for statistical analysis? Why?

(d) Reestimate the bivariate OLS model from part (a) but exclude four outliers with very high wages and outliers with height below 40 inches. Briefly compare results to earlier results.

(e) What happens when the sample size is smaller? To answer this question, reestimate the bivariate OLS model from above (that excludes outliers), but limit the analysis to the first 800 observations.[29] Which changes more from the results with the full sample: the estimated coefficient on height or the estimated standard error of the coefficient on height? Explain.

4. Table 3.6 lists the variables in the WorkWomen.dta and WorkMen.dta data sets, which are based on Chakraborty, Holter, and Stepanchuk (2012).

TABLE 3.6 Variables for Divorce Rate and Hours Worked

Variable name	Description
ID	Unique number for each country in the data set
country	Name of the country
hours	Average yearly labor (in hours) for gender specified in data set
divorcerate	Divorce rate per thousand
taxrate	Average effective tax rate

---

[29] To do this in Stata, include `if _n <800` at the end of the Stata regress command. Because some observations have missing data and others are omitted as outliers, the actual sample size in the regression will fall a bit lower than 800. The `_n` notation is Stata's way of indicating the observation number, which is the row number of the observation in the data set.

Answer the following questions about the relationship between hours worked and divorce rates.

(a) For each data set (for women and for men), create a scatterplot of hours worked on the Y-axis and divorce rates on the X-axis.

(b) For each data set, estimate an OLS regression in which hours worked is regressed on divorce rates. Report the estimated regression equation and interpret the coefficients. Explain any differences in coefficients.

(c) What are the fitted value and residual for men in Germany?

(d) What are the fitted value and residual for women in Spain?

5. Use the data in Table 3.6 to answer the following questions about the relationship between hours worked and tax rates:

(a) For each data set (for women and for men), create a scatterplot of hours worked on the Y-axis and tax rates on the X-axis.

(b) For each data, set estimate an OLS regression in which hours worked is regressed on tax rates. Report the estimated regression equation and interpret the coefficients. Explain any differences in coefficients.

(c) What are the fitted value and residual for men in the United States?

(d) What are the fitted value and residual for women in Italy?

Hypothesis Testing and Interval Estimation: Answering Research Questions

4

Sometimes the results of an experiment are obvious. In 1881, Louis Pasteur administered an anthrax vaccine to 24 sheep and selected 24 other sheep to be a control group. He exposed all 48 sheep to a deadly dose of anthrax and asked visitors to come back in two days. By then, 21 of the unvaccinated sheep had died. Two more unvaccinated sheep died before the visitors' eyes, and the last unvaccinated sheep died the next day. Of the vaccinated sheep, only one died and its symptoms were inconsistent with anthrax. Nobody needed fancy econometrics to conclude the vaccine worked; they only needed masks to cover the smell.

Mostly, though, the conclusions from an experiment are not so obvious. What if the death toll had been two unvaccinated sheep and one vaccinated sheep? That well could have happened by chance. What if five unvaccinated sheep died and no vaccinated sheep died? That outcome would seem less likely to have happened simply by chance. But would it be enough for us to believe that the vaccine treatment can prevent anthrax?

Questions like these pervade all econometric analysis. We're trying to answer questions, and while it's pretty easy to see whether a policy is associated with more of a given outcome, it's much harder to know at what point we should become convinced the relationship is real, rather than the result of the hurly-burly randomness of real life.

▶ **hypothesis testing**
A process assessing whether the observed data is or is not consistent with a claim of interest.

Hypothesis testing is the infrastructure statistics provides for answering these questions. Hypothesis testing allows us to assess whether the observed data is or is not consistent with a claim of interest. The process does not yield 100 percent definitive answers; rather, it translates our statistical estimates into statements like "We are quite confident that the vote share of the incumbent U.S. president's party goes up when the economy is good" or "We are quite confident that tall people get paid more."

91

The standard statistical way to talk about hypotheses is a bit of an acquired taste. Suppose there is no effect (i.e. $\beta_1 = 0$). What is the probability that when we run OLS on the data we actually have, we will see a coefficient as large as what we actually observe? That is, suppose we want to test the claim that $\beta_1 = 0$. If this claim were true (meaning $\beta_1 = 0$), what is the probability of observing a $\hat{\beta}_1 = 0.4$ or 7.2 or whatever result our OLS produced? If this probability of observing the $\hat{\beta}_1$ we actually observe is very small when $\beta_1 = 0$, then we can reasonably infer that the hypothesis that $\beta_1 = 0$ is probably not true.

Intuitively we know that if a treatment has no effect, the probability of seeing a huge difference is low and the chance of seeing a small difference is large. The magic of stats–and it is quite remarkable—is that we can quantify the probabilities of seeing any observed effect given that the effect really is zero.

In this chapter we discuss the tools of hypothesis testing. Section 4.1 lays out the core logic and terminology. Section 4.2 covers the workhorse of hypothesis testing, the *t* test. Section 4.3 introduces *p* values, which are a useful by-product of the hypothesis testing enterprise. Section 4.4 discusses statistical power, a concept that's sometimes underappreciated despite its cool name. Power helps us appreciate the difference between finding no relationship because there is no relationship and finding no relationship because we don't have enough data. Section 4.5 discusses some of the very real limitations to the hypothesis testing approach and Section 4.6 then introduces the confidence interval approach to estimation, which avoids some of the problems of hypothesis testing.

Much of the material in this chapter will be familiar to those who have had a probability and statistics course. Learning this material or tuning up our understanding of it will put us in great position to understand OLS as it is practiced.

4.1   Hypothesis Testing

We want to use statistics to answer questions, and the main way to do so is to use OLS to assess hypotheses. In this section, we introduce the null and alternative hypotheses, apply the concepts to our presidential election example, and then develop the important concept of significance level.

▶ **null hypothesis** A hypothesis of no effect.

Hypothesis testing begins with a **null hypothesis**, which is typically a hypothesis of no effect. Consider the height and wage example from page 73:

$$Wage_i = \beta_0 + \beta_1 Adult\ height_i + \epsilon_i \qquad (4.1)$$

The standard null hypothesis is that height has no effect on wages. Or, more formally,

$$H_0 : \beta_1 = 0$$

where the subscript zero after the H indicates that this is the null hypothesis.

Statistical tools do not allow us to prove or disprove a null hypothesis. Instead, we "reject" or "fail to reject" the null hypotheses. When we reject a null hypothesis, we are actually saying that the probability of seeing the $\hat{\beta}_1$ that we estimated is very low if the null hypothesis is true. For example, it is unlikely we will observe a large $\hat{\beta}_1$ with a small standard error if the truth is $\beta_1 = 0$. If we do nonetheless observe a large $\hat{\beta}_1$ with a small standard error, we will reject the null hypothesis and refer to the coefficient as **statistically significant**.

▶ **statistically significant** A coefficient is statistically significant when we reject the null hypothesis that it is zero.

When we fail to reject a null hypothesis, we are saying that the $\hat{\beta}_1$ we observe would not be particularly unlikely if the null hypothesis were true. For example, we typically reject the null hypothesis when we observe a small $\hat{\beta}_1$. That outcome would not be surprising at all for $\beta_1 = 0$. We can also fail to reject null hypotheses when uncertainty is high. That is, a large $\hat{\beta}_1$ may not be too surprising even when $\beta_1 = 0$ if the variance of $\hat{\beta}_1$ is large relative to the value of $\hat{\beta}_1$. We formalize this logic when we discuss t statistics in the next section.

The heart of proper statistical analysis is to recognize that we might be making a mistake. When we reject a null hypothesis we are concluding that given the $\hat{\beta}_1$ we observe, it is *unlikely* that $\beta_1 = 0$. We are not saying it is impossible.

When we fail to reject a null hypothesis we are saying that given the $\hat{\beta}_1$ we observe, it would not surprise us if $\beta_1 = 0$. We are definitely not saying that we *know* that $\beta_1 = 0$ when we fail to reject the null. Instead, the situation is like a "not guilty" verdict from a jury; the accused may be guilty, but the evidence is not sufficient to convict.

▶ **Type I error** A hypothesis-testing error that occurs when we reject a null hypothesis that is in fact true.

▶ **Type II error** A hypothesis-testing error that occurs when we fail to reject a null hypothesis that is in fact false.

We characterize possible mistakes in two ways. **Type I errors** occur when we reject a null hypothesis that is in fact true. If we say height increases wages, but actually it doesn't, we're committing a Type I error. **Type II errors** occur when we fail to reject a null hypothesis that is in fact false. If we say that there is no relationship between height and wages, but there actually is one, we're committing a Type II error. Table 4.1 summarizes this terminology.

Standard hypothesis testing focuses heavily on Type I error. That is, the approach is built around specifying an acceptable level of Type I error and proceeding from there. We should not forget Type II error, though. In many situations we must take the threat of Type II error seriously; we consider some when we discuss statistical power in Section 4.4.

▶ **alternative hypothesis** An alternative hypothesis is what we accept if we reject the null.

If we reject the null hypothesis, we accept the **alternative hypothesis**. We do not prove the alternative hypothesis is true. Rather, the alternative hypothesis is the idea we hang onto when we have evidence that is inconsistent with the null hypothesis.

TABLE 4.1 Type I and Type II Errors

	$\beta_1 \neq 0$	$\beta_1 = 0$
Reject H_0	Correct inference	**Type I error**: wrongly reject null
Fail to reject H_0	**Type II error**: wrongly fail to reject null	Correct inference

▶ **one-sided alternative hypothesis** An alternative to the null hypothesis that has a direction. For Example, $H_A : \beta_1 > 0$ or $H_A : \beta_1 < 0$.

An alternative hypothesis is either one sided or two sided. A **one-sided alternative hypothesis** has a direction. For example, if we have theoretical reasons to believe that being taller increases wages, then the alternative hypothesis for the following model

$$Wage_i = \beta_0 + \beta_1 Adult\ height_i + \epsilon_i \tag{4.2}$$

would be written as $H_A : \beta_1 > 0$.

A **two-sided alternative hypothesis** has no direction. For example, if we think height affects wages but we're not sure whether tall people get paid more or less, the alternative hypothesis would be $H_A : \beta_1 \neq 0$. If we've done enough thinking to run a statistical model, it seems reasonable to believe that we should have at least an idea of the direction of the coefficient on our variable of interest, implying that two-sided alternatives might be rare. They are not, however, in part because they are more statistically cautious, as we will discuss shortly.

▶ **two-sided alternative hypothesis** An alternative to the null hypothesis that indicates the coefficient is not equal to 0 (or some other specified value). For example, $H_A : \beta_1 \neq 0$.

Formulating appropriate null and alternative hypotheses allows us to translate substantive ideas into statistical tests. For published work, it is generally a breeze to identify null hypotheses: just find the $\hat{\beta}$ that the authors jabber on most about. The main null hypothesis is almost certainly that that coefficient is zero.

OLS coefficients under the null hypothesis for the presidential election example

With a null hypothesis in hand, we can move toward serious econometric analysis. Let's consider the presidential election example that opened Chapter 3. To identify a null hypothesis, we first need a model, such as

$$Vote\ share_t = \beta_0 + \beta_1 Change\ in\ income_t + \epsilon_t \tag{4.3}$$

where $Vote\ share_t$ is percent of the vote received by the incumbent president's party in year t and the independent variable, $Change\ in\ income_t$, is the percent change in real disposable income in the United States in the year before the presidential election. The null hypothesis is that there is no effect H_0: $\beta_1 = 0$.

What is the distribution of $\hat{\beta}_1$ under the null hypothesis? Pretty simple: it is a normally distributed random variable centered on zero. This is because OLS produces unbiased estimates and, if the true value of β_1 is zero, then an unbiased distribution of $\hat{\beta}_1$ will be centered on zero.

How wide is the distribution of $\hat{\beta}_1$ under the null hypothesis? In contrast; that is, to the mean of the distribution, which we know under the null, the width depends on the data and the standard error implied by the data. In other words, we allow the data to tell us the standard error of the $\hat{\beta}_1$ estimate under the null hypothesis.

TABLE 4.2	Effect of Income Changes on Presidential Elections	
Variable	Coefficient	Standard error
Change in income	2.29	0.52
Constant	45.91	1.69
$N = 17$		

Table 4.2 shows the results for the model. Of particular interest for us at this point is that the standard error of the $\hat{\beta}_1$ estimate is 0.52. This number tells us how wide the distribution of the $\hat{\beta}_1$ will be under the null.

With this information we can picture the distribution of $\hat{\beta}_1$ under the null. Specifically, Figure 4.1 shows the probability density function of $\hat{\beta}_1$ under the null hypothesis, which is a normal probability density centered at zero with a

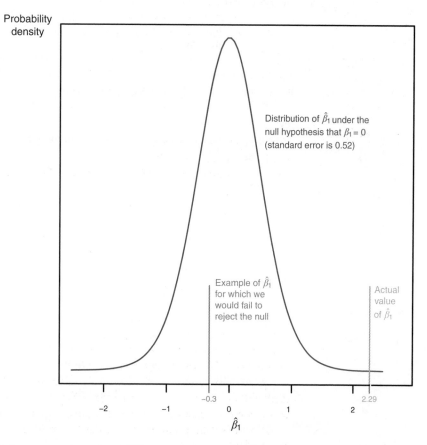

Probability density

Distribution of $\hat{\beta}_1$ under the null hypothesis that $\beta_1 = 0$ (standard error is 0.52)

Example of $\hat{\beta}_1$ for which we would fail to reject the null

Actual value of $\hat{\beta}_1$

−0.3

−2   −1   0   1   2   2.29

$\hat{\beta}_1$

FIGURE 4.1: Distribution of $\hat{\beta}_1$ under the Null Hypothesis for Presidential Election Example

standard deviation of 0.52. We also refer to this as the *distribution* of $\hat{\beta}_1$ under the null hypothesis. We introduced probability density functions in Section 3.2 and discuss them in further detail in the appendix starting on page 524.

Figure 4.1 illustrates the key idea of hypothesis testing. The actual value of $\hat{\beta}_1$ that we estimated is 2.29. That number seems pretty unlikely, doesn't it? Under the null hypothesis, most of the distribution of $\hat{\beta}_1$ is to the left of the $\hat{\beta}_1$ observed. We formalize things in the next section, but intuitively it's reasonable to think that the observed value $\hat{\beta}_1$ is so unlikely if the null is true that, well, the null hypothesis is probably not true.

Now name a value of $\hat{\beta}_1$ that would lead us not to reject the null hypothesis. In other words, name a value of $\hat{\beta}_1$ that is perfectly likely under the null hypothesis. We showed one such example in Figure 4.1: the line at $\hat{\beta}_1 = -0.3$. A value like this would be completely unsurprising if the null hypothesis were true. Hence, if we observed such a value for $\hat{\beta}_1$ we would deem it to be consistent with the null hypothesis and we would not reject the null hypothesis.

Significance level

Given that our strategy is to reject the null hypothesis when we observe a $\hat{\beta}_1$ that is quite unlikely under the null hypothesis, the natural question is: just *how* unlikely does $\hat{\beta}_1$ have to be? We get to choose the answer to this question. In other words, we get to decide our standard for what we deem to be sufficiently unlikely to reject the null hypothesis. We'll call this probability the **significance level** and denote it with α (the Greek letter alpha). A significance level determines how unlikely a result has to be under the null hypothesis for us to reject the null hypothesis. A very common significance level is 5 percent (meaning $\alpha = 0.05$).

▶ **significance level**

For each hypothesis test, we set a significance level that determines how unlikely a result has to be under the null hypothesis for us to reject the null hypothesis. The significance level is the probability of committing a Type I error for a hypothesis test.

If we set $\alpha = 0.05$, then we reject the null when we observe a $\hat{\beta}_1$ so large that we would expect a 5 percent chance of seeing the observed value or higher under only the null hypothesis. Setting $\alpha = 0.05$ means that there is a 5 percent chance that we would see a value high enough to reject the null hypothesis even when the null hypothesis is true, meaning that α is the probability of making a Type I error.

If we want to be more cautious (in the sense of requiring a more extreme result to reject the null hypothesis), we can choose $\alpha = 0.01$, in which case we will reject the null if we have a 1 percent or lower chance of observing a $\hat{\beta}_1$ as large as we actually did.

Reducing α is not completely costless, however. As the probability of making a Type I error decreases, the probability of making a Type II error increases. In other words, the more we say we're going to need really strong evidence to reject the null hypothesis (which is what we say when we make α small), the more likely it is that we'll fail to reject the null hypothesis when the null hypothesis is wrong (which is the Type II error).

REMEMBER THIS

1. A null hypothesis is typically a hypothesis of no effect, written as H_0: $\beta_1 = 0$.

   - We reject a null hypothesis when the statistical evidence is inconsistent with the null hypothesis. A coefficient estimate is statistically significant if we reject the null hypothesis that the coefficient is zero.

   - We fail to reject a null hypothesis when the statistical evidence is consistent with the null hypothesis.

   - Type I error occurs when we wrongly reject a null hypothesis.

   - Type II error occurs when we wrongly fail to reject a null hypothesis.

2. A alternative hypothesis is the hypothesis we accept if we reject the null hypothesis.

   - We choose a one-sided alternative hypothesis if theory suggests either $\beta_1 > 0$ or $\beta_1 < 0$.

   - We choose a two-sided alternative hypothesis if theory does not provide guidance as to whether β_1 is greater than or less than zero.

3. The significance level (α) refers to the probability of a Type 1 error for our hypothesis test. We choose the value of the significance level, typically 0.01 or 0.05.

4. There is a trade-off between Type I and Type II errors. If we lower α, we decrease the probability of making a Type I error but increase the probability of making a Type II error.

Discussion Questions

1. Translate each of the following questions into a bivariate model with a null hypothesis that could be tested. There is no single answer for each.

   (a) "What causes test scores to rise?"

   (b) "How can Republicans increase support among young voters?"

   (c) "Why did unemployment spike in 2008?"

2. For each of the following, identify the null hypothesis, draw a picture of the distribution of $\hat{\beta}_1$ under the null, identify values of $\hat{\beta}_1$ that would lead you to reject or fail to reject the null, and explain what it would mean to commit Type I and Type II errors in each case.

   (a) We want to know if height increases wages.

   (b) We want to know if gasoline prices affect the sales of SUVs.

   (c) We want to know if handgun sales affect murder rates.

4.2 *t* Tests

▶ **t test** A hypothesis test for hypotheses about a normal random variable with an estimated standard error.

The most common tool we use for hypothesis testing in OLS is the **t test**. There's a quick rule of thumb for *t* tests: if the absolute value of $\frac{\hat\beta_1}{\text{se}(\hat\beta_1)}$ is bigger than 2, reject the null hypothesis (recall that $\text{se}(\hat\beta_1)$ is the standard error of our coefficient estimate). If not, don't. This section provide the logic and tools of *t* testing, which will enable us to be more precise, but this rule of thumb is pretty much all there is to it.

$\hat\beta_1$ and standard errors

To put our *t* tests in context, let's begin by stating that we have calculated $\hat\beta_1$ and are trying to figure out whether $\hat\beta_1$ would be highly surprising if the null hypothesis were true. A challenge is that the scale of our $\hat\beta_1$ could be anything. In our presidential election model, we estimated $\hat\beta_1$ to be 2.29. Is that estimate surprising under the null? As we saw in Figure 4.1, a $\hat\beta_1$ that big is unlikely to appear when the standard error of $\hat\beta_1$ is only 0.52. What if the standard error of $\hat\beta_1$ were 2.0? The distribution of $\hat\beta_1$ under the null hypothesis would still be centered at zero, but it would be really wide, as in Figure 4.2. In this case, it really wouldn't be so surprising to see a $\hat\beta_1$ of 2.29 even if the null hypothesis that $\beta_1 = 0$ were true.

What we really care about is not the $\hat\beta_1$ coefficient estimate by itself but, rather, how large the $\hat\beta_1$ coefficient is relative to its standard error. In other words, we are unlikely to observe a $\hat\beta_1$ coefficient that is much bigger than its standard error, which would place it outside the range of the most likely outcomes for a normal distribution.

Therefore we use a test statistic that consists of the estimated coefficients divided by the estimated standard deviation of the coefficient: $\frac{\hat\beta_1}{\text{se}(\hat\beta_1)}$. Thus our test statistic reflects how many standard errors above or below zero the estimated coefficient is. If the $\hat\beta_1$ is 6 and $\text{se}(\hat\beta_1)$ is 2, our test statistic will be 3 because the estimated coefficient is 3 standard errors above zero. If the standard error had been 12 instead, the value of our test statistic would have been 0.5.

The *t* distribution

Dividing $\hat\beta_1$ by its standard error solves the scale problem but introduces another challenge. We know $\hat\beta_1$ is normally distributed, but what is the distribution of $\frac{\hat\beta_1}{\text{se}(\hat\beta_1)}$? The $\text{se}(\hat\beta_1)$ is also a random variable because it depends on the estimated $\hat\beta_1$. It's a tricky question and now is a good time to turn to our friends at Guinness Brewery for help. Really. Not for what you might think, but for work they did in the early twentieth century demonstrating that the distribution of $\frac{\hat\beta_1}{\text{se}(\hat\beta_1)}$ follows

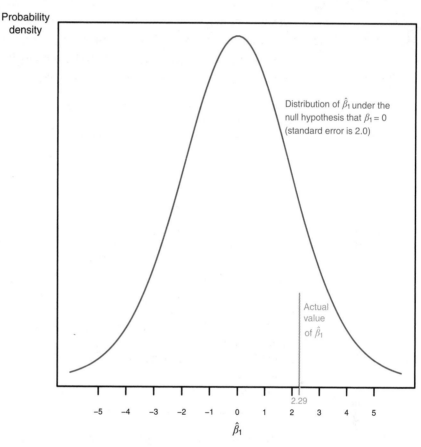

FIGURE 4.2: Distribution of $\hat{\beta}_1$ under the Null Hypothesis with Larger Standard Error for Presidential Election Example

t distribution A distribution that looks like a normal distribution, but with fatter tails. The exact shape of the distribution depends on the degrees of freedom. This distribution converges to a normal distribution for large sample sizes.

a distribution we call the *t* distribution.[1] The **t distribution** is bell shaped like a normal distribution but has "fatter tails."[2] We say it has fat tails because the values on the far left and far right have higher probabilities than what we find for the normal distribution. The extent of these chubby tails depends on the sample size; as the sample size gets bigger, the tails melt down to become the same as the normal distribution. What's going on is that we need to be more cautious about

_____

[1] Like many statistical terms, *t* distribution and *t* test have quirky origins. William Sealy Gosset devised the test in 1908 when he was working for Guinness Brewery in Dublin. His pen name was "Student." There already was an *s* test (now long forgotten), so Gosset named his test and distribution after the second letter of his pen name. The standard error of $\hat{\beta}_1$ follows a statistical distribution called a χ^2 distribution and the ratio of a normally distributed random variable and a χ^2 random variable follows a *t* distribution. More details are in the appendix on page 532. For now, just note that the Greek letter χ (chi) is pronounced like "ky," as in Kyle.

[2] That's a statistical term. Seriously.

rejecting the null because it is possible that by chance, our estimate of $se(\hat{\beta}_1)$ will be too small, which will make $\frac{\hat{\beta}_1}{se(\hat{\beta}_1)}$ appear to be really big. When we have small amounts of data, the issue is serious because we will be quite uncertain about $se(\hat{\beta}_1)$; when we have lots of data, we'll be more confident about our estimate of $se(\hat{\beta}_1)$ and, as we'll see, the fat tails of the t distribution fade away and the t distribution and normal distribution become virtually indistinguishable.

The specific shape of a t distribution depends on the degrees of freedom, which is sample size minus the number of parameters. A bivariate OLS model estimates two parameters ($\hat{\beta}_0$ and $\hat{\beta}_1$), which means, for example, that the degrees of freedom for a bivariate OLS model with a sample size of 50 is $50 - 2 = 48$.

Figure 4.3 on page opposite displays three different t distributions; a normal distribution is plotted in the background of each panel as a dotted

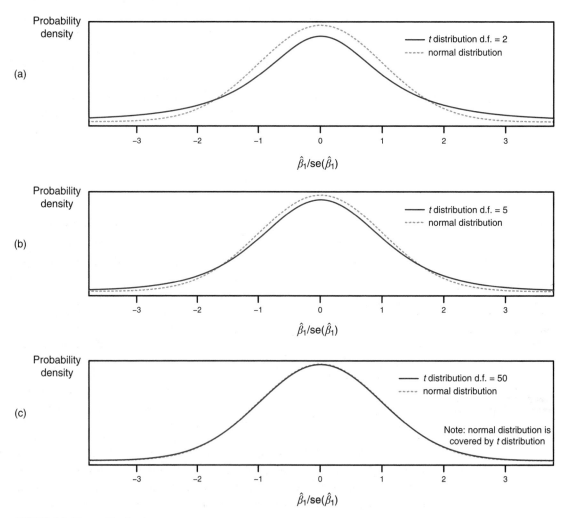

FIGURE 4.3: Three t Distributions

TABLE 4.3 Decision Rules for Various Alternative Hypotheses

Alternative hypothesis	Decision rule
H_A: $\beta_1 \neq 0$ (two-sided alternative)	Reject H_0 if $\left\| \frac{\hat{\beta}_1}{\text{se}(\hat{\beta}_1)} \right\| >$ appropriate critical value
H_A: $\beta_1 > 0$ (one-sided alternative)	Reject H_0 if $\frac{\hat{\beta}_1}{\text{se}(\hat{\beta}_1)} >$ appropriate critical value
H_A: $\beta_1 < 0$ (one-sided alternative)	Reject H_0 if $\frac{\hat{\beta}_1}{\text{se}(\hat{\beta}_1)} < -1$ times appropriate critical value

line. Panel (a) shows a t distribution with degrees of freedom (d.f.) equal to 2. Check out those fat tails. The probability of observing a value as high as 3 is higher for the t distribution than for the normal distribution. The same thing goes for the probability of observing a value as low as −3. Panel (b) of Figure 4.3 shows a t distribution with degrees of freedom equal to 5. If we look closely, we can see some chubbiness in the tails because the t distribution has higher probabilities at, for example, values greater than 2. We have to look pretty closely to see that, though. Panel (c) shows a t distribution with degrees of freedom equal to 50. It is visually indistinguishable from a normal distribution and, in fact, covers up the normal distribution so we cannot see it.

Critical values

critical value In hypothesis testing, a value above which a $\hat{\beta}_1$ would be so unlikely that we reject the null.

Once we know the distribution of $\frac{\hat{\beta}_1}{\text{se}(\hat{\beta}_1)}$, we can come up with a **critical value**. A critical value is the threshold for our test statistic. Loosely speaking, we reject the null hypothesis if $\frac{\hat{\beta}_1}{\text{se}(\hat{\beta}_1)}$ (the test statistic) is greater than the critical value; if $\frac{\hat{\beta}_1}{\text{se}(\hat{\beta}_1)}$ is below the critical value, we fail to reject the null hypothesis.

More precisely, our specific decision rule depends on the nature of the alternative hypothesis. Table 4.3 displays the specific rules. Rather than trying to memorize these rules, it is better to concentrate on the logic behind them. If the alternative hypothesis is two sided, then big values of $\hat{\beta}_1$ relative to the standard error incline us to reject the null. We don't particularly care if they are very positive or very negative. If the alternative hypothesis is that $\beta > 0$, then only large, positive values of $\hat{\beta}_1$ will incline us to reject the null hypothesis in favor of the alternative hypothesis. Observing a very negative $\hat{\beta}_1$ would be odd, but certainly it would not incline us to believe that the true value of β is greater than zero. Similarly, if the alternative hypothesis is that $\beta < 0$, then only very negative values of $\hat{\beta}_1$ will incline us to reject the null hypothesis in favor of the alternative hypothesis. We refer to the *appropriate* critical value in the table because the actual value of the critical value will depend on whether the test is one sided or two sided, as we discuss shortly.

The critical value for t tests depends on the t distribution and identifies the point at which we decide the observed $\frac{\hat{\beta}_1}{se(\hat{\beta}_1)}$ is unlikely enough under the null hypothesis to justify rejecting the null hypothesis.

Critical values depend on the significance level α we choose, our degrees of freedom, and whether the alternative is one sided or two sided. Figure 4.4 depicts critical values for various scenarios. We assume the sample size is large in each, allowing us to use the normal approximation to the t distribution.

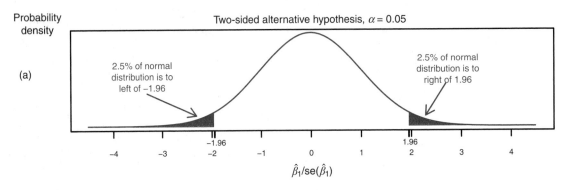

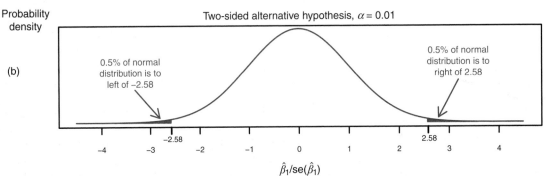

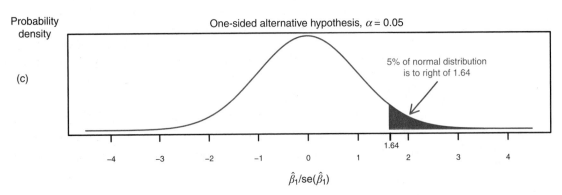

FIGURE 4.4: Critical Values for Large-Sample t Tests

Panel (a) of Figure 4.4 shows critical values for $\alpha = 0.05$ and a two-sided alternative hypothesis. The distribution of the t statistic is centered at zero under the null hypothesis that $\beta_1 = 0$. For a two-sided alternative hypothesis, we want to identify ranges that are far from zero and unlikely under the null hypothesis. For $\alpha = 0.05$, we want to find the range that constitutes the least-likely 5 percent of the distribution under the null. This 5 percent is the sum of the 2.5 percent on the far left and the 2.5 percent on the far right. Values in these ranges are not impossible, but they are unlikely. For a large sample size, the critical values that mark off the least-likely 2.5 percentage regions of the distribution are -1.96 and 1.96.

Panel (b) of Figure 4.4 depicts another two-sided alternative hypothesis; this time $\alpha = 0.01$. Now we're saying that to reject the null hypothesis, we're going to need to observe an even more unlikely $\hat{\beta}_1$ under the null hypothesis. The critical value for a large sample size is 2.58. This number defines the point at which there is a 0.005 probability (which is half of α) of being higher than than the critical value and there is a 0.005 probability of being less than the negative of it.

The picture and critical values differ a bit for a one-tailed test in which we look only at one side of the distribution. In panel (c) of Figure 4.4, $\alpha = 0.05$ and H_A: $\beta_1 > 0$. Here, 5 percent of the distribution is to the right of 1.64, meaning that we will reject the null hypothesis in favor of the alternative that $\beta_1 > 0$ if $\frac{\hat{\beta}_1}{se(\hat{\beta})} > 1.64$.

Note that the one-sided critical value for $\alpha = 0.05$ is lower than the two-sided critical value. One-sided critical values will always be lower for any given value of α, meaning that it is easier to reject the null hypothesis for a one-sided alternative hypothesis than for a two-sided alternative hypothesis. Hence, using critical values based on a two-sided alternative is statistically cautious insofar as we are less likely to appear overeager to reject the null if we use a two-sided alternative.

Table 4.4 displays critical values of the t distribution for one-sided and two-sided alternative hypotheses for common values of α. When the degrees of freedom are very small (typically owing to a small sample size), the critical values are relatively large. For example, with 2 degrees of freedom and $\alpha = 0.05$, we need to see a t stat above 2.92 to reject the null.[3] With 10 degrees of freedom, we need to see a t stat above 1.81 to reject the null. With 100 degrees of freedom, we need a t stat above 1.66 to reject the null. As the degrees of freedom get higher, the t distribution looks more and more like a normal distribution; for infinite degrees of freedom, it is exactly like a normal distribution, producing identical critical values. For degrees of freedom above 100, it is reasonable to use critical values from the normal distribution as a good approximation.

We compare $\frac{\hat{\beta}_1}{se(\hat{\beta}_1)}$ to our critical value and reject if the magnitude is larger than the critical value. We refer to the ratio of $\frac{\hat{\beta}_1}{se(\hat{\beta}_1)}$ as the *t* **statistic** (or "*t* stat," as the kids say). The t statistic is so named because that ratio will be compared

▶ *t* **statistic** The test statistic used in a *t* test. It is equal to $\frac{\hat{\beta}_1 - \beta^{Null}}{se(\hat{\beta}_1)}$.

---

[3] It's unlikely that we would seriously estimate a model with 2 degrees of freedom. For a bivariate OLS model, that would mean estimating a model with just four observations.

TABLE 4.4 **Critical Values for _t_ Distribution**

	α (1-sided) ⇒	0.05	0.025	0.01	0.005
	α (2-sided) ⇒	0.10	0.050	0.02	0.01
	2	2.92	4.30	6.97	9.92
	5	2.01	2.57	3.37	4.03
	10	1.81	2.23	2.76	3.17
Degrees of freedom	15	1.75	2.13	2.60	2.95
	20	1.73	2.09	2.53	2.85
	50	1.68	2.01	2.40	2.68
	100	1.66	1.98	2.37	2.63
	∞	1.64	1.96	2.32	2.58

A t distribution with ∞ degrees of freedom is the same as a normal distribution.

to a critical value that depends on the t distribution in the manner just outlined. Tests based on two-sided alternative tests with $\alpha = 0.05$ are very common. When the sample size is large, the critical value for such a test is 1.96. Hence the rule of thumb is that a t statistic bigger than 2 is statistically significant at conventional levels.

t Statistics for the height and wage example

To show t testing in action, Table 4.5 provides the results of the height and wages models from Chapter 3 but now adds t statistics. As before, we show results by using standard errors estimated by the equation that requires errors to be

TABLE 4.5 **Effect of Height on Wages with _t_ Statistics**

Variable	Assuming homoscedasticity	Allowing heteroscedasticity
Adult height	0.412	0.412
	(0.0976)	(0.0953)
	[$t = 4.225$]	[$t = 4.325$]
Constant	−13.093	−13.093
	(6.897)	(6.691)
	[$t = 1.898$]	[$t = 1.957$]
N	1,910	1,910
$\hat{\sigma}^2$	142.4	142.4
$\hat{\sigma}$	11.93	11.93
R^2	0.009	0.009

Standard errors in parentheses.

homoscedastic and standard errors estimated via an equation that allows errors to be heteroscedastic. The coefficients across models are identical.

The column on the left shows that the *t* statistic from the homoscedastic model for the coefficient on adult height is 4.225, meaning that $\hat{\beta}_1$ is 4.225 standard deviations away from zero. The *t* statistic from the heteroscedastic model for the coefficient on adult height is 4.325, which is essentially the same as in the homoscedastic model. For simplicity, we'll focus on the homoscedastic model results.

Is this coefficient on adult height statistically significant? To answer that question, we'll need a critical value. To pick a critical value, we need to choose a one-sided or two-sided alternative hypothesis and a significance level. Let's start with a two-sided test and $\alpha = 0.05$.

For a *t* distribution we also need to know the degrees of freedom. Recall that to find the degrees of freedom, we take the sample size and substract the number of parameters estimated. The smaller the sample size, the more uncertainty we have about our standard error estimate, hence the larger we make our critical value. Here, the sample size is 1,910 and we estimate two parameters, so the degrees of freedom are 1,908. For a sample this large, we can reasonably use the critical values from the last row of Table 4.4. The critical value for a two-sided test with $\alpha = 0.05$ and a high number for degrees of freedom is 1.96. Because our *t* statistic of 4.225 is higher than 1.96 we reject the null hypothesis. It's that easy.

Other types of null hypothesis

Finally, it's worth noting that we can extend the *t* test logic to cases in which the null hypothesis refers to some value other than zero. Such cases are not super common, but not unheard of. Suppose, for example, that our null hypothesis is $H_0: \beta_1 = 7$ versus $H_A: \beta_1 \neq 7$. In this case, we simply need to check how many standard deviations $\hat{\beta}_1$ is away from 7. So we compare $\frac{\hat{\beta}_1 - 7}{\text{se}(\hat{\beta}_1)}$ against the standard critical values we have already developed. More generally, to test a null hypothesis that $H_0: \beta_1 = \beta^{Null}$ we look at $\frac{\hat{\beta}_1 - \beta^{Null}}{\text{se}(\hat{\beta}_1)}$, where β^{Null} is the value of β indicated in the null hypothesis.

REMEMBER THIS

1. We use a *t* test to test the null hypotheses $H_0: \beta_1 = 0$. The steps are as follows:

    (a) Choose a one-sided or two-sided alternative hypothesis.

    (b) Set a significance level, α, usually equal to 0.01 or 0.05.

    (c) Find a critical value based on the *t* distribution. This value depends on α, whether the alternative hypothesis is one sided or two sided, and the degrees of freedom (equal to sample size minus number of parameters estimated).

(d) Use OLS to estimate parameters.

- For a two-sided alternative hypothesis, we reject the null hypothesis if $\left|\frac{\hat{\beta}_1}{se(\hat{\beta}_1)}\right| >$ the critical value. Otherwise, we fail to reject the null hypothesis.

- For a one-sided alternative hypothesis that $\beta_1 > 0$, we reject the null hypothesis if $\frac{\hat{\beta}_1}{se(\hat{\beta}_1)} >$ the critical value.

- For a one-sided alternative hypothesis that $\beta_1 < 0$, we reject the null hypothesis if $\frac{\hat{\beta}_1}{se(\hat{\beta}_1)} < -1$ times the critical value.

2. We can test any hypothesis of the form $H_0: \beta_1 = \beta^{Null}$ by using $\frac{\hat{\beta}_1 - \beta^{Null}}{se(\hat{\beta}_1)}$ as the test statistic for a t test.

Review Questions

1. Refer to the results in Table 4.2 on page 95.

    (a) What is the t statistic for the coefficient on change in income?

    (b) What are the degrees of freedom?

    (c) What is the critical value for a two-sided alternative hypothesis and $\alpha = 0.01$? Do we accept or reject the null?

    (d) What is the critical value for a one-sided alternative hypothesis and $\alpha = 0.05$? Do we accept or reject the null?

2. Which is bigger: the critical value from one-sided tests or two-sided tests? Why?

3. Which is bigger: the critical value from a large sample or a small sample? Why?

4.3   *p* Values

▶ **p value** The probability of observing a coefficient as high as we actually observed if the null hypothesis were true.

The **p value** is a useful by-product of the hypothesis testing framework. It indicates the probability of observing a coefficient as high as we actually did if the null hypothesis were true. In this section we explain how to calculate p values and why they're useful.

As a practical matter, the thing to remember is that we reject the null if the p value is less than α. Our rule of thumb here is "small p value means reject": low p values are associated with rejecting the null, and high p values are associated with failing to reject the null hypothesis.

Although p values can be calculated for any null hypothesis, w
most common null hypotheses in which $\beta_1 = 0$. Most statistical s
a two-sided p value, which indicates the probability that a coefficient is l...
magnitude (either positively or negatively) than the coefficient we observe.

Panel (a) of Figure 4.5 shows the p value calculation for the $\hat{\beta}_1$ estimate in
the wage and height example we discussed on page 104. The t statistic is 4.23.

Probability
density

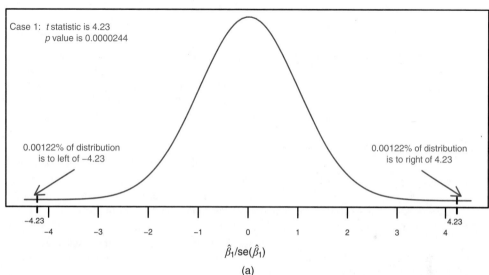

Case 1: t statistic is 4.23
p value is 0.0000244

0.00122% of distribution
is to left of −4.23

0.00122% of distribution
is to right of 4.23

−4.23
−4   −3   −2   −1   0   1   2   3   4   4.23

$\hat{\beta}_1/se(\hat{\beta}_1)$

(a)

Probability
density

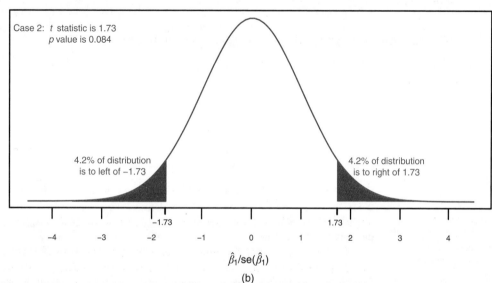

Case 2: t statistic is 1.73
p value is 0.084

4.2% of distribution
is to left of −1.73

4.2% of distribution
is to right of 1.73

−1.73   1.73
−4   −3   −2   −1   0   1   2   3   4

$\hat{\beta}_1/se(\hat{\beta}_1)$

(b)

FIGURE 4.5: Two Examples of p Values

The p value is calculated by finding the likelihood of getting a t statistic larger in magnitude than is observed under the null hypothesis. There is a 0.0000122 probability that the t statistic will be larger than 4.23. (In other words, there is a tiny probability we would observe a t statistic as high as 4.23 if the null hypothesis were true.) Because the normal distribution is symmetric, there is also a 0.0000122 probability that the t statistic will be less than −4.23. Hence the p value will be twice the probability of being above the observed t statistic, or 0.0000244.[4] We see a very small p value, meaning that if β_1 were actually equal to 0, the observed $\hat{\beta}_1$ would have been really, really unlikely.

Suppose, however, that our $\hat{\beta}_1$ were 0.09 (instead of the 0.41 it actually was). The t statistic would be $\frac{0.09}{0.52} = 1.73$. Panel (b) of Figure 4.5 shows the p value in this case. There is a 0.042 probability of observing a t statistic greater than 1.73 under the null hypothesis and a 0.042 probability of observing a t statistic less than −1.73 under the null, so the p value in this case would be 0.084. In this case, just by looking at the p value, we could reject the null for $\alpha = 0.10$ but fail to reject the null for $\alpha = 0.05$.

p values are helpful because they show us not only whether we reject the null hypothesis, but also whether we *really* reject the null or just barely reject the null. For example, a p value of 0.0001 indicates only a 0.0001 probability of observing the $\hat{\beta}_1$ as large as what we observe if the $\beta_1 = 0$. In this case, we are not only rejecting, we are decisively rejecting. Seeing a coefficient large enough to produce such a p value is highly, highly unlikely if $\beta_1 = 0$. On the other hand, if the p value is 0.049, we are just barely rejecting the null for $\alpha = 0.05$ and would, relatively speaking, have less confidence that the null is false. For $\alpha = 0.05$, we just barely fail to reject the null hypothesis with a p value of 0.051.

Since any statistical package that conducts OLS will provide p values, we typically don't need to calculate them ourselves. Our job is to know what they mean. Calculating p values is straightforward, though, especially for large sample sizes. The Computing Corner provides details.[5]

---

[4] Here we are calculating two-sided p values, which are the output most commonly reported by statistical software. If $\frac{\hat{\beta}_1}{se(\hat{\beta}_1)}$ is greater than zero, then the two-sided p value is twice the probability of being greater than that value. If $\frac{\hat{\beta}_1}{se(\hat{\beta}_1)}$ is less than zero, the two-sided p value is twice the probability of being less than that value. A one-sided p value is simply half the two-sided p value.

[5] For a two-sided p value we want to know the probability of observing a t statistic higher than the absolute value of the t statistic we actually observe under the null hypothesis. This is $2 \times \left[1 - \Phi\left(\left|\frac{\hat{\beta}_1}{se(\hat{\beta}_1)}\right|\right)\right]$, where Φ is the capital Greek letter Phi (pronounced like the "fi" in "wi-fi") and $\Phi()$ indicates the normal cumulative density function (CDF). (We see the normal CDF in our discussion of statistical power below; page 526 supplies more details). If the alternative hypothesis is $H_A: \beta_1 > 0$, the p value is the probability of observing a t statistic higher than the observed t statistic under the null hypothesis: $1 - \Phi\left(\frac{\hat{\beta}_1}{se(\hat{\beta}_1)}\right)$. If the alternative hypothesis is $H_A: \beta_1 < 0$, the p value is the probability of observing a t statistic less than the observed t statistic under the null hypothesis: $\Phi\left(\frac{\hat{\beta}_1}{se(\hat{\beta}_1)}\right)$.

REMEMBER THIS

The p value is the probability of observing a coefficient as large in magnitude as actually observed if the null hypothesis is true.

1. The lower the p value, the less consistent the estimated $\hat{\beta}_1$ is with the null hypothesis.
2. We reject the null hypothesis if the p value is less than α.
3. A p value can be useful to indicate the weight of evidence against a null hypothesis.

4.4   Power

The hypothesis testing infrastructure we've discussed so far is designed to deal with the possibility of Type I error, which occurs when we reject a null hypothesis that is actually true. When we set the significance level, we are setting the probability of making a Type I error. Obviously, we'd really rather not believe the null is false when it is true.

Type II errors aren't so hot either, though. We make a Type II error when β is really something other than zero and we fail to reject the null hypothesis that β is zero. In this section we explain statistical power, the statistical concept associated with Type II errors. We open by discussing the importance and meaning of Type II error, then show how to calculate power and how to create power curves. We finish by discussing when we should care about power.

Incorrectly failing to reject the null hypothesis

Type II error can be serious. For example, suppose there's a new medicine that really saves lives, but in the analysis the U.S. Food and Drug Administration relies on, the $\hat{\beta}_1$ estimate of the drug's efficacy is not statistically significant. If on the basis of that analysis the FDA fails to approve the drug, people will die unnecessarily. That's not "Oops"; that's horrific. Even when the stakes are lower, imagine how stupid we'd feel if we announced that a policy doesn't work when in fact it does work—we just happened to get a random realization of $\hat{\beta}_1$ that was not high enough to be statistically significant.

Type II error happens because it is possible to observe values of $\hat{\beta}_1$ that are less than the critical value even if β_1 (the true value of the parameter) is greater than zero. This is more likely to happen when the standard error of $\hat{\beta}_1$ is high.

Figure 4.6 shows the probability of Type II error for three different values of β. In these plots, we assume a large sample (allowing us to use the normal distribution for critical values) and test $H_0: \beta_1 = 0$ against a one-sided alternative hypothesis $H_A: \beta_1 > 0$, with $\alpha = 0.01$. In this case, the critical value is 2.32, which

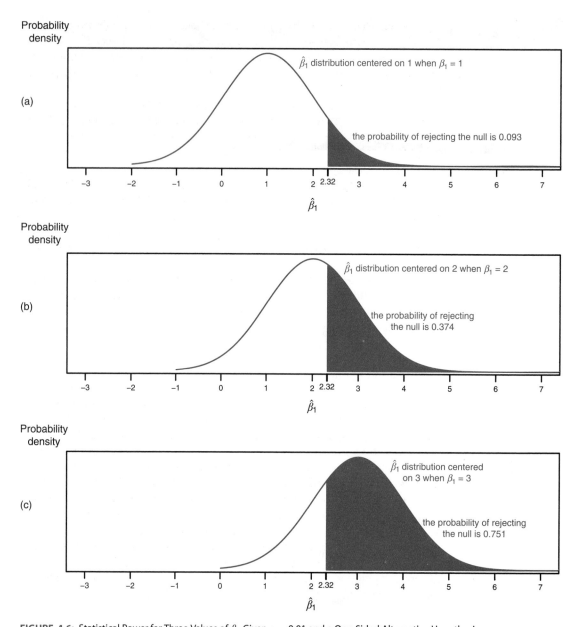

FIGURE 4.6: Statistical Power for Three Values of β_1 Given $\alpha = 0.01$ and a One-Sided Alternative Hypothesis

means that we reject the null hypothesis if we observe $\frac{\hat{\beta}_1}{\text{se}(\hat{\beta}_1)}$ greater than 2.32. For simplicity, we'll suppose $\text{se}(\hat{\beta}_1)$ is 1.

Panel (a) of Figure 4.6 displays the probability of Type II error if the true value of β equals 1. In this case, the distribution of $\hat{\beta}_1$ will be centered at 1. Only 9.3 percent of this distribution is to the right of 2.32, meaning that we have only a 9.3 percent chance of rejecting the null hypothesis. In other words, even though the null hypothesis actually is false—we're assuming $\beta_1 = 1$, not 0—we have only a roughly 1 in 10 chance of rejecting the null. In other words, our test is not particularly able to provide statistically significant results when the true value of β is 1.

Panel (b) of Figure 4.6 displays the probability of Type II error if the true value of β equals 2. In this case, the distribution of $\hat{\beta}_1$ will be centered at 2. Here 37.4 percent of the distribution is to the right of 2.32. Better, but not by much: even though $\beta_1 > 0$, we have a roughly 1 in 3 chance of rejecting the null hypothesis that $\beta_1 = 0$.

Panel (c) of Figure 4.6 displays the probability of Type II error if the true value of β equals 3. In this case, the distribution of $\hat{\beta}_1$ will be centered at 3. Here 75.1 percent of the distribution is to the right of 2.32. We're making progress, but still far from perfection. In other words, the true value of β must be near or above 3 before we have a 75.1 percent chance of rejecting the null when we should.

These examples illustrate why we use the somewhat convoluted "fail to reject the null" terminology; when we observe a $\hat{\beta}_1$ less than the critical value, it is still quite possible that the true value is not zero. Failure to find an effect is not the same as finding no effect.

Calculating power

> **power** The ability of our data to reject the null. A high-powered statistical test will reject the null with a very high probability when the null is false; a low-powered statistical test will reject the null with a low probability when the null is false.

The main tool for thinking about whether we are making Type II errors is **power**. The statistical definition of power differs from how we use the the word in ordinary conversation. Power in the statistical sense refers to the ability of our data to reject the null. A high-powered statistical test will reject the null with a very high probability when the null is false; a low-powered statistical test will reject the null with a low probability when the null is false. Think of statistical power like the power of a microscope. Using a powerful microscope allows us to distinguish small differences in an object, differences that are there but invisible to us when we look through a low-powered microscope.

To calculate power, we begin by noting that the probability we reject the null for any true value of β_1^{True} is the probability that the t statistic is greater than the critical value. We can write this condition as follows (where the condition following the vertical line is what we're assuming to be true):

$$\Pr(\text{Reject null given } \beta_1 = \beta_1^{True}) = \Pr\left(\frac{\hat{\beta}_1}{\text{se}(\hat{\beta}_1)} > \text{Critical value} \mid \beta_1 = \beta_1^{True}\right)$$

(4.4)

In other words, the power is the probability that the t statistic is higher than the critical value. This probability will depend on the actual value of β_1, since we know that the distribution of $\hat{\beta}_1$ will depend on the true value of β_1.

To make these calculations easier, we need some additional steps. First, note that the probability that the t statistic is bigger than the critical value (as described in Equation 4.4) is equal to 1 minus the probability that the t statistic is less than the critical value, yielding

$$\text{Pr(Reject null given } \beta_1 = \beta_1^{True}) = 1 - \text{Pr}\left(\frac{\hat{\beta}_1}{\text{se}(\hat{\beta}_1)} < \text{Critical value} \,|\, \beta_1 = \beta_1^{True}\right)$$

$$(4.5)$$

The key element of this equation is $\text{Pr}(\frac{\hat{\beta}_1}{\text{se}(\hat{\beta}_1)} < \text{Critical value} \,|\, \beta_1 = \beta_1^{True})$. This mathematical term seems complicated, but we actually know a fair bit about it. For a large sample size, the t statistic $\left(\text{which is } \frac{\hat{\beta}_1}{\text{se}(\hat{\beta}_1)}\right)$ will be normally distributed with a variance of 1 around the true value divided by the standard error of the estimated coefficient. And, from the properties of the normal distribution (see page 531 for a review), we know the probability that the t statistic will be less than the critical value will therefore be

$$\text{Pr(Reject null given } \beta_1 = \beta_1^{True}) = 1 - \Phi\left(\text{Critical value} - \frac{\beta_1^{True}}{\text{se}(\hat{\beta}_1)}\right)$$

where as before $\Phi()$ indicates the normal cumulative density function (see page 526 for more details). This quantity will vary depending on the true value of β_1 we wish to use in our power calculations.[6]

Deciding what true value to use in calculating power can be puzzling. There really is no specific value that we should look at; fact, the point is that we can pick any value and calculate the power. We might pick a value of β_1 that indicates a substantial real-world effect and find the probability of rejecting the null for that value. If the probability is low (meaning power is low), we should be a bit skeptical because we may not have enough data to reject the null for such a low true value. If the probability is high (meaning power is high), we can be confident that if the true β_1 is that value, then we probably can reject the null hypothesis.

Power curves

▶ **power curve**
Characterizes the probability of rejecting the null for each possible value of the parameter.

Even better than picking a single value to use to calculate power, we can look at power over a range of possible true values of β_1. A **power curve** characterizes the probability of rejecting the null for each possible value of the parameter. Figure 4.7 displays two power curves. The solid line on top is the power curve for when $\text{se}(\hat{\beta}_1) = 1.0$ and $\alpha = 0.01$. On the horizontal axis are

---

[6] And we can make the calculation a bit easier by using the fact that $1 - \Phi(-Z) = \Phi(Z)$ to write the power as $\Phi\left(\frac{\beta_1^{True}}{\text{se}(\hat{\beta}_1)} - \text{Critical value}\right)$.

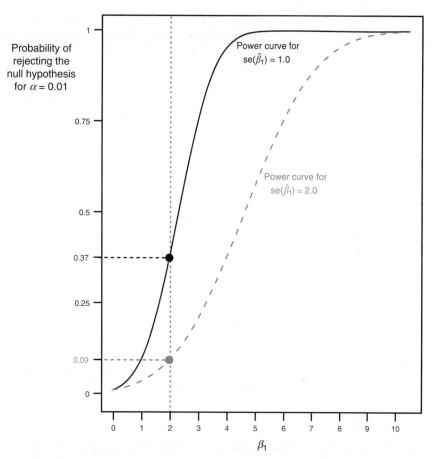

FIGURE 4.7: Power Curves for Two Values of se($\hat{\beta}_1$)

hypothetical values of β_1. The line shows the probability of rejecting the null for a one-tailed test of H_0: $\beta_1 = 0$ versus H_A: $\beta_1 > 0$ for $\alpha = 0.01$ and a sample large enough to permit us to use the normal approximation to the t distribution. To reject the null under these conditions requires a t stat greater than 2.32 (see Table 4.4). This power curve plots for each possible value of β_1 the probability that $\frac{\hat{\beta}}{se(\hat{\beta})}$ (which in this case is $\frac{\hat{\beta}}{1.0}$) is greater than 2.32. This curve includes the values we calculated in Figure 4.6 but now also covers all values of β_1 between 0 and 10.

Look first at the values of β_1 that are above zero, but small. For these values, the probability of rejecting the null is quite small. In other words, even though the null hypothesis is false for these values (since $\beta_1 > 0$), we're unlikely to reject the null that $\beta_1 = 0$. As β_1 increases, this probability increases and by around $\beta_1 = 4$, the probability of rejecting the null approaches 1.0. That is, if the true value of β_1 is 4 or bigger, we will reject the null with almost certainty.

The dashed line in Figure 4.7 displays a second power curve for which the standard error is bigger, here equal to 2.0. The significance level is the same as for the first power curve, $\alpha = 0.01$. We immediately see that the statistical power is lower. For every possible value of β_1, the probability of rejecting the null hypothesis is lower than when $se(\hat{\beta}_1) = 1.0$ because there is more uncertainty with the higher standard error for the estimate. For this standard error, the probability of rejecting the null when β_1 equals 2 is 0.09. So even though the null is false, we will have a very low probability of rejecting it.[7]

When to care about power

One of the main determinants of $se(\hat{\beta}_1)$ is sample size (see page 64). Hence a useful rule of thumb is that hypothesis tests based on large samples are usually high in power and hypothesis tests based on small samples are usually low in power. In Figure 4.7, we can think of the solid line as the power curve for a large sample and the dashed line as the power curve for a smaller sample. More generally, though, statistical power is a function of the variance of $\hat{\beta}_1$ and all the factors that affect it.

> **null result** A finding in which the null hypothesis is not rejected.

Power is particularly relevant when someone presents a **null result**, a finding in which the null hypothesis is not rejected. For example, someone may say class size is not related to test scores or that an experimental treatment does not work. In this case, we need to ask what the power of the test was. It could be, for example, that the sample size is very small, such that the probability of rejecting the null is small even for substantively large values of β_1.

▶ REMEMBER THIS

Statistical power refers to the probability of rejecting a null hypothesis for a given value of β_1.

1. A power curve shows the probability of rejecting the null for a range of possible values of β_1.

2. Large samples typically produce high-power statistical tests. Small samples typically produce low-power statistical tests.

3. It is particularly important to discuss power in the presentation of null results that fail to reject the null hypothesis.

---

[7] What happens when β_1 actually is zero? In this case, the null hypothesis is true and power isn't the right concept. Instead, the probability of rejecting the null here is the probability of rejecting the null when it is true. In other words, the probability of rejecting the null when $\beta_1 = 0$ is the probability of committing a Type I error, which is the α level we set.

Review Questions

1. For each of the following, indicate the power of the test of the null hypothesis $H_0 : \beta_1 = 0$ against the alternative hypothesis of $H_A : \beta_1 > 0$ for a large sample size and $\alpha = 0.01$ for the given true value of β_1. We'll assume $se(\hat{\beta}_1) = 0.75$. Draw a sketch to help explain your numbers.

   (a) $\beta_1^{True} = 1$

   (b) $\beta_1^{True} = 2$

2. Suppose the estimated $se(\hat{\beta}_1)$ doubled. What will happen to the power of the test for the two cases in question 1? First answer in general terms and then calculate specific answers.

3. Suppose $se(\hat{\beta}_1) = 2.5$. What is the probability of committing a Type II error for each of the true values given for β_1 in question 1?

Straight Talk about Hypothesis Testing

The ins and outs of hypothesis testing can be confusing. There are t distributions, degrees of freedom, one-sided tests, two-sided tests, lions, tigers, and bears. Such confusion is unfortunate for two reasons. First, the essence is simple: high t statistics indicate that the $\hat{\beta}_1$ we observe would be quite unlikely if $\beta_1 = 0$. Second, as a practical matter, computers make hypothesis testing super easy. They crank out t stats and p values lickety-split.

Sometimes these details distract us from the big picture: hypothesis testing is not the whole story. In this section we discuss four important limits to the hypothesis testing framework.

First, and most important, all hypothesis testing tools we develop—all of them!—are predicated on the assumption of no endogeneity. If there is endogeneity, these tools are useless. If the input is junk, even a fancy triple-backflip-somersault hypothesis test produces junk. We discussed endogeneity in Section 1.2 and will cover it in detail in Chapter 5.

Second, hypothesis tests can be misleadingly decisive. Suppose we have a sample of 1,000 and we are interested in a two-sided hypothesis test for $\alpha = 0.05$. If we observe a t statistic of 1.95, we will fail to reject the null. If we observe a t statistic of 1.97, we will reject the null. The world is telling us essentially the same thing in both cases, but the hypothesis testing approach gives us dramatically different answers.

Third, a hypothesis test can mask important information. Suppose the t statistic on one variable is 2 and the t statistic for another is 25. In both cases, we reject the null. But there's a big difference. We're kinda-sorta confident the null is not correct when the t stat is 2. We're damn sure the null sucks when the t stat is 25. Hypothesis testing alone does not make such a distinction. We should. The p values we'll discussed earlier are helpful, as are the confidence intervals we'll discuss shortly.

Fourth, hypothesis tests and their focus on statistical significance can distract us from **substantive significance**. A substantively significant coefficient is one that, well, matters; it indicates that the independent variable has a meaningful effect on the dependent variable. Although deciding how big a coefficient must be for us to believe it matters, it can be a bit subjective. This is a conversation we need to have. And statistical significance is not always a good guide. Remember that t stats depend a lot on the $se(\hat{\beta}_1)$, and the $se(\hat{\beta}_1)$ in turn depends on sample size and other factors (see page 64). If we have a really big sample, and these days it is increasingly common to have sample sizes in the millions, the standard error will be tiny and our t stat might be huge even for a substantively trivial $\hat{\beta}_1$ estimate. In these cases, we may reject the null even when the $\hat{\beta}_1$ coefficient suggests a minor effect.

> ▶ **substantive significance** If a reasonable change in the independent variable is associated with a meaningful change in the dependent variable, the effect is substantively significant. Some statistically significant effects are not substantively significant, especially for large data sets.

For example, suppose we look at average test scores for every elementary classroom in the country as a function of the salary of the teachers. We could conceivably get a statistically significant coefficient that implied, say, an increase of 0.01 point out of 100 for every $100,000 we pay teachers. Statistically significant, yes; substantively significant, not so much.

Or, conversely, we could have a small sample size that would lead to a large standard error on $\hat{\beta}_1$ and, say, to a failure to reject the null. But the coefficient could be quite big, suggesting perhaps a meaningful relationship. Of course, we wouldn't want to rush to conclude that the effect is really big, but it's worth appreciating that the data in such a case is indicating the possibility of a substantively significant relationship. In this instance, getting more data would be particularly valuable.

▶ REMEMBER THIS

Statistical significance is not the same as substantive significance.

1. A coefficient is *statistically significant* if we reject the null hypothesis.

2. A coefficient is *substantively significant* if the variable has a meaningful effect on the dependent variable.

3. With large data sets, substantively small effects can sometimes be statistically significant.

4. With small data sets, substantively large effects can sometimes be statistically insignificant.

Confidence Intervals

▶ **confidence interval**
Defines the range of true values that are consistent with the observed coefficient estimate. Confidence intervals depend on the point estimate, $\hat{\beta}_1$, and the measure of uncertainty, $se(\hat{\beta}_1)$.

▶ **point estimate** Point estimates describe our best guess as to what the true value is.

One way to get many of the advantages of hypothesis testing without the stark black/white, reject/fail-to-reject dichotomies of hypothesis testing is to use **confidence intervals**. A confidence interval defines the range of true values that are most consistent with the observed coefficient estimate. A confidence interval contrasts with a **point estimate**, which is a single number (such as $\hat{\beta}_1$).

This section explains how confidence intervals are calculated and why they are useful. The intuitive way to think about confidence intervals is that they give us a range in which we're confident the true parameter lies. An approximate rule of thumb is that the confidence interval for a $\hat{\beta}_1$ estimate goes from 2 standard errors of $\hat{\beta}_1$ below $\hat{\beta}_1$ to 2 standard errors of $\hat{\beta}_1$ above $\hat{\beta}_1$. That is, the confidence interval for an estimate $\hat{\beta}_1$ will approximately cover $\hat{\beta}_1 - 2 \times se(\hat{\beta}_1)$ to $\hat{\beta}_1 + 2 \times se(\hat{\beta}_1)$.

The full explanation of confidence intervals involves statistical logic similar to that for t stats. The starting point is the realization that we can assess the probability of observing the $\hat{\beta}_1$ for any "true" β_1. For some values of β_1, our observed $\hat{\beta}_1$ wouldn't be surprising. Suppose, for example, we observe a coefficient of 0.41 with a standard error of 0.1, as we did in Table 3.2. If the true value were 0.41, a $\hat{\beta}_1$ near 0.41 wouldn't be too surprising. If the true value were 0.5, we'd be a wee bit surprised, perhaps, but not shocked, to observe $\hat{\beta}_1 = 0.41$. For some values of β_1, though, the observed $\hat{\beta}_1$ would be surprising. If the true value were 10, for example, we'd be gobsmacked to observe $\hat{\beta}_1 = 0.41$ with a standard error of 0.1. Hence, if we see $\hat{\beta}_1 = 0.41$ with a standard error of 0.1, we're pretty darn sure the true value of β_1 isn't 10.

Confidence intervals generalize this logic to identify the range of true values that would be reasonably likely to produce the $\hat{\beta}_1$ that we observe. They identify that range of true values for which the observed $\hat{\beta}_1$ and $se(\hat{\beta}_1)$ would not be too unlikely. We get to say what we mean by "unlikely" by choosing our significance level, which is typically $\alpha = 0.05$ or $\alpha = 0.01$. We'll often refer to **confidence levels**, which are $1 - \alpha$. The upper bound of a 95 percent confidence interval is the value of β_1 that yields less than a 2.5 percent probability of observing a $\hat{\beta}_1$ equal to or lower than the $\hat{\beta}_1$ actually observed. The lower bound of a 95 percent confidence interval is the value of β_1 that yields less than an $\frac{\alpha}{2} = 0.025$ probability of observing a $\hat{\beta}_1$ equal to or higher than the $\hat{\beta}_1$ actually observed.

▶ **confidence levels**
Term referring to confidence intervals and based on $1 - \alpha$.

Figure 4.8 illustrates the meaning of a confidence interval. Suppose $\hat{\beta}_1 = 0.41$ and $se(\hat{\beta}_1) = 0.1$. For any given true value of β, we can calculate the probability of observing the $\hat{\beta}_1$ we actually did observe. Panel (a) shows that if β_1 really were 0.606, the distribution of $\hat{\beta}_1$ would be centered at 0.606, and we would see a value as low as 0.41 (what we actually observe for $\hat{\beta}_1$) only 2.5 percent of the time. Panel (b) shows that if β_1 really were 0.214, the distribution of $\hat{\beta}_1$ would be centered at 0.214 and we would see a value as high as 0.41 (what we actually observe for $\hat{\beta}_1$) only 2.5 percent of the time. In other words, our

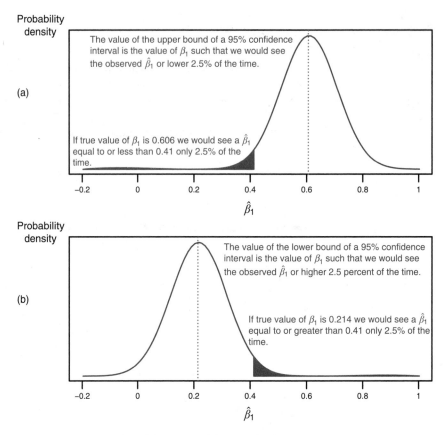

FIGURE 4.8: Meaning of Confidence Interval for Example of 0.41 ± 0.196

95% confidence interval ranges from 0.214 to 0.606 and includes the values that of β_1 that plausibly generate the $\hat{\beta}_1$ we actually observed.[8]

Figure 4.8 does not tell us how to calculate the upper and lower bounds of a confidence interval. A confidence interval is $\hat{\beta}_1 -$ critical value $\times \operatorname{se}(\hat{\beta}_1)$ to $\hat{\beta}_1 +$ critical value $\times \operatorname{se}(\hat{\beta}_1)$. For large samples and $\alpha = 0.05$, the critical value is 1.96, giving rise to the rule of thumb that a 95 percent confidence interval is approximately $\hat{\beta}_1 \pm 2 \times$ the standard error of $\hat{\beta}_1$. In our example, where $\hat{\beta}_1 = 0.41$ and $\operatorname{se}(\hat{\beta}_1) = 0.1$, we can be 95 percent confident that the true value is between 0.214 and 0.606.

---

[8] Confidence intervals can also be defined with reference to random sampling. Just as an OLS coefficient estimate is random, so too is a confidence interval. Just as a coefficient may randomly be far from true value, so too may a confidence interval fail to cover the true value. The point of confidence intervals is that it is unlikely that a confidence interval will fail to include the true value. For example, if we draw many samples from some population, 95 percent of the confidence intervals generated from these samples will include the true coefficient.

TABLE 4.6 Calculating Confidence Intervals for Large Samples

Confidence level	Critical value	Confidence interval	Example $\hat{\beta}_1 = 0.41$ and se$(\hat{\beta}_1) = 0.1$
90%	1.64	$\hat{\beta}_1 \pm 1.64 \times$ se$(\hat{\beta}_1)$	$0.41 \pm 1.64 \times 0.1 = 0.246$ to 0.574
95%	1.96	$\hat{\beta}_1 \pm 1.96 \times$ se$(\hat{\beta}_1)$	$0.41 \pm 1.96 \times 0.1 = 0.214$ to 0.606
99%	2.58	$\hat{\beta}_1 \pm 2.58 \times$ se$(\hat{\beta}_1)$	$0.41 \pm 2.58 \times 0.1 = 0.152$ to 0.668

Table 4.6 shows some commonly used confidence intervals for large sample sizes. The large sample size allows us to use the normal distribution to calculate critical values. A 90 percent confidence interval for our example is 0.246 to 0.574. The 99 percent confidence interval for a $\hat{\beta}_1 = 0.41$ and se$(\hat{\beta}_1) = 0.1$ is 0.152 to 0.668. Notice that the higher the confidence level, the wider the confidence interval.

Confidence intervals are closely related to hypothesis tests. Because confidence intervals tell us the range of possible true values that are consistent with what we've seen, we simply need to note whether the confidence interval on our estimate includes zero. If it does not, zero was not a value that would be likely to produce the data and estimates we observe; we can therefore reject H_0: $\beta_1 = 0$.

Confidence intervals do more than hypothesis tests, though, because they provide information on the likely location of the true value. If the confidence interval is mostly positive, but just barely covers zero, we would fail to reject the null hypothesis; we would also recognize that the evidence suggests the true value is likely positive. If the confidence interval does not cover zero but is restricted to a region of substantively unimpressive values of β_1, we can conclude that while the coefficient is statistically different from zero, it seems unlikely that the true value is substantively important.

REMEMBER THIS

1. A confidence interval indicates a range of values in which the true value is likely to be, given the data.

   - The lower bound of a 95 percent confidence interval will be a value of β_1 such that there is less than a 2.5 percent probability of observing a $\hat{\beta}_1$ as *high* as the $\hat{\beta}_1$ actually observed.

   - The upper bound a 95 percent confidence interval will be a value of β_1 such that there is less than a 2.5 percent probability of observing a $\hat{\beta}_1$ as *low* as the $\hat{\beta}_1$ actually observed.

2. A confidence interval is calculated as $\hat{\beta}_1 \pm t$-critical value $\times$ se$(\hat{\beta}_1)$, where the t-critical value is the critical value from the t table. It depends on the sample size and α, the significance level. For large samples and $\alpha = 0.05$, the t-critical value is 1.96.

Conclusion

"Statistical inference" refers to the process of reaching conclusions based on the data. Hypothesis tests, particularly *t* tests, are central to inference. They're pretty easy. Honestly, a well-trained parrot could probably do simple *t* tests. Look at the damn *t* statistic! Is it bigger than 2? Then squawk "reject"; if not, squawk "fail to reject."

We can do much more. With *p* values and confidence intervals, we can characterize our findings with some nuance. With power tests, we can recognize the likelihood of failing to see effects that are there. Taken as a whole, then, these tools help us make inferences from our data in a sensible way.

After reading and discussing this chapter, we should be able to do the following.

- Section 4.1: Explain the conceptual building blocks of hypothesis testing, including null and alternative hypotheses and Type I and Type II errors.

- Section 4.2: Explain the steps in using *t* tests to test hypotheses.

- Section 4.3: Explain *p* values.

- Section 4.4: Explain statistical power. Describe when it is particularly relevant.

- Section 4.5: Explain the limitations of hypothesis testing.

- Section 4.6: Explain confidence intervals. Explain the rule of thumb for approximating a 95 percent confidence interval.

Further Reading

Ziliak and McCloskey (2008) provide a book-length attack on the hypothesis testing framework. Theirs is hardly the first such critique, but it may be the most fun.

An important, and growing, school of thought in statistics called Bayesian statistics produces estimates of the following form: "There is an 8.2 percent probability that β is less than zero." Happily, there are huge commonalities across Bayesian statistics and the approach used in this (and most other) introductory books. Simon Jackman's *Bayesian Analysis for the Social Sciences* (2009) is an excellent guide to Bayesian statistics.

Key Terms

Alternative hypothesis (93)
Confidence interval (117)
Confidence levels (117)
Critical value (101)
Hypothesis testing (91)
Null hypothesis (92)
Null result (114)
One-sided alternative
    hypothesis (94)

p Value (106)
Point estimate (117)
Power (111)
Power curve (112)
Significance level (96)
Statistically significant (93)
Substantive significance
    (116)
t Distribution (99)

t Statistic (103)
t Test (98)
Two-sided alternative
    hypothesis (94)
Type I error (93)
Type II error (93)

Computing Corner

Stata

1. To find the critical value from a *t* distribution for a given a and $N - k$
   degrees of freedom, use the inverse *t* tail function in Stata: `display
   invttail(n-k, a)`.[9] The `display` command tells Stata to print the
   results on the screen.

   - To calculate the critical value for a one-tailed *t* test with $n - k = 100$
     and $\alpha = 0.05$, type `display invttail(100, 0.05)`.

   - To calculate the critical value for a two-tailed *t* test with $n - k = 100$
     and $\alpha = 0.05$, type `display invttail(100, 0.05/2)`.

2. To find the critical value from a normal distribution for a given a, use the
   inverse normal function in Stata. For a two-sided test with $\alpha = 0.05$, type
   `display invnormal(1-0.05/2)`. For a one-sided test with $\alpha = 0.01$,
   type `display invnormal(1-0.01)`.

3. The regression command in Stata (e.g., `reg Y X1 X2`) reports two-sided
   p values and confidence intervals. To generate the *p* values from the *t*
   statistic only, use `display 2*ttail(DF, abs(TSTAT))`, where DF is

---

[9] This is referred to as an *inverse t function* because we provide a percent (the α) and it returns a value
of the *t* distribution for which α percent of the distribution is larger in magnitude. For non-inverse *t*
function, we typically provide some value for *t* and the function tells us how much of the distribution
is larger in magnitude. The tail part of the function command indicates that we're dealing with the far
ends of the distribution.

the degrees of freedom and TSTAT is the observed value of the t statistic.[10] For a two-sided p value for a t statistic of 4.23 based on 1,908 degrees of freedom, type display 2*ttail(1908, 4.23).

4. Use the following code to create a power curve for $\alpha = 0.01$ and a one-sided alternative hypothesis covering 71 possible values of the true β_1 from 0 to 7:

```
set obs 71
gen BetaRange = (_n-1)/10 /* Sequence of possible betas from 0 to 7 */
scalar stderrorBeta = 1.0 /* Standard error of beta-hat */
gen PowerCurve = normal(BetaRange/stderrorBeta - 2.32)
          /* Probability t statistic is greater than critical value */
          /* for each value in BetaRange/stderrorBeta */
graph twoway (line PowerCurve BetaRange)
```

1. In R, inverse probability distribution functions start with q (no reason why, really; it's just a convention). To calculate the critical value for a two-tailed t test with $n - k = 100$ and $\alpha = 0.05$, use the inverse t distribution command. For the inverse t function, type qt(1-0.05/2, 100). To find the one-tailed critical value for a t distribution for $\alpha = 0.01$ and 100 degrees of freedom: qt(1-0.01, 100).

2. To find the critical value from a normal distribution for a given a, use the inverse normal function in R. For a two-sided test: qnorm(1-a/2). For a one-sided test: display qnorm(1-a).

3. The p value reported in summary(lm(Y ~ X1)) is a two-sided p value. To generate the p values from the t statistic only, use 2*(1-pt(abs(TSTAT), DF)), where TSTAT is the observed value of the t statistic and DF is the degrees of freedom. For example, for a two-sided p value for a t statistic of 4.23 based on 1,908 degrees of freedom, type 2*(1-pt(abs(4.23), 1908)).

4. To calculate confidence intervals by means of the regression results from the *Simpsons* data on page 83, use the confint command. For example, the 95 percent confidence intervals for the coefficient estimates in the donut regression model from the Chapter 3 Computing Corner (page 83) is

---

[10] The ttail function in Stata reports the probability of a t-distributed random variable being higher than a t statistic we provide (which we denote here as TSTAT). This syntax contrasts to the convention for normal distribution functions, which typically report the probability of being less than the t statistic we provide.

```
confint(OLSResults, level = 0.95)

                     2.5%      97.5%
     (Intercept)   86.605    158.626
     donuts         4.878     13.329
```

5. Use the following code to create a power curve for $\alpha = 0.01$ and a one-sided alternative hypothesis covering 71 possible values of the true β_1 from 0 to 7:

```
BetaRange = seq(0, 7, 0.1)
    # Sequence of possible betas from 0 to 7
    # separated by 0.1 (e.g. 0, 0.1, 0.2, ...)
stderrorBeta = 1
    # Standard error of beta-hat
PowerCurve = pnorm(BetaRange/stderrorBeta -2.32)
    # Probability t statistic is greater than critical value
    # for each value in BetaRange/stderrorBeta}
plot(BetaRange, PowerCurve, xlab="Beta",
        ylab="Probability reject null", type="l")
```

Exercises

1. Persico, Postlewaite, and Silverman (2004) analyzed data from the National Longitudinal Survey of Youth (NLSY) 1979 cohort to assess the relationship between height and wages for white men. Here we explore the relationship between height and wages for the full sample, which includes men and women and all races. The NLSY is a nationally representative sample of 12,686 young men and women who were 14 to 22 years old when they were first surveyed in 1979. These individuals were interviewed annually through 1994 and biannually since then. Table 4.7 describes the variables from heightwage.dta we'll use for this question.

   (a) Create a scatterplot of adult wages against adult height. What does this plot suggest about the relationship between height and wages?

TABLE 4.7 Variables for Height and Wage Data in the United States

Variable name	Description
wage96	Hourly wages (in dollars) in 1996
height85	Adult height: height (in inches) measured in 1985

(b) Estimate an OLS regression in which adult wages is regressed on adult height for all respondents. Report the estimated regression equation and interpret the results, explaining in particular what the p value means.

(c) Assess whether the null hypothesis that the coefficient on *height*81 equals 0 is rejected at the 0.05 significance level for one-sided and for two-sided hypothesis tests.

2. In this problem, we will conduct statistical analysis on the sheep experiment discussed at the beginning of the chapter. We will create variables and use OLS to analyze their relationships. Death is the dependent variable and treatment is the independent variable. For all models, the treatment variable will equal one for the first 24 observations and zero for the last 24 observations.

(a) Suppose, as in the example, that only one sheep in the treatment group died and all sheep in the control group died. Is the treatment coefficient statistically significant? What is the (two-sided) p value? What is the confidence interval?

(b) Suppose now that only one sheep in the treatment group died and only 10 sheep in the control group died. Is the treatment coefficient statistically significant? What is the (two-sided) p value? What is the confidence interval?

(c) Continue supposing that only one sheep in the treatment group died. What is the minimal number of sheep in the control group that needed to die for the treatment effect to be statistically significant? (Solve by trial and error.)

3. Voters care about the economy, often more than any other issue. It is not surprising, then, that politicians invariably argue that their party is best for the economy. Who is right? In this exercise we'll look at the U.S. economic and presidential party data in PresPartyEconGrowth.dta to test if there is any difference in economic performance between Republican and Democratic presidents. We will use two different dependent variables:

- *ChangeGDPpc* is the change in real per capita GDP in each year from 1962 to 2013 (in inflation-adjusted U.S. dollars, available from the World Bank).

- *Unemployment* is the unemployment rate each year from 1947 to 2013 (available from the U.S. Bureau of Labor Statistics).

Our independent variable is *LagDemPres*. This variable equals 1 if the president in the previous year was a Democrat and 0 if the president in the previous year was a Republican. The idea is that the president's policies do not take effect immediately, so and the economic growth in a given year may be influenced by who was president the year before.[11]

(a) Estimate a model with unemployment as the dependent variable and *LagDemPres* as the independent variable. Interpret the coefficients.

(b) Estimate a model with GDP per capita as the dependent variable and *LagDemPres* as the independent variable. Interpret the coefficients. Explain why the sample size differs from the first model.

(c) Choose an α level and alternative hypothesis and indicate for each model above whether you accept or reject the null hypothesis.

(d) Explain in your own words what the p value means for the *LagDemPres* variable in each model.

(e) Create a power curve for the model with GDP per capita as the dependent variable for $\alpha = 0.01$ and a one-sided alternative hypothesis. Explain what the power curve means by indicating what the curve means for true $\beta_1 = 200$, 400, and 800. Use the code in the Computing Corner, but with the actual standard error of $\hat{\beta}_1$ from the regression output.[12]

(f) Discuss the implications of the power curve for the interpretation of the results for the model in which change in GDP per capita was the dependent variable.

4. Run the simulation code in the initial part of the education and salary question from Chapter 3 (page 87).

(a) Generate t statistics for the coefficient on education for each simulation. What are the minimal and maximal values of these t statistics?

---

[11] Other ways of considering the question are addressed in the large academic literature on presidents and the economy. See, among others, Bartels (2008), Campbell (2011), Comiskey and Marsh (2012), and Blinder and Watson (2013).

[12] In Stata, start with the following lines to create a list of possible true values of β_1 and then set the "stderrorBeta" variable to be equal to the actual standard error of $\hat{\beta}_1$. *Note*: The first line clears all data; you will need to reload the data set if you wish to run additional analyses. If you have created a syntax file, it will be easy to reload and rerun what you have done so far.

```
clear
set obs 201
gen BetaRange = 4*(_n-1) /* Sequence of true beta values from 0 to 800 */
```

(b) Generate two-sided p values for the coefficient on education for each simulation. What are the minimal and maximal values of these p values?

(c) In what percent of the simulations do we reject the null hypothesis that $\beta_{Education} = 0$ at the $\alpha = 0.05$ level with a two-sided alternative hypothesis?

(d) Rerun the simulations, but set the true value of $\beta_{Education}$ to zero. (Do this in the gen Salary = 20000 + 1000*Ed + StdDev*rnormal() line of code by changing 1,000 to 0.) Do this for 500 simulations and report what percent of time we reject the null at the $\alpha = 0.05$ level with a two-sided alternative hypothesis.

5. We will continue the analysis of height and wages in Britain from the Exercises in Chapter 3, page 89.

(a) Estimate the model with income at age 33 as the dependent variable and height at age 33 as the independent variable. (Exclude observations with wages above 400 British pounds per hour and height less than 40 inches.) Interpret the t statistics on the coefficients.

(b) Explain the p values for the two estimated coefficients.

(c) Show how to calculate the 95 percent confidence interval for the coefficient on height.

(d) Do we accept or reject the null hypothesis that $\beta_1 = 0$ for $\alpha = 0.01$ and a two-sided alternative? Explain your answer.

(e) Do we accept or reject the null hypothesis that $\beta_0 = 0$ (the constant) for $\alpha = 0.01$ and a two-sided alternative? Explain.

(f) Limit the sample size to the first 800 observations.[13] Do we accept or reject the null hypothesis that $\beta_1 = 0$ for $\alpha = 0.01$ and a two-sided alternative? Explain if/how/why this answer differs from the earlier hypothesis test about β_1.

6. The data set MLBattend.dta contains Major League Baseball attendance records for 32 teams from the 1970s through 2000. This problem uses the power calculation described in Section 4.4 (page 111).

---

[13] In Stata, do this by adding & _n < 800 to the end of the "if" statement at the end of the "regress" command.

(a) Estimate a regression in which home attendance rate is the dependent variable and runs scored is the independent variable. Report your results and interpret all coefficients.

(b) Use the standard error from your results to calculate the statistical power of a test of H_0: $\beta_{runs\_scored} = 0$ vs H_A: $\beta_{runs\_scored} > 0$ with $\alpha = 0.05$ (assuming a large sample for simplicity) for three cases:

    (i) $\beta_{runs\_scored} = 100$

    (ii) $\beta_{runs\_scored} = 400$

    (iii) $\beta_{runs\_scored} = 1,000$

(c) Suppose we had much less data than we actually do, such that the standard error on the coefficient on β_{runs_scored} were 900 (which is much larger than what we estimated). Use the standard error of $\beta_{runs\_scored} = 900$ to calculate the statistical power of a test of H_0: $\beta_{runs\_scored} = 0$ vs H_A: $\beta_{runs\_scored} > 0$ with $\alpha = 0.05$ (assuming a large sample for simplicity) for three cases:

    (i) $\beta_{runs\_scored} = 100$

    (ii) $\beta_{runs\_scored} = 400$

    (iii) $\beta_{runs\_scored} = 1,000$

(d) Suppose we had much more data than we actually do, such that the standard error on the coefficient on β_{runs_scored} were 200 (which is much smaller than what we estimated). Use the standard error of $\beta_{runs\_scored} = 200$ to calculate the statistical power of a test of H_0: $\beta_{runs\_scored} = 0$ vs. H_A: $\beta_{runs\_scored} > 0$ with $\alpha = 0.05$ (assuming a large sample for simplicity) for three cases:

    (i) $\beta_{runs\_scored} = 100$

    (ii) $\beta_{runs\_scored} = 400$

    (iii) $\beta_{runs\_scored} = 1,000$

(e) Discuss the differences across the power calculations for the different standard errors.

5 Multivariate OLS: Where the Action Is

It's pretty easy to understand why we need to go beyond bivariate OLS: observational data is lousy with endogeneity. It's almost always the case that X is correlated with ϵ in observational data and if we ignore that reality, we may come up with some pretty silly results.

For example, suppose we've been tasked to figure out how sales responds to temperature. Easy, right? We can run a bivariate model such as

$$Sales_t = \beta_0 + \beta_1 Temperature_t + \epsilon_t$$

where $Sales_t$ is sales in billions of dollars during month t and $Temperature_t$ is the average temperature in the month. Figure 5.1 shows monthly data for New Jersey for about 20 years. We've also added the fitted line from a bivariate regression. It's negative, implying that people shop less as temperatures rise.

Is that the full story? Could there be endogeneity? Is something correlated with temperature and associated with more shopping? Think about shopping in the United States. When is it at its most frenzied? Right before Christmas. Something that happens in December . . . when it's cold. In other words, we think there is something in the error term (Christmas shopping season) that is correlated with temperature. That's a recipe for endogeneity.

In this chapter, we learn how to control for other variables so that we can avoid (or at least reduce) endogeneity and thereby see causal associations more clearly. Multivariate OLS is the tool that makes this possible. In our shopping example, multivariate OLS helps us see that once we account for the December effect, higher temperatures are associated with *higher* sales.

▶ **multivariate OLS**
OLS with multiple independent variables.

Multivariate OLS refers to OLS with multiple independent variables. We're simply going to add variables to the OLS model developed in the previous

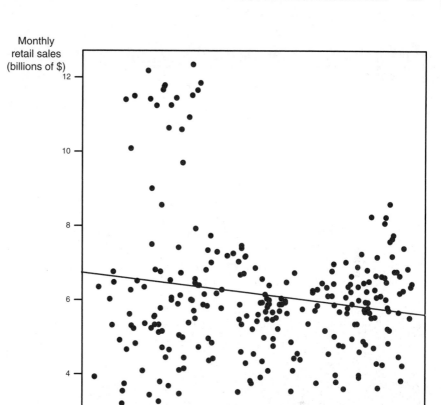

Monthly retail sales (billions of $)

Average monthly temperature (in degrees Fahrenheit)

FIGURE 5.1: Monthly Retail Sales and Temperature in New Jersey from 1992 to 2013

chapters. What do we gain? Two things: bias reduction and precision. When we reduce bias, we get more accurate parameter estimates because the coefficient estimates are on average less skewed away from the true value. When we increase precision, we reduce uncertainty because the distribution of coefficient estimates is more closely clustered toward the true value.

In this chapter we explain how to use multivariate OLS to fight endogeneity. Section 5.1 introduces the model and shows how controlling for multiple variables can lead to better estimates. Section 5.2 discusses omitted variable bias, which occurs when we fail to control for variables that affect Y and are correlated with included variables. Section 5.3 shows how the omitted variable bias framework can be used to understand what happens when we use poorly measured variables. Section 5.4 explains the precision of our estimates in multivariate OLS. Section 5.5 concludes the chapter with a more big-think discussion of how to decide which variables should go in a model.

Using Multivariate OLS to Fight Endogeneity

Multivariate OLS allows us to control for multiple independent variables at once. This section presents two situations in which controlling for additional variables has a huge effect on the results. Then we discuss the mechanics of the multivariate estimation process.

Multivariate OLS in action: retail sales

The sales and temperature example is useful for getting the hang of multivariate analysis. Panel (a) of Figure 5.2 has the same data as Figure 5.1, but we've indicated the December observations with triangles. Clearly New Jerseyites shop more in December; it looks like the average sales are around $11 billion in December versus average sales of around $6 billion per month in other months. After we have taken into account that December sales run about $5 billion higher than other months, is there a temperature effect?

The idea behind multivariate OLS is to net out the December effect and then look at the relationship between sales and temperature. That is, suppose we subtracted the $5 billion bump from all the December observations and then

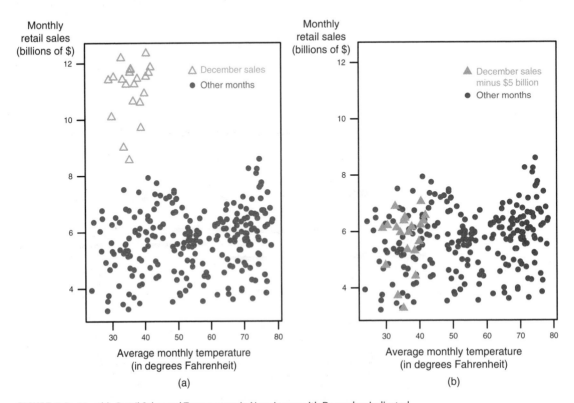

FIGURE 5.2: Monthly Retail Sales and Temperature in New Jersey with December Indicated

considered the relationship between temperature and sales. That is what we've done in panel (b) of Figure 5.2, where each December observation is now $5 billion lower than before. When we look at the data this way, the negative relationship between temperature and sales seems to go away; it may even be that the relationship is now positive.

In essence, multivariate OLS nets out the effects of other variables when it controls for additional variables. When we actually implement multivariate OLS, we (or, really, computers) do everything at once, controlling for the December effect while estimating the effect of temperature even as we are simultaneously controlling for temperature while estimating the December effect.

Table 5.1 shows the results for both a bivariate and a multivariate model for our sales data. In the bivariate model, the coefficient on temperature is –0.019. The estimate is statistically significant because the t-statistic is above 2. The implication is that people shop less as it gets warmer or, in other words, folks like to shop in the cold. When we use multivariate OLS to control for December (by including the December variable that equals one for observations from the month of December and zero for all other observations), the coefficient on temperature becomes positive and statistically significant. Our conclusion has flipped! Heat brings out the cash. Whether this relationship exists because people like shopping when it's warm or are going out to buy swimsuits and sunscreen, we can't say. We can say, though, that our initial bivariate finding that people shop less as the temperature rises is not robust to controlling for holiday shopping in December.

The way we interpret multivariate OLS regression coefficients is slightly different from how we interpret bivariate OLS regression coefficients. We still say that a one-unit increase in X is associated with a $\hat{\beta}_1$ increase in Y, but now

TABLE 5.1	Bivariate and Multivariate Results for Retail Sales Data	
	Bivariate	Multivariate
Temperature	−0.019*	0.014*
	(0.007)	(0.005)
	[$t = 2.59$]	[$t = 3.02$]
December		5.63*
		(0.26)
		[$t = 21.76$]
Constant	7.16*	4.94*
	(0.41)	(0.26)
	[$t = 17.54$]	[$t = 18.86$]
N	256	256
$\hat{\sigma}$	1.82	1.07
R^2	0.026	0.661

Standard errors in parentheses.

* *indicates significance at $p < 0.05$, two-tailed.*

we need to add, "holding constant the other factors in the model." We therefore interpret our multivariate results as "Controlling for the December shopping boost, increases in temperature are associated with more shopping." In particular, the multivariate estimate implies that controlling for the surge in shopping in December, a one-degree increase in average monthly temperature is associated with an increase in retail sales of $0.014 billion (also known as $14 million).

Unless we're stalling for time, we don't have to say the full long version every time we talk about multivariate OLS results; people who understand multivariate OLS will understand the longer, technically correct interpretation. We can also use the fancy-pants phrase **ceteris paribus**, which means all else being equal, as in "Ceteris paribus, the effect on retail shopping in New Jersey of a one-degree increase in temperature is $14 million."

> **ceteris paribus** All else being equal. A phrase used to describe multivariate regression results as a coefficient is said to, account for change in the dependent variable with all other independent variables held constant.

The way economists talk about multivariate results takes some getting used to. When economists say things like *holding all else constant* or *holding all else equal*, they are simply indicating that the model contains other variables, which have been statistically controlled for. What they really mean is more like *netting out the effect of other variables in the model.* The logic behind saying that other factors are constant is that once we have netted out the effects of these other variables, it is as if the values of these variables are equal for every observation. The language doesn't exactly sparkle with clarity, but the idea is not particularly subtle. Hence, when someone says something like "Holding X_2 constant, the estimated effect of a one-unit change in X_1 is $\hat{\beta}_1$," we need simply to translate the remark as "Accounting for the effect of X_2, the effect of X_1 is estimated to be $\hat{\beta}_1$."

Multivariate OLS in action: height and wages

Here's another example that shows what happens when we add variables to a model. We use the data on height and wages introduced in Chapter 3 (page 74). The bivariate model was

$$Wages_i = \beta_0 + \beta_1 Adult\ height_i + \epsilon_i \tag{5.1}$$

where $Wages_i$ was the wages of men in the sample in 1996 and the adult height was measured in 1985.

This is observational data, and the reality is that with such data, the bivariate model is suspect. There are many ways something in the error term could be correlated with the independent variable.

The authors of the height and wages study identified several additional variables to include in the model, focusing in particular on one: adolescent height. They reasoned that people who were tall as teenagers might have developed more confidence and participated in more high school activities, and that this experience may have laid the groundwork for higher wages later.

If teen height is actually boosting adult wages in the way the researchers suspected, it is possible that the bivariate model with only adult height (Equation 5.1) will suggest a relationship even though the real action was to be found between adolescent height and wages. How can we tell what the real story is?

Multivariate OLS comes to the rescue. It allows us to simply "pull" adolescent height out of the error term and into the model by including it as an additional variable in the model. The model becomes

$$Wages_i = \beta_0 + \beta_1 Adult\ height_i + \beta_2 Adolescent\ height_i + \epsilon_i \qquad (5.2)$$

where β_1 reflects the effect on wages of being one inch taller as an adult when including adolescent height in the model and β_2 reflects the effect on wages of being one inch taller as an adolescent when adult height is included in the model.

The coefficients are estimated by using logic similar to that for bivariate OLS. We'll discuss estimation momentarily. For now, though, let's concentrate on the differences between bivariate and multivariate results. Both are presented in Table 5.2. The first column shows the coefficient and standard error on $\hat{\beta}_1$ for the bivariate model with only adult height in the model; these are identical to the results presented in Chapter 3 (page 75). The coefficient of 0.41 implies that each inch of height is associated with an additional 41 cents per hour in wages.

	Bivariate	Multivariate	
		(a)	(b)
Adult height	0.41*	0.003	0.03
	(0.10)	(0.20)	(0.20)
	[$t = 4.23$]	[$t = 0.02$]	[$t = 0.17$]
Adolescent height		0.48*	0.35
		(0.19)	(0.19)
		[$t = 2.49$]	[$t = 1.82$]
Athletics			3.02*
			(0.56)
			[$t = 5.36$]
Clubs			1.88*
			(0.28)
			[$t = 6.69$]
Constant	−13.09	−18.14*	−13.57
	(6.90)	(7.14)	(7.05)
	[$t = 1.90$]	[$t = 2.54$]	[$t = 1.92$]
N	1,910	1,870	1,851
$\hat{\sigma}$	11.9	12.0	11.7
R^2	0.01	0.01	0.06

TABLE 5.2 **Bivariate and Multiple Multivariate Results for Height and Wages Data**

Standard errors in parentheses.

* *indicates significance at $p < 0.05$, two-tailed.*

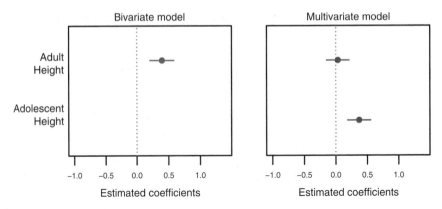

FIGURE 5.3: 95 Percent Confidence Intervals for Coefficients in Adult Height, Adolescent Height, and Wage Models

The second column shows results from the multivariate analysis; they tell quite a different story. The coefficient on adult height is, at 0.003, essentially zero. In contrast, the coefficient on adolescent height is 0.48, implying that, controlling for adult height, adult wages were 48 cents higher per hour for each inch taller someone was when younger. The standard error on this coefficient is 0.19 with a t statistic that is higher than 2, implying a statistically significant effect.

Figure 5.3 displays the confidence intervals implied by the coefficients and their standard errors. The dots are placed at the coefficient estimate (e.g., 0.41 for the coefficient on adult height in the bivariate model and 0.003 for the coefficient on adolescent height in the multivariate model). The solid lines indicate the range of the 95 percent confidence interval. As discussed in Chapter 4 (page 119), confidence intervals indicate the range of true values of β most consistent with the observed estimate; they are calculated as $\hat{\beta} \pm 1.96 \times \text{se}(\hat{\beta})$.

The confidence interval for the coefficient on adult height in the bivariate model is clearly positive and relatively narrow, and it does not include zero. However, the confidence interval for the coefficient on adult height includes zero in the multivariate model. In other words, the multivariate model suggests that the effect of adult height on wages is small or even zero when we control for adolescent height. In contrast, the confidence interval for adolescent height is positive, reasonably wide, and far from zero when we control for adult height. These results suggest that the effect of adolescent height on wages is large and the relationship we see is unlikely to have arisen simply by chance.

In this head-to-head battle of the two height variables, adolescent height wins: the coefficient on it is large, and its confidence interval is far from zero. The coefficient on adult height, however, is puny and has a confidence interval that clearly covers zero. In other words, the multivariate model we have estimated is telling us that being tall as a kid matters more than being tall as a grown-up. This conclusion is quite thought provoking. It appears that the height premium in wages does not reflect a height fetish by bosses; instead, it reflects the human capital developed in youth extracurricular activities. Eat your veggies, make the volleyball team, get rich.

Estimation process for multivariate OLS

Multivariate OLS allows us to keep adding independent variables; that's where the "multi" comes from. Whenever we think of another variable that could plausibly be in the error term and could be correlated with the independent variable of interest, we simply add it to the model (thereby removing it from the error term and eliminating it as a possible source of endogeneity). Lather. Rinse. Repeat. Do this long enough and we may be able to wash away sources of endogeneity lurking in the error term. The model will look something like

$$Y_i = \beta_0 + \beta_1 X_{1i} + \beta_2 X_{2i} + \cdots + \beta_k X_{ki} + \epsilon_i \tag{5.3}$$

where each X is another variable and k is the total number of independent variables. Often a single variable is of primary interest, or perhaps a subset of variables. We refer to the other independent variables as **control variables**, as these are included to control for factors that could affect the dependent variable and also could be correlated with the independent variables of primary interest. Control variables and control groups are different: a *control variable* is an additional variable we include in a model, while a *control group* is the group to which we compare the treatment group in an experiment.[1]

▶ **control variable** An independent variable included in a statistical model to control for some factor that is not the primary factor of interest.

The authors of the height and wage study argue that adolescent height in and of itself was not causing increased wages. Their view is that adolescent height translated into opportunities that provided skills and experience that increased ability to get high wages later. They view increased participation in clubs and sports activities as a channel for adolescent height to improve wage-increasing human capital. In statistical terms, the claim is that participation in clubs and athletics was a factor in the error term of a model with only adult height and adolescent height. If either height variable turns out to be correlated with any of the factors in the error term, we could have endogeneity.

With the right data, we can check the claim that the effect of adolescent height on adult wages is due, at least in part, to the effect of adolescent height

---

[1] The control variable and control group concepts are related. In an experiment, a control variable is set to be the same for all subjects of the experiment, to ensure that the only difference between treated and untreated groups is the experimental treatment. If we were experimenting on samples in petri dishes, for example, we could treat temperature as a control variable. We would make sure that the temperature is the same for all petri dishes used in the experiment. Hence, the *control group* has everything similar to the treatment group except the treatment. In observational studies, we cannot determine the values of other factors; we can, however, try to net out these other factors, such that once we have taken them into account, the treated and untreated groups should be the same. In the Christmas shopping example, the dummy variable for December is our control variable. The idea is that once we net out the effect of Christmas on shopping patterns in the United States, retail sales should differ based only on differences in the temperature. If we worry (as we should) that factors in addition to temperature still matter, we should include other control variables until we feel confident that the only remaining difference is due to the variable of interest.

on participation in developmentally helpful activities. In this case, the researchers had measures of the number of clubs each person participated in (excluding athletics and academic/honor society clubs), as well as a dummy variable that indicated whether each person participated in high school athletics.

The right-most column of Table 5.2 therefore presents "multivariate (b)" results from a model that also includes measures of participation in activities as a young person. If adolescent height truly translates into higher wages because tall adolescents have more opportunities to develop leadership and other skills, we would expect part of the adolescent height effect to be absorbed by the additional variables. As we see in the right-most column, this is part of the story. The coefficient on adolescent height in the multivariate (b) column goes down to 0.35 with a standard error of 0.19, which is statistically insignificant. The coefficients on the athletics and clubs variables are 3.02 and 1.88, respectively, with t stats of 5.36 and 6.69, implying highly statistically significant effects.

By the way, notice the R^2 values at the bottom of the table. They are 0.01, 0.01, and 0.06. Terrible, right? Recall that R^2 is the square of the correlation of observed and fitted observations. (Or, equivalently, these R^2 numbers indicate the proportion of the variance of wages explained by the independent variables.) These values mean that the even in the best-fitting model, the correlation of observed and fitted values of wages is about 0.245 (because $\sqrt{0.06} = 0.245$). That's not so hot, but we shouldn't care. That's not how we evaluate models. As discussed in Chapter 3 (page 71), we evaluate the strength of estimated relationships based on coefficient estimates and standard errors, not based on directly looking at R^2.

As practical people, we recognize that measuring every possible source of endogeneity in the error term is unlikely. But if we can measure more variables and pull more factors out of the error term, our estimates typically will become less biased and will be distributed more closely to the true value. We provide more details when we discuss omitted variable bias in the next section.

Given how important it is to control for additional variables, we may reasonably wonder about how exactly multivariate OLS controls for multiple variables. Basically, the estimation of the multivariate model follows the same OLS principles used in the bivariate OLS model. Understanding the estimation process is not essential for good analysis per se, but understanding it helps us get comfortable with the model and its fitted values.

First, write out the equation for the residual, which is the difference between actual and fitted values:

$$\hat{\epsilon}_i = Y_i - \hat{Y}_i$$
$$= Y_i - (\hat{\beta}_0 + \hat{\beta}_1 X_{1i} + \hat{\beta}_2 X_{2i} + \cdots + \hat{\beta}_k X_{ki})$$

Second, square the residuals (for the same reasons given on page 49):

$$\hat{\epsilon}_i^2 = (Y_i - (\hat{\beta}_0 + \hat{\beta}_1 X_{1i} + \hat{\beta}_2 X_{2i} + \cdots + \hat{\beta}_k X_{ki}))^2$$

Multivariate OLS then finds the $\hat{\beta}$'s that minimize the sum of the squared residuals over all observations. We let computers do that work for us.

The name "ordinary least squares" (OLS) describes the process: *ordinary* because we haven't gotten to the fancy stuff yet, *least* because we're minimizing the deviations between fitted and actual values, and *squares* because there was a squared thing going on in there. Again, it's an absurd name. It's like calling a hamburger a "kill-with-stun-gun-then-grill-and-put-on-a-bun." OLS is what people call it, though, so we have to get used to it.

REMEMBER THIS

1. Multivariate OLS is used to estimate a model with multiple independent variables.

2. Multivariate OLS fights endogeneity by pulling variables from the error term into the estimated equation.

3. As with bivariate OLS, the multivariate OLS estimation process selects $\hat{\beta}$'s in a way that minimizes the sum of squared residuals.

Discussion Questions

1. *Mother Jones* magazine blogger Kevin Drum (2013a, b, c) offers the following scenario. Suppose we gathered records of a thousand school children aged 7 to 12, used a bivariate model, and found that heavier kids scored better on standardized math tests.

   (a) Based on these results, should we recommend that kids eat lots of potato chips and french fries if they want to grow up to be scientists?

   (b) Write down a model that embodies Drum's scenario.

   (c) Propose additional variables for this model.

   (d) Would inclusion of additional controls bolster the evidence? Would doing so provide definitive proof?

2. Researchers from the National Center for Addiction and Substance Abuse at Columbia University (2011) suggest that time spent on Facebook and Twitter increases risks of smoking, drinking, and drug use. They found that compared with kids who spent no time on social networking sites, kids who visited the sites each day were five times likelier to smoke cigarettes, three times more likely to drink alcohol, and twice as likely to smoke pot. The researchers argue that kids who use social media regularly see others engaged in such behaviors and then emulate them.

(a) Write down the model implied by the description of the Columbia study and discuss the factors that are in error term.

(b) What specifically has to be true about these factors for their omission to cause bias? Discuss whether these conditions will be true for the factors you identify.

(c) Discuss which factors could be measured and controlled for and which would be difficult to measure and control for.

3. Suppose we are interested in knowing the relationship between hours studied and scores on a Spanish exam.

(a) Suppose some kids don't study at all but ace the exam, leading to a bivariate OLS result that studying has little or no effect on the score. Would you be convinced by these results?

(b) Write down a model and discuss your answer to (a) in terms of the error term.

(c) What if some kids speak Spanish at home? Discuss implications for a bivariate model that does not include this factor and a multivariate model that controls for this factor.

5.2 Omitted Variable Bias

Another way to think about how multivariate OLS fights bias is by looking at what happens when we fail to soak up one of the error term variables. That is, what happens if we omit a variable that should be in the model? In this section we show that omitting a variable that affects Y and is correlated with X_1 will lead to a biased estimate of $\hat{\beta}_1$.

Let's start with a case in which the true model has two independent variables, X_1 and X_2:

$$Y_i = \beta_0 + \beta_1 X_{1i} + \beta_2 X_{2i} + v_i \quad (5.4)$$

We assume (for now) that the error in this true model, v_i, is uncorrelated with X_{1i} and X_{2i}. (The Greek letter v, or nu, is pronounced "new"—even though it looks like a v.) As usual with multivariate OLS, the β_1 parameter reflects how much higher Y_i would be if we increased X_{1i} by one; β_2 reflects how much higher Y_i would be if we increased X_{2i} by one.

What happens if we omit X_2 and estimate the following model?

$$Y_i = \beta_0^{\text{OmitX}_2} + \beta_1^{\text{OmitX}_2} X_{1i} + \epsilon_i \quad (5.5)$$

where β^{OmitX_2} indicates the coefficient on X_{1i} we get when we omit variable X_2 from the model. How close will $\hat{\beta}_1^{\text{OmitX}_2}$ be to β_1 in Equation 5.4? In other words, will $\hat{\beta}_1^{\text{OmitX}_2}$ be an unbiased estimator of β_1? Or, in English: will our estimate of the effect of X_1 suck if we omit X_2? We ask questions like this every time we analyze observational data.

It's useful to first characterize the relationship between the two independent variables, X_1 and X_2. To do this, we use an **auxiliary regression** equation. An auxiliary regression is a regression that is not directly the one of interest but yields information helpful in analyzing the equation we really care about. In this case, we can assess how strongly X_1 and X_2 are related by means of the equation

▶ **auxiliary regression**
A regression that is not directly the one of interest but is related to and yields information helpful in analyzing the equation we really care about.

$$X_{2i} = \delta_0 + \delta_1 X_{1i} + \tau_i \tag{5.6}$$

where δ_0 ("delta") and δ_1 are coefficients for this auxiliary regression and τ_i ("tau," rhymes with what you say when you stub your toe) is how we denote the error term (which acts just like the error term in our other equations, but we want to make it clear that we're dealing with a different equation). We assume τ_i is uncorrelated with v_i and X_1.

This equation for X_{2i} is not based on a causal model. Instead, we are using a regression model to indicate the relationship between the included variable (X_1) and the excluded variable (X_2). If $\delta_1 = 0$, then X_1 and X_2 are not related. If δ_1 doesn't equal zero, then X_1 and X_2 are related.

If we substitute the equation for X_{2i} (Equation 5.6) into the main equation (Equation 5.4), then do some rearranging and a bit of relabeling, we get

$$\begin{aligned} Y_i &= \beta_0 + \beta_1 X_{1i} + \beta_2(\delta_0 + \delta_1 X_{1i} + \tau_i) + v_i \\ &= (\beta_0 + \beta_2\delta_0) + (\beta_1 + \beta_2\delta_1)X_{1i} + (\beta_2\tau_i + v_i) \\ &= \beta_0^{OmitX_2} + \beta_1^{OmitX_2} X_{1i} + \epsilon_i \end{aligned}$$

This means that

$$\beta_1^{OmitX_2} = \beta_1 + \beta_2\delta_1 \tag{5.7}$$

where β_1 and β_2 come from the main equation (Equation 5.4) and δ_1 comes from the equation for X_{2i} (Equation 5.6).[2]

Given our assumption that τ and v are not correlated with any independent variable, we can use our bivariate OLS results to know that $\hat{\beta}_1^{OmitX_2}$ will be distributed normally with mean of $\beta_1 + \beta_2\delta_1$. In other words, when we omit X_2, the distribution of the estimated coefficient on X_1 will be skewed away from β_1 by a factor $\beta_2\delta_1$. This is **omitted variable bias**.

▶ **omitted variable bias** Bias that results from leaving out a variable that affects the dependent variable and is correlated with the independent variable.

In other words, when we omit X_2, the coefficient on X_1 (which is $\beta_1^{OmitX_2}$) will pick up not only β_1, which is the effect of X_1 on Y, but also β_2, which is the effect of the omitted variable X_2 on Y. The extent to which $\beta_1^{OmitX_2}$ picks up the effect of X_2 depends on δ_1, which characterizes how strongly X_2 and X_1 are related.

---

[2] Note that in the derivation, we replace $\beta_2\tau_i + v_i$ with ϵ_i. If, as we're assuming here, τ_i and v_i are uncorrelated with each other and uncorrelated with X_1, then errors of the form $\beta_2\tau_i + v_i$ will also be uncorrelated with each other and uncorrelated with X_1.

This result is consistent with our intuition about endogeneity: when X_2 is omitted and thereby relegated to the error, we won't be able to understand the true relationship between X_1 and Y to the extent that X_2 is correlated with X_1.[3]

Two conditions must hold for omitted variable bias to occur. The first is that $\beta_2 \neq 0$. If this condition does not hold, $\beta_2 = 0$ and $\beta_2 \delta_1 = 0$, which means that the bias term in Equation 5.7 goes away and there is no omitted variable bias. In other words, if the omitted variable X_2 has no effect on Y_i (which is the implication of $\beta_2 = 0$), there will be no omitted variable bias. Perhaps this is obvious; we probably weren't worried that our wage and height models in Section 5.1 were biased because we failed to include a variable for the whether the individual likes baked beans. Nonetheless, it is useful to be clear that omitted variable bias requires omission of a variable that affects the dependent variable.

The second condition for omitted variable bias to occur is that $\delta_1 \neq 0$. The parameter δ_1 from Equation 5.6 tells us how strongly X_1 and X_2 are related. If X_1 and X_2 are not related, then $\delta_1 = 0$. This, in turn, means $\hat{\beta}_1^{\mathrm{OmitX_2}}$ will be an unbiased estimate of β_1 from Equation 5.4, the true effect of X_1 on Y even though we omitted X_2 from the model. In other words, if the omitted variable is not correlated with the included variable, . . . no harm and no foul.

This discussion relates perfectly to our theme of endogeneity. If a variable is omitted, it ends up in the error term. If the omitted variable hanging out in the error term is correlated with the included variable (which means $\delta_1 \neq 0$), then we have endogeneity and we have bias. We now have an equation that tells us the extent of the bias. If, on the other hand, the omitted variable hanging out in the error term is not correlated with the included variable (which means $\delta_1 = 0$), we do not have endogeneity and we do not have bias. Happy, happy, happy.

If either of these two conditions holds, there is no omitted variable bias. In most cases, though, we can't be sure that at least one condition holds because we don't actually have a measure of the omitted variable. In that case, we can use omitted variable bias concepts to speculate on the magnitude of the bias. The magnitude of bias depends on how much the omitted variable explains Y (which is determined by β_2) and how much the omitted variable is related to the included variable (which is reflected in δ_1). Sometimes we can come up with possible bias but believe that β_2 or δ_1 is small, meaning that we shouldn't lose too much sleep over bias. On the other hand, in other cases, we might think β_2 and δ_1 are huge. Hello, insomnia.

Omitted variable bias in more complicated models

Chapter 14 covers additional topics related to omitted variable bias. On page 493 we discuss how to use the bias equation to anticipate whether omission of a variable will cause the estimated coefficient to be higher or lower than it should be. On page 494 we discuss the more complicated case in which the true model and the estimated model have more variables. These situations are a little harder to predict than the case we have discussed. As a general matter, bias usually (but not always) goes down when we add variables that explain the dependent variable.

---

[3] We derive this result more formally on page 489.

> **REMEMBER THIS**

1. Two conditions must both be true for omitted variable bias to occur:

    a) The omitted variable affects the dependent variable.

    - Mathematically: $\beta_2 \neq 0$ in Equation 5.4.

    - An equivalent way to state this condition is that X_{2i} really should have been in Equation 5.4 in the first place.

    b) The omitted variable is correlated with the included independent variable. Mathematically: $\delta_1 \neq 0$ in Equation 5.6.

2. Omitted variable bias is more complicated in models with more independent variables, but the main intuition applies.

CASE STUDY   ## Does Education Support Economic Growth?

Does more education lead to more economic growth? A standard way to look at this question is via so-called growth equations in which the average growth of countries over some time period is the dependent variable. Hanushek and Woessmann (2012) put together a data set on economic growth of 50 countries from 1960 to 2000. The basic model is

$$\text{Growth from 1960 to 2000}_i$$
$$= \beta_0 + \beta_1 \text{Average years of education}_i$$
$$+ \beta_2 \text{GDP per capita in 1960}_i + \epsilon_i$$

The data is structured such that even though information on the economic growth in these countries for each year is available, we are looking only at the average growth rate across the 40 years from 1960 to 2000. Thus each country gets only a single observation. We control for GDP per capita in 1960 because of a well-established phenomenon that countries that were wealthier in 1960 have a slower growth rate. The poor countries simply have more capacity to grow economically. The main independent variable of interest at this point is average years of education; it measures education across countries.

The results in the left-hand column of Table 5.3 suggest that additional years of schooling promote economic growth. The $\hat{\beta}_1$ estimate implies that each additional average year of schooling within a country is associated with 0.44 percentage point higher annual economic growth. With a t statistic of 4.22, this is a highly statistically

TABLE 5.3 Using Multiple Measures of Education to Study Economic Growth and Education

	Without math/science test scores	With math/science test scores
Avg. years of school	0.44*	0.02
	(0.10)	(0.08)
	[$t = 4.22$]	[$t = 0.28$]
Math/science test scores		1.97*
		(0.24)
		[$t = 8.28$]
GDP in 1960	−0.39*	−0.30*
	(0.08)	(0.05)
	[$t = 5.19$]	[$t = 6.02$]
Constant	1.59*	−4.76*
	(0.54)	(0.84)
	[$t = 2.93$]	[$t = 5.66$]
N	50	50
$\hat{\sigma}$	1.13	0.72
R^2	0.36	0.74

Standard errors in parentheses.

* indicates significance at $p < 0.05$, two-tailed.

significant result. By using the standard error and techniques from page 119, we can calculate the confidence interval to be from 0.24 to 0.65.

Sounds good: more education, more growth. Nothing more to see here, right? Not to Hanushek and Woessmann. Their intuition was that not all schooling is equal. They were skeptical that simply sitting in class and racking up the years improves economically useful skills and argued that we should assess whether *quality* of education made a difference, not simply the quantity of it. As their measure of quality, they used average math and science test scores.

Before getting to their updated model, it's useful to get a feel for the data. Panel (a) of Figure 5.4 is a scatterplot of economic growth and average years of schooling. There's not an obvious relationship. (We observe a strong positive coefficient in the first column of Table 5.3 because GDP in 1960 was also controlled for.) Panel (b) of Figure 5.4 is a scatterplot of economic growth and average test scores. The observations with high test scores often were accompanied by high economic growth, suggesting a relationship between the two.

Could the real story be that test scores explain growth, not years in school? If so, why is there a significant coefficient on years of schooling in the first column of Table 5.3? We know the answer: omitted variable bias. As discussed on page 138, if we omit a variable that matters (and we suspect that test scores matter), the estimate of the effect of the variable that is included will be biased *if* the omitted variable is correlated with the included variable. To address this issue, look at panel (c) of Figure 5.4, a scatterplot of average test scores and average years of schooling.

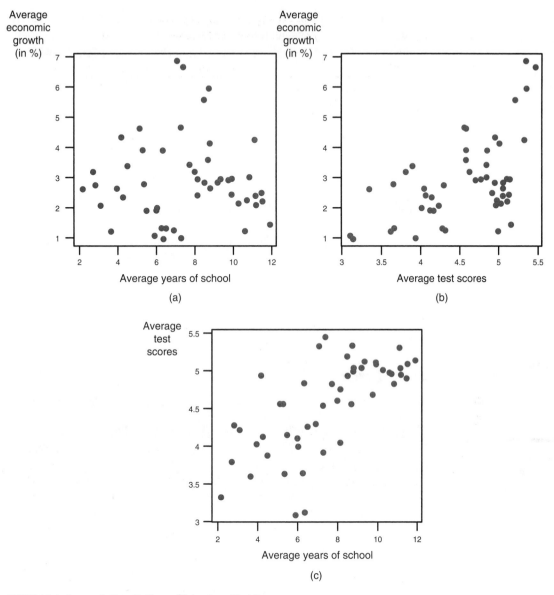

FIGURE 5.4: Economic Growth, Years of School, and Test Scores

Yes, indeed, these variables look quite correlated, as observations with high years of schooling also tend to be accompanied by high test scores. Hence the omission of test scores could be problematic.

Therefore it makes sense to add test scores to the model as in the right-hand column of Table 5.3. The coefficient on years of schooling differs markedly from before. It is now very close to zero. The coefficient on average test scores, on the other hand, is 1.97 and statistically significant, with a t statistic of 8.28.

Because the scale of the test score variable is not immediately obvious, we need to do a bit of work to interpret the substantive significance of the coefficient estimate. Based on descriptive statistics (not reported), the standard deviation of the test score variable is 0.61. The results therefore imply that increasing average test scores by a standard deviation is associated with an increase of $0.61 \times 1.97 =$ 1.20 percentage points in the average annual growth rate *per year* over these 40 years. This increase is large when we are talking about growth compounding over 40 years.[4]

Notice the very different story we have across the two columns. In the first one, years of schooling is enough for economic growth. In the second specification, quality of education, as measured with math and science test scores, matters more. The second specification is better because it shows that a theoretically sensible variable matters a lot. Excluding this variable, as the first specification does, risks omitted variable bias. In short, these results suggest that education is about quality, not quantity. High test scores explain economic growth better than years in school. Crappy schools do little; good ones do a lot. These results don't end the conversation about education and economic growth, but they do move it ahead a few more steps.

5.3 Measurement Error

> **measurement error**
> Measurement error occurs when a variable is measured inaccurately.

We can apply omitted variable concepts to understand the effects of **measurement error** on our estimates. Measurement error is pretty common; it occurs when a variable is measured inaccurately.

In this section we define the problem, show how to think of it as an omitted variables problem, and then characterize the nature of the bias caused when independent variables are measured with error.

Quick: how much money is in your bank account? It's pretty hard recall the exact amount (unless it's zero!). So a survey of wealth relying on people to recall their savings is probably going to have at least a little error and maybe a lot (especially because people get squirrelly about talking about money and some overreport and some underreport). And many, perhaps even most, variables could have error. Just think how hard it would be to accurately measure spending on education or life expectancy or attitudes toward Justin Bieber in an entire country.

Measurement error in the dependent variable

OLS will do just fine if the measurement error is only in the dependent variable. In this case, the measurement error is simply part of the overall error term.

---

[4] Since the scale of the test score variable is different from the years in school variable, we cannot directly compare the two coefficients. Section 7.3 shows how to make such comparisons.

The bigger the error, the bigger the variance of the error term. We know that in bivariate OLS, a larger variance of the error term leads to a larger $\hat{\sigma}^2$, which increases the variance of $\hat{\beta}$ (see page 64). This intuition carries over to multivariate OLS, as we'll see in Section 5.4.

Measurement error in the independent variable

OLS will not do so well if the measurement error is in an independent variable. In this case, the OLS estimate will systematically underestimate the magnitude of the coefficient. To see why, suppose the true model is

$$Y_i = \beta_0 + \beta_1 X_{1i}^* + \epsilon_i$$

where the asterisk in X_{1i}^* indicates that we do not observe this variable directly. For this section, we assume that ϵ_i is uncorrelated with X_{1i}^*, which lets us concentrate on measurement error.

Instead we observe our independent variable with error; that is, we observe some X_1 that is a function of the true value X_1^* and some error. For example, suppose we observe reported savings rather than actual savings:

$$X_{1i} = X_{1i}^* + v_i \tag{5.8}$$

We keep things simple here by assuming that the measurement error (v_i) has a mean of zero and is uncorrelated with the true value.

Notice that we can rewrite X_{1i}^* as the observed value (X_{1i}) minus the measurement error:

$$X_{1i}^* = X_{1i} - v_i$$

Substitute for X_{1i}^* in the true model, do a bit of rearranging, and we get

$$\begin{aligned} Y_i &= \beta_0 + \beta_1 (X_{1i} - v_i) + \epsilon_i \\ &= \beta_0 + \beta_1 X_{1i} - \beta_1 v_i + \epsilon_i \end{aligned} \tag{5.9}$$

The trick here is to think of this example as an omitted variable problem, where v_i is the omitted variable. We don't observe the measurement error directly, right? If we could observe it, we would fix our darn measure of X_1. So what we do is treat the measurement error as an unobserved variable that, by definition, we must omit; then we can see how this particular form of omitted variable bias plays out. Unlike the case of a generic omitted variable bias problem, we know two things that allow us to be more specific than in the general omitted variable case: the coefficient on the omitted term (v_i) is β_1 and v_i relates to X_1 as in Equation 5.8.

We go step by step through the logic and math in Chapter 14 (page 495). The upshot is that as the sample size gets very large, the estimated coefficient when the independent variable is measured with error is

$$\text{plim } \hat{\beta}_1 = \beta_1 \frac{\sigma^2_{X_1^*}}{\sigma^2_v + \sigma^2_{X_1^*}}$$

where plim is the probability limit, as discussed in Section 3.5.

Notice that $\hat{\beta}_1$ converges to the true coefficient times a quantity that has to be less than 1.

The equation becomes quite intuitive if we look at two extreme scenarios. If σ^2_v is zero, the measurement error has no variance and must always equal zero (given our assumption that it is a mean-zero random variable). In this case, $\frac{\sigma^2_{X_1^*}}{\sigma^2_v + \sigma^2_{X_1^*}}$ will equal one (assuming $\sigma_{X_1^*}$ is not zero, which is simply assuming that X_1^* varies). In other words, if there is no error in the measured value of X_1 (which is what $\sigma^2_v = 0$ means), then plim $\hat{\beta}_1 = \beta_1$, and our estimate of β_1 will converge to the true value as the sample gets larger. This conclusion makes sense: no measurement error, no problem. OLS will happily produce an unbiased estimate.

On the other hand, if σ^2_v is huge relative to $\sigma_{X_1^*}$, the measurement error varies a lot in comparison to X_1^*. In this case, $\frac{\sigma^2_{X_1^*}}{\sigma^2_v + \sigma^2_{X_1^*}}$ will be less than 1 and could be near zero, which means that the probability limit of $\hat{\beta}_1$ will be smaller than the true value. This result also makes sense: if the measurement of the independent variable is junky, how could we see the true effect of that variable on Y?

attenuation bias A form of bias in which the estimated coefficient is closer to zero than it should be.We refer to this particular example of omitted variable bias as **attenuation bias** because when we omit the measurement error term from the model, our estimate of $\hat{\beta}_1$ deviates from the true value by a multiplicative factor between zero and one. This means that $\hat{\beta}_1$ will be closer to zero than it should be when X_1 is measured with error. If the true value of β_1 is a positive number, we see values of $\hat{\beta}_1$ less than they should be. If the true value of β_1 is negative, we see values of $\hat{\beta}_1$ larger (meaning closer to zero) than they should be.

REMEMBER THIS

1. Measurement error in the *dependent variable* does not bias $\hat{\beta}$ coefficients but does increase the variance of the estimates.

2. Measurement error in an *independent variable* causes attenuation bias. That is, when X_1 is measured with error, $\hat{\beta}_1$ will generally be closer to zero than it should be.

   - The attenuation bias is a consequence of the omission of the measurement error from the estimated model.

   - The larger the measurement error, the larger the attenuation bias.

5.4 Precision and Goodness of Fit

Precision is crucial for hypothesis tests and confidence intervals. In this section we show that var($\hat{\beta}$) in multivariate OLS inherits the intuitions of var($\hat{\beta}$) in bivariate OLS but also is influenced by the extent to which the multiple independent variables covary together. We also discuss goodness of fit in the multivariate model and, in particular, what happens when we include independent variables that don't explain the dependent variable at all.

Variance of coefficient estimates

The variance of coefficient estimates for the multivariate model is similar to the variance of $\hat{\beta}_1$ for the bivariate model. As with variance of $\hat{\beta}_1$ in bivariate OLS, the equation we present applies when errors are homoscedastic and not correlated with each other. Complications arise when errors are heteroscedastic or correlated with each other, but the intuitions we're about to develop still apply.

We denote the coefficient of interest as $\hat{\beta}_j$ to indicate that it's the coefficient associated with the jth independent variable. The variance of the coefficient on the jth independent variable is

$$\text{var}(\hat{\beta}_j) = \frac{\hat{\sigma}^2}{N \, \text{var}(X_j)(1 - R_j^2)} \tag{5.10}$$

This equation is similar to the equation for variance of $\hat{\beta}_1$ in bivariate OLS (Equation 3.9, page 62). The new bit relates to the $(1 - R_j^2)$ in the denominator. Before elaborating on R_j^2, let's note the parts from the bivariate variance equation that carry through to the multivariate context.

- In the numerator we see $\hat{\sigma}^2$, which means that the higher the variance of the regression, the higher the variance of the coefficient estimate. Because $\hat{\sigma}^2$ measures the average squared deviation of the fitted value from the actual value $\left(\hat{\sigma}^2 = \frac{\sum_{i=1}^{N}(Y_i - \hat{Y}_i)^2}{N-k}\right)$, all else equal, the better our variables are able to explain the dependent variable, the more precise will our estimate of $\hat{\beta}_j$ be. This point is particularly relevant for experiments. In their ideal form, experiments do not need to add control variables to avoid bias.[5] Including control variables when analyzing experiments is still useful, however, because they improve the fit of the model, thus reducing $\hat{\sigma}^2$ and therefore giving us more precise coefficient estimates.

---

[5] We discuss experiments in their real-world form in Chapter 10.

- In the denominator we see the sample size, N. As for the bivariate model, as we get more data, this term in the denominator gets bigger, making the var($\hat{\beta}_j$) smaller. In other words, more data means more precise estimates.

- The greater the variation of X_j (as measured by $\frac{\sum_{i=1}^{N}(X_{ij}-\bar{X}_j)^2}{N}$ for large samples), the bigger the denominator will be. The bigger the denominator, the smaller var($\hat{\beta}_j$) will be.

Multicollinearity

The new element in Equation 5.10 compared to the earlier variance equation is the $(1 - R_j^2)$. Notice the j subscript. We use the subscript to indicate that R_j^2 is the R^2 from an auxiliary regression in which X_j is the dependent variable and all the other independent variables in the full model are the independent variables in the auxiliary model. The R^2 without the j is still the R^2 for the main equation, as discussed on page 72.

There is a different R_j^2 for each independent variable. For example, if our model is

$$Y_i = \beta_0 + \beta_1 X_{1i} + \beta_2 X_{2i} + \beta_3 X_{3i} + \epsilon_i \tag{5.11}$$

there will be three different R_j^2's:

- R_1^2 is the R^2 from $X_{1i} = \gamma_0 + \gamma_1 X_{2i} + \gamma_2 X_{3i} + \epsilon_i$ where the γ parameters are estimated coefficients from OLS. We're not really interested in the value of these parameters. We're not making any causal claims about this model—just using them to understand the correlation of independent variables (which is measured by the R_j^2). (We're being a bit loose notationally, reusing the γ and ϵ notation in each equation.)

- R_2^2 is the R^2 from $X_{2i} = \gamma_0 + \gamma_1 X_{1i} + \gamma_2 X_{3i} + \epsilon_i$

- R_3^2 is the R^2 from $X_{3i} = \gamma_0 + \gamma_1 X_{1i} + \gamma_2 X_{2i} + \epsilon_i$

These R_j^2 tell us how much the other variables explain X_j. If the other variables explain X_j very well, the R_j^2 will be high and—here's the key insight—the denominator will be smaller. Notice that the denominator of the equation for var($\hat{\beta}_j$) has $(1 - R_j^2)$. Remember that R^2 is always between 0 and 1; so as R_j^2 gets bigger, $1 - R_j^2$ gets smaller, which in turn makes var($\hat{\beta}_j$) bigger. The intuition is that if variable X_j is virtually indistinguishable from the other independent variables, it should in fact be hard to tell how much that variable affects Y and we will, therefore, have a larger var($\hat{\beta}_j$).

In other words, when an independent variable is highly related to other independent variables, the variance of the coefficient we estimate for that variable will be high. We use a fancy term, **multicollinearity**, to refer to situations in which independent variables have strong linear relationships. The term comes from "multi" for multiple variables and "co-linear" because they vary together in a linear fashion. The polysyllabic jargon should not hide a simple fact: *The variance of our estimates increases when an independent variable is closely related to other independent variables.*

The term $\frac{1}{1-R_j^2}$ is referred to as the **variance inflation factor** (VIF). It measures how much variance is inflated owing to multicollinearity relative to a case in which there is no multicollinearity.

It's really important to understand what multicollinearity does and does not do. It does not cause bias. It doesn't even cause the standard errors of $\hat{\beta}_1$ to be incorrect. It simply causes the standard errors to be bigger than they would be if there were no multicollinearity. In other words, OLS is on top of the whole multicollinearity thing, producing estimates that are unbiased with appropriately calculated uncertainty. It's just that when variables are strongly related to each other we're going to have more uncertainty—the distributions of $\hat{\beta}_1$ will be wider, meaning that it will be harder to learn from the data.

What, then, should we do about multicollinearity? If we have a lot of data, our standard errors may be small enough to allow reasonable inferences about the coefficients on the collinear variables. In that case, we do not have to do anything. OLS is fine and we're perfectly happy. Both our empirical examples in this chapter are consistent with this scenario. In the height and wages analysis in Table 5.2, adult height and adolescent height are highly correlated (at 0.86, actually). And yet, the actual effects of these two variables are so different that we can parse out their differential effects with the amount of data we have. In the education and economic growth analysis in Table 5.3, the years of school and test score variables are correlated at 0.81. And yet, the effects are different enough to let us parse out the differential effects of these two variables with the data we have.

However, if we have substantial multicollinearity, we may get very large standard errors on the collinear variables, preventing us from saying much about any one variable. Some are tempted in such cases to drop one or more of the highly multicollinear variables and focus only on the results for the remaining variables. This isn't quite fair, however, since we may not have solid evidence to indicate which variables we should drop and which we should keep. A better approach is to be honest: we should just say that the collinear variables taken as a group seem to matter or not and that we can't parse out the individual effects of these variables.

For example, suppose we are interested in predicting undergraduate grades as a function of two variables: scores from a standardized math test and scores from a standardized verbal reasoning test. Suppose also that these test score variables are highly correlated and that when we run a model with both variables as independent variables, both are statistically insignificant in part because the

---

▶ **multicollinearity**
Variables are multicollinear if they are correlated. The consequence of multicollinearity is that the variance of $\hat{\beta}_1$ will be higher than it would have been in the absence of multicollinearity. Multicollinearity does not cause bias.

▶ **variance inflation factor** A measure of how much variance is inflated owing to multicollinearity.

standard errors will be very high owing to the high R_j^2 values. If we drop one of the test scores, the remaining test score variable may be statistically significant, but it would be poor form to believe, then, that only that test score affected undergraduate grades. Instead, we should use the tools we present later (Section 7.4, page 226), which allow us to assess whether both variables taken together explain grades. At that point, we may be able to say that we know standardized test scores matter, but we cannot say much about the relative effect of math versus verbal test scores. So even though it'd be more fun to say which test score matters, the statistical evidence to justify the statement may simply not be there.

▶ **perfect multicollinearity**
Occurs when an independent variable is completely explained by other independent variables.

A lethal dose of multicollinearity, called **perfect multicollinearity**, occurs when an independent variable is completely explained by other independent variables. If this happens, $R_j^2 = 1$ and the var($\hat{\beta}_1$) blows up because $(1 - R_j^2)$ is in the denominator (in the sense that the denominator becomes zero, which is a big no-no). In this case, statistical software either will refuse to estimate the model or will automatically delete enough independent variables to extinguish perfect multicollinearity. A silly example of perfect multicollinearity is including the same variable twice in a model.

Goodness of fit

Let's talk about the regular old R^2, the one without a j subscript. As with the R^2 for a bivariate OLS model, the R^2 for a multivariate OLS model measures goodness of fit and is the square of the correlation of the fitted values and actual values (see Section 3.7).[6] As before, it can be interesting to know how well the model explains the dependent variable, but this information is often not particularly useful. A good model can have a low R^2 and a biased model can have a high R^2.

There is one additional wrinkle for R^2 in the multivariate context. Adding a variable to a model necessarily makes the R^2 go up, at least by a tiny bit. To see why, notice that OLS minimizes the sum of squared errors. If we add a new variable, the fit cannot be worse than before because we can simply set the coefficient on this new variable to be zero, which is equivalent to not having the variable in the model in the first place. In other words, every time we add a variable to a model, we do no worse and, as a practical matter, we do at least a little better even if the variable doesn't truly affect the dependent variable. Just by chance, estimating a non-zero coefficient on this variable will typically improve the fit for a couple of observations. Hence R^2 always is the same or larger as we add variables.

Devious people therefore think, "Aha, I can boost my R^2 by adding variables." First of all, who cares? R^2 isn't directly useful for much. Second of all, that's cheating. Therefore most statistical software program report so-called

---

[6] The model needs to have a constant term for this interpretation to work—and for R^2 to be sensible.

▶ **adjusted R^2** The R^2 with a penalty for the number of variables included in the model. Widely reported, but rarely useful.

adjusted R^2 results. This measure is based on the R^2 but lowers the value depending on how many variables are in the model. The adjustment is ad hoc, and different people do it in different ways. The idea behind the adjustment is perfectly reasonable, but it's seldom worth getting too worked up about adjusting per se. It's like electronic cigarettes. Yes, smoking them is less bad than smoking regular cigarettes, but, really, why do it at all?

Inclusion of irrelevant variables

▶ **irrelevant variable** A variable in a regression model that should not be in the model, meaning that its coefficient is zero. Including an irrelevant variable does not cause bias, but it does increase the variance of the estimates.

The equation for the variance of $\hat{\beta}_j$ is also helpful for understanding what happens when we include an **irrelevant variable**—that is, when we add a variable to the model that shouldn't be there. Whereas our omitted variable discussion was about what happens when we exclude a variable that should be in the model, here we want to know what happens when we include a variable that should *not* be in the model.

Including an irrelevant variable does not cause bias. It's as if we'd written down a model and the correct coefficient on the irrelevant variable happened to be zero. That doesn't cause bias, it's just another variable. We should get an unbiased estimate of that coefficient, and including the irrelevant variable will not create endogeneity.

It might seem therefore that the goal is simply to add as many variables as we can get our hands on. That is, the more we control for, the less likely there are to be factors in the error term that are correlated with the independent variable of interest. The reality is different. Including an irrelevant variable is not harmless. Doing so makes our estimates less precise because this necessarily increases R_j^2, since R^2 always go up when variables are added.[7] This conclusion makes sense: the more we clutter up our analysis with variables that don't really matter, the harder it is to see a clear relationship between a given variable and the dependent variable.

Review Questions

1. How much will other variables explain X_j when X_j is a randomly assigned treatment? Approximately what will R_j^2 be?

2. Suppose we are designing an experiment in which we can determine the value of all independent variables for all observations. Do we want the independent variables to be highly correlated or not? Why or why not?

---

[7] Our earlier discussion was about the regular R^2, but it also applies to any R^2 (from the main equation or an auxiliary equation). R^2 goes up as the number of variables increases.

REMEMBER THIS

1. If errors are not correlated with each other and are homoscedastic, the variance of the $\hat{\beta}_j$ estimate is

$$\text{var}(\hat{\beta}_j) = \frac{\hat{\sigma}^2}{N \times \text{var}(X_j)(1 - R_j^2)}$$

2. Four factors influence the variance of multivariate $\hat{\beta}_j$ estimates.

    (a) Model fit: The better the model fits, the lower will be $\hat{\sigma}^2$ and $\text{var}(\hat{\beta}_j)$.

    (b) Sample size: The more observations, the lower will be $\text{var}(\hat{\beta}_j)$.

    (c) Variation in X: The more the X_j variable varies, the lower will be $\text{var}(\hat{\beta}_j)$.

    (d) Multicollinearity: The less the other independent variables explain X_j, the lower will be R_j^2 and $\text{var}(\hat{\beta}_j)$.

3. Independent variables are multicollinear if they are correlated.

    (a) The variance of $\hat{\beta}_1$ is higher when there is multicollinearity than when there is no multicollinearity.

    (b) Multicollinearity does not bias $\hat{\beta}_1$ estimates.

    (c) The $\text{se}(\hat{\beta}_1)$ produced by OLS accounts for multicollinearity.

    (d) An OLS model cannot be estimated when there is perfect multicollinearity, that is, when an independent variable is perfectly explained by one or more of the other independent variables.

4. Inclusion of irrelevant variables occurs when variables that do not affect Y are included in a model.

    (a) Inclusion of irrelevant variables causes the variance of $\hat{\beta}_1$ to be higher than if the variables were not included.

    (b) Inclusion of irrelevant variables does not cause bias.

5. The variance of $\hat{\beta}_j$ is more complicated when errors are correlated or heteroscedastic, but the intuitions about model fit, sample size, variance of X, and multicollinearity still apply.

| CASE STUDY | Institutions and Human Rights |

Governments around the world all too often violate basic human rights. What deters such abuses? Many believe that an independent judiciary constrains governments from bad behavior.

This hypothesis offers a promising opportunity for statistical analysis. Our dependent variable can be *Human rights*$_{st}$, a measure of human rights for country s at time t based on rights enumerated in United Nations treaties. Our independent variable can be *Judicial independence*$_{st}$, which measures judicial independence for country s at time t based on the tenure of judges and the scope of judicial authority.[8]

We pretty quickly see that a bivariate model will be insufficient. What factors are in the error term? Could they be correlated with judicial independence? Experience seems to show that human rights violations occur less often in wealthy countries. Wealthy countries also tend to have more independent judiciaries. In other words, omission of country wealth plausibly satisfies conditions for omitted variable bias to occur: the variable influences the dependent variable and is correlated with the independent variable in question.

In looking at the effect of judicial independence on human rights, therefore it is a good idea to control for wealth. The left-hand column of Table 5.4 presents results from such a model. Wealth is measured by per capita GDP. The coefficient on judicial independence is 11.37, suggesting that judicial independence does indeed improve human rights. The t statistic is 2.53, so we reject the null hypothesis that the effect of judicial independence is zero.

Is this the full story? Is an omitted variable that affects human rights (the dependent variable) somehow correlated with judicial independence (the key independent variable)? If this is true, omitting this other variable could result in the showing of a spurious association between judicial independence and human rights protection.

New York University professor Anna Harvey (2011) proposes exactly such a critique. She argues that democracy might protect human rights and that the degree of democracy in a country could be correlated with judicial independence.

Before we discuss what Harvey found, let's think about what would have to be true if omitting a measure of democracy is indeed causing bias under our

---

[8] This example is based on La Porta et al. (2004). Measurement of abstract concepts like human rights and judicial independence is not simple. See Harvey (2011) for more details.

TABLE 5.4 **Effects of Judicial Independence on Human Rights**

	Without democracy variable	With democracy variable
Judicial independence	11.37*	1.03
	(4.49)	(3.15)
	[$t = 2.53$]	[$t = 0.33$]
Log GDP per capita	9.77*	1.07
	(1.36)	(4.49)
	[$t = 7.20$]	[$t = 0.82$]
Democracy		24.93*
		(2.77)
		[$t = 9.01$]
Constant	−22.68	30.97*
	(12.57)	10.15
	[$t = 1.80$]	[$t = 3.05$]
N	63	63
$\hat{\sigma}$	17.6	11.5
R^2	0.47	0.78
$R^2_{Judicialind.}$		0.153
R^2_{LogGDP}		0.553
$R^2_{Democracy}$		0.552

Standard errors in parentheses.

* *indicates significance at $p < 0.05$, two-tailed.*

conditions given on page 141. First, the level of democracy in a country actually needs to affect the dependent variable, human rights (this is the $\beta_2 \neq 0$ condition). Is that true here? Very plausibly. We don't know beforehand, of course, but it certainly seems possible that torture tends not to be a great vote-getter. Second, democracy needs to be correlated with the independent variable of interest, which in this case is judicial independence. This we know is almost certainly true: democracy and judicial independence definitely seem to go together in the modern world. In Harvey's data, democracy and judicial independence correlate at 0.26: not huge, but not nuthin'. Therefore we have a legitimate candidate for omitted variable bias.

The right-hand column of Table 5.4 shows that Harvey's intuition was right. When the democracy measure is added, the coefficients on both judicial independence and GDP per capita fall precipitously. The coefficient on democracy, however, is 24.93, with a t statistic of 9.01, a highly statistically significant estimate.

Statistical significance is not the same as substantive significance. Let's try to interpret our results in a more meaningful way. If we generate descriptive statistics for our variable that depends on human rights, we see that it ranges from 17 to

99, with a mean of 67 and a standard deviation of 24. Doing the same for the democracy variable indicates a range of 0 to 2 with a mean of 1.07 and a standard deviation of 0.79. A coefficient of 24.93 implies that a change in the democracy measures of one standard deviation is associated with a $24.93 \times 0.79 = 19.7$ increase on the human rights scale. Given that the standard deviation change in the dependent variable is 24, this is a pretty sizable association between democracy and human rights.[9]

This is a textbook example of omitted variable bias.[10] When democracy is not accounted for, judicial independence is strongly associated with human rights. When democracy is accounted for, however, the effect of judicial independence fades to virtually nothing. And, this is not just about statistics. How we view the world is at stake, too. The conclusion from the initial model was that courts protect human rights. The additional analysis suggests that democracy protects human rights.

The example also highlights the somewhat provisional nature of social scientific conclusions. Someone may come along with a variable to add or another way to analyze the same data that will change our conclusions. That is the nature of the social scientific process. We do the best we can, but we leave room (sometimes a little, sometimes a lot) for a better way to understand what is going on.

Table 5.4 also includes some diagnostics to help us think about multicollinearity, for surely such factors as judicial independence, democracy, and wealth are correlated. Before looking at specific diagnostics, we should note that collinearity of independent variables does not cause bias. It doesn't even cause the variance equation to be wrong. Instead, multicollinearity simply causes the variance to be higher than it would be without collinearity among the independent variables.

Toward the bottom of the table we see that $R^2_{Judicialind.}$ is 0.153. This value is the R^2 from an auxiliary regression in which judicial independence is the dependent variable and the GDP and democracy variables are the independent variables. This value isn't particularly high, and if we plug it into the equation for the variance inflation factor (VIF), which is just the part of the variance of $\hat{\beta}_j$ associated with multicollinearity, we see that the VIF for the judicial independence variable is $\frac{1}{1-R^2_j} = \frac{1}{1-0.153} = 1.18$. In other words, the variance of the coefficient on the judicial independence variable is 1.18 times larger than it would have been if the judicial independence variable were completely uncorrelated with the other independent variables in the model. That's pretty small. The R^2_{LogGDP} is 0.553. This value corresponds to a VIF of 2.24, which is higher but still not in a range people

---

[9] Determining exactly what is a substantively large effect can be subjective. There's no rule book on what is "large." Those who have worked in a substantive area for a long time often get a good sense of effects qualify as "large." An effect might be considered large if it is larger than the effect of other variables that people think are important. Or an effect might be considered large if we know that the benefit is estimated to be much higher than the cost. In the human rights case, we can get a sense of what a 19.7 change in human rights scale means by looking at pairs of countries that differed by around 20 points on that scale. Pakistan was 22 points higher than North Korea. Decide if it would make a difference to vacation in North Korea or Pakistan. If it would make a difference, then 19.7 is a large difference; if not, then it's not.

[10] Or, it is now, . . .

get too worried about. And, just to reiterate, this is not a problem to be corrected. Rather, we are simply noting that one source of variance of the coefficient estimate on GDP is multicollinearity. Another source is the sample size and another is the fit of the model (indicated by $\hat{\sigma}$, which indicates that the fitted values are, on average, roughly 11.5 units away from the actual values).

<table>
<tr><td>5.5</td><td></td></tr>
</table>

5.5 Model Specification

▶ **model specification**
The process of deciding which variables should go in a statistical model.

Multivariate OLS allows us to included multiple independent variables. Common sense boosted by our irrelevant variable results in the preceding section suggests that we cannot include every variable we can find.

That means we have to choose. We call the selection process **model specification** because it consists of specifying the variables we want to include in the model.[11] This process is tricky. Political scientist Phil Schrodt (2010) has noted that most experienced statistical analysts have witnessed cases in which "even minor changes in model specification can lead to coefficient estimates that bounce around like a box full of gerbils on methamphetamines." This is an exaggeration—perhaps a box of caffeinated chinchillas is more like it—but there is a certain truth behind his claim.

In this section we discuss three dangers in model specification and how to conduct and report results in a way that minimizes these dangers.

Model fishing

▶ **model fishing**
Occurs when researchers add and subtract variables until they get just the answers they were looking for.

An invidious problem in model specification is **model fishing**: the addition and subtraction of variables until the researchers get the answer they were looking for. Sometimes a given result may emerge under just the right conditions—perhaps when variables X_1 and X_4 are included and X_2 and X_3 are excluded—and this is the only result that the model fisher gives us.

One reason model fishing is possible is because the coefficient on any given variable can change depending on what other variables are in the model. We have already discussed how omitted variable bias can affect coefficients. We have also discussed how multicollinearity drives up variance of our estimates, meaning that the $\hat{\beta}_1$ estimates will tend to bounce around more when the independent variables are highly correlated with one another.

---

[11] Model specification also includes deciding on the functional form of the model. We discuss functional form in Chapter 7.

A second source of changing results is that sample size can change as we include more variables. Sometimes we're missing observations for some variables. For example, in survey data it is quite common for a pretty good chunk of people to decline to answer questions about their annual income. If we include a variable like income, OLS will include only observations for people who fessed up about how much money they make. If only half of the survey respondents answered, including increase as a control variable will cut our sample size in half. This change in the sample can cause coefficient estimates to jump around because, as we talked about with regard to sampling distributions (on page 53), coefficients will differ for each sample. In some instances, the effects on a coefficient estimate can be large.

A third danger in model specification arises when we are tempted to include so-called *post-treatment variables*. These are variables that are themselves affected by the independent variable of interest. For example, King (1991) discusses a study of the effect of oil prices on perceptions of oil shortages based on surveys over several years. We may be tempted to include a measure of media stories on oil because media stories very plausibly affect public perceptions. On the other hand, the media stories themselves may be a consequence of the oil price increase, meaning that if we include a media variable in the model, we may be underestimating the effect of oil prices on public opinion.

Ideally, we avoid post-treatment variables. In an experimental context, for example, we should control only for variables measured before the experiment or variables that do not change (such as sex and race). In observational studies, it can be tricky to irrefutably categorize variables as post-treatment, but it's worthwhile to try to focus on pretreatment controls and to report results with and without variables that themselves may be affected by the independent variable we're most interested in.[12]

Creating and reporting credible results

There are certain good practices that mitigate some of the dangers inherent in model specification. The first is to adhere to the replication standard. Some people see how coefficient estimates can change dramatically depending on specification and become statistical cynics. They believe that statistics can be manipulated to give any answer. Such thinking lies behind the aphorism "There are three kinds of lies: lies, damned lies, and statistics." A better response is skepticism, a belief that statistical analysis should be transparent to be believed. In this view, the saying should be "There are three kinds of lies: lies, damned lies, and statistics that can't be replicated."

A second good practice is to present results from multiple specifications in a way that allows readers to understand which steps of the specification

---

[12] See King (1991) for more on post-treatment variables (and a critique of R^2). Even pretreatment variables can be problematic; Elwert and Winship (2014) discuss recent results in causal inference suggesting that controlling for pretreatment variables with certain characteristics can cause bias, as well.

are the crucial ones for the conclusion being offered. Coefficients will change when variables are added or excluded; that is, after all, the point of multivariate analysis. For the analysis to be credible, though, it needs to be clear about which specification decisions drive the results. Readers need to know whether the results are robust to a number of reasonable specification choices or depend narrowly on one set of choices about which variables to include.

All statistical analysis should, as a matter of course, report multiple specifications, typically from a simple model to more complicated models. The results on height and wages reported in Table 5.2 offer one example, and we'll see more throughout the book.

REMEMBER THIS

1. An important part of model specification is choosing what variables to include in the model.

2. Reasons that results can very across model specifications include

   (a) Exclution of a variable may cause omitted variable bias that affects coefficients on included variables.

   (b) Inclusion of a variable may increase multicollinearity and lead to highly variable coefficient estimates.

   (c) Inclusion of a variable with missing data can change the sample and in some cases, change coefficient estimates.

   (d) Inclusion of a post-treatment variable can improperly soak up effects of a treatment variable.

3. Researchers should adhere to the replication standard by reporting multiple specifications, both to demonstrate the robustness of results and to highlight variables associated with changes in coefficients.

Conclusion

Multivariate OLS is a huge help in our fight against endogeneity because it allows us to add variables to our models. Doing so cuts off at least part of the correlation between an independent variable and the error term because the included variables are no longer in the error term. For observational data, multivariate OLS is very necessary, although we seldom can wholly defeat endogeneity simply by including variables. For experimental data not suffering from attrition, balance, or compliance problems, we can beat endogeneity without multivariate OLS. However, multivariate OLS makes our estimates more precise.

Multivariate OLS can be usefully regarded as an effort to avoid omitted variable bias. Omitting a variable causes problems when *both* the following are true: the omitted variable affects the dependent variable and is correlated with the included independent variable.

While we are most concerned with the factors that bias estimates, we have also identified four factors that make our estimates less precise. Three were the same as with bivariate OLS: poor model fit, limited variation in the independent variable, and small data sets. A precision-killing factor new to multivariate OLS is multicollinearity. When independent variables are highly correlated, they get in one another's way and make it hard for us to know which one has which effect. The result is not bias, but imprecision.

We're well on our way to understanding multivariate OLS when we can nail the following:

- Section 5.1: Write down the multivariate regression equation and explain all its elements (dependent variable, independent variables, coefficients, intercept, and error term). Explain how adding a variable to a multivariate OLS model can help fight endogeneity.

- Section 5.2: Explain omitted variable bias, including the two conditions necessary for omitted variable bias to exist.

- Section 5.3: Explain what measurement error in dependent and independent variables does to our coefficient estimates.

- Section 5.4: Produce the equation for the variance of $\hat{\beta}_1$ and explain the elements of it, including $\hat{\sigma}^2$, $\sum_{i=1}^{N}(X_{ij} - \overline{X}_j)^2$, and R_j^2. Use this equation to explain the consequences of multicollinearity and inclusion of irrelevant variables.

- Section 5.5: Explain good practices regarding model specification.

Further Reading

King, Keohane, and Verba (1994) provide an intuitive and useful discussion of omitted variable bias.

Goldberger (1991) has a terrific discussion of multicollinearity. His point is that the real problem with multicollinear data is that the estimates will be imprecise. We defeat imprecise data with more data; hence the problem of multicollinearity is not having enough data, a state of affairs Goldberger tongue-in-cheekily calls "micronumerosity."

Morgan and Winship (2014) provide a fascinating alternative way of thinking about controlling for multiple variables. They spend a fair bit of time discussing the strengths and weaknesses of multivariate OLS and providing alternatives.

Statistical results can often be more effectively presented as figures instead of tables. Kastellec and Leoni (2007) provide a nice overview of the advantages and options for such an approach.

Key Terms

Adjusted R^2 (151)
Attenuation bias (146)
Auxiliary regression (139)
Ceteris paribus (132)
Control variable (135)
Irrelevant variable (151)

Measurement error (144)
Model fishing (156)
Model specification (156)
Multicollinearity (149)
Multivariate OLS (128)
Omitted variable bias (139)

Perfect multicollinearity
(150)
Variance inflation factor
(149)

Computing Corner

Stata

1. To estimate a multivariate OLS model, we simply extend the syntax from bivariate OLS (described on page 81). The syntax is
   ```
   reg Y X1 X2 X3
   ```
   For heteroscedasticity-consistent standard errors, simply add the robust subcommand (as discussed on page 68):
   ```
   reg Y X1 X2 X3, robust
   ```

2. There are two ways to assess multicollinearity.

   - Calculating the R_j^2 for each variable. For example, calculate the R_1^2 via
     ```
     reg X1 X2 X3
     ```
     and calculate the R_2^2 via
     ```
     reg X2 X1 X3
     ```

   - Stata also provides a variance inflation factor command that estimates $\frac{1}{1-R_j^2}$ for each variable. This command needs to be run immediately after the main model of interest. For example,
     ```
     reg Y X1 X2 X3
     vif
     ```
     would provide the variance inflation factor for all variables from the main model. A VIF of 5, for example, indicates that the variance is five times higher than it would be if there were no multicollinearity.

R

1. To estimate a multivariate OLS model, we simply extend the syntax described on page 83. The syntax is

    `OLSResults = lm(Y ~ X1 + X2 + X3)`

    For heteroscedasticity-consistent standard errors, install and load the AER package and use the `coeftest` and `vcov` commands as follows, as discussed on page 85:

    `coeftest(OLSResults, vcov = vcovHC(OLSResults, type = "HC1"))`

2. To assess multicollinearity, calculate the R_j^2 for each variable. For example, calculate the R_1^2 via

    `AuxReg1 = lm(X1 ~ X2 + X3)`

    and calculate the R_2^2 via

    `AuxReg2 = lm(X2 ~ X1 + X3)`

Exercises

1. Table 5.5 describes variables from heightwage.dta we will use in this problem. We have seen this data in Chapter 3 (page 73) and in Chapter 4 (page 123).

    (a) Estimate two OLS regression models: one in which adult wages is regressed on adult height for all respondents, the other in which adult wages is regressed on adult height *and* adolescent height for

TABLE 5.5 Variables for Height and Wages Data in the United States

Variable name	Description
wage96	Hourly wages (in dollars) in 1996
height85	Adult height: height (in inches) measured in 1985
height81	Adolescent height: height (in inches) measured in 1981
athlets	Participation in high school athletics (1 = yes, 0 = no)
clubnum	Number of club memberships in high school, excluding athletics and academic/vocational clubs
siblings	Number of siblings
age	Age in 1996
male	Male (1 = yes, 0 = no)

all respondents. Discuss differences across the two models. Explain why the coefficient on adult height changed.

(b) Assess the multicollinearity of the two height variables using (i) a plot, (ii) the variance inflation factor command, and (iii) an auxiliary regression. Run the plot once without a jitter subcommand (e.g., `scatter X1 X2`), and once with it (e.g., `scatter X1 X2, jitter(3)`), and choose the more informative of the two plots. (Note that in the auxiliary regression it's useful to limit the sample to observations for which *wage96* is not missing, to ensure that the R^2 from the auxiliary regression will be based on the same number of observations as the regression used for the `vif` command. The syntax is `if wage96 !=.` where the exclamation means "not" and the period is how Stata marks missing values.)

(c) Notice that IQ is omitted from the model. Is this a problem? Why or why not?

(d) Notice that eye color is omitted from the model. Is this a problem? Why or why not?

(e) You're the boss! Use the data in this file to estimate a model that you think sheds light on an interesting relationship. The specification decisions include deciding whether to limit the sample and what variables to include. Report only a single additional specification. Describe in no more than two paragraphs why this is an interesting way to assess the data.

2. Use the MLBattend.dta data on Major League Baseball attendance records for 32 teams from the 1970s through 2000 (see Chapter 4, page 126). We are interested in the factors that impact baseball game attendance.

(a) Estimate a regression in which home attendance rate is the dependent variable and wins, runs scored, and runs allowed are the independent variables. Report your results, identify variables that are statistically significant, and interpret all significant coefficients.

(b) Suppose someone argues that we need to take into account the growth of the U.S. population between 1970 and 2000. This particular data set does not have a population variable, but it does have a variable called *Season*, which indicates what season the data is from (e.g., *Season* equals 1969 for observations from 1969 and *Season* equals 1981 for observations from 1981, etc.). What are the conditions that need to be true for omission of the season variable to bias other coefficients? Do you think they hold in this case?

(c) Estimate a second regression by using the dependent and independent variables from part (a), but including *Season* as an additional independent variable to control for trends on overall attendance over time. Report your results and discuss the differences between these results and those observed in part (a).

(d) What is the relationship between *Season* and *Runs_scored*? Assess with an auxiliary regression and a scatterplot. Discuss the implications for the results in part (c).

3. Do cell phones distract drivers and cause accidents? Worried that this is happening, many states over the last 10 years have passed legislation to reduce distracted driving. Fourteen states now have laws making handheld cell phone use while driving illegal and 44 states have banned texting while driving. This problem looks more closely at the relationship between cell phones and traffic fatalities. Table 5.6 describes the variables in the data set Cellphone_2012_homework.dta.

(a) While we don't know how many people are using their phones while driving, we can find the number of cell phone subscriptions in a state (in thousands). Estimate a bivariate model with traffic deaths as the dependent variable and number of cell phone subscriptions as the independent variable. Briefly discuss the results. Do you suspect endogeneity? If so, why?

(b) Add population to the model. What happens to the coefficient on cell phone subscriptions? Why?

(c) Add total miles driven to the model. What happens to the coefficient on cell phone subscriptions? Why?

TABLE 5.6 Variables for Cell Phones and Traffic Deaths Data

Variable name	Description
year	Year
State	State name
state_numeric	State name (numeric representation of state)
numberofdeaths	Number of traffic deaths
cell_subscription	Number of cell phone subscriptions (in thousands)
population	Population within a state
total_miles_driven	Total miles driven within a state for that year (in millions of miles)

TABLE 5.7 **Variables for Speeding Ticket Data**

Variable name	Description
MPHover	Miles per hour over the speed limit
Amount	Assessed fine for the ticket
Age	Age of driver

(d) Based on the model in part (c), calculate the variance inflation factor for population and total miles driven. Why are they different? Discuss implications of this level of multicollinearity for the coefficient estimates and the precision of the coefficient estimates.

4. What determines how much drivers are fined if they are stopped for speeding? Do demographics like age, gender, and race matter? To answer this question, we'll investigate traffic stops and citations in Massachusetts using data from Makowsky and Stratmann (2009). Even though state law sets a formula for tickets based on how fast a person was driving, police officers in practice often deviate from the formula. Table 5.8 describes data in speeding_tickets_text.dta that includes information on all traffic stops. An amount for the fine is given only for observations in which the police officer decided to assess a fine.

   (a) Estimate a bivariate OLS model in which ticket amount is a function of age. Is age statistically significant? Is endogeneity possible?

   (b) Estimate the model from part (a), also controlling for miles per hour over the speed limit. Explain what happens to the coefficient on age and why.

   (c) Suppose we had only the first thousand observations in the data set. Estimate the model from part (b) and report on what happens to the standard errors and t statistics when we have fewer observations. (In Stata, use `if _n < 1001` at the end of the regression command to limit the sample to the first thousand observations. Because the amount is missing for drivers who were not fined, the sample size will be much smaller than $1,000$.)

5. We will continue the analysis of height and wages in Britain from Exercise 3 in Chapter 3 (page 89). We want to know if the relationship between height and wages in the United States also occurs among

TABLE 5.8	Variables for Height and Wages Data in Britain
Variable name	**Description**
gwage33	Hourly wages (in British pounds) at age 33
height33	Height (in inches) measured at age 33
height16	Height (in inches) measured at age 16
height07	Height (in inches) measured at age 7
momed	Education of mother, measured in years
daded	Education of father, measured in years
siblings	Number of siblings
Ht16Noisy	Height (in inches) measured at age 16 with measurement error added in

British men. Table 5.8 describes the data set heightwage_british_males_-
multivariate.dta which contains data on males in Britain from Persico,
Postlewaite, and Silverman (2004).[13]

(a) Persico, Postlewaite, and Silverman (2004) argue that adolescent
    height is most relevant because it is height at these ages that affects
    the self-confidence to develop interpersonal skills at a young age.
    Estimate a model with wages at age 33 as the dependent variable
    and both height at age 33 and at age 16 as independent variables.
    What happens to the coefficient on height at age 33? Explain what
    is going on here.

(b) Let's keep going. Add height at age 7 to the above model and discuss
    the results. Be sure to note changes in sample size (and its possible
    effects), and discuss the implications of adding a variable with the
    statistical significance observed for the "height at age 7" variable.

(c) Is there multicollinearity in the model from part (b)? Qualify the
    degree of multicollinearity and indicate its consequences. Specify
    whether the multicollinearity will bias coefficients or have some
    other effect.

(d) Perhaps characteristics of parents affect height (some force kids to
    eat veggies, while others give them only french fries and Fanta). Add
    the two parental education variables to the model and discuss results.
    Include only height at age 16 (meaning we do not include the height

---

[13] For the reasons discussed in the homework problem in Chapter 3 on page 89, we limit the data set
to observations with height greater than 40 inches and self-reported income less than 400 British
pounds per hour. We also exclude observations of individuals who grew shorter from age 16 to age
33. Excluding these observations doesn't substantially affect the results we see here, but since it's
reasonable to believe there is some kind of nontrivial measurement error for these cases, we exclude
them for the analysis for this question.

at ages 33 and 7 for this question—although feel free to include them too on your own; the results are interesting).

(e) Perhaps kids had their food stolen by greedy siblings. Add the number of siblings to the model and discuss results.

(f) We have included a variable, *Ht16Noisy*, which is the height measured at age 16 with some random error included. In other words, it does not equal the actual measured height at age 16, but is a "noisy" measure of height at age 16. Estimate the model using the variable *Ht16Noisy* instead of *height*16 and discuss any changes in coefficient on the height variable. Relate the changes to theoretical expectations about measurement error discussed in the chapter.

Dummy Variables: Smarter Than You Think

6

Picture, if you will, a frenzied home crowd at a sporting event. That has to help the home team, right? The fans sure act like it will. But does it really? This is a question begging for data analysis.

Let's look at Manchester City in English Premier League soccer in 2012–13. Panel (a) of Figure 6.1 shows the goal differential for Manchester City's 38 games, distinguishing between home and away games. The average goal differential for away games is about 0.32 (meaning the team scored on average 0.32 more goals than their opponents when playing away from home). The average goal differential for home games is about 1.37, meaning that the goal differential is more than 1 goal higher at home. Well done, obnoxious drunk fans! Panel (b) in Figure 6.1 shows the goal differential for Manchester United. The average goal differential for away games is about 0.90 and the average goal differential for home games is about 1.37 (coincidentally the same value as for Manchester City). These numbers mean that the home field advantage for Manchester United is only about 0.47. C'mon Manchester United fans—yell louder!

We can use OLS to easily generate such estimates and conduct hypothesis tests. And we can do much more. We can estimate such difference of means while controlling for other variables, and we can see whether covariates have different effects at home and away. The key step is using a dummy variable, a variable that equals either zero or one, as the independent variable.

In this chapter we show the many powerful uses of dummy variables in OLS models. Section 6.1 shows how to use a bivariate OLS model for difference of means. Section 6.2 shows how to use multivariate OLS to control for other variables when conducting a difference of means test. In Section 6.3 we use dummy variables to control for categorical variables, which indicate category membership in one of multiple categories. Religion and race are classic categorical variables. Section 6.4 discusses how dummy variable

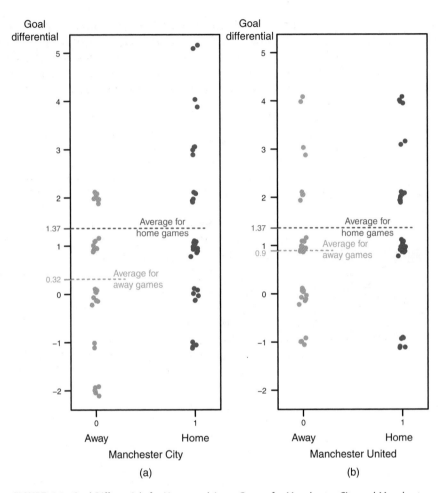

FIGURE 6.1: Goal Differentials for Home and Away Games for Manchester City and Manchester United

interactions allow us to estimate different slopes for different groups. This chapter covers dummy *independent* variables; Chapter 12 covers dummy *dependent* variables.

6.1 Using Bivariate OLS to Assess Difference of Means

Researchers frequently want to know how two groups differ. In experiments, researchers are curious about whether the treatment group differed from the control group. In observational studies, researchers want to compare outcomes between categories: men versus women, college grads versus high school grads, Ohio State versus Michigan. These comparisons are often referred to as

▶ **difference of means test** A test that involves comparing the mean of Y for one group (e.g., the treatment group) against the mean of Y for another group (e.g., the control group). These tests can be conducted with bivariate and multivariate OLS and other statistical procedures.

difference of means tests because they involve comparing the mean of Y for one group (e.g., the treatment group) against the mean of Y for another group (e.g., the control group). In this section, we show how to use the bivariate regression model and OLS to make such comparisons. We also work through an example about opinions on President Barack Obama.

Regression model for difference of means tests

Consider a typical experiment. There is a treatment group which is a randomly selected group of individuals who received a treatment. There is also a control group, which received no treatment. We use a **dummy variable** to represent whether an individual was or was not in the treatment group. A dummy variable equals either zero or one for each observation. Dummy variables are also referred to as **dichotomous variables**. Typically, the dummy variable is 1 for those in the treatment group and 0 for those in the control group.

A bivariate OLS model that assesses the effect of an experimental treatment is

▶ **dummy variable** A dummy variable equals either zero or one for all observations. Dummy variables are sometimes referred to as *dichotomous variables.*

$$Y_i = \beta_0 + \beta_1 Treatment_i + \epsilon_i \tag{6.1}$$

where Y_i is the dependent variable, β_0 is the intercept, β_1 is the effect of being treated, and $Treatment_i$ is our independent variable ("X_i"). This variable is 1 if person i received the experimental treatment and 0 otherwise. As usual, ϵ_i is the error term. Because this is an experiment (one that we assume does not suffer from attrition, balancing, or compliance problems), ϵ_i will be uncorrelated with $Treatment_i$, thereby satisfying the exogeneity condition.

▶ **dichotomous variable** A dichotomous variable takes on one of two values, almost always zero or one, for all observations. Also known as a *dummy variable.*

The standard interpretation of $\hat{\beta}_1$ from bivariate OLS applies here: a one-unit increase in the independent variable is associated with a $\hat{\beta}_1$ increase in Y_i. (See page 52 on the standard OLS interpretation.) Equation 6.1 implies that getting the treatment (going from 0 to 1 on $Treatment_i$) is associated with a $\hat{\beta}_1$ increase in Y_i.

When our independent variable is a dummy variable, as with our $Treatment_i$ variable, we can also treat $\hat{\beta}_1$ as an estimate of the difference of means of our dependent variable Y across the two groups. To see why, note first that the fitted value for the control group (for whom $Treatment_i = 0$) is

$$\hat{Y}_i = \hat{\beta}_0 + \hat{\beta}_1 Treatment_i$$
$$= \hat{\beta}_0 + \hat{\beta}_1 \times 0$$
$$= \hat{\beta}_0$$

In other words, $\hat{\beta}_0$ is the predicted value of Y for individuals in the control group. It is not surprising that the value of $\hat{\beta}_0$ that best fits the data is simply the average of Y_i for individuals in the control group.[1]

---

[1] The proof is a bit laborious. We show it in the appendix on page 541.

The fitted value for the treatment group (for whom $Treatment_i = 1$) is

$$\hat{Y}_i = \hat{\beta}_0 + \hat{\beta}_1 Treatment_i$$
$$= \hat{\beta}_0 + \hat{\beta}_1 \times 1$$
$$= \hat{\beta}_0 + \hat{\beta}_1$$

In other words, $\hat{\beta}_0 + \hat{\beta}_1$ is the predicted value of Y for individuals in the treatment group. The best predictor of this value is simply the average of Y for individuals in the treatment group. Because $\hat{\beta}_0$ is the average of individuals in the control group, $\hat{\beta}_1$ is the *difference* in averages between the treatment and control groups. If $\hat{\beta}_1 > 0$, then the average Y for those in the treatment group is higher than for those in the control group. If $\hat{\beta}_1 < 0$, then the average Y for those in the treatment group is lower than for those in the control group. If $\hat{\beta}_1 = 0$, then the average Y for those in the treatment group is no different from the average of Y for those in the control group.

In other words, our slope coefficient ($\hat{\beta}_1$) is, in the case of a bivariate OLS model with a dummy independent variable, a measure of the difference in means across the two groups. The standard error on this coefficient tells us how much uncertainty we have and determines the confidence interval for our estimate of $\hat{\beta}_1$.

Figure 6.2 graphically displays the difference of means test in bivariate OLS with a scatterplot of data. It looks a bit different from our previous scatterplots (e.g., Figure 3.1 on page 46) because here the independent variable takes on only two values: 0 or 1. Hence the observations are stacked at 0 and 1. In our example the values of Y when $X = 0$ are generally lower than the values of Y when $X = 1$. The parameter $\hat{\beta}_0$ corresponds to the average of Y for all observations for which $X = 0$. The average for the treatment group (for whom $X = 1$) is $\hat{\beta}_0 + \hat{\beta}_1$. The *difference* in averages across the groups is $\hat{\beta}_1$. A key point is that the standard interpretation of coefficients in bivariate OLS still applies: A one-unit change in X (e.g., going from $X = 0$ to $X = 1$) is associated with a $\hat{\beta}_1$ change in Y.

This is excellent news. Whenever our independent variable is a dummy variable—as it typically is for experiments and often is for observational data—we can simply run bivariate OLS and the $\hat{\beta}_1$ coefficient tells us the difference of means. The standard error on this coefficient tells us how precisely we have measured this difference and allows us to conduct a hypothesis test and determine a confidence interval.

OLS produces difference of means tests for observational data as well. The model and interpretation are the same; the difference is how much we worry about whether the exogeneity assumption is satisfied. Typically, exogeneity will be seriously in doubt for observational data. And sometimes OLS can be useful in estimating the difference of means as a descriptive statistic without a causal interpretation.

Difference of means tests can be conducted without using OLS. Doing so is totally fine, of course; in fact, OLS and non-OLS difference of means tests assuming the same variances across groups produce *identical* estimates and standard errors. The advantage of the OLS approach is that we can use it within a framework that also does all the other things OLS does, such as adding multiple variables to the model.

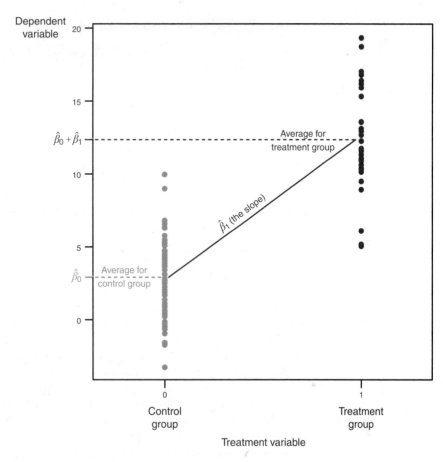

FIGURE 6.2: Bivariate OLS with a Dummy Independent Variable

Difference of means and views about President Obama

Table 6.1 provides an example. The left-hand column presents results from a
model of feelings toward President Obama from a December 2011 public opinion
survey. The dependent variable is respondents' answers to a request to rate the
president on a "feeling thermometer," scale of 0 to 100, where 0 is feeling very
cold toward him and 100 is feeling very warm toward him. The independent
variable is a dummy variable called *Democrat* that is 1 for respondents who
identify themselves as Democrats and 0 for those who do not. The *Democrat*
variable equals 0 for all non-Democrats (a group that includes Republicans,
independents, supporters of other parties, and nonpartisans). The results indicate
that Democrats rate Obama 41.82 points higher than non-Democrats, an effect
that is highly statistically significant.[2]

---

[2] A standard OLS regression model produces a standard error and a *t* statistic that are equivalent to
the standard error and *t* statistic produced by a difference of means test in which variance is assumed
to be the same across both groups. An OLS model with heteroscedasticity-consistent standard errors
(as discussed in Section 3.6) produces a standard error and *t* statistic that are equivalent to a

TABLE 6.1	Feeling Thermometer Toward Barack Obama	
	Treatment = Democrat	Treatment = Not Democrat
Democrat	41.82*	
	(1.09)	
	[t = 38.51]	
Not Democrat		−41.82*
		(1.09)
		[t = 38.51]
Constant	23.38*	65.20*
	(0.78)	(0.76)
	[t = 30.17]	[t = 85.72]
N	2,183	2,183
R^2	0.40	0.40

Standard errors in parentheses.

* *indicates significance at p < 0.05, two-tailed.*

Difference of means tests convey the same essential information when the coding of the dummy variable is flipped. The column on the right in Table 6.1 shows results from a model in which *NotDemocrat* was the independent variable. This variable is the opposite of the *Democrat* variable, equaling 1 for non-Democrats and 0 for Democrats. The numerical results are different, but they nonetheless contain the same information. The constant is the mean evaluation of Obama by Democrats. In the first specification this mean is $\hat{\beta}_0 + \hat{\beta}_1 = 23.38 + 41.82 = 65.20$. In the second specification it is simply $\hat{\beta}_0$ because this is the mean value for the excluded category. In the first equation the coefficient on *Democrat* is 41.82, indicating that Democrats evaluated Obama 41.82 points higher than non-Democrats. In the second equation the coefficient on *NonDemocrat* is negative, −41.82, indicating that non-Democrats evaluated Obama 41.82 points lower than Democrats.

Figure 6.3 scatterplots the data and highlights the estimated differences in means between non-Democrats and Democrats. Dummy variables can be a bit tricky to plot because the values of the independent variable are only 0 or 1, causing the data to overlap such that we can't tell whether a given dot in the scatterplot indicates 2 or 200 observations. A trick of the trade is to **jitter** each observation by adding a small random number to each observation for the independent and dependent variables. The jittered data gives the cloudlike images in the figure that help us get a decent sense of the data. We jitter *only* the data that is plotted; we do not jitter the data when running the statistical analysis. The Computing Corner at the end of this chapter shows how to jitter data for plots.[3]

▶ **jitter** A process used in scatterplotting data. A small random number is added to each observation for purposes of plotting only. This procedure produces cloudlike images, which overlap less than the unjittered data, hence providing a better sense of the data.

difference of means test in which variance differs across groups. The Computing Corner shows how to estimate these models.

[3] We discussed jittering data earlier, on page 73.

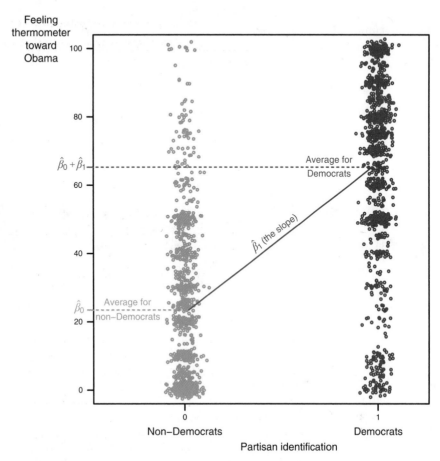

FIGURE 6.3: Scatterplot of Obama Feeling Thermometers and Party Identification

Non-Democrats' feelings toward Obama clearly run lower: that group shows many more observations at the low end of the feeling thermometer scale. The non-Democrats' average feeling thermometer rating is 23.38. Feelings toward Obama among Democrats are higher, with an average of 65.20. When interpreted correctly, both the specifications in Table 6.1 tell this same story.

REMEMBER THIS

A difference of means test assesses whether the average value of the dependent variable differs between two groups.

1. We often are interested in the difference of means between treatment and control groups or between women and men or between other groupings.

2. Difference of means tests can be implemented in bivariate OLS by using a dummy independent variable.

$$Y_i = \beta_0 + \beta_1 Treatment_i + \epsilon_i$$

(a) The estimate of the mean for the control group is $\hat{\beta}_0$.

(b) The estimate of the mean for the treatment group is $\hat{\beta}_0 + \hat{\beta}_1$.

(c) The estimate for differences in means between groups is $\hat{\beta}_1$.

Review Questions

1. Approximately what are the averages of Y for the treatment and control groups in each panel of Figure 6.4? Approximately what is the estimated difference of means in each panel?

2. Approximately what are the values of $\hat{\beta}_0$ and $\hat{\beta}_1$ in each panel of Figure 6.4?

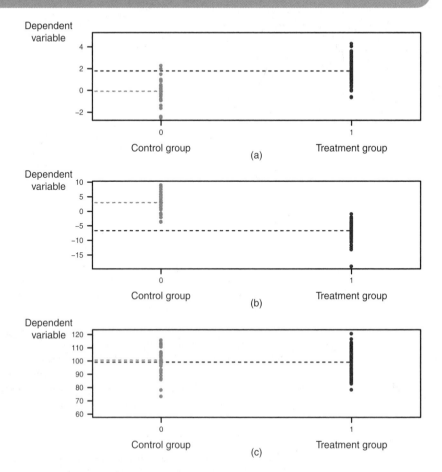

FIGURE 6.4: Three Difference of Means Tests for Review Questions

| CASE STUDY | Sex Differences in Heights |

As an example of OLS difference in means, let's look at the difference in heights between men and women. We already know men are, on average, taller, but it is interesting to know just how much taller and how confident we can be of the estimate. In this case, the dependent variable is height and the independent variable is gender. We can code the "treated" value as either being male or female; for now, we'll use a male dummy variable that is 1 if the person is male and 0 if the person is female.[4] Later, we'll come back and do the analysis again with a female dummy variable.

Figure 6.5 displays a scatterplot of height and gender. As expected, men are taller on average than women; the men-blob is clearly higher than the women-blob.

That's not very precise, though, so we'll use an OLS model to provide a specific estimate of the difference in heights between men and women. The model is

$$Height_i = \beta_0 + \beta_1 Male_i + \epsilon_i$$

The estimated coefficient $\hat{\beta}_0$ tells us the average height for the group for which the dummy variable is zero, which in this case is women. The estimated coefficients $\hat{\beta}_0 + \hat{\beta}_1$ tell us the average height for the group for which the dummy variable is 1, which in this case is men. The *difference* between the two groups is estimated as $\hat{\beta}_1$.

The results are reported in Table 6.2. The average height of women is $\hat{\beta}_0$, which is 64.23 inches. The average height for men is $\hat{\beta}_0 + \hat{\beta}_1$, which is $64.23 + 5.79 = 70.02$ inches. The *difference* between the two groups is estimated as $\hat{\beta}_1$, which is 5.79 inches.

This estimate is quite precise. The *t* statistic for *Male* is 103.4, which allows us to reject the null hypothesis. We can also use our confidence interval algorithm from page 119 to produce a 95 percent confidence interval for $\hat{\beta}_1$ of 5.68 to 5.90 inches. In other words, we are 95 percent confident that the difference of means of height between men and women is between 5.68 and 5.9 inches.

Figure 6.6 adds the information from Table 6.2 to the scatterplot. We can see that $\hat{\beta}_0$ is estimating the middle of the women-blob, $\hat{\beta}_0 + \hat{\beta}_1$ is estimating the middle of the men-blob, and the difference between the two is $\hat{\beta}_1$. We can interpret the estimated effect of going from zero to one on the independent variable (which is equivalent to going from female to male) is to add 5.79 inches on average.

---

[4] Sometimes people will name a variable like this "gender." That's annoying! Readers will have to dig through the paper to figure out whether 1 indicates males or females.

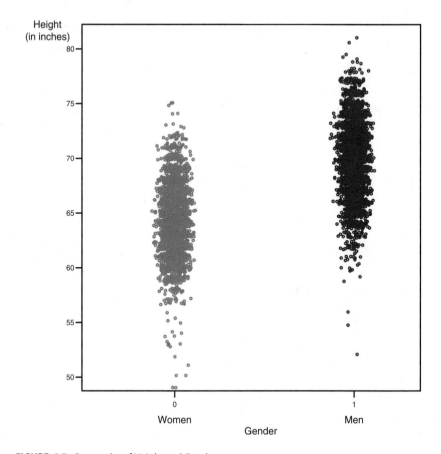

FIGURE 6.5: Scatterplot of Height and Gender

We noted earlier that it is reasonable to code the treatment as being female. If we replace the male dummy variable with a female dummy variable, the model becomes

$$Height_i = \beta_0 + \beta_1 Female_i + \epsilon_i$$

TABLE 6.2	Difference of Means Test for Height and Gender
Constant	64.23*
	(0.04)
	[$t = 1,633.6$]
Male	5.79*
	(0.06)
	[$t = 103.4$]
N	10,863

Standard errors in parentheses.

* indicates significance at $p < 0.05$, two-tailed.

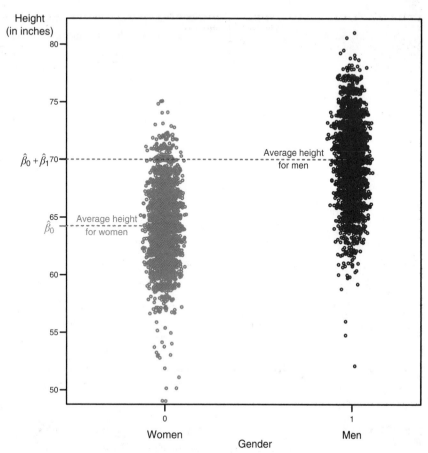

FIGURE 6.6: Another Scatterplot of Height and Gender

Now the estimated coefficient $\hat{\beta}_0$ will tell us the average height for men (the group for which *Female* = 0). The estimated coefficients $\hat{\beta}_0 + \hat{\beta}_1$ will tell us the average height for women and the *difference* between the two groups is estimated as $\hat{\beta}_1$.

The results with the female dummy variable are in the right-hand column of Table 6.3. The numbers should look familiar because we are learning the same information from the data. It is just that the accounting is a bit different. What is the estimate of the average height for men? It is $\hat{\beta}_0$ in the right-hand column, which is 70.02. Sound familiar? That was the number we got from our initial results (reported again in the left-hand column of Table 6.3); in that case we had to add $\hat{\beta}_0 + \hat{\beta}_1$ because when the dummy variable indicated men, we needed both coefficients to get the average height for men. What is the difference between males and females estimated in the right-hand column? It is –5.79, which is the same as before, only negative. The underlying fact is that women are estimated to be 5.79 inches shorter on average. If we have coded our dummy variable as *Female* = 1, then going from

TABLE 6.3	Another Way to Show Difference of Means Test Results for Height and Gender	
	Treatment = male	Treatment = female
Male	5.79*	
	(0.06)	
	[t = 103.4]	
Female		−5.79*
		(0.06)
		[t = 103.4]
Constant	64.23*	70.02*
	(0.04)	(0.04)
	[t = 1,633.6]	[t = 1,755.9]
N	10,863	10,863

Standard errors in parentheses.

* *indicates significance at p < 0.05, two-tailed.*

0 to 1 on the independent variable is associated with a decline of 5.79 inches on average. If we have coded our dummy variable as *Male* = 1, then going from 0 to 1 on the independent variable is associated with an increase of 5.79 inches on average.

6.2   Dummy Independent Variables in Multivariate OLS

We can easily extend difference of means tests to multivariate OLS. The extension is useful because it allows us to control for other variables when assessing whether two groups are different.

For example, earlier in this chapter we assessed the home field advantage of Manchester City while controlling for the quality of the opponent. Using multivariate OLS we can estimate

$$Goal\ differential_i = \beta_0 + \beta_1 Home_i + \beta_2 Opponent\ quality_i + \epsilon_i \qquad (6.2)$$

where *Opponent quality$_i$* measures the opponent's overall goal differential in all other games. The $\hat{\beta}_1$ estimate will tell us, controlling for opponent quality, whether the goal differential was higher for Manchester City for home games. The results are in Table 6.4.

The generic for such a model is

$$Y_i = \beta_0 + \beta_1 Dummy_i + \beta_2 X_i + \epsilon_i \qquad (6.3)$$

It is useful to think graphically about the fitted lines from this kind of model. Figure 6.7 shows the data for Manchester City's results in 2012–13. The

TABLE 6.4	Manchester City Example with Dummy and Continuous Independent Variables
Home field	1.026*
	(0.437)
	$[t = 2.35]$
Opponent quality	−0.025*
	(0.009)
	$[t = 2.69]$
Constant	0.266
	(0.309)
	$[t = 0.86]$
N	38
R^2	0.271
$\hat{\sigma}$	1.346

Standard errors in parentheses.

* *indicates significance at $p < 0.05$, two-tailed.*

observations for home games (for which the *Home* dummy variable is 1) are black dots; the observations for away games (for which the *Home* dummy variable is 0) are gray dots.

As discussed on page 174, the intercept for the $Home_i = 0$ observations (the away games) will be $\hat{\beta}_0$ and the intercept for the $Home_i = 1$ observations (the home games) will be $\hat{\beta}_0 + \hat{\beta}_1$, which equals the intercept for away games plus the bump (up or down) for home games. Note that the coefficient indicating the difference of means is the coefficient on the dummy variable. (Note also that the β we should look at depends on how we write the model. For this model, β_1 indicates the difference of means controlling for the other variable, but it would be β_2 if we wrote the model to have β_2 multiplied by the dummy variable.)

The innovation is that our difference of means test here also controls for another variable—in this case, opponent quality. Here the effect of a one-unit increase in opponent quality is $\hat{\beta}_2$; this effect is the same for the $Home_i = 1$ and $Home_i = 0$ groups. Hence the fitted lines are parallel, one for each group separated by $\hat{\beta}_1$, the differential bump associated with being in the $Home_i = 1$ group. In Figure 6.7, $\hat{\beta}_1$ is greater than zero, but it could be less than zero (in which case the dashed line for $\hat{\beta}_0 + \hat{\beta}_1$ for the $Home_i = 1$ group would be below the $\hat{\beta}_0$ line) or equal to zero (in which case the two dashed lines would overlap exactly).

We can add independent variables to our heart's content, allowing us to assess the difference of means between the $Home_i = 1$ and $Home_i = 0$ groups in a manner that controls for the additional variables. Such models are incredibly common.

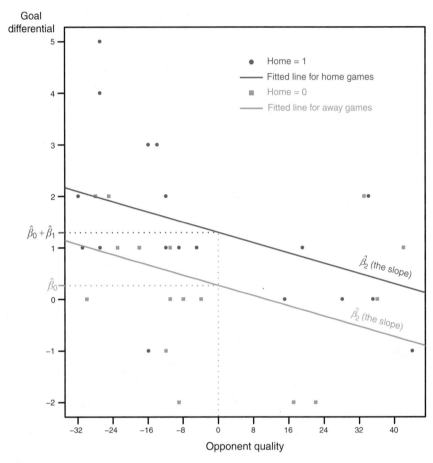

FIGURE 6.7: Fitted Values for Model with Dummy Variable and Control Variable: Manchester City Example

REMEMBER THIS

1. Including a dummy variable in a multivariate regression allows us to conduct a difference of means test while controlling for other factors with a model such as

$$Y_i = \beta_0 + \beta_1 Dummy_i + \beta_2 X_i + \epsilon_i$$

2. The fitted values from this model will be two parallel lines, each with a slope of $\hat{\beta}_1$ and separated by $\hat{\beta}_2$ for all values of X.

6.3 Transforming Categorical Variables to Multiple Dummy Variables

▶ **categorical variable**
Has two or more categories but does not have an intrinsic ordering. Also known as a *nominal variable*.

▶ **ordinal variable** A variable that expresses rank but not necessarily relative size.

Categorical variables (also known as *nominal variables*) are common in data analysis. They have two or more categories, but the categories have no intrinsic ordering. Information on religion is often contained in a categorical variable: 1 for Buddhist, 2 for Christian, 3 for Hindu, and so forth. Race, industry, and many more attributes also appear as categorical variables. Categorical variables differ from dummy variables in that categorical variables have multiple categories. Categorical variables differ from **ordinal variables** in that ordinal variables express rank but not necessarily relative size. An example of an ordinal variable is a one indicating answers to a survey question that is coded 1 = strongly disagree, 2 = disagree, 3 = agree, 4 = strongly agree.[5]

In this section, we show how to use dummy variables to analyze categorical variables. We illustrate the technique with an example about wage differentials across regions in the United States.

Categorical variables in regression models

We might suspect that wages in the United States are different in different regions. Are they higher in the Northeast? Or are they higher in the South? Suppose we have data on wages and on region. It should be easy to figure this out, right? Well, yes, as long as we appreciate how to analyze categorical variables. Categorical

---

[5] It is possible to treat ordinal independent variables in the same way as categorical variables in the manner we describe here. Or, it is common to simply include ordinal independent variables directly in a regression model and interpret a one-unit increase as movement from one category to another.

variables indicate membership in some category. They are common in policy analysis. For example, suppose our region variable is coded such that 1 indicates a person is from the Northeast, 2 indicates a person is from the Midwest, 3 indicates a person is from the South, and 4 indicates a person is from the West.

How should we incorporate categorical variables into OLS models? Should we estimate the model with this equation?

$$Wage_i = \beta_0 + \beta_1 X_{1i} + \beta_2 Region_i + \epsilon_i \tag{6.4}$$

(Here $Wage_i$ is the wages of person i and $Region_i$ is the region person i lives in, as just defined.)

No, no, and no. Though the categorical variable may be coded numerically, it has no inherent order, which means the units are not meaningful. The Midwest is not "1" more than the Northeast; the South is not "1" more than the Midwest.

So what do we do with categorical variables? Dummy variables save the day. We simply convert categorical variables into a series of dummy variables, a different one for each category. If region is the nominal variable, we simply create a Northeast dummy variable (1 for people from the Northeast, 0 otherwise), a Midwest dummy variable (1 for midwesterners, 0 otherwise), and so on.

The catch is that we cannot include dummy variables for every category—if we did, we would have perfect multicollinearity (as we discussed on page 150). Hence we exclude one of the dummy variables and treat that category as the **reference category** (also called the *excluded category*), which means that coefficients on the included dummy variables indicate the difference between the category designated by the dummy variable and the reference category.

We've already been doing something like this with dichotomous dummy variables. When we used the male dummy variable in our height and wages example on page 175, we did not include a female dummy variable, meaning that females were the reference category and the coefficient on the male dummy variable indicated how much taller men were. When we used the female dummy variable, men were the reference category and the coefficient on the female dummy variable indicated how much shorter females were on average.

▶ **reference category**
When a model includes dummy variables indicating the multiple categories of a nominal variable, we need to exclude a dummy variable for one of the groups, which we refer to as the reference category. The coefficients on all the included dummy variables indicate how much higher or lower the dependent variable is for each group relative to the reference category. Also referred to as the *excluded category*.

Categorical variables and regional wage differences

To see how categorical variables work in practice, we will analyze women's wage data in 1996 across the Northeast, Midwest, South, and West in the United States. We won't, of course, include a single region variable. Instead, we create dummy variables for each region and include all but one of them in the OLS regression. For example, if we treat *West* as the excluded category, we estimate

$$Wages_i = \beta_0 + \beta_1 Northeast_i + \beta_2 Midwest_i + \beta_3 South_i + \epsilon_i$$

TABLE 6.5 Using Different Excluded Categories for Wages and Region

	(a) Exclude West	(b) Exclude South	(c) Exclude Midwest	(d) Exclude Northeast
Northeast	2.02*	4.15*	3.61*	
	(0.59)	(0.506)	(0.56)	
	$[t = 3.42]$	$[t = 8.19]$	$[t = 6.44]$	
Midwest	−1.59*	0.54		−3.61*
	(0.534)	(0.44)		(0.56)
	$[t = 2.97]$	$[t = 1.23]$		$[t = 6.44]$
South	−2.13*		−0.54	−4.15*
	(0.48)		(0.44)	(0.51)
	$[t = 4.47]$		$[t = 1.23]$	$[t = 8.19]$
West		2.13*	1.59*	−2.02*
		(0.48)	(0.53)	(0.59)
		$[t = 4.47]$	$[t = 2.97]$	$[t = 3.42]$
Constant	12.50*	10.37*	10.91*	14.52*
	(0.40)	(0.26)	(0.36)	(0.43)
	$[t = 31.34]$	$[t = 39.50]$	$[t = 30.69]$	$[t = 33.53]$
N	3,223	3,223	3,223	3,223
R^2	0.023	0.023	0.023	0.023

Standard errors in parentheses.

* *indicates significance at $p < 0.05$, two-tailed.*

The results for this regression are in column (a) of Table 6.5. The $\hat{\beta}_0$ result (indicated in the "Constant" line in the table) tells us that the average wage per hour for women in the West (the excluded category) was $12.50. Women in the Northeast are estimated to receive $2.02 more per hour than those in the West, or $14.52 per hour. Women in the Midwest earn $1.59 less than women in the West, which works out to $10.91 per hour. And women in the South receive $2.13 less than women in the West, or $10.37 per hour.

Column (b) of Table 6.5 shows the results from the same data, but with South as the excluded category instead of West. The $\hat{\beta}_0$ result tells us that the average wage per hour for women in the South (the excluded category) was $10.37. Women in the Northeast get $14.52 per hour, which is $4.15 per hour more than women in the South. Women in the Midwest receive $0.54 per hour more than women in the South (which works out to $10.91 per hour) and women in the West get $2.13 per hour more than women in the South (which works out to $12.50 per hour). The key pattern is that the estimated amount that women in each region get is the same in columns (a) and (b). Columns (c) and (d) have Midwest and Northeast, respectively, as the excluded categories and, with calculations like those we just did, we can see that the estimated average wages for each region are the same in all specifications.

Hence it is important to always remember that the coefficient estimates themselves are meaningful only with reference to the excluded category. Even though the coefficients on each dummy variable change across the specifications, the underlying estimates for wages in each region do not. Think of the difference between Fahrenheit and Celsius—the temperature is the same, but the numbers on the two thermometers are different.

Thus we don't need to worry about which category should be excluded. It simply doesn't matter. The difference is due to the reference category we are using. In the first specification, we are comparing wages in the Northeast, Midwest, and South to the West; in the second specification, we are comparing wages in the Northeast, Midwest, and West to the South. The coefficient on Midwest is negative in the first specification and positive in the second because women in the Midwest earn *less* than women in the West [the reference category in specification (a)] and *more* than women in the South [the reference category in specification (b)]. In both specifications (and the subsequent two), women in the Midwest are estimated to earn $10.91 per hour.

REMEMBER THIS

To use dummy variables to control for categorical variables, we include dummy variables for every category except one.

1. The excluded category is the reference point, and all the coefficients on the included dummy variables indicate how much higher or lower each group is than the excluded category.

2. Coefficients differ depending on which excluded category is used, but when interpreted appropriately, the fitted values for each category do not change across specifications.

Review Questions

1. Suppose we wanted to conduct a cross-national study of opinion in North America and have a variable named "Country" that is coded 1 for respondents from the United States, 2 for respondents from Mexico, and 3 for respondents from Canada. Write a model and explain how to interpret the coefficients.

2. For the results in Table 6.6 on page 185, indicate what the coefficients are in boxes (a) through (j).

TABLE 6.6 **Hypothetical Results for Wages and Region When Different Categories Are Excluded**

	Exclude West	Exclude South	Exclude Midwest	Exclude Northeast
Constant	125.0	95.0	(d)	(g)
	(0.9)	(1.1)	(1.0)	(0.9)
Northeast	−5.0	(a)	(e)	
	(1.3)	(1.4)	(1.3)	
Midwest	−10.0	(b)		(h)
	(1.4)	(1.5)		(1.3)
South	−30.0		(f)	(i)
	(1.4)		(1.5)	(1.4)
West		(c)	10.0	(j)
		(1.4)	(1.4)	(1.3)
N	1,000	1,000	1,000	1,000
R^2	0.3	0.3	0.3	0.3

Standard errors in parentheses.

CASE STUDY   When Do Countries Tax Wealth?

Taxes are a big deal. They affect how people allocate their time, how much money the government has, and potentially, how much inequality exists in society. If we can figure out why some tax policies are chosen over others, we'll have some insight into why economies and societies look the way they do.

Inheritance taxes are a particularly interesting tax policy because of the clear potential for conflict between rich and poor. Because these policies have a bigger negative impact on the rich than on those who are less well off (you've got to be pretty rich to have lots of money to pass on), we might expect that democracies with more middle and low income voters would be more likely to have high inheritance taxes.

Scheve and Stasavage (2012) investigated the sources of inheritance taxes by looking at tax policy and other characteristics of 19 countries for which data is available from 1816 to 2000; these countries include most of the major economies over that period of time. Specifically, the researchers looked at the relationship between inheritance taxes and who was allowed to vote. Keep in mind that early democracies generally limited voting to (mostly white) men with property, so a reasonable measure of how many people could vote is whether the government limited suffrage to property owners or included all men (with or without property).

TABLE 6.7 **Difference of Means of Inheritance Taxes for Countries with Universal Male Suffrage, 1816–2000**

Universal male suffrage	19.33*
	(1.81)
	[$t = 10.66$]
Constant	4.75*
	(1.45)
	[$t = 3.27$]
N	563

Standard errors are in parentheses.

* indicates significance at $p < 0.05$, two-tailed.

Hence, at least for earlier times, universal male suffrage was a policy that broadened the electorate from a narrow slice of property holders to a larger group of nonproperty holders—and, thus, less wealthy citizens.

To assess if universal male suffrage led to increases in inheritance taxes, we can begin with the following model:

$$Inheritance\ tax_{it} = \beta_0 + \beta_1 Universal\ male\ suffrage_{i,t-1} + \varepsilon_{it} \qquad (6.5)$$

The data is measured every five years. The dependent variable is the top inheritance tax rate, and the independent variable is a dummy variable for whether all men were eligible to vote in at least half of the previous five years.[6]

Table 6.7 shows initial results that corroborate our suspicion. The coefficient on our universal male suffrage dummy variable is 19.33, with a t statistic of 10.66, indicating strong statistical significance. The results mean that countries without universal male suffrage had an average inheritance tax of 4.75 ($\hat{\beta}_0$) percent and that countries with universal male suffrage had an average inheritance tax of 24.07 ($\hat{\beta}_0 + \hat{\beta}_1$) percent.

These results are from a bivariate OLS analysis of observational data. It is likely that unmeasured factors lurking in the error term are correlated with the universal suffrage dummy variable, which would induce endogeneity.

One possible source of endogeneity could be that major advances in universal male suffrage happened at the same time inheritance taxes were rising throughout the world, whatever the state of voting was. Universal male suffrage wasn't really a thing until around 1900 but then took off quickly, and by 1921, a majority of

---

[6] Measuring these things can get tricky; see the original paper for details. Most countries had an ignominious history of denying women the right to vote until the late nineteenth or early twentieth century (New Zealand was one of the first to extend the right to vote to women, in 1893) and of denying or restricting voting by minorities until even later. Scheve and Stasavage used statistical tools we will cover later, including fixed effects (introduced in Chapter 8) and lagged dependent variables (explained in Chapter 13).

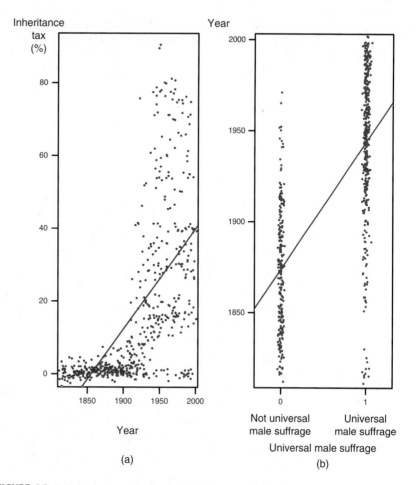

FIGURE 6.8: Relation between Omitted Variable (Year) and Other Variables

the countries had universal male suffrage (at least in theory). In other words, it seems quite possible that something in the error term (a time trend) is correlated both with inheritance taxes and with universal suffrage. So what appears to be a relationship between suffrage and taxes may be due to the fact that suffrage increased at a time when inheritance taxes were going up rather than to a causal effect of suffrage.

Figure 6.8 presents evidence consistent with these suspicions. Panel (a) shows the relationship between year and the inheritance tax. The line is the fitted line from a bivariate OLS regression model in which inheritance tax was the dependent variable and year was the independent variable. Clearly, the inheritance tax was higher as time went on.

Panel (b) of Figure 6.8 shows the relationship between year and universal male suffrage. The data are jittered for ease of viewing, and the line is from a bivariate model. Obviously, this is not a causal model; it instead shows that the mean value for the year variable was much higher when universal male suffrage equaled 1 than when universal male suffrage equaled 0. Taken together with panel (a), we have evidence that the two conditions for omitted variable bias are satisfied: The year variable is associated with the dependent variable and with the independent variable.

What to do next is simple enough—include a year variable with the following model:

$$\text{Inheritance tax}_{it} = \beta_0 + \beta_1 \text{Universal male suffrage}_{i,t-1} + \beta_2 \text{Year}_{it} + \varepsilon_{it} \qquad (6.6)$$

where *Year* equals the value of the year of the observation. This model allows us to assess whether a difference exists between countries with universal male suffrage and countries without universal male suffrage even after we control for a year trend that may have affected all countries.

Table 6.8 shows the results. The bivariate column is the same as in Table 6.7. The multivariate (a) column adds the year variable. Whoa! Huge difference. Now the coefficient on universal male suffrage is –0.38, with a tiny t statistic. In terms of difference of means testing, we can now say that, controlling for a year trend, the average inheritance tax in countries with universal male suffrage was not statistically different from that in countries without universal male suffrage.

Scheve and Stasavage argue that war was a more important factor behind increased inheritance taxes. When a country mobilizes to fight, leaders not only need money to fund the war, they also need a societal consensus in favor of it. Ordinary people may feel stretched thin, with their sons conscripted and their taxes increased. An inheritance tax could be a natural outlet that provides the government with more money while creating a sense of fairness within society.

Column (b) in the multivariate results includes a dummy variable indicating that the country was mobilized for war for more than half of the preceding five years. The coefficient on the war variable is 14.05, with a t statistic of 4.68, meaning that there is a strong connection between war and inheritance taxes. The coefficient on universal suffrage is negative but not quite statistically significant (with a t statistic of 1.51). The coefficient on year continues to be highly statistically significant, indicating that the year trend persists even when we control for war.

Many other factors could affect the dependent variable and be correlated with one or more of the independent variables. There could, for example, be regional variation, as perhaps Europe tended to have more universal male suffrage and higher inheritance taxes. Therefore we include dummy variables for Europe, Asia, and Australia/New Zealand in column (c). North America is the excluded category, which means, for example, that European inheritance taxes were 5.65 percentage points lower than in North America once we control for the other variables.

The coefficient on the war variable in column (c) is a bit lower than in column (b) but still very significant. The universal male suffrage variable is close to zero and statistically insignificant. These results therefore suggest that the results in column (b) are robust to controlling for continent.

Column (d) shows what happens when we use Australia/New Zealand as our excluded category instead of North America. The coefficients on the war and

TABLE 6.8 Multivariate OLS Analysis of Inheritance Taxes

	Bivariate	Multivariate			
		(a)	(b)	(c)	(d)
Universal male suffrage	19.33*	−0.38	−3.24	0.69	0.69
	(1.81)	(2.10)	(2.15)	(2.22)	(2.22)
	[$t = 10.66$]	[$t = 0.18$]	[$t = 1.51$]	[$t = 0.31$]	[$t = 0.31$]
Year		0.28*	0.30*	0.28*	0.28*
		(0.20)	(0.02)	(0.02)	(0.02)
		[$t = 14.03$]	[$t = 15.02$]	[$t = 13.75$]	[$t = 13.75$]
War			14.05*	11.76*	11.76*
			(3.00)	(2.94)	(2.94)
			[$t = 4.68$]	[$t = 4.01$]	[$t = 4.01$]
Europe				−5.65*	2.19
				(2.38)	(2.57)
				[$t = 2.37$]	[$t = 0.85$]
Asia				10.87*	18.71*
				(3.18)	(3.45)
				[$t = 3.41$]	[$t = 5.42$]
Australia/New Zealand				−7.84*	
				(3.32)	
				[$t = 2.36$]	
North America					7.84*
					(3.32)
					[$t = 2.36$]
Constant	4.75*	−516.48*	−565.60*	−513.79*	−521.63*
	(1.45)	(37.18)	(37.99)	(38.33)	(37.92)
	[$t = 3.27$]	[$t = 13.89$]	[$t = 14.89$]	[$t = 13.41$]	[$t = 13.78$]
N	563	563	563	563	563

Standard errors in parentheses.

* indicates significance at $p < 0.05$, two-tailed.

suffrage variables are identical to those in column (c). Remember that changing the excluded category affects only how we interpret the coefficients on the dummy variables associated with the categorical variable in question.

The coefficients on the region variables, however, do change with the new excluded category. The coefficient on Europe in column (d) is 2.19 and statistically insignificant. Wait a minute! Wasn't the coefficient on Europe −5.65 and statistically significant in column (c)? Yes, but in column (c), Europe was being compared to North America and Europe's average inheritance taxes were (controlling for the other variables) 5.65 percentage points lower than North American inheritance taxes. In column (d), Europe is being compared to Australia/New Zealand and the coefficient indicates that European inheritance taxes were 2.19 percentage points higher than in Australia/New Zealand.

The relative relationship between Europe and North America is the same in both specifications as the coefficient on the North America dummy variable is 7.84 in column (d), which is 5.65 higher than the coefficient on Europe in column (d).

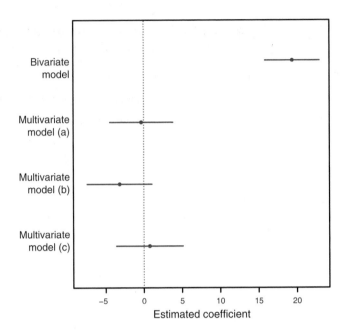

FIGURE 6.9: Confidence Intervals for Universal Male Suffrage Variable in Table 6.8

We can go through such a thought process for each of the coefficients and see the bottom line: As long as we know how to use dummy variables for categorical variables, the substantive results are exactly the same in multivariate columns (c) and (d).

Figure 6.9 shows the 95 percent confidence intervals for the coefficient on the universal suffrage variable for the bivariate and multivariate models. As discussed in Section 4.6, confidence intervals indicate the range of possible true values most consistent with the data. In the bivariate model, the confidence interval ranges from 15.8 to 22.9. This confidence interval does not cover zero, which is another way of saying that the coefficient is statistically significant. When we move to the multivariate models, however, the 95 percent confidence intervals shift dramatically downward and cover zero, indicating that the estimated effect is no longer statistically significant. We don't need to plot the results from column (d) because the coefficient on the suffrage variable is identical to that in column (c).

6.4 Interaction Variables

Dummy variables can do even more work for us. Perhaps being in the $Dummy_i = 1$ group does more than give each individual a bump up or down. Group membership might *interact* with another independent variable, changing the way the independent variable affects Y. Perhaps, for example, discrimination does not simply mean that all men get paid more by the same amount. It could be that work experience for men is more highly rewarded than work experience for women. We address this possibility with models in which a dummy independent variable interacts with (meaning "is multiplied by") a continuous independent variable.[7]

The following OLS model allows the effect of X to differ across groups:

$$Y_i = \beta_0 + \beta_1 X_i + \beta_2 Dummy_i + \beta_3 Dummy_i \times X_i + \epsilon_i \qquad (6.7)$$

The third variable is produced by multiplying the $Dummy_i$ variable times the X_i variable. In a spreadsheet, we would simply create a new column that is the product of the $Dummy$ and X columns. In statistical software, we generate a new variable, as described in the Computing Corner of this chapter.

For the $Dummy_i = 0$ group, the fitted value equation simplifies to

$$\begin{aligned}
\hat{Y}_i &= \hat{\beta}_0 + \hat{\beta}_1 X_i + \hat{\beta}_2 Dummy_i + \hat{\beta}_3 Dummy_i \times X_i \\
&= \hat{\beta}_0 + \hat{\beta}_1 X_i + \hat{\beta}_2 (0) + \hat{\beta}_3 (0) \times X_i \\
&= \hat{\beta}_0 + \hat{\beta}_1 X_i
\end{aligned}$$

In other words, the estimated intercept for the $Dummy_i = 0$ group is $\hat{\beta}_0$ and the estimated slope is $\hat{\beta}_1$.

For the $Dummy_i = 1$ group, the fitted value equation simplifies to

$$\begin{aligned}
\hat{Y}_i &= \hat{\beta}_0 + \hat{\beta}_1 X_i + \hat{\beta}_2 Dummy_i + \hat{\beta}_3 Dummy_i \times X_i \\
&= \hat{\beta}_0 + \hat{\beta}_1 X_i + \hat{\beta}_2 (1) + \hat{\beta}_3 (1) \times X_i \\
&= (\hat{\beta}_0 + \hat{\beta}_2) + (\hat{\beta}_1 + \hat{\beta}_3) X_i
\end{aligned}$$

In other words, the estimated intercept for the $Dummy_i = 1$ group is $\hat{\beta}_0 + \hat{\beta}_2$ and the estimated slope is $\hat{\beta}_1 + \hat{\beta}_3$.

Figure 6.10 shows a hypothetical example for the following model of salary as a function of experience for men and women:

$$Salary_i = \beta_0 + \beta_1 Experience_i + \beta_2 Male_i + \beta_3 Male_i \times Experience_i + \epsilon_i \quad (6.8)$$

The dummy variable here is an indicator for men and the continuous variable is a measure of years of experience. The intercept for women (the $Dummy_i = 0$ group) is $\hat{\beta}_0$ and the intercept for men (the $Dummy_i = 1$ group) is $\hat{\beta}_0 + \hat{\beta}_2$. The $\hat{\beta}_2$ coefficient indicates the salary bump that men get even at 0 years of experience. The slope for women is $\hat{\beta}_1$ and the slope for men is $\hat{\beta}_1 + \hat{\beta}_3$. The $\hat{\beta}_3$ coefficient indicates the extra salary men get for each year of experience over and above the salary increase women get for another year of experience. In this figure, the initial gap between the salaries of men and women is modest (equal to $\hat{\beta}_2$) but due to a positive $\hat{\beta}_3$, the salary gap becomes quite large for people with many years of experience.

---

[7] Interactions between continuous variables are created by multiplying two continuous variables together. The general logic is the same. Kam and Franceze (2007) provide an in-depth discussion of all kinds of interactions.

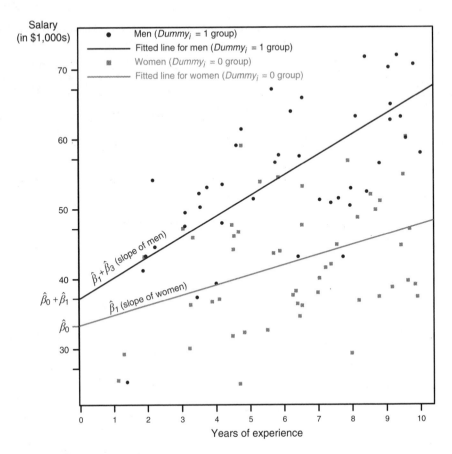

FIGURE 6.10: Interaction Model of Salaries for Men and Women

We have to be careful when we interpret $\hat{\beta}_3$, the coefficient on $Dummy_i \times X_i$. It is the differential slope for the $Dummy_i = 1$ group, meaning that $\hat{\beta}_3$ tells us how different the effect of X is for the $Dummy_i = 1$ group compared to the $Dummy_i = 0$ group. $\hat{\beta}_3$ is positive in Figure 6.10, meaning that the slope of the fitted line for the $Dummy_i = 1$ group is steeper than the slope of the line for the $Dummy_i = 0$ group.

If $\hat{\beta}_3$ were zero, the slope of the fitted line for the $Dummy_i = 1$ group would be no steeper than the slope of the line for the $Dummy_i = 0$ group, meaning that the slopes would be the same for both the $Dummy_i = 0$ and $Dummy_i = 1$ groups. If $\hat{\beta}_3$ were negative, the slope of the fitted line for the $Dummy_i = 1$ group would be less steep than the slope of the line for the $Dummy_i = 0$ group (or even negative).

Interpreting interaction variables can be a bit tricky sometimes: the $\hat{\beta}_3$ can be negative, but the effect of X on Y for the $Dummy_i = 1$ group still might be positive. For example, if $\hat{\beta}_1 = 10$ and $\hat{\beta}_3 = -3$, the slope for the $Dummy_i = 1$ group would be positive because the slope is the sum of the coefficients and therefore equals 7. The negative $\hat{\beta}_3$ indicates that the slope for the $Dummy_i$ group is less than the

TABLE 6.9 **Interpreting Coefficients in Dummy Interaction Model:**
$$Y_i = \beta_0 + \beta_1 X_i + \beta_2 D_i + \beta_3 X_i \times D_i$$

	$\hat{\beta}_3 < 0$	$\hat{\beta}_3 = 0$	$\hat{\beta}_3 > 0$
$\hat{\beta}_1 < 0$	Slope for $D_i = 0$ group is negative. Slope for $D_i = 1$ group is more negative.	Slope for $D_i = 0$ group is negative. Slope for $D_i = 1$ is same.	Slope for $D_i = 0$ group is negative. Slope for $D_i = 1$ is less negative and will be positive if $\hat{\beta}_1 + \hat{\beta}_3 > 0$.
$\hat{\beta}_1 = 0$	Slope for $D_i = 0$ is zero and slope for $D_i = 1$ group is negative.	Slope for both groups is zero.	Slope for $D_i = 0$ group is zero and slope for $D_i = 1$ group is positive.
$\hat{\beta}_1 > 0$	Slope for $D_i = 0$ group is positive. Slope for $D_i = 1$ is less positive and will be negative if $\hat{\beta}_1 + \hat{\beta}_3 < 0$.	Slope for $D_i = 0$ group is positive. Slope for $D_i = 1$ is same.	Slope for $D_i = 0$ group is positive. Slope for $D_i = 1$ is more positive.

slope for the other group; it does not tell us whether the effect of X is positive or negative, though. We must look at the sum of the coefficients to know that.

Table 6.9 summarizes how to interpret coefficients when dummy interaction variables are included.

The standard error of $\hat{\beta}_3$ is useful for calculating confidence intervals for the difference in slope coefficients across the two groups. Standard errors for some quantities of interest are tricky, though. To generate confidence intervals for the effect of X on Y, we need to be alert. For the $Dummy_i = 0$ group, the effect is simply $\hat{\beta}_1$ and we can simply use the standard error of $\hat{\beta}_1$. For the $Dummy_i = 1$ group, the effect is $\hat{\beta}_1 + \hat{\beta}_3$; the standard error of the effect is more complicated because we must account for the standard error of both $\hat{\beta}_1$ and $\hat{\beta}_3$ in addition to any correlation between $\hat{\beta}_1$ and $\hat{\beta}_3$ (which is associated with the correlation of X_1 and X_3). The appendix provides more details on how to do this on page 542.

REMEMBER THIS

Interaction variables allow us to estimate effects that depend on more than one variable.

1. A dummy interaction is created by multiplying a dummy variable times another variable.

2. Including a dummy interaction in a multivariate regression allows us to conduct a difference of means test while controlling for other factors with a model such as

$$Y_i = \beta_0 + \beta_1 X_i + \beta_2 Dummy_i + \beta_3 Dummy_i \times X_i + \epsilon_i \tag{6.9}$$

3. The fitted values from this model will be two lines. For the model as written, the slope for the group for which $Dummy_i = 0$ will be $\hat{\beta}_1$. The slope for the group for which $Dummy_i = 1$ will be $\hat{\beta}_1 + \hat{\beta}_3$.

4. The coefficient on a dummy interaction variable indicates the estimated *difference* in slopes between two groups.

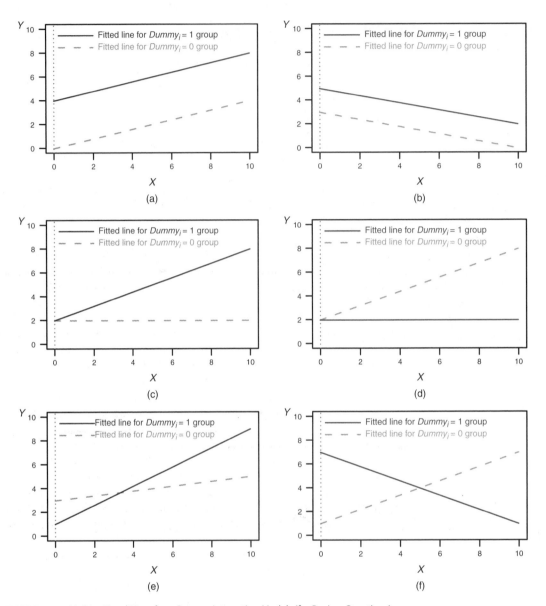

FIGURE 6.11: Various Fitted Lines from Dummy Interaction Models (for Review Questions)

Review Questions

1. For each panel in Figure 6.11, indicate whether each of $\beta_0, \beta_1, \beta_2,$ and β_3 is less than, equal to, or greater than zero for the following model:

$$Y_i = \beta_0 + \beta_1 X_i + \beta_2 Dummy_i + \beta_3 Dummy_i \times X_i + \epsilon_i$$

2. Express the value of $\hat{\beta}_3$ in panel (d) in terms of other coefficients.

3. True or false: If $\hat{\beta}_3 < 0$, an increase in X for the treatment group is associated with a decline in Y.

CASE STUDY **Energy Efficiency**

Energy efficiency promises a double whammy of benefits: reduce the amount of energy used and we can both save the world and save money. What's not to love?

But do energy-saving devices really deliver? The skeptic in us should worry that energy savings may be overpromised. In this case study, we analyze the energy used to heat a house before and after the homeowner installed a programmable thermostat. The attraction of a programmable thermostat is that it allows the user to preset temperatures at energy-efficient levels, especially for the middle of the night when the house doesn't need to be as warm (or, for hot summer nights, as cool).

Figure 6.12 is a scatterplot of monthly observations of the gas used in a house (measured in therms) and heating degree-days (HDD), a measure of how cold it was in the month.[8] We've marked the months without a programmable thermostat as squares and the months with the programmable thermostat with circles.

Visually, we immediately see that heating goes up as the heating degree days increase (which happens when the temperature drops). Not a huge surprise. We also can see the possibility that the programmable thermostat lowered gas usage because the observations with the programmable thermostat seem lower. However, it is not clear how large the effect is and whether it is statistically significant.

We need a model to get a more precise answer. What model is best? Let's start with a very basic difference of means model:

$$Therms_i = \beta_0 + \beta_1 Programmable\ Thermostat_i + \epsilon_i$$

The results for this model, in column (a) of Table 6.10, indicate that the homeowner used 13.02 fewer therms of energy in months of using the programmable thermostat than in months before he acquired it. Therms cost about $1.59 at this

---

[8] For each day, the heating degree-days is measured as number of degrees that a day's average temperature is below 65 degrees Fahrenheit, the temperature below which buildings may need to be heated. The monthly measure adds up the daily measures and provides a rough measure of the amount of heating needed in the month. If the temperature is above 65 degrees, the heating degree-days measure will be zero.

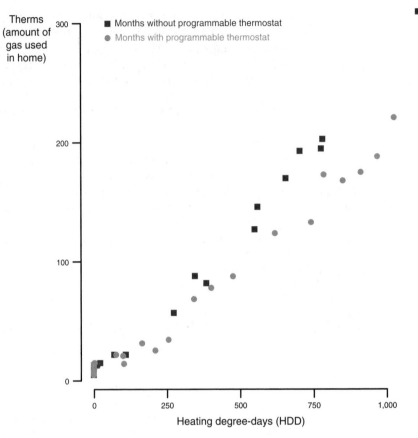

FIGURE 6.12: Heating Used and Heating Degree-Days for Homeowner Who Installed a Programmable Thermostat

time, so the homeowner saved roughly $20.70 per month on average. That's not bad. However, the effect is not statistically significant (not even close, really, as the *t* statistic is only 0.54), so based on this result we should be skeptical that the thermostat saved money.

The difference of means model does not control for anything else, and we know that the coefficient on the programmable thermostat variable will be biased if there is some other variable that matters and is correlated with the programmable thermostat variable. In this case, we know unambiguously that heating degree-days matters, and it is plausible that the heating degree-days differed in the months with and without the programmable thermostat. Hence a better model is clearly

$$Therms_i = \beta_0 + \beta_1 Programmable\ Thermostat_i + \beta_2 HDD_i + \epsilon_i$$

The results for this model are in column (b) of Table 6.10. The heating degree variable is hugely (massively, superlatively) statistically significant. Including it also leads to a higher coefficient on the programmable thermostat variable, which is now 20.05. The standard error on the programmable thermostat variable also goes down a ton because of the much smaller $\hat{\sigma}$, which in turn is due to the much better fit we get by including the heating degree-days variable. The effect of the programmable thermostat variable is statistically significant and, given a cost of $1.59 per therm, the savings is about $31.87 per month. Because a programmable thermostat costs about $60 plus installation, the programmable thermostat should pay for itself pretty quickly.

However, something about these results should nag at us: they are about gas usage only, which in this house goes overwhelmingly to heating (with the rest used to heat water and for the stove). Does it make sense that the programmable thermostat should save $30 in the middle of the summer? The furnace is never on and, well, that means cooking a lot fewer scrambled eggs on the stove to save that much money.

It makes more sense to think about the effect of the thermostat as interactive. That is, the colder it is, the more energy the programmable thermostat can save. Therefore we also estimate the following model that includes an interaction between the thermostat dummy and heating degree-days (HDD):

$$Therms_i = \beta_0 + \beta_1 Programmable\ thermostat_i + \beta_2 HDD_i$$
$$+ \beta_3 Programmable\ thermostat_i \times HDD_i + \epsilon_i$$

TABLE 6.10 **Data from Programmable Thermostat and Home Heating Bills**

	(a)	(b)	(c)
Programmable thermostat	−13.02	−20.05*	−0.48
	(23.94)	(4.49)	(4.15)
	[$t = 0.54$]	[$t = 4.46$]	[$t = 0.11$]
HDD		0.22*	0.26*
(Heating degree-days)		(0.006)	(0.007)
		[$t = 34.42$]	[$t = 38.68$]
Programmable thermostat × HDD			−0.062*
			(0.009)
			[$t = 7.00$]
Constant	81.52*	14.70*	4.24
	(17.49)	(3.81)	(3.00)
	[$t = 4.66$]	[$t = 3.86$]	[$t = 1.41$]
N	45	45	45
$\hat{\sigma}$	80.12	15.00	10.25
R^2	0.007	0.966	0.985

Standard errors in parentheses.

* *indicates significance at $p < 0.05$, two-tailed.*

The results for this model are in column (c) of Table 6.10, where the coefficient on *Programmable thermostat* indicates the difference in therms when the other variables are zero. Because both variables include heating degree-days, the coefficient on *Programmable thermostat* indicates the effect of the thermostat when heating degree-days are zero (meaning the weather is warm for the whole month). The coefficient of −0.48 with a *t* statistic of 0.11 indicates there is no significant bump down in energy usage across all months. This might seem to be bad news, but is it good news for us, given that we have figured out that the programmable thermostat shouldn't reduce heating costs when the furnace isn't running?

The overall effect of the thermostat is $\hat{\beta}_1 + \hat{\beta}_3 \times HDD$. Although we have already seen that $\hat{\beta}_1$ is insignificant, the coefficient on *Programmable thermostat* $\times HDD$, −0.062, is highly statistically significant, with a *t* statistic of 7.00. For every increase in HDD, the programmable thermostat lowered the therms used by 0.062. In a month with the heating degree-days variable equal to 500, we estimate that the homeowner changed energy used by $\hat{\beta}_1 + \hat{\beta}_2 500 = -0.48 - 0.062 \times 500 = -31.48$ therms after the programmable thermostat was installed (lowering the bill by $50.05, at $1.59 per therm). In a month with the heating degree-days variable equal to 1,000, we estimate that the homeowner changed energy use by $-0.48 - 0.062 \times 1000 = -62.48$ therms lowering the bill by $99.34, at $1.59 per therm. Suddenly we're talking real money. And we're doing so from a model that makes intuitive sense because the savings should indeed differ depending on how cold it is.[9]

This case provides an excellent example of how useful—and distinctive—the dummy variable models we've presented in this chapter can be. In panel (a) of Figure 6.13 we show the fitted values based on model (b) in Table 6.10, which controls for heating degree-days but models the effect of the thermostat as a constant difference across all values of heating degree-days. The effect of the programmable thermostat is statistically significant and rather substantial, but it doesn't ring true because it suggests that savings from reduced use of gas for the furnace are the same in a swettering summer month and in a frigid winter month. Panel (b) of Figure 6.13 shows the fitted values based on model (c) in Table 6.10, which allows the effect of the thermostat to vary depending on the heating degree-days. This is an interactive model that yields fitted lines with different slopes. Just by inspection, we can see the fitted lines for model (c) fit the data better. The effects are statistically significant and substantial and, perhaps most important, make more sense because the effect of the programmable thermostat on heating gas used increases as the month gets colder.

---

[9] We might be worried about correlated errors given that this is time series data. As discussed on page 68, the coefficient estimates are not biased if the errors are correlated, but standard OLS standard errors might not be appropriate. In Chapter 13 we show how to estimate models with correlated errors. For this data set, the results get a bit stronger.

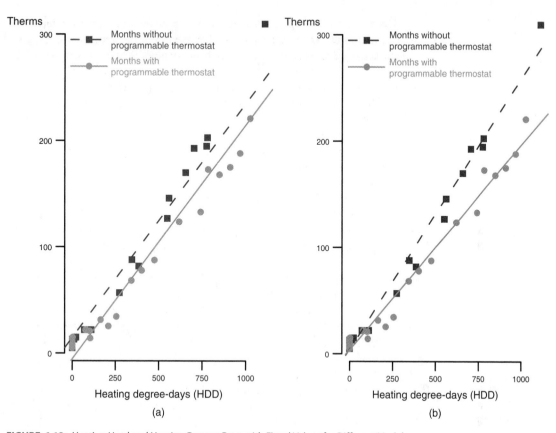

FIGURE 6.13: Heating Used and Heating Degree-Days with Fitted Values for Different Models

Conclusion

Dummy variables are incredibly useful. Despite a less-than-flattering name, they do some of the most important work in all of statistics. Experiments almost always are analyzed with treatment group dummy variables. A huge proportion of observational studies care about or control for dummy variables such as gender or race. And, when we interact dummy variables with continuous variables, we can investigate whether the effects of certain variables differ by group.

We have mastered the core points of this chapter when we can do the following:

- Section 6.1: Write down a model for a difference of means test using bivariate OLS. Which parameter measures the estimated difference? Sketch a diagram that illustrates the meaning of this parameter.

- Section 6.2: Write down a model for a difference of means test using multivariate OLS. Which parameter measures the estimated difference? Sketch a diagram that illustrates the meaning of this parameter.

- Section 6.3: Explain how to incorporate categorical variables in OLS models. What is the excluded category? Explain why coefficient estimates change when the excluded category changes.

- Section 6.4: Write down a model that has a dummy variable (D) interaction with a continuous variable (X). How do we explain the effect of X on Y? Sketch the relationship for $D_i = 0$ observations and $D_i = 1$ observations.

Further Reading

Brambor, Clark, and Golder (2006) and Kam and Franceze (2007) provide excellent discussions of interactions, including the appropriate interpretation of models with two continuous variables interacted. Braumoeller (2004) does a good job of injecting caution into the interpretation of coefficients on lower-order terms in models that include interaction variables.

Key Terms

Categorical variable (181)
Dichotomous variable (169)
Difference of means test
  (169)

Dummy variable (169)
Excluded category (182)
Jitter (172)
Nominal variable (181)

Ordinal variable (181)
Reference category (182)

Computing Corner

Stata

1. A difference of means test in OLS is simply `reg Y Dum` where `Dum` is the name a dummy variable. This command will produce an identical estimate, standard error, and t statistic as `ttest Y, by(Dum)`. To allow the variance to differ across the two groups, the OLS model is `reg Y Dum, robust` and the stand-alone t test is `ttest Y, by(Dum) unequal`.

2. To create an interaction variable named "*DumInteract*", simply type `gen DumInteract = Dum * X`, where `Dum` is the name of the dummy variable and `X` is the name of the continuous variable.

3. Page 542 discusses how to generate a standard error in Stata for the effect of X on Y for the $Dummy_i = 1$ group.

R

1. A difference of means test in OLS is simply `lm(Y ~ Dum)`. This command will produce an identical estimate, standard error, and t statistic as `t.test(Y[Dum==1], Y[Dum==0], var.equal = TRUE)`. To allow the variance to differ across the two groups, the stand-alone t test is `t.test(Y[Dum==1], Y[Dum==0], var.equal = FALSE)`. The OLS version of this model takes a bit more work, as it involves estimating the heteroscedasticity-consistent standard error model described on page 85. It is

```
OLSResults = lm(Y ~ Dum)
coeftest(OLSResults, vcov = vcovHC(OLSResults, type = "HC1"))
```

2. To create an interaction variable named "DumInteract," simply type `DumInteract = Dum * X`, where `Dum` is the name of the dummy variable and `X` is the name of the continuous variable.

3. Page 542 discusses how to generate a standard error in R for the effect of X on Y for the $Dummy_i = 1$ group.

Exercises

1. Use data from heightwage.dta that we used in Chapter 5 (page 161).

   (a) Estimate an OLS regression model with adult wages as the dependent variable and adult height, adolescent height, and a dummy variable for males as the independent variables. Does controlling for gender affect the results?

   (b) Generate a female dummy variable. Estimate a model with both a male dummy variable and a female dummy variable. What happens? Why?

   (c) Reestimate the model from part (a) *separately* for males and females. Do these results differ from the model in which male was included as a dummy variable? Why or why not?

   (d) Estimate a model in which adult wages is the dependent variable and there are controls for adult and adolescent height in addition to dummy variable interactions of male times each of the two height variables. Compare the results to the results from part (c).

(e) Estimate a model in which adult wages is the dependent variable and there are controls for male, adult height, adolescent height, and two dummy variable interactions of male times each of the two height variables. Compare the results to the results from part (c).

(f) Every observation is categorized into one of four regions based on where the subjects lived in 1996. The four regions are Northeast (*norest*96) Midwest (*norcen*96), South (*south*96), and West (*west*96). Add dummy variables for regions to a model explaining wages in 1996 as a function of height in 1981, male, and male times height in 1981. First exclude West, then exclude South, and explain the changes to the coefficients on the height variables and the regional dummy variables.

2. These questions are based on "The Fed may be politically independent, but it is not politically indifferent," a paper by William Clark and Vincent Arel-Bundock (2013). The paper explores the relationship between elections and the federal funds rate (FFR). Often a benchmark for financial markets, the FFR is the average interest rate at which federal funds trade in a day. The rate is set by the U.S. central bank, the Federal Reserve, aka the Fed. Table 6.11 describes the variables from fed_2012_kkedits.dta that we use in this problem.

(a) Create two scatterplots, for years in which a Democrat was president and one for years in which a Republican was president, showing the relationship between the federal funds rate and the quarters since the previous election. Comment on the differences in the relationships. The variable *Election* is coded 0 to 15, representing each quarter from one election to the next. For each presidential term, the value *Election* is zero in the first quarter containing the election and 15 in the quarter before the next election.

TABLE 6.11 Variables for Monetary Policy Data

Variable	Description
FEDFUNDS	Effective federal funds rate (in percent)
lag_FEDFUNDS	Lagged effective federal funds rate (in percent)
Democrat	Democrat = 1, Republican = 0
Election	Quarters since previous election (0–15)
Inflation	Annualized inflation rate (1 percent inflation = 1.00)
DATE	Date

(b) Create an interaction variable between *Election* and *Democrat* to test whether closeness to elections has the same effect on Democrats and Republicans. Run a model with the federal funds rate as the dependent variable, allowing the effect of the *Election* variable to vary by party of the president.

    (i) What change in federal fund rates is associated with a one-unit increase in the *Election* variable when the president is a Republican?

    (ii) What change in federal fund rates is associated with a one-unit increase in the *Election* variable when the president is a Democrat?

(c) Is the effect of *Election* statistically significant under Republicans? (Easy.) Is the effect of *Election* statistically significant under Democrats? (Not so easy.) How can the answer be determined? Run any additional tests if necessary.

(d) Graph two fitted lines for relationship between elections and interest rates, one for Republicans and one for Democrats. (Use the `twoway` and `lfit` commands with appropriate `if` statements; label by hand.) Briefly describe the relationship.

(e) Rerun the model from part (b) controlling for both the interest rate in the previous quarter (lag_FEDFUND) and inflation and discuss results, focusing on (i) effect of election for Republicans, (ii) the differential effect of election for Democrats, (iii) impact of lagged federal funds rate, and (iv) inflation. Simply report the statistical significance of the coefficient estimates; don't go through the entire analysis from part (c).

3. This problem uses the cell phone and traffic data set described in Chapter 5 (page 163) to analyze the relationship between cell and texting bans and traffic fatalities. We add two variables: *cell_ban* is coded 1 if it is illegal to operate a handheld cell phone while driving and 0 otherwise; *text_ban* is coded 1 if it is illegal to text while driving and 0 otherwise.

(a) Add the dummy variables for cell phone bans and texting bans to the model from Chapter 5 (page 163). Interpret the coefficients on these dummy variables.

(b) Based on the the results from part (a), how many lives would be saved if California banned cell phone use while driving? How

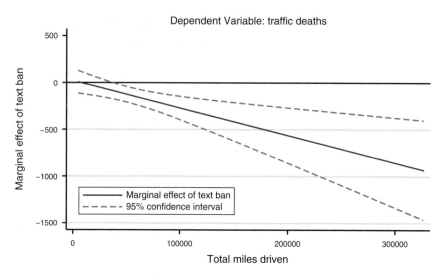

FIGURE 6.14: Marginal Effect of Text Ban as Total Miles Changes

many lives would be saved if Wyoming had a such a ban? Discuss implications for the proper specification of the model.

(c) Estimate a model in which total miles is interacted with both the cell phone ban and the prohibition of texting variables. What is the estimated effect of a cell phone ban for California? For Wyoming? What is the effect of a texting ban for California? For Wyoming? What is the effect of total miles?

(d) This question uses material from page 193. Figure 6.14 displays the effect of the cell phone ban as a function of total miles. The dashed lines depict confidence intervals. Identify the points on the fitted lines for the estimated effects for California and Wyoming from the results in part (c). Explain the conditions under which the cell phone ban has a statistically significant effect.[10]

4. In this problem we continue analyzing the speeding ticket data first introduced in Chapter 5 (page 164). The variables we use are in Table 6.12.

(a) Implement a simple difference of means test that uses OLS to assess whether the fines for men and women are different. Do we have any reason to expect endogeneity? Explain.

---

[10] Brambor, Clark, and Golder (2006) provide Stata code to create a plot like this for models with interaction variables.

TABLE 6.12 Variables for Speeding Ticket Data

Variable name	Description
MPHover	Miles per hour over the speed limit
Amount	Assessed fine for the ticket
Age	Age of driver
Female	Equals 1 for women and 0 for men
Black	Equals 1 for African-Americans and 0 otherwise
Hispanic	Equals 1 for Hispanics and 0 otherwise
StatePol	Equals 1 if ticketing officer was state patrol officer
OutTown	Equals 1 if driver from out of town and 0 otherwise
OutState	Equals 1 if driver from out of state and 0 otherwise

(b) Implement a difference of means test for men and women that controls for age and miles per hour. Do we have any reason to expect endogeneity? Explain.

(c) Building from the model just described, also assess whether fines are higher for African-Americans and Hispanics compared to non-Hispanic whites. Explain what the coefficients on these variables mean.

(d) Look at standard errors on coefficients for the Female, Black, and Hispanic variables. Why they are different?

(e) Within a single OLS model, assess whether miles over the speed limit has a differential effect on the fines for women, African-Americans, and Hispanics.

5. There is a consensus among economists that increasing government spending and cutting taxes boost economic growth during recessions. Do regular citizens share in this consensus? We care because political leaders often feel pressure to do what voters want, regardless of its probable effectiveness.

To get at this issue, a 2012 YouGov survey asked people questions about what would happen to unemployment if taxes were raised or government spending increased. Answers were coded into three categories based on consistency with the economic consensus. On the tax question, people who said raising taxes would raise unemployment were coded as "3" (the correct answer), people who said raising taxes would have no effect on unemployment were coded as "2," and people who said raising taxes would lower unemployment were coded as "1." On the spending question, people who said raising government spending would lower unemployment were coded as "3" (the correct answer), people who said raising spending would have no effect on unemployment were coded as "2," and people who said raising spending would raise unemployment were coded as "1."

(a) Estimate two bivariate OLS models in which political knowledge predicts the answers. In one model, use the tax dependent variable; in the other model, use the spending dependent variable. The model will be

$$Answer_i = \beta_0 + \beta_1 Political\ knowledge_i + \epsilon_i$$

where $Answer_i$ is the correctness of answers, coded as described. We measure political knowledge based on how many of nine factual questions about government each person answered correctly. (Respondents were asked to identify the Vice President, the Chief Justice of the United States, and so forth.) Interpret the results.

(b) Add partisan affiliation to the model by estimating the following model for each of the two dependent variables (the tax and spending variables):

$$Answer_i = \beta_0 + \beta_1 Political\ knowledge_i + \beta_2 Republican_i + \epsilon_i$$

where $Republican_i$ is 1 for people who self-identify with the Republican party and 0 for everyone else.[11] Explain your results.

(c) The effect of party may go beyond simply giving all Republicans a bump up or down in their answers. It could be that political knowledge *interacts* with being Republican such that knowledge has different effects on Republicans and non-Republicans. To test this, estimate a model that includes a dummy interaction term:

$$Answer_i = \beta_0 + \beta_1 Political\ knowledge_i + \beta_2 Republican_i$$
$$+ \beta_3 Political\ knowledge_i \times Republican_i + \epsilon_i$$

Explain the results and compare/contrast to the initial bivariate results.

---

[11] We could use tools for categorical variables discussed in Section 6.3 to separate non-Republicans into Democrats and Independents. Our conclusions would be generally similar in this particular example.

Transforming Variables, Comparing Variables

7

What makes people happy? Relationships? Wisdom? Money? Chocolate? Figure 7.1 provides an initial look at this question by displaying the self-reported life satisfaction of U.S. citizens from the World Values Survey (2008). Each data point is the average value reported by survey respondents in a two-year age group. The scores range from 1 ("dissatisfied") to 10 ("satisfied").[1] There is a pretty clear pattern: people start off reasonably satisfied at age 18 and then reality hits, making them less satisfied until their mid-40s. Happily, things brighten from that point onward, and old folks are generally the happiest bunch. (Who knew?) This pattern is not an anomaly: other surveys at other times and in other countries reveal similar patterns.

The relationship is U-shaped (or smile shaped, if you will).[2] Given what we've done so far, it may not be obvious how to make OLS estimate such a model. However, OLS is actually quite flexible, and this chapter shows off some of the cool tricks OLS can do, including estimating non-linear relationships like the one we see in the life satisfaction data. The unifying theme is that each of these tricks involves a transformation of the data or the model to do useful things.

The particular tasks we tackle in this chapter are estimating non-linear models and comparing coefficients. Section 7.1 shows how to estimate non-linear effects with polynomial models. In Section 7.2 we produce a different kind of non-linear model by using logged variables, which are particularly helpful in characterizing effects in percentage terms. Section 7.3 demonstrates

---

[1] We have used multivariate OLS to net out the effect of income, religiosity, and children from the life satisfaction scores.

[2] To my knowledge there is no study of chocolate and happiness, but I'm pretty sure it would be an upside down U: people might get happier the more they eat for a while, but at some point, more chocolate has to lead to unhappiness, as it did for the kid in *Willy Wonka*.

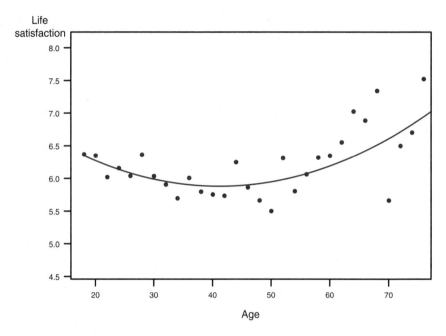

FIGURE 7.1: Average Life Satisfaction by Age in the United States

how standardizing variables can make OLS coefficients more comparable. Section 7.4 shows formal tests of whether coefficients differ from each other. The technique illustrated can be used for any hypothesis involving multiple coefficients.

7.1 Quadratic and Polynomial Models

The world doesn't always move in straight lines and, happily, neither do OLS estimates. In this section we explain the difference between linear and non-linear models in the regression context and then introduce quadratic and polynomial models as flexible tools to deal with non-linear models.

Linear versus non-linear models

The standard OLS model is remarkably flexible. It can, for example, estimate non-linear effects. This idea might seem a little weird at first. Didn't we say at the outset (page 46) that OLS is also known as linear regression? How can we estimate non-linear effects with a linear regression model? The reason is a bit pedantic, but here goes: when we refer to a "linear" model, we mean linear in parameters, which means that the β's aren't squared or cubed or logged or subject to some other non-linearity.

This means that OLS can't handle models like the following[3]:

$$Y_i = \beta_0 + \beta_1^2 X_{1i} + \epsilon_i$$
$$Y_i = \beta_0 + \sqrt{\beta_1} X_{1i} + \beta_2 X_{1i} + \epsilon_i$$

The X's, though, are fair game: we can square, cube, log, or otherwise transform X's to produce fitted *curves* instead of fitted *lines*. Therefore both the following models are OK in OLS because each β simply multiplies itself times some independent variable that may or not be non-linear:

$$Y_i = \beta_0 + \beta_1 X_{1i} + \beta_2 X_{1i}^2 + \epsilon_i$$
$$Y_i = \beta_0 + \beta_1 \sqrt{X_{1i}} + \beta_2 X_{1i}^7 + \epsilon_i$$

Non-linear relationships are common in the real world. Figure 7.2 shows data on life expectancy and GDP per capita for all countries in the world. We immediately sense that there is a positive relationship: The wealthier countries definitely have higher life expectancy. But we also see that the relationship is a curve, rather than a line, because life expectancy rises rapidly at the lower levels of GDP per capita, but then flattens out. Based on this data, it's pretty reasonable to expect an annual increase of $1,000 in per capita GDP to have a fairly substantial effect on life expectancy in a country with low GDP per capita, while an increase of $1,000 in per capita GDP for a very wealthy country would have only a negligible effect on life expectancy. Therefore we want to get beyond estimating straight lines alone.

Figure 7.3 shows the life expectancy data with two different kinds of fitted lines. Panel (a) shows a fitted line from a standard OLS model:

$$Life\ expectancy_i = \beta_0 + \beta_1 GDP_i + \epsilon_i \tag{7.1}$$

The fit isn't great. The fitted line is lower than the data for many of the observations with low GDP values. For observations with high GDP levels, the fitted line dramatically overestimates life expectancy. As bad as it is, this is the best possible straight line in terms of minimizing squared error.

Polynomial models

▶ **polynomial model**
A model that includes values of X raised to powers greater than one.

We can generate a better fit by using a **polynomial model**. Polynomial models include not only an independent variable, but also the independent variable raised to some power. By using a polynomial model, we can produce fitted value lines that curve.

---

[3] The world doesn't end if we really want to estimate a model that is non-linear in the β's. We just need something other than OLS to estimate the model. In Chapter 12 we discuss probit and logit models, which are non-linear in the β's.

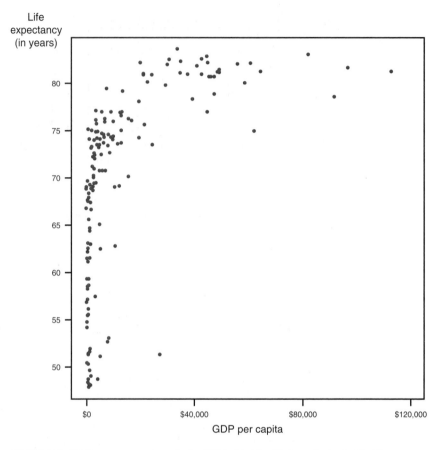

FIGURE 7.2: Life Expectancy and per Capita GDP in 2011 for All Countries in the World

▶ **quadratic model** A model that includes X and X^2 as independent variables.

The simplest example of a polynomial model is a **quadratic model** that includes X and X^2. The model looks like this:

$$Y_i = \beta_0 + \beta_1 X_{1i} + \beta_2 X_{1i}^2 + \epsilon_i \tag{7.2}$$

For our life expectancy example, a quadratic model is

$$Life\ expectancy_i = \beta_0 + \beta_1 GDP_i + \beta_2 GDP_i^2 + \epsilon_i \tag{7.3}$$

Panel (b) of Figure 7.3 plots this fitted curve. It better captures the non-linearity in the data as life expectancy rises rapidly at low levels of GDP and then levels off. The fitted curve is not perfect. The predicted life expectancy is still a bit low for low values of GDP, and the turn to negative effects seems more dramatic than the data warrant. We'll see how to generate fitted lines that flatten out without turning down when we cover logged models later in this chapter.

Interpreting coefficients in a polynomial model is different from this procedure in a standard OLS model. Note that the effect of X changes depending on the value of X. In panel (b) of Figure 7.3, the effect of GDP on life expectancy

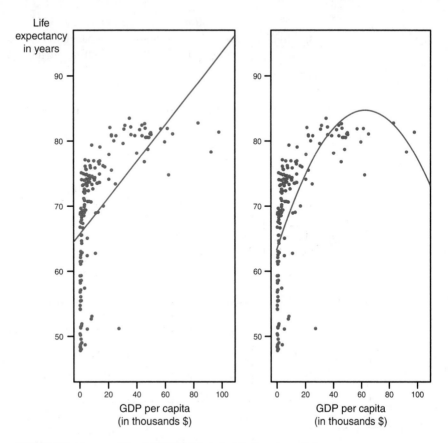

FIGURE 7.3: Linear and Quadratic Fitted Lines for Life Expectancy Data

is large for low values of GDP. That is, when GDP goes from $0 to $20,000, the fitted value for life expectancy increases relatively rapidly. The effect of GDP on life expectancy is smaller as GDP gets higher: the change in fitted life expectancy when GDP goes from $40,000 to $60,000 is much smaller than the change in fitted life expectancy when GDP goes from $0 to $20,000. The predicted effect of GDP even turns negative when GDP goes above $60,000.

We need some calculus to get the specific equation for the effect of X on Y. We refer to the effect of X on Y as $\frac{\partial Y}{\partial X_1}$:

$$\frac{\partial Y}{\partial X_1} = \beta_1 + 2\beta_2 X_1 \tag{7.4}$$

This equation means that when we interpret results from a polynomial regression, we can't look at individual coefficients in isolation; instead, we need to know how the coefficients on X_1 and X_1^2 come together to produce the estimated curve.[4]

---

[4] Equation 7.4 is the result of using standard calculus tools to take the derivative of Y in Equation 7.2 with respect to X_1. The derivative is the slope evaluated at a given value of X_1. For a linear model, the slope is always the same and is $\hat{\beta}_1$. The ∂Y in the numerator refers to the change in Y; the ∂X_1 in the

Figure 7.4 illustrates more generally the kinds of relationships that a quadratic model can account for. Each panel illustrates a different quadratic function. In panel (a), the effect of X is getting bigger as X gets bigger. In panel

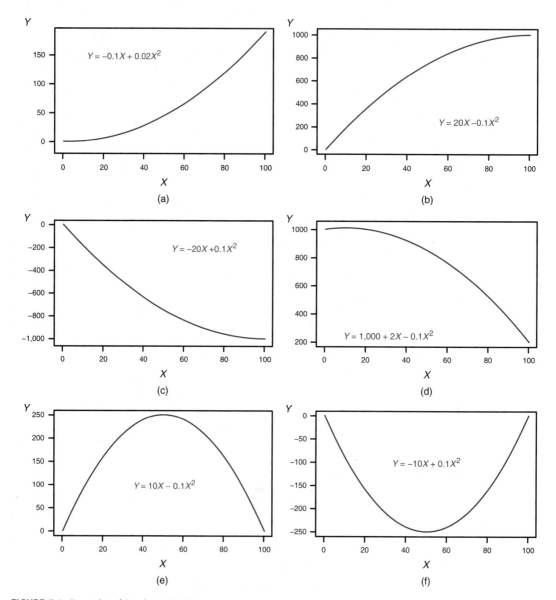

FIGURE 7.4: Examples of Quadratic Fitted Curves

denominator refers to the change in X_1. The fraction $\frac{\partial Y}{\partial X_1}$ therefore refers to the change in Y divided by the change in X_1, which is the slope.

(b), the effect of X on Y is getting smaller. In both the top panels, Y gets bigger as X gets bigger, but the relationships have a quite different feel.

In panels (c) and (d), there are negative relationships between X and Y: the more X, the less Y. Again, though, we see very different types of relationships. In panel (c), there is a leveling out, while in panel (d), the negative effect of X on Y accelerates as X gets bigger.

A quadratic OLS model can even estimate relationships that change directions. In panel (e), Y initially gets bigger as X increases, but then it levels out; eventually, increases in X decrease Y. In panel (f), we see the opposite pattern, with Y getting smaller as X rises for small values of X and, eventually, Y rising with X.

One of the nice things about using a quadratic specification in OLS is that we don't have to know ahead of time whether the relationship is curving down or up, flattening out, or getting steeper. The data will tell us. We can simply estimate a quadratic model and, if the relationship is like that in panel (a), the estimated OLS coefficients will yield a curve like the one in the panel; if the relationship is like that in panel (f), OLS will produce coefficients that best fit the data. So if we have data that looks like any of the patterns in Figure 7.4, we can get fitted lines that reflect the data simply by estimating a quadratic OLS model.

Polynomial models with cubed or higher-order terms can account for patterns that wiggle and bounce even more than those in the quadratic model. It's relatively rare to use higher-order polynomial models, which often simply aren't supported by the data. In addition, using higher-order terms without strong theoretical reasons can be a bit fishy—as in raising the specter of the model fishing we warned about on page 156. A control variable with a high order can be more defensible; ideally, however, our main results do not depend on untheorized high-order polynomial control variables.

REMEMBER THIS

OLS can estimate non-linear effects via polynomial models.

1. A polynomial model includes X raised to powers greater than 1. The general form is

$$Y_i = \beta_0 + \beta_1 X_i + \beta_2 X_i^2 + \beta_3 X_i^3 + \ldots + \beta_k X_i^k + \epsilon_i$$

2. The most commonly used polynomial model is the quadratic model:

$$Y_i = \beta_0 + \beta_1 X_i + \beta_2 X_i^2 + \epsilon_i$$

- The effect of X_i in a quadratic model varies depending on the value of X.
- The estimated effect of a one-unit increase in X_i in a quadratic model is $\hat{\beta}_1 + 2\hat{\beta}_2 X$.

Discussion Questions

1. For each of the following, discuss whether you expect the relationship to be linear or non-linear. Sketch the relationship you expect with a couple of points on the X-axis, labeled to identify the nature of any non-linearity you anticipate.

   (a) Age and income in France

   (b) Height and speed in the Boston Marathon

   (c) Height and rebounds in the National Basketball Association

   (d) IQ and score on a college admissions test in Japan

   (e) IQ and salary in Japan

   (f) Gas prices and oil company profits

   (g) Sleep and your score on your econometrics final exam

CASE STUDY   **Global Warming**

Climate change may be one of the most important long-term challenges facing humankind. We'd really like to know if temperatures have been increasing and, if so, at what rate.

Figure 7.5 shows global temperatures since 1880. Panel (a) plots global average temperatures by year over time. Temperature is measured in deviation from average pre-industrial temperature. The more positive the value, the more temperature has increased. Clearly there is an upward trend. But how should we characterize this trend?

Panel (b) of Figure 7.5 includes the fitted line from a bivariate OLS model with *Year* as the independent variable:

$$Temperature_i = \beta_0 + \beta_1 Year_i + \epsilon_i$$

The linear model fits reasonably well, although it seems to be underestimating recent temperatures and overestimating temperatures in the 1970s.

Column (a) of Table 7.1 shows the coefficient estimates for the linear model. The estimated $\hat{\beta}_1$ is 0.006, with a standard error of 0.0003. The t statistic of 18.74 indicates a highly statistically significant coefficient. The result suggests that the earth has been getting 0.006 degree warmer each year since 1879 (when the data series begins).

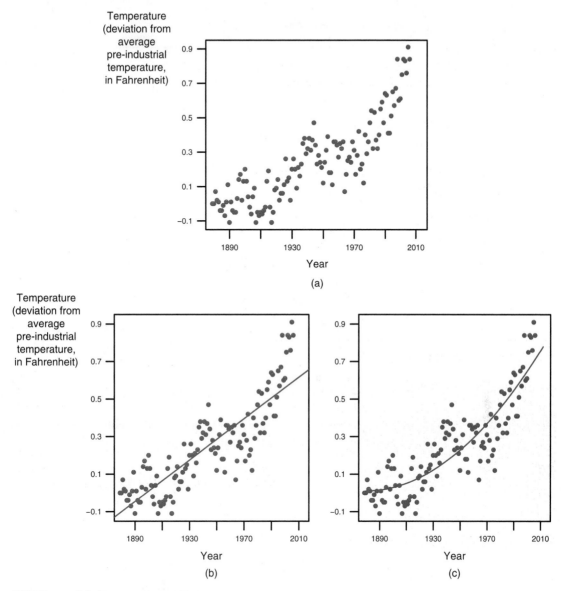

FIGURE 7.5: Global Temperature over Time

The data looks pretty non-linear, so we also estimate the following quadratic OLS model:

$$Temperature_i = \beta_0 + \beta_1 Year_i + \beta_2 Year_i^2 + \epsilon_i$$

in which *Year* and *Year*^{2} are independent variables. This model allows us to assess whether the temperature change has been speeding up or slowing down by allowing us to estimate a curve in which the change per year in recent years is, depending on the data, larger or smaller than the change per year in earlier years. We have plotted the fitted line in panel (c) of Figure 7.5; notice that it is a curve that

TABLE 7.1	Global Temperature, 1879–2012	
	(a)	(b)
Year	0.006*	−0.166*
	(0.0003)	(0.031)
	[$t = 18.74$]	[$t = 5.31$]
$Year^2$		0.000044*
		(0.000008)
		[$t = 5.49$]
Constant	−10.46*	155.68*
	(0.57)	(30.27)
	[$t = 18.31$]	[$t = 5.14$]
N	128	128
R^2	0.73	0.78

Standard errors in parentheses.

* *indicates significance at $p < 0.05$, two-tailed.*

is getting steeper over time. It fits the data even better with less underestimation in recent years and less overestimation in the 1970s.

Column (b) of Table 7.1 reports results from the quadratic model. The coefficients on *Year* and *Year²* have *t* stats greater than 5, indicating clear statistical significance.

The coefficient on *Year* is −0.166, and the coefficient on *Year²* is 0.000044. What the heck do those numbers mean? At a glance, not much. Recall, however, that in a quadratic model an increase in *Year* by 1 will be associated with a $\hat{\beta}_1 + 2\hat{\beta}_2 Year_i$ increase in estimated average global temperature. This means the predicted change from an increase in *Year* by 1 in 1900 is:

$$-0.166 + 2 \times 0.000044 \times 1900 = 0.0012 \text{ degree}$$

The predicted change in temperature from an increase in *Year* by 1 in 2000 is:

$$-0.166 + 2 \times 0.000044 \times 2000 = 0.01 \text{ degree}$$

In the quadratic model, in other words, the predicted effect of *Year* changes over time. In particular, the estimated rate of warming in 2000 (0.01 degree per year) is around eight times the estimated rate of warming in 1900 (0.0012 degree per year).

We won't pay much attention at this point to the standard errors because errors are almost surely autocorrelated, which would make the standard errors reported by OLS incorrect, probably too small. We address autocorrelation and other time series aspects of this data in Chapter 13.

Review Questions

Figure 7.6 contains hypothetical data on investment by consumer electronics companies as a function of their profit margins.

1. For each panel, describe the model you think best explains the data.

2. Sketch a fitted line for each panel.

3. For each panel, approximate the predicted effect on R & D investment of changing profits from 0 to 1 percent and from changing profits from 3 to 4 percent.

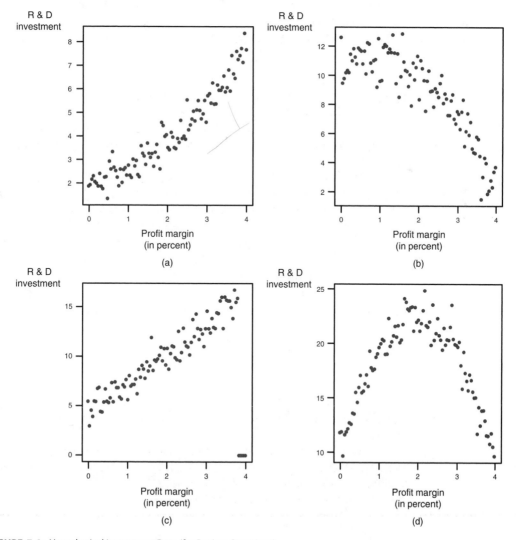

FIGURE 7.6: Hypothetical Investment Data (for Review Questions)

7.2   Logged Variables

Empirical analysts, especially in economics, often use logged variables. Logged variables allow for non-linear relationships but have cool properties that allow us to interpret estimated effects in percentage terms. In this section we discuss logs and how they work in OLS models, and we show how they work in our height and wages example. Although we present several different ways to use logged variables, the key thing to remember is that if there's a log, there's a percentage interpretation of some sort going on.

Logs in regression models

We'll work with so-called *natural logs*, which revolve around the constant e, which equals approximately 2.71828. Like $\pi \approx 3.14$, e is one of those numbers that pops up all over in math. Recall that if $e^2 = 7.38$, then $\ln(7.38) = 2$. (The notation "ln" refers to natural log.) In other words, the natural log of some number k is the exponent to which we have to raise e to obtain k. The fact that $\ln(3) = 1.10$ means that $e^{1.10} = 3$ (with rounding).

For our purposes, we won't be using the mathematical properties of logs too much.[5] We instead note that using logged variables in OLS equations can allow us to characterize non-linear relationships that are broadly similar to panels (b) and (c) of Figure 7.4. In that sense, these models don't differ dramatically from polynomial models.

One difference from the quadratic models is that models with logged variables have an additional, very attractive feature. The estimated coefficients can be interpreted directly in percentage terms. That is, with the right logged model we can produce results that tell us how much a one percent increase in X affects Y. Often this is a good way to think about empirical questions. For example, suppose we have wage data for a large number of people across many years and we want to know how inflation affects wages. We might begin with an OLS model something like

$$Wages_{it} = \beta_0 + \beta_1 Inflation_t + \epsilon_{it} \tag{7.5}$$

where wages per hour for person i in year t is the dependent variable and the inflation rate in year t is the independent variable. The estimated $\hat{\beta}_1$ in this model would tell us the increase in wages per hour that would be associated with a one-unit increase in inflation. At first glance, this might seem like an OK model. On second glance, we realize it is absurd. Suppose the model produces $\hat{\beta}_1 = 1.25$; that result would say that everyone—whatever their wage level—would get another \$1.25 for every one point increase in inflation. That conclusion is actually kind of weird: such a model is, by design, saying that for every one percent increase in inflation, the richest CEO gets another buck and a quarter per hour, as does the lowliest temp.

---

[5] We derive the marginal effects in log models in the appendix (page 542).

▶ log-linear model A model in which the dependent variable is transformed by taking its natural log.

What we really want is a model that allows us to estimate what percent of people's salary changes with inflation. Using logged variables makes this possible. For example, we could estimate a **log-linear model** in which the dependent variable is transformed by taking the natural log of it. Such a model would look like

$$\ln(Wages_{it}) = \beta_0 + \beta_1 Inflation_t + \epsilon_{it} \tag{7.6}$$

It turns out, through the magic of calculus (presented on page 542), that the $\hat{\beta}_1$ in this model can be interpreted as the percentage change in Y associated with a one-unit increase in X. In other words, if $\hat{\beta}_1 = 0.82$, we would say that a one-unit increase in inflation is associated with a 0.82 percentage increase in wages. The CEO would get a 0.82 percent increase of her high wages; the temp would get a 0.82 percent increase of his low wages. These are very different dollar amounts.

▶ linear-log model A model in which the dependent variable is not logged, but the independent variable is.

We can also estimate a **linear-log model** in which the dependent variable is not logged, but the independent variable is. Such a model would look like

$$Y_i = \beta_0 + \beta_1 \ln X_i + \epsilon_i \tag{7.7}$$

Here, β_1 indicates the effect of a one percent increase in X on Y. We need to divide the estimated coefficient by 100 to convert it to units of Y. This is one of the odd hiccups in models with logged variables: the units can be a bit tricky. While we can memorize the way units work in these various models, the safe course of action here is to simply accept that we'll probably have to look up how units in logged models work when we use logged models after being away from them for a bit.

Figure 7.7 shows a fitted line from a linear-log model using the GDP and life expectancy data we saw earlier in Figure 7.3. One nice feature of the fitted line from this model is that the fitted values keep rising by smaller and smaller amounts as GDP per capita increases. This pattern contrasts to the fitted values in the quadratic model, which declined for high values of GDP per capita. The estimated coefficient in the linear-log model on GDP per capita (measured in thousands of dollars) is 5.1. This implies that a one percent increase in GDP per capita is associated with an increase in life expectancy of 0.051 years. For a country with a GDP per capita of $100,000, an increase of GDP per capita of $1,000 will increase life expectancy by only about one-twentieth (0.05) of a year. For a country with a GDP per capita of $10,000, however, an increase of GDP per capita of $1,000 is a 10 percent increase, implying that the estimated effect is to increase life expectancy by about one-half of a year. A $1,000 increase in GDP per capita for a country with GDP per capita of $1,000 would a 100 percent increase, implying that the fitted value of life expectancy would rise by about 5 years.

▶ log-log model A model in which the dependent variable and the independent variables are logged.

▶ elasticity The percent change in Y associated with a percent change in X.

At the pinnacle of loggy-ness is the so-called **log-log model**. This model allows us to estimate **elasticity** in economic models. Elasticity is the percent change in Y associated with a percent change in X. For example, if we want to know the elasticity of demand for airline tickets, we can get data on sales and

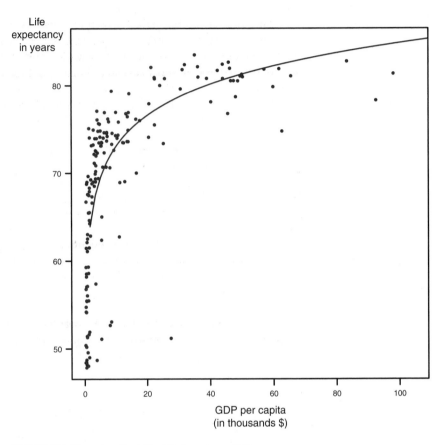

FIGURE 7.7: Linear-Log Model for Life Expectancy Data

prices and estimate the following model:

$$\ln(\textit{Ticket sales}_{it}) = \beta_0 + \beta_1 \ln(\textit{Price}_{it}) + \epsilon_{it} \tag{7.8}$$

where the dependent variable is the natural log of monthly ticket sales on routes (e.g., New York to Tokyo) and the independent variable is the natural log of the monthly average price of the tickets on those routes. $\hat{\beta}_1$ estimates the percentage change of sales when ticket prices go up by one percent.[6]

Another hiccup we notice with logged models is that the values of the variable being logged must be greater than zero. The reason is that the mathematical log function is undefined for values less than or equal to zero.[7] Hence, logged models

_____

[6] A complete analysis would account for the fact that prices are also a function of the quantity of tickets sold. We address these type of models in Section 9.6.

[7] Recall that (natural) log of k is the exponent to which we have to raise e to obtain k. There is no number that we can raise e to and get zero. We can get close by raising e to minus a huge number; for example, $e^{-100} = \frac{1}{e^{100}}$, which is very close to zero, but not quite zero.

work best with economic variables such as sales, quantities, and prices. Even there, though, it is not uncommon to see an observation with zero sales or zero wages, and we're forced to omit such observations.[8]

Logged models are super easy to estimate; we'll see how in the Computing Corner. The key is interpretation. If the model has a logged variable or variables, we know the coefficients reflect a percentage of some sort, with the exact interpretation depending on which variables are logged.

Logs in height and wages example

Table 7.2 takes us back to the height and wage data we discussed on page 133. It reports results from four regressions. In the first specification nothing is logged. Interpretation of $\hat{\beta}_1$ is old hat: a one-inch increase in adolescent height is associated with a $0.412 increase in predicted hourly wages.

The second column reports results from a linear-log model in which the dependent variable is not logged and the independent variable is logged. The interpretation of $\hat{\beta}_1$ is that a one percent increase in X (which is adolescent height in this case) is associated with a $\frac{29.316}{100} = \$0.293$ increase in hourly wages. The dividing by 100 is a bit unusual, but no big deal once we get used to it.

The third column reports results from a model in which the dependent variable has been logged but the independent variable has not been logged. The

TABLE 7.2 Different Logged Models of Relationship between Height and Wages

	No log	Linear-log	Log-linear	Log-log
Adolescent height	0.412*		0.033*	
	(0.098)		(0.015)	
	[$t = 4.23$]		[$t = 2.23$]	
Log adolescent height		29.316*		2.362*
		(6.834)		(1.021)
		[$t = 4.29$]		[$t = 2.31$]
Constant	−13.093	−108.778*	0.001	−7.754
	(6.897)	(29.092)	(1.031)	(4.348)
	[$t = 1.90$]	[$t = 3.74$]	[$t = 0.01$]	[$t = 1.78$]
N	1,910	1,910	1,910	1,910
R^2	0.009	0.010	0.003	0.003

Standard errors in parentheses.

* indicates significance at $p < 0.05$, two-tailed.

---

[8] Some people recode these numbers as something very close to zero (such as 0.0000001) on the reasoning that the log function is defined for low positive values and the essential information (that the variable is near zero) in such observations is not lost. However, it's always a bit sketchy to be changing values (even from zero to a small number), so tread carefully.

interpretation of $\hat{\beta}_1$ here is that a one-inch increase in height is associated with a 3.3 percent increase in wages.

The fourth column reports a log-log model in which both the dependent variable and the independent variable have been logged. The interpretation of $\hat{\beta}_1$ here is that a 1 percent increase in height is associated with a 2.362 percent increase in wages. Note that in the log-linear column, the probability is on a scale of 0 to 1, and in the log-log column, the probability is on a 0 to 100 scale. Yeah, that's a pain; it's just how the math works out.

So which model is best? Sadly, there is no magic bullet that will always hit the perfect model here, another hiccup when we work with logged models. We can't simply look at the R^2 because those values are not comparable: in the first two models the dependent variable is Y and in the last two the dependent variable is $\ln(Y)$. As is often the case, some judgment will be necessary. If we're dealing with an economic problem of estimating price elasticity, a log-log model is natural. In other contexts, we have to decide whether the causal mechanism makes more sense in percentage terms and whether it applies to the dependent and/or independent variables.

REMEMBER THIS

1. How to interpret logged models:

   Log-linear: $\ln Y_i = \beta_0 + \beta_1 X_i + \epsilon_i$ A one-unit increase in X is associated with a β_1 percent change in Y (on a 0–1 scale).

   Linear-log: $Y_i = \beta_0 + \beta_1 \ln X_i + \epsilon_i$ A one percent increase in X is associated with a $\frac{\beta_1}{100}$ change in Y.

   Log-log: $\ln Y_i = \beta_0 + \beta_1 \ln X_i + \epsilon_i$ A one percent increase in X is associated with a β_1 percent change in Y (on a 0–100 scale).

2. Logged models have some challenges not found in other models (the Three Hiccups):

   (a) The scale of the $\hat{\beta}$ coefficients varies depending on whether the model is log-linear, linear-log, or log-log.

   (b) We cannot log variables that have values less than or equal to zero.

   (c) There is no simple test for choosing among log-linear, linear-log, and log-log models.

7.3 Standardized Coefficients

We frequently want to compare coefficients. That is, we want to say whether X_1 or X_2 has a bigger effect on Y. If the variables are on the same scale, this task is pretty easy. For example, in the height and wages model, both adolescent and adult height are measured in inches, so we can naturally compare the estimated effects of an inch of adult height versus an inch of adolescent height.

Challenge of comparing coefficients

When the variables are not on the same scale, we have a tougher time making a direct comparison. Suppose we want to understand the economics of professional baseball players' salaries. Players with high batting averages get on base a lot, keeping the offense going and increasing the odds of scoring. Players who hit home runs score right away, sometimes in bunches. Which group of players earns more? We might first address question this by estimating

$$Salary_i = \beta_0 + \beta_1 Batting\ average_i + \beta_2 Home\ runs_i + \epsilon_i$$

The results are in Table 7.3. The coefficient on batting average is 12,417,629.72. That's huge! The coefficient on home runs is 129,627.36. Also big. But nothing like the coefficient on batting average. Batting average must have a much bigger effect on salaries than home runs, right?

Umm, no. These variables aren't comparable. Batting averages typically range from 0.200 to 0.350 (meaning most players get a hit between 20 and 35 percent of the time). Home runs per season range from 0 to 73 (with a lot more 0s

TABLE 7.3 Determinants of Major League Baseball Salaries, 1985–2005

Batting average	12,417,629.72*
	(940,985.99)
	[$t = 13.20$]
Home runs	129,627.36*
	(2,889.77)
	[$t = 44.86$]
Constant	−2,869,439.40*
	(244,241.12)
	[$t = 11.75$]
N	6,762
R^2	0.30

Standard errors in parentheses.

* *indicates significance at $p < 0.05$, two-tailed.*

than 73s!). Each OLS coefficient in the model tells us what happens if we increase the variable by "1." For batting average, that's an impossibly large increase (going from probability of getting a hit of 0 to a probability of 1.0). Increasing the home run variable by "1" happens every time someone hits a home run. In other words, "1" means something very different for two variables and we'd be nuts to directly compare the regression coefficients on the variables.

Standardizing coefficients

▶ **standardize**

Standardizing a variable converts it to a measure of standard deviations from its mean.

A convenient trick is to **standardize** the variables. To do so, we convert variables to standard deviations from their means. That is, instead of having a variable that indicates a baseball player's batting average, we have a variable that indicates how many standard deviations above or below the average batting average a player was. Instead of having a variable that indicates home runs, we have a variable that indicates how many standard deviations above or below the average number of home runs a player hit. The attraction of standardizing variables is that a one-unit increase for both standardized independent variables will be a standard deviation.

We often (but not always) standardize the dependent variable as well. If we do so, the coefficient on a standardized independent variable can be interpreted as "Controlling for the other variables in the model, a one standard deviation increase in X is associated with a $\hat{\beta}_1$ standard deviation increase in the dependent variable."

We standardize variables using the following equation:

$$Variable^{Standardized} = \frac{Variable - \overline{Variable}}{sd(Variable)} \tag{7.9}$$

where $\overline{Variable}$ is the average of the variable for all units in the sample and sd($Variable$) is the standard deviation of the variable.

Table 7.4 reports the means and standard deviations of the variables for our baseball salary example. Table 7.5 then uses these means and standard deviations to report the unstandardized and standardized values of salary, batting average, and home runs for three selected players. Player 1 earned $5.85 million. Given that the standard deviation of salaries in the data set was $2,764,512, the standardized value of this player's salary is $\frac{5,850,000 - 2,024,616}{2,764,512} = 1.38$. In other words, player 1 earned 1.38 standard deviations more than the average salary. This player's batting average was 0.267, which is exactly the average. Hence his standardized batting

TABLE 7.4 **Means and Standard Deviations of Baseball Variables**

Variable	Mean	Standard deviation
Salary	$2,024,616	$2,764,512
Batting average	0.267	0.031
Home runs	12.11	10.31

TABLE 7.5 Means and Standard Deviations of Baseball Variables for Three Players

Player ID	Salary	Unstandardized Batting average	Home runs	Salary	Standardized Batting average	Home runs
1	5,850,000	0.267	43	1.38	0.00	2.99
2	2,000,000	0.200	4	−0.01	−2.11	−0.79
3	870,000	0.317	33	−0.42	1.56	2.03

average is zero. He hit 43 home runs, which is 2.99 standard deviations above the mean number of home runs.

Table 7.6 displays standardized OLS results along with the unstandardized results from Table 7.3. Here we leave the dependent variable in unstandardized form because we want to interpret results in terms of dollars earned. The standardized results allow us to reasonably compare the effects on salary of batting average and home runs. We see in Table 7.4 that a standard deviation of batting average is 0.031. The **standardized coefficients** tell us that an increase of one standard deviation of batting average is associated with an increase in salary of 0.14 standard deviation. So, for example, a player raising his batting average by 0.031, from 0.267 to 0.298, can expect an increase in salary of $0.14 \times \$2,764,512 = \$387,032$. A player who increases his home runs by one standard deviation (which Table 7.4 tells us is 10.31 home runs), can expect a 0.48 standard deviation increase in salary (which is $0.48 \times \$2,764,512 = \$1,326,966$). In other words, home runs have a bigger bang for the buck. Eat your steroid-laced Wheaties, kids.[9]

While results from OLS models with standardized variables seem quite different, all they really do is rescale the original results. The model fit is the

▶ **standardized coefficient** The coefficient on an independent variable that has been standardized.

TABLE 7.6 Standardized Determinants of Major League Baseball Salaries, 1985–2005

	Unstandardized	Standardized
Batting average	12,417,629.72*	0.14*
	(940,985.99)	(0.01)
	[$t = 13.20$]	[$t = 13.20$]
Home runs	129,627.36*	0.48*
	(2,889.77)	(0.01)
	[$t = 44.86$]	[$t = 44.86$]
Constant	−2,869,439.40*	0.00
	(244,241.12)	(0.01)
	[$t = 11.75$]	[$t = 0.00$]
N	6,762	6,762
R^2	0.30	0.30

Standard errors in parentheses.

* indicates significance at $p < 0.05$, two-tailed.

---

[9] That's a joke! Wheaties are gross.

same whether standardized or unstandardized variables are used. Notice that the R^2 is identical. Also, the conclusions about statistical significance are the same in the unstandardized and standardized regressions; we can see that by comparing the t statistics in the unstandardized and standardized results. Think of the standardization as something like international currency conversion. In unstandardized form, the coefficients are reported in different currencies, but in standardized form, the coefficients are reported in a common currency. The underlying real prices are the same whether they are reported in dollars, euros, or baht, though.

REMEMBER THIS

Standardized coefficients allow the effects of two independent variables to be compared.

1. When the independent variable, X_k, and dependent variable are standardized, an increase of one standard deviation in X_k is associated with a $\hat{\beta}_k$ standard deviation increase in the dependent variable.

2. Statistical significance and model fit are the same for unstandardized and standardized results.

7.4 Hypothesis Testing about Multiple Coefficients

The standardized coefficients on batting average and home runs look quite different. But are they statistically significantly different from each other? The t statistics in Table 7.6 tell us that each is statistically significantly different from zero but nothing about whether they are different from each other.

Answering this kind of question is trickier than it was for the t tests because we're dealing with more than one estimated coefficient. Uncertainty is associated with both estimates, and to make things worse, the estimates may covary in ways that we need to take into account. In this section we discuss F tests as a solution to this challenge, explain two different types of commonly used hypotheses about multiple coefficients, and then show how to use R^2 results to implement these tests, including an example for our baseball data.[10]

F tests

▶ **F test** A type of hypothesis test commonly used to test hypotheses involving multiple coefficients.

There are several ways to test hypotheses involving multiple coefficients. We focus on an **F test**. This test shares features with hypothesis tests discussed earlier (page 97). When using a F test, we define null and alternative hypotheses, set a significance level, and compare a test statistic to a critical value. The F test is different in that we use a new test statistic and compare it to a critical value

---

[10] It is also possible to use t tests to compare multiple coefficients, but F tests are more widely used for this purpose.

derived from an F distribution rather than a t distribution or a normal distribution. We provide more information on the F distribution in the appendix (page 532).

▶ **F statistic** The test statistic used in conducting an F test.

The new test statistic is an **F statistic**. It is based on R^2 values from two separate OLS specifications. We'll first discuss these OLS models and then describe the F statistic in more detail.

▶ **unrestricted model** An unrestricted model is the model in an F test that imposes no restrictions on the coefficients.

The first specification is the **unrestricted model**, which is simply the full model. For example, if we have three independent variables, our full model might be

$$Y_i = \beta_0 + \beta_1 X_{1i} + \beta_2 X_{2i} + \beta_3 X_{3i} + \epsilon_i \tag{7.10}$$

The model is called unrestricted because we are imposing no restrictions on what the values of $\hat{\beta}_1, \hat{\beta}_2$, and $\hat{\beta}_3$ will be.

▶ **restricted model** The model in an F test that imposes the restriction that the null hypothesis is true.

The second specification is the so-called **restricted model** in which we force the computer to give us results that comport with the null hypothesis. It's called restricted because we are restricting the estimated values of $\hat{\beta}_1, \hat{\beta}_2$, and $\hat{\beta}_3$ to be consistent with the null hypothesis.

How do we do that? Sounds hard. Actually, it isn't. We simply take the relationship implied by the null hypothesis and impose it on the unrestricted model. We can divide hypotheses involving multiple coefficients into two general cases.

Case 1: Multiple coefficients equal zero under the null hypothesis

It is fairly common to be interested in a null like $H_0 : \beta_1 = \beta_2 = 0$. This is a null that both coefficients are zero; we reject it if we observe evidence that one or both coefficients are not equal to zero. This type of hypothesis is particularly useful when we have multicollinear variables. In such circumstances, the multicollinearity may drive up the standard errors of the $\hat{\beta}$ estimates, giving us very imprecise (and probably statistically insignificant) estimates for the individual coefficients. By testing the null that both the multicollinear variables equal zero, we can at least learn if one (or both) of them is non-zero, even as we can't say which one it is because the two are so closely related.

In this case, imposing the null hypothesis means making sure that our estimates of β_1 and β_2 are both zero. The process is actually easy-schmeasy: Just set the coefficients to zero and see that the resulting model is simply a model without variables X_1 and X_2. Specifically, the restricted model for $H_0 : \beta_1 = \beta_2 = 0$ is

$$\begin{aligned} Y_i &= \beta_0 + \beta_1 X_{1i} + \beta_2 X_{2i} + \beta_3 X_{3i} + \epsilon_i \\ &= \beta_0 + 0 \times X_{1i} + 0 \times X_{2i} + \beta_3 X_{3i} + \epsilon_i \\ &= \beta_0 + \beta_3 X_{3i} + \epsilon_i \end{aligned}$$

Case 2: One or more coefficients equal each other under the null hypothesis

In a more complicated—and interesting—case, we want to test whether the effect of one variable is larger than the effect of another. In this case, the null hypothesis will be that both coefficients are the same. For example, if we want to know if the effect of X_1 is bigger than the effect of X_2, the null hypothesis will be $H_0 : \beta_1 = \beta_2$. Note that such a hypothesis test makes sense only if the scales of X_1 and X_2 are the same or the two variables have been standardized.

In this case, imposing the null hypothesis to create the restricted equation involves rewriting the unrestricted equation so that the two coefficients are the same. We can do so, for example, by replacing β_2 with β_1 (because they are equal under the null). After some cleanup, we have a model in which $\beta_1 = \beta_2$. Specifically, the restricted model for $H_0 : \beta_1 = \beta_2$ is

$$
\begin{aligned}
Y_i &= \beta_0 + \beta_1 X_{1i} + \beta_2 X_{2i} + \beta_3 X_{3i} + \epsilon_i \\
&= \beta_0 + \beta_1 X_{1i} + \beta_1 X_{2i} + \beta_3 X_{3i} + \epsilon_i \\
&= \beta_0 + \beta_1 (X_{1i} + X_{2i}) + \beta_3 X_{3i} + \epsilon_i
\end{aligned}
$$

In this restricted model, increasing X_1 or X_2 by one unit increases Y_i by β_1. To estimate this model, we need only create a new variable $X_1 + X_2$ and include it as an independent variable instead of X_1 and X_2 separately.

The cool thing is that if we increase X_1 by one unit, $X_{1i} + X_{2i}$ goes up by 1 and we expect a β_1 increase in Y. At the same time, if we increase X_2 by one unit, $X_{1i} + X_{2i}$ goes up by 1 and we expect a β_1 increase in Y. Presto! We have an equation in which the effect of X_1 and X_2 will necessarily be the same.

F tests using R^2 values

The statistical fits of the unrestricted and restricted model are measured with $R^2_{Unrestricted}$ and $R^2_{Restricted}$. These are simply the R^2 values from each separate model. The $R^2_{Unrestricted}$ will always be higher because the model without restrictions can generate a better model fit than the same model subject to some restrictions. This conclusion is a little counterintuitive at first, but note that $R^2_{Unrestricted}$ will be higher than $R^2_{Restricted}$ even when the null hypothesis is true. This is because in estimating the unrestricted equation, the software not only has the option of estimating both coefficients to be whatever the value is under the null (hence assuring the same fit as in the restricted model), but also any other deviation, large or small, that improves the fit.

The *extent* of difference between $R^2_{Unrestricted}$ and $R^2_{Restricted}$ depends on whether the null hypothesis is or is not true. If we are testing $H_0 : \beta_1 = \beta_2 = 0$ and β_1 and β_2 really are zero, then restricting them to be zero won't cause the $R^2_{Restricted}$ to be too far from $R^2_{Unrestricted}$ because the optimal values of $\hat{\beta}_1$ and $\hat{\beta}_2$ really are around zero. If the null is false and β_1 and β_2 are much different from zero, there will be a huge difference between $R^2_{Unrestricted}$ and $R^2_{Restricted}$ because setting them to non-zero values, as happens only in the unrestricted model, improves fit substantially.

Hence the heart of an F test is the difference between $R^2_{Unrestricted}$ and $R^2_{Restricted}$. When the difference is small, imposing the null doesn't do too much damage to the model fit. When the difference is large, imposing the null damages model fit a lot.

An F test is based on the F statistic:

$$F_{q,N-k} = \frac{(R^2_{Unrestricted} - R^2_{Restricted})/q}{(1 - R^2_{Unrestricted})/(N-k)} \tag{7.11}$$

The q term refers to how many constraints are in the null hypothesis. That's just a fancy way of saying how many equal signs are in the null hypothesis. So for $H_0: \beta_1 = \beta_2$, the value of q is 1. For $H_0: \beta_1 = \beta_2 = 0$, the value of q is 2. The $N - k$ term is a degrees of freedom term, like what we saw with the t distribution. This is the sample size minus the number of parameters estimated in the unrestricted model. (For example, k for Equation 7.11 will be 3 because we estimate $\hat{\beta}_0$, $\hat{\beta}_1$, and $\hat{\beta}_2$.) We need to know these terms because the shape of the F distribution depends on the sample size and the number of constraints in the null, just as the t distribution shifted based on the number of observations.

The F statistic has the difference of $R^2_{Unrestricted}$ and $R^2_{Restricted}$ in it and also includes some other bits to ensure that the F statistic is distributed according to an F distribution. The F distribution describes the relative probability of observing different values of the F statistic under the null hypothesis. It allows us to know the probability that the F statistic will be bigger than any given number when the null is true. We can use this knowledge to identify critical values for our hypothesis tests; we'll describe how shortly.

How we approach the alternative hypotheses depends on the type of null hypothesis. For case 1 null hypotheses (in which multiple coefficients are zero under the null hypothesis), the alternative hypothesis is that at least one coefficient is not zero. In other words, the null hypothesis is that they all are zero and the alternative is the negation of that, which is that one or more of the coefficients is not zero.

For case 2 null hypotheses (in which two or more coefficients are equal under the null hypothesis), it is possible to have a directional alternative hypothesis that one coefficient is larger than the other. The critical value remains the same, but we add a requirement that the coefficients actually go in the direction of the specified alternative hypothesis. For example, if we are testing $H_0: \beta_1 = \beta_2$ versus $H_A: \beta_1 > \beta_2$, we reject the null in favor of the alternative hypothesis if the F statistic is bigger than the critical value *and* $\hat{\beta}_1$ is actually bigger than $\hat{\beta}_2$.

This all may sound complicated, but the process isn't that hard, really. (And, as we show in the Computing Corner, statistical software makes it easy.) The crucial step is formulating a null hypothesis and using it to create a restricted equation. This process is not very hard. If we're dealing with a case 1 null hypothesis (that multiple coefficients are zero), we simply drop the variables listed in the null in the restricted equation. If we're dealing with a case 2 null hypothesis (that two or more coefficients are equal to each other), we simply create a new variable that is the sum of the variables and use it in the restricted equation instead of the individual variables.

F tests and baseball salaries

To see F testing in action, let's return to our standardized baseball salary model and first test the following case 1 null hypothesis: $H_0 : \beta_1 = \beta_2 = 0$. The unrestricted equation is

$$Salary_i = \beta_0 + \beta_1 Std. \ batting \ average_i + \beta_2 Std. \ home \ runs_i + \epsilon_i$$

The $R^2_{Unrestricted}$ is 0.2992 (it's usually necessary to be more precise than the 0.30 reported in Table 7.6).

For the unrestricted model, we simply drop the variables listed in the null hypothesis, yielding

$$Salary_i = \beta_0 + \epsilon_i$$

This is a bit of a silly model, producing an $R^2_{Restricted} = 0.00$ (because R^2 is always zero when there are no independent variables to explain the dependent variable). We calculate the F statistic by substituting these values, along with q (which is 2 because there are two equals signs in the null hypothesis) and $N - k$, which is the sample size (6,762) minus 3 (because there are three coefficients estimated in the unrestricted model), which is 6,759. The result is

$$F_{q,N-k} = \frac{(R^2_{Unrestricted} - R^2_{Restricted})/q}{(1 - R^2_{Unrestricted})/(N - k)}$$
$$= \frac{(0.2992 - 0.00)/2}{(1 - 0.2992)/6,759}$$
$$= 1,442.846$$

The critical value (which we show how to identify in the Computing Corner, pages 237 and 238) is 3.00. Since the F statistic is (way!) higher than the critical value, we reject the null handily.

We can also easily test whether the standardized effect of home runs is bigger than the standardized effect of batting average. The unrestricted equation is, as before,

$$Salary_i = \beta_0 + \beta_1 Std. \ batting \ average_i + \beta_2 Std. \ home \ runs_i + \epsilon_i$$

The $R^2_{Unrestricted}$ continues to be 0.2992. For the restricted model, we simply replace the individual batting average and home run variables with a variable that is the sum of the two variables:

$$Salary_i = \beta_0 + \beta_1 Std.\ batting\ average_i + \beta_2 Std.\ home\ runs_i + \epsilon_i$$
$$= \beta_0 + \beta_1 Std.\ batting\ average_i + \beta_1 Std.\ home\ runs_i + \epsilon_i$$
$$= \beta_0 + \beta_1 (Std.\ batting\ average_i + Std.\ home\ runs_i) + \epsilon_i$$

The $R^2_{Restricted}$ turns out to be 0.2602. We calculate the F statistic by substituting these values, along with q (which is 1 because there is one equal sign in the null hypothesis) and $N - k$, which continues to be 6,759. The result is

$$F_{q,N-k} = \frac{(R^2_{Unrestricted} - R^2_{Restricted})/q}{(1 - R^2_{Unrestricted})/(N-k)}$$
$$= \frac{(0.2992 - 0.2602)/1}{(1 - 0.2992)/6,759}$$
$$= 376.14$$

The critical value (which we show how to identify in the Computing Corner, pages 237 and 238) is 3.84. Here, too, the F statistic is vastly higher than the critical value, and we reject the null hypothesis that $\beta_1 = \beta_2$ as well.

REMEMBER THIS

1. F tests are useful to test hypotheses involving multiple coefficients. To implement an F test for the following model

$$Y_i = \beta_0 + \beta_1 X_{1i} + \beta_2 X_{2i} + \beta_3 X_{3i} + \epsilon_i$$

proceed through the four steps listed.

   (a) Estimate an unrestricted model that is the full model.

   (b) Write down the null hypothesis.

   (c) Estimate a restricted model by using the conditions in the null hypothesis to restrict the full model,

   - Case 1: When the null hypothesis is that multiple coefficients equal zero, we create a restricted model by simply dropping the variables listed in the null hypothesis.

   - Case 2: When the null hypothesis is that two or more coefficients are equal, we create a restricted model by replacing the variables listed in the null hypothesis with a single variable that is the sum of the listed variables.

(d) Use the R^2 values from the unrestricted and restricted models to generate an F statistic using Equation 7.11 and compare the F statistic to the critical value from the F distribution.

2. The bigger the difference between $R^2_{Unrestricted}$ and $R^2_{Restricted}$, the more the null hypothesis is reducing fit and, therefore, the more likely we are to reject the null.

CASE STUDY **Comparing Effects of Height Measures**

We assessed the effect of height on income in Chapter 5 (page 133). The final specification had independent variables measuring adult height, adolescent height, and participation in clubs and athletics:

$$Wages_i = \beta_0 + \beta_1 Adult\ height_i + \beta_2 Adolescent\ height_i$$
$$+ \beta_3 Clubs_i + \beta_4 Athletics_i + \epsilon_i$$

Let's test two different null hypotheses with multiple coefficients. First, let's test a case 1 null that neither height variable has an effect on wages. This null is H_0: $\beta_1 = \beta_2 = 0$. The restricted equation for this null will be

$$Wages_i = \beta_0 + \beta_3 Clubs_i + \beta_4 Athletics_i + \epsilon_i \tag{7.12}$$

Table 7.7 presents results necessary to test this null. We use an F test that requires R^2 values from two specifications. The first column presents the unrestricted model; at the bottom is the $R^2_{Unrestricted}$, which is 0.06086. The second column presents the restricted model; at the bottom is the $R^2_{Restricted}$, which is 0.05295. There are two restrictions in this null, meaning $q = 2$. The sample size is 1,851 and the number of parameters in the unrestricted model is 5, meaning $N - k = 1,846$.

Hence, for H_0: $\beta_1 = \beta_2 = 0$,

$$F_{q,N-k} = \frac{(R^2_{Unrestricted} - R^2_{Restricted})/q}{(1 - R^2_{Unrestricted})/(N - k)}$$

$$F_{2,1846} = \frac{(0.06086 - 0.05295)/2}{(1 - 0.06086)/1846}$$

$$= 7.77$$

We have to use software (or tables) to find the critical value. We'll discuss that process in the Computing Corner (pages 237 and 238). For $q = 2$ and $N - k = 1,846$, the critical value for $\alpha = 0.05$ is 3.00. Because our F statistic as just calculated is

TABLE 7.7 **Unrestricted and Restricted Models for F Tests**

	Unrestricted model	Restricted model for $H_0: \beta_1 = \beta_2 = 0$	Restricted model for $H_0: \beta_1 = \beta_2$
Adult height	0.03		
	(0.20)		
	$[t = 0.17]$		
Adolescent height	0.35		
	(0.19)		
	$[t = 1.82]$		
Number of clubs	1.88*	1.91*	1.89*
	(0.28)	(0.28)	(0.28)
	$[t = 6.87]$	$[t = 6.77]$	$[t = 6.71]$
Athletics	3.02*	3.28*	3.03*
	(0.56)	(0.56)	(0.56)
	$[t = 5.36]$	$[t = 5.85]$	$[t = 5.39]$
Adult height plus adolescent height			0.19*
			(0.05)
			$[t = 3.85]$
Constant	−13.57	13.17*	−13.91*
	(7.05)	(0.41)	(7.04)
	$[t = 1.92]$	$[t = 32.11]$	$[t = 1.98]$
N	1,851	1,851	1,851
R^2	0.06086	0.05295	0.06050

Standard errors in parentheses.

* indicates significance at $p < 0.05$, two-tailed.

bigger than that, we can reject the null. In other words, the data is telling us that if the null were true, we would be very unlikely to see such a big difference in fit between the unrestricted and restricted models.[11]

Second, let's test the following case 2 null, $H_0: \beta_1 = \beta_2$. The first column in Table 7.7 still presents the unrestricted model; at the bottom is the $R^2_{Unrestricted}$, which is 0.06086. The restricted model is different for this null. Following the logic of discussed on page 228, it is

$$Wages_i = \beta_0 + \beta_1(Adult\ height_i + Adolescent\ height_i) + \beta_3 Clubs_i + \beta_4 Athletics_i + \epsilon_i$$
$$(7.13)$$

The third column in Table 7.7 present the results for this restricted model; at the bottom is the $R^2_{Restricted}$, namely 0.0605. There is one restriction in this null, meaning $q = 1$. The sample size is still 1,851 and the number of parameters in the unrestricted model is still 5, meaning $N - k = 1,846$.

---

[11] The specific value of the F statistic provided by automated software F tests will differ from our presentation because the automated software tests do not round to three digits, as we have done.

Hence, for $H_0: \beta_1 = \beta_2$,

$$F_{q,N-k} = \frac{(R^2_{Unrestricted} - R^2_{Restricted})/q}{(1 - R^2_{Unrestricted})/(N-k)}$$

$$F_{1,1846} = \frac{(0.06086 - 0.06050)/1}{(1 - 0.06086)/1846}$$

$$= 0.71$$

We again have to use software (or tables) to find the critical value. For $q = 1$ and $N - k = 1,846$, the critical value for $\alpha = 0.05$ is 3.85. Because our F statistic as calculated here is less than the critical value, we fail to reject the null that the two coefficients are equal. The coefficients are quite different in the unrestricted model (0.03 and 0.35), but notice that the standard errors are large enough to prevent us from rejecting the null that either coefficient is zero. In other words, we have a lot of uncertainty in our estimates. The F test formalizes this uncertainty by forcing OLS to give us the same coefficient on both height variables and, when we do this, the overall model fit is pretty close to the model fit achieved when the coefficients are allowed to vary across the two variables. If the null is true, this result is what we would expect, because imposing the null would not lower R^2 by very much. If the null were false, then imposing the null probably would have caused a more substantial reduction in $R^2_{Restricted}$.

Conclusion

This chapter has worked through some of the practical capabilities of the very powerful OLS model. First, the world is not necessarily linear, and the multivariate model can accommodate a vast array of non-linear relationships. Polynomial models, of which quadratic models are the most common, can produce fitted lines with increasing returns, diminishing returns, and U-shaped and upside-down U-shaped relationships. Logged models allow for effects to be interpreted in percentage terms.

Often we care not only about individual variables but also about how variables relate to each other. Which variable has a bigger effect? As a first cut, we can standardize variables to make them plausibly comparable. If and when the variables are comparable, we can use F tests to determine which effect is larger. This is possible because F tests allow us to test hypotheses about multiple coefficients.

We have mastered the core points of this chapter we can do the following:

- Section 7.1: Explain polynomial models and quadratic models. Sketch the various kinds of relationships that a quadratic model can estimate. Show how to interpret coefficients from a quadratic model.

- Section 7.2: Explain three different kinds of logged models. Show how to interpret coefficients in each.

- Section 7.3: Use standardized variables to compare coefficients. Show how to standardize a variable. Explain how to interpret the coefficient on a standardized independent variable.

- Section 7.4: Explain how to test a hypothesis about multiple coefficients. Use an F test to test the following null hypotheses for the model

$$Y_i = \beta_0 + \beta_1 X_{1i} + \beta_2 X_{2i} + \epsilon_i.$$

- $H_0 : \beta_1 = \beta_2 = 0$

- $H_0 : \beta_1 = \beta_2$

Further Reading

Empirical papers using logged variables are very common; see, for example, Card (1990). Zakir Hossain (2011) discusses the use of *Box-Cox* tests to help decide which functional form (linear, log-linear, linear-log, or log-log) is best. Achen (1982, 77) critiques standardized variables, in part because they depend on the standard errors of independent variables in the sample.

Key Terms

Elasticity (219)
F test (226)
F statistic (227)
Linear-log model (219)
Log-linear model (219)

Log-log model (219)
Polynomial model (209)
Quadratic model (210)
Restricted model (227)
Standardize (224)

Standardized coefficient (225)
Unrestricted model (227)

Computing Corner

Stata

1. To estimate a quadratic model in Stata, simply generate a new variable equal to the square of the variable (e.g., gen X1Squared = X1^2) and include it in a regression (e.g., `reg Y X1 X1Squared X2`).

2. To estimate a linear-logged model in Stata, simply generate a new variable equal to the log of the independent variable (e.g., gen X1Log

= log(X1)) and include it in a regression (e.g., reg Y X1Log X2).
Log-linear and log-log models proceed similarly.

3. In Stata, there is an easy way and a hard way to generate standardized
regression coefficients. Here's the easy way: type , beta at the end
of a regression command. For example, reg salary BattingAverage
Homeruns, beta.

salary	Coef.	Std. Err.	t	P>|t|	Beta
BattingAverage	1.24e+07	940986	13.20	0.000	.1422752
Homeruns	129627.4	2889.771	44.86	0.000	.4836231
_cons	-2869439	244241.1	-11.75	0.000	.

The standardized coefficients are listed on the right under "Beta."

The hard way isn't very hard. Use Stata's egen comment to create
standardized versions of every variable in the model:
egen BattingAverage_std = std(BattingAverage)
egen Homeruns_std = std(Homeruns)
egen Salary_std = std(Salary)
Then run a regression with these standardized variables:
reg Salary_std BattingAverage_std Homeruns_std

Salary_std	Coef.	Std. Err.	t	P>|t|
BattingAverage_std	.1422752	.0107814	13.20	0.000
Homeruns_std	.4836231	.0107814	44.86	0.000
_cons	-2.82e-09	.0101802	-0.00	1.000

The standardized coefficients are listed, as usual, under "Coef." Notice
that they are identical to the results from using the , beta command.

4. Stata has a very convenient way to conduct F tests for hypotheses
involving multiple coefficients. Simply estimate the unrestricted model,
then type test, and then key in the coefficients involved and restriction
implied by the null. For example, to test the null hypothesis that the
coefficients on *Height*81 and *Height*85 are both equal to zero, type the
following:
reg Wage Height81 Height85 Clubs Athletics
test Height81 = Height85 = 0
To test the null hypothesis that the coefficients on *Height*81 and *Height*85
are equal to each other, type the following:
reg Wage Height81 Height85 Clubs Athletics
test Height81 = Height85

Rounding will cause this code to produce F statistics slightly different from those on page 232.

5. The OLS output in Stata automatically reports results for an F test of the hypothesis that the coefficients on all variables all equal zero. This is sometimes referred to as "the" F test.

6. To find the critical value from an F distribution for a given a, q, and $N - k$, use the inverse F function in Stata. The display function will print this on the screen:

```
display invF(q, N-k, 1-a)
```

For example, to calculate the critical value on page 232 for H_0: $\beta_1 = \beta_2 = 0$, type `display invF(2, 1846, 0.95)`

R

1. To estimate a quadratic model in R, simply generate a new variable equal to the square of the variable (e.g., `X1Squared = X1^2`) and include it in a regression (e.g., `lm(Y ~ X1 X1Squared X2)`).

2. To estimate a linear-logged model in R, simply generate a new variable equal to the log of the independent variable (e.g., `X1Log = log(X1)`) and include it in a regression (e.g., `lm(Y ~ X1 X1Log X2)`). Log-linear and log-log models proceed similarly.

3. R offers us an easy way and a hard way to generate standardized regression coefficients. Here's the easy way: use the `scale` command in R. This command will automatically create standardized variables on the fly:

```
summary(lm(scale(Sal) ~ scale(BatAvg)+ scale(HR)))
```

A harder but perhaps more transparent approach is to create standardized variables and then use them to estimate a regression model. Standardized variables can be created manually (e.g., `Sal_std = (bb$salary - mean(bb$salary))/ sqrt(var(bb$salary))`. Standardize all variables, and simply use those variables to run an OLS model.

```
summary(lm(Sal_std ~ BatAvg_std + HR_std))
```

	Estimate	Std. Error	t value	Pr(>|t|)
(Intercept)	-0.000	0.010	0.00	1.00
BatAvg_std	0.142	0.011	13.20	0.00
HR_std	0.483	0.011	44.86	0.00

4. There are automated functions available on the Web to do F tests for hypotheses involving multiple coefficients, but they require a fair amount of work as front to get them working. Here we present a manual approach for the tests on page 232.

```
Unrestricted    = lm(Wage~ Height81 + Height85 + Clubs + Athletics)
    # Unrestricted model with all variables
Restricted1     = lm(Wage~  Clubs + Athletics)
    # Restricted model for null that height coefficients are both zero
HeightsAdded    = Height81 + Height85
    # Creates a new variable that is sum of two height variables
Restricted2     = lm(Wage~  HeightsAdded + Clubs + Athletics)
    # Restricted model for null that height coefficients equal each other
```

R stores R^2 values and degrees of freedom information for each model. We can access this information by using the summary command followed by a dollar sign and the appropriate name. To see the various values of R^2 for the unrestricted and restricted models, type
summary(Unrestricted)$r.squared.
summary(Restricted1)$r.squared.
summary(Restricted2)$r.squared.
To see the degrees of freedom for the unrestricted model, type
summary(Unrestricted1)$df[2].
We'll have to keep track of q on our own.

To calculate the F statistic for $H_0 : \beta_1 = \beta_2 = 0$ as described on page 232, type

```
((summary(Unrestricted)$r.squared - summary(Restricted1)$r.squared)/2) /
((1-summary(Unrestricted)$r.squared)/summary(Unrestricted)$df[2])
```

This code will produce slightly different F statistics than on page 232 due to rounding.

5. The OLS output in R automatically reports results for an F test of the hypothesis that the coefficients on all variables all equal zero. This is sometimes referred to as "the" F test.

6. To find the critical value from an F distribution for a given a, q, and $N - k$, type qf(1-a, df1=q, df2= N-k).
For example, to calculate the critical value on page 232 for $H_0 : \beta_1 = \beta_2 = 0$, type qf(.95, df1=2, df2=1846).

Exercises

1. The relationship between political instability and democracy is important and likely to be quite complicated. Do democracies manage conflict in a way that reduces instability or do they stir up conflict? Use the data set called Instability_PS data.dta from Zaryab Iqbal and Christopher Zorn (2008) to answer the following questions. The data set covers 157 countries between 1946 and 1997. The unit of observation is the country-year. The variables are listed in Table 7.8.

   (a) Estimate a bivariate model with instability as the dependent variable and democracy as the independent variable. Because the units of the variables are not intuitive, use standardized coefficients to interpret. Briefly discuss the estimated relationship and whether you expect endogeneity.

   (b) To combat endogeneity, include a variable for lagged GDP. Discuss changes in results, if any.

   (c) Perhaps GDP is better conceived of in log terms. Estimate a model with logged-lagged GDP and interpret the coefficient on this GDP variable.

   (d) Suppose we are interested in whether instability was higher or lower during the Cold War. Run two models. In the first, add a Cold War dummy variable to the preceding specification. In the second model, add a logged Cold War dummy variable to the above specification. Discuss what happens.

   (e) It is possible that a positive relationship exists between democracy and political instability because in more democratic countries,

TABLE 7.8 Variables for Political Instability Data

Variable	Description
Ccode	Country code
Year	Year
Instab	Index of instability (revolutions, crises, coups, etc.); ranges from −4.65 to +10.07
Coldwar	Cold War year (1 = yes, 0 = no)
Gdplag	GDP in previous year
Democracy	Democracy score in previous year, ranges from 0 (most autocratic) to 100 (most democratic)

people feel freer to engage in confrontational political activities such as demonstrations. It may be, however, that this relationship is positive only up to a point or that more democracy increases political instability more at lower levels of political freedom. Estimate a quadratic model, building off the specification above. Use a figure to depict the estimated relationship and use calculus to indicate the point at which the sign on democracy changes.

2. Use globaled.dta, the data set on education and growth from Hanushek and Woessmann (2009) for this question. The variables are given in Table 7.9.

   (a) Use standardized variables to assess whether the effect of test scores on economic growth is larger than the effect of years in school. At this point, simply compare the different effects in a meaningful way. We'll do statistical tests next. The dependent variable is GDP growth per year. For this part, control for average test scores, average years of schooling between 1960 and 2000, and GDP per capita in 1960.

   (b) Now conduct a statistical test of whether the (appropriately comparable) effects of test scores and years in school on economic growth are different. Do this test in two ways: (i) use the `test` command in Stata and (ii) generate values necessary to use an F-test equation. Report differences/similarities in results.

   (c) Now control for openness of economy and security of property rights. Which matters more: test scores or property rights? Use appropriate statistical evidence in your answer.

TABLE 7.9 **Variables for Global Education Data**

Variable	Description
name	Country name
code	Country code
ypcgr	Average annual growth rate (GDP per capita), 1960–2000
testavg	Average combined math and science standardized test scores, 1964–2003
edavg	Average years of schooling, 1960–2000
ypc60	GDP per capita in 1960
region	Region
open	Openness of the economy scale
proprts	Security of property rights scale

3. We will continue the analysis of height and wages in Britain from Exercise 5 in Chapter 5. We'll use the data set heightwage_british_all_ multivariate.dta, which includes men and women and the variables listed in Table 7.10.[12]

(a) Estimate a model explaining wages at age 33 as a function of female, height at age 16, mother's education, father's education, and number of siblings. Use standardized coefficients to assess whether height or siblings has a larger effect on wages.

(b) Use bivariate OLS to implement a difference of means test across males and females. Do this twice: once with female as the dummy variable and the second time with male as the dummy variable (the male variable needs to be generated). Interpret the coefficient on the gender variable in each model and compare results across models.

(c) Now do the same test, but with log of wages at age 33 as the dependent variable. Use female as the dummy variable. Interpret the coefficient on the female dummy variable.

(d) How much does height explain salary differences across genders? Estimate a difference of means test across genders, controlling for height at age 33 and at age 16. Explain the results.

(e) Does the effect of height vary across genders? Use tools of this chapter to test for differential effects of height across genders. Use

TABLE 7.10 Variables for Height and Wages Data in Britain

Variable name	Description
gwage33	Hourly wages (in British pounds) at age 33
height33	Height (in inches) measured at age 33
height16	Height (in inches) measured at age 16
momed	Education of mother, measured in years
daded	Education of father, measured in years
siblings	Number of siblings
female	Female indicator variable (1 for women, 0 for men)
LogWage33	Log of hourly wages at age 33

[12] For the reasons discussed in the homework problem in Chapter 3 on page 89, we limit the data set to observations with height greater than 40 inches and self-reported income less than 400 British pounds per hour. We also exclude observations of individuals who grew shorter from age 16 to age 33. Excluding these observations doesn't really affect the results, but the observations themselves are just odd enough to make us think that these cases may suffer from nontrivial measurement error.

logged wages at age 33 as the dependent variable, and control for height at age 16 and the number of siblings. Explain the estimated effect of height at age 16 for men and for women.

4. Use the MLBattend.dta we used in Chapter 4 (page 126) and Chapter 5 (page 162). Which matters more for attendance: winning or runs scored? [To keep us on the same page, use *home_attend* as the dependent variable and control for *wins*, *runs_scored*, *runs_allowed*, and *season*.]

5. In this problem we continue analyzing the speeding ticket data introduced in Chapter 5 (page 164). The variables we will use are listed in Table 7.11.

(a) Is the effect of age on fines non-linear? Assess this question by estimating a model with a quadratic age term, controlling for *MPHover*, *Female*, *Black*, and *Hispanic*. Interpret the coefficients on the age variables.

(b) Sketch the relationship between age and ticket amount from the foregoing quadratic model: calculate the fitted value for a white male with 0 *MPHover* (probably not many people going zero miles over the speed limit got a ticket, but this simplifies calculations a lot) for ages equal to 20, 25, 30, 35, 40, and 70. [*Note*: Either calculate these by hand (or in Excel) from the estimated coefficients or use Stata's display function. To display the fitted value for a 0-year-old white male in Stata, use `display _b[_cons]+ _b[_Age]*0+ _b[_AgeSq]*0^2.`]

(c) Use Equation 7.4 to calculate the marginal effect of age at ages 20, 35, and 70. Describe how these marginal effects relate to your sketch.

TABLE 7.11 **Variables for Speeding Ticket Data**

Variable name	Description
MPHover	Miles per hour over the speed limit
Amount	Assessed fine for the ticket
Age	Age of driver
Female	Equals 1 for women and 0 for men
Black	Equals 1 for African-Americans and 0 otherwise
Hispanic	Equals 1 for Hispanics and 0 otherwise
StatePol	Equals 1 if ticketing officer was state patrol officer
OutTown	Equals 1 if driver from out of town and 0 otherwise
OutState	Equals 1 if driver from out of state and 0 otherwise

(d) Calculate the age that is associated with the lowest predicted fine based on the quadratic OLS model results given earlier.

(e) Do drivers from out of town and out of state get treated differently? Do state police and local police treat nonlocals differently? Estimate a model that allows us to assess whether out-of-towners and out-of-staters are treated differently *and* whether state police respond differently to out-of-towners and out-of-staters. Interpret the coefficients on the relevant variables.

(f) Test whether the two state police interaction terms are jointly significant. Briefly explain the results.

PART II

The Contemporary Econometric Toolkit

Using Fixed Effects Models to Fight Endogeneity in Panel Data and Difference-in-Difference Models

8

Do police reduce crime? It certainly seems plausible that they get some bad guys off the street and deter others from breaking laws. It is, however, hardly a foregone conclusion. Maybe cops don't get out of their squad cars enough to do any good. Maybe police officers do some good, but not as much universal prekindergarten does.

It is natural to try to answer the question by using OLS to analyze data on crime and police in cities over time. The problem is we probably won't be able to measure many factors that are associated with crime, factors such as drug use and gang membership. These factors will go in the error term and will probably correlate highly with the number of police officers as police are hired specifically to deal with such problems. A naïve OLS model therefore risks finding police cause crime because the places with lots of crime-causing factors in the error term will also have large police forces.

In this chapter we introduce fixed effects models as a simple yet powerful way to fight such endogeneity. Fixed effects models boil down to models that have dummy variables that control for otherwise unexplained unit-level differences in outcomes across units. They can be applied to data on individuals, cities, states, countries, and many other units of observation. Often they produce profoundly different—and more credible—results than basic OLS models.

There are two contexts in which the fixed effect logic is particularly useful. In the first, we have **panel data**, which consists of multiple observations for a specific set of units. Observing annual crime rates in a set of cities over 20 years is an example. So too is observing national unemployment rates for every year from 1946 to the present for all advanced economies. Anyone analyzing such data needs to use fixed effects models to be taken seriously.

The logic behind the fixed effect approach also is important when we conduct *difference-in-difference analysis*, which is particularly helpful in the evaluation

▶ **panel data** Has observations for multiple units over time.

of policy changes. We use this model to compare changes in units affected by some policy change to changes in units not affected by the policy. We show how difference-in-difference methods rely on the logic of fixed models and, in some cases, use the same tools as panel data analysis.

In this chapter, we show the power and ease of implementing fixed effects models. Section 8.1 uses a panel data example to illustrate how basic OLS can fail when the error term is correlated with the independent variable. Section 8.2, shows how fixed effects can come to the rescue in this case (and others). It describes how to estimate fixed effects models by using dummy variables or so-called *de-meaned data*. Section 8.3 explains the mildly miraculous ability of fixed effects models to control for variables even as the models are unable to estimate coefficients associated with these variables. This ability is a blessing in that we control for these variables; it is a curse in that we sometimes are curious about such coefficients. Section 8.4 extends fixed effect logic to so-called two-way fixed effects models that control for both unit- and time-related fixed effects. Section 8.5 discusses difference-in-difference methods that rely on the fixed effect logic and are widely used in policy analysis.

8.1   The Problem with Pooling

In this section we show how using basic OLS to analyze crime data in U.S. cities over time can lead us dangerously astray. Understanding the problem helps us understand the merits of the fixed effects approach we present in Section 8.2.

We explore a data set that covers robberies per capita and police officers per capita in 59 large cities in the United States from 1951 to 1992.[1] Table 8.1 presents OLS results from estimation of the following simple model:

$$Crime_{it} = \beta_0 + \beta_1 Police_{i,t-1} + \epsilon_{it} \tag{8.1}$$

where $Crime_{it}$ is crime in city i at time t and $Police_{i,t-1}$ is a measure of the number of police on duty in city i in the preceding year. It's common to use lagged police because under some conditions the number of police in a given year might be simultaneously determined by the number of crimes in that year. We revisit this point in Section 8.4. For now, let's take it as a fairly conventional modeling choice in analyses of the effect of police on crime. Notice also that the subscripts contain both i's and t's. This notation is new and will become important later.

---

[1] This data is from Marvell and Moody (1996). Their paper discusses a more comprehensive analysis of this data.

	Pooled OLS
Lag police, per capita	2.37*
	(0.07)
	[$t = 32.59$]
N	1,232

TABLE 8.1 Basic OLS Analysis of Burglary and Police Officers

Standard errors in parentheses.

* indicates significance at $p < 0.05$, two-tailed.

▶ **pooled model** Treats all observations as independent observations.

We'll refer to this model as a **pooled model**. In a pooled model, an observation is completely described by its X variables; that some observations came from one city and others from another city is ignored. For all the computer knew when running that model, there were N separate cities producing the data.

Table 8.1 shows the results. The coefficient on the police variable is *positive* and very statistically significant. Yikes. More cops, more crime. Weird. In fact, for every additional police officer per capita, there were 2.37 more robberies per capita. Were we to take these results at face value, we would believe that cities could eliminate more than two robberies per capita for every police officer per capita they fired.

Of course, we don't believe the pooled results. We worry that there are unmeasured factors lurking in the error term that could be correlated with the number of police, thereby causing bias. The error term in Equation 8.1 contains gangs, drugs, economic hopelessness, broken families, and many more conditions. If any of those factors is correlated with the number of police in a given city, we have endogeneity. Given that police are more likely to be deployed when and where there are gangs, drugs, and economic desolation, endogeneity in our model seems inevitable.

In this chapter we try to eliminate some of this endogeneity by focusing on aspects of the error associated with each city. To keep our discussion relatively simple, we'll turn our attention to five California cities: Los Angeles, San Francisco, Oakland, Fresno, and Sacramento. Figure 8.1 plots their per capita robbery and police data from 1971 to 1992.

Consistent with the OLS results on all cities, the message seems clear that robberies are more common when there are more police. However, we actually have more information than Figure 8.1 displays. We know which city each observation comes from. Figure 8.2 replots the data from Table 8.1, but in a way that differentiates by city. The underlying data is *exactly* the same, but the observations for each city have different shapes. The observations for Fresno are the circles in the lower left, the observations for Oakland are the triangles in the top middle, and so forth. What does the relationship between police and crime look like now?

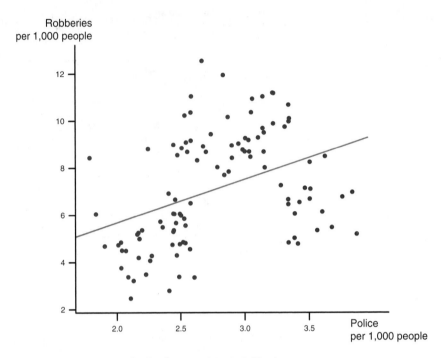

FIGURE 8.1: Robberies and Police for Large Cities in California

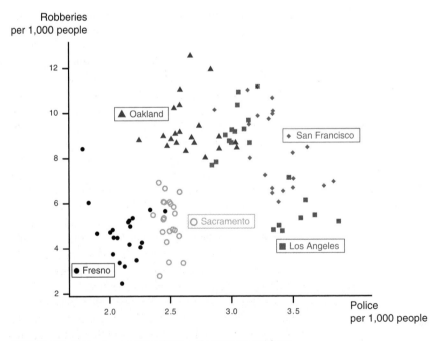

FIGURE 8.2: Robberies and Police for Specified Cities in California

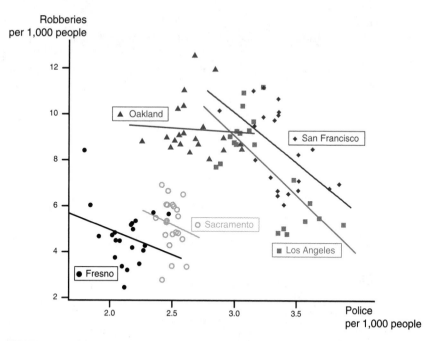

FIGURE 8.3: Robberies and Police for Specified Cities in California with City-Specific Regression Lines

It's still a bit hard to see, so Figure 8.3 adds a fitted line for each city. These are OLS regression lines estimated on a city-by-city basis. All are negative, some dramatically so (Los Angeles and San Francisco). The claim that police reduce crime is looking much better. Within each individual city, robberies tend to decline as police increase.

The difference between the pooled OLS results and these city-specific regression lines presents a puzzle. How can the pooled OLS estimates suggest a conclusion so radically different from Figure 8.3? The reason is the villain of this book—endogeneity.

Here's how it happens. Think about what's in the error term ϵ_{it} in Equation 8.1: gangs, drugs, and all that. These factors almost certainly affect the crime across cities and are plausibly correlated with the number of police because cities with bigger gang or drug problems hire more police officers. Many of these elements in the error term are also stable within each city, at least in our 20-year time frame. A city that has a culture or history of crime in year 1 probably has a culture or history of crime in year 20 as well. This is the case in our selected cities: San Francisco has lots of police and many robberies, while Fresno has not so many police and not so many robberies.

And here's what creates endogeneity: these city-specific baseline levels of crime are correlated with the independent variable. The cities with the most robberies (Oakland, Los Angeles, and San Francisco) have the most police. The cities with fewest robberies (Fresno and Sacramento) have the fewest police. If we are not able to find another variable to control for whatever is causing these differential levels of baselines—and if it is something hard to measure like history or culture or gangs or drugs, we may not be able to—then standard OLS will have endogeneity-induced bias and will lead us to the spurious inference we highlighted at the start of the chapter.

Test score example

The problem we have identified here occurs in many contexts. Let's look at another example to get comfortable with identifying factors that can cause endogeneity. Suppose we want to assess whether private schools produce better test scores than public schools and we begin with the following pooled model:

$$Test\ scores_{it} = \beta_0 + \beta_1 Private\ school_{it} + \epsilon_{it} \tag{8.2}$$

where $Test\ scores_{it}$ is test scores of student i at time t and $Private\ school_{it}$ is a dummy variable that is 1 if student i is in a private school at time t. This model is for a (hypothetical) data set in which we observe test scores for specific children over a number of years.

The following three simple questions help us identify possibly troublesome endogeneity.

What is in the error term?   Test performance depends potentially not only on whether a child went to a private school (a variable in the model) but also on his or her intelligence and diligence, the teacher's ability, family support, and many other factors in the error term. While we can hope to measure some of these factors, it is a virtual certainty that we will not be able to measure them all.

Are there any stable unit-specific elements in the error term?   Intelligence, diligence, and family support are likely to be quite stable for individual students across time.

Are the stable unit-specific elements in the error term likely to be correlated with the independent variable?   It is quite likely that family support, at least, is correlated with attendance at private schools, since families with the wealth and/or interest in private schools are likely to provide other kinds of educational support to their children. This tendency is by no means set in stone, however: countless kids with good family support go to public schools, and there are certainly kids with no family support who end up in private schools. On average, though, it is reasonable to suspect that kids in private schools have more family support. If this is the case, then what may seem to be a causal effect of private schools on test scores may be little more than an indirect effect of family support on test scores.

REMEMBER THIS

1. A pooled model with panel data ignores the panel nature of the data. The equation is

$$Y_{it} = \beta_0 + \beta_1 X_{it} + \epsilon_{it}$$

2. A common source of endogeneity in the use of a pooled model to analyze panel data is that the specific units have different baseline levels of Y, and these levels are correlated with X. For example, cities with higher crime (meaning high unit-specific error terms) also tend to have more police, creating a correlation in a pooled model between the error term and the police independent variable.

8.2 Fixed Effects Models

In this section we introduce fixed effects as a way to deal with at least part of the endogeneity described in Section 8.1. We define the term and then show two ways to estimate basic fixed effects models.

▶ **fixed effect** A parameter associated with a specific unit in a panel data model. For a model $Y_{it} = \beta_0 + \beta_1 X_{1it} + \alpha_i + v_{it}$, the α_i parameter is the fixed effect for unit i.

Starting with Equation 8.1, we divide the error term, ϵ_{it}, into a **fixed effect**, α_i, and a random error term, v_{it} (the Greek letter, nu, pronounced "new"). Our focus here is on α_i; we'll assume the v_{it} part of the error term is well behaved—that is, it is homoscedastic and not correlated with other errors or with any independent variable. We rewrite our model as

$$Crime_{it} = \beta_0 + \beta_1 Police_{i,t-1} + \epsilon_{it}$$
$$= \beta_0 + \beta_1 Police_{i,t-1} + \alpha_i + v_{it}$$

More generally, **fixed effects models** look like

$$Y_{it} = \beta_0 + \beta_1 X_{1it} + \alpha_i + v_{it} \tag{8.3}$$

▶ **fixed effects model** A model that controls for unit-specific effects. These fixed effects capture differences in the dependent variable associated with each unit.

A fixed effects model is simply a model that contains a parameter like α_i that captures differences in the dependent variable associated with each unit and/or period.

The fixed effect α_i is the part of the unobserved error that has the same value for every observation for unit i. It basically reflects the average value of the dependent variable for unit i, after we have controlled for the independent variables. The unit is the unit of observation. In our city crime example, the unit of observation is the city.

Even though we write down only a single parameter (α_i), we're actually representing a different value for each unit. That is, this parameter takes on a potentially different value for each unit. In the city crime model, therefore, the value of α_i will be different for each city. If Pittsburgh has a higher average number of robberies than Portland, the α_i for Pittsburgh will be higher than the α_i for Portland.

The amazing thing about the ~~fixed effects parameter is that it allows us to control for a vast array of unmeasured attributes of units in the data set.~~ These could correspond to historical, geographical, or institutional factors. Or these attributes could relate to things we haven't even thought of. The key is that the fixed effect term allows different units to have different baseline levels of the dependent variable.

Why is it useful to model fixed effects in this way? When fixed effects are in the error term, as in the pooled OLS model, they can cause endogeneity and bias. But if we can pull them out of the error term, we will have overcome this source of endogeneity. We do this by controlling for the fixed effects, which will take them out of the error term so that they no longer can be a source for the correlation of the error term and an independent variable. This strategy is similar to the one we pursued with multivariate OLS: we identified a factor in the error term that could cause endogeneity and pulled it out of the error term by controlling for the variable in the regression.

How do we pull the fixed effects out of the error term? Easy! We simply estimate a different intercept for each unit. This will work as long as we have multiple observations for each unit. In other words, we can pull fixed effects out of the error term when we have panel data.

Least squares dummy variable approach

▶ **least squares dummy variable (LSDV) approach** An approach to estimating fixed effects models in the analysis of panel data.

There are two ways to estimate fixed effects models. In the **least squares dummy variable (LSDV) approach**, we create dummy variables for each unit and include these dummy variables in the model:

$$Y_{it} = \beta_0 + \beta_1 X_{1it} + \beta_2 D_{1i} + \beta_3 D_{2i} + \cdots + \beta_P D_{P-1,i} + \nu_{it} \qquad (8.4)$$

where D_{1i} is a dummy variable that equals 1 if the observation is from the first unit (which in our crime example is city), D_{2i} is a dummy variable that equals 1 if the observation is from the second unit, and so on to the $(P-1)$th unit. We exclude the dummy for one unit because we can't have a dummy variable for every unit if we include β_0, for reasons we discussed earlier (page 182).[2] The data will look like the data in Table 8.2, which gives the city, year, the dependent and independent variables, and the first three dummy variables. In the Computing Corner, we show how to quickly create these dummy variables.

With this simple step we have just soaked up anything (*anything*) that is in the error term that is fixed within unit over the time period of the panel.

---

[2] It doesn't really matter which unit we exclude. We exclude the Pth unit for convenience; plus it is fun to try to pronounce $(P-1)$th.

TABLE 8.2   **Example of Robbery and Police Data for Cities in California**

City	Year	Robberies per 1,000	Police per 1,000 (lagged)	D_1 (Fresno dummy)	D_2 (Oakland dummy)	D_3 (San Francisco dummy)
Fresno	1991	6.03	1.83	1	0	0
Fresno	1992	8.42	1.78	1	0	0
Oakland	1991	10.35	2.57	0	1	0
Oakland	1992	11.94	2.82	0	1	0
San Francisco	1991	9.50	3.14	0	0	1
San Francisco	1992	11.02	3.14	0	0	1

We are really just running OLS with loads of dummy variables. In other words, we've seen this before. Specifically, on page 182 we showed how to use multiple dummy variables to account for categorical variables. Here the categorical variable is whatever the unit of observation denotes (in our city crime data, it's city).

De-meaned approach

▶ **de-meaned approach**   An approach to estimating fixed effects models for panel data involving subtracting average values within units from all variables.

We shouldn't let the old-news feel of the LSDV approach lead us to underestimate fixed effects models. They're actually doing a lot of work, work that we can better appreciate when we consider a second way to estimate fixed models, the **de-meaned approach**. It's an odd term—it sounds like we're trying to humiliate data—but it describes well what we're doing. (Data is pretty shameless anyway.) When using the de-meaned approach, we subtract the unit-specific averages from both independent and dependent variables. The approach allows us to control for the fixed effects (the α_i terms) without estimating coefficients associated with dummy variables for each unit.

Why might we want to do this? Two reasons. First, it can be a bit of a hassle creating dummy variables for every unit and then wading through results with so many variables. For example, use the LSDV approach to estimate a country-specific fixed effects model describing voting in the United Nations, we might need roughly 200 dummy variables.

Second, the inner workings of the de-meaned estimator reveal the intuition behind fixed effects models. This reason is more important. The de-meaned model looks like

$$Y_{it} - \overline{Y}_{i.} = \beta_1(X_{it} - \overline{X}_{i.}) + \tilde{v}_{it} \tag{8.5}$$

where $\overline{Y}_{i.}$ is the average of Y for unit i over all time periods in the data set and $\overline{X}_{i.}$ is the average of X for unit i over all time periods in the data set. The dot notation indicates when an average is calculated. $\overline{Y}_{i.}$ is the average for unit i averaged over all time periods (values of). In our crime data, $\overline{Y}_{Fresno.}$ is the average crime in Fresno over the time frame of our data, and $\overline{X}_{Fresno}$. is the average police per capita in Fresno over the time frame of our data.[3]

Estimating a model using this transformed data will produce *exactly* the same coefficient and standard error estimates for $\hat{\beta}_1$ as produced by the LSDV approach.

The de-meaned approach allows us to see that fixed effects models convert data to deviations from mean levels for each unit and variable. In other words, fixed effects models are about differences *within* units, not differences *across* units. In the pooled model for our city crime data, the variables reflect differences in police and robberies in Los Angeles relative to police and robberies in Fresno. In the fixed effects model, the variables are transformed to reflect how much robberies in Los Angeles differ from average levels in Los Angeles as a function of how much police in Los Angeles differ from average levels of police in Los Angeles.

An example shows how this works. Recall the data on crime earlier, where we saw that estimating the model with a pooled model led to very different coefficients than with the fixed effects model. The reason for the difference was, of course, that the pooled model was plagued by endogeneity and the fixed effects model was not. How does the fixed effects model fix things? Figure 8.4 presents illustrative data for two made-up cities, Fresnomento and Los Frangelese. In panel (a), the pooled data is plotted as in Figure 8.1, with each observation number indicated. The relationship between police and robberies looks positive and, indeed, the OLS $\hat{\beta}_1$ is positive.

In panel (b) of Figure 8.4, we plot the same data after it has been de-meaned. Table 8.3 shows how we generated the de-meaned data. Notice, for example, that observation 1 is from Los Frangelese in 2010. The number of police (the value of X_{it}) was 4, which is one of the bigger numbers in the X_{it} column. When we compare this number to the average number of police per thousand people in Los Frangelese (which was 5.33), though, it is low. In fact, the de-meaned value of the police variable for Los Frangelese in 2010 is -1.33, indicating that the police per thousand people was actually 1.33 *lower* than the average for Los Frangelese in the time period of the data.

Although the raw values of Y get bigger as the raw values of X get bigger, the relationship between $Y_{it} - \overline{Y}_{i\cdot}$ and $X_{it} - \overline{X}_{i\cdot}$ is quite different. Panel (b) of Figure 8.4 shows a clear negative relationship between the de-meaned X and the de-meaned Y.[4]

---

[3] The de-meaned equation is derived by subtracting the same thing from both sides of Equation 8.3. Specifically, note that the average dependent variable for unit i over time is $\overline{Y}_{i\cdot} = \beta_0 + \beta_1\overline{X}_{i\cdot} + \overline{\alpha}_{i\cdot} + \overline{v}_{i\cdot}$. If we subtract the left-hand side of this equation from the left-hand side of Equation 8.3 and the right-hand side of this equation from the right-hand side of Equation 8.3, we get $Y_{it} - \overline{Y}_{i\cdot} = \beta_0 + \beta_1 X_{it} + \alpha_i + v_{it} - \beta_0 - \beta_1\overline{X}_{i\cdot} - \overline{\alpha}_{i\cdot} - \overline{v}_{i\cdot}$. The α terms cancel because $\overline{\alpha}_i$ equals α_i (the average of fixed effects for each unit are, by definition, the same for all observations of a given unit in all time periods). Rearranging terms yields something that is almost Equation 8.5. For simplicity, we let $\tilde{v}_{it} = v_{it} - \overline{v}_{i\cdot}$; this new error term will inherit the properties of v_{it} (e.g., being uncorrelated with the independent variable and having a mean of zero).

[4] One issue that can seem confusing at first—but really isn't—is how to interpret the coefficients. Because the LSDV and de-meaned approaches produce identical estimates, we can stick with our relatively straightforward way of explaining LSDV results even when we're describing results from a de-meaned model. Specifically, we can simply say that a one-unit change in X_1 is associated with a

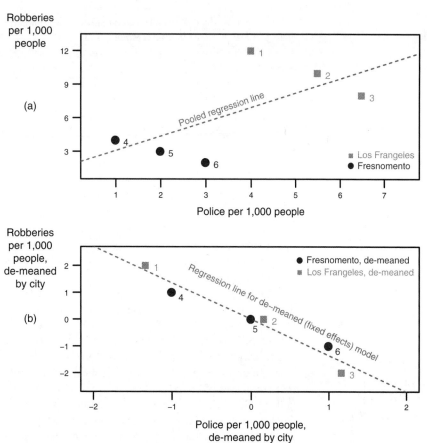

FIGURE 8.4: Robberies and Police for Hypothetical Cities in California

TABLE 8.3 Robberies and Police Data for Hypothetical Cities in California

Observation number	City	Year	X_{it}	$\bar{X}_{i\cdot}$	$X_{it} - \bar{X}_{i\cdot}$	Y_{it}	$\bar{Y}_{i\cdot}$	$Y_{it} - \bar{Y}_{i\cdot}$
1	Los Frangelese	2010	4	5.33	−1.33	12	10	2
2	Los Frangelese	2011	5.5	5.33	0.17	10	10	0
3	Los Frangelese	2012	6.5	5.33	1.17	8	10	−2
4	Fresnomento	2010	1	2	−1	4	3	1
5	Fresnomento	2011	2	2	0	3	3	0
6	Fresnomento	2012	3	2	1	2	3	−1

$\hat{\beta}_1$ increase in Y when we control for unit fixed effects. This interpretation is similar to how we interpret multivariate OLS coefficients, which makes sense because the fixed effects model is really just an OLS model with lots of dummy variables.

TABLE 8.4 Burglary and Police Officers, Pooled versus Fixed Effects Models

	Pooled OLS	Fixed effects (one-way)
Lag police (per capita)	2.37*	1.49*
	(0.07)	(0.17)
	$[t = 32.59]$	$[t = 8.67]$
N	1,232	1,232
Number of cities	59	59

Standard errors in parentheses.

* *indicates significance at $p < 0.05$, two-tailed.*

In practice, we seldom calculate the de-meaned variables ourselves. There are easy ways to implement the model in Stata and R. We describe these techniques in the Computing Corner at the end of the chapter.

Table 8.4 shows the results for a basic fixed effects model for our city crime data. We include the pooled results from Table 8.1 for reference. The coefficient on police per capita falls from 2.37 to 1.49 once we've included fixed effects. The drop in the coefficient suggests that there were indeed more police officers in cities with higher baseline levels of crime. So the fixed effects were real: that is, some cities have higher average robberies per capita even when we control for the number of police, and these effects may be correlated with the number of police officers. The fixed effects model controls for these city-specific averages and leads to a smaller coefficient on police officers.

However, the coefficient still suggests that every police officer per capita is associated with 1.49 more robberies. This estimate seems quite large and is highly statistically significant. We'll revisit this data in Section 8.4 with models that account for additional important factors.

We should note that we do not indicate whether results in Table 8.4 were estimated with LSDV or the de-meaned approach. Why? Because it doesn't matter. Either one would produce identical coefficients and standard errors on the police variable.

REMEMBER THIS

1. A fixed effects model includes an α_i term for every unit:

$$Y_{it} = \beta_0 + \beta_1 X_{1it} + \alpha_i + \epsilon_{it}$$

2. The fixed effects approach allows us to control for any factor that is fixed within unit for the entire panel, regardless of whether we observe this factor.

3. There are two ways to produce identical fixed effects coefficient estimates for the model.

     (a) In the least squares dummy variable (LSDV) approach, we simply include dummy variables for each unit except an excluded reference category.

     (b) In the de-meaned approach, we transform the data such that the dependent and independent variables indicate deviations from the unit mean.

Discussion Questions

What factors influence student evaluations of professors in college courses? Are instructors who teach large classes evaluated less favorably? Consider using the following model to assess the question based on a data set of evaluations of instructors across multiple classes and multiple years:

$$Evaluation_{it} = \beta_0 + \beta_1 Number\ of\ students_{it} + \epsilon_{it}$$

where $Evaluation_{it}$ is the average evaluation by students of instructor i in class t, and $Number\ of\ students_{it}$ is the number of students in the class of instructor i's class t.

- What is in the error term?

- Are there any stable, unit-specific elements in the error term?

- Are any stable, unit-specific elements in the error term likely to be correlated with the independent variable?

8.3   Working with Fixed Effects Models

Fixed effects models are relatively easy to implement. In practice, though, several elements take a bit of getting used to. In this section we explore the consequences of using fixed effects models when they're necessary and when they're not. We also explain why fixed effects models cannot estimate some relationships even as they control for them.

It's useful to consider possible downsides of using fixed effects models. What if we control for fixed effects when $\alpha_i = 0$ for all units? In this case, the fixed effects are all zero and they cannot cause bias. Could including fixed effects in this case cause bias? The answer is no, for the same reasons we discussed earlier (in Chapter 5, page 151): controlling for irrelevant variables does not cause bias. Rather, bias occurs when errors are correlated with independent variables. As a general matter, however, including extra variables does not cause errors to be correlated with independent variables.[5]

If the fixed effects are non-zero, we of course want to control for them. We should note, however, that just because some (or many!) α_i are non-zero, our fixed effects model and our pooled model will not necessarily produce different results. Recall that bias occurs when errors are correlated with an independent variable. The fixed effects could exist, but they are not necessarily correlated with the independent variables. To cause bias, in other words, fixed effects must not only exist, they must be correlated with the independent variables. It's not unusual to observe instances in real data where fixed effects exist but don't cause bias. In such cases, the coefficients from the pooled and fixed effects models are similar.[6]

The prudent approach to analyzing panel data is therefore to control for fixed effects. If the fixed effects are zero, we'll get unbiased results even with the controls for fixed effects. If the fixed effects are non-zero, we'll get unbiased results that will differ or not from pooled results depending on whether the fixed effects are correlated with the independent variable.

A downside to fixed models is that they make it impossible to estimate effects for certain variables that might be of interest. As is often the case, there is no free lunch (although it's a pretty cheap lunch).

Specifically, fixed effects models cannot estimate coefficients on any variables that are fixed for all individuals over the entire time frame. Suppose, for example, that in the process of analyzing our city crime data we wonder if northern cities are more crime prone. We studiously create a dummy variable $North_i$ that equals 1 if a city is in a northern state and 0 otherwise and set about estimating the following model:

$$Crime_{it} = \beta_0 + \beta_1 Police_{i,t-1} + \beta_2 North_i + \alpha_i + v_{it}$$

Sadly, this approach won't work. The reason is easiest to see by considering the fixed effects model in de-meaned terms. The *North* variable will be converted to $North_{it} - \overline{North}_{i\cdot}$. What is the value of this de-meaned variable for a city in the North? The $North_{it}$ part will equal 1 for all time periods for such a city. But wait, this means that $\overline{North}_{i\cdot}$ will also be 1 because that is the average of this variable for this northern city. That means the value of the de-meaned *North* variable will

---

[5] Controlling for fixed effects when all the $\alpha_i = 0$ will lead to larger standard errors, though. So if we can establish that there is no sign of a non-zero α_i for any unit, we may wish to also estimate a model without fixed effects. To test for unit-specific fixed effects, we can implement an F test following the process discussed in Chapter 7 (page 231). The null hypothesis is $H_0 : \alpha_1 = \alpha_2 = \alpha_3 = \cdots = 0$. The alternative hypothesis is that at least one of the fixed effects is non-zero. The unrestricted model is a model with fixed effects (most easily thought of as the LSDV model that has dummy variables for each specific unit). The restricted model is a model without any fixed effects, which is simply the pooled OLS model. We provide computer code on pages 277 and 278.

[6] A so-called Hausman test can be used to test whether fixed effects are causing bias. If the results indicate no sign of bias when fixed effects are not controlled for, we can use the random effects model discussed in Chapter 15 on page 507.

be 0 for any city in the North. What is the value for the de-meaned North variable for a non-northern city? Similar logic applies: the $North_{it}$ part will equal 0 for all time periods and so too will $\overline{North}_i$. for a non-nothern city. The de-meaned North variable will therefore also be 0 for non-northern cities. In other words, the de-meaned *North* variable will be 0 for all cities in all years. The first job of a variable is to vary. If it doesn't, well, that ain't no variable! Hence it will not be possible to estimate a coefficient on this variable.[7]

More generally, a fixed effects model (estimated with either LSDV or the de-meaned approach) cannot estimate a coefficient on a variable if the variable does not change within units for all units. So even though the variable varies across cities (e.g., the $North_i$ variable is 1 for some cities and 0 for other cities), we can't estimate a coefficient on it because within cities it does not vary. This issue arises in many other contexts. In panel data in which individuals are the unit of observation, fixed effects models cannot estimate coefficients on variables such as gender or race that do not vary within individuals. In panel data on countries, the effect of variables such as area or being landlocked cannot be estimated when there is no variation within country for any country in the data set.

Not being able to include such a variable does *not* mean fixed effects models do not control for it. The unit-specific fixed effect is controlling for *all* factors that are fixed within a unit for the span of the data set. The model cannot parse out which of these unchanging factors have which effect, but it does control for them via the fixed effects parameters.

Some variables might be fixed within some units but variable within other units. Those we can estimate. For example, a dummy variable that indicates whether a city has more than a million people will not vary for many cities that have been above or below one million in population for the entire span of the panel data. However, if at least some cities have risen above one million or declined below one million during the period covered in the panel data, then the variable can be used in a fixed effects model.

Panel data models need not be completely silent with regard to variables that do not vary. We can investigate how unchanging variables interact with variables that do change. For example, we can estimate β_2 in the following model:

$$Crime_{it} = \beta_0 + \beta_1 Police_{i,t-1} + \beta_2(North_i \times Police_{i,t-1}) + \alpha_i + \nu_{it}$$

The $\hat{\beta}_2$ will tell us how different the coefficient on the police variable is for northern cities.

Sometimes people are tempted to abandon fixed effects because they care about variables that do not vary within unit. That's cheating. The point of choosing a fixed effects model is to avoid the risk of bias, which could creep in if something

---

[7] Because we know that LSDV and de-meaned approaches produce identical results, we know that we will not be able to estimate a coefficient on the *North* variable in an LSDV model as well. This is the result of perfect multicollinearity: the *North* variable is perfectly explained as the sum of the dummy variables for the northern cities.

fixed within individuals across the panel happened to be correlated with an independent variable. Bias is bad, and we can't just close our eyes to it to get to a coefficient we want to estimate. The best-case scenario is that we run a fixed effects model and test for whether we need the fixed effects, find that we do not, and then proceed guilt free. But let's not get our hopes up. We usually need the fixed effects.

REMEMBER THIS

1. Fixed effects models do not cause bias when implemented in situations in which $\alpha_i = 0$ for all units.

2. ~~Pooled OLS models are biased only when fixed effects are correlated with the independent variable.~~

3. Fixed effects models cannot estimate coefficients on variables that do not vary within at least some units. Fixed effects models do control for these factors, though, as they are subsumed within the unit-specific fixed effect.

Discussion Questions

1. Suppose we have panel data on voter opinions toward government spending in 2010, 2012, and 2014. Explain why we can or cannot estimate the effect of each of the following in a fixed effects model.

    (a) Gender

    (b) Income

    (c) Race

    (d) Party identification

2. Suppose we have panel data on the annual economic performance of 100 countries from 1960 to 2015. Explain why we can or cannot estimate the effect of each of the following in a fixed effects model.

    (a) Average years of education

    (b) Democracy, which is coded 1 if political control is determined by competitive elections

    (c) Country size

    (d) Proximity to the equator

3. Suppose we have panel data on the annual economic performance of the 50 U.S. states from 1960 to 2015. Explain why we can or cannot estimate the effect of each of the following in a fixed effects model.

   (a) Average years of education

   (b) Democracy, which is coded 1 if political control is determined by competitive elections

   (c) State size

   (d) Proximity to Canada

8.4 Two-Way Fixed Effects Model

▶ **one-way fixed effects model** A panel data model that allows for fixed effects at the unit level.

▶ **two-way fixed effects model** A panel data model that allows for fixed effects at the unit and time levels.

So far we have presented models in which there is a fixed effect for the unit of observation. We refer to such models as **one-way fixed effects model**. We can generalize the approach to a **two-way fixed effects model** in which we allow for fixed effects not only at the unit level but also at the time level. That is, just as some cities might have more crime than others (due to unmeasured history of violence or culture), some years might have more crime than others as a result of unmeasured factors. Therefore we add a time fixed effect to our model, making it

$$Y_{it} = \beta_0 + \beta_1 X_{1it} + \alpha_i + \tau_t + \nu_{it} \tag{8.6}$$

where we've taken Equation 8.3 from page 253 and added τ_t (the Greek letter tau—rhymes with "wow"), which accounts for differences in crime for all units in year t. This notation provides a shorthand way to indicate that each separate time period gets its own τ_t effect on the dependent variable (in addition to the α_i effect on the dependent variable for each individual unit of observation in the data set).

Similar to our one-way fixed effects model, the single parameter for a time fixed effect indicates the average difference for all observations in a given year, after we have controlled for the other variables in the model. A positive fixed effect for the year 2008 (α_{2008}) would indicate that, controlling for all other factors, the dependent variable was higher for all units in the data set in 2008. A negative fixed effect for the year 2014 (α_{2014}) would indicate that, controlling for all other factors, the dependent variable was lower for all units in the data set in 2014.

There are lots of situations in which we suspect that a time fixed effect might be appropriate:

- The whole world suffered an economic downturn in 2008 because of a financial crisis. Hence any model with economic dependent variables could merit a time fixed effect to soak up this distinctive characteristic of the economy in 2008.

- Approval of political institutions went way up in the United States after the terrorist affects of September 11, 2001. This was clearly a time-specific factor that affected the entire country.

We can estimate a two-way fixed model in several different ways. The simplest approach is to extend the LSDV approach to include dummy variables both for units and for time periods. We can even use a two-way de-meaned approach.[8] We can even use a hybrid LSDV/de-meaned approach; we show how in the Computing Corner.

Table 8.5 shows the huge effect of using a two-way fixed effects model on our analysis of city crime data. For reference, the first two columns show the pooled OLS and one-way fixed effects results. The third column displays the results for a two-way fixed effects model controlling only for police per capita. In contrast to the pooled and one-way models, the coefficient is small (0.14) and statistically insignificant, suggesting that both police spending and crime were high in certain years. Robberies were common in some years throughout the country (possibly, perhaps, owing to the crack epidemic that was more serious in some years than others). Once we had controlled for that fact, however, we were able to net out a source of substantial bias.

The fourth and final column reports two-way fixed effects results from a model that also controls for the lagged per capita robbery rate in each city in order to control for city-specific trends in crime. The estimate from this model implies that an increase of one police officer per 100,000 people is associated with a decrease of 0.202 robbery per capita. The effect is marginally statistically significant.[9]

---

[8] The algebra is a bit more involved than for a one-way model, but the result has a similar feel:

$$Y_{it} - \overline{Y}_{i.} - \overline{Y}_{.t} + \overline{Y}_{..} = \beta_1 (X_{it} - \overline{X}_{i.} - \overline{X}_{.t} + \overline{X}_{..}) + \tilde{v}_{it} \tag{8.7}$$

where the dot notation indicates what is averaged over. Thus $\overline{Y}_{i.}$ is the average value of Y for unit i over time, $\overline{Y}_{.t}$ is the average value of Y for all units at time t, and $\overline{Y}_{..}$ is the average over all units and all time periods. Don't worry, we almost certainly won't have to create these variables ourselves; we're including the dot convention just to provide a sense of how a one-way fixed effects model extends to a two-way fixed effects model.

[9] The additional control variable is called a *lagged dependent variable*. Inclusion of such a variable is common in analysis of panel data. These variables often are highly statistically significant, as is the case here. Control variables of these types raise some complications, which we address in Chapter 15 on advanced panel data models.

TABLE 8.5 **Burglary and Police Officers, For Multiple Models**

	Pooled OLS	Fixed effects (one-way)		Fixed effects (two-way)
Lag police	2.37*	1.49*	0.14	−0.212
(per capita)	(0.07)	(0.17)	(0.17)	(0.11)
	[$t = 32.59$]	[$t = 8.67$]	[$t = 0.86$]	[$t = 1.88$]
Lag robberies	—	—	—	0.79*
(per capita)	—	—	—	(0.02)
	—	—	—	[$t = 41.63$]
N	1,232	1,232	1,232	1,232
Number of cities	59	59	59	59

Standard errors in parentheses.

* *indicates significance at $p < 0.05$, two-tailed.*

It is useful to take a moment to appreciate that not all models are created equal. A cynic might look at the results in Table 8.5 and conclude that statistics can be made to say anything. But this is not the right way to think about the results. The models do indeed produce different results, but there are reasons for the differences. One of the models is better. A good statistical analyst will know this. We can use statistical logic to explain why the pooled results are suspect. We know pretty much what is going on: certain fixed effects in the error term of the pooled model are correlated with the police variable, thereby biasing the pooled OLS coefficients. So although there is indeed output from statistical software that could be taken to imply that police cause crime, we know better. Treating all results as equivalent is not serious statistics; it's just pressing buttons on a computer. Instead of supporting statistical cynicism, this example testifies to the benefits of appropriate analysis.

REMEMBER THIS

1. A two-way fixed effects model accounts for both unit- and time-specific errors.

2. A two-way fixed effects model is written as

$$Y_{it} = \beta_0 + \beta_1 X_{1it} + \beta_2 X_{2it} + \alpha_i + \tau_t + \nu_{it}$$

3. A two-way fixed effects model can be estimated with an LSDV approach (which has dummy variables for each unit and each period in the data set), with a de-meaned approach, or with a combination of the two.

CASE STUDY   ## Trade and Alliances

Does trade follow the flag? That is, does international trade flow more heavily between countries that are allies? Or do economic factors alone determine trade? On the one hand, it seems reasonable to suppose that national security alliances boost trade by fostering good relations and stability. On the other hand, isn't pretty much everything in the United States made in China?

A basic panel model to test for the effect of alliances on trade is

$$Bilateral\ trade_{it} = \beta_0 + \beta_1 Alliance_{it} + \alpha_i + \epsilon_{it} \qquad (8.8)$$

▶ **dyad** An entity that consists of two elements. For the trade data set, a dyad indicates a pair of countries and the data indicates how much trade flows between the members of the dyad.

where *Bilateral trade_{it}* is total trade volume between countries in **dyad** *i* at time *t*. A dyad is a unit that consists of two elements. Here, a dyad indicates a pair of countries, and the data indicates how much trade flows between them. For example, the United States and Canada form one dyad, the United States and Japan form another dyad, and so on. *Alliance_{it}* is a dummy variable that is 1 if countries in the dyad are entered into a security alliance at time *t*. The α_i term captures the amount by which trade in dyad *i* is higher or lower over the entire course of the panel.

Because the unit of observation is a country-pair dyad, fixed effects here entail factors related to a pair of countries. For example, the fixed effect for the United States–New Zealand dyad in the trade model may be higher because of the shared language. The fixed effect for the China–India dyad might be negative because the countries are separated by mountains (which they happen to fight over, too).

As we consider whether a fixed effects model is necessary, we need to think about whether the dyad-specific fixed effects could be correlated with the independent variables. Dyad-specific fixed effects could exist because of a history of commerce between two countries, a favorable trading geography (not divided by mountains, for example), economic complementarities of some sort, and so on. These factors could also make it easier or harder to form alliances.

Table 8.6 reports results from Green, Kim, and Yoon (2001) based on data covering trade and alliances from 1951 to 1992. The dependent variable is the amount of trade between the two countries in a given dyad in a given year. In addition to the alliance measure, the independent variables are *GDP* (total gross domestic product of the two countries in the dyad), *Population* (total population of the two countries in the dyad), *Distance* (distance between the capitals of the two countries), and *Democracy* (the minimum value of a democracy ranking for the two countries in the dyad: the higher the value, the more democracy).

The dependent and continuous independent variables are logged. Logging variables is a common practice in this literature; the interpretation is that a one

TABLE 8.6	Bilateral Trade, Pooled versus Fixed Effects Models		
	Pooled OLS	Fixed effects, one way	Fixed effects, two way
Alliance	−0.745*	0.777*	0.459*
	(0.042)	(0.136)	(0.134)
	[$t = 17.67$]	[$t = 5.72$]	[$t = 3.43$]
GDP (logged)	1.182*	0.810*	1.688*
	(0.008)	(0.015)	(0.042)
	[$t = 156.74$]	[$t = 52.28$]	[$t = 39.93$]
Population (logged)	−0.386*	0.752*	1.281*
	(0.010)	(0.082)	(0.083)
	[$t = 39.70$]	[$t = 9.19$]	[$t = 15.47$]
Distance (logged)	−1.342*		
	(0.018)		
	[$t = 76.09$]		
Democracy (logged)	0.075*	−0.039*	−0.015*
	(0.002)	(0.003)	(0.003)
	[$t = 35.98$]	[$t = 13.42$]	[$t = 5.07$]
Observations	93,924	93,924	93,924
Dyads	3,079	3,079	3,079

Standard errors are in parentheses.

* *indicates significance at $p < 0.05$, two-tailed.*

percent increase in any independent variable is associated with a $\hat{\beta}$ percent increase in trade volume. (We discussed logged variables on page 222.)

The results are remarkable. In the pooled model, *Alliance* is associated with a 0.745 percentage point decline in trade. In the one-way fixed effects model, the estimate completely flips and is associated with a 0.777 *increase* in trade. In the two-way fixed effects model, the estimated effect remains positive and significant but drops to 0.459. The coefficients on *Population* and *Democracy* also flip, while being statistically significant across the board.

These results are shocking. If someone said, "I'm going to estimate an OLS model of bilateral trade relations," we'd be pretty impressed, right? But actually, that model produces results that lead to results almost completely opposite from those produced by the more appropriate fixed effects models.

There are other interesting things going on as well. The coefficient on *Distance* disappears in the fixed effects models. Yikes! What's going on? The reason, of course, is that the distance between two countries does not change. Fixed effects models cannot estimate a coefficient on distance because distance does not vary within the dyad over the course of the panel. Does that mean that the effect of distance is not controlled for? That would seem to be a problem, since distance certainly affects trade. It's not a problem, though, because even though fixed effects models cannot estimate coefficients on variables that do not vary within unit of observation (which is dyad pairs of countries in this data set), the effects of these variables are controlled for via the fixed effect. And, even better, not only is the effect of distance controlled for, so too are hard-to-measure factors such as being on a trade route or having cultural affinities. That's what the fixed effect is—a big ball of all the effects that are the same within units for the period of the panel.

Not all coefficients flip. The coefficient on *GDP* is relatively stable, indicating that unlike the variables that do flip signs from the pooled to fixed effects specifications, *GDP* does not seem to be correlated with the unmeasured fixed effects that influence trade between countries.

8.5 Difference-in-Difference

▶ **difference-in-difference model** A model that looks at differences in changes in treated units compared to untreated units.

The logic of fixed effects plays a major role in **difference-in-difference models**, which look at differences in changes in treated units in comparison to untreated units and are particularly useful in policy evaluation. In this section we explain the logic of this approach, show how to use OLS to estimate these models, and then link the approach to the two-way fixed effects models we developed for panel data.

Difference-in-difference logic

To understand difference-in-difference logic, let's consider a policy evaluation of "stand your ground" laws, which have the effect of allowing individuals to use lethal force when they reasonably believe they are threatened.[10] Does a law that removes the duty to retreat when life or property is being threatened prevent homicides by making would-be aggressors reconsider? Or do such laws increase homicides by escalating violence?

Naturally, we would start by looking at the change in homicides in a state that passed a stand your ground law. This approach is what every policy maker in the history of time uses to assess the impact of a policy change. Suppose we find homicides rising in the states that passed the law. Is that fact enough to lead us to conclude that the law increases crime?

It doesn't take a ton of thinking to realize that such evidence is pretty weak. Homicides could rise or fall for a lot of reasons, many of them completely unrelated to stand your ground laws. If homicides went up not only in the state that passed the law, but in all states—even states that made no policy change—we can't seriously blame the law for the rise in homicides. Or, if homicides declined everywhere, we shouldn't attribute the decline in a particular state to the law.

What we really want to do is to look at differences in the state that passed the policy in comparison to differences in similar states that did not pass such a

---

[10] See McClellan and Tekin (2012) and Cheng and Hoekstra (2013).

law. To use experimental language, we want to look at the difference in treated states versus the difference in control states. We can write this difference of differences as

$$\Delta Y_T - \Delta Y_C \qquad (8.9)$$

where ΔY_T is the change in the dependent variable in treated states (those that passed a stand your ground law) and ΔY_C is the change in the dependent variable in the untreated states, which did not pass such a law. We call this approach the difference-in-difference approach because we look at the difference between differences in treated and control states.

Using OLS to estimate difference-in-difference models

It is perfectly reasonable to generate a difference-in-difference estimate by calculating the changes in treated and untreated states and taking the difference. We'll use OLS to produce the same result, however. The advantage is that OLS will also spit out standard errors on our estimate. We can also easily add control variables when we use OLS.

Specifically, we'll use the following OLS model:

$$Y_{it} = \beta_0 + \beta_1 Treated_i + \beta_2 After_t + \beta_3 (Treated_i \times After_t) + \epsilon_{it} \qquad (8.10)$$

where $Treated_i$ equals 1 for a treated state and 0 for a control state, $After_t$ equals 1 for all after observations (from both control and treated units), and $Treated_i \times After_t$ is an interaction of $Treated_i$ and $After_t$. This interaction variable will equal 1 for treated states in the post-treatment period and 0 for all other observations.

The control states have some mean level of homicides, which we denote with β_0; the treated states have some mean level of homicides, and we denote these with $\beta_0 + \beta_1 Treated_i$. If β_1 is positive, the mean level for the treated states is higher than in control states. If β_1 is negative, the mean level for the treated states is lower. If β_1 is zero, the mean level for the treated states is the same as in control states. Since this preexisting difference of mean levels was by definition there before the law was passed, the law can't be the cause of differences. Instead, these differences represented by β_1 are simply the preexisting differences in the treated and untreated states. This parameter is analogous to a unit fixed effect, although here it is for the entire group of treated states, rather than individual units.

The model captures national trends with the $\beta_2 After_t$ term. The dependent variable for all states, treated and not, changes by β_2 in the after period. This parameter is analogous to a time fixed effect, but it's for the entire post-treatment period rather than individual time periods.

The key coefficient is β_3. This is the coefficient on the interaction between $Treated_i$ and $After_t$. This variable equals 1 only for treated units in the after period.

The coefficient tells us there is an additional change in the treated states after the policy went into effect, once we have controlled for preexisting differences between the treated and control states (β_1) and differences in the before and after periods for all states (β_2).

If we work out the fitted values for changes in treated and control states, we can see how this regression model produces a difference-in-difference estimate. First, note that the fitted value for treated states in the after period is $\beta_0 + \beta_1 + \beta_2 + \beta_3$ (because $Treated_i$, $After_t$, and $Treated_i \times After_t$ all equal 1 for treated states in the after period). Second, note that the fitted value for treated states in the before period is $\beta_0 + \beta_1 + \beta_3$, so the change for fitted states is $\beta_2 + \beta_3$. The fitted value for control states in the after period is $\beta_0 + \beta_2$ (because $Treated_i$ and $Treated_i \times After_t$ equal 0 for control states). The fitted value for control states in the before period is β_0, so the change for control states is β_2. The difference in differences of treated and control states will therefore be β_3. Presto!

Figure 8.5 displays two examples that illustrate the logic of difference-in-difference models. In panel (a), there is no treatment effect. The dependent

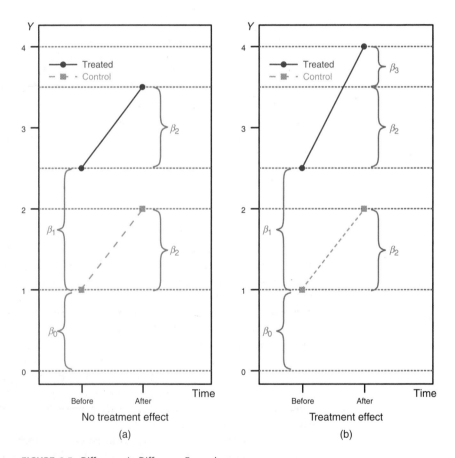

FIGURE 8.5: Difference-in-Difference Examples

variables for the treated and control states differ in the before period by β_1. Then the dependent variable for both the treated and control units rose by β_2 in the after period. In other words, Y was bigger for the treated unit than for the control by the same amount before and after the treatment. The implication is that the treatment had no effect, even though Y went up in treatment states after they passed the law.

Panel (b) shows an example with a treatment effect. The dependent variables for the treated and control states differ in the before period by β_1. The dependent variable for both the treated and control units rose by β_2 in the after period, but the value of Y for the treated unit rose yet another β_3. In other words, the treated group was β_1 bigger than the control before the treatment and $\beta_1 + \beta_3$ bigger than the control after the treatment. The implication is that the treatment caused a β_3 bump over and above the differences across unit and time that are accounted for in the model.

Consider how the difference-in-difference approach would assess outcomes in our stand your ground law example. If homicides declined in states with such laws more than in states without them, the evidence supports the claim that the law prevented homicides. Such an outcome could happen if homicides went down by 10 in states with the law but decreased by only 2 in other states. Such an outcome could also happen if homicides actually went up by 2 in states with stand your ground laws but went up by 10 in other states. In both instances, the difference-in-difference estimate is −8.

One great thing about using OLS to estimate difference-in-difference models is that it is easy to control for other variables with OLS. Simply include them as covariates and do what we've been doing. In other words, simply add a $\beta_4 X_{it}$ term (and additional variables, if appropriate), yielding the following difference-in-difference model:

$$Y_{it} = \beta_0 + \beta_1 Treated_i + \beta_2 After_t + \beta_3 (Treated_i \times After_t) + \beta_4 X_{it} + \epsilon_{it} \quad (8.11)$$

Difference-in-difference models for panel data

A difference-in-difference model works not only with panel data but also with **rolling cross section data**. Rolling cross section data consists of data from each treated and untreated region; the individual observations come from different individuals across time periods. An example of a rolling cross section of data is a repeated national survey of people's experience with their health insurance over multiple years. We could look to see if state-level decisions about Medicaid coverage in 2014 led to different changes in treated states relative to untreated states. For such data we can easily create dummy variables indicating whether the observation did or did not come from the treated state and whether the observation was in the before or after period. The model can take things from there.

If we have panel data, we can estimate a more general form of a difference-in-difference model that looks like a two-way fixed effects model:

▶ **rolling cross section data** Repeated cross sections of data from different individuals at different points in time.

$$Y_{it} = \alpha_i + \tau_t + \beta_3(Treated_i \times After_t) + \beta_4 X_{it} + \epsilon_{it} \tag{8.12}$$

where

- the α_i terms (the unit-specific fixed effects) capture differences that exist across units both before and after the treatment.

- the τ_t terms (the time-specific fixed effects) capture differences that exist across all units in every period. If homicide rates are higher in 2007 than in 2003, then the τ_t for 2007 will be higher than the τ_t for 2003.

- $Treated_i \times After_t$ is an interaction of a variable indicating whether a unit is a treatment unit (meaning in our case that $Treated_i = 1$ for states that passed stand your ground laws) and $Post_t$, which indicates whether the observation occurred post-treatment (meaning in our case that the observation occurred after the state passed a stand your ground law). This interaction variable will equal 1 for treated states in the post-treatment period and 0 for all other observations.

Our primary interest is the coefficient on $Treated_i \times After_t$ (which we call β_3 to be consistent with earlier equations). As in the difference-in-difference model without fixed effects, this parameter indicates the effect of the treatment.

Table 8.7 refers to a 2012 analysis of stand your ground laws by Georgia State University economists Chandler McClellan and Erdal Tekin. They implemented a state and time fixed effect version of a difference-in-difference model and found that the homicide rate per 100,000 residents went up by 0.033 after the passage of the stand your ground laws. In other words, controlling for the preexisting differences in state homicide rates (via state fixed effects) and national trends in homicide rates (via time fixed effects) and additional controls related to race, age,

TABLE 8.7 Effect of Stand Your Ground Laws on Homicide Rate per 100,000 Residents

Variable	Coefficient
Stand your ground laws	0.033*
	(0.013)
	[$t = 2.54$]
State fixed effects	Included
Period fixed effects	Included

Standard errors are in parentheses.

* *indicates significance at $p < 0.05$, two-tailed.*

Includes controls for racial, age, and urban demographics. Adapted from Appendix Table 1 of McClellan and Tekin (2012).

and percent of residents living in urban areas, they found that the homicide rates went up by 0.033 after states implemented these laws.[11]

REMEMBER THIS

A difference-in-difference model estimates the effect of a change in policy by comparing changes in treated units to changes in control units.

1. A basic difference-in-difference estimator is $\Delta Y_T - \Delta Y_C$, where ΔY_T is the change in the dependent variable for the treated unit and ΔY_C is the change in the dependent variable for a control unit.

2. Difference-in-difference estimates can be generated from the following OLS model:

$$Y_{it} = \beta_0 + \beta_1 Treated_i + \beta_2 After_t + \beta_3(Treated_i \times After_t) + \beta_4 X_{it} + \epsilon_{it}$$

3. For panel data, we can use a two-way fixed effects model to estimate difference-in-difference effects.

$$Y_{it} = \alpha_i + \tau_t + \beta_3(Treated_i \times After_t) + \beta_4 X_{it} + \epsilon_{it}$$

where the α_i fixed effects capture differences in units that existed both before and after treatment and the τ_t captures differences common to all units in each time period.

Discussion Question

1. For each of the following examples, explain how to create (i) a simple difference-in-difference estimate of policy effects and (ii) a fixed effects difference-in-difference model.

   (a) California implemented a first-in-the-nation program of paid family leave in 2004. Did this policy increase use of maternity leave?[a]

   (b) Fourteen countries engaged in "expansionary austerity" policies in response to the 2008 financial crisis. Did these austerity policies work? (For simplicity, treat austerity as a dummy variable equal to 1 for countries that engaged in it and 0 for others.)

   (c) Some neighborhoods in Los Angeles changed zoning laws to make it easier to mix commercial and residential buildings. Did these changes reduce crime?[b]

---

[a] See Rossin-Slater, Ruhm, and Waldfogel (2013).
[b] See Anderson, Macdonald, Bluthenthal, and Ashwood (2013).

---

[11] Cheng and Hoekstra (2013) found similar results.

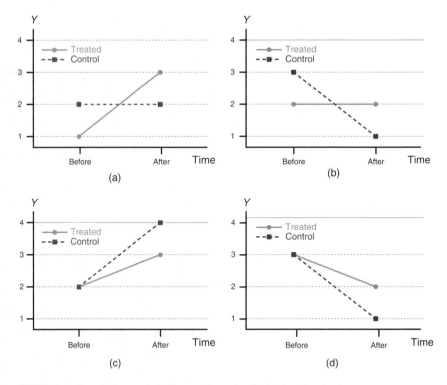

FIGURE 8.6: More Difference-in-Difference Examples (for Review Question)

Review Question

1. For each of the four panels in Figure 8.6, indicate the values of $\beta_0, \beta_1, \beta_2,$ and β_3 for the basic difference-in-difference OLS model:

$$Y_{it} = \beta_0 + \beta_1 Treated_i + \beta_2 After_t + \beta_3(Treated_i \times After_t) + \epsilon_{it}$$

Conclusion

Again and again we've emphasized the importance of exogeneity. If X is uncorrelated with ϵ we get unbiased estimates and we are happy. Experiments are sought after because the randomization in them ensures—or at least aids—exogeneity. With OLS we can—sometimes, maybe, almost, sort of, kind of—approximate endogeneity by soaking up so much of the error term with measured variables that what remains correlates little or not at all with X.

Realistically, though, we know that we will not be able to measure everything. Real variables with real causal force will almost certainly lurk in the error term. Are we stuck? Turns out, no (or, at least, not yet). We've got a few more tricks up our sleeve. One of the best tricks is to use fixed effects tools. Although uncomplicated, the fixed effects approach can knock out a whole class of unmeasured (and even unknown) variables that lurk in the error term. Simply put, any factor that is fixed across time periods for each unit or fixed across units for each time period can be knocked out of the error term. Fixed effects tools are powerful and, as we have seen in real examples, they can produce results that differ dramatically from those produced by basic OLS models.

We will have mastered the material in this chapter when we can do the following.

- Section 8.1: Explain how a pooled model can be problematic in the analysis of panel data.

- Section 8.2: Write down a fixed effects model and explain the fixed effect. Give examples of the kinds of factors subsumed in a fixed effect. Explain how to estimate a fixed effects model with LSDV and de-meaned approaches.

- Section 8.3: Explain why coefficients on variables that do not vary within a unit cannot be estimated in fixed effects models. Explain how these variables are nonetheless controlled for in fixed effects models.

- Section 8.4: Explain a two-way fixed effects model.

- Section 8.5: Explain the logic behind a difference-in-difference estimator. Provide and explain an OLS model that generates a difference-in-difference estimate.

Further Reading

Chapter 15 discusses advanced panel data models. Baltagi (2005) is a more technical survey of panel data methods.

Green, Kim, and Yoon (2001) provide a nice discussion of panel data methods in international relations. Wilson and Butler (2007) reanalyze articles that did not use fixed effects and find results changed, sometimes dramatically.

If we use pooled OLS to analyze panel data sets, we are quite likely to have errors that are correlated within unit in the manner discussed on page 68. This correlation of errors will not cause OLS $\hat{\beta}_1$ estimates to be biased, but it will make the standard OLS equation for the variance of $\hat{\beta}_1$ inappropriate. While fixed effects models typically account for a substantial portion of the correlation of errors, there is also a large literature on techniques to deal with the correlation of errors in panel data and difference-in-difference models. We discuss one portion of this literature when we cover random effects models in Chapter 15. Bertrand, Duflo, and Mullainathan (2004) show that standard error estimates for difference-in-difference estimators can be problematic in the presence of autocorrelated errors if there are multiple periods both before and after the treatment.

Hausman and Taylor (1981) discuss an approach for estimating parameters on time-invariant covariants.

Key Terms

De-meaned approach (255)

Difference-in-difference model (268)

Dyad (266)

Fixed effect (253)

Fixed effects model (253)

Least squares dummy variable (LSDV) approach (254)

One-way fixed effects model (263)

Panel data (247)

Pooled model (249)

Rolling cross section data (271)

Two-way fixed effects model (263)

Computing Corner

Stata

1. To use the LSDV approach to estimate a panel data model, we run an OLS model with dummy variables for each unit.

   (a) Generate dummy variables for each unit:
   `tabulate City, generate(CityDum)`
   This command generates a variable called "CityDum1" that is 1 for observations from the first city listed in "City" and 0 otherwise, a variable called "CityDum2" that is 1 for observations from the second city listed in "City," and so on.

   (b) Estimate the model with the command `regress Y X1 X2 X3 CityDum2 - CityDum50`. The notation of `CityDum2 - CityDum50` tells Stata to include each of the city dummies from CityDum2 to CityDum50. As we discussed in Chapter 7, we need an excluded category. By starting at CityDum2 in our list of dummy variables, we are setting the first city as the excluded reference category.

(c) To use an *F* test to test whether fixed effects are all zero, the unrestricted model is the model with the dummy variables we just estimated. The restricted model is a regression model without the dummy variables (also known as the pooled model):
`regress Y X1 X2 X3.`

2. To use the de-meaned approach to estimate a one-way fixed effects model, type
`xtreg Y X1 X2 X3, fe i(City)`
The subcommand of `, fe` tells Stata to estimate a fixed effects model. The `i(City)` subcommand tells Stata to use the City variable to identify the city for each observation.

3. To estimate a two-way fixed model:

   (a) Create dummy variables for years:
   `tabulate Year, gen(Yr)`
   This command generates a variable called "Yr1" that is 1 for observations in the first year and 0 otherwise, a variable called "Yr2" that is 1 for observations in the second year and 0 otherwise, and so on.

   (b) Run Stata's built-in, one-way fixed effects model and also include the dummies for the years:
   `xtreg Y X1 X2 X3 Yr2-Yr10, fe i(City)`
   where `Yr2-Yr10` is a shortcut way of including every Yr variable from Yr2 to Yr10.

4. There are several ways to implement difference-in-difference models.

   (a) To implement a basic difference-in-difference model, type `reg Y Treat After TreatAfter X2` where *Treat* indicates membership in treatment group, *After* indicates the after period, *TreatAfter* is the interaction of the two variables, and *X2* is one (or more) control variables.

   (b) To implement a panel data version of a difference-in-difference model, type `xtreg Y TreatAfter X2 Yr2-Yr10, fe i(City)`.

   (c) To plot the basic difference-in-difference results, plot separate fitted lines for the treated and untreated groups:
   `graph twoway (lfit Y After if Treat ==0) (lfit Y After if Treat ==1).`

R

1. To use the LSDV approach to estimate a panel data model, we run an OLS model with dummy variables for each unit.

   (a) It's possible to name and include dummy variables for every unit, but doing this can be a colossal pain when we have lots of units. It is usually easiest to use the `factor` command, which will automatically include dummy variables for each unit. The code is `lm(Y ~ X1 + factor(unit))`. This command will estimate a model in which there is a dummy variable for every unique value unit indicated in the *unit* variable. For example, if our data looked like Table 8.2, including a `factor(city)` term in the regression code would lead to the inclusion of dummy variables for each city.

   (b) To implement an F test on the hypothesis that all fixed effects (both unit and time) are zero, the unrestricted equation is the full model and the restricted equation is the model with no fixed effects.
   `Unrestricted = lm(Y ~ X1 + factor(unit)+ factor (time))`
   `Restricted = lm(Y ~ X1)`
   Go back to page 238 for more details on how to implement an F test in R.

2. To estimate a one-way fixed effects model by means of the de-meaned approach, use one of several add-on packages that automate the steps in panel data analysis. We discussed how to install an R package in Chapter 3 on page 85. For fixed effects models, we can use the `plm` command from the "plm" package.

   (a) Install the package by typing `install.packages("plm")`. Once installed on a computer, the package can be brought into R's memory with the `library(plm)` command.

   (b) The `plm` command works like the `lm` command. We indicate the dependent variable and the independent variables for the main equation. We need to indicate what the units are with the `index=c("city", "year")` command. These are the variable names that indicate your units and time variables, which will vary depending on the data set. Put all your variables into a *data frame* and then refer to that data frame in the `plm` command.[12] For a one-way fixed effects model, include `model="within"`.

```
library(plm)
All.data = data.frame(Y, X1, X2, city, time)
plm(Y ~ X1 + X2, data=All.data, index=c("city"),
model="within")
```

3. To estimate a two-way fixed effects model, we have two options.

   (a) We can simply include time dummies as covariates in a one-way fixed effects model.
   ```
   plm(Y ~ X1 + X2 + factor(year), data=All.data,
   index=c("city"), model="within")
   ```

   (b) We can use the `plm` command and indicate the unit and time variables with the `index=c("city", "year")` command. These are the variable names that indicate your units and time variables, which will vary depending on your data set. We also need to include the subcommand `effect="twoways"`.
   ```
   plm(Y  ~  X1 + X2, data=All.data, index=c("city",
   "year"), model="within", effect="twoways")
   ```

4. There are several ways to implement difference-in-difference models.

   (a) To implement a basic difference-in-difference model, type `lm(Y ~ Treat + After + TreatAfter + X2)`, where *Treat* indicates membership in the treatment group, *After* indicates that the period is the after period, *TreatAfter* is the interaction of the two variables, and *X2* is one (or more) control variables.

   (b) To implement a panel data version of a difference-in-difference model, type
   ```
   lm(Y ~ TreatAfter + factor(Unit)+ factor(Year) + X2).
   ```

   (c) To plot the basic difference-in-difference results, plot separate fitted lines for the treated and untreated groups.
   ```
   plot(After, Y, type="n")
   abline(lm(Y[Treat==0] ~ After[Treat==0]))
   abline(lm(Y[Treat==1] ~ After[Treat==1]))
   ```

---

[12] A data frame is a convenient way to package data in R. Not only can you put variables together in one named object, but you can include text variables like names of countries.

Exercises

1. Researchers have long been interested in the relationship between economic factors and presidential elections. The PresApproval.dta data set includes data on presidential approval polls and unemployment rates by state over a number of years. Table 8.8 lists the variables.

   (a) Use pooled data for all years to estimate a pooled OLS regression explaining presidential approval as a function of state unemployment rate. Report the estimated regression equation and interpret the results.

   (b) Many political observers believe politics in the South are different. Add *South* as an additional independent variable and reestimate the model from part (a). Report the estimated regression equation. Do the results change?

   (c) Reestimate the model from part (b), controlling for state fixed effects by using the de-meaned approach. How does this approach affect the results? What happens to the *South* variable in this model? Why? Does this model control for differences between southern and other states?

   (d) Reestimate the model from part (c) controlling for state fixed effects using the LSDV approach. (Do not include a *South* dummy variable). Compare the coefficients and standard errors for the unemployment variable.

   (e) Estimate a two-way fixed effects model. How does this model affect the results?

2. How do young people respond to economic conditions? Are they more likely to pursue public service when jobs are scarce? To get at this question, we'll analyze data in PeaceCorps.dta, which contains variables

TABLE 8.8 Variables for Presidential Approval Data

Variable name	Description
State	State name
StCode	State numeric ID
Year	Year
PresApprov	Percent positive presidential approval
UnemPct	State unemployment rate
South	Southern state (1 = yes, 0 = no)

TABLE 8.9 **Variables for Peace Corps Data**

Variable name	Description
state	State name
year	Year
stateshort	First three letters of state name (for labeling scatterplot)
appspc	Applications to the Peace Corps from each state per capita
unemployrate	State unemployment rate

on state economies and applications to the Peace Corps. Table 8.9 lists the variables.

(a) Before looking at the data, what relationship do you hypothesize between these two variables? Explain your hypothesis.

(b) Run a pooled regression of Peace Corps applicants per capita on the state unemployment rate and year dummies. Describe and critique the results.

(c) Plot the relationship between the state economy and Peace Corps applications. Does any single state stick out? How may this outlier affect the estimate on unemployment rate in the pooled regression in part (b)? Create a scatterplot without the unusual state and comment briefly on the difference from the scatterplot with all observations.

(d) Run the pooled model from part (b) without the outlier. Comment briefly on the results.

(e) Use the LSDV approach to run a two-way fixed effects model without the outlier. Do your results change from the pooled analysis? Which results are preferable?

(f) Run a two-way fixed effects model without the outlier; use the fixed effects command in Stata or R. Compare to the LSDV results.

3. We wish to better understand the factors that contribute to a student's favorable overall evaluation of an instructor. The data set TeachingEval_-HW.dta contains average faculty evaluation scores, class size, a dummy variable indicating required courses, and the percent of grades that were A– and above. Table 8.10 lists the variables.

(a) Estimate a model ignoring the panel structure of the data. Use overall evaluation of the instructor as the dependent variable and the

TABLE 8.10 Variables for Instructor Evaluation Data

Variable name	Description
Eval	Average course evaluation on a 5-point scale
Apct	Percent of students who receive an A or A- in the course
Enrollment	Number of students in the course
Required	A dummy variable indicating if the course was required
InstrID	A unique identifying number for each instructor
CourseID	A unique identifying number for each course
Year	Academic year

   class size, required, and grades variables as independent variables.
   Report and briefly describe the results.

   (b) Explain what a fixed effect for each of the following would control
   for: instructor, course, and year.

   (c) Use the equation from part (a) to estimate a model that includes
   a fixed effect for instructor. Report your results and explain any
   differences from part (a).

   (d) Now estimate a two-way fixed effects model with year as an
   additional fixed effect. Report and briefly describe your results.

4. In 1993 Georgia initiated a HOPE scholarship program to let state
   residents who had at least a B average in high school attend public college
   in Georgia for free. The program is not need based. Did the program
   increase college enrollment? Or did it simply transfer funds to families
   who would have sent their children to college anyway? Dynarski (2000)
   used data on young people in Georgia and neighboring states to assess this
   question.[13] Table 8.11 lists the variables.

   (a) Run a basic difference-in-difference model. What is the effect of the
   program?

   (b) Calculate the percentage of people in the sample in college from
   the following four groups: (i) Before 1993/non-Georgia, (ii) Before
   1993/Georgia, (iii) After 1992/non-Georgia, (iv) After 1992/Geor-
   gia. First, use the mean function (e.g., in Stata use `mean Y if
   X1 == 0 & X2 == 0`). Second, use the coefficients from the OLS
   output in part (a).

---

[13] For simplicity we will not use the sample weights used by Dynarski. The results are stronger,
however, when these sample weights are used.

TABLE 8.11 Variables for the HOPE Scholarship Data

Variable name	Description
InCollege	A dummy variable equal to 1 if the individual is in college
AfterGeorgia	A dummy variable equal to 1 for Georgia residents after 1992
Georgia	A dummy variable equal to 1 if the individual is a Georgia resident
After	A dummy variable equal to 1 for observations after 1992
Age	Age
Age18	A dummy variable equal to 1 if the individual is 18 years old
Black	A dummy variable equal to 1 if the individual is African-American
StateCode	State codes
Year	Year of observation
Weight	Weight used in Dynarski (2000)

(c) Graph the fitted lines for the Georgia group and non-Georgia samples.

(d) Use panel data formulation for a difference-in-difference model to control for all year and state effects.

(e) Add covariates for 18-year-olds and African-Americans to the panel data formulation. What is the effect of the HOPE program?

(f) The way the program was designed, Georgia high school graduates with a B or higher average and annual family income over $50,000 could qualify for HOPE by filling out a simple one-page form. Those with lower income were required to apply for federal aid with a complex four-page form and had any federal aid deducted from their HOPE scholarship. Run separate basic difference-in-difference models for these two groups and comment on the substantive implication of the results.

5. Table 8.12 describes variables in TexasSchools.dta, a data set covering 1,020 Texas school board districts and teachers' salaries in them from 2003 to 2009. Anzia (2012) used this data to estimate the effect of election timing on teachers' salaries in Texas. Some believe that teachers will be paid more when school board members are elected in "off-cycle" elections, when only school board members are up for election. The idea is that teachers and their allies will mobilize for these elections, while many other citizens will tune out. In this view, teachers' salaries will be relatively lower when school boards are elected in "on-cycle" elections in which people also vote for state and national offices; turnout will be

TABLE 8.12 **Variables for the Texas School Board Data**

Variable name	Description
LnAvgSalary	The average salary of teachers in the district, adjusted for inflation and logged
OnCycle	A dummy variable which equals one for districts where school boards were elected "on-cycle" (i.e., they were elected at same time people were voting on other offices). A zero indicates that the school board was elected "off-cycle," meaning that school board members, were elected in a separate election.
CycleSwitch	A dummy variable indicating that the district switched from off-cycle to on-cycle elections starting in 2007
AfterSwitch	A dummy variable indicating year > 2006
AfterCycleSwitch	*CycleSwitch×AfterSwitch*, an interaction of the cycle switch variable (the treatment) of the after switch variable (indicates post-treatment time periods)
DistNumber	District ID number
Year	Year

higher in on-cycle elections, and teachers and teachers unions will have relatively less influence.

From 2003 to 2006 all districts in the sample elected their school board members off-cycle. A change in state policies in 2006 led some, but not all, districts to elect their school board members on-cycle from 2007 onward. The districts that switched then stayed switched for the period 2007–2009, and no other district switched.

(a) Estimate the pooled model of $LnAvgSalary_{it} = \beta_0 + \beta_1 OnCycle_{it} + \epsilon_{it}$. Discuss whether there is potential bias here. Consider in particular the possibility that teachers unions are most able to get off-cycle elections in districts where they are strongest. Could such a situation create bias? Explain why or why not.

(b) Estimate a standard difference-in-difference model using the fact that a subset of districts switched their school board elections to "on-cycle" in 2007 and all subsequent elections in the data set. No one else switched at any other time. Before 2007 all districts used "off-cycle" elections. Explain the results. What is the effect of election time on teachers' salaries? Can we say anything about the types of districts that switched? Can we say anything about salaries in all districts in the years after the switch?

(c) Run a one-way fixed effects model in which the fixed effect relates to individual school districts. Interpret the results and explain whether this model accounts for time trends that could affect all districts.

(d) Now use a two-way fixed effects model to estimate a difference-in-difference approach. Interpret the results and explain whether this model accounts for (i) differences in preexisting attributes of the switcher districts and nonswitcher districts and (ii) differences in the post-switch years that affected all districts regardless of whether they switched.

(e) Suppose that we tried to estimate the two-way fixed effects model on only the last three years of the data (2007, 2008, and 2009). Would we be able to estimate the effect of *OnCycle* for this subset of the data? Why or why not?

6. This problem uses a panel version of the data set described in Chapter 5 (page 163) to analyze the effect of cell phone and texting bans on traffic fatalities. Use deaths per mile as the dependent variable because this variable accounts for the pattern we saw earlier that miles driven is a strong predictor of the number of fatalities. Table 8.13 describes the variables in the data set Cellphone_panel_homework.dta; it covers all states plus Washington, DC, from 2006 to 2012.

(a) Estimate a pooled OLS model with deaths per mile as the dependent variable and cell phone ban and text ban as the two independent variables. Briefly interpret the results.

(b) Describe a possible state fixed effect that could cause endogeneity and bias in the model from part (a).

(c) Estimate a one-way fixed effects model that controls for state-level fixed effects. Include deaths per mile as the dependent variable and cell phone ban and text ban as the two independent variables. Does

TABLE 8.13 **Variables in the Cell Phones and Traffic Deaths Data**

Variable name	Description
year	Year
State	State name
state_numeric	State name (numeric representation of state)
population	Population within a state
DeathsPerBillionMiles	Deaths per billion miles driven in state
cell_ban	Coded 1 if handheld cell phone while driving ban is in effect; 0 otherwise
text_ban	Coded 1 if texting while driving ban is in effect; 0 otherwise
cell_per10thous_pop	Number of cell phone subscriptions per 10,000 people in state
urban_percent	Percent of state residents living in urban areas

the coefficient on cell phone ban change in the manner you would expect based on your answer from part (a)?

(d) Describe a possible year fixed effect that could cause endogeneity and bias in the fixed effects model in part (c).

(e) Use the hybrid de-meaned approach discussed in the chapter to estimate a two-way fixed effects model. Include deaths per mile as the dependent variable and cell phone ban and text ban as the two independent variables. Does the coefficient on cell phone ban change in the manner you would expect based on your answer in part (d)?

(f) The model in part (e) is somewhat sparse with regard to control variables. Estimate a two-way fixed effects model that includes control variables for cell phones per 10,000 people and percent urban. Briefly describe changes in inference about the effect of cell phone and text bans.

(g) Estimate the same two-way fixed effects model by using the least squares dummy variable (LSDV) approach. Compare the coefficient and t statistic on the cell phone variable to the results from part (f).

(h) Based on the LSDV results, identify states with large positive and negative fixed effects. Explain what these mean (being sure to note the excluded category) and speculate about how the positive and negative fixed effect states differ. (It is helpful to connect the state number to state name; in Stata, do this with the command `list state state_numeric if year ==2012`.)

Instrumental Variables: Using Exogenous Variation to Fight Endogeneity

9

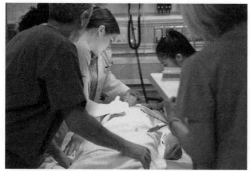

Medicaid is the U.S. government health insurance program for low-income people. Does it save lives? If so, how many? These are important but challenging questions. The challenge is, you guessed it, endogeneity. People enrolled in Medicaid differ from those not enrolled, not only in terms of income but also on many other factors. Some factors such as age, race, and gender are fairly easy to measure. Other factors, such as health, lifestyle, wealth, and medical knowledge, are difficult to measure, however.

The danger is that these unmeasured factors may be correlated with enrollment in Medicaid. Who is more likely to enroll: a poor sick person or a poor healthy person? Probably the sick people are more likely to be enrolled, which means that comparing health outcomes of enrollees and non-enrollees could show differences not only due to Medicaid, but also due to one or more underlying conditions that preceded the decision to enroll in Medicaid.

We must therefore be cautious—or clever—when we analyze Medicaid. This chapter goes with clever. We show how we can use *instrumental variables* to navigate around endogeneity. This approach is relatively advanced, but its logic is pretty simple. The idea is to find exogenous variation in X and use only that variation to estimate the effect of X on Y. For the Medicaid question, we want to look for some variation in enrollment in the program that is unrelated to the health outcomes of individuals. One way is to find a factor that changed enrollment but was unrelated to health or lifestyle or any other factor that affects the health outcome variable. In this chapter we show how to incorporate instrumental variables using a technique called **two-stage least squares (2SLS)**. In Chapter 10 we'll use 2SLS to analyze randomized experiments in which not everyone complies with assigned treatment.

▶ **two-stage least squares (2SLS)** Uses exogenous variation in X to estimate the effect of X on Y.

Like many powerful tools, 2SLS can be a bit dangerous. We won't cut off a finger using it, but if we aren't careful we could end up with worse estimates than we would have produced with OLS. And, also like many powerful tools, the approach is not cheap. In this case, the cost is that the estimates produced by 2SLS are typically quite a bit less precise than OLS estimates.

In this chapter we provide the instruction manual for this tool. Section 9.1 presents an example in which an instrumental variables approach proves useful. Section 9.2 gives the basics for the 2SLS model. Section 9.3 discusses what to do when we have multiple instruments. Section 9.4 reveals what happens to 2SLS estimates when the instruments are flawed. Section 9.5 explains why 2SLS estimates tend to be less precise than OLS estimates. Section 9.6 applies 2SLS tools to so-called *simultaneous equation models* in which X causes Y, but Y also causes X.

9.1 2SLS Example

Before we work through the steps of the 2SLS approach, we introduce the logic of 2SLS with an example about police and crime by *Freakonomics* author Steve Levitt (1997, 2002). Having seen the question of whether police reduce crime before (on page 249), we know full well that an observational study almost certainly suffers from endogeneity. Why? It is highly likely that components in the error term that cause crime—factors such as drug use, gang warfare, and demographic changes—also are related to how many police officers a city has. After all, it is just common sense that communities that expect more crime hire more police. Equation 9.1 shows the basic model:

$$Crime_{it} = \beta_0 + \beta_1 Police_{i,t-1} + \epsilon_{it} \tag{9.1}$$

Levitt's (2002) idea is that while some police are hired for endogenous reasons (city leaders expect more crime, so hire more police), other police are hired for exogenous reasons (the city simply has more money to spend). In particular, Levitt argues that the number of firefighters in a city reflects voters' tastes for public services, union power, and perhaps political patronage. These factors also partially predict the size of the police force and are not directly related to crime. In other words, to the extent that changes in the number of firefighters predict changes in police numbers, those changes in the numerical strength of a police force are exogenous because they have nothing to do with crime. The idea, then, is to isolate the portion of changes in the police force associated with changes in the number of firefighters and see if crime went down (or up) in relation to those changes.

We'll work through the exact steps of the process soon. For now we can get a sense of how instrumental variables can matter by looking at Levitt's results. The left column of results in Table 9.1 shows the coefficient on police estimated

TABLE 9.1 Levitt (2002) Results on Effect of Police Officers on Violent Crime

	OLS with year dummies only	OLS with year and city dummies	2SLS
Lagged police officers per capita (logged)	0.562*	−0.076	−0.435
	(0.056)	(0.061)	(0.231)
	[*t* = 10.04]	[*t* = 1.25]	[*t* = 1.88]

Standard errors in parentheses.

* *indicates significance at p < 0.05, two-tailed.*

All models include controls for prison population, per capita income, abortion, city size, and racial demographics.

Results from Levitt (2002).

via a standard OLS estimation of Equation 9.1 based on an OLS analysis with covariates and year dummy variables but no city fixed effects. The coefficient is positive and significant, implying that police *cause* crime. Yikes!

However, we're pretty sure that endogeneity distorts simple OLS results in this context. The second column shows that the results change dramatically when city fixed effects are included. As discussed in Chapter 8, fixed effects account for the tendency of cities with chronically high crime to also have larger police forces. The estimated effect of police is negative, but small and statistically insignificant at usual levels.

The third column shows the results obtained when the instrumental variables technique is used. The coefficient on police is negative and almost statistically significant. This result differs dramatically from the OLS result without city fixed effects and nontrivially from the fixed effects results.

Levitt's analysis essentially treats changes in firefighters as a kind of experiment. He estimates the number of police that cities add when they add firefighters and assesses whether crime changed in conjunction with these particular changes in police. Levitt is using the firefighter variable as an **instrumental variable**, a variable that explains the endogenous independent variable of interest (which in this case is the log of the number of police per capita) but does not directly explain the dependent variable (which in this case is violent crimes per capita).

The example also highlights some limits to instrumental variables methods. First, the increase in police associated with changes in firefighters may not really be exogenous. That is, can we be sure that the firefighter variable is truly independent of the error term in Equation 9.1? It is possible, for example, that reelection-minded political leaders provide other public services when they boost the number of firefighters—goodies such as tax cuts, roads, and new stadiums—and that these policy choices may affect crime (perhaps by improving economic growth). In that case, we worry that our exogenous bump in police is actually associated with factors that also affect crime, and that those factors may be in the error term. Therefore, as we develop the logic of instrumental

▶ **instrumental variable** Explains the endogenous independent variable of interest but does not directly explain the dependent variable.

variables, we also spend a lot of time worrying about the exogeneity of our instruments.

A second concern is that we may reasonably worry that changes in firefighters do not account for much of the variation in police forces. In that case, the exogenous change we are measuring will be modest and may lead to imprecise estimates. We see this in Table 9.1, where the standard error based on an instrumental variables approach is more than four times larger than the standard errors in the other models.

REMEMBER THIS

1. An instrumental variable is a variable that explains the endogenous independent variable of interest but does not directly explain the dependent variable.

2. When we use the instrumental variables approach, we focus on changes in Y due to the changes in X that are attributable to changes in the instrumental variable.

3. Major challenges associated with using instrumental variables include the following.

   (a) It is often hard to find an appropriate instrumental variable that is exogenous.

   (b) Estimates based on instrumental variables are often imprecise.

9.2 Two-Stage Least Squares (2SLS)

We implement the instrumental variables approach with the two-stage least squares (2SLS) approach. As you can see from the name, it's still a least squares approach, meaning that the underlying calculations are still based on minimizing the sum of squared residuals as in OLS. The new element is that 2SLS has—you guessed it—two stages, unlike standard OLS, which only has one stage.

In this section we distinguish endogenous and instrumental variables, explain the two stages of 2SLS, discuss the characteristics of good instrumental variables, and describe the challenges of finding good instrumental variables.

Endogenous and instrumental variables

The main equation in 2SLS is the same as in OLS:

$$Y_i = \beta_0 + \beta_1 X_{1i} + \beta_2 X_{2i} + \epsilon_i \tag{9.2}$$

where Y_i is our dependent variable, X_{1i} is our main variable of interest, and X_{2i} is a control variables (and we could easily add additional control variables).

The difference is that X_{1i} is an endogenous variable, which means that it is correlated with the error term. Our goal with 2SLS is to replace the endogenous X_{1i} with a different variable that measures only the portion of X_{1i} that is not related to the error term in the main equation.

We model X_{1i} as

$$X_{1i} = \gamma_0 + \gamma_1 Z_i + \gamma_2 X_{2i} + v_i \tag{9.3}$$

where Z_i is a new variable we are adding to the analysis, X_{2i} is the control variable in Equation 9.2, the γ's are coefficients that determine how well Z_i and X_{2i} explain X_{1i}, and v_i is an error term. (Recall that γ is the Greek letter gamma and v is the Greek letter nu.) We call Z our instrumental variable; this variable is the star of this chapter, hands down. It is the variable Z that is the source of our exogenous variation in X_{1i}.

In Levitt's police and crime example, "police officers per capita" is the endogenous variable (X_1 in our notation) and "firefighters" is the instrumental variable (Z in our notation). The instrumental variable is the variable that causes the endogenous variable to change for reasons unrelated to the error time. In other words, in Levitt's model, Z (firefighters) explains X_{1i} (police per capita) but is not correlated with the error term in the equation explaining Y (crime).

There are, not surprisingly, two steps to 2SLS. First, we generate fitted values of X, which we call (as is our habit) $\hat{X}_{1i}$, by estimating $\hat{\gamma}$ values based on Equation 9.3 and use them in the following equation:

$$\hat{X}_{1i} = \hat{\gamma}_0 + \hat{\gamma}_1 Z_i + \hat{\gamma}_2 X_{2i}$$

Notice that $\hat{X}_{1i}$ is a function only of Z, X_2, and the γ's. That fact has important implications for what we are trying to do. The error term when X_{1i} is the dependent variable is v_i; it is almost certainly correlated with ϵ_i, the error term in the Y_i equation. That is, drug use and criminal history are likely to affect both the number of police (X_1) and crime (Y). This means the actual value of X_1 is correlated with ϵ; the *fitted* value $\hat{X}_{1i}$, on the other hand, is *only* a function of Z, X_2, and the γ's. So even though police forces in reality may be ebbing and flowing as related to drug use and other factors in the error term of Equation 9.2, the fitted value $\hat{X}_{1i}$ will not change. Our $\hat{X}_{1i}$ will ebb and flow only with changes in Z and X_2, which means our fitted value of X has been purged of the association between X and ϵ.

All control variables from the second-stage model must be included in the first stage. We want our instrument to explain variation in X_1 over and above any variation that can be explained by the other independent variables.

In the second stage, we estimate our outcome equation, but (key point here) we use $\hat{X}_{1i}$—the fitted value of X_{1i}—rather than the actual value of X_{1i}. In other words, instead of using X_{1i}, which we suspect is endogenous (correlated with ϵ_i), we use the measure of $\hat{X}_{1i}$, which has been purged of X_{1i}'s association with error. Specifically, the second stage of the 2SLS model is

$$Y_i = \beta_0 + \beta_1 \hat{X}_{1i} + \beta_2 X_{2i} + \epsilon_i \tag{9.4}$$

The little hat on $\hat{X}_{1i}$ is a big deal. Once we appreciate why we're using it and how to generate it, 2SLS becomes easy. We are now estimating how much the exogenous variation in X_{1i} affects Y. Notice also that there is no Z in Equation 9.4. By the logic of 2SLS, Z affects Y only indirectly, by affecting X.

Control variables play an important role, just as in OLS. If a factor that affects Y is correlated with Z, we need to include it in the second-stage regression. Otherwise, the instrument may soak up some of the effect of this omitted factor rather than merely exogenous variation in X_1. For example, suppose that cities in the South started facing more arson and hence hired more firefighters. In that case, Levitt's firefighter instrument for police officers will also contain variation due to region. If we do not control for region in the second-stage regression, some of the region effect may work its way through the instrument, potentially creating a bias.

Actual estimation via 2SLS is a bit more involved than simply running OLS with $\hat{X}_1$ because $\hat{X}_{1i}$ is itself an estimate, and the standard errors need to be adjusted to account for this. In practice, though, statistical packages do this adjustment automatically with their 2SLS commands.[1]

Two characteristics of good instruments

The success of 2SLS hinges on the instrument. Good instruments satisfy two conditions. These conditions are conceptually simple but, in practice, they are hard to meet.

First, an instrument must actually explain the endogenous variable of interest. That is, our endogenous variable, X_1, must vary in relation to our instrument, Z. This is the **inclusion condition**: a condition that Z needs to exert a meaningful effect in the first-stage equation that explains X_{1i}. In Levitt's police example, police forces must actually rise and fall as firefighter numbers change. This claim is plausible but not guaranteed. We can easily check this condition for any potential instrument, Z, by estimating the first-stage model of the form of Equation 9.3. If the coefficient on Z is statistically significant, we have satisfied this condition. For reasons we explain later (in Sections 9.4 and 9.5), the more Z_i explains X_{1i}, the better.

Second, an instrument must be uncorrelated with the error term in the main equation, Equation 9.2. This condition is the **exclusion condition** because it implies that, since the instrument exerts no direct effect on Y, it can be excluded from the second-stage equation. In other words, by saying that an instrument is uncorrelated with ϵ, we are saying that it reflects no part of the error term in the main equation hence can be excluded from it. Recall the various factors in the error term in a crime model: drug use, gang warfare, demographic changes, and

> **inclusion condition**
> For 2SLS, a condition that the instrument exert a meaningful effect in the first-stage equation in which the endogenous variable is the dependent variable.

> **exclusion condition**
> For 2SLS, a condition that the instrument exert no direct effect in the second-stage equation. This condition cannot be tested empirically.

[1] When there is a single endogenous independent variable and a single instrument, the 2SLS estimator reduces to $\hat{\beta}_1 = \frac{\text{cov}(Z,Y)}{\text{cov}(Z,X)}$ (Murnane and Willett 2011, 229). While it may be computationally simpler to use this ratio of covariances to estimate $\hat{\beta}_1$, it becomes harder to see the intuition about exogenous variation if we do so. In addition, the 2SLS estimator is more general: it allows for multiple independent variables and instruments.

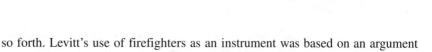

so forth. Levitt's use of firefighters as an instrument was based on an argument that the number of firefighters in a city was uncorrelated with these elements of the error term.

Unfortunately, there is no direct test of whether Z is uncorrelated with ϵ. The whole point of the error term is that it covers unmeasured factors. We simply cannot directly observe whether Z is correlated with these unmeasured factors.

A natural instinct is to try to test the exclusion condition by including Z directly in the second stage, but this won't work. If Z is a good instrument, it will explain X_{1i}, which in turn will affect Y. We will observe some effect of Z on Y, which will be the effect of Z on X_{1i}, which in turn can have an effect on Y. Instead, the discussion of the exclusion condition will need to be primarily conceptual rather than statistical. We will need to justify our assertion that Z does not affect Y directly, without statistical analysis. Yes, that's a bummer and, frankly, a pretty weird position to be in for a statistical analyst. Life is like that sometimes.[2]

Figure 9.1 illustrates the two conditions necessary for Z to be an appropriate instrument. The inclusion condition is that Z explains X. We test this simply by regressing X on Z. The exclusion restriction is that Z does not cause Y. The exclusion condition is tricky to test because if the inclusion condition holds, Z causes X, which in turn may cause Y. In this case there would be an observed relationship between Z and Y but only via Z's effect on X. Hence we can't test the exclusion restriction statistically and must make substantive arguments about why we believe Z has no direct effect on Y.

Finding a good instrument is hard

Finding an instrument that satisfies the exclusion condition is really hard with observational data. Economists Josh Angrist and Alan Krueger provided a famous example in a 1991 study of the effect of education on wages. Because the personal traits that lead a person to get more education (smarts, diligence, family wealth) are often the traits that lead to financial success, education is very likely to be endogenous when one is explaining wages. Therefore the researchers sought an instrument for education, a variable that would explain years of schooling but have nothing to do with wages. They identified a very clever possibility: quarter of birth.

Although this idea seems crazy at first, it actually makes sense. Quarter of birth satisfies the inclusion condition because how much schooling a person gets depends, in part, on the month the person was born. Most school districts have

---

[2] A test called the Hausman test (or the Durbin-Wu-Hausman test) is sometimes referred to as a test of endogeneity. We should be careful to recognize that this is not a test of the exclusion restriction. Instead, the Hausman test assesses whether X is endogenous. It is not a test of whether Z is exogenous. Hausman derived the test by noting that if Z is exogenous and X is endogenous, then OLS and 2SLS should produce very different $\hat{\beta}$ estimates. If Z is exogenous and X is exogenous, then OLS and 2SLS should produce similar $\hat{\beta}$ estimates. The test involves assessing how different the $\hat{\beta}$ estimates are from OLS and 2SLS. Crucially, we need to assume that Z is exogenous for this test. That's the claim we usually want to test, so the Hausman test of endogeneity is often less valuable than it sounds.

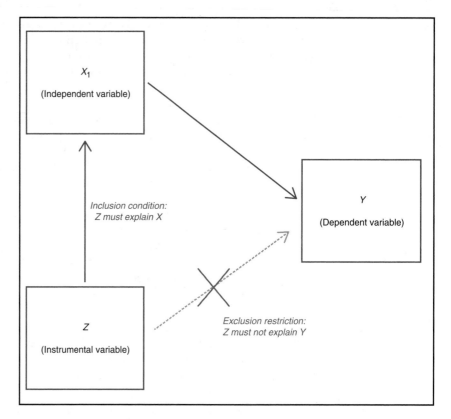

FIGURE 9.1: Conditions for Instrumental Variables

laws that say that young people have to stay in school until they are 16. For a school district that starts kids in school based on their age on September 1, kids born in July would be in eleventh grade when they turn 16, whereas kids born in October (who started a year later) would be only in tenth grade when they turn 16. Hence kids born in July can't legally drop out until they are in the eleventh grade, but kids born in October can drop out in the tenth grade. The effect is not huge, but with a lot of data (and Angrist and Krueger had a lot of data), this effect is statistically significant.

Quarter of birth also seems to satisfy the exclusion condition because birth month doesn't seem to be related to such unmeasured factors that affect salary as smarts, diligence, and family wealth. (Astrologers disagree, by the way.)

However, Bound, Jaeger, and Baker (1995) showed that quarter of birth has been associated with school attendance rates, behavioral difficulties, mental health, performance on tests, schizophrenia, autism, dyslexia, multiple sclerosis, region, and income. [Wealthy families, for example, have fewer babies in the winter (Buckles and Hungerman 2013). Go figure.] That this example may fail the exclusion condition is disappointing: if quarter of birth doesn't satisfy the exclusion condition, it's fair to say a lot of less clever instruments may be in trouble as well. Hence, we should be exercise due caution in using instruments, being sure both to implement the diagnostics discussed next and to test theories with multiple instruments or analytical strategies.

REMEMBER THIS

Two-stage least squares uses exogenous variation in X to estimate the effect of X on Y.

1. In the first stage, the endogenous independent variable is the dependent variable and the instrument, Z, is an independent variable:

$$X_{1i} = \gamma_0 + \gamma_1 Z_i + \gamma_2 X_{2i} + v_i$$

2. In the second stage, $\hat{X}_{1i}$ (the fitted values from the first stage) is an independent variable:

$$Y_i = \beta_0 + \beta_1 \hat{X}_{1i} + \beta_2 X_{2i} + \epsilon_i$$

3. A good instrument, Z, satisfies two conditions:

   - Z must be a statistically significant determinant of X_1. In other words, it needs to be included in the first stage of the 2SLS estimation process.

   - Z must be uncorrelated with the error term in the main equation, which means that Z must not directly influence Y. In other words, an instrument must be properly excluded from the second stage of the 2SLS estimation process. This condition *cannot* be directly assessed statistically.

4. When we use observational data, it is difficult to find an instrument that incontrovertibly satisfies the exclusion condition.

Discussion Questions

1. Some people believe cell phones and platforms like Twitter, which use related technology, have increased social unrest by making it easier to organize protests or acts of violence. Pierskalla and Hollenbach (2013) used data from Africa to test this view. In its most basic form, the model was

$$Violence_i = \beta_0 + \beta_1 Cell\ phone\ coverage_i + \epsilon_i$$

where $Violence_i$ is data on organized violence in city i and $Cell\ phone\ coverage_i$ measures availability of mobile coverage in city i.

(a) Explain why endogeneity may be a concern.

(b) Consider a measure of regulatory quality as an instrument for cell phone coverage. This proposed variable is based on a separate study of telecommunications policy in African countries that found that regulatory quality increased cell phone availability. Explain how to test whether this variable satisfies the inclusion condition.

(c) Does the regulatory quality variable satisfy the exclusion condition? Can we test whether this condition holds?

2. Do political protests affect election results? Consider the following model, which is a simplified version of the analysis presented in Madestam, Shoag, Veuger, and Yanagizawa-Drott (2013):

$$Republican\ vote_i = \beta_0 + \beta_1 Tea\ Party\ protest\ turnout_i + \epsilon_i$$

where *Republican vote$_i$* is the vote for the Republican candidate for Congress in district i in 2010 and *Tea Party protest turnout$_i$* measures the number of people who showed up at Tea Party protests in district i on April 15, 2009, a day of planned protests across the United States.

(a) Explain why endogeneity may be a concern.

(b) Consider local rainfall on April 15, 2009, as an instrument for Tea Party protest turnout. Explain how to test whether the rain variable satisfies the inclusion condition.

(c) Does the local rainfall variable satisfy the exclusion condition? Can we test whether this condition holds?

3. Do economies grow more when their political institutions are better? Consider the following simple model:

$$Economic\ growth_i = \beta_0 + \beta_1 Institutional\ quality_i + \epsilon_i$$

where *Economic growth$_i$* is the growth of country i and *Institutional quality$_i$* is a measure of the quality of governance of country i.

(a) Explain why endogeneity may be a concern.

(b) Acemoglu, Johnson, and Robinson (2001) proposed country-specific mortality rates faced by European soldiers, bishops, and sailors in their countries' colonies in the seventeenth, eighteenth, and nineteenth centuries as an instrument for current institutions. The logic is that European powers were more likely to set up worse institutions in places where the people they sent over kept dying. In these places, the institutions were oriented more toward extracting resources than toward creating a stable, prosperous society. Explain how to test whether the settler mortality variable satisfies the inclusion condition.

(c) Does the settler mortality variable satisfy the exclusion condition? Can we test whether this condition holds?

CASE STUDY   Emergency Care for Newborns

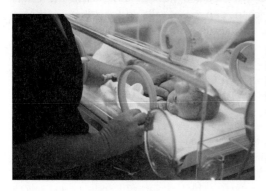

Are neonatal intensive care unit (NICU) facilities effective? These high-tech medical facilities deal with the most at-risk pregnancies and work to keep premature babies alive and healthy. It seems highly likely they help because they attract some of the best people in medicine and have access to the most advanced technology.

A naïve analyst using observational data might not think so, however. Suppose we analyze birth outcomes with the following simple model

$$Death_i = \beta_0 + \beta_1 NICU_i + \epsilon_i \tag{9.5}$$

where *Death* equals 1 if the baby passed away and *NICU* equals 1 if the delivery occurred in a high-level NICU facility.

It is highly likely that the coefficient in this case would be positive. It is beyond doubt that the riskiest births go to the NICU, so clearly the key independent variable (*NICU*) will be correlated with factors associated with a higher risk of death. In other words, we are quite certain endogeneity would bias the coefficient upward. We could, of course, add covariates that indicate risk factors in the pregnancy. Doing so would reduce the endogeneity by taking factors correlated with *NICU* out of the error term and putting them in the equation. We would, nonetheless, still worry that cases that are riskier than usual in reality, but perhaps in ways that are difficult to measure, would still be more likely to end up in NICUs, with the result that endogeneity would be hard to fully purge with multivariate OLS.

Perhaps experiments could be helpful. They are, after all, designed to ensure exogeneity. They are also completely out of bounds in this context. It is shocking to even consider randomly assigning mothers and newborns to NICU and non-NICU facilities. It won't and shouldn't happen.

So are we done? Do we have to accept multivariate OLS as the best we can do? Not quite. Instrumental variables, and 2SLS in particular, give us hope for producing more accurate estimates. What we need is something that explains exogenous variation in use of NICU. That is, can we identify a variable that explains usage of NICUs but is not correlated with pregnancy risk factors?

Lorch, Baiocchi, Ahlberg, and Small (2012) identified a good prospect: distance to a NICU. Specifically, they created a dummy variable we'll call *Near NICU*, which equals 1 for mothers who could get to NICU in at most 10 minutes more than it took to get to a regular hospital. The idea is that mothers who lived closer to a NICU-equipped hospital would be more likely to deliver there. At the same time, distance to a NICU should not directly affect birth outcomes; it should affect birth outcomes only to the extent that it affects utilization of NICUs.

Does this variable satisfy the conditions necessary for an instrument? The first condition is that the instrumental variable explains the endogenous variable, which in this case is whether the mother delivered at a NICU. Table 9.2 shows the results from a multivariate analysis in which the dependent variable was a dummy variable indicating delivery at a NICU and the main independent variable was the variable indicating that the mother lived near a NICU.

Clearly, mothers who live close to a NICU hospital are more likely to deliver at such a hospital. The estimated coefficient on *Near NICU* is highly statistically significant with a *t* statistic exceeding 178. Distance does a very good job explaining NICU usage. Table 9.2 shows coefficients for two other variables as well (the actual analysis has 60 control variables). Gestational age indicates how far along the pregnancy was at the time of delivery. ZIP code poverty indicates the percent of people in a ZIP code living below the poverty line. Both these control variables are significant, with babies that are gestationally older less likely to be delivered in NICU hospitals and women from high-poverty ZIP codes more likely to deliver in NICU hospitals.

The second condition that a good instrument must satisfy is that its variable not be correlated with the error term in the second stage. This is the exclusion condition, which holds that we can justifiably exclude the instrument from the second stage. Certainly it seems highly unlikely that the mere fact of living near a NICU would help a baby unless the mother used that facility. However, living near a NICU might be correlated with a risk factor. What if NICUs tended to be in large urban hospitals in poor areas? In that case, living near one could be correlated with poverty, which in turn might itself be a pregnancy risk factor. Hence it is crucial in this analysis that poverty be a control variable in both the first and second stages. In the first stage, controlling for poverty allows us to identify how much more likely

TABLE 9.2 Influence of Distance on NICU Utilization (First-Stage Results)	
Near NICU	0.040*
	(0.0002)
	[$t = 178.05$]
Gestational age	−0.021*
	(0.0006)
	[$t = 34.30$]
ZIP code poverty	0.623*
	(0.026)
	[$t = 23.83$]
N	192,077

Standard errors in parentheses.

* *indicates significance at $p < 0.05$, two-tailed.*

The model includes a total of 60 controls for pregnancy risk and demographics factors. Results based on Lorch, Baiocchi, Ahlberg, and Small (2012).

TABLE 9.3	Influence of NICU Utilization on Baby Mortality		
	Bivariate OLS	Multivariate OLS	2SLS
NICU utilization	0.0109*	−0.0042*	−0.0058*
	(0.0006)	(0.0006)	(0.0016)
	[$t = 17.68$]	[$t = 6.72$]	[$t = 3.58$]
Gestational age		−0.0141*	−0.0141*
		(0.0002)	(0.0002)
		[$t = 79.87$]	[$t = 78.81$]
ZIP code poverty		0.0113	0.0129
		(0.0076)	(0.0078)
		[$t = 1.48$]	[$t = 1.66$]
N	192,077	192,077	192,077

Standard errors in parentheses.

* *indicates significance at $p < 0.05$, two-tailed.*

The multivariate and 2SLS models include many controls for pregnancy risk and demographic factors. Results based on Lorch, Baiocchi, Ahlberg, and Small (2012).

women are to go to a NICU without ignoring neighborhood poverty. In the second stage, controlling for poverty allows us to control for the effect of this variable to prevent conflating it with the effect of actually going to a NICU-equipped hospital.

Table 9.3 presents results for assessing the effect of giving birth in a NICU hospital. The first column shows results from a bivariate model predicting whether the baby passes away as a function of whether the delivery was in a NICU hospital. The coefficient is positive and highly significant, meaning that babies delivered in NICU hospitals are more likely to die. For the reasons discussed earlier, we would never believe this conclusion due to obvious endogeneity, but it provides a useful baseline to appreciate the pitfalls of failing to account for endogeneity.

The second column shows that adding covariates changes the results considerably: the effect of giving birth in a NICU is now associated with lower chance of death. The effect is statistically significant, with a t statistic of 6.72. Table 9.3 reports results for two covariates, gestational age and ZIP code poverty. The highly statistically significant coefficient on gestational age indicates that babies that have been gestating longer are less likely to die. The effect of ZIP code poverty is not quite statistically significant. The full analysis included many more variables on risk and demographic factors.

We're still worried that the multivariate OLS result could be biased upward (i.e., less negative than it should be) if unmeasured pregnancy risk factors sent women to the NICU hospitals. The results in the 2SLS address this concern by focusing on the exogenous change in utilization of NICU hospitals associated with living near them. The coefficient on living near a NICU continues to be negative, and at −0.0058 it is almost 50 percent greater in magnitude than the multivariate OLS results (in this case, almost 50 percent more negative). This is the coefficient on the fitted value of NICU utilization that is generated by using the coefficients estimated in Table 9.2. The estimated coefficient on NICU utilization is statistically significant, but with a smaller t statistic than multivariate OLS, consistent with the fact that 2SLS results are typically less precise than OLS results.

Review Questions

Table 9.4 provides results on regressions used in a 2SLS analysis of the effect of alcohol consumption on grades. This is from hypothetical data on grades, standardized test scores, and average weekly alcohol consumption from 1,000 undergraduate students at universities in multiple states. The beer tax variable measures the amount of tax on beer in the state in which the student attends university. The test score is the composite SAT score from high school. Grades are measured as grade point average in the student's most recent semester.

1. Identify the first-stage model and the second-stage model. What is the instrument?

2. Is the instrument a good instrument? Why or why not?

3. Is there evidence about the exogeneity of the instrument in the table? Why or why not?

4. What would happen if we included the beer tax variable in the grades model?

5. Do the (hypothetical!) results here present sufficient evidence to argue that alcohol has no effect on grades?

TABLE 9.4 **Regression Results for Models Relating to Drinking and Grades**

	Dependent Variable	
	Drinks per week	Grades
Standardized test score	−0.001*	0.01*
	(0.002)	(0.001)
	[$t = 5.00$]	[$t = 10.00$]
Beer tax	−2.00	
	(1.50)	
	[$t = 1.33$]	
Drinks per week		−1.00
(fitted)		(1.00)
		[$t = 1.00$]
Constant	4.00*	2.00*
	(1.00)	(1.00)
	[$t = 4.00$]	[$t = 2.00$]
N	1,000	1,000
R^2	0.20	0.28

Standard errors in parentheses.

* *indicates significance at $p < 0.05$, two-tailed.*

9.3   Multiple Instruments

Sometimes we have multiple potential instrumental variables that we think predict X but not Y. In this section we explain how to handle multiple instruments and the additional diagnostic tests that become possible when we have more than one instrument.

2SLS with multiple instruments

When we have multiple instruments, we proceed more or less as before but include all instruments in the first stage. So if we had three instruments (Z_1, Z_2, and Z_3), the first stage would be

$$X_{1i} = \gamma_0 + \gamma_1 Z_{1i} + \gamma_2 Z_{2i} + \gamma_3 Z_{3i} + \gamma_4 X_{2i} + v_i \qquad (9.6)$$

If these are all valid instruments, we have multiple sources of exogeneity that could improve the fit in the first stage.

When we have multiple instruments, the best way to assess whether the instruments adequately predict the endogenous variable is to use an F test for the null hypothesis that the coefficients on all instruments in the first stage are zero. For our example, the F test would test $H_0 : \gamma_1 = \gamma_2 = \gamma_3 = 0$. We presented the F test in Chapter 7 (page 229). In this case, rejecting the null would lead us to accept that at least one of the instruments helps explain X_{1i}. We discuss a rule of thumb for this test shortly on page 304.

Overidentification tests

▶ **overidentification test**   A test used for 2SLS models having more than one instrument. The logic of the test is that the estimated coefficient on the endogenous variable in the second-stage equation should be roughly the same when each individual instrument is used alone.

Having multiple instruments also allows us to implement an **overidentification test**. The name of the test comes from the fact that we say that an instrumental variable model is identified if we have an instrument that can explain X without directly influencing Y. When we have more than one instrument, the equation is overidentified; that sounds a bit ominous, like something will explode.[3] Overidentification is actually a good thing. Having multiple instruments allows us to do some additional analysis that will shed light on the performance of the instruments.

The references in this chapter's Further Reading section and the appendix point to a number of formal tests regarding multiple instruments. The tests can get a bit involved, but the core intuition is rather simple. If each instrument is valid—that is, if each satisfies the two conditions for instruments—then using each one alone should produce an unbiased estimate of β_1. Therefore, as an overidentification test, we can simply estimate the 2SLS model with each individual instrument alone. The coefficient estimates should look pretty much the same, given that each instrument alone under these circumstances produces an unbiased estimator. Hence, if each of these models produces coefficients that are

---

[3] Everyone out now! The model is going to blow any minute . . . it's way overidentified!

similar, we can feel pretty confident that each is a decent instrument (or that they all are equally bad, which is the skunk at the garden party for overidentification tests).

If the instruments produce vastly different $\hat{\beta}_1$ coefficient estimates, we have to rethink our instruments. This can happen if one of the instruments violates the exclusion condition. The catch is that we don't know which instrument is the bad one. Suppose $\hat{\beta}_1$ found by using Z_1 as an instrument is very different from $\hat{\beta}_1$ with Z_2 used as an instrument. Is Z_1 a bad instrument? Or is the problem with Z_2? Overidentification tests can't say.

An overidentification test is like having two clocks. If the clocks show different times, we know at least one is wrong, and possibly both. If both clocks show the same time, we know they're either both right or both wrong in same exact way.

Overidentification tests are relatively uncommon, not because they aren't useful but because it's hard to find one good instrument, let alone two or more.

REMEMBER THIS

An instrumental variable is *overidentified* when there are multiple instruments for a single endogenous variable.

1. To estimate a 2SLS model with multiple valid instruments, simply include all of them in the first stage.

2. To use overidentification tests to assess instruments, run 2SLS models separately with each instrumental variable. If the second-stage coefficients on the endogenous variable in question are similar across models, this result is evidence that all the instruments are valid.

9.4   Quasi and Weak Instruments

2SLS estimates are fragile. In this section, we show how they can go bad if Z is correlated with ϵ or if Z performs poorly in the first stage.

Quasi-instrumental variables are not strictly exogenous

As discussed earlier, observational data seldom provide instruments for which we can be sure that the correlation of Z and ϵ is literally zero. Sometimes we will be considering the use of instruments that we believe correlate with ϵ just a little bit or, at least, a lot less than X_1 correlates with ϵ. Such instruments are called **quasi-instruments**.

It can sometimes be useful to estimate a 2SLS model with a quasi-instrument because a bit of correlation between Z and ϵ does not necessarily render 2SLS useless. To see why, let's consider a simple case: one independent variable and one instrument. We examine the probability limit of $\hat{\beta}_1$ because the properties of probability limits are easier to work with than expectations in this context.[4] For reference, we first note that the probability limit for the OLS estimate of $\hat{\beta}_1$ is

$$\text{plim } \hat{\beta}_1^{OLS} = \beta_1 + \text{corr}(X_1, \epsilon)\frac{\sigma_\epsilon}{\sigma_X} \tag{9.7}$$

where plim refers to the probability limit and corr indicates the correlation of the two variables in parentheses. If $\text{corr}(X_1, \epsilon)$ is zero, then the probability limit of $\hat{\beta}_1^{OLS}$ is β_1. That's a good thing! If $\text{corr}(X_1, \epsilon)$ is non-zero, the OLS of $\hat{\beta}_1$ will converge to something other than β_1 as the sample size gets very large. That's not good.

If we use a quasi-instrument to estimate a 2SLS, the probability limit for the 2SLS estimate of $\hat{\beta}_1$ is

$$\text{plim } \hat{\beta}_1^{2SLS} = \beta_1 + \frac{\text{corr}(Z, \epsilon)}{\text{corr}(Z, X_1)}\frac{\sigma_\epsilon}{\sigma_{X_1}} \tag{9.8}$$

If $\text{corr}(Z, \epsilon)$ is zero, then the probability limit of $\hat{\beta}_1^{2SLS}$ is β_1.[5] Another good thing! Otherwise the 2SLS estimate of $\hat{\beta}_1$ will converge to something other than β_1 as the sample size gets very large.

Equation 9.8 has two very different implications. On the one hand, the equation can be grounds for optimism about 2SLS. Comparing the probability limits from the OLS and 2SLS models shows that if there is only a small correlation between Z and ϵ and a high correlation between Z and X_1, then 2SLS will perform better than OLS when the correlation of X and ϵ is large. This can happen when an instrument does a great job predicting X but has a wee bit of correlation with the error in the main equation. In other words, quasi-instruments may help us get estimates that are closer to the true value.

On the other hand, the correlation of the Z and X_1 in the denominator of Equation 9.8 implies that when the instrument does a poor job of explaining X_1, even a small amount of correlation between Z and ϵ can become magnified by virtue of being divided by a very small number. In the education and wages

---

[4] Section 3.5 introduces probability limits, which may be useful here.
[5] The form of this equation is from Wooldridge (2009), based on Bound, Jaeger, and Baker (1995).

example, the month of birth explained so little of the variation in education that the danger was substantial distortion of the 2SLS estimate if even a dash of correlation existed between month of birth and ϵ.

Weak instruments do a poor job of predicting X

▶ **weak instrument**
An instrumental variable that adds little explanatory power to the first-stage regression in a 2SLS analysis.

The possibility that our instrument may have some correlation with ϵ means that with 2SLS, we must be on guard against problems associated with **weak instruments**—those that add little explanatory power to the first-stage regression. Equation 9.8 showed that when we have a weak instrument, a small amount of correlation of the instrument and error term can lead to 2SLS to produce $\hat{\beta}_1$ estimates that diverge substantially from the true value.

Weak instruments create additional problems, as well. Technically, 2SLS produces consistent, but biased, estimates of $\hat{\beta}_1$. This means that even though the 2SLS estimate is converging toward the true value β_1 as the sample gets large, the expected value of the estimate for any given sample will not be β_1. In particular, the expected value of $\hat{\beta}_1$ from 2SLS will be skewed toward the $\hat{\beta}_1$ from OLS. The extent of this bias decreases as the sample gets bigger. This means that in small samples, 2SLS tends to look more like OLS than we would like. This problem worsens as the fit in the first-stage model worsens.

We might be tempted therefore to try to pump up the fit of our first-stage model by including additional instruments. Unfortunately, it's not that simple. The bias of 2SLS associated with small samples also worsens as the number of instruments increases, creating a trade-off between the number of instruments and the explanatory power of the instruments in the first stage. Each additional instrument brings at least a bit more explanatory power, but also a bit more small-sample bias. The details are rather involved; see references discussed in the Further Reading section for more details.

It is therefore important to diagnose weak instruments by looking at how well Z explains X_1 in the first-stage regression. When we use multivariate regression, we'll want to know how much more Z explains X_1 than the other variables in the model. We'll look for large t statistics for the Z variable in the first stage. The typical rule of thumb is that the t statistic should be greater than 3. A rule of thumb for multiple instruments is that the F statistic should be at least 10 for the test of the null hypothesis that the coefficients on all instruments are all zero in the first-stage regression. This rule of thumb is not a statistical test but, rather, a guideline for what to aim for in seeking a first-stage model that fits well.[6]

---

[6] The rule of thumb is from Staiger and Stock (1997). We can, of course, run an F test even when we have only a single instrument. A cool curiosity is that the F statistic in this case will be the square of the t statistic. This means that when we have only a single instrument, we can simply look for a t statistic that is bigger than $\sqrt{10}$, which we approximate (roughly!) by saying the t statistic should be bigger than 3. The appendix provides more information on the F distribution on page 507.

REMEMBER THIS

1. A quasi-instrument is an instrument that is correlated with the error term in the main equation. If the correlation of the quasi-instrument (Z) and the error term (ϵ) is small relative to the correlation of the quasi-instrument and the endogenous variable (X), then as the sample size gets very large, the 2SLS estimate based on Z will converge to something closer to the true value than the OLS estimate.

2. A weak instrument does a poor job of explaining the endogenous variable (X). Weak instruments magnify the problems associated with quasi-instruments and also can cause bias in small samples.

3. All 2SLS analyses should report tests of independent explanatory power of the instrumental variable or variables in first-stage regression. A rule of thumb is that the F statistic should be at least 10 for the hypothesis that the coefficients on all instruments in the first-stage regression are zero.

9.5 Precision of 2SLS

To calculate proper standard errors for 2SLS, we need to account for the fact that the fitted $\hat{X}_1$ values are themselves estimates. Any statistical program worth its salt does this automatically, so we typically will not have to worry about the nitty-gritty of calculating precision for 2SLS.

We should appreciate, however, that standard errors for 2SLS estimates differ in interesting ways from OLS standard errors. In this section we show why they run bigger and how this result is largely related to the fit of the first-stage regression.

The variance of 2SLS estimates is similar to the variance of OLS estimates. Recall from page 147 that the variance of a coefficient estimate in OLS is

$$\text{var}(\hat{\beta}_j) = \frac{\hat{\sigma}^2}{N\text{var}(X_j)(1 - R_j^2)} \tag{9.9}$$

where $\hat{\sigma}^2$ is the variance of ϵ (which is estimated as $\hat{\sigma}^2 = \frac{\sum(Y_i - \hat{Y}_i)^2}{N-k}$) and R_j^2 is the R^2 from a regression of X_j on all the other independent variables ($X_j = \gamma_0 + \gamma_1 X_1 + \gamma_2 X_2 + \cdots$).

For a 2SLS estimate, the variance of the coefficient on the instrumented variable is

$$\text{var}(\hat{\beta}_1^{2SLS}) = \frac{\hat{\sigma}^2}{N\text{var}(\hat{X}_1)(1 - R_{\hat{X}_1^{NoZ}}^2)} \tag{9.10}$$

where $\hat{\sigma}^2 = \frac{\sum(Y_i - \hat{Y}_i)^2}{N-k}$ using fitted values from 2SLS estimation, and $R_{\hat{X}_1^{NoZ}}^2$ is the R^2 from a regression of $\hat{X}_1$ on all the other independent variables ($\hat{X}_1 = \gamma_0 + \gamma_2 X_2 + \cdots$) but not the instrumental variable (we'll return to $R_{\hat{X}_1^{NoZ}}^2$ soon).

As with OLS, variance is lower when there is a good model fit (meaning a low $\hat{\sigma}^2$) and a large sample size (meaning a large N in the denominator).

The new points for the 2SLS variance equation relate to our use of $\hat{X}_{1i}$ instead of X_{1i} in the equation. There are two important implications.

- The denominator of Equation 9.10 contains $\text{var}(\hat{X}_1)$, which is the variance of the fitted value, $\hat{X}_1$ (notice the hat). If the fitted values do not vary much, then $\text{var}(\hat{X}_1)$ will be relatively small. That's a problem because to produce a small variance, this quantity should be big. In other words, we want the fitted values for our endogenous variable to vary a lot. A poor fit in the first-stage regression can lead the fitted values to vary little; a good fit will lead the fitted variables to vary more.

- The $R_{\hat{X}_1^{NoZ}}^2$ term in Equation 9.10 is the R^2 from

$$\hat{X}_{1i} = \pi_0 + \pi_1 X_{2i} + \eta_i \tag{9.11}$$

  where we use π, the Greek letter pi, as coefficients and η, the Greek letter eta (which rhymes with β), to emphasize that this is a new model, different from earlier models. Notice that Z is not in this regression, meaning that the R^2 from it explains the extent to which $\hat{X}_1$ is a function of the other independent variables. If this R^2 is high, $\hat{X}_1$ is explained by X_2, but not by Z, which will push up $\text{var}(\hat{\beta}_{\hat{X}_1}^{2SLS})$.

The point here is not to learn how to calculate standard error estimates by hand. Computer programs do the chore perfectly well. The point is to understand the sources of variance in 2SLS. In particular, it is useful to see the importance of the ability of Z to explain X_1. If Z lacks this ability, our $\hat{\beta}_1^{2SLS}$ estimates will be imprecise.

As for goodness of fit, the conventional R^2 for 2SLS is basically broken. It is possible for it to be negative. If we really need a measure of goodness of fit, the square of the correlation of the fitted values and actual values will do. However, as we discussed when we introduced R^2 on page 71, the validity of the results does not depend on the overall goodness of fit.

REMEMBER THIS

1. Four factors influence the variance of 2SLS $\hat{\beta}_j$ estimates.

   (a) Model fit: The better the model fits, the lower will be $\hat{\sigma}^2$ and $\text{var}(\hat{\beta}_j^{2SLS})$.

   (b) Sample size: The more observations, the lower will be $\text{var}(\hat{\beta}_j^{2SLS})$.

   (c) The overall fit of the first-stage regression: The better the fit of the first-stage model, the higher will be $\text{var}(\hat{X}_1)$ and the lower the $\text{var}(\hat{\beta}_1^{2SLS})$ will be.

   (d) The explanatory power of the instrument in explaining X:

   - If Z is a weak instrument (i.e., if it does a poor job of explaining X_1 when we control for the other X variables), then $R^2_{\hat{X}_1^{NoZ}}$ will be high because $\hat{X}_1$ will depend almost completely on the other independent variables. The result will be a high $\text{var}(\hat{\beta}_1^{2SLS})$.

   - If Z explains X_1 when we control for the other X variables, then $R^2_{\hat{X}_1^{NoZ}}$ will be low, which will lower $\text{var}(\hat{\beta}_1^{2SLS})$.

2. R^2 is not meaningful for 2SLS models.

9.6 Simultaneous Equation Models

▶ **simultaneous equation model** A model in which two variables simultaneously cause each other.

One particular source of endogeneity occurs in **simultaneous equation models** in which X causes Y and Y also causes X. In this section we explain these models, as well as why endogeneity is inherent in them and how to use 2SLS to estimate them.

Endogeneity in simultaneous equation models

Simultaneous causation is funky, but not crazy. Examples abound:

- In equilibrium, price in a competitive market is a function of quantity supplied. Quantity supplied is also a function of price.

- Effective government institutions may spur economic growth. At the same time, strong economic growth may produce effective government institutions.

- Individual views toward the Affordable Care Act ("ObamaCare") may be influenced by what a person thinks of President Obama. At the same time, views of President Obama may be influenced by what a person thinks of the Affordable Care Act.

The labels X and Y don't really work anymore when the variables cause each other because no variable is only an independent variable or only a dependent variable. Therefore we use the following equations to characterize basic model of simultaneous causality:

$$Y_{1i} = \beta_0 + \beta_1 Y_{2i} + \beta_2 W_i + \beta_3 Z_{1i} + \epsilon_{1i} \qquad (9.12)$$

$$Y_{2i} = \gamma_0 + \gamma_1 Y_{1i} + \gamma_2 W_i + \gamma_3 Z_{2i} + \epsilon_{2i} \qquad (9.13)$$

The first dependent variable, Y_1, is a function of Y_2 (the other dependent variable), W (a variable that affects both dependent variables), and Z_1 (a variable that affects only Y_1). The second dependent variable, Y_2, is a function of Y_1 (the other dependent variable), W (a variable that affects both dependent variables), and Z_2 (a variable that affects only Y_2).

Figure 9.2 illustrates the framework characterized by Equations 9.12 and 9.13. Y_1 and Y_2 cause each other. W causes both Y_1 and Y_2 but the Y variables have no effect on W. Z_1 causes *only* Y_1 and Z_2 causes *only* Y_2.

With simultaneity comes endogeneity. Let's consider Y_{2i}, which is an independent variable in Equation 9.12. We know from Equation 9.13 that Y_{2i} is a function of Y_{1i}, which in turn is a function of ϵ_{1i}. Thus Y_{2i} must be correlated with ϵ_{1i} and therefore we have endogeneity in Equation 9.12 because an independent variable is correlated with the error. The same reasoning applies for Y_{1i} in Equation 9.13.

Simultaneous equations are a bit mind-twisting at first. It really helps to work through the logic for ourselves. Consider the classic market equilibrium case in which price depends on quantity supplied and vice versa. Suppose we look only at price as a function of quantity supplied. Because quantity supplied depends on price, such a model is really looking at price as a function of something (quantity supplied) that is itself a function of price. Of course, quantity supplied will explain price—it is determined in part by price.

As a practical matter, the approach to estimating simultaneous equation models is quite similar to what we did for instrumental variable models. Only now we have two equations, so we'll do 2SLS twice. We just need to make sure, for reasons we describe shortly, that our first-stage regression does not include the other endogenous variable.

Let's say we're more interested in the Y_1 equation; the logic goes through in the same way for both equations, of course.

In this case, we want to estimate Y_1 as a function of Y_2, W, and Z_1. Because Y_2 is the endogenous variable, we'll want to find an instrument for it with a variable that predicts Y_2 but does not predict Y_1. We have such a variable in this case. It is Z_2, which is in the Y_2 equation but not the Y_1 equation.

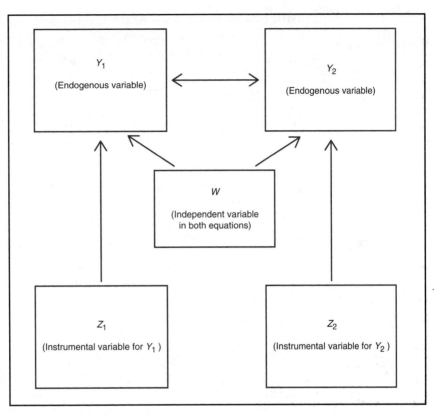

FIGURE 9.2: Simultaneous Equation Model

Using 2SLS for simultaneous equation models

The tricky thing is that Y_2 is a function of Y_1. If we were to run a first-stage model for Y_2 and to include Y_1 and then put the fitted value into the equation for Y_1, we would have a variable that is a function of Y_1 explaining Y_1. Not cool. Instead, we work with a **reduced form equation** for Y_2. In a reduced form equation, Y_1 is only a function of the nonendogenous variables (which are the W and Z variables, not the Y variables). For this reason, the first-stage regression will be

> ▶ **reduced form equation** In a reduced form equation Y_1 is only a function of the nonendogenous variables (which are the X and Z variables, not the Y variables).

$$Y_{2i} = \pi_0 + \pi_1 W_i + \pi_2 Z_{1i} + \pi_3 Z_{2i} + \epsilon_i \qquad (9.14)$$

We use the Greek letter π to indicate our coefficients because they will differ from the coefficients in Equation 9.13, since Equation 9.14 does not include Y_1. We show in the appendix (page 543) how the reduced form relates to Equations 9.12 and 9.13.

The second-stage regression will be

$$Y_{1i} = \beta_0 + \beta_1 \hat{Y}_{2i} + \beta_2 W_i + \beta_3 Z_{1i} + \epsilon_{1i} \qquad (9.15)$$

where $\hat{Y}_{2i}$ is the fitted value from the first-stage regression (Equation 9.14).

Identification in simultaneous equation models

▶ **identified** A
statistical model is
identified on the basis of
assumptions that allow
us to estimate the
model.

For simultaneous equation models to work, they must to be **identified**; that is, we need certain assumptions in order to be able to estimate the model. For 2SLS with one equation, we need at least one instrument that satisfies both the inclusion and exclusion conditions. When we have two equations, we need at least one instrument for each equation. To estimate both equations here, we need at least one variable that belongs in Equation 9.12 but not in Equation 9.13 (which is Z_1 in our notation) and at least one variable that belongs in Equation 9.13 but not in Equation 9.12 (which is Z_2 in our notation).

Happily, we can identify equations separately. So even if we don't have an instrument for each equation, we can nonetheless plow ahead with the equation for which we do have an instrument. So if we have only a variable that works in the second equation and not in the first equation, we can estimate the first equation (because the instrument allows us to estimate a fitted value for the endogenous variable in the first equation). If we have only a variable that works in the first equation and not in the second equation, we can estimate the second equation (because the instrument allows us to estimate a fitted value for the endogenous variable in the second equation).

In fact, we can view the police and crime example discussed in Section 9.1 as a simultaneous equation model, with police and crime determining each other simultaneously. To estimate the effect of police on crime, Levitt needed an instrument that predicted police but not crime. He argued that his firefighter variable fit the bill and then used that instrument in a first-stage model for predicting police forces, generating a fitted value of police that he then used in the model for predicting crime. We discussed this model as a single equation, but the analysis would be unchanged if we viewed it as a single equation of a simultaneous equation system.

REMEMBER THIS

We can use instrumental variables to estimate coefficients for the following simultaneous equation model:

$$Y_{1i} = \beta_0 + \beta_1 Y_{2i} + \beta_2 W_i + \beta_3 Z_{1i} + \epsilon_{1i}$$
$$Y_{2i} = \gamma_0 + \gamma_1 Y_{1i} + \gamma_2 W_i + \gamma_3 Z_{2i} + \epsilon_{2i}$$

1. Use the following steps to estimate the coefficients in the first equation.

   • In the first stage, we estimate a model in which the endogenous variable is the dependent variable and all W and Z variables are the independent variables. Importantly, the other endogenous variable (Y_1) is not included in this first stage:

   $$Y_{2i} = \pi_0 + \pi_1 W_i + \pi_2 Z_{1i} + \pi_3 Z_{2i} + v_i$$

- In the second stage, we estimate a model in which the fitted values from the first stage, $\hat{Y}_{2i}$, is an independent variable:

$$Y_{1i} = \beta_0 + \beta_1 \hat{Y}_{2i} + \beta_2 W_i + \beta_3 Z_{1i} + \epsilon_{1i}$$

2. We proceed in a similar way to estimate coefficients for the second equation in the model.

- First, estimate a model with Y_{1i} as the dependent variable and the W and Z variables (but not Y_2!) as independent variables.

- Estimate the final model by using $\hat{Y}_{1i}$ instead of Y_{1i} as an independent variable.

CASE STUDY   ## Supply and Demand Curves for the Chicken Market

Even though nothing defines the field of economics like supply and demand, estimating supply and demand curves can be tricky. We can't simply estimate an equation in which quantity supplied is the dependent variable and price is an independent variable because price itself is a function of how much is supplied. In other words, quantity and price are simultaneously determined.

Our simultaneous equation framework can help us navigate this challenge. First, though, let's be clear about what we're trying to do. We want to estimate two relationships: a supply function and a demand function. Each of these characterizes the relationship between price and amount, but they do so in pretty much opposite ways. We expect the quantity supplied to increase as the price increases. After all, we suspect a producer will say, "You'll pay more? I'll make more!" On the other hand, we expect the quantity demanded to decrease when the price increases, as consumers will say, "It costs more? I'll buy less!"

As we pose the question, we can see this won't be easy as we typically observe one price and one quantity for each period. How are we going to get two different slopes out of this same information?

If we only had information on price and quantity, we could not, in fact, estimate the supply and demand functions. In that case, we should shut the computer off and go to bed. If we have other information, however, that satisfies our conditions for instrumental variables, then we can potentially estimate both supply and demand functions. Here's how.

Let's start with the supply side and write down equations for quantity and price supplied:

$$Quantity_t = \beta_0 + \beta_1 Price_t + \beta_2 W_t + \beta_3 Z_{1t} + \varepsilon_{1t}$$
$$Price_t = \gamma_0 + \gamma_1 Quantity_t + \gamma_2 W_t + \gamma_3 Z_{2t} + \varepsilon_{2t}$$

where W is a variable in both equations and Z_{1t} and Z_{2t} are instrumental variables that appear in only one of the equations.

As always with simultaneous equation models, the key is the instruments. These are variables that belong in one but not the other equation. For example, to estimate the quantity equation, we need an instrumental variable for the price equation. Such a variable will affect the price but will not directly affect the supply. For example, the income of the potential demanders should directly affect how much they are willing to pay but have no direct effect on the amount supplied other than through the price mechanism. The price of a substitute or complement good may also affect how much of the product people want. If the price of ice cream cones skyrockets, for example, maybe people are less interested in buying ice cream; if the price of gas plummets, perhaps people are more interested in buying trucks. The prices of other goods do not directly affect the supply of the good in question other than via changing the price that people are willing to pay for something.

Okay. We've got a plan. Now we can go out and do this for every product, right? Actually, it's pretty hard to come up with a nice, clean example of supply and demand where everything works the way economic theory says it should. Epple and McCallum (2006) pored through 26 textbooks and found that none of them presented a supply and demand model estimated with simultaneous equations that produced statistically significant and theoretically sensible results. Epple and McCallum were, however, able to come up with one example using data on chicken.[7]

The supply is the overall supply of chicken from U.S. producers, and the demand is the amount of chicken consumed by U.S. consumers. For the supply equation, Epple and McCallum proposed several instruments, including change in income, change in price of beef (a substitute), and the lagged price. They argue that each of these variables is a valid instrument because it affects the pri are willing to pay without directly affecting the quantity supplied fun words, they say can include each of these variables in the price equ in the supply equation. Clearly, these claims are open to question, es regard to lagged price, but we'll work with their assumptions to sh model works.

We include other variables in the supply equation that plausibly affe ply of chicken, including the price of chicken feed and the lagged value tion. We also include a time trend, which can capture changes in techn transportation affecting production over time. The supply equation there

$$Chicken\ produced_t = \beta_0 + \beta_1 Price_t + \beta_2 Feed\ price_t + \beta_3 Chicken\ produced_{t-1}$$
$$+\beta_4 Time_t + \varepsilon_{1t}$$

where $Price_t$ is instrumented with change in income, change in the price of beef, and the lagged price.

We can do a similar exercise when estimating the demand function. We still work with quantity and price equations. However, now we're looking for factors

---

[7] We simplify things a fair bit; see the original article and Brumm, Epple, and McCallum (2008) for a more detailed discussion.

TABLE 9.5	Price and Quantity Supplied Equations for U.S. Chicken Market	Price equation (first stage)	Quantity supplied equation (second stage)
Endogenous variable	Price of chicken (logged)		0.203* (0.099) [t = 2.04]
Control variables	Price of chicken feed (logged)	0.188* (0.072) [t = 2.62]	−0.141* (0.048) [t = 2.94]
	Time	−0.162 (0.009) [t = 1.83]	−0.018* (0.006) [t = 3.03]
	Lag production (logged)	0.323 (0.185) [t = 1.74]	0.640* (0.116) [t = 5.53]
Instrumental variables	Change in income (logged)	1.35* (0.614) [t = 2.21]	
	Change in price of beef (logged)	0.435* (0.178) [t = 2.44]	
	Lag price of chicken (logged)	0.644* (0.124) [t = 5.18]	
	Constant	−1.73 (1.07) [t = 1.62]	1.98* (0.634) [t = 3.12]
	N	40	40
	F test of H_0: coefficients on instruments = 0	11.16	

Standard errors in parentheses.

* indicates significance at $p < 0.05$, two-tailed.

that affect the price via the supply side but do not directly affect how much chicken people will want to consume. Epple and McCallum proposed the price of chicken feed, the amount of meat (non-chicken) demanded for export, and the lagged amount of the amount produced as instrumental variables that satisfy these conditions. For example, the price of feed will affect how much it costs to produce chicken, but it should not affect the amount consumed except by affecting the price. This leads to the following model:

$$Chicken\ demanded_t = \gamma_0 + \gamma_1 Price_t + \gamma_2 Beef\ price_t + \gamma_3 Chicken\ demanded_{t-1} + \gamma_4 Income_t + \gamma_5 Time_t + \varepsilon_{2t}$$

where $Price_t$ is instrumented with price of chicken feed, the change in meat exports, and the lagged production.

There are two additional challenges. First, we will log variables in order to generate price elasticities. We discussed reasons why in Section 7.2. Hence, every variable except the time trend will be logged. Second, we're dealing with time series data. We saw a bit about time series data when we covered autocorrelation in

TABLE 9.6 Price and Quantity Demanded Equations for U.S. Chicken Market

		Price equation (first stage)	Quantity demanded equation (second stage)
Endogenous variable	Price of chicken (logged)		−0.257* (0.076) [t = 3.37]
Control variables	Change in income (logged)	1.718* (0.502) [t = 3.42]	0.408 (0.219) [t = 1.86]
	Change in price of beef (logged)	0.330* (0.161) [t = 2.05]	0.232* (0.079) [t = 2.94]
	Time	−0.00038 (0.0002) [t = 1.95]	−0.002* (0.00008) [t = 2.32]
Instrumental variables	Price of chicken feed (logged)	0.212* (0.074) [t = 2.89]	
	Change in meat exports (logged)	0.081* (0.034) [t = 2.36]	
	Lag price of chicken (logged)	−0.135* (0.037) [t = 3.61]	
	N	39	39
	F test of H_0: coefficients on instruments = 0	10.86	

Standard errors in parentheses.

* indicates significance at $p < 0.05$, two-tailed.

Section 3.6, and we'll discuss time series data in much greater detail in Chapter 13. For now, we simply note that a concern with strong time dependence led Epple and McCallum to conclude the best approach was to use *differenced variables* for the demand equation. Differenced variables measure the change in a variable rather than the level. Hence, the value of a differenced variable for year 2 of the data is the change from period 1 to period 2 rather than the amount in period 2.

Table 9.5 on page 313 shows the results for the supply equation. The first-stage results are from a reduced form model in which the price is the dependent variable and all the control variables and instruments are the independent variables. Notably, we do not include the quantity as a control variable in this first-stage regression. Each of the instruments is statistically significant, and the *F* statistic for the null hypothesis that all coefficients on the instruments equal zero is 11.16, which satisfies the rule of thumb that the *F* statistic for the test regarding all instruments should be over 10.

The second-stage supply equation uses the fitted value of the price of chicken. We see that the elasticity is 0.203, meaning that a one percent change in price is associated with a 0.203 percent increase in production. We also see that a one percent increase in the price of chicken feed, a major input, is associated with a 0.141 percent reduction in quantity of chicken produced.

Table 9.6 on page 314 shows the results for the demand equation. The first-stage price equation uses the price of chicken feed, meat exports, and the lagged price of chicken as instruments. Chicken feed prices should affect suppliers but not directly affect the demand side. The volume of meat exports should affect suppliers' output, but not what consumers in the United States want. Our dependent variable in the second stage is the amount of chicken consumed by people in the United States.

Each instrument performs reasonably well, with the t statistics above 2. The F statistic for the null hypothesis that all coefficients are zero is 10.86, which satisfies our first-stage inclusion condition.

The second-stage demand equation reported in Table 9.6 is quite sensible. A one percent increase in price is associated with a 0.257 percent *decline* in amount demanded. This is pretty neat. Whereas Table 9.5 showed an *increase* in quantity supplied as price rises, Table 9.6 shows a *decrease* in quantity demanded as price rises. This is precisely what economic theory says should happen.

The other coefficients in Table 9.6 make sense as well. A one percent increase in incomes is associated with a 0.408 percent increase in consumption, although this is not quite statistically significant. In addition, the amount of chicken demanded increases as the price of beef rises. In particular, if beef prices go up by one percent, people in the U.S. eat 0.232 percent more chicken. Think of that coefficient as basically a Chick-fil-A commercial, but with math.

Conclusion

Two-stage least squares is a great tool for fighting endogeneity. It provides us a means to use exogenous changes in an endogenous independent variable to isolate causal effects. It's easy to implement, both conceptually (two simple regressions) and practically (let the computer do it).

The problem is that a fully convincing 2SLS can be pretty elusive. In observational data in particular, it is very difficult to come up with a perfect or even serviceable instrument because the assumption that the instrument is uncorrelated with the error term is unverifiable statistically and often arguable in practice. The method also often produces imprecise estimates, which means that even a good instrument might not tell us much about the relationship we are studying. Even imperfect instruments, though, can be useful because they can be less prone to bias than OLS, especially if they perform well in first-stage models.

When we can do the following, we can be confident we understand instrumental variables and 2SLS:

- Section 9.1: Explain the logic of instrumental variables models.

- Section 9.2: Explain the first- and second-stage regressions in 2SLS. What two conditions are necessary for an instrument to be valid?

- Section 9.3: Explain how to use multiple instruments in 2SLS.

- Section 9.4: Explain quasi-instruments and weak instruments and their implications for 2SLS analysis. Identify results from the first-stage that must be reported.

- Section 9.5: Explain how the first-stage results affect the precision of the second-stage results.

- Section 9.6: Explain what simultaneity is and why it causes endogeneity. Describe how to use 2SLS to estimate simultaneous equations, noting the difference from non-simultaneous models.

Further Reading

local average treatment effect (LATE) The causal effect for those people affected by the instrument only. Relevant if the effect of X on Y varies within the population.

monotonicity Monotonicity requires that the effect of the instrument on the endogenous variable go in the same direction for everyone in a population.

stable unit treatment value assumption (SUTVA) The condition that an instrument has no spillover effect.

Murray (2006a) summarizes the instrumental variables approach and is particularly good at discussing finite sample bias and many statistical tests that are useful in diagnosing whether instrumental variables conditions are met. Baiocchi, Cheng, and Small (2014) provide an intuitive discussion of instrumental variables in health research.

One topic that has generated considerable academic interest is the possibility that the effect of X differs within a population. In this case, 2SLS estimates the **local average treatment effect (LATE)**, which is the causal effect only for those affected by the instrument. This effect is considered "local" in the sense of describing the effect for the specific class of individuals for whom the endogenous X_1 variable was influenced by the exogenous Z variable.[8]

In addition, scholars who study instrumental variables methods discuss the importance of **monotonicity**, which is a condition under which the effect of the instrument on the endogenous variable goes in the same direction for everyone in a population. This condition rules out the possibility that an increase in Z causes some units to increase X and other units to decrease X. Finally, scholars also discuss the **stable unit treatment value assumption (SUTVA)**, the condition under which the treatment doesn't vary in unmeasured ways across individuals and there are no spillover effects that might be anticipated—for example, if an untreated neighbor of someone in the treatment group somehow benefits from the treatment via the neighbor who is in the group.

---

[8] Suppose, for example, that the effect of education on future wages differs for students who like school (they learn a lot in school, so more school leads to higher wages) and students who hate school (they learn little in school, so more school does not lead to higher wages for them). If we use month of birth as an instrument, the variation in years of schooling we are looking at is only the variation among people who would or would not drop out of high school after their sophomore year, depending on when they turned 16. The effect of schooling for those folks might be pretty small, but that's what the 2SLS approach will estimate.

Imbens (2014) and Chapter 4 of Angrist and Pischke (2009) discuss these points in detail and provide mathematical derivations. Sovey and Green (2011) discuss these and related points, with a focus on the instrumental variables in political science.

Key Terms

Exclusion condition (292)

Identified (310)

Inclusion condition (292)

Instrumental variable (289)

Overidentification test (301)

Quasi-instrument (303)

Reduced form equation (309)

Simultaneous equation model (307)

Two-stage least squares (2SLS) (287)

Weak instrument (304)

Computing Corner

Stata

1. To estimate a 2SLS model in Stata, use the `ivregress 2sls` command (ivregress stands for instrumental variable regression). It works like the `reg` command in Stata, but now the endogenous variable (X_1 in the example below) is indicated, along with the instrument (Z in our notation in this chapter) in parentheses. The `, first` subcommand tells Stata to also display the first-stage regression, something we should always do:

   ```
   ivregress 2sls Y X2 X3(X1 = Z), first
   ```

2. It is important to assess the explanatory power of the instruments in the first-stage regression.

   - The rule of thumb when there is only one instrument is that the t statistic on the instrument in the first stage should be greater than 3. The higher, the better.

   - When there are multiple instruments, run an F test using the `test` command. The rule of thumb is that the F statistic should be larger than 10.

     ```
     reg X1 Z1 Z2 X2 X3
     test Z1=Z2=0
     ```

3. To estimate a simultaneous equation model, we simply use the `ivregress 2sls` command:

   ```
   ivregress 2sls Y1 W1 Z1 (Y2 = Z2), first
   ivregress 2sls Y2 W1 Z2 (Y1 = Z1), first
   ```

R

1. To estimate a 2SLS model in R, we can use the `ivreg` command from the AER package.

   - See page 85 on how to install the AER package. Recall that we need to tell R to use the package with the `library` command below for each R session in which we use the package.

   - Other packages provide similar commands to estimate 2SLS models; they're generally pretty similar, especially for standard 2SLS models.

   - The `ivreg` command operates like the `lm` command. We indicate the dependent variable and the independent variables for the main equation. The new bit is that we include a vertical line, after which we note the independent variables in the first stage. R figures out that whatever is in the first part but not the second is an endogenous variable. In this case, X1 is in the first part but not the second and therefore is the endogenous variable:
   ```
   library(AER)
   ivreg(Y ~ X1 + X2 + X3 | Z1 + Z2 + X2 + X3)
   ```

2. It is important to assess the explanatory power of the instruments in the first-stage regression.

   - If there is only one instrument, the rule of thumb is that the t statistic on the instrument in the first stage should be greater than 3. The higher, the better.
   ```
   lm(X1 ~ Z1 + X2 + X3)
   ```

   - When there are multiple instruments, run an F test with an unrestricted equation that includes that instruments and a restricted equation that does not. The rule of thumb is that the F statistic should be greater than 10. See page 238 on how to implement an F test in R.
   ```
   Unrestricted = lm(X1 ~ Z1 + Z2 + X2 + X3)
   Restricted = lm(X1 ~ X2 + X3)
   ```

3. We can also use the `ivreg` command to estimate a simultaneous equation model. Indicate the full model and then, after the vertical line, indicate the reduced form variables that will be included (which is all variables but the other dependent variable):
   ```
   library(AER)
   ivreg(Y1 ~ Y2 + W1 + Z1 | Z1 + W1 + Z2)
   ivreg(Y2 ~ Y1 + W1 + Z2 | Z1 + W1 + Z2)
   ```

Exercises

1. Does economic growth reduce the odds of civil conflict? Miguel, Satyanath, and Sergenti (2004) use an instrumental variables approach to assess the relationship between economic growth and civil war. They provide data (available in RainIV.dta) on 41 African countries from 1981 to 1999, including the variables listed in Table 9.7.

    (a) Estimate a bivariate OLS model in which the occurrence of civil conflict is the dependent variable and lagged GDP growth is the independent variable. Comment on the results.

    (b) Add control variables for initial GDP, democracy, mountains, and ethnic and religious fractionalization to the model in part (a). Do these results establish a causal relationship between the economy and civil conflict?

    (c) Consider lagged rainfall growth as an instrument for lagged GDP growth. What are the two conditions needed for a good instrument? Describe whether and how we test the two conditions. Provide appropriate statistical results.

    (d) Explain in your own words how instrumenting for GDP with rain could help us identify causal effect of the economy on civil conflict.

    (e) Use the dependent and independent variables from part (b), but now instrument for lagged GDP growth with lagged rainfall growth. Comment on the results.

    (f) Redo the 2SLS model in part (e), but this time use dummy variables to add country fixed effects. Comment on the quality of the

TABLE 9.7 Variables for Rainfall and Economic Growth Data

Variable name	Description
InternalConflict	Coded 1 if civil war with greater than 25 deaths; 0 otherwise
LaggedGDPGrowth	Lagged GDP growth
InitialGDPpercap	GDP per capita at the beginning of the period of analysis, 1979.
Democracy	A measure of democracy (called a "polity" score); values range from −10 to 10
Mountains	Percent of country that is mountainous terrain
EthnicFrac	Ethnic-linguistic fractionalization
ReligiousFrac	Religious fractionalization
LaggedRainfallGrowth	Lagged estimate of change in millimeters of precipitation from previous year

instrument in the first stage and the results for the effect of lagged economic growth in the second stage.

(g) (funky) Estimate the first stage from the 2SLS model in part (f) and save the residuals. Then estimate a regular OLS model that includes the same independent variables from part (f) and country dummies. Use lagged GDP growth (do not use fitted values), and now include the residuals from the first stage you just saved. Compare the coefficient on lagged GDP growth you get here to the coefficient on that variable in the 2SLS. Discuss how endogeneity is being handled in this specification.

2. Can television inform people about public affairs? It's a tricky question because the nerds (like us) who watch public-affairs-oriented TV are pretty well informed to begin with. Therefore political scientists Albertson and Lawrence (2009) conducted a field experiment in which they randomly assigned people to treatment and control conditions. Those assigned to the treatment condition were told to watch a specific television broadcast about affirmative action and that they would be interviewed about what they had seen. Those in the control group were not told about the program but were told that they would be re-interviewed later. The program they studied aired in California prior to the vote on Proposition 209, a controversial proposition relating to affirmative action. Their data (available in NewsStudy.dta) includes the variables listed in Table 9.8.

(a) Estimate a bivariate OLS model in which the information the respondent has about Proposition 209 is the dependent variable and whether the person watched the program is the independent variable. Comment on the results, especially whether and how they might be biased.

(b) Estimate the model in part (a), but now include measures of political interest, newspaper reading, and education. Are the results different? Have we defeated endogeneity?

TABLE 9.8 **Variables for News Program Data**

Variable name	Description
ReadNews	Political news reading habits (never = 1 to every day = 7)
PoliticalInterest	Interest in political affairs (not interested = 1 to very interested = 4)
Education	Education level (eighth grade or less = 1 to advanced graduate degree = 13)
TreatmentGroup	Assigned to watch program (treatment = 1; control = 0)
WatchProgram	Actually watched program (watched = 1, did not watch = 0)
InformationLevel	Information about Proposition 209 prior to election (none = 1 to great deal = 4)

(c) Why might the assignment variable be a good instrument for watching the program? What test or tests can we run?

(d) Estimate a 2SLS model from using assignment to the treatment group as an instrument for whether a given respondent watched the program. Use the additional independent variables from part (b). Compare the first-stage results to results in part (c). Are they similar? Are they identical? (*Hint*: Compare sample sizes.)

(e) What do the 2SLS results suggest about the effect of watching the program on information levels? Compare the results to those in part (b). Have we defeated endogeneity?

3. Suppose we want to understand the demand curve for fish. We'll use the following demand curve equation:

$$Quantity_t^D = \beta_0 + \beta_1 Price_t + \epsilon_t^D$$

Economic theory suggests $\beta_1 < 0$. Following standard practice, we estimate elasticity of demand with respect to price by means of log-log models.

(a) To see that prices and quantities are endogenous, draw supply and demand curves and discuss what happens when the demand curve shifts out (which corresponds to a change in the error term of the demand function). Note also what happens to price in equilibrium and discuss how this event creates endogeneity.

(b) The data set fishdata.dta (from Angrist, Graddy, and Imbens 2000) provides data on prices and quantities of a certain kind of fish (called whiting) over 111 days at the Fulton Street Fish Market, which then existed in Lower Manhattan. The variables are indicated in Table 9.9. The price and quantity variables are logged. Estimate a

TABLE 9.9 Variables for Fish Market Data

Variable name	Description
Price	Daily price of fish (logged)
Supply	Daily supply of fish (logged)
Stormy	Dummy variable indicating a storm at sea based on height of waves and wind speed at sea
Day1	Dummy variable indicating Monday
Day2	Dummy variable indicating Tuesday
Day3	Dummy variable indicating Wednesday
Day4	Dummy variable indicating Thursday
Rainy	Dummy variable indicating rainy day at the fish market
Cold	Dummy variable indicating cold day at the fish market

naïve OLS model of demand in which quantity is the dependent variable and price is the independent variable. Briefly interpret results and then discuss whether this analysis is useful.

(c) Angrist, Graddy, and Imbens suggest that a dummy variable indicating a storm at sea is a good instrumental variable that should affect the supply equation but not the demand equation. *Stormy* is a dummy variable that indicates a wave height greater than 4.5 feet and wind speed greater than 18 knots. Use 2SLS to estimate a demand function in which *Stormy* is an instrument for *Price*. Discuss first-stage and second-stage results, interpreting the most relevant portions.

(d) Reestimate the demand equation but with additional controls. Continue to use *Stormy* as an instrument for price, but now also include covariates that account for the days of the week and the weather on shore. Discuss first-stage and second-stage results, interpreting the most relevant portions.

4. Does education reduce crime? If so, spending more on education could be a long-term tool in fight against crime. The file inmates.dta contains data used by Lochner and Moretti in their 2004 article in *The American Economic Review* on the effects of education on crime. Table 9.10 describes the variables.

(a) Estimate a model with prison as the dependent variable and *education*, *age*, and *African-American* as independent variables. Make this a fixed effects model by including dummies for state of

TABLE 9.10 Variables for Education and Crime Data

Variable name	Description
prison	Dummy variable equals 1 if the respondent is in prison
educ	Years of schooling
age	Age
AfAm	Dummy variable for African-Americans
state	State of residence (FIPS codes)
year	Census year
ca9	Dummy equals 1 if state compulsory schooling equals 9 years
ca10	Dummy equals 1 if state compulsory schooling equals 10 years
ca11	Dummy equals 1 if state compulsory schooling is 11 or more years

FIPS codes are Federal Information Processing Codes for states (and also countries).

residence (state) and year of census data (year). Report and briefly describe the results.

(b) Based on the OLS results, can we causally conclude that increasing education will reduce crime? Why is it difficult to estimate the effect of education on criminal activity?

(c) Lochner and Moretti use 2SLS to improve upon their OLS estimates. They use changes in compulsory attendance laws (set by each state) as an instrument. The variable $ca9$ indicates that compulsory schooling is equal to 9 years, $ca10$ indicates that compulsory schooling is equal to 10 years, and $ca11$ is 11 or more years. The control group is 8 or fewer years. Does this set of instruments satisfy the two conditions for good instruments?

(d) Estimate a 2SLS model using the instruments just described and the control variables from the OLS model above (including state and year dummy variables). Briefly explain the results.

(e) 2SLS is known for being less precise than OLS. Is that true here? Is this a problem for the analysis in this case? Why or why not?

5. Does economic growth lead to democracy? This question is at the heart of our understanding of how politics and the economy interact. The answer also exerts huge influence on policy: if we believe economic growth leads to democracy, then we may be more willing to pursue economic growth first and let democracy come later. If economic growth does not lead to democracy, then perhaps economic sanctions or other tools may make sense if we wish to promote democracy. Acemoglu, Johnson, Robinson, and Yared (2008) analyzed this question by using data on democracy and GDP growth from 1960 to 2000. The data is in the form of five-year panels—one observation for each country every five years. Table 9.11 describes the variables.

TABLE 9.11 Variables for Income and Democracy Data

Variable name	Description
democracy_fh	Freedom House measure of democracy (range from 0 to 1)
log_gdp	Log real GDP per capita
worldincome	Trade-weighted log GDP
year	Year
YearCode	Order of years of data set (1955 = 1, 1960 = 2, 1965 = 3, etc.)
CountryCode	Numeric code for each country

(a) Are countries with higher income per capita more democratic? Run a pooled regression model with democracy (*democracy_fh*) as the dependent variable and logged GDP per capita (*log_gdp*) as the independent variable. Lag *log_gdp* so that the model reflects that income at time $t - 1$ predicts democracy at time t. Describe the results. What are the concerns with this model?

(b) Rerun the model from part (a), but now include fixed effects for year and country. Describe the model. How does including these fixed effects change the results?

(c) To better establish causality, the authors use 2SLS. One of the instruments that they use is changes in the income of trading partners (*worldincome*). They theorize that the income of a given country's trading partners should predict its own GDP but should not directly affect the level of democracy in the country. Discuss the viability of this instrument with specific reference to the conditions that instruments need to satisfy. Provide evidence as appropriate.

(d) Run a 2SLS model that uses *worldincome* as an instrument for logged GDP. Remember to lag both. Compare the coefficient and standard error to the OLS and panel data results.

Experiments: Dealing with **10** Real-World Challenges

In the 2012 presidential election, the Obama campaign team was famously teched up. Not just in iPhones and laptops, but also in *analytics*. They knew how to do all the things we're talking about in this book: how to appreciate the challenges of endogeneity, how to analyze data effectively, and perhaps most important of all, how to design randomized experiments to answer the questions they were interested in.

One thing they did was work their e-mail list almost to exhaustion with a slew of fund-raising pitches over the course of the campaign. These pitches were not random—or, wait, actually they were *random* in the sense that the campaign tested them ruthlessly by means of experimental methods (Green 2012). On June 26, 2012, for example, they sent e-mail messages with randomly selected subject lines, ranging from the minimalist "Change" to the sincere "Thankful every day" to the politically scary "I will be outspent." The campaign then tracked which subject lines generated the most donations. The "I will be outspent" message kicked butt, producing almost five times the donations the "Thankful every day" subject line did. As a result, the campaign sent millions of people e-mails with the "I will be outspent" subject line and, according to the campaign, raised millions of dollars more than they would have if they had used one of the other subject lines tested.

Of course, campaigns are not the only organizations that use randomized experiments. Governments and researchers interested in health care, economic development, and many other public policy issues use them all the time. And experiments are important in the private sector as well. Capital One, one of the largest credit card companies in the United States, grew from virtually nothing largely on the strength of a commitment to experiment-driven decision making. Google, Amazon, Facebook, and eBay also experiment relentlessly.

Randomized experiments pose an alluring solution to our quest for exogeneity. Let's create it! That is, let's use randomization to ensure that our independent variable of interest will be uncorrelated with the error term. As we discussed in Section 1.3, if our independent variable is uncorrelated with everything, it is uncorrelated with the error term. Hence, if the independent variable is random, it is exogenous and unbiased inference will be a breeze.

In theory, analysis of randomized experiments should be easy. We randomly pick a group of subjects to be the treatment group, treat them, and then look for differences in the results from an untreated control group.[1] As discussed in Section 6.1, we can use OLS to estimate a difference of means model with an equation of the form:

$$Y_i = \beta_0 + \beta_1 Treatment_i + \epsilon_i \qquad (10.1)$$

where Y_i is the outcome we care about and $Treatment_i$ equals one for subjects in the treatment group.

In reality, randomized experiments face a host of challenges. Not only are they costly, potentially infeasible, and sometimes unethical, as discussed in Section 1.3, they run into several challenges that can undo the desired exogeneity of randomized experiments. This chapter focuses on these challenges. Section 10.1 discusses the challenges raised by possible dissimilarity of the treatment and control groups. If the treatment group differs from the control group in ways other than the treatment, we can't be sure whether it's the treatment or other differences that explain differences across these groups. Section 10.2 moves on to the challenges raised by non-compliance with assignment to an experimental group. Section 10.3 shows how to use the 2SLS tools from Chapter 9 to deal with non-compliance. Section 10.4 discusses the challenge posed to experiments by attrition, a common problem that arises when people leave an experiment. Section 10.5 changes gears to discuss natural experiments, which occur without intervention by researchers.

▶ **ABC issues** Three issues that every experiment needs to address: attrition, balance, and compliance.

We refer to the attrition, balance, and compliance challenges facing experiments as **ABC issues**.[2] Every analysis of experiments should discuss these ABC issues explicitly.

---

[1] Often the control group is given a placebo treatment of some sort. In medicine, this is the well-known sugar pill. In social science, a placebo treatment may be an experience that shares the form of the treatment but not the content. For example, in a study of advertising efficacy, a placebo group might be shown a public service ad. The idea is that the mere act of viewing an ad, any ad, could affect respondents and that ad designers want their ad to cause changes over and above that baseline effect.

[2] We actually discuss balance first, followed by compliance and then attrition, because this order follows the standard sequence of experimental analysis. We'll stick with calling them ABC issues because BCA doesn't sound as cool as ABC.

10.1 Randomization and Balance

When we run experiments, we worry that randomization may fail to produce comparable treatment and control groups, in which case the treatment and control groups might differ in more ways than just the experimental treatment. If the treatment group is older, for example, we worry that the differences between the results posted by the treatment and control groups could be due to age rather than the treatment or lack of it.

In this section we discuss how to try to ensure that treatment and control groups are equivalent, explain how treatment and control groups can differ, show how to detect such differences, and tell what to do if there are differences.

Blocking to ensure similar treatment and control groups

blocking Picking treatment and control groups so that they are equal in covariates.

Ideally, researchers will be able to ensure that their treatment and control groups are similar. They do this by **blocking**, which is a way of ensuring that the treatment and control groups picked will be the same for selected covariates. A simple form of blocking is to separate the sample into men and women and randomly pick treatment and control subjects within those blocks. This ensures that the treatment and control groups will not differ by sex. Unfortunately, there are limits to blocking. Sometimes it just won't work in the context of an experiment being carried out in the real world. Or, more pervasively, practical concerns arise because it gets harder and harder to make blocking work as we increase the number of variables we wish to block. For example, if we want to ensure that treatment and control groups are the same in each age group and in both sexes, we must pick subsets of women in each age group and men in each age group. If we add race to our wish list, then we'll have even smaller individuals in targeted blocks to randomize within. Eventually, things get very complicated, and our sample size can't provide people in every block. The Further Reading section at the end of the chapter points to articles with more guidance on blocking.

Why treatment and control groups may differ

Differences in treatment and control groups can arise both when no blocking is possible and when blocking is not able to account for all variables. Sometimes the randomization procedures may simply fail. This may happen because some experimental treatments are quite valuable. A researcher may want random allocation of a prized treatment (e.g., free health care, access to a new cancer drug, or admission to a good school). It is possible that the family of a sick person or ambitious schoolchild will be able to get that individual into the treatment group. Or perhaps the people implementing the program aren't quite on board with randomization and put some people in or out of the treatment group for their own reasons. Or maybe the folks doing the randomization screwed up.

In other cases, the treatment and control groups may differ simply due to chance. Suppose we want to conduct a random experiment on a four-person family of mom, dad, big sister, and little brother. Even if we pick the two-person treatment and control groups randomly, we'll likely get groups that differ in important ways. Maybe the treatment group will be dad and little brother; too many guys there. Or maybe the treatment group will be mom and dad; too many middle-aged people there. In these cases, any outcome differences between the treatment and control groups would be due not only to the treatment but also possibly to the sex or age differences. Of course, the odds that the treatment and control groups differ substantially fall rapidly as the sample size increases (a good reason to have a big sample!). The chance that such differences occur never completely disappears, however.

Checking for balance

▶ **balance** Treatment and control groups are balanced if the distributions of control variables are the same for the treatment and control groups.

Therefore an important first step in analyzing an experiment is to check for **balance**. Balance exists when the treatment and control groups are similar in all measurable ways. The core diagnostic for balance involves comparing difference of means for all possible independent variables between those assigned to the treatment and control groups. We accomplish this by using our OLS difference of means test (as discussed on page 168) to assess for each X variable whether the treatment and control groups are different. Thus we start with

$$X_i = \gamma_0 + \gamma_1 TreatmentAssigned_i + v_i \tag{10.2}$$

where $TreatmentAssigned_i$ is 1 for those assigned to the treatment group and 0 for those assigned to the control group. We use γ (gamma) to indicate the coefficients and v (nu) to indicate the error term. We do not use β and ϵ here, to emphasize that the model differs from the main model (Equation 10.1). We estimate Equation 10.2 for each potential independent variable; each equation will produce a different $\hat{\gamma}_1$ estimate. A statistically significant $\hat{\gamma}_1$ estimate indicates that the X variable differed across those assigned to the treatment and control groups.[3]

Ideally, we won't see any statistically significant $\hat{\gamma}_1$ estimates; this outcome would indicate that the treatment and control groups are balanced. If the $\hat{\gamma}_1$ estimates are statistically significant for many X variables, we do not have balance in our experimentally assigned groups, which suggests systematic interference with the planned random assignments.

We should keep statistical power in mind when we evaluate balance tests. As discussed earlier on page 109, statistical power relates to the probability

---

[3] More advanced balance tests also allow us to assess whether the variance of a variable is the same across treatment and control groups. See, for example, Imai (2005).

of rejecting the null hypothesis when we should. Power is low in small data sets, since when there are few observations, we are unlikely to find statistically significant differences in treatment and control groups even when there are differences. In contrast, power is high for large data sets; that is, we may observe statistically significant differences even when the actual differences are substantively small. Hence, balance tests are sensitive not only to whether there are differences across treatment and control groups, but also to the factors that affect power. We should therefore be cautious in believing we have achieved balance in a small sample set, and we should be sure to assess the substantive importance of any differences we see in large samples.

What if the treatment and control groups differ for only one or two variables? Such an outcome is not enough to indicate that randomization failed. Recall that even when there is no difference between treatment and control groups, we will reject the null hypothesis of no difference 5 percent of the time when $\alpha = 0.05$. Thus, for example, if we look at at 20 variables, it would be perfectly natural for the means of the treatment and control groups to differ statistically significantly for one of those variables.

Good results on balancing tests also suggest (without proving) that balance has been achieved even on the variables we can't measure. Remember, the key to experiments is that no unmeasured factor in the error term is correlated with the independent variable. Given that we cannot see the darn things in the error term, it seems a bit unfair to expect us to have any confidence about what's going on in there. However, if balance has been achieved for everything we can observe, we can reasonably (albeit cautiously) speculate that the treatment and control groups are also balanced for factors we cannot observe.

What to do if treatment and control groups differ

If we do find imbalances, we should not ignore them. First, we should assess the magnitude of the difference. Even if only one X variable differs across treatment and control groups, a huge difference could be a sign of a deeper problem. Second, we should control for even smallish differences in treatment and control groups in our analysis, lest we conflate outcome differences in Y across treatment and control groups and differences in some X for which treatment and control groups differ. In other words, when we have imbalances it is a good idea to use multivariate OLS, even though in theory we need only bivariate OLS when our independent variable is randomly assigned. For example, if we find that the treatment and control groups differ in age, we should estimate

$$Y_i = \beta_0 + \beta_1 Treatment_i + \beta_2 Age_i + \epsilon_i$$

In adding control variables, we should be careful to control only for variables that are measured before the treatment or do not vary over time. If we control for a variable measured after the treatment, it is possible that it will be affected by the treatment itself, thereby making it hard to figure out the actual effect of treatment.

For example, suppose we are analyzing an experiment in which job training was randomly assigned within a certain population. In assessing whether the training helped people get jobs, we would not want to control for test scores measured after the treatment because the scores could have been affected by the training. Since part of the effect of treatment may be captured by this post-treatment variable, including such a post-treatment variable will muddy the analysis.

> # REMEMBER THIS
>
> 1. Experimental treatment and control groups are balanced if the average values of independent variables are not substantially different for people assigned to treatment and control groups.
>
> 2. We check for balance by conducting difference of means tests for all possible independent variables.
>
> 3. When we assess the effect of a treatment, it is a good idea to control for imbalanced variables.

CASE STUDY   Development Aid and Balancing

One of the most important challenges in modern times is figuring out how best to fight the grinding poverty that bedevils much of the world's population. Some think that alleviating poverty is simply a question of money: spend enough and poverty goes away. Others are skeptical, wondering if the money spent by governmental and nongovernmental organizations actually does any good.

Using observational studies to settle this debate is dicey. Such studies estimate something like the following equation:

$$Health_{it} = \beta_0 + \beta_1 Aid_{it} + \beta_2 X_{it} + \epsilon_{it} \qquad (10.3)$$

where $Health_{it}$ is the health of person i at time t, Aid_{it} is the amount of foreign aid going to person i's village, and X_{it} represents one or more variables that affect health. The problem is that the error may be correlated with aid. Aid may flow to places where people are truly needy, with economic and social problems that go beyond any simple measure of poverty. Or resources may flow to places that are actually better off and better able to attract attention than simple poverty statistics would suggest.

In other words, aid is probably endogenous. And because we cannot know if aid is positively or negatively correlated with the error term, we have to admit that we don't know whether the actual effects are larger or smaller than what we observe with the observational analysis. That's not a particularly satisfying study.

If the government resources flowed exogenously, however, we could analyze health and other outcomes and be much more confident that we are measuring the effect of the aid. One example of a confidence-inspiring study is the Progresa experiment in Mexico, described in Gertler (2004). In the late 1990s the Mexican government wanted to run a village-based health care program, but realized it did not have enough resources to cover all villages at once. The government decided the fairest way to pick villages was to pick them randomly and *voila!* an experiment was born. Government authorities randomly selected 320 villages as treatment cases and implemented the program there. The Mexican government also monitored 185 control villages, where no new program was implemented. In the program, eligible families received a cash transfer worth about 20 to 30 percent of household income if they participated in health screening and education activities including immunizations, prenatal visits, and annual health checkups.

Before assessing whether the treatment worked, analysts needed to assess whether randomization worked. Were villages indeed selected randomly and, if so, were they similar with regard to factors that could influence health? Table 10.1 provides results for balancing tests for the Progresa program. The first column has the $\hat{\gamma}_0$ estimates from Equation 10.2 for various X variables. These are the averages of the variable in question for the young children in the control villages. The second column displays the $\hat{\gamma}_1$ estimates, which indicate how much higher or lower the

TABLE 10.1 Balancing Tests for the Progresa Experiment: Differences of Means Tests Using OLS

Dependent variable	$\hat{\gamma}_0$	$\hat{\gamma}_1$	t stat ($\hat{\gamma}_1$)	p value ($\hat{\gamma}_1$)
1. Age (in years)	1.61	0.01	0.11	0.91
2. Male	0.49	0.02	1.69	0.09
3. Child was ill in last 4 weeks	0.32	0.01	0.29	0.77
4. Father's years of education	3.84	−0.04	0.03	0.98
5. Mother's years of education	3.83	−0.33	1.87	0.06
6. Father speaks Spanish	0.93	0.01	1.09	0.28
7. Mother speaks Spanish	0.92	0.02	0.77	0.44
8. Own house	0.91	0.01	0.73	0.47
9. House has electricity	0.71	−0.07	1.69	0.09
10. Hectares of land owned	0.79	0.02	0.59	0.55
11. Male daily wage rate (pesos)	31.22	−0.74	0.90	0.37
12. Female daily wage rate (pesos)	27.84	−0.58	0.69	0.49
Sample size:	7,825			

Results from 12 different OLS regressions in which the dependent variable is as listed at left. The coefficients are from the model $X_i = \gamma_0 + \gamma_1 Treatment_i + v_i$ (see Equation 10.2).

average of the variable in question is for children in the treatment villages. For example, the first line indicates that the children in the treatment village were 0.01 year older than the children in the control village. The t statistic is very small for this coefficient and the p value is high, indicating that this difference is not at all statistically significant. For the second row, the male variable equals 1 for boys and 0 for girls. The average of this variable indicates the percent of the sample that were boys. In the control villages, 49 percent of the children were males; 51 percent ($\hat{y}_0 + \hat{y}_1$) of the children in the treatment villages were male. This 2 percent difference is statistically significant at the 0.10 level (given that $p < 0.10$). The most statistically significant difference we see is in mother's years of education, for which the p value is 0.06. In addition, houses in the treatment group were less likely to have electricity ($p = 0.09$).

The study author took the results to indicate that balance had been achieved. We see, though, that achieving balance is an art, rather than a science, because for 12 variables, only one or perhaps two would be expected to be statistically significant at the $\alpha = 0.10$ level if there were, in fact, no differences across the groups. These imbalances should not be forgotten; in this case, the analysts controlled for all the listed variables when they estimated treatment effects.

And, by the way, did the Progresa program work? In a word, yes. Results from difference of means tests revealed that kids in the treatment villages were sick less often, taller, and less likely to be anemic.

10.2 Compliance and Intention-to-Treat Models

> **compliance** The condition of subjects receiving the experimental treatment to which they were assigned.

Many social science experiments also have to deal with **compliance** problems, which arise when some people assigned to a treatment do not experience the treatment to which they were assigned. A compliance problem can happen, for example, when someone is randomly assigned to receive a phone call asking for a chairitable donation. If the person does not answer the phone, we say (perhaps a bit harshly) that he failed to comply with the experimental treatment.

In this section we show how non-compliance can create endogeneity. Then we present a schematic for thinking about the problem and introduce so-called *intention-to-treat* models as one way to deal with the problem.

Non-compliance and endogeneity

Non-compliance is often non-random, opening a back door for endogeneity to weasel its way into experiments because the people who comply with a treatment may differ systematically from the people who do not. This is precisely the problem we use experiments to avoid.

Educational voucher experiments illustrate how endogeneity can sneak in with non-compliance. These experiments typically start when someone ponies up a ton of money to send poor kids to private schools. Because there are more poor kids than money, applicants are randomly chosen in a lottery to receive vouchers to attend private schools. These are the kids in the treatment group. The kids who aren't selected in the lottery are the control group.[4] After a year of schooling (or more), the test scores of the treatment and control groups are compared to see whether kids who had vouchers for private schools did better. Because being in a voucher school is a function of a random lottery, we can hope that the only systematic difference between the treatment and control groups is whether the children in the treatment group attended the private school. If so, it is fair to say that the treatment caused any differences in outcomes we observe.

Non-compliance complicates matters. Not everyone who receives the voucher uses it to attend private school. In a late 1990s New York City voucher experiment discussed by Howell and Peterson (2004), for example, 74 percent of families who were offered vouchers used them in the first year. That number fell to 62 percent and 53 percent after two and three years of the program, respectively. Kids with vouchers might end up not attending a private school for lots of reasons. They might find the private school unwelcoming or too demanding. Their family might move. Some of these causes are plausibly related to academic performance: a child who finds private school too demanding is likely to be less academically ambitious than one who does not have that reaction. In that case, the kids who actually use vouchers to attend private school (the "compliers" in our terminology) are not a randomly selected group; rather, they are a group that could differ systematically from kids who decline to use the vouchers. The result can be endogeneity, because the variable of interest (attending private school) might be correlated with factors in the error term (such as academic ambition) that explain test performance.

Schematic representation of the non-compliance problem

Figure 10.1 provides a schematic of the non-compliance problem (Imai 2005). At the top level, a researcher randomly assigns subjects to receive the treatment or not. If a subject is assigned to receive a treatment, $Z_i = 1$; if a subject is not assigned to receive a treatment, $Z_i = 0$. Subjects assigned treatment who actually receive it are the compliers, and for them $T_i = 1$, where T indicates whether the person actually received the treatment. The people who are assigned to treatment ($Z_i = 1$) but do not actually receive it ($T_i = 0$) are the non-compliers.

For everyone in the control group, Z_i equals 0, indicating that those kids were not assigned to receive the treatment. We don't observe compliance for people in the control group because they're not given a chance to comply. Hence the dashed

---

[4] Researchers in this area are careful to analyze only students who actually applied for the vouchers because the students (and parents) who apply for vouchers for private schools almost certainly differ systematically from students (and parents) who do not.

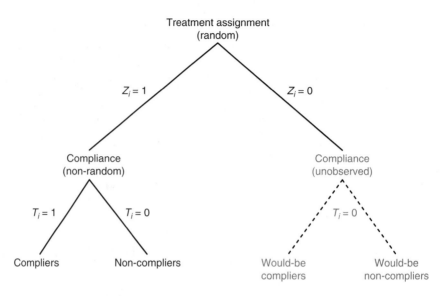

Treatment assignment
(random)

$Z_i = 1$

$Z_i = 0$

Compliance
(non-random)

Compliance
(unobserved)

$T_i = 1$ $T_i = 0$

$T_i = 0$

Compliers   Non-compliers

Would-be
compliers

Would-be
non-compliers

FIGURE 10.1: Compliance and Non-compliance in Experiments

lines in Figure 10.1 indicate that we can't know who among the control group are would-be compliers and would-be non-compliers.[5]

We can see the mischief caused by non-compliance when we think about how to compare treatment and control groups in this context. We could compare the students who actually went to the private school ($T_i = 1$) to those who didn't ($T_i = 0$). Note, however, that the $T_i = 1$ group includes only compliers—students who, when given the chance to go to a private school, took it. These students are likely to be more academically ambitious than the non-compliers. The $T_i = 0$ group includes non-compliers (for whom $Z_i = 1$ and $T_i = 0$) and those not assigned to treatment (for whom $Z_i = 0$). This comparison likely stacks the deck in favor of finding that the private schools improve test scores because this $T_i = 1$ group has a disproportionately high proportion of educationally ambitious students.

Another option is to compare the compliers (the $Z_i = 1$ and $T_i = 1$ students) to the whole control group (the $Z_i = 0$ students). This method, too, is problematic. The control group has two types of students—would-be compliers and would-be non-compliers—while the treatment group in this approach only has compliers. Any differences found with this comparison could be attributed either to the effect of the private school or to the absence of non-compliers from the complier group, whereas the control group includes both complier types and non-complier types.

---

[5] An additional wrinkle in the real world is that people from the control group may find a way to receive the treatment without being assigned to treatment. For example, in the New York voucher experiment just discussed, 5 percent of the control group ended up in private schools without having received a voucher.

Intention-to-treat models

▶ intention-to-treat (ITT) analysis ITT analysis addresses potential endogeneity that arises in experiments owing to non-compliance. We compare the means of those assigned treatment and those not assigned treatment, irrespective of whether the subjects did or did not actually receive the treatment.

A better approach is to conduct an **intention-to-treat (ITT) analysis**. To conduct an ITT analysis, we compare the means of those assigned treatment (the whole $Z_i = 1$ group, which consists of those who complied and did not comply with the treatment) to those not assigned treatment (the $Z_i = 0$ group consisting of would-be compliers and would-be non-compliers). The ITT approach sidesteps non-compliance endogeneity at the cost of producing estimates that are statistically conservative (meaning that we expect the estimated coefficients to be smaller than the actual effect of the treatment).

To understand ITT, let's start with the non-ITT model we really care about:

$$Y_i = \beta_0 + \beta_1 Treatment_i + \epsilon_i \tag{10.4}$$

For individuals who receive no treatment ($Treatment_i = 0$), we expect Y_i to equal some baseline value, β_0. For individuals who have received the treatment ($Treatment_i = 1$), we expect Y_i to be $\beta_0 + \beta_1$. This simple bivariate OLS model allows us to test for the difference of means between treatment and control groups.

The problem, as we have discussed, is that non-compliance creates correlation between treatment and the error term because the type of people who comply with the treatment may differ systematically from non-compliers.

The idea behind the ITT approach is to look for differences between the whole treatment group (whether they complied or not) and the whole control group. The model is

$$Y_i = \delta_0 + \delta_1 Z_i + v_i \tag{10.5}$$

In this model, Z is 1 for individuals assigned to the treatment group. We use δ to highlight our use of assignment to treatment as the independent variable rather than actual treatment. In this model, δ is an intention-to-treat estimator because it estimates the difference between all the people we intended to treat and all the people we did not intend to treat.

Note that Z is uncorrelated with the error term. It reflects assignment to treatment (rather than actual compliance with treatment); hence none of the compliance issues are able to sneak in correlation with anything, including the error term. Therefore the coefficient estimate associated with the treatment assignment variable will not be clouded by other factors that could explain both the dependent variable and compliance. For example, if we use ITT analysis to explain the relationship between test scores and attending private schools, we do not have to worry that our key independent variable is also capturing the individuals who, being more academically ambitious kids, may have been more likely to use the private school vouchers. ITT avoids this problem by comparing all kids given a chance to use the vouchers to all kids not given that chance.

ITT is not costless, however. When there is non-compliance, ITT will underestimate the treatment effect. This means the ITT estimate, $\hat{\delta}_1$, is a lower-bound estimate of β, the estimate of the effect of the treatment itself from Equation 10.4. In other words, we expect the magnitude of the $\hat{\delta}_1$ parameter estimated from Equation 10.5 to be smaller than or equal to the β_1 parameter in Equation 10.4.

To see why, consider the two extreme possibilities zero compliance and full compliance. If there is zero compliance, such that no one assigned treatment complied ($T_i = 0$ for all $Z_i = 1$), then δ_1 has to be 0 because there is no difference between the treatment and control groups. (No one took the treatment!) At the other extreme, if everyone assigned treatment ($Z_i = 1$) also complied ($T_i = 1$), then the *Treatment$_i$* variable in Equation 10.4 will be identical to Z_i (treatment assignment) in Equation 10.5. In this instance, $\hat{\beta}_1$ will be an unbiased estimator of β_1 because there are no non-compliers messing up the exogeneity of the random experiment. In this case, $\hat{\beta}_1 = \hat{\delta}_1$ because the variables in the models are identical.

Hence we know that the ITT estimate of $\hat{\delta}_1$ is going to be somewhere between zero and an unbiased estimator of the true treatment effect. The lower the compliance, the more the ITT estimate will be biased toward zero. The ITT estimator is still preferable to $\hat{\beta}_1$ from a model with treatment received when there are non-compliance problems; this is because $\hat{\beta}_1$ can be biased when compliers differ from non-compliers, causing endogeneity to enter the model.

The ITT approach is a cop-out, but in a good way. When we use it, we're being conservative in the sense that the estimate will be prone to underestimate the magnitude of the treatment effect. If the ITT approach reveals an effect, it will be due to treatment, not to endogenous non-compliance issues.

Researchers regularly estimate ITT effects. Sometimes whether someone did or didn't comply with a treatment is not known. For example, if the experimenter mailed advertisements to randomly selected households, it will be very hard, if not impossible, to know who actually read the ads (Bailey, Hopkins, and Rogers 2015).

Or sometimes the ITT effect is the most relevant quantity of interest. Suppose, for example, we know that compliance will be spotty and we want to build non-compliance into our estimate of a program's effectiveness. Miguel and Kremer (2004) analyzed an experiment in Kenya that provided medical treatment for intestinal worms to children at randomly selected schools. Some children in the treated schools, however, missed school the day the medicine was administered. An ITT analysis in this case compares kids assigned to treatment (whether or not they were in school on that day) to kids not assigned to treatment. Because some kids will always miss school for a treatment like this, policy makers may care more about the ITT estimated effect of the treatment because ITT takes into account both the treatment effect and the less-than-perfect compliance.

REMEMBER THIS

1. In an experimental context, a person assigned to receive a treatment who actually receives the treatment is said to comply with the treatment.

2. When compliers differ from non-compliers, non-compliance creates endogeneity.

3. Intention-to-treat (ITT) analysis compares people assigned to treatment (whether they complied or did not) to people in the control group.

   • ITT is not vulnerable to endogeneity due to non-compliance.

   • ITT estimates will be smaller in magnitude than the true treatment effect. The more numerous the non-compliers, the closer to zero will be the ITT estimates.

Discussion Questions

1. Will there be balance problems if there is non-compliance? Why or why not?

2. Suppose there is non-compliance but no signs of balance problems. Does this mean the non-compliance must be harmless? Why or why not?

3. For each of the following scenarios, discuss (i) whether non-compliance is likely to be an issue, (ii) the likely implication of non-compliance for comparing those who received treatment to the control group, and (iii) what exactly an ITT variable would consist of.

   (a) Suppose an international aid group working in a country with low literacy rates randomly assigned children to a treatment group that received one hour of extra reading help each day and a control group that experienced only the standard curriculum. The dependent variable is a reading test score after one year.

   (b) Suppose an airline randomly upgraded some economy class passengers to business class. The dependent variable is satisfaction with the flight.

   (c) Suppose the federal government randomly selected a group of school districts that could receive millions of dollars of aid for revamping their curriculum. The control group receives nothing from the program. The dependent variable is test scores after three years.

10.3 Using 2SLS to Deal with Non-compliance

An even better way to deal with non-compliance is to use 2SLS to directly estimate the effect of treatment. The key insight is that randomized treatment assignment is a great instrument. Randomized assignment satisfies the exclusion condition (that Z is uncorrelated with ϵ) because it is uncorrelated with everything, including the error term. Random assignment also usually satisfies the inclusion condition because being randomly assigned to treatment typically predicts whether a person got the treatment.

In this section we build on material from Section 9.2 to show how to use 2SLS to deal with non-compliance. We accomplish this by working through an example and by showing the sometimes counterintuitive way we use variables in this model.

Example of using 2SLS to deal with non-compliance

To see how to use 2SLS to analyze an experiment with non-compliance, let's look at an experimental study of get-out-the-vote efforts. Political consultants often joke that they know half of what they do works, they just don't know which half. An experiment might help figure out which half (or third or quarter!) works.

We begin by laying out what an observational study of campaign effectiveness looks like. A simple model is

$$Turnout_i = \beta_0 + \beta_1 \ Campaign \ contact_i + \epsilon_i \qquad (10.6)$$

where $Turnout_i$ equals 1 for people who voted and 0 for those who did not.[6] The independent variable is whether or not someone was contacted by a campaign.

What is in the error term? Certainly political interest will be, because more politically attuned people are more likely to vote. We'll have endogeneity if political interest (incorporated in the error term) is correlated with contact by a campaign (the independent variable). We will probably have endogeneity because campaigns do not want to waste time contacting people who won't vote. Hence, we'll have endogeneity unless the campaign is incompetent (or, ironically, run by experimentalists).

Such endogeneity could corrupt the results easily. Suppose we find a positive association between campaign contact and turnout. We should worry that the relationship is due not to the campaign contact but to the kind of people who were contacted—namely, those who were more likely to vote before they were contacted. Such concerns make it very hard to analyze campaign effects with observational data.

---

[6] The dependent variable is a dichotomous variable. We discuss such dependent variables in more detail in Chapter 12.

Professors Alan Gerber and Don Green (2000, 2005) were struck by these problems with observational studies and have almost single-handedly built an empire of experimental studies in American politics.[7] As part of their signature study, they randomly assigned citizens to receive in-person visits from a get-out-the-vote campaign. In their study, all the factors that affect turnout would be uncorrelated with assignment to receive the treatment.[8]

Compliance is a challenge in such studies. When campaign volunteers knocked on doors, not everyone answered. Some people weren't home. Some were in the middle of dinner. Maybe a few ran out the back door screaming when they saw a hippie volunteer ringing their doorbell.

Non-compliance, of course, could affect the results. If the more socially outgoing types answered the door (hence receiving the treatment) and the more reclusive types did not (hence not receiving the treatment even though they were assigned to it), the treatment variable as delivered would depend not only on the random assignment but also on how outgoing a person was. If more outgoing people are more likely to vote, then treatment as delivered will be correlated with the sociability of the experimental subject, and we will have endogeneity.

To get around this problem, Gerber and Green used treatment assignment as an instrument. This variable, which we've been calling Z_i, indicates whether a person was randomly selected to receive a treatment. This variable is well suited to satisfy the requisite conditions for a good instrument discussed in Section 9.2. First, Z_i should be included in the first stage because being randomly assigned to be contacted by the campaign does indeed increase campaign contact. Table 10.2 shows the results from the first stage of Gerber and Green's turnout experiment. The dependent variable, treatment delivered, is 1 if the person actually talked to the volunteer canvasser. The independent variable is whether the person was or was not assigned to treatment.

TABLE 10.2 **First-Stage Regression in Campaign Experiment: Explaining Contact**

Personal visit assigned ($Z = 1$)	0.279*
	(0.003)
	[$t = 95.47$]
Constant	0.000
	(0.000)
	[$t = 0.00$]
N	29,380

Standard errors in parentheses.

* *indicates significance at $p < 0.05$, two-tailed.*

---

[7] Or should we say double handedly? Or, really, quadruple handedly?

[8] The study also looked at other campaign tactics, such as phone calls and mailing postcards. These didn't work as well as the personal visits; for simplicity, we focus on the in-person visits.

TABLE 10.3 Second-Stage Regression in Campaign Experiment: Explaining Turnout	
Personal visit ($\hat{T}$)	0.087*
	(0.026)
	[$t = 3.34$]
Constant	0.448*
	(0.003)
	[$t = 138.38$]
N	29,380

The dependent variable is 1 for individuals who voted. The independent variable is the fitted value from the first stage.

Standard errors in parentheses.

* indicates significance at $p < 0.05$, two-tailed.

These results suggest that 27.9 percent of those assigned to be visited were actually visited. In other words, 27.9 percent of the treatment group complied with the treatment. This estimate is hugely statistically significant, in part owing to the large sample size. The intercept is 0.0, implying that no one in the non-contact-assigned group was contacted by this particular get-out-the-vote campaign.

The treatment assignment variable Z_i also is highly likely to satisfy the 2SLS exclusion condition because the randomized treatment assignment variable Z_i affects Y only through people actually getting campaign contact. Being assigned to be contacted by the campaign in and of itself does not affect turnout. Note that we are not saying that the people who actually complied (received a campaign contact) are random, for all the reasons just given in relation to concerns about compliance come into play here. We are simply saying that when we put a check next to randomly selected names indicating they that should be visited, these folks were indeed randomly selected. That means that Z is uncorrelated with ϵ and can, therefore, be excluded from the main equation.

In the second-stage regression, we use the fitted values from the first-stage regression as the independent variable. Table 10.3 shows that the effect of a personal visit is to increase probability of turning out to vote by 8.7 percentage points. This estimate is statistically significant, as we can see from the t stat, 3.34. We could improve the precision of the estimates by adding covariates, but doing so is not necessary to avoid bias.

Understanding variables in 2SLS models of non-compliance

Understanding the way the fitted values work is useful for understanding how 2SLS works here. Table 10.4 shows the three different ways we are using to measure campaign contact for three hypothetical observations. In the first column is treatment assignment. Volunteers were to visit Laura and Bryce but not Gio. This selection was randomly determined. In the second column is actual contact,

TABLE 10.4	Various Measures of Campaign Contact in 2SLS Model for Selected Observations		
Name	Contact-assigned (Z)	Contact-delivered (T)	Contact-fitted ($\hat{T}$)
Laura	1	1	0.279
Bryce	1	0	0.279
Gio	0	0	0.000

which is observed contact by the campaign. Laura answered the door when the campaign volunteer knocked, but Bryce did not. (No one went to poor Gio's door.) The third column displays the fitted value from the first-stage equation for the treatment variable. These fitted values depend only on contact assignment. Laura and Bryce were assigned to be called randomly ($Z = 1$), so both their fitted values were $\hat{X} = 0.0 + 0.279 \times 1 = 0.279$ even though Laura was actually contacted and Bryce wasn't. Gio was not assigned not to be visited ($Z = 0$), so his fitted contact values was $\hat{X} = 0.0 + 0.279 \times 0 = 0.0$.

2SLS uses the "contact-fitted" ($\hat{T}$) variable. It is worth taking the time to really understand $\hat{T}$, which might be the weirdest thing in the whole book.[9] Even though Bryce was not contacted, his $\hat{T}_i$ is 0.279, just the same as Laura, who was in fact visited. Clearly, this variable looks very different from actual observed campaign contact. Yes, this is odd, but it's a feature, not a bug. The core inferential problem, as we've noted, is endogeneity in actual observed contact. Bryce might be avoiding contact because he loathes politics. That's why we don't want to use observed contact as a variable—it would capture not only the effect of contact, but also the fact that the type of people who get contact in observational data are different. The fitted value, however, varies only according the Z—something that is exogenous. In other words, by looking at the bump up in expected contact associated with being in the randomly assembled contact-assigned group, we have isolated the exogenous bump up in contact associated with the exogenous factor and can assess whether it is associated with a corresponding bump up in voting turnout.

REMEMBER THIS

1. 2SLS is useful for analyzing experiments when there is imperfect compliance with the experimental treatment.

2. Assignment to treatment typically satisfies the inclusion and exclusion conditions necessary for instruments in 2SLS analysis.

---

[9] Other than the ferret thing in Chapter 3—also weird.

Minneapolis Domestic Violence Experiment

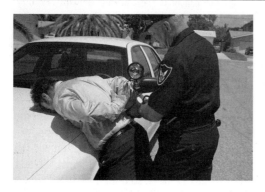

Instrumental variables can be used to analyze an ambitious and, at first glance, very unlikely experiment. It deals with domestic violence, a social ill that has long challenged police and others trying to reduce it. This may sound like a crazy place for an experiment, but stay tuned because it turns out not to be.

The goal is to figure out what police should do when they come upon a domestic violence incident. Police can either take a hard line and arrest suspects whenever possible or they can be conciliatory and decline to make an arrest as long as no one is in immediate danger. Either approach could potentially be more effective: arresting suspects creates clear consequences for offenders, while not arresting them may possibly defuse the situation.

So what should police do? This is a great question to answer empirically. A model based on observational data would look like

$$\text{Arrested later}_i = \beta_0 + \beta_1 \text{Arrested initially}_i + \beta_2 X_i + \epsilon_i \tag{10.7}$$

where *Arrested later* is 1 if the person is arrested at some later date for domestic violence, *Arrested initially* is 1 if the suspect was arrested at the time of the initial domestic violence report, and *X* refers to other variables, such as whether a weapon or drugs were involved in the first incident.

Why might there be endogeneity? (That is, why might we suspect a correlation between *Arrested initially* and the error term?) Elements in the error term include person-specific characteristics. Some people who have police called on them are indeed nasty; let's call them the bad eggs. Others are involved in a once-in-a-lifetime incident; in the overall population of people who have police called on them, they are the (relatively) good eggs. Such personality traits are in the error term of the equation predicting domestic violence in the future.

We could also easily imagine that people's good or bad eggness will affect whether they were arrested initially. Police who arrive at the scene of a domestic violence incident involving a bad egg will, on average, find more threat; police who arrive at the scene of an incident involving a (relatively) good egg will likely find the environment less threatening. We would expect police to arrest the bad egg types more often, and we would expect these folks to have more problems in the future. Observational data could therefore suggest that arrests make things worse because those arrested are more likely to be bad eggs and therefore more likely to be rearrested.

The problem is endogeneity. The correlation of the *Arrested initially* variable and the personal characteristics in the error term prevents observational data from isolating the effect of the policy (arrest) from the likelihood that this policy will, at least sometimes, be differentially applied across types of people.

An experiment is promising here, at least in theory. If police randomly choose to arrest people when domestic violence has been reported, then our arrest variable would no longer be correlated with the personal traits of the perpetrators. Of course this idea is insane, right? Police can't randomly arrest people (can they?). Believe it or not, researchers in Minneapolis created just such an experiment. More details are in Angrist (2006); we'll simplify the experiment a bit. The Minneapolis researchers gave police a note pad to document incidents. The note pad had randomly colored pages; the police officer was supposed to arrest or not arrest the perpetrator based on the color of the page.

Clearly, perfect compliance is impossible and undesirable. No police department could tell its officers to arrest or not based simply on the color of pages in a notebook. Some circumstances are so dangerous that an arrest must be made, notebook be damned. Endogeneity concerns arise because the type of people arrested under these circumstances (the bad eggs) are different from those not arrested.

2SLS can rescue the experimental design. We'll show first how randomization in experiments satisfies the 2SLS conditions and then show how 2SLS works and how it looks versus other approaches.

The inclusion condition is that Z explains X. In this case, the condition requires that assignment to the arrest treatment actually predict being arrested. Table 10.5 shows that those assigned to be arrested were 77.3 percentage points more likely to be arrested, even when the reported presence of a weapon or drugs at the scene

TABLE 10.5 **First-Stage Regression in Domestic Violence Experiment: Explaining Arrests**

Arrest assigned ($Z = 1$)	0.773*
	(0.043)
	[$t = 17.98$]
Weapon	0.064
	(0.045)
	[$t = 1.42$]
Drugs	0.088*
	(0.040)
	[$t = 2.20$]
Constant	0.216
N	314

Standard errors in parentheses.

* *indicates significance at $p < 0.05$, two-tailed.*

TABLE 10.6	Selected Observations for Minneapolis Domestic Violence Experiment		
Observation	Arrest-assigned (Z)	Arrest-delivered (T)	Arrest-fitted ($\hat{T}$)
1	1	1	0.989
2	1	0	0.989
3	0	1	0.216
4	0	0	0.216

is controlled for. The effect is massively statistically significant, with a t statistic of 17.98. The intercept was not directly reported in the original paper, but from other information in the paper we can determine that $\hat{\gamma}_0 = 0.216$ in our first-stage regression.

Assignment to the arrest treatment is very plausibly uncorrelated with the error term. This condition is not testable and must instead be argued based on nonstatistical evidence. Here the argument is pretty simple: the instrument was randomly generated and therefore not correlated with anything, in the error term or otherwise.

Before we present the 2SLS results, let's be clear about the variable used in the 2SLS model as opposed to the variables used in other approaches. Table 10.6 shows the three different ways to measure arrest. The first (Z) is whether an individual was assigned to the arrest treatment. The second (T) is whether a person was in fact arrested. The third ($\hat{T}$) is the fitted value of arrest based on Z. We report four examples, assuming that no weapons or drugs were reported in the initial incident. Person 1 was assigned to be arrested and in fact was arrested. His fitted value is $\hat{\gamma}_0 + \hat{\gamma}_1 \times 1 = 0.216 + 0.773 = 0.989$. Person 2 was assigned to be arrested and was not arrested. His fitted value is the same as person 1's: $\hat{\gamma}_0 + \hat{\gamma}_1 \times 1 = 0.216 + 0.773 = 0.989$. Person 3 was not assigned to be arrested but was in fact arrested. He was probably pretty nasty when the police showed up. His fitted value is $\hat{\gamma}_0 + \hat{\gamma}_1 \times 0 = 0.216 + 0 = 0.216$. Person 4 was not assigned to be arrested and was not arrested. He was probably relatively calm when the police showed up. His fitted value is $\hat{\gamma}_0 + \hat{\gamma}_1 \times 0 = 0.216 + 0 = 0.216$. Even though we suspect that persons 3 and 4 are very different types of people, the fitted values are the same, which is a good thing because factors associated with actually being arrested (the bad eggness) that are correlated with the error term in the equation predicting future arrests are purged from the $\hat{T}$ variable.

Table 10.7 shows the results from three different ways to estimate a model in which *Arrested later* is the dependent variable. The models also control for whether a weapon or drugs had been reported in the initial incident. The OLS model uses treatment delivered (T) as the independent variable. The ITT model uses treatment assigned (Z) as the independent variable. The 2SLS model uses the fitted value of treatment ($\hat{T}$) as the independent variable.

TABLE 10.7	**Using Different Estimators to Analyze the Results of the Domestic Violence Experiment**		
	OLS	**ITT**	**2SLS**
Arrest	−0.070	−0.108*	−0.140*
	(0.038)	(0.041)	(0.053)
	[$t = 1.84$]	[$t = 2.63$]	[$t = 2.64$]
Weapon	0.010	0.004	0.005
	(0.043)	(0.042)	(0.043)
	[$t = 0.23$]	[$t = 0.10$]	[$t = 0.12$]
Drugs	0.057	0.052	0.064
	(0.039)	(0.038)	(0.039)
	[$t = 1.46$]	[$t = 1.37$]	[$t = 1.64$]
N	314	314	314

Dependent variable is a dummy variable indicating rearrest.

Standard errors in parentheses.

* indicates significance at $p < 0.05$, two-tailed.

The first column shows that OLS estimates a decrease of 7 percentage points in probability of a rearrest later. The independent variable was whether someone was actually arrested. This group includes people who were randomly assigned to be arrested and people in the no-arrest-assigned treatment group who were arrested anyway. We worry about bias when we use this variable because we suspect that the bad eggs were more likely to get arrested.[10]

The second column shows that ITT estimates that being assigned to the arrest treatment lowers the probability of being arrested later by 10.8 percentage points. This result is more negative than the OLS estimate and is statistically significant. The ITT model avoids endogeneity because treatment assignment cannot be correlated with the error term. The approach will understate the true effect when there was non-compliance, either because some people not assigned to the treatment got it or because everyone who was assigned to the treatment actually received it.

The third column shows the 2SLS results. In this model, the independent variable is the fitted value of the treatment. The estimated coefficient on arrest is even more negative than the ITT estimate, indicating that the probability of rearrest for individuals who were arrested is 14 percentage points lower than for individuals who were not initially arrested. The magnitude is double the effect estimated by OLS. This result implies that the city of Minneapolis can, on average, reduce the probability of another incident by 14 percentage points by arresting individuals on the initial call. 2SLS is the best model because it accounts for non-compliance and

---

[10] The OLS model reported here is still based on partially randomized data because many were arrested owing to the randomization in the police protocol. If we had purely observational data with no randomization, the bias of OLS would be worse, as it's likely that only bad eggs would have been arrested.

provides an unbiased estimate of the effect that arresting someone initially had on likelihood of a future arrest.

This study was quite influential and spawned similar investigations elsewhere; see Berk, Campbell, Klap, and Western (1992) for more details.

10.4 Attrition

▶ **attrition** Occurs when people drop out of an experiment altogether such that we do not observe the dependent variable for them.

Another challenge for experiments is **attrition**—people dropping out of an experiment altogether, preventing us from observing the dependent variable for them. Attrition can happen when experimental subjects become frustrated with the experiment and discontinue participation, when they are too busy to respond, and when they move away or die. Attrition can occur in both treatment and control groups.

In this section we explain how attrition can infect randomized experiments with endogeneity, show how to detect problematic attrition, and describe three ways to counteract the effects of attrition.

Attrition and endogeneity

Attrition opens a back door for endogeneity to enter our experiments when it is non-random. Suppose we randomly give people free donuts. If some of these subjects eat so many donuts that they can't rise from the couch to answer the experimenter's phone calls, we no longer have data for these folks. This is a problem, because the missing observations would have told of people who got lots of donuts and had a pretty bad health outcome. Losing these observations will make donuts look less bad and thereby bias our conclusions.

Attrition is real. In the New York City school choice experiment discussed earlier, researchers intended to track test scores of students in the treatment and control groups over time. A surprising number of students, however, could not be tracked. Some had moved away, some were absent on test days, and some probably got lost in the computer system.

And attrition can be non-random. In the New York school choice experiment, 67 percent of African-American students in the treatment group took the test in year 2 of the experiment, while only 55 percent of African-American students in the control group took the test in year 2. We should wonder if these groups are comparable and should worry about the possibility that test differentials discovered were due to differential attrition rather than to the effects of private schooling.

Detecting problematic attrition

Detecting problematic attrition is therefore an important part of any experimental analysis. First, we should assess whether attrition was related to treatment. Commonsensically, we can simply look at attrition rates in treatment and control groups. Statistically, we could estimate the following model:

$$Attrition_i = \delta_0 + \delta_1 Treatment_i + v_i \qquad (10.8)$$

where $Attrition_i$ equals 1 for observations for which we do not observe the dependent variable and equals 0 when we observe the dependent variable. A statistically significant $\hat{\delta}_1$ would indicate differential attrition across treatment and control groups.

We can add some nuance to our evaluation of attrition by looking for differential attrition patterns in the treatment and control groups. Specifically, we can investigate whether the treatment variable interacted with one or more covariates in a model explaining attrition. In our analysis of a randomized charter school experiment we might explore whether high test scores in earlier years were associated with differential attrition in the treatment group. If we use the tools for interaction variables discussed in Section 6.4, the model would be

$$Attrition_i = \delta_0 + \delta_1 Treatment_i + \delta_2 EarlyTestScores_i$$
$$+ \delta_3 Treatment \times EarlyTestScores_i + v_i$$

where $EarlyTestScores_i$ is the pre-experimental test score of student i. If δ_3 is not equal to zero, then the treatment would appear to have had a differential effect on kids who were good students in the pre-experimental period. Perhaps kids with high test scores were really likely to stick around in the treated group (which means they attended charter schools), while the good students in the control group (who did not attend a charter school) were less likely to stick around (perhaps moving to a different school district and thereby making unavailable their test scores for the period after the experiment had run). In this situation, treated and control groups would differ on the early test score measure, something that should show up in a balance test limited to those who remained in the sample.

Dealing with attrition

There is no magic bullet to zap attrition, but three strategies can prove useful. The first is simply to control for variables associated with attrition in the final analysis. Suppose we found that kids with higher pretreatment test scores were more likely to stay in the experiment. We would be wise to control for pretreatment test scores with multivariate OLS. However, this strategy cannot counter unmeasured sources of attrition that could be correlated with treatment status and post-treatment test scores.

▶ **trimmed data set** A trimmed data set is one for which observations are removed in a way offsets that potential bias due to attrition.

A second approach to attrition is to use a **trimmed data set**, which will make the groups more plausibly comparable. A trimmed data set offsets potential bias due to attrition because certain observations are removed. Suppose we observe 10 percent attrition in the treated group and 5 percent attrition in the control group. We should worry that weak students were dropping out of the treatment group, making the comparison between treated and untreated invalid because the treated group may have shed some of its weakest students. A statistically conservative approach here would be to trim the control group by removing another 5 percent of the weakest students before doing our analysis so that now both groups in the data have 10 percent attrition rates. This practice is statistically conservative in the sense that it makes it harder to observe a statistically significant treatment effect because it is unlikely that literally all of those who dropped out from the treatment group were the worst students.

▶ **selection model**
Simultaneously accounts for whether we observe the dependent variable and what the dependent variable is.

A third approach to attrition is to use **selection models**. The most famous selection model is called a Heckman selection model (1979). In this approach, we would model both the process of being observed (which is a dichotomous variable equaling 1 for those for whom we observe the dependent variable and 0 for others) and the outcome (the model with the dependent variable of interest, such as test scores). These models build on the probit model we shall discuss in Chapter 12. More details are in the Further Reading section at the end of this chapter.

▶ **REMEMBER THIS**

1. Attrition occurs when individuals drop out of an experiment, causing us to lack outcome data for them.

2. Non-random attrition can cause endogeneity even when treatment is randomly assigned.

3. We can detect problematic attrition by looking for differences in attrition rates across treated and control groups.

4. Attrition can be addressed by using multivariate OLS, trimmed data sets, or selection models.

Discussion Question

Suppose each of the following experimental populations suffered from attrition. Speculate on the likely implications of not accounting for attrition in the analysis.

1. Researchers were interested in the effectiveness of a new drug designed to lower cholesterol. They gave a random set of patients the drug; the rest got a placebo pill.

2. Researchers interested in rehabilitating former prisoners randomly assigned some newly released prisoners to an intensive support group. The rest received no such access. The dependent variable was an indicator for returning to prison within five years.

CASE STUDY   Health Insurance and Attrition

In the United States, health care consumes about one-sixth of the entire economy and is arguably the single biggest determinant of future budget deficits in the country.

Figuring out how to deliver high-quality care more efficiently is therefore one of the biggest policy questions we face. One option that attracts a lot of interest is to change the way we pay for health care. We could, for example, make consumers pay more for medical care, to encourage them to use only what they really need. In such an approach, health insurance would cover the really big catastrophic items (think heart transplant), but would cover less of the more mundane, potentially avoidable items (think flu visits).

To know whether such an approach will work, we need to answer two questions. First, are health care outcomes the same or better when costs to the consumer are higher? It's not much of a reform if it saves money by making us sicker. Second, do medical expenditures go down when people have to pay more for medical services?

Because there are many health insurance plans on the private market, we could imagine using observational data to answer these questions. We could see whether people on relatively stingy health insurance plans (that pay only for very major costs) are as healthy as others who spend less on routine health care.

Such an approach really wouldn't be very useful though. Why? You guessed it:

> Insurance is endogenous; those who expect to demand more services have a clear incentive to obtain more complete insurance, either by selecting a more generous option at the place of employment, by working for an employer with a generous insurance plan, or by purchasing privately more generous coverage (Manning et al. 1987, 252).

In other words, because sick people probably seek out better health care coverage, a non-experimental analysis of health coverage and costs would be likely to show that health care costs more for those with better coverage. That wouldn't mean the generous coverage *caused* costs to go up; such a relationship could simply be the endogeneity talking.

Suppose we don't have a good measure of whether someone has diabetes. We would expect that people with diabetes seek out generous coverage because they expect to rack up considerable medical expenses. The result would be a correlation between the error term and type of health plan, with people in the generous health plan having lower health outcomes (because of all those people with diabetes who signed up for the generous plan). Or maybe insurance companies figure out a way to measure whether people have diabetes and not let them into generous insurance plans, which would mean the people in the generous plans would be healthier than others. Here too the diabetes in the error term would be correlated with the type of health plan, although in the other direction.

Thus we have a good candidate for a randomized experiment, which is exactly what ambitious researchers at RAND designed in the 1970s. They randomly assigned people to various health plans including a free plan that covered medical care at no cost and various cost-sharing plans that had different levels of co-payments. With randomization, the type of people assigned to a free plan should be expected to be the same as the type of people assigned to a cost-sharing plan. The only expected difference between the groups is their health plans; hence to the extent that the groups differed in utilization or health outcomes, the differences could be attributed to differences in the health plans.

The RAND researchers found that medical expenses were 45 percent higher for people in plans with no out-of-pocket medical expenses than for those who had stingy insurance plans (which required people to pay 95 percent of costs, up to a $1,000 yearly maximum). In general, health outcomes were no worse for those in the stingy plans.[11] This experiment has been incredibly influential—it is the reason we pay $10 or whatever when we check out of the doctor's office.

Attrition is a crucial issue in evaluating the RAND experiment. Not everyone stayed in the experiment. Inevitably in such a large study, some people moved, some died, and others opted out of the experiment because they were unhappy with the plan they were randomly placed in. The threat to the validity of this experiment is that this attrition may have been non-random. If the type of people who stayed with one plan differed systematically from the type of people who stayed with another plan, comparing health outcomes or utilization rates across these groups may be inappropriate, given that the groups differ both in their health plans *and* in the type of people who remain in the wake of attrition.

Aron-Dine, Einav, and Finkelstein (2013) reexamined the RAND data in light of attrition and other concerns. They showed that 1,894 people had been randomly assigned to the free plan. Of those, 114 (5 percent) were non-compliers who declined to participate. Of the remainder who participated, 89 (5 percent) left the experiment. These low numbers for non-compliance and attrition are not very surprising. The free plan was gold plated, covering everything. The cost-sharing plan requiring the highest out-of-pocket expenditures had 1,121 assigned participants. Of these 269 (24 percent) declined the opportunity to participate and another 145 (17 percent) left the experiment. These patterns contrast markedly from the non-compliance and attrition patterns for the free plan.

What kind of people would we expect to leave a cost-sharing plan? Probably people who ended up paying a lot of money under the plan. And what kind of people would end up paying a lot of money under a cost-sharing plan? Sick people, most likely. So that means we have reason to worry that the free plan had all kinds of people, but the cost-sharing plans had a sizable hunk of

---

[11] Outcomes for people in the stingy plans were worse for some subgroups and some conditions, leading the researchers to suggest programs targeted at specific conditions rather than providing fee-free service for all health care.

sick people who pulled out. So any finding that the cost-sharing plans yielded the same health outcomes could have one of two causes: the plans did not have different health impacts *or* the free plan was better but had a sicker population.

Aron-Dine, Einav, and Finkelstein (2013) therefore conducted an analysis on a trimmed data set based on techniques from Lee (2009). They dropped the highest spenders in the free-care plan until they had a data set with the same proportion of observations from those assigned to the free plan and to the costly plan. Comparing these two groups is equivalent to assuming that those who left the costly plan were the patients requiring the most expensive care; since this is unlikely to be completely true, the results from such a comparison are considered a lower bound—actual differences between the groups would be larger if some of the people who dropped out from the costly plan were not among the most expensive patients. The results indicated that the effect of the cost-sharing plan was still negative, meaning that it lowered expenditures. However, the magnitude of the effect was less than the magnitude reported in the initial study, which did little to account for differential attrition across the various types of plans.

Review Questions

Consider a hypothetical experiment in which researchers evaluated a program that paid teachers a substantial bonus if their students' test scores rose. The researchers implemented the program in 50 villages and also sought test score data in 50 randomly selected villages.

Table 10.8 on the next page provides results from regressions using data available to the researchers. Each column shows a bivariate regression in which *Treatment* was the independent variable. This variable equaled 1 for villages where teachers were paid for student test scores and 0 for the control villages.

Researchers also had data on average village income, village population and whether or not test scores were available (a variable that equals 1 for villages that reported test scores and 0 for villages that did not report test scores.)

1. Is there a balance problem? Use specific results in the table to justify your answer.

2. Is there an attrition problem? Use specific results in the table to justify your answer.

3. Did the treatment work? Justify your answer based on results here and discuss what, if any, additional information you would like to see.

TABLE 10.8 Regression Results for Models Relating Teacher Payment Experiment (for Review Questions)

	Dependent Variable			
	Test scores	Village population	Village income	Test score availability
Treatment	24.0*	−20.00	500.0*	0.20*
	(8.00)	(100.0)	(200.0)	(0.08)
	[$t = 3.00$]	[$t = 0.20$]	[$t = 2.50$]	[$t = 2.50$]
Constant	50.0*	500.0*	1000.0*	0.70*
	(10.00)	(100.0)	(200.0)	(0.05)
	[$t = 5.00$]	[$t = 5.00$]	[$t = 5.00$]	[$t = 14.00$]
N	80	100	100	100

Standard errors in parentheses.

* *indicates significance at $p < 0.05$, two-tailed.*

10.5 Natural Experiments

As a practical matter, experiments cannot cover every research question. As we discussed in Section 1.3, experiments we might think up are often infeasible, unethical, or unaffordable.

Sometimes, however, an experiment may fall into our laps. That is, we might find that the world has essentially already run a **natural experiment** that pretty much looks like a randomized experiment, but we didn't have to muck about actually implementing it. In a natural experiment, a researcher identifies a situation in which the values of the independent variable have been determined by a random, or at least exogenous, process.

▶ **natural experiment**
Occurs when a researcher identifies a situation in which the values of the independent variable have been determined by a random, or at least exogenous, process.

In this section we discuss some of the clever ways researchers have been able to use natural experiments to answer interesting research questions.

In an ideal natural experiment, an independent variable is exogenously determined, leaving us with treatment and control groups that look pretty much as they would look if we had intentionally designed a random experiment. One example is in elections. In 2010, a hapless candidate named Alvin Greene won the South Carolina Democratic primary election to run for the U.S. Senate. Greene had done no campaigning and was not exactly an obvious senatorial candidate: He had been involuntarily discharged from both the army and the air force and had been unemployed since leaving the military. He was also under indictment for showing pornographic pictures to a college student. Yet he won 59 percent of the vote in the 2010 primary against a former state legislator. While some wondered if something nefarious was going on, many pointed to a more mundane possibility: when voters don't know much about candidates, they might pick the first name they see. Greene was first on the ballot and perhaps that's why he did so well.[12]

---

[12] Greene went on to get only 28 percent of the vote in the general election but vowed to run for President anyway.

An experimental test of this proposition would involve randomly rotating the ballot order of candidates and seeing if candidates who appear first on the ballot do better. Conceptually that's not too hard, but practically it is a lot to ask, given that election officials are pretty protective of how they run elections. In the 1998 Democratic primary in New York City, however, election officials decided on their own to rotate the order of candidates' names by precinct. Political scientists Jonathan Koppell and Jennifer Steen got wind of this decision and analyzed the election as a natural experiment. Their 2004 paper found that in 71 of 79 races, candidates received more votes in precincts where they were listed first. In seven of those races the differences were enough to determine the election outcome. That's pretty good work for an experiment the researchers didn't even set up.

Researchers have found other clever opportunities for natural experiments. An important question is whether economic stimulus packages of tax cuts and government spending increases that were implemented in response to the 2008 recession boosted growth. At a first glance, such analysis should be easy. We know how much the federal government cut taxes and increased spending. We also know how the economy performed. Of course, things are not so simple because, as former chair of the Council of Economic Advisers Christina Romer (2011) noted, "Fiscal actions are often taken in response to other things happening in the economy." When we look at the relationship between two variables, like consumer spending and the tax rebate, we "need to worry that a third variable, like the fall in wealth, is influencing both of them. Failing to take account of this omitted variable leads to a biased estimate of the relationship of interest."

One way to deal with this challenge is to find *exogenous* variation in stimulus spending that is not correlated with any of the omitted variables we worry about. This is typically very hard, but sometimes natural experiments pop up. For example, Parker et al. (2013) noted that the 2008 stimulus consisted of tax rebate checks that were sent out in stages according to the last two digits of recipients' Social Security numbers. Thus the timing was effectively random for each family. After all, the last two digits are essentially randomly assigned to people when they are born. This means that the timing of the government spending by family was exogenous. An analyst's dream come true! The researchers found that family spending among those that got a check was almost $500 more than those who did not, bolstering the case that the fiscal stimulus boosted consumer spending.

REMEMBER THIS

1. In a natural experiment, the values of the independent variable have been determined by a random, or at least exogenous, process.

2. Natural experiments are widely used and can be analyzed with OLS, 2SLS, or other tools.

CASE STUDY   Crime and Terror Alerts

One need not have true randomness for a natural experiment. One needs only exogeneity, something quite different from randomness, as the following example makes clear. It is about the effect of police on crime. As discussed earlier (page 250), observational data used to estimate the following model

$$Crime_{st} = \beta_0 + \beta_1 Police_{st} + \epsilon_{st} \qquad (10.9)$$

are likely to suffer from endogeneity and risks statistical catastrophe because one of the variables is likely to be endogenous.

Could we use experiments to test the relationship? Sure. All we need to do is head down to the police station and ask that officers be assigned to different places at random. The idea is not completely crazy and, frankly, it is the kind of thing police should consider doing. It's not an easy sell, though. Can you imagine the outrage if a shocking crime occurred in an area that had randomly been assigned a low number of officers?

Economists Jonathan Klick and Alexander Tabarrok identified in 2005 a clever natural experiment that looks much like the randomized experiment we proposed. They noticed that Washington, DC, deployed more police when the terror alert level was high. A high terror alert was not random; presumably it had been prompted by some cause, somewhere. The condition was exogenous, though. Whatever leads terrorists to threaten carnage, it was not associated with factors that lead local criminals in Washington, DC, to rob a liquor store. In other words, it was highly unlikely that terror alerts are correlated with the things in the error term causing endogeneity, as we have discussed. It was as if someone had designed a study in which extra police would be deployed at random times, only in this case the "random" times were essentially selected by terrorist suspects with no information about crime in DC, rather than by a computerized random number generator, as typically would be used in an academic experiment.

Klick and Tabarrok therefore assessed whether crime declined when the terror alert level was high. Table 10.9 reports their main results: crimes decreased when the terror alert level went up. The researchers also controlled for subway ridership, to account for the possibility that if more people (and tourists in particular) were around, there might be more targets for crime. The effect of the high terror alerts was still negative. Because this variable was exogenous to crime in the capital and could, Klick and Tabarrok argued, affect crime only by means of the increased police presence, they asserted that their result provided pretty good evidence that police can reduce crime. They used ordinary least squares, but the tools of analysis were really less important than the vision of finding something that caused exogenous changes to police deployment and then tracking changes in crime. Again, this is a pretty good day's work for an experiment the people who analyzed it didn't run.

TABLE 10.9 Effect of Terror Alerts on Crime		
High terror alert	−7.32*	−6.05*
	(2.88)	(2.54)
	[$t = 2.54$]	[$t = 2.38$]
Subway ridership		17.34*
		(5.31)
		[$t = 3.27$]
N	506	506

Dependent variable is total number of crimes in Washington, DC, from March 12 to July 30, 2003.

Standard errors in parentheses.

* indicates significance at $p < 0.05$, two-tailed.

Conclusion

Experiments are incredibly promising for statistical inference. To find out if X causes Y, do an experiment. Change X for a random subset of people. Compare what happens to Y for the treatment and control groups. The approach is simple, elegant, and has been used productively countless times.

For all their promise, though, experiments are like movie stars—idealized by many but tending to lose some luster in real life. Movie stars' teeth are a bit yellow, and they aren't particularly witty without a script. By the same token, experiments don't always achieve balance; they sometimes suffer from non-compliance and attrition; and in many circumstances they aren't feasible, ethical, or generalizable.

For these reasons, we need to take particular care when examining experiments. We need to diagnose and, if necessary, respond to ABC issues (attrition, balance and compliance). Every experiment needs to assess balance to ensure that the treatment and control groups do not differ systematically except for the treatment. Many social science experiments also have potential non-compliance problems, since people can choose not to experience the randomly assigned treatment. Non-compliance can induce endogeneity if we use *Treatment delivered* as the independent variable, but we can get back to unbiased inference if we use ITT or 2SLS to analyze the experiment. Finally, at least some people invariably leave the experiment, which can be a problem if the attrition is related to the treatment. Attrition is hard to overcome but it must be diagnosed and, if it is a problem, we should at least use multivariate OLS or trimmed data to lessen the validity-degrading effects.

The following steps provide a general guide to implementing and analyzing a randomized experiment:

1. Identify a target population.

2. Randomly pick a subset of the population and give them the treatment. The rest are the control group.

3. Diagnose possible threats to internal validity.

   (a) Assess balance with difference of means tests for all possible independent variables.

   (b) Assess compliance by looking at what percent of those assigned to treatment actually experienced it.

   (c) Assess non-random attrition by looking for differences in observation patterns across treatment and control groups.

4. Gather data on the outcome variable Y and assess differences between treated and control groups.

   (a) If there is perfect balance and compliance and no attrition, use bivariate OLS. Multivariate OLS also will be appropriate and will provide more precise estimates.

   (b) If there are imbalances, use multivariate OLS, controlling for variables that are unbalanced across treatment and control groups.

   (c) If there is imperfect compliance, use ITT analysis and 2SLS.

   (d) If there is attrition, use multivariate OLS, trim the data, or use a selection model.

We are on track to understand social science experiments if we can

- Section 10.1: Explain how to assess whether randomization was successful with balancing tests.

- Section 10.2: Explain how imperfect compliance can create endogeneity. What is the ITT approach, and how does it avoid conflating treatment effects and non-compliance effects? How do ITT estimates relate to the actual treatment effects?

- Section 10.3: Explain how 2SLS can be useful for experiments with imperfect compliance.

- Section 10.4: Explain how attrition can create endogeneity. What are some steps we can take to diagnose and deal with attrition?

- Section 10.5: Explain natural experiments.

Further Reading

Experiments are booming in the social sciences. Gerber and Green (2012) provide a comprehensive guide to field experiments. Banerjee and Duflo (2011) give an excellent introduction to experiments in the developing world, and Duflo, Glennerster, and Kremer (2008) provide an experimental toolkit that's useful for experiments in the developing world and beyond. Dunning (2012) has published a detailed guide to natural experiments. A readable guide by Manzi (2012) is also a critique of randomized experiments in social science and business. He refers (2012, 190) to a report to Congress in 2008 that identified policies that demonstrated significant results in randomized field trials.

Attrition is one of the harder things to deal with, and different analysts take different approaches. Gerber and Green (2012, 214) discuss their approaches to dealing with attrition. The large literature on selection models includes, for example, Das, Newey, and Vella (2003). Some experimentalists resist using selection models because those models rely heavily on assumptions about the distributions of error terms and functional form.

Imai, King, and Stuart (2008) discuss how to use blocking to get more efficiency and less potential for bias in randomized experiments.

Key Terms

ABC issues (326)

Attrition (346)

Balance (328)

Blocking (327)

Compliance (332)

Intention-to-treat (ITT)
   analysis (335)

Natural experiment (352)

Selection model (348)

Trimmed data set (347)

Computing Corner

Stata

1. To assess balance, estimate a series of bivariate regression models with all "X" variables as dependent variables and treatment assignment as independent variables:

```
reg X1 TreatmentAssignment
reg X2 TreatmentAssignment
```

2. To estimate an ITT model, estimate a model with the outcome of interest as the dependent variable and treatment assignment as the main independent variable. Other variables can be included, especially if there are balance problems.

```
reg Y TreatmentAssignment X1 X2
```

3. To estimate a 2SLS model, estimate a model with the outcome of interest as the dependent variable and treatment assignment as an instrument for *Treatment delivered*. Other variables can be included, especially if there are balance problems.
   ```
   ivregress Y (Treatment = TreatmentAssignment) X1 X2
   ```

R

1. To assess balance, estimate a series of bivariate regression models with all "*X*" variables as dependent variables and treatment assignment as independent variables:
   ```
   lm(X1 ~ TreatmentAssignment)
   lm(X2 ~ TreatmentAssignment)
   ```

2. To estimate an ITT model, estimate a model with the outcome of interest as the dependent variable and treatment assignment as the main independent variable. Other variables can be included, especially if there are balance problems.
   ```
   lm(Y ~ TreatmentAssignment+ X1 + X2)
   ```

3. To estimate a 2SLS model, estimate a model with the outcome of interest as the dependent variable and treatment assignment as an instrument for *Treatment delivered*. Other variables can be included, especially if there are balance problems. As discussed on page 318, we'll use the `ivreg` command from the AER library:
   ```
   library(AER)
   ivreg(Y ~ Treatment + X2 | TreatmentAssignment + X2)
   ```

Exercises

1. In an effort to better understand the effects of get-out-the-vote messages on voter turnout, Gerber and Green (2005) conducted a randomized field experiment involving approximately 30,000 individuals in New Haven, Connecticut, in 1998. One of the experimental treatments was randomly assigned in-person visits in which a volunteer visited the person's home and encouraged him or her to vote. The file GerberGreenData.dta contains the variables described in Table 10.10.

   (a) Estimate a bivariate model of the effect of actual contact on voting. Is the model biased? Why or why not?

   (b) Estimate compliance by estimating what percentage of treatment-assigned people actually were contacted.

TABLE 10.10 **Variables for Get-out-the-Vote Experiment from Gerber and Green (2005)**

Variable	Description
Voted	Voted in the 1998 election (voted = 1)
ContactAssigned	Assigned to in-person contact (assigned = 1)
ContactObserved	Actually contacted via in-person visit (treated = 1)
Ward	Ward number
PeopleHH	Household size

(c) Use ITT to estimate the effect of being assigned treatment on whether someone turned out to vote. Is this estimate likely to be higher or lower than the actual effect of being contacted? Is it subject to endogeneity?

(d) Use 2SLS to estimate the effect of contact on voting. Compare the results to the ITT results. Justify your choice of instrument.

(e) We can use ITT results and compliance rates to generate a Wald estimator, which is an estimate of the treatment effects calculated by dividing the ITT effect by the coefficient on the treatment assignment variable in the first-stage model of the 2SLS model. (If no one in the non-treatment-assignment group gets the treatment, this coefficient will indicate the compliance rate; more generally, this coefficient indicates the net effect of treatment assignment on probability of treatment observed.) Calculate this quantity by using the results in part (b) and (c) and compare to the 2SLS results. It helps to be as precise as possible. Are they different? Discuss.

(f) Create dummy variables indicating whether respondents lived in Ward 2 and Ward 3. Assess balance for Wards 2 and 3 and also for the people-per-household variables. Is imbalance a problem? Why or why not? Is there anything we should do about it?

(g) Estimate a 2SLS model including controls for Ward 2 and Ward 3 residence and the number of people in the household. Do you expect the results to differ substantially? Why or why not? Explain how the first-stage results differ from the balance tests described earlier.

2. In Chapter 9 (page 320) we considered an experiment in which people were assigned to a treatment group that was encouraged to watch a television program on affirmative action. We will revisit that analysis, paying attention to experimental challenges.

(a) Check balance in treatment versus control for all possible independent variables.

(b) What percent of those assigned to the treatment group actually watched the program? How is your answer relevant for the analysis?

(c) Are the compliers different from the non-compliers? Provide evidence to support your answer.

(d) In the first round of the experiment, 805 participants were interviewed and assigned to either the treatment or the control condition. After the program aired, 507 participants were re-interviewed about the program. With only 63 percent of the participants re-interviewed, what problems are created for the experiment?

(e) In this case data (even pretreatment data) is available only for the 507 people who did not leave the sample. Is there anything we can do?

(f) We estimated a 2SLS model earlier (page 320). Calculate a Wald estimator by dividing the ITT effect by the coefficient on the treatment assignment variable in the first-stage model of the 2SLS model. (If no one in the non-treatment-assigned group gets the treatment, this coefficient will indicate the compliance rate; more generally, this coefficient indicates the net effect of treatment assignment on probability of treatment observed.) In all models, control for measures of political interest, newspaper reading, and education. Compare the results for the effect of watching the program to OLS (using actual treatment) and 2SLS estimates.

3. In their paper "Are Emily and Greg More Employable than Lakisha and Jamal? A Field Experiment on Labor Market Discrimination," Marianne Bertrand and Sendhil Mullainathan (2004) discuss the results of their field experiment on randomizing names on job resumes. To assess whether employers treated African-American and white applicants similarly, they had created fictitious resumes and randomly assigned white-sounding names (e.g., Emily and Greg) to half of the resumes and African-American-sounding names (e.g., Lakisha and Jamal) to the other half. They sent these resumes in response to help-wanted ads in Chicago and Boston and collected data on the number of callbacks received. Table 10.11 describes the variables in the data set resume_HW.dta.

TABLE 10.11	Variables for Resume Experiment
Variable	**Description**
education	0 = not reported; 1 = some high school; 2 = high school graduate; 3 = some college; 4 = college graduate or more
yearsexp	Number of years of work experience
honors	1 = resume mentions some honors
volunteer	1 = resume mentions some volunteering experience
military	1 = Applicant has some military experience
computerskills	1 = resume mentions computer skills
afn_american	1 = African-American-sounding name; 0 = white-sounding name
call	1 = applicant was called back ; 0 applicant not called back
female	1 = female; 0 = male
h_quality	1 = High-quality resume; 0 = low-quality resume

(a) What would be the concern of looking at the number of callbacks by race from an observational study?

(b) Check balance between the two groups (resumes with African-American-sounding names and resumes with white-sounding names) on the following variables: education, years of experience, volunteering experience, honors, computer skills, and gender. The treatment is whether the resume had or did not have an African-American sounding name as indicated by the variable *afn_american*.

(c) What would compliance be in the context of this experiment? Is there a potential non-compliance problem?

(d) What variables do we need to use 2SLS to deal with non-compliance?

(e) Calculate the intention-to-treat (ITT) for receiving a callback from the resumes. The variable call is coded 1 if a person received a callback and 0 otherwise. Use OLS with *call* as the dependent variable.

(f) We're going to add covariates shortly. Discuss the implications of adding covariates to this analysis of a randomized experiment.

(g) Rerun the analysis from part (e) with controls for education, years of experience, volunteering experience, honors, computer skills, and gender. Report the results and briefly describe the effect of having an

African-American-sounding name and if/how the estimated effect changed from the earlier results.

(h) The authors were also interested to see whether race had a differential effect for high-quality resumes and low-quality resumes. They created a variable *h_quality* that indicated a high-quality resume based on labor market experience, career profile, existence of gaps in employment, and skills. Use the controls from part (g) plus the high-quality indicator variable to estimate the effect of having an African-American-sounding name for high- and low-quality resumes.

4. Improving education in Afghanistan may be key to bringing development and stability to that country. In 2007 only 37 percent of primary-school-age children in Afghanistan attended schools, and there is a large gender gap in enrollment (with girls 17 percentage points less likely to attend school). Traditional schools in Afghanistan serve children from numerous villages. Some believe that creating more village-based schools can increase enrollment and students' performance by bringing education closer to home. To assess this belief, researchers Dana Burde and Leigh Linden (2013) conducted a randomized experiment to test the effects of adding village-based schools. For a sample of 12 equal-sized village groups, they randomly selected 5 groups to receive a village-based school. One of the original village groups could not be surveyed and was dropped, resulting in 11 village groups with 5 treatment villages in which a new school was built and 6 control villages in which no new school was built.

This question focuses on the treatment effects for the fall 2007 semester, which began after the schools had been provided. There were 1,490 children across the treatment and control villages. Table 10.12 displays the variables in the data set schools_experiment_HW.dta.

(a) What issues are associated with studying the effects of new schools in Afghanistan that are not randomly assigned?

(b) Why is checking balance an important first step in analyzing a randomized experiment?

(c) Did randomization work? Check the balance of the following variables: age of child, girl, number of sheep family owns, length of time family lived in village, farmer, years of education for household head, number of people in household, and distance to nearest school.

(d) On page 68 we noted that if errors are correlated, the standard OLS estimates for the standard error of $\hat{\beta}$ are incorrect. In this case,

TABLE 10.12   **Variables for Afghan School Experiment**

Variable	Description
formal_school	Enrolled in school
testscores	Fall test scores (normalized); tests were to be given to all children whether in school or not
treatment	Assigned to village-based school $= 1$; otherwise $= 0$
age	Age of child
girl	Girl $= 1$; Boy $= 0$
sheep	Number of sheep owned
duration_village	Duration family has lived in village
farmer	Farmer $= 1$
education_head	Years of education of head of household
number_ppl_hh	Number of people living in household
distance_nearest_school	Distance to nearest school
f07_test_observed	Equals 1 if test was observed for fall 2007
Clustercode	Village code
f07_hh_id	Household ID

we might expect errors to be correlated within village. That is, knowing the error for one child in a given village may provide some information about the error for another child in the same village. The way to generate standard errors that account for correlated errors within some unit is to use the `, cluster(ClusterName)` command at the end of Stata's regression command. In this case, the cluster is the village, as indicated with the variable *Clustercode*. Redo the balance tests from part (c) with clustered standard errors. Do the coefficients change? Do the standard errors change? Do our conclusions change?

(e) Calculate the effect on fall enrollment of being in a treatment village. Use OLS, and report the fitted value of the school attendance variable for control and treatment villages, respectively.

(f) Calculate the effect on fall enrollment of being in a treatment village, controlling for age of child, sex, number of sheep family owns, length of time family lived in village, farmer, years of education for household head, number of people in household, and distance to nearest school. Use the standard errors that account for within-village correlation of errors. Is the coefficient on treatment substantially different from the bivariate OLS results? Why or why not? Briefly note any control variables that are significantly associated with attending school.

(g) Calculate the effect on fall test scores of being in a treatment village. Use the model that calculates standard errors that account for within-village correlation of errors. Interpret the results.

(h) Calculate the effect on test scores of being in a treatment village, controlling for age of child, sex, number of sheep family owns, length of time family lived in village, farmer, years of education for household head, number of people in household, and distance to nearest school. Use the standard errors that account for within-village correlation of errors. Is the coefficient on treatment substantially different from the bivariate OLS results? Why or why not? Briefly note any control variables that are significantly associated with higher test scores.

(i) Compare the sample size for the enrollment and test score data. What concern does this comparison raise?

(j) Assess whether attrition was associated with treatment. Use the standard errors that account for within-village correlation of errors.

Regression Discontinuity: Looking for Jumps in Data

11

▶ **discontinuity**

Occurs when the graph of a line makes a sudden jump up or down.

So far, we've been fighting endogeneity with two strategies. One is to soak up as much endogeneity as we can by including control variables or fixed effects, as we have done with OLS and panel data models. The other is to create or find exogenous variation via randomization or instrumental variables.

In this chapter we offer a third way to fight endogeneity: looking for discontinuities. A **discontinuity** is a point at which a graph suddenly jumps up or down. Potential discontinuities arise when a treatment is given in a mechanical way to observations above some cutoff. Jumps in the dependent variable at the cutoff point indicate the causal effects of treatments under reasonably general conditions.

Suppose, for example, that we want to know whether drinking alcohol causes grades to go down. An observational study might be fun, but worthless: it's a pretty good bet that the kind of people who drink a lot also have other things in their error term (e.g., lack of interest in school) that also account for low grades. An experimental study might even be more fun, but pretty unlikely to get approved (or finished . . .).

But we still have some tricks to get at the effect of drinking. Consider the U.S. Air Force Academy, where the drinking age is strictly enforced. Students over 21 are allowed to drink; those under 21 are not allowed to drink and face expulsion if caught. If we can compare the performance on final exams of those students who had just turned 21 to those who had not, we might be able to identify the causal effect of drinking.

Carrell, Hoekstra, and West (2010) made this comparison, and Figure 11.1 summarizes their results. Each circle shows average test score for Air Force Academy students grouped by age. The circle on the far left shows the average test score for students who were 270 days before their 21st birthday when they took their test. The circle on the far right shows the average test score for students who reached their 21st birthday 270 days before their test. In the middle are those who had just turned 21.

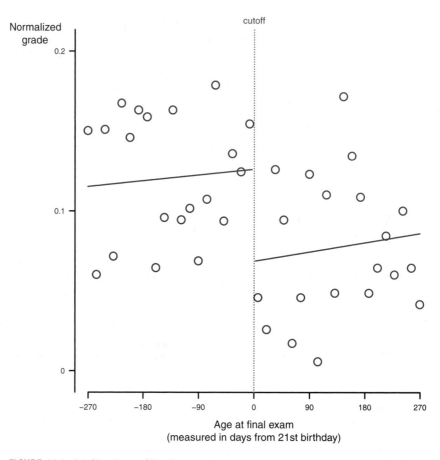

FIGURE 11.1: Drinking Age and Test Scores

We've included fit lines to help make the pattern clear. Those who had not yet turned 21 scored higher. There is a discontinuity at the zero point in the figure (corresponding to students taking a test on their 21st birthday). If we can't come up with another explanation for test scores to change at this point, we have pretty good evidence that drinking hurts grades.

▶ **regression discontinuity (RD)**

Regression discontinuity techniques use regression analysis to identify possible discontinuities at the point at which some treatment applies.

Regression discontinuity (RD) analysis formalizes this logic by using regression analysis to identify possible discontinuities at the point of application of the treatment. For the drinking age case, RD analysis involves fitting an OLS model that allows us to see if there is a discontinuity at the point students become legally able to drink.

Regression discontinuity analysis has been used in a variety of contexts in which a treatment of interest is determined by a strict cutoff. Card, Dobkin, and Maestas (2009) used RD to analyze the effect of Medicare on health because Medicare eligibility kicks in the day someone turns 65. Lee (2008) used RD to study the effect of incumbency on reelection to Congress because incumbents are decided by whoever gets more votes. Lerman (2009) used RD to assess the effect of being in a high-security prison on inmate aggression because the security level of the prison to which a convict is sent depends directly on a classification score determined by the state.

RD can be an excellent option in the design of research studies. Standard observational data may not provide exogeneity. Good instruments are hard to come by. Experiments can be expensive or infeasible. And even when experiments can work, they can seem unfair or capricious to policy makers, who may not like the idea of allocating a treatment randomly. In RD, the treatment is assigned according to a rule, which to many people seems more reasonable and fair than random assignment.

RD models can work in the analysis of individuals, states, counties, and other units. In this chapter we mostly discuss RD as applied to individuals, but the technique works perfectly well to analyze other units that have treatment assigned by a cutoff rule of some sort.

This chapter explains how to use RD models to estimate causal effects. Section 11.1 presents the core RD model. Section 11.2 then presents ways to more flexibly estimate RD models. Section 11.3 shows how to limit the data sets and create graphs that are particularly useful in the RD context. The RD approach is not bulletproof, though and Section 11.4 discusses the vulnerabilities of the approach and how to diagnose them.

11.1   Basic RD Model

In this section we introduce RD models by explaining the important role of the assignment variable in the model. We then translate the RD model into a convenient graphical form and explain the key condition necessary for the model to produce unbiased results.

The assignment variable in regression discontinuity models

▶ **assignment variable**
An assignment variable determines whether someone receives some treatment. People with values of the assignment variable above some cutoff receive the treatment; people with values of the assignment variable below the cutoff do not receive the treatment.

The necessary ingredient in a regression discontinuity model is an **assignment variable** that determines whether someone does or does not receive a treatment. People with values of the assignment variable above some cutoff receive the treatment; people with values of the assignment variable less than the cutoff do not receive the treatment.

As long as the only thing that changes at the cutoff is that the person gets the treatment, then any jump up or down in the dependent variable at the cutoff will reflect the causal effect of the treatment.

One way to understand why is to look at observations very, very close to the cutoff. The only difference between those just above and just below the cutoff is the treatment. For example, Medicare eligibility kicks in when someone turns 65. If we compare the health of people one minute before their 65th birthday to the health of people who turned 65 one minute ago, we could reasonably believe that the only difference between those two groups is that the federal government provides health care for some but not others.

That's a pretty extreme example, though. As a practical matter, we typically don't have data on very many people very close to our cutoff. Because statistical precision depends on sample size (as we discussed on page 152), we typically can't expect very useful estimates unless we expand our data set to include observations some degree above and below the cutoff. For Medicare, for example, perhaps we'll need to look at people days, weeks, or months from their 65th birthday to get a reasonable sample size. Thus the treated and untreated will differ not only in whether they got the treatment but also in the assignment variable. People 65 years and 2 months old not only can get Medicare, they are also older than people 2 months shy of their 65th birthday. While 4 months doesn't seem like a lot for an individual, health declines with age in the whole population, and some people will experience a bad turn during those few months.

Regression discontinuity models therefore control for treatment and the assignment variable. In its most basic form, a regression discontinuity model looks like

$$Y_i = \beta_0 + \beta_1 T_i + \beta_2 (X_{1i} - C) + \epsilon_i \tag{11.1}$$

where

$$T_i = 1 \text{ if } X_{1i} \geq C$$
$$T_i = 0 \text{ if } X_{1i} < C$$

where T_i is a dummy variable indicating whether person i received the treatment and $X_{1i} - C$ is our assignment variable, which indicates how much above or below the cutoff an observation is. For reasons we'll explain soon, it is useful to use an assignment variable of this form (that indicates how much above or below the cutoff a person was).

Graphical representation of regression discontinuity models

Figure 11.2 displays a scatterplot of data and fitted lines for a typical RD model. This picture captures the essence of RD. If we understand it, we understand RD models. The distance to the cutoff variable, $X_{1i} - C$, is along the horizontal axis. In this particular example, $C = 0$, meaning that the eligibility for the treatment kicked in when X_1 was zero. Those with X_1 above zero got the treatment; those with X_1 below zero did not get the treatment. Starting from the left, we see that the dependent variable rises as $X_{1i} - C$ gets bigger and, whoa, jumps up at the cutoff point (when $X_1 = 0$). This jump at the cutoff, then, is the estimated causal effect of the treatment.

The parameters in the model are easy to locate in the figure. The most important parameter is β_1, which is the effect of being in the treatment group. This is the jump at the heart of RD analysis. The slope parameter, $\hat{\beta}_2$, captures the relationship between the distance to the cutoff variable and the dependent variable. In this basic version of the RD model, this slope is the same above and below the cutoff.

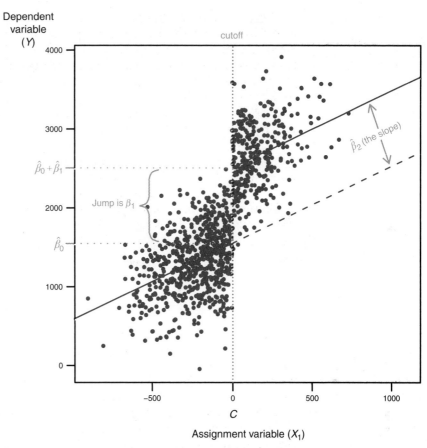

FIGURE 11.2: Basic Regression Discontinuity Model, $Y_i = \beta_0 + \beta_1 T_i + \beta_2 (X_{1i} - C)$

Figure 11.3 displays more examples of results from RD models. In panel (a), β_1 is positive, just as in Figure 11.2, but β_2 is negative, creating a downward slope for the assignment variable. In panel (b), the treatment has no effect, meaning that $\beta_1 = 0$. Even though everyone above the cutoff received the treatment, there is no discernible discontinuity in the dependent variable at the cutoff point. In panel (c), β_1 is negative because there is a jump downward at the cutoff, implying that the treatment lowered the dependent variable.

The key assumption in regression discontinuity models

The key assumption for RD to work is that the error term itself does not jump at the point of the discontinuity. In other words, we're assuming that when the assignment variable crosses the cutoff, the error term, whatever is in it, will be continuous without any jumps up or down. We discuss in Section 11.4 how this condition can be violated.

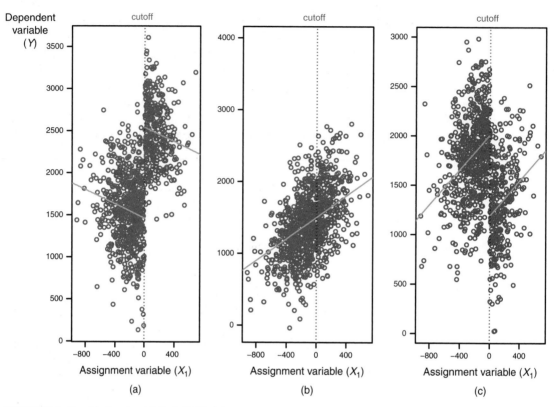

FIGURE 11.3: Possible Results with Basic RD Model

One of the cool things about RD is that even if the error term is correlated with the assignment variable, the estimated effect of the treatment is still valid. To see why, suppose $C = 0$, the error and assignment variable are correlated, and we characterize the correlation as follows:

$$\epsilon_i = \rho X_{1i} + v_i \tag{11.2}$$

where the Greek letter rho (ρ, pronounced row) captures how strongly the error and X_{1i} are related and v_i is a random term that is uncorrelated with X_{1i}. In the Medicare example, mortality is the dependent variable, the treatment T is Medicare (which kicks in the second someone turns 65), age is the assignment variable, and health is in the error term. It is totally reasonable to believe that health is related to age, and we use Equation 11.2 to characterize such a relationship.

If we estimate the following model, which does not control for the assignment variable (X_{1i})

$$Y_i = \beta_0 + \beta_1 T_i + \epsilon_i$$

there will be endogeneity because the treatment, T, depends on X_{1i}, which is correlated with the error. In the Medicare example, if we predict mortality as a function of Medicare only, the Medicare variable will pick up not only the effect of the program, but also the effect of health, which is in the error term, which is correlated with age, which is, in turn, correlated with Medicare.

If we control for X_{1i}, however, the correlation between T and ϵ disappears. To see why, we begin with the basic RD model (Equation 11.1). For simplicity, we assume $C = 0$. Using Equation 11.2 to substitute for ϵ yields

$$Y_i = \beta_0 + \beta_1 T_i + \beta_2 X_{1i} + \epsilon_i$$
$$= \beta_0 + \beta_1 T_i + \beta_2 X_{1i} + \rho X_{1i} + \nu_i$$

We can rearrange and relabel $\beta_2 + \rho$ as $\tilde{\beta}_2$, producing

$$Y_i = \beta_0 + \beta_1 T_i + (\beta_2 + \rho)X_{1i} + \nu_i$$
$$= \beta_0 + \beta_1 T_i + \tilde{\beta}_2 X_{1i} + \nu_i$$

Notice that we have an equation in which the error term is now ν_i (the part of Equation 11.2 that is uncorrelated with anything). Hence, the treatment variable, T, in the RD model is uncorrelated with the error term even though the assignment variable is correlated with the error term. This means that OLS will provide an unbiased estimate of β_1, the coefficient on T_i.

Meanwhile, the coefficient we estimate on the X_{1i} assignment variable is $\tilde{\beta}_2$ (notice the squiggly on top), a combination of β_2 (with no squiggly on top; the actual effect of X_{1i} on Y) and ρ (the degree of correlation between X_{1i} and the error term in the original model, ϵ).

Thus we do not put a lot of stock into the estimate of the variable on the assignment variable because the coefficient combines the actual effect of the assignment variable and the correlation of the assignment variable and the error. That's OK, though, because our main interest is in the effect of the treatment, β_1.

REMEMBER THIS

A regression discontinuity (RD) analysis can be used when treatment depends on an assignment variable being above some cutoff C.

1. The basic model is

$$Y_i = \beta_0 + \beta_1 T_i + \beta_2 (X_{1i} - C) + \epsilon_i$$
$$T_i = 1 \text{ if } X_{1i} \geq C$$
$$T_i = 0 \text{ if } X_{1i} < C$$

2. RD models require that the error term be continuous at the cutoff. That is, the value of the error term must not jump up or down at the cutoff.

3. RD identifies a causal effect of treatment because the assignment variable soaks up the correlation of error and treatment.

Discussion Questions

1. Many school districts pay for new school buildings with bond issues that must be approved by voters. Supporters of these bond issues typically argue that new buildings improve schools and thereby boost housing values. Cellini, Ferreira, and Rothstein (2010) used RD to test whether passage of school bonds caused housing values to rise.

   (a) What is the assignment variable?

   (b) Explain how to use a basic RD approach to estimate the effect of school bond passage on housing values.

   (c) Provide a specific equation for the model.

2. U.S. citizens are eligible for Medicare the day they turn 65 years old. Many believe that people with health insurance are less likely to die prematurely because they will be more likely to seek treatment and doctors will be more willing to conduct tests and procedures for them. Card, Dobkin, and Maestas (2009) used RD to address this question.

   (a) What is the assignment variable?

   (b) Explain how to use a basic RD approach to estimate the effect of Medicare coverage on the probability of dying prematurely.

   (c) Provide a specific equation for the model. (Don't worry that the dependent variable is a dummy variable; we'll deal with that issue later on page 402.)

11.2 More Flexible RD Models

In a basic version RD model, the slope of the line is the same on both sides of the cutoff for treatment. This might not be the case in reality. In this section we show how to implement more flexible RD models that allow the slope to vary or allow for a non-linear relationship between the assignment variable and outcomes.

Varying slopes model

Most RD applications allow the slope to vary above and below the threshold. By incorporating tools we discussed in Section 6.4, the following will produce estimates in which the slope is different below and above the threshold:

$$Y_i = \beta_0 + \beta_1 T_i + \beta_2 (X_{1i} - C) + \beta_3 (X_{1i} - C) T_i + \epsilon_i$$

$$T_i = 1 \text{ if } X_{1i} \geq C$$

$$T_i = 0 \text{ if } X_{1i} < C$$

The new term at the end of the equation is an interaction between T and $X_1 - C$. The coefficient on that interaction, β_3, captures how different the slope is for observations where X_1 is greater than C. The slope for untreated observations (for whom $T_i = 0$) will simply be β_2, which is the slope for observations to the left of the cutoff. The slope for the treated observations (for whom $T_i = 1$) will be $\beta_2 + \beta_3$, which is the slope for observations to the right of the cutoff. (Recall our discussion in Chapter 6, page 193, regarding the proper interpretation of coefficients on interactions.)

Figure 11.4 displays examples in which the slopes differ above and below the cutoff. In panel (a), $\beta_2 = 1$ and $\beta_3 = 2$. Because β_3 is greater than zero, the slope is steeper for observations to the right of the cutoff. The slope for observations to the left of the cutoff is 1 (the value of β_2) and the slope for observations to the right of the cutoff is $\beta_2 + \beta_3 = 3$.

In panel (b) of Figure 11.4, β_3 is zero, meaning that the slope is the same (and equal to β_2) on both sides of the cutoff. In panel (c), β_3 is less than zero, meaning that the slope is less steep for observations for which X_1 is greater than C. Note that just because β_3 is negative, the slope for observations to the right of the cutoff need not be negative (although it may be). A negative value of β_3 simply means that the slope is less steep for observations to the right of the cutoff. In panel (c), $\beta_3 = -\beta_2$, which is why the slope is zero to the right of the cutoff.

In estimating an RD model with varying slopes, is important to use $X_{1i} - C$ instead of X_{1i} for the assignment variable. In this model, we're estimating two separate lines. The intercept for the line for the untreated group is $\hat{\beta}_0$ and the intercept for the line for the treated group is $\hat{\beta}_0 + \hat{\beta}_1$. If we used X_{1i} as the assignment variable (instead of $X_{1i} - C$), the $\hat{\beta}_1$ estimate would indicate the differences in treated and control when X_{1i} is zero even though we care about the difference between treated and control when X_{1i} equals the cutoff. By using $X_{1i} - C$ instead of X_{1i} for the assignment variable, we have ensured that $\hat{\beta}_1$ will indicate the difference between treated and control when $X_{1i} - C$ is zero, which occurs, of course, when $X_{1i} = C$.

Polynomial model

Once we start thinking about how the slope could vary across different values of X_1, it is easy to start thinking about other possibilities. Hence more technical RD

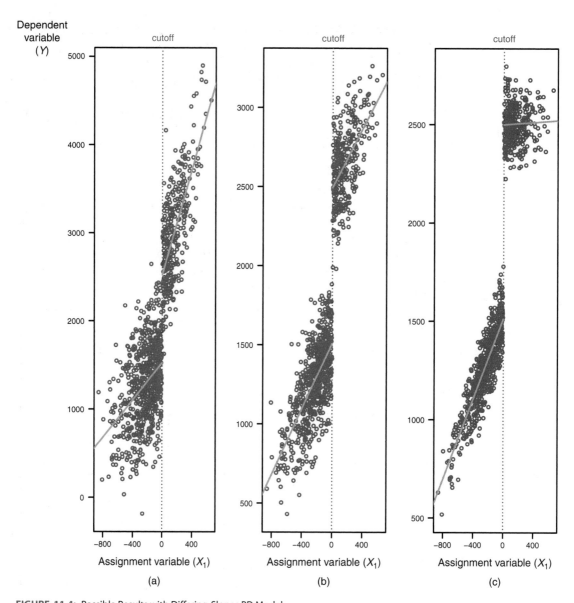

Dependent variable (Y)

Assignment variable (X_1)

(a)   (b)   (c)

FIGURE 11.4: Possible Results with Differing-Slopes RD Model

analyses spend a lot of effort estimating relationships that are even more flexible than the varying slopes model. One way to estimate more flexible relationships between the assignment variable and outcome is to use our polynomial regression model from Chapter 7 (page 208) to allow the relationship between X_1 to Y to wiggle and curve. The RD insight is that however wiggly that line gets, we're still looking for a jump (a discontinuity) at the point where the treatment kicks in.

For example, we can use polynomial models to allow the estimated lines to curve differently above and below the treatment threshold with a model like the following:

$$Y_i = \beta_0 + \beta_1 T_i + \beta_2(X_{1i} - C) + \beta_3(X_{1i} - C)^2 + \beta_4(X_{1i} - C)^3$$
$$+ \beta_5(X_{1i} - C)T_i + \beta_6(X_{1i} - C)^2 T_i + \beta_7(X_{1i} - C)^3 T_i + \epsilon_i$$
$$T_i = 1 \text{ if } X_{1i} \geq C$$
$$T_i = 0 \text{ if } X_{1i} < C$$

Figure 11.5 shows two relationships that can be estimated with such a polynomial model. In panel (a), the value of Y accelerates as X_1 approaches the

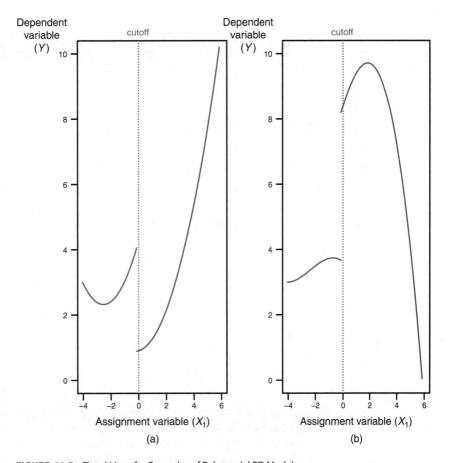

FIGURE 11.5: Fitted Lines for Examples of Polynomial RD Models

cutoff, dips at the point of treatment, and accelerates again from that lower point. In panel (b), the relationship appears relatively flat for values of X_1 below the cutoff. There is a fairly substantial jump up in Y at the cutoff. After that, Y rises sharply with X_1 and then falls sharply.

It is virtually impossible to predict funky non-linear relationships like these ahead of time. The goal is to find a functional form for the relationship between $X_1 - C$ and outcomes that soaks up any relation between $X_1 - C$ and outcomes to ensure that any jump at the cutoff reflects only the causal effect of the treatment. This means we can estimate the polynomial models and see what happens even without full theory about how the line should wiggle.

With this flexibility comes danger, though. Polynomial models are quite sensitive and sometimes can produce jumps at the cutoff that are bigger than they should be. Therefore we should always report simple linear models, too, to avoid seeming to be fishing around for a non-linear model that gives us the answer we'd like.

REMEMBER THIS

When we conduct RD analysis, it is useful to allow for a more flexible relationship between assignment variable and outcome.

- A varying slopes model allows the slope to vary on different sides of the treatment cutoff:

$$Y_i = \beta_0 + \beta_1 T_i + \beta_2 (X_{1i} - C) + \beta_3 (X_{1i} - C) T_i + \epsilon_i$$

- We can also use polynomial models to allow for non-linear relationships between the assignment and outcome variables.

Review Question

For each panel in Figure 11.6, indicate whether each of β_1, β_2, and β_3 is less than, equal to, or greater than zero for the varying slopes RD model:

$$Y_i = \beta_0 + \beta_1 T_i + \beta_2 (X_{1i} - C) + \beta_3 (X_{1i} - C) T_i + \epsilon_i$$

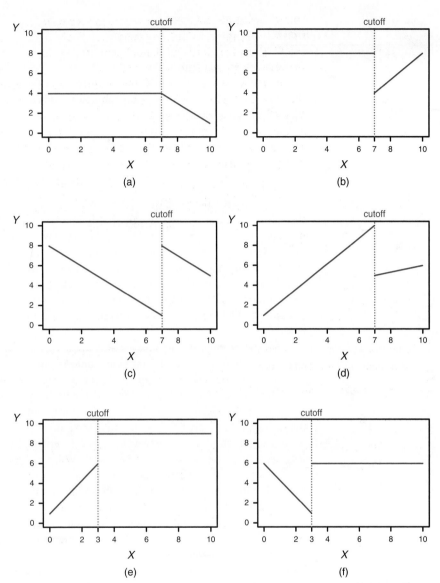

FIGURE 11.6: Various Fitted Lines for RD Model of Form $Y_i = \beta_0 + \beta_1 T_i + \beta_2(X_{1i} - C) + \beta_3(X_{1i} - C)T_i$ (for Review Question)

11.3 Windows and Bins

There are other ways to make RD models flexible. An intuitive approach is to simply focus on a subset of the data near the threshold. In this section we show the benefits and costs of that approach and introduce binned graphs as a useful tool for all RD analysis.

Adjusting the window

> **window** A window is the range of observations we analyze in a regression discontinuity analysis. The smaller the window, the less we need to worry about non-linear functional forms.

As we discussed earlier, polynomial models can be a bit hard to work with. An easier alternative (or at least supplement) to polynomial models is to narrow the **window** that is, the range of the assignment variable to which we limit our analysis. Accordingly, we look only at observations with values of the assignment variable in this range. Ideally, we'd make the window very, very small near the cutoff. For such a small window, we'd be looking only at the observations just below and just above the cutoff. These observations would be very similar, and hence the treatment effect would be the difference in Y for the untreated (those just below the cutoff) and the treated (those just above the cutoff).

A smaller window allows us to worry less about the functional form on both sides of the cutoff. Figure 11.7 provides some examples. In panels (a) and (b), we show the same figures as in Figure 11.5, but highlight a small window. To the right of each of these panels we show just the line in the highlighted smaller window. While the relationships are quite non-linear for the full window, we can see that they are approximately linear in the smaller windows. For example, when we look only at observations of X_1 between -1 and 1 for panel (a), we see two more or less linear lines on each side of the cutoff. When we look only at observations of X_1 between -1 and 1 for panel (b), we see a more or less flat line below the cutoff and line with a positive slope above the cutoff. So even though the actual relationships between the assignment variable and Y are non-linear in both panels, a reasonably simple varying slopes model should be more than sufficient when we focus on the smaller window. A smaller window for these cases allows us to feel more confident that our results do not depend on sensitive polynomial models, but instead reflect differences between treated and untreated observations near the cutoff.

> **binned graphs** Used in regression discontinuity analysis. The assignment variable is divided into bins, and the average value of the dependent variable is plotted for each bin. The plots allow us to visualize a discontinuity at the treatment cutoff.

As a practical matter, we usually don't have very many observations in a small window near the cutoff. To have any hope of having any statistical power, then, we'll need to make the window large enough to cover a reasonable number of observations.

Binned graphs

A convenient trick that helps us understand non-linearities and discontinuities in our RD data is to create **binned graphs**. Binned graphs look like scatterplots

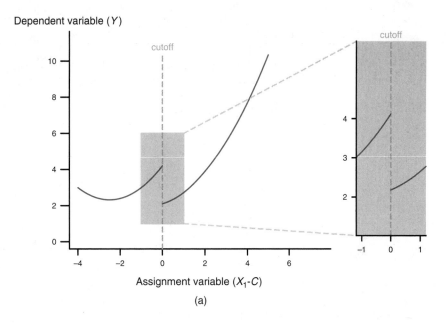

(a)

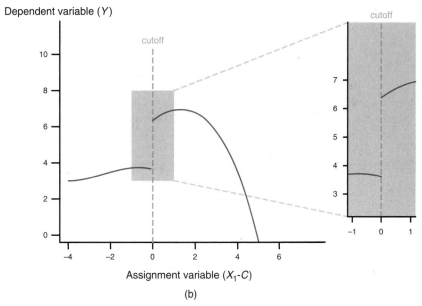

(b)

FIGURE 11.7: Smaller Windows for Fitted Lines for Polynomial RD Model in Figure 11.5

but are a bit different. To construct a bin plot, we divide the X_1 variable into multiple regions (or "bins") above and below the cutoff; then we calculate the average value of Y within each of those regions. When we plot the data we get

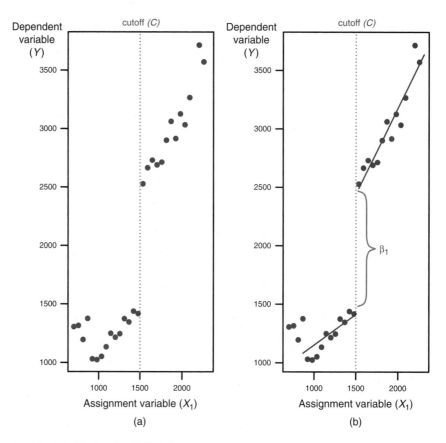

FIGURE 11.8: Bin Plots for RD Model

something that looks like panel (a) of Figure 11.8. Notice that there is a single observation for each bin, producing a graph that's cleaner than a scatterplot of all observations.

The bin plot provides guidance for selecting the right RD model. If the relationship is highly non-linear or seems dramatically different above and below the cutpoint, the bin plot will let us know. In panel (a) of Figure 11.8, we see a bit of non-linearity because there is a U-shaped relationship between X_1 and Y for values of X_1 below the cutoff. This relationship suggests that a quadratic could be appropriate or, even simpler, the window could be narrowed to focus only on the range of X_1 where the relationship is more linear. Panel (b) of Figure 11.8 shows the fitted lines based on an analysis that used only observations for which X_1 is between 900 and 2200. The implied treatment effect is the jump in the data indicated by β_1 in the figure. We do not actually use the binned data to estimate the model; we use the original data in our regressions.

REMEMBER THIS

1. It is useful to look at smaller window sizes when possible by considering only data close to the treatment cutoff.

2. Binned graphs help us visualize the discontinuity and the possibly non-linear relationship between assignment variable and outcome.

CASE STUDY   ## Universal Prekindergarten

"Universal prekindergarten" is the name of a policy of providing high-quality, free school to 4-year olds. If it works as advocates say, universal pre-K will counteract socioeconomic disparities, boost productivity, and decrease crime.

But does it work? Gormley, Phillips, and Gayer (2008) used RD to evaluate one piece of the puzzle by looking at the impact of universal pre-K on test scores in Tulsa, Oklahoma. They could do so because children born on or before September 1, 2001, were eligible to enroll in the program in 2005–06, while children born after this date had to wait until the next school year to enroll.

Figure 11.9 is a bin plot for this analysis. The dependent variable is test scores from a letter-word identification test that measures early writing skills. The children took the test a year after the older kids started pre-K. The kids born before September 1 spent the year in pre-K; the kids born after September 1 spent the year doing whatever it is 4-year-olds do when not in pre-K.

The horizontal axis shows age measured in days from the pre-K cutoff date. The data is binned in groups of 14 days so that each data point shows the average test scores for children with ages in a 14-day range. While the actual statistical analysis uses all observations, the binned graph helps us better see the relationship between the cutoff and test scores than would a scatterplot of all observations.

One of the nice features of RD is that the plot often tells the story. We'll do formal statistical analysis in a second, but in this case, as in many RD examples, we know how the story is going to end just from the bin plot.

There's no mistaking the data: there is a jump in test scores precisely at the point of discontinuity. There's a clear relationship of kids scoring higher as they get older (as we can see from the positive slope on age), but right at the age-related cutoff for the pre-K program there is a substantial jump up. The kids above the cutoff went to pre-K. The kids who were below the cutoff did not. If the program

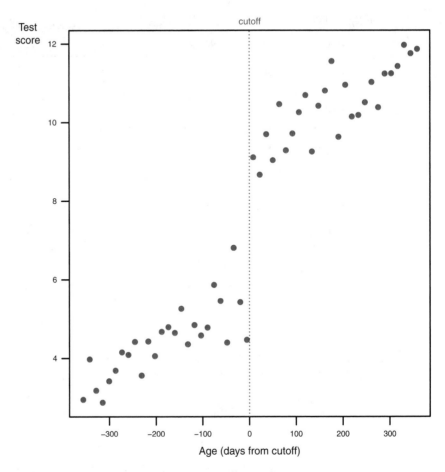

FIGURE 11.9: Binned Graph of Test Scores and Pre-K Attendance

had no effect, the kids who didn't go to pre-K would score lower than the kids who did, simply because they were younger. But unless the program boosted test scores, there is no obvious reason for a discontinuity to be located right at the cutoff.

Table 11.1 shows statistics results for the basic and varying slopes RD models. For the basic model, the coefficient on the variable for pre-K is 3.492 and highly significant, with a t statistic of 10.31. The coefficient indicates the jump that we see in Figure 11.9. The age variable is also highly significant. No surprise there, as older children did better on the test.

In the varying slopes model, the coefficient on the treatment is virtually unchanged from the basic model, indicating a jump of 3.479 in test scores for the kids who went to pre-K. The effect is highly statistically significant, with a t statistic of 10.23. The coefficient on the interaction is insignificant, indicating that the slope on age is the same for kids who had pre-K and those who didn't.

TABLE 11.1	RD Analysis of Prekindergarten	
	Basic	Varying slopes
Pre-K	3.492*	3.479*
	(0.339)	(0.340)
	$[t = 10.31]$	$[t = 10.23]$
Age – C	0.007*	0.007*
	(0.001)	(0.001)
	$[t = 8.64]$	$[t = 6.07]$
Pre-K × (Age – C)		0.001
		(0.002)
		$[t = 0.42]$
Constant	5.692*	5.637*
	(0.183)	(0.226)
	$[t = 31.07]$	$[t = 24.97]$
N	2,785	2,785
R^2	0.323	0.323

Standard errors in parentheses.

* indicates significance at $p < 0.05$, two-tailed.

The conclusion? Universal pre-K increased school readiness in Tulsa.

11.4 Limitations and Diagnostics

The RD approach is a powerful tool. It allows us to generate unbiased treatment effects as long as treatment depends on some threshold and the error term is continuous at the treatment threshold. However, RD can go wrong, and in this section we discuss situations in which RD doesn't work and how to detect these breakdowns. We also discuss limitations on how broadly we can generalize RD results.

Imperfect assignment

One drawback to the RD approach is that it's pretty rare to have an assignment variable that decisively determines treatment. If we're looking at the effect of going to a certain college, for example, we probably cannot use RD because admission was based on multiple factors, none them cut and dried. Or if we're trying to assess the effectiveness of a political advertising campaign, it's unlikely that the campaign simply advertised in cities where its poll results were less than some threshold; instead, the managers probably selected certain criteria to identify where they might advertise and then decided exactly where to run ads on the basis of a number of factors (including gut feel).

▶ **fuzzy RD models**

Regression discontinuity models in which the assignment variable imperfectly predicts treatment.

In the Further Reading section we point to readings on so-called **fuzzy RD models**, which can be used when the assignment variable imperfectly predicts treatment. Fuzzy RD models can be useful when there is a point at which treatment becomes much more likely but isn't necessarily guaranteed. For example, a college might look only at people with test scores of 160 or higher. Being above 160 may not guarantee admission, but there is a huge leap in probability of admission for those who score 160 instead of 159.

Discontinuous error distribution at threshold

A bigger problem for RD models occurs when the error can be discontinuous at the treatment threshold. Real people living their lives may do things that create a jump in the error term at the discontinuity. For example, suppose that a high school GPA above 3.0 makes students eligible for a tuition discount at their state university. This seems like a promising RD design: use high school GPA as the assignment variable and set a threshold at 3.0. We can then see, for example, whether graduation rates (Y) are higher for students who got the tuition discount.

The problem is that the high school students (and teachers) know the threshold and how close they are to it. Students who plan ahead and really want to go to college will make damn sure that their high school GPA is north of 3.0. Students who are drifting through life and haven't gotten around to thinking about college won't be so careful. Therefore we could expect that when we are looking at students with GPAs near 3.0, the more ambitious students pile up on one side and the slackers pile up on the other. If we think ambition influences graduation (it does!), then ambition (something in the error term) jumps at the discontinuity, messing up the RD design.

Therefore any RD analysis should discuss whether the only thing happening at the discontinuity is the treatment. Do the individuals always know about the cutoff? Sometimes they don't. Perhaps a worker training program enrolls people who score over some number on a screening test. The folks taking the test probably don't know what the number is, so they're unlikely to be able to game the system. Even if people know the score they need, it's often reasonable to assume that they'll do their best because presumably they won't know precisely how much effort will be enough to exceed the cutoff. If the test can be retaken, though, the more ambitious folks might keep taking it until they pass, while the less ambitious will head home to binge-watch *Breaking Bad*. In such a situation, something in the error term (ambition) would jump at the cutoff because the ambitious people would tend to be above the cutoff and the less ambitious people would be below it.

Diagnostic tests for RD models

Given the vulnerabilities of the RD model, two diagnostic tests are important to assess the appropriateness of the RD approach. First, we want to know if the assignment variable itself acts peculiar at the cutoff. If the values of the assignment variable cluster just above the cutoff, we should worry that people know about the cutoff and are able to manipulate things to get over it. In such a situation, it's quite plausible that the people who are able to just get over the cutoff differ from those who do not, perhaps because the former have more ambition (as in our GPA example), or better contacts, better information, or other advantages. To the extent that these factors also affect the dependent variable, we'll violate the assumption that the error term does not have a discrete jump at the cutoff.

The best way to assess whether there is clustering on one side of the cutoff is to create a histogram of the assignment variable, looking for it to show unusual activity at the cutoff point. Panel (a) in Figure 11.10 is a histogram of assignment values in a case with no obvious clustering. The frequency of values in each bin for the assignment variable bounces around a bit here and there, but it's mostly smooth and there is no clear jump up or down at the cutoff. In contrast, the histogram in panel (b) shows clear clustering just above the cutoff. When faced with data like panel (b), it's pretty reasonable to suspect that the word is out about the cutoff, and people have figured out how to get over the threshold.[1]

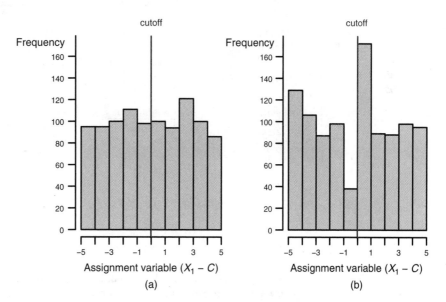

FIGURE 11.10: Histograms of Assignment Variable for RD Analysis

---

[1] Formally testing for discontinuity of the assignment variable at the cutoff is a bit tricky. McCrary (2008) has more details. Usually, a visual assessment provides a good sense of what is going on, although it's a good idea to try different bin sizes to make sure that what you're seeing is not an artifact of one particular choice for bin size.

The second diagnostic test involves assessing whether other variables act weird at the discontinuity. For RD to be valid, we want only Y to jump at the point where T equals 1, nothing else. If some other variable jumps at the discontinuity, we may wonder if people are somehow self-selecting (or being selected) based on unknown additional factors. If so, it could be that the jump at Y is being caused by these other factors jumping at the discontinuity, not the treatment. A basic diagnostic test of this sort looks like

$$X_{2i} = \gamma_0 + \gamma_1 T_i + \gamma_2 (X_{1i} - C) + v_i$$
$$T_i = 1 \text{ if } X_{1i} \geq C$$
$$T_i = 0 \text{ if } X_{1i} < C$$

A statistically significant $\hat{\gamma}_1$ coefficient from this model means that X_2 jumps at the treatment discontinuity, which casts doubt on the main assumption of the RD model—namely, that the only thing happening at the discontinuity is movement from the untreated to the treated category.

A significant $\hat{\gamma}_1$ from this diagnostic test doesn't necessarily kill the RD, but we would need to control for X_2 in the RD model and explain why this additional variable jumps at the discontinuity. It also makes sense to use varying slopes models, polynomial models, and smaller window sizes in conducting balance tests.

Including any variable that jumps at the discontinuity is only a partial fix, though, because if we observe a difference at the cutoff in a variable we can measure, it's plausible that there is also a difference at the cutoff in a variable we can't measure. We can measure education reasonably well; it's a lot harder to measure intelligence, and it's extremely hard to measure conscientiousness. If we see that people are more educated at the cutoff, we'll worry that they are also more intelligent and conscientious—that is, we'll worry that at the discontinuity, our treated group may differ from the untreated group in ways we can't measure.

Generalizability of RD results

An additional limitation of RD is that it estimates a very specific treatment effect, also known as the local average treatment effect (LATE). This concept comes up for instrumental variables models as well (as discussed in the Further Reading Section of chapter 9 on page 316). The idea is that the effects of the treatment may differ within the population: a training program might work great for some types of people but do nothing for others. The treatment effect estimated by RD is the effect of the treatment on folks who have X_1 equal to the threshold. Perhaps the treatment would have no effect on people with very low values of the assignment variable. Or perhaps the treatment effect grows as the assignment variable grows. RD will not be able to speak to these possibilities because we observe only the treatment happening at one cutoff. Hence it is possible that the RD results will not generalize to the whole population.

REMEMBER THIS

To assess the appropriateness of RD:

1. Qualitatively assess whether people have control over the assignment variable.

2. Conduct diagnostic tests.

   • Assess the distribution of the assignment variable by using a histogram to see if there is clustering on one side of the cutoff.

   • Run RD models, and use other covariates as dependent variables. The treatment should not be associated with any discontinuity in any covariate.

CASE STUDY   **Alcohol and Grades**

The Air Force Academy alcohol and test score example that began the chapter provides a great example of how RD and RD diagnostics work. Table 11.2 shows the actual RD results behind Figure 11.1 from page 366. The first-column results are based on a varying slopes model in which the key variable is the dummy variable indicating that a student was older than 21 when he or she took the exam. This model also controlled for the assignment variable, age, allowing the effect of age to vary before and after people turned 21. The dependent variable is standardized test scores; thus the results in the first column indicate that turning 21 decreased test scores by 0.092 standard deviation. This effect is highly statistically significant, with a t statistic of 30.67. Adding controls strengthens the results, as reported in the second column. The results are quite similar when we allow the age variable to affect test scores non-linearly by including a quadratic function of age in the model.

Are we confident that the only thing that happens at the discontinuity is that students become eligible to drink? That is, are we confident that there is no discontinuity in the error term at the point people turn 21? First, we want to think about the issue qualitatively. Obviously, people can't affect their age, so there's little worry that anyone is manipulating the assignment variable. And while it is possible, for example, that good students decide to drop out just after their 21st birthday, which would mean that the students we observe who just turned 21 are more likely to be bad students, it doesn't seem particularly likely.

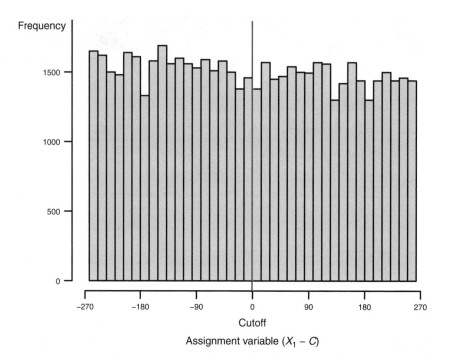

FIGURE 11.11: Histogram of Age Observations for Drinking Age Case Study

We can also run diagnostic tests. Figure 11.11 shows the frequency of observations for students above and below the age cutoff. There is no sign of manipulation of the assignment variable: the distribution of ages is mostly constant, with some apparently random jumps up and down.

We can also assess whether other covariates showed discontinuities at the 21st birthday. Since as discussed earlier, the defining RD assumption is that the only discontinuity at the cutoff is in the dependent variable, we hope to see no

TABLE 11.2 **RD Analysis of Drinking Age and Test Scores**

	Varying slopes	Varying slopes with control variables	Quadratic with control variables
Discontinuity at 21	-0.092^*	-0.114^*	-0.106^*
	(0.03)	(0.02)	(0.03)
	$[t = 30.67]$	$[t = 57.00]$	$[t = 35.33]$
N	$38,782$	$38,782$	$38,782$

Standard errors in parentheses.

All three specifications control for age, allowing the slope to vary on either side of the cutoff. The second and third specifications control for semester, SAT scores, and other demographics factors.

* indicates significance at $p < 0.05$, two-tailed.

From Carrell, Hoekstra, and West (2010).

TABLE 11.3 RD Diagnostics for Drinking Age and Test Scores

	SAT math	SAT verbal	Physical fitness score
Discontinuity at 21	2.371	1.932	0.025
	(2.81)	(2.79)	(0.04)
	[$t = 0.84$]	[$t = 0.69$]	[$t = 0.63$]
N	38,782	38,782	38,782

Standard errors in parentheses.

All three specifications control for age, allowing the slope to vary on either side of the cutoff.

From Carrell, Hoekstra, and West (2010).

statistically significant discontinuities when other variables are used as dependent variables. The model we're testing is

$$Covariate_i = \gamma_0 + \gamma_1 T_i + \gamma_2 (Age_i - C) + v_i$$

$$T_i = 1 \text{ if } X_{1i} \geq C$$

$$T_i = 0 \text{ if } X_{1i} < C$$

Table 11.3 shows results for three covariates: SAT math scores, SAT verbal scores, and physical fitness. For none of these covariates is $\hat{\gamma}_1$ statistically significant, suggesting that there is no jump in covariates at the point of the discontinuity, a conclusion that is consistent with the idea that the only thing changing at the discontinuity is the treatment.

Conclusion

Regression discontinuity is a powerful statistical tool. It works even when the treatment we are trying to analyze is correlated with the error. It works because the assignment variable—a variable that determines whether a unit gets the treatment—soaks up endogeneity. The only assumption we need is that there is no discontinuity in the error term at the cutoff in the assignment variable X_1.

If we have such a situation, the basic RD model is super simple. It is just an OLS model with a dummy variable (indicating treatment) and a variable indicating distance to the cutoff. More complicated RD models allow for more complicated relationships between the assignment variable and the dependent variable. No matter the model, however, the heart of the RD remains looking for a jump in the value of Y at the cutoff point for assignment to treatment. As long as there is no discontinuity in relationship between error and the outcome at the cutoff, we can attribute any jump in the dependent variable to the effect of the treatment.

RD is an essential part of any econometric toolkit. Regression discontinuity can fill in a hole when panel data, instrumental variable, or experimental techniques aren't up to the task. RD analysis is also quite clean. Anybody can pretty much see the answer by looking at a binned graph, and the statistical models are relatively simple to implement and explain.

RD is not without pitfalls, however. If people can manipulate their score on the assignment variable, then the RD estimate no longer captures just the effect of treatment; it also captures the effects of whatever qualities are overrepresented among the folks who were able to boost their assignment score above the threshold. For this reason, it is very important to report diagnostics that help us sniff out possible discontinuities in the error term at the cutoff.

We are on the right track when we can do the following:

- Section 11.1: Write down a basic RD model and explain all terms, including treatment variable, assignment variable, and cutoff. Explain how RD models overcome endogeneity.

- Section 11.2: Write down and explain RD models with varying slopes and non-linear relationships.

- Section 11.3: Explain why it is useful to look at a smaller window. Explain a binned graph and how it differs from a conventional scatterplot.

- Section 11.4: Explain conditions under which RD might not be appropriate. Explain qualitative and statistical diagnostics for RD models.

Further Reading

Imbens and Lemieux (2008) and Lee and Lemieux (2010) go into additional detail on regression discontinuity designs, including discussions of fuzzy RD models. Bloom (2012) gives another useful overview of RD methods. Cook (2008) provides a history of RD applications. Buddlemeyer and Skofias (2003) compare performance of regression discontinuity and experiments and find that RD works well as long as discontinuity is rigorously enforced.

See Grimmer, Hersh, Feinstein, and Carpenter (2010) for an example of using diagnostics to critique RD studies with election outcomes as an RD assignment variable.

Key Terms

Assignment variable (367)
Binned graphs (378)
Discontinuity (365)

Fuzzy RD models (384)
Regression discontinuity
  (RD) (366)

Window (378)

Computing Corner

To estimate an RD model in Stata, create a dummy treatment variable and an $X_1 - C$ variable and use the syntax for multivariate OLS.

1. The following commands create variables needed for RD. It is helpful to create a *scalar variable* named cutoff that is simply a variable with a single value (in contrast to a typical variable, which has a list of values). For this example we assume the cutoff is 10. The variable T indicates treatment; in many datasets it will already exist. The variable Assign is the assignment variable.

```
scalar cutoff = 10
gen T = 0
replace T = 1 if X1 > cutoff
gen Assign = X1 - cutoff
```

2. Basic RD is a simple OLS model:

```
reg Y T Assign
```

3. To estimate a model with varying slopes, first create an interaction variable and then run OLS:

```
gen AssignxT = Assign * T
reg Y T Assign AssignxT
```

4. To create a scatterplot with the fitted lines from a varying slopes RD model, use the following:

```
graph twoway (scatter Y Assign) (lfit Y Assign if T == 0) /*
*/ (lfit Y Assign if T == 1)
```

R

To estimate an RD model in R, we create a dummy treatment variable and a $X_1 - C$ variable and use the syntax for multivariate OLS.

1. The following commands create variables needed for RD. It is useful to create a scalar variable named cutoff that is a simply a variable with a single value (in contrast to a typical variable that has a list of values). For this example we assume the cutoff is 10. The variable T indicates treatment; in many datasets it will already exist. The variable Assign is the assignment variable.

```
cutoff = 10
T = 0
T[X1 > cutoff] = 1
Assign = X1 - cutoff
```

2. Basic RD is a simple OLS model:
   ```
   RDResults = lm(Y ~ T + Assign)
   ```

3. To estimate a model with varying slopes, first create an interaction variable and then run OLS:
   ```
   AssignxT = Assign*T
   RDResults = lm(Y ~ T + Assign + AssignxT)
   ```

Exercises

1. As discussed on page 381, Gormley, Phillips, and Gayer (2008) used RD to evaluate the impact of pre-K on test scores in Tulsa. Children born on or before September 1, 2001, were eligible to enroll in the program in 2005–06, while children born after this date had to wait to enroll until the 2006–07 school year. Table 11.4 lists the variables. The pre-K data set covers 1,943 children just beginning the program in 2006–07 (preschool entrants) and 1,568 children who had just finished the program and began kindergarten in 2006–07 (preschool alumni).

   (a) Why should there be a jump in the dependent variable right at the point where a child's birthday renders him or her eligible to have participated in preschool the previous year (2005–06) rather than the current year (2006–07)? Should we see jumps at other points as well?

   (b) Assess whether there is a discontinuity at the cutoff for the free-lunch status, gender, and race/ethnicity covariates.

TABLE 11.4 **Variables for Prekindergarten Data**

Variable	Description
age	Days from the birthday cutoff. The cutoff value is coded as 0; negative values indicate days born after the cutoff; positive values indicate days born before the cutoff
cutoff	Treatment indicator (1 = born before cutoff, 0 = born after cutoff)
wjtest01	Woodcock-Johnson letter-word identification test score
female	Female (1 = yes, 0 = no)
black	Black (1 = yes, 0 = no)
white	White (1 = yes, 0 = no)
hispanic	Hispanic (1 = yes, 0 = no)
freelunch	Eligible for free lunch based on low income in 2006–07 (1 = yes, 0 = no)

(c) Repeat the tests for covariate discontinuities, restricting the sample to a one-month (30-day) window on either side of the cutoff. Do the results change? Why or why not?

(d) Use letter-word identification test score as the dependent variable to estimate a basic RD model controlling for treatment status (born before the cutoff) and the assignment variable (age measured as days from the cutoff). What is the estimated effect of the preschool program on letter-word identification test scores?

(e) Estimate the effect of pre-K by using an RD specification that allows the relationship to vary on either side of the cutoff. Do the results change? Should we prefer this model? Why or why not?

(f) Add controls for lunch status, gender, and race/ethnicity to the model. Does adding these controls change the results? Why or why not?

(g) Reestimate the model from part (e), limiting the window to one month (30 days) on either side of the cutoff. Do the results change? How do the standard errors in this model compare to those from the model using the full data set?

2. Gormley, Phillips, and Gayer (2008) also used RD to evaluate the impact of Head Start on test scores in Tulsa. Children born on or before September 1, 2001, were eligible to enroll in the program in 2005–06, while children born after this date could not enroll until the 2006–07 school year. The variable names and definitions are the same as in Table 11.4, although in this case the data refers to 732 children just beginning the program in 2006–07 (Head Start entrants) and 470 children who had just finished the program and were beginning kindergarten in 2006–07 (Head Start alumni).

(a) Assess whether there is a discontinuity at the cutoff for the free-lunch status, gender, and race/ethnicity covariates.

(b) Repeat the tests for covariate discontinuities, restricting the sample to a one-month (30-day) window on either side of the cutoff. Do the results change? Why or why not?

(c) Use letter-word identification test score as the dependent variable to estimate a basic RD model. What is the estimated effect of the preschool program on letter-word identification test scores?

(d) Estimate the effect of Head Start by using an RD specification that allows the relationship to vary on either side of the cutoff. Do the results change? Should we prefer this model? Why or why not?

(e) Add controls for lunch status, gender, and race/ethnicity to the model. Do the results change? Why or why not?

(f) Reestimate the model from part (e), limiting the window to one month (30 days) on either side of the cutoff. Do the results change? How do the standard errors in this model compare to those from the model using the full data set?

3. Congressional elections are decided by a clear rule: whoever gets the most votes in November wins. Because virtually every congressional race in the United States is between two parties, whoever gets more than 50 percent of the vote wins.[2] We can use this fact to estimate the effect of political party on ideology. Some argue that Republicans and Democrats are very distinctive; others argue that members of Congress have strong incentives to respond to the median voter in their districts, regardless of party. We can assess how much party matters by looking at the ideology of members of Congress in the 112th Congress (which covered the years 2011 and 2012). Table 11.5 lists the variables.

(a) Suppose we try to explain congressional ideology as a function of political party only. Explain how endogeneity might be a problem.

TABLE 11.5 **Variables for Congressional Ideology Data**

Variable	Description
GOP2party2010	The percent of the vote received by the Republican congressional candidate in the district in 2010. Ranges from 0 to 1.
GOPwin2010	Dummy variable indicating Republican won; equals 1 if *GOP2party2010* > 0.5.
Ideology	The conservativism of the member of Congress as measured by Carroll et al. (2009, 2014). Ranges from –0.779 to 1.293. Higher values indicate more conservative voting in Congress.
ChildPoverty	Percentage of district children living in poverty. Ranges from 0.03 to 0.49.
MedianIncome	Median income in the district. Ranges from $23,291 to $103,664.
Obama2008	Percent of vote for Barack Obama in the district in 2008 presidential election. Ranges from 0.23 to 0.95.
WhitePct	Percent of the district that is non-Hispanic white. Ranges from 0.03 to 0.97.

[2] We'll look only at votes going to the two major parties, Democrats and Republicans, to ensure a nice 50 percent cutoff.

(b) How can an RD model fight endogeneity when we are trying to assess if and how party affects congressional ideology?

(c) Generate a scatterplot of congressional ideology against *GOP2party* and based on this plot discuss what you think the RD will indicate.

(d) Write down a basic RD model for this question and explain the terms.

(e) Estimate a basic RD model and interpret coefficients.

(f) Create an adjusted assignment variable (equal to *GOP2party2010* −0.50) and use it to estimate a varying slopes RD model and interpret the coefficients. Create a graphic that has a scatterplot of the data and fitted lines from the model. Calculate the fitted values for four observations: a Democrat with *GOP2party2010* = 0, a Democrat with *GOP2party2010* = 0.5, a Republican with *GOP2party2010* = 0.5, and a Republican with *GOP2party2010* = 1.0).

(g) Reestimate the varying slopes model, but use the unadjusted variable (and unadjusted interaction). Compare the coefficient estimates to your results in part (f). Calculate the fitted values for four observations: a Democrat with *GOP2party2010* = 0, a Democrat with *GOP2party2010* = 0.5, a Republican with *GOP2party2010* = 0.5, and a Republican with *GOP2party2010* = 1.0). Compare to the fitted values in part (f).

(h) Assess whether there is clustering of the dependent variable just above the cutoff.

(i) Assess whether there are discontinuities at GOPVote = 0.50 for *ChildPoverty, MedianIncome, Obama2008, and WhitePct*. Discuss the implications of your findings.

(j) Estimate a varying slopes model controlling for *ChildPoverty, MedianIncome, Obama2008, and WhitePct*. Discuss these results in light of your findings from the part (i).

(k) Estimate a quadratic RD model and interpret the results.

(l) Estimate a varying slopes model with a window of GOP vote share from 0.4 to 0.6. Discuss any meaningful differences in coefficients and standard errors from the earlier varying slopes model.

(m) Which estimate is the most credible?

TABLE 11.6 **Variables for Head Start Data**

Variable	Description
County	County indicator
Mortality	County mortality rate for children aged 5 to 9 from 1973 to 1983, limited to causes plausibly affected by Head Start
Poverty	Poverty rate in 1960: transformed by subtracting cutoff; also divided by 10 for easier interpretation
HeadStart	Dummy variable indicating counties that received Head Start assistance: counties with poverty greater than 59.2 are coded as 1; counties with poverty less than 59.2 are coded as 0
Bin	The "bin" label for each observation based on dividing the poverty into 50 bins

4. Ludwig and Miller (2007) use a discontinuity in program funding for Head Start to test the impacts on child mortality rates. In the 1960s, the federal government helped 300 of the poorest counties in the United States write grants for Head Start programs. Only counties where poverty was greater than 59.2 percent received this assistance. This problem explores the effects of Head Start on child mortality rates. Table 11.6 lists the variables.

   (a) Write out an equation for a basic RD design to assess the effect of Head Start assistance on child mortality rates. Draw a picture of what you expect the relationship to look like. Note that in this example, treatment occurs for low values of the assignment variable.

   (b) Explain how RD can identify a causal effect of Head Start assistance on mortality.

   (c) Estimate the effect of Head Start on mortality rate by using a basic RD design.

   (d) Estimate the effect of Head Start on mortality rate by using a varying slopes RD design.

   (e) Estimate a basic RD model with (adjusted) poverty values that are between –0.8 and 0.8. Comment on your findings.

   (f) Implement a quadratic RD design. Comment on the results.

   (g) Create a scatterplot of the mortality and poverty data. What do you see?

(h) Use the following code to create a binned graph of the mortality and poverty data. What do you see?[3]

```
egen BinMean = mean(Mortality), by(Bin)
graph twoway (scatter BinMean Bin, ytitle("Mortality") /*
*/ xtitle("Poverty") msize(large) xline(0.0) )/*
*/ (lfit BinMean Bin if HeadStart == 0, clcolor(blue)) /*
*/ (lfit BinMean Bin if HeadStart == 1, clcolor(red))
```

(i) Rerun the quadratic model and save predicted values as *FittedQuadratic*. Include the fitted values in the graph from part (h) by adding (scatter FittedQuadratic Poverty) to the code above. Explain the results.

---

[3] The trick to creating a binned graph is associating each observation with a bin label that is in the middle of the bin. Stata code that created the *Bin* variable is (where we use semi-colon to indicate line breaks to save space) scalar BinNum = 50; scalar BinMin = -6; scalar BinMax = 3; scalar BinLength = (BinMax-BinMin)/BinNum; gen Bin = BinMin + BinLength*(0.5+(floor((Poverty-BinMin)/BinLength))). The *Bin* variable here sets the value for each observation to the middle of the bin; there are likely to be other ways to do it.

PART III

Limited Dependent Variables

Dummy Dependent Variables $\quad$ **12**

Think of a baby born just ... now. Somewhere in the world it has happened. This child's life will be punctuated by a series of dichotomous events. Was she born prematurely? Will she go to pre-K? Will she attend a private school? Will she graduate from high school? Will she get a job? Get married? Buy a car? Have a child? Vote Republican? Have health care? Live past 80 years old?

When we use data to analyze such phenomena—and many others—we need to confront the fact that the outcomes are **dichotomous**. They either happened or didn't, meaning that our dependent variable is either 1 (happened) or 0 (didn't happen). Although we can continue to use OLS for dichotomous dependent variables, the probit and logit models we introduce in this chapter often fit the data better. Probit and logit models come with a price, though: they are more complicated to interpret.

▶ **dichotomous**
Divided into two parts. A dummy variable is an example of a dichotomous variable.

This chapter explains how to deal with dichotomous dependent variables. Section 12.1 shows how to use OLS to estimate these models. OLS does fine, but there are some things that aren't quite right. Hence Section 12.2 introduces *latent variable models* to help us analyze dichotomous outcomes. Section 12.3 then presents the workhorse probit and logit models. These models differ from OLS, and Section 12.4 explains how. Section 12.5 then presents the somewhat laborious process of interpreting coefficients from these models. Probit and logit models have several cool properties, but ease of interpretation is not one of them. Section 12.6 shows how to test hypotheses involving multiple coefficients when we're working with probit and logit models.

<table>
<tr><td>

> **linear probability model (LPM)** Used when the dependent variable is dichotomous. This is an OLS model in which the coefficients are interpreted as the change in probability of observing $Y_i = 1$ for a one-unit change in X.

</td></tr>
</table>

12.1 Linear Probability Model

The easiest way to analyze a dichotomous dependent variable is to use the **linear probability model** (**LPM**). This is a fancy way of saying, "Just run your darn OLS model already."[1] The LPM has witnessed a bit of a renaissance lately as people have realized that despite some clear defects, it often conveniently and effectively characterizes the relationships between independent variables and outcomes. If there is no endogeneity (a big if, as we know all too well), then the coefficients will be the right sign and will generally imply a substantive relationship similar to that estimated by the more complicated probit and logit models we'll discuss later in this chapter.

In this section we show how the LPM model works and describe its limitations.

LPM and the expected value of Y

One nice feature of OLS is that it generates the best estimate of the expected value of Y as a linear function of the independent variables. In other words, we can think of OLS as providing us

$$E[Y_i \,|\, X_1, X_2] = \beta_0 + \beta_1 X_{1i} + \beta_2 X_{2i}$$

where $E[Y_i \,|\, X_1, X_2]$ is the expected value of Y_i given the values of X_{1i} and X_{2i}. This term is also referred to as the conditional value of Y.[2]

When the dependent variable is dichotomous, the expected value of Y is equal to the probability that the variable equals 1. For example, consider a dependent variable that is 1 if it rains and 0 if it doesn't. If there is a 40 percent chance of rain, the expected value of this variable is 0.40. If there is an 85 percent chance of rain, the expected value of this variable is 0.85. In other words, because $E[Y \,|\, X] = Probability(Y = 1 \,|\, X)$, OLS with a dependent variable provides

$$\Pr(Y = 1 \,|\, X_1, X_2) = \beta_0 + \beta_1 X_{1i} + \beta_2 X_{2i}$$

The interpretation of $\hat{\beta}_1$ from this model is that a one-unit increase in X_1 is associated with a $\hat{\beta}_1$ increase in the probability of observing $Y = 1$.

---

[1] We discussed dichotomous *independent* variables in Chapter 7.

[2] The terms *linear* and *non-linear* can get confusing. A linear model is one of the form $Y_i = \beta_0 + \beta_1 X_{1i} + \beta_1 X_{2i} + \cdots$ where none of the parameters to be estimated is multiplied, divided, or raised to powers of other parameters. In other words, all the parameters enter in their own little plus term. In a non-linear model, some of the parameters are multiplied, divided, or raised to powers of other parameters. Linear models can estimate some non-linear relationships (by creating terms that are functions of the independent variables, not the parameters). We described this process in Section 7.1. Such polynomial models will not, however, solve the deficiencies of OLS for dichotomous dependent variables. The models that do address the problems, the probit and logit models we cover later in this chapter, are complex functions of other parameters and are therefore necessarily non-linear models.

TABLE 12.1	**LPM Model of the Probability of Admission to Law School**
GPA	0.032*
	(0.003)
	$[t = 12.29]$
Constant	−2.28*
	(0.206)
	$[t = 11.10]$
N	514
R^2	0.23
Minimum $\hat{Y}_i$	−0.995
Maximum $\hat{Y}_i$	0.682

Standard errors in parentheses.

* indicates significance at $p < 0.05$, two-tailed.

Table 12.1 displays the results from an LPM model of the probability of admission into a competitive Canadian law school (see Bailey, Rosenthal and Yoon 2015). The independent variable is college grade point average (GPA) (measured on a 100-point scale, as is common in Canada). The coefficient on GPA is 0.032, meaning that an increase in one point on the 100-point GPA scale is associated with a 3.2 percent increase in the probability of admission into this law school.

Figure 12.1 is a scatterplot of the law school admissions data. It includes the fitted line from the LPM model. The scatterplot looks different from a typical regression model scatterplot because the dependent variable is either 0 or 1, creating two horizontal lines of observations. Each point is a light vertical line, and when there are many observations, the scatterplot appears as a dark bar. We can see that folks with GPAs under 80 mostly do not get admitted, while people with GPAs above 85 tend to get admitted.

The expected value of Y based on the LPM model is a straight line with a slope of 0.032. Clearly, as GPAs rise, the probability of admission rises as well. The difference from OLS is that instead of interpreting $\hat{\beta}_1$ as the increase in the value of Y associated with a one-unit increase in X, we now interpret $\hat{\beta}_1$ as the increase in the probability Y equals one associated with a one-unit increase in X.

Limits to LPM

While Figure 12.1 is generally sensible, it also has a glaring flaw. The fitted line goes below zero. In fact, the fitted line goes far below zero. The poor soul with a GPA of 40 has a fitted value of −0.995. This is nonsensical (and a bit sad). Probabilities must lie between 0 and 1. For a low enough value of X, the predicted

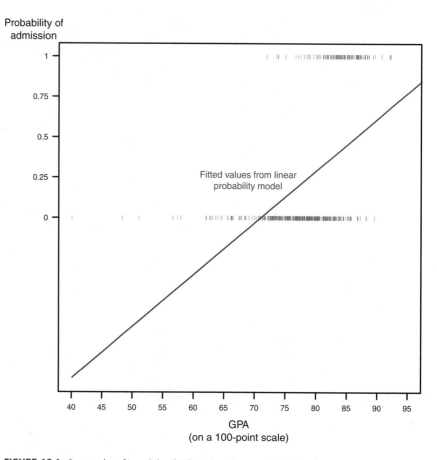

FIGURE 12.1: Scatterplot of Law School Admissions Data and LPM Fitted Line

value falls below zero; for a high enough value of X, the predicted value exceeds one.[3]

That LPM sometimes provides fitted values that make no sense isn't the only problem. We could, after all, simply say that any time we see a fitted value below 0, we'll call that a 0 and any time we see a fitted value above 1 we'll call that a 1. The deeper problem is that fitting a straight line to data with a dichotomous dependent variable runs the risk of misspecifying the relationship between the independent variables and the dichotomous dependent variable.

Figure 12.2 illustrates an example of LPM's problem. Panel (a) depicts a fitted line from an LPM model that uses law school admissions data based on the six hypothetical observations indicated. The line is reasonably steep,

---

[3] In this particular figure, the fitted probabilities do not exceed 1 because GPAs can't go higher than 100. In other cases, though, the independent variable may not have such a clear upper bound. Even so, it is extremely common for LPM fitted values to be less than 0 for some observations and greater than 1 for other observations.

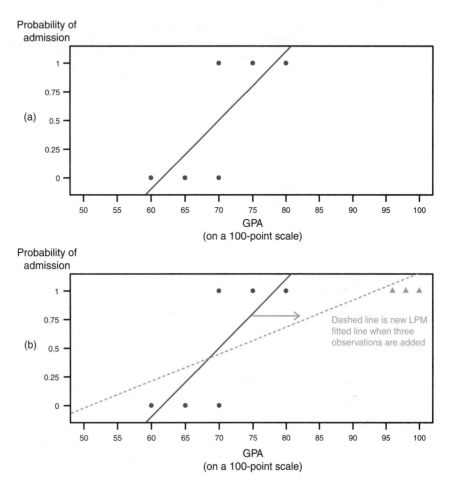

FIGURE 12.2: Misspecification Problem in an LPM

implying a clear relationship. Now suppose that we add three observations from applicants with very high GPAs, all of whom were admitted. These observations are the triangles in the upper right of panel (b). Common sense suggests these observations should strengthen our belief that GPAs predict admission into law school. Sadly, LPM lacks common sense. The figure shows that the LPM fitted line with the new observations (the dashed line) is flatter than the original estimate, implying that the estimated relationship is weaker than the relationship we estimated in the original model with less data.

What's that all about? Once we come to appreciate that the LPM needs to fit a linear relationship, it's pretty easy to understand. If these three new applicants had higher GPAs, from an LPM perspective, we should expect them to have a higher probability of admission than the applicants in the initial sample. But the dependent variable can't be higher than 1, so the LPM interprets the new data as suggesting a weaker relationship. In other words, because these applicants had higher independent variables but not higher dependent variables, the LPM model suggests that the independent variable is not driving the dependent variable higher.

What really is going on is that once GPAs are high enough, students are pretty much certain to be admitted. In other words, we expect a non-linear relationship—the probability of admission rises with GPAs up to a certain level, then levels off as most applicants whose GPAs are above that level are admitted. The probit and logit models we develop next allow us to capture precisely this possibility.[4]

In LPM's defense, it won't systematically estimate positive slopes when the actual slope is negative. And we should not underestimate its convenience and practicality. Nonetheless, we should worry that LPM may leave us with an incomplete view of the relationship between the independent and dichotomous dependent variables.

REMEMBER THIS

The linear probability model (LPM) uses OLS to estimate a model with a dichotomous dependent variable.

1. The coefficients are easy to interpret: a one-unit increase in X_j is associated with a β_j increase in the probability that Y equals 1.

2. Limitations of the LPM include the following:

   - Fitted values of $\hat{Y}_i$ may be greater than 1 or less than 0.

   - Coefficients from an LPM model may mischaracterize the relationship between X and Y.

12.2 Using Latent Variables to Explain Observed Variables

Given the limits to the LPM model, our goal is to develop a model that will produce fitted values between zero and one. In this section, we describe the S curves that achieve this goal and introduce latent variables as a tool that will help us estimate S curves.

---

[4] LPM also has a heteroscedasticity problem. As discussed earlier, heteroscedasticity is a less serious problem than endogeneity, but heteroscedasticity forces us to cast a skeptical eye toward standard errors estimated by LPM. There is a fix for this problem, but the process is so complicated that we might as well run the probit or logit models described shortly. For more details, see Long (1997, 39).

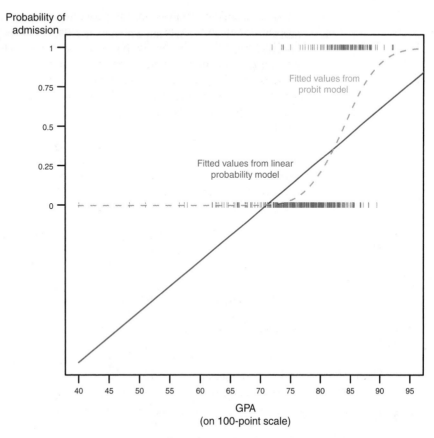

FIGURE 12.3: Scatterplot of Law School Admissions Data and LPM- and Probit-Fitted Lines

S-curves

Figure 12.3 shows the law school admissions data. The LPM fitted line, in all its negative probability glory is there, but we have also added a fitted curve from a probit model. The probit-fitted line looks like a tilted letter "S," and so the relationship between X and the dichotomous dependent variable is non-linear. We explain how to generate such a curve over the course of this chapter, but for now let's note some of its nice features.

For applicants with GPAs below 70 or so, the probit-fitted line has flattened out. This means that no matter how low students' GPAs go, their fitted probability of admission will not go below zero. For applicants with very high GPAs, increasing scores lead to only small increases in the probability of admission. Even if GPAs were to go very, very high, the probit-fitted line flattens out, and no one will have a predicted probability of admission greater than one.

Not only does the S-shaped curve of the probit-fitted line avoid nonsensical probability estimates, it also reflects the data better in several respects. First, there is a range of GPAs in which the effect on admissions is quite high. Look in the range from around 80 to around 90. As GPA rises in this range, the effect on probability of admission is quite high, much higher than implied by the LPM fitted line. Second, even though the LPM fitted values for the high GPAs are logically possible (because they are between 0 and 1), they don't reflect the data particularly well. The person with the highest GPA in the entire sample (a GPA of 92), is predicted by the LPM model to have only a 68 percent probability of admission. The probit model, in contrast, predicts a 96 percent probability of admission for this GPA star.

Latent variables

▶ **latent variable** For a probit or logit model, an unobserved continuous variable reflecting the propensity of an individual observation of Y_i to equal 1.

To generate such non-linear fitted lines, we're going to think in terms of a **latent variable**. Something is latent if you don't see it. A latent variable is something we don't see, at least not directly. We'll think of the observed dummy dependent variable (which is zero or one) as reflecting an underlying continuous latent variable. If the value of an observation's latent variable is high, then the dependent variable for that observation is likely to be one; if the value of an observation's latent variable is low, then the dependent variable for that observation is likely to be zero. In short, we're interested in a latent variable that is an unobserved continuous variable reflecting the propensity of an individual observation of Y_i to equal 1.

Here's an example. Pundits and politicians obsess over presidential approval. They know that a president's reelection and policy choices are often tied to the state of his approval. Presidential approval is typically measured with a yes-or-no question: do you approve of the way the president is handling his job? That's our dichotomous dependent variable, but we know full well that the range of responses to the president covers far more than two choices. Some people froth at the mouth in anger at the mention of the president. Others think "Meh." Others giddily support the president.

It's useful to think of these different views as different latent attitudes toward the president. We can think of the people who hate the president as having very negative values of a latent presidential approval variable. People who are so-so about the president have values of a latent presidential approval variable near zero. People who love the president have very positive values of a latent presidential approval variable.

We think in terms of a latent variable because it is easy to write down a model of the propensity to approve of the president. It looks like an OLS model. Specifically, Y_i^* (pronounced "Y-star") is the latent propensity to be a 1 (an ugly phrase, but that's really what it is). It depends on some independent variable X and the β's.

$$Y_i^* = \beta_0 + \beta_1 X_{1i} + \epsilon_i \tag{12.1}$$

We'll model the observed dichotomous dependent variable as a function of this unobserved latent variable. We observe $Y_i = 1$ (notice the lack of a star) for people whose latent feelings are above zero.[5] If the latent variable is less than zero, we observe $Y_i = 0$. (We ignore nonanswers to keep things simple.)

This latent variable approach is consistent with how the world works. There are folks who approve of the president but differ in the degree to which they approve; they are all ones in the observed variable (Y) but vary in the latent variable (Y^*). There are folks who disapprove of the president but differ in the degree of their disapproval; they are all zeros in the observed variable (Y) but vary in the latent variable (Y^*).

Formally, we connect the latent and observed variables as follows. The observed variable is

$$Y_i = \begin{cases} 0 & \text{if } Y_i^* < 0 \\ 1 & \text{if } Y_i^* \geq 0 \end{cases}$$

Plugging in Equation 12.1 for Y_i^*, we observe $Y_i = 1$ if

$$\beta_0 + \beta_1 X_i + \epsilon_i \geq 0$$
$$\epsilon_i \geq -\beta_0 - \beta_1 X_{1i}$$

In other words, if the random error term is greater than or equal to $-\beta_0 - \beta_1 X_i$, we'll observe $Y_i = 1$. This implies

$$\Pr(Y_i = 1 \mid X_1) = \Pr(\epsilon_i \geq -\beta_0 - \beta_1 X_{1i})$$

With this characterization, the probability that the dependent variable is one is necessarily bounded between 0 and 1 because it is expressed in terms of the probability that the error term is greater or less than some number. Our task in the next section is to characterize the distribution of the error term as a function of the β parameters.

REMEMBER THIS

Latent variable models are helpful to analyze dichotomous dependent variables.

1. The latent (unobserved) variable is

$$Y_i^* = \beta_0 + \beta_1 X_i + \epsilon_i$$

2. The observed variable is

$$Y_i = \begin{cases} 0 & \text{if } Y_i^* < 0 \\ 1 & \text{if } Y_i^* \geq 0 \end{cases}$$

---

[5] Because the latent variable is unobserved, we have the luxury of using zero to label the point in the latent variable space at which folks become ones.

12.3 │ Probit and Logit Models

Both the probit model and the logit model allow us to estimate the relationship between X and Y in a way that forces the fitted values to lie between zero and one, thereby producing estimates that more accurately capture the full relationship between X and Y than do LPM models.

The probit and logit models are effectively very similar, but they differ in the equations they use to characterize the error term distributions. In this section we explain the equations behind each of these two models.

Probit model

▶ **probit model** A way to analyze data with a dichotomous dependent variable. The key assumption is that the error term is normally distributed.

The key assumption in a **probit model** is that the error term (ϵ_i) is itself normally distributed. We've worked with the normal distribution a lot because the central limit theorem (from page 57) implies that with enough data, OLS coefficient estimates are normally distributed no matter how ϵ is distributed. For the probit model, we're saying that ϵ itself is normally distributed. So while normality of $\hat{\beta}_1$ is a proven *result* for OLS, normality of ϵ is an *assumption* in the probit model.

Before we explain the equation for the probit model, it is useful to do a bit of bookkeeping. We have shown that $\Pr(Y_i = 1 | X_1) = \Pr(\epsilon_i \geq -\beta_0 - \beta_1 X_{1i})$, but this equation can be hard to work with, given the widespread convention in probability of characterizing the distribution of a random variable in terms of the probability that it is less than some value. Therefore, we're going to do a quick trick based on the symmetry of the normal distribution: because the distribution is symmetrical when it has the same shape on each side of the mean, the probability of seeing something larger than some number is the same as the probability of seeing something less than the negative of that number. Figure 12.4 illustrates this property. In panel (a), we shade the probability of being greater than -1.5. In panel (b), we shade the probability of being less than 1.5. The symmetry of the normal distribution backs up what our eyes suggest: the shaded areas are equal in size, indicating equal probabilities. In other words, $\Pr(\epsilon_i > -1.5) = \mathrm{Prob}(\epsilon_i < 1.5)$. This fact allows us to rewrite $\Pr(Y_i = 1 | X_1) = \Pr(\epsilon_i \geq -\beta_0 - \beta_1 X_{1i})$ as

$$\Pr(Y_i = 1 | X_1) = \Pr(\epsilon_i \leq \beta_0 + \beta_1 X_{1i})$$

▶ **cumulative distribution function (CDF)** Indicates how much of normal distribution is to the left of any given point.

There isn't a huge conceptual issue here, but now it's much easier to characterize the model with conventional tools for working with normal distributions. In particular, stating the condition in this way simplifies our use of the **cumulative distribution function (CDF)** of a standard normal distribution. The CDF tells us how much of normal distribution is to the left of any given point. Feed the CDF a number, and it will tell us the probability that a standard normal random variable is less than that number.

Figure 12.5 on page 412 shows examples for several values of $\beta_0 + \beta_1 X_{1i}$. In panel (a), the portion of a standard normal probability density to the left of -0.7

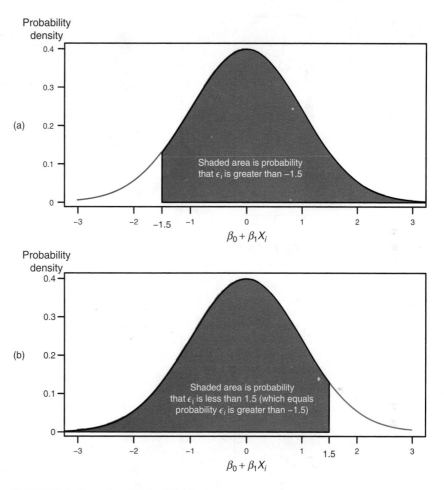

FIGURE 12.4: Symmetry of Normal Distribution

is shaded. Below that, in panel (d), the CDF function with the value of the CDF at -0.7 is highlighted. The value is roughly 0.25, which is the area of the normal curve that is to the left of -0.7 in panel (a).

Panel (b) shows a standard normal density curve with the portion to the left of $+0.7$ shaded. Clearly, this is more than half the distribution. The CDF below it, in panel (e), shows that in fact roughly 0.75 of a standard normal density is to the left of $+0.7$. Panel (c) shows a standard normal PDF with the portion to the left of 2.3 shaded. Panel (f), below that, shows a CDF and highlights its CDF value at 2.3, which is about 0.99. Notice that the CDF can't be less than 0 or more than 1 because it is impossible to have less than 0 percent or more than 100 percent of the area of the normal density to the left of any number.

Since we know $Y_i = 1$ if $\epsilon_i \leq \beta_0 + \beta_1 X_{1i}$, the probability $Y_i = 1$ will be the CDF defined at the point $\beta_0 + \beta_1 X_{1i}$.

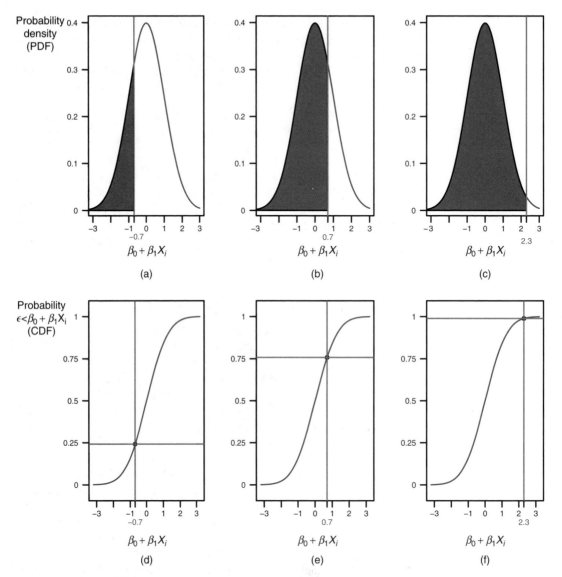

FIGURE 12.5: PDFs and CDFs

The notation we'll use for the normal CDF is $\Phi()$ (the Greek letter Φ is pronounced "fi," as in wi-fi) which indicates the probability that a normally distributed random variable (ϵ in this case) is less than the number in parentheses. In other words,

$$\text{Prob}(Y_i = 1) = \text{Prob}(\epsilon_i \leq \beta_0 + \beta_1 X_{1i})$$
$$= \Phi(\beta_0 + \beta_1 X_{1i})$$

The probit model produces estimates of β that best fit the data. To the extent possible, that is, probit estimates will produce $\hat{\beta}$'s that lead to high predicted probabilities for observations that actually were 1s. Likewise, to the extent possible, probit estimates will produce $\hat{\beta}$'s that lead to low predicted probabilities for observations that actually were 0s. We discuss estimation after we introduce the logit model.

Logit model

logit model A way to analyze data with a dichotomous dependent variable. The error term in a logit model is logistically distributed. Pronounced "low–jit".

Logit models also allow us to estimate parameters for a model with a dichotomous dependent variable in a way that forces the fitted values to lie between 0 and 1. They are functionally very similar to probit models. The difference from a probit model is the equation that characterizes the error term. The equation differs dramatically from the probit equation, but it turns out that this difference has little practical import.

In a logit model

$$\text{Prob}(Y_i = 1) = \text{Prob}(\epsilon_i \leq \beta_0 + \beta_1 X_{1i})$$

$$= \frac{e^{\beta_0 + \beta_1 X_i}}{1 + e^{\beta_0 + \beta_1 X_{1i}}} \quad (12.2)$$

To get a feel for the logit equation, consider what happens when $\beta_0 + \beta_1 X_{1i}$ is humongous. In the numerator, e is raised to that big number, which leads to a super big number. In the denominator will be that same number plus 1, which is pretty much the same number. Hence the probability will be very, very close to 1. But no matter how big $\beta_0 + \beta_1 X_{1i}$ gets, the probability will never exceed 1.

If $\beta_0 + \beta_1 X_{1i}$ is super negative, the numerator of the logit function will have e raised to a huge negative number, which is the same as one over e raised to a big number, which is essentially zero. The denominator will have that number plus one, meaning that the fraction is very close to $\frac{0}{1}$, and therefore the probability that $Y_i = 1$ will be very, very close to zero. No matter how negative $\beta_0 + \beta_1 X_{1i}$ gets, the probability will never go below zero.[6]

The probit and logit models are rivals, but friendly rivals. When properly interpreted, they yield virtually identical results. Do not sweat the difference. Simply pick probit or logit and get on with life. Back in the early days of computers, the logit model was often preferred because it is computationally easier than the probit model. Now powerful computers make the issue moot.

---

[6] If $\beta_0 + \beta_1 X_{1i}$ is zero, then $\text{Prob}(Y_i = 1) = 0.5$. It's a good exercise to work out why. The logit function can also be written as

$$\text{Prob}(Y_i = 1) = \frac{1}{1 + e^{-(\beta_0 + \beta_1 X_{1i})}}$$

> ## REMEMBER THIS
>
> The probit and logit models are very similar. Both estimate S-shaped fitted lines that are always above 0 and below 1.
>
> 1. In a probit model,
>
> $$\text{Prob}(Y_i = 1) = \Phi(\beta_0 + \beta_1 X_{1i})$$
>
> where $\Phi()$ is the standard normal CDF indicating the probability that a standard normal random variable is less than the number in parentheses.
>
> 2. In a logit model,
>
> $$\text{Prob}(Y_i = 1) = \frac{e^{\beta_0 + \beta_1 X_{1i}}}{1 + e^{\beta_0 + \beta_1 X_{1i}}}$$

Discussion Questions

1. Come up with an example of a dichotomous dependent variable of interest, and do the following:

    (a) Describe the latent variable underlying the observed dichotomous variable.

    (b) Identify a continuous independent variable that may explain this dichotomous dependent variable. Create a scatterplot of what you expect observations of the independent and dependent variables to be.

    (c) Sketch and explain the relationship you expect between your independent variable and the probability of observing the dichotomous dependent variable of 1.

2. Come up with another example of a dichotomous dependent variable of interest; this time, identify a dichotomous independent variable, as well, and finish up by doing the following.

    (a) Create a scatterplot of what you expect observations of the independent and dependent variables to be.

    (b) Sketch and explain the relationship you expect between your independent variable and the probability of observing the dichotomous dependent variable of 1.

12.4 Estimation

So how do we select the best $\hat{\beta}$ for the data given? The estimation process for the probit and logit models is called **Maximum likelihood estimation (MLE)**. It is more complicated than estimating coefficients using OLS. Understanding the inner workings of MLE is not necessary to implement or understand probit and logit models. Such an understanding can be helpful for more advanced work, however, and we discuss the technique in more detail in the appendix, starting on page 544.

▶ **maximum likelihood estimation (MLE)** The estimation process used to generate coefficient estimates for probit and logit models, among others.

In this section we explain the properties of MLE estimates, describe the fitted values produced by probit and logit models, and show how goodness of fit is measured in MLE models.

Properties of MLE estimates

Happily, many major statistical properties of OLS estimates carry over to MLE estimates. For large samples, the parameter estimates are normally distributed and consistent if there is no endogeneity. That means we can interpret statistical significance and create confidence intervals and p values much as we have done with OLS models. One modest difference is that we use z **tests** rather than t tests for MLE models. A z test compares test statistics to critical values based on the normal distribution. Because the t distribution approximates the normal distribution in large samples, z tests and t tests are very similar, practically speaking. The critical values will continue to be the familiar values we used in OLS. In particular, we can continue to rely on the rule of thumb that a coefficient is statistically significant if it is more than twice as large as its standard error.

▶ **z test** A hypothesis test involving comparison of a test statistic and a critical value based on a normal distribution.

Fitted values from the probit model

The estimated $\hat{\beta}$'s from a probit model will produce fitted lines that best fit the data. Figure 12.6 shows examples. Panel (a) shows a classic probit-fitted line. The observed data are indicated with short vertical lines. For low values of X, Y is mostly zero, with a few exceptions. There is a range of X that has a pretty even mix of $Y = 0$ and $Y = 1$ observations; then for high values of X, all Y's are one. The estimated $\hat{\beta}_0$ coefficient is -3, indicating that low values of X are associated with low probabilities that $Y = 1$. The estimated $\hat{\beta}_1$ coefficient is positive because higher values of X are associated with a high probability of observing $Y = 1$.

To calculate fitted values for the model depicted in panel (a) of Figure 12.6, we need to supply a value of X and use the coefficient estimates in the probit equation. Since $\hat{\beta}_0 = -3$ and $\hat{\beta}_1 = 2$, the fitted probability of observing $Y = 1$ when $X = 0$ is

$$\hat{Y}_i = \text{Prob}(Y_i = 1)$$
$$= \Phi(\hat{\beta}_0 + \hat{\beta}_1 X_i)$$
$$= \Phi(-3 + 2 \times 0)$$
$$= \Phi(-3)$$
$$= 0.001$$

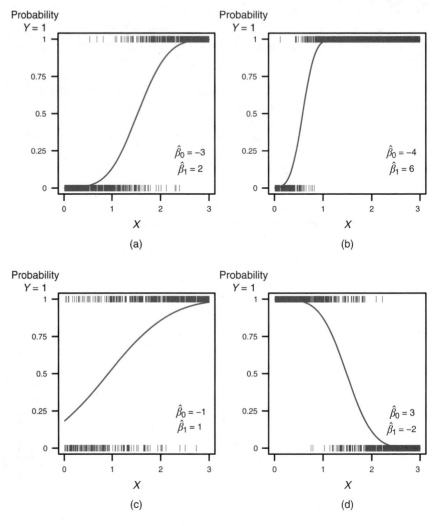

FIGURE 12.6: Examples of Data and Fitted Lines Estimated by Probit

Based on the same coefficient estimates, the fitted probability of observing $Y = 1$ when $X = 1.5$ is

$$\hat{Y}_i = \Phi(-3 + 2 \times 1.5)$$
$$= \Phi(0)$$
$$= 0.5$$

Panel (b) of Figure 12.6 shows a somewhat similar relationship, but the transition between the $Y = 0$ and $Y = 1$ observations is starker. When X is less than about 0.5, the Y's are all zero; when X is greater than about 1.0, the Ys are all one. This pattern of data indicates a strong relationship between X and Y, and $\hat{\beta}_1$ is, not surprisingly, larger in panel (b) than in panel (a). The fitted line is quite steep.

Panel (c) of Figure 12.6 shows a common situation in which the relationship between X and Y is rather weak. The estimated coefficients produce a fitted line that is pretty flat; we don't even see the full S-shape emblematic of probit models. If we were to display the fitted line for a much broader range of X values, we would see the S-shape because the fitted probabilities would flatten out at zero for sufficiently negative values of X and would flatten out at one for sufficiently positive values of X. Sometimes, as in this case, the flattening of a probit-fitted line occurs outside the range of observed values of X.

Panel (d) shows a case of a positive $\hat{\beta}_0$ coefficient and negative $\hat{\beta}_1$. This case best fits the pattern of the data in which $Y = 1$ for low values of X and $Y = 0$ for high values of X.

Fitted values from the logit model

For logit, the fitted values are calculated as

$$\hat{Y}_i = \frac{e^{\hat{\beta}_0 + \hat{\beta}_1 X_{1i} + \hat{\beta}_2 X_{2i} + \cdots}}{1 + e^{\hat{\beta}_0 + \hat{\beta}_1 X_{1i} + \hat{\beta}_2 X_{2i} + \cdots}}$$

Yes, that's pretty ugly. Usually (but not always) there is a convenient way to get statistical software to generate fitted values if we ask nicely. We'll discuss how in this chapter's Computing Corner.

Goodness of fit for MLE models

▶ **log likelihood** The log of the probability of observing the Y outcomes we report, given the X data and the $\hat{\beta}$'s.

The overall fit of a probit or logit model is reported with a **log likelihood** statistic, often written as "log L." This statistic is a by-product of the MLE estimation process. The log likelihood is the log of the probability of observing the Y outcomes we did with the given X data and $\hat{\beta}$'s. It is an odd way to report how well the model fits because, well, it is incomprehensible. The upside of the incomprehensibility of this fit statistic is that we are less likely to put too much emphasis on it, in contrast to the more accessible R^2 for OLS models, which is sometimes overemphasized (as we discussed in Section 3.7).

The log likelihood is useful in hypothesis tests involving multiple coefficients. Just as R^2 feeds into the F statistic (as discussed on page 231), the log likelihood feeds into the test statistic used when we are interested in hypotheses involving multiple coefficients in probit or logit models as we discuss later in Section 12.6.

> ## REMEMBER THIS
>
> 1. Probit and logit models are estimated via maximum likelihood estimation (MLE) instead of OLS.
>
> 2. We can assess the statistical significance of MLE estimates of $\hat{\beta}$ by using z tests, which closely resemble t tests in large samples for OLS models.

TABLE 12.2 Sample Probit Results for Review Questions		
	(a)	(b)
X_1	0.5	1.0
	(0.1)	(1.0)
X_2	−0.5	−3.0
	(0.1)	(1.0)
Constant	0.00	3.0
	(0.1)	(0.0)
N	500	500
$\log L$	−1000	−1200

Standard errors in parentheses.

Review Questions

1. For each panel in Figure 12.6, identify the value of X that produces $\hat{Y}_i = 0.5$. Use the probit equation.

2. Based on Table 12.2, indicate whether the following statements are true, false, or indeterminate.

   (a) The coefficient on X_1 in column (a) is statistically significant.

   (b) The coefficient on X_1 in column (b) is statistically significant.

   (c) The results in column (a) imply that a one-unit increase in X_1 is associated with a 50-percentage-point increase in the probability that $Y = 1$.

   (d) The fitted probability found by using the estimate in column (a) for $X_{1i} = 0$ and $X_{2i} = 0$ is 0.

   (e) The fitted probability found by using the estimate in column (b) for $X_{1i} = 0$ and $X_{2i} = 0$ is approximately 1.

3. Based on Table 12.2, indicate the fitted probability for the following:

   (a) Column (a) and $X_{1i} = 4$ and $X_{2i} = 0$.

   (b) Column (a) and $X_{1i} = 0$ and $X_{2i} = 4$.

   (c) Column (b) and $X_{1i} = 0$ and $X_{2i} = 1$.

12.5 Interpreting Probit and Logit Coefficients

The LPM model may have its problems, but it is definitely easy to interpret: a one-unit increase in X is associated with a $\hat{\beta}_1$ increase in the probability that $Y = 1$.

Probit and logit models have their strengths, but being easy to interpret is not one of them. This is because the $\hat{\beta}$'s feed into the complicated equations defining the probability of observing $Y = 1$. These complicated equations keep the predicted values above zero and less than one, but they can do so only by allowing the effect of X to vary across values of X.

In this section we explain how the estimated effect of X_1 on Y in probit and logit models depends not only on the value of X_1, but also on the value of the other independent variables. We then describe approaches to interpreting the coefficient estimates from these models.

The effect of X_1 depends on the value of X_1

Figure 12.7 displays the fitted line from the probit model of law school admission. Increasing GPA from 70 to 75 leads to a small change in predicted probability (about 3 percentage points). Increasing GPA from 85 to 90 is associated with a substantial increase in predicted probability (about 30 percentage points). The

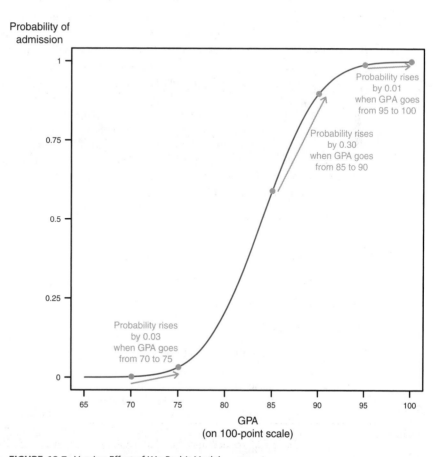

FIGURE 12.7: Varying Effect of X in Probit Model

change in predicted probability then gets small—really small—when we increase GPA from 95 to 100 (about 1 percentage point).

This is certainly a more complicated story than in OLS, but it's perfectly sensible. Increasing a very low GPA really doesn't get a person seriously considered for admission. For a middle range of GPAs, increases are indeed associated with real increases in probability of being admitted. After a certain point, however, higher GPAs have little effect on the probability of being admitted because the likelihood that anyone with such a high GPA would be rejected is slim.

The effect of X_1 depends on the values of the other independent variables

There's another wrinkle: the other variables. In probit and logit models, the effect of increasing X_1 varies not only over values of X_1, but also over values of the other variables in the model. Suppose, for example, that we're analyzing law school admission in terms of college GPAs and standardized Law School Admission Test (LSAT) test scores. The effect of GPAs actually depends on the value of the LSAT test score. If an applicant's LSAT test score is very high, the predicted probability will be near 1 based on that alone and there will be very little room for a higher GPA to affect the predicted probability of being admitted to law school. If an applicant's LSAT test score is low, then there will be a lot more room for a higher GPA to affect the predicted probability of admission.

We know that the estimated effect of X_1 on the probability $Y = 1$ depends on the values of X_1 and the other independent variables, but this creates a knotty problem: how do we convey the magnitude of the estimated effect? In other words, how do we substantively interpret probit and logit coefficients?

There are several reasonable ways to approach this issue. Here we focus on simulations. If X_1 is a continuous variable, we summarize the effect of X_1 on the probability $Y = 1$ by calculating the average increase that would occur in fitted probabilities if we were to increase X_1 by one standard deviation for every observation. First we use the estimated $\hat{\beta}$'s to calculate the fitted values for all observations. Then, we add one standard deviation to the value of X_1 for each observation and calculate new fitted values for all observations. The average difference in these two fitted values across all observations is the simulated effect of increasing X_1 by one standard deviation. The bigger $\hat{\beta}_1$, the bigger this simulated effect will be.

It is not set in stone that we add one standard deviation. Sometimes it may make sense to calculate these quantities by simply using an increase of one or some other amount.

These simulations make the coefficients interpretable in a commonsense way. We can say things like, "The estimates imply that increasing GPA by one standard deviation is associated with an average increase of 15 percentage points in predicted probability of being admitted to law school." That's a mouthful, but much more meaningful than the $\hat{\beta}$ itself.

If X_1 is a dummy variable, we summarize the effect of X_1 slightly differently. We calculate what the average increase in fitted probabilities would be if the value of X_1 for every observation were to go from zero to one. We first use the estimated $\hat{\beta}$'s to calculate the fitted values for all observations, setting $X_1 = 0$ for all observations and using the observed values for all other independent variables. Then we calculate the fitted values for all observations, setting $X_1 = 1$ for all observations while still using the observed values for all other independent variables. The average difference in these two fitted values across all observations is the estimated effect of the dummy variable X_1 going from zero to one.

Our approach is called the *observed-value, discrete-differences approach* to estimating the effect of an independent variable on the probability $Y = 1$. "Observed value" comes from our use of these observed values in the calculation of simulated probabilities. The alternative to the observed-value approach is the *average-case approach*, which creates a single composite observation whose independent variables equal sample averages. We discuss the average-case approach in the appendix on page 546.

The "discrete-difference" part of our approach involves the use of specific differences in the value of X_1 when simulating probabilities. The alternative to the discrete-differences approach is the *marginal-effects approach*, which calculates the effect of changing X_1 by a minuscule amount. This calculus-based approach is a bit more involved (but easy with a simple trick) and produces results that are generally similar to the approach we present. We discuss the marginal-effects approach in the appendix on page 546 and show how to implement the approach in this chapter's Computing Corner on pages 437 and 439.

Interpreting logit coefficients proceeds in the same way, only we use the logit equation (Equation 12.2) instead of the probit equation. For example, for an observed-value, discrete-differences simulation of the effect of a continuous variable, we calculate logit-fitted values for all observations and then, when the variable has increased by one standard deviation, calculate logit-fitted values. The average difference in fitted values is the simulated effect of an increase in the variable of one standard deviation.

REMEMBER THIS

1. Use the observed-value, discrete-differences method, to interpret probit coefficients as follows.

- If X_1 is continuous:

    (a) For each observation, calculate P_{1i} as the standard fitted probability from the probit results.

$$P_{1i} = \Phi(\hat{\beta}_0 + \hat{\beta}_1 X_{1i} + \hat{\beta}_2 X_{2i} + \hat{\beta}_3 X_{3i} + \cdots)$$

(b) For each observation, calculate P_{2i} as the fitted probability when the value of X_{1i} is increased by one standard deviation (σ_{X_1}) for each observation:

$$P_{2i} = \Phi(\hat{\beta}_0 + \hat{\beta}_1(X_{1i} + \sigma_{X_1}) + \hat{\beta}_2 X_{2i} + \hat{\beta}_3 X_{3i} + \cdots)$$

(c) The simulated effect of increasing X_1 by one standard deviation is the average difference $P_{2i} - P_{1i}$ across all observations.

- If X_1 is a dummy variable:

  (a) For each observation, calculate P_{1i} as the fitted probability but with X_{1i} set to 0 for all observations:

  $$P_{0i} = \Phi(\hat{\beta}_0 + \hat{\beta}_1 \times 0 + \hat{\beta}_2 X_{2i} + \hat{\beta}_3 X_{3i} + \cdots)$$

  (b) For each observation, calculate P_{1i} as the fitted probability but with X_{1i} set to 1 for all observations:

  $$P_{1i} = \Phi(\hat{\beta}_0 + \hat{\beta}_1 \times 1 + \hat{\beta}_2 X_{2i} + \hat{\beta}_3 X_{3i} + \cdots)$$

  (c) The simulated effect of going from 0 to 1 for the dummy variable X_1 is the average difference $P_{1i} - P_{0i}$ across all observations.

2. To interpret logit coefficients by using the observed-value, discrete-differences method, proceed as with the probit model, but use the logit equation to generate fitted values.

Review Questions

Suppose we have data on restaurants in Los Angeles and want to understand what causes them to go out of business. Our dependent variable is a dummy variable indicating bankruptcy in the year of the study. One dependent variable is the years of experience running a restaurant of the owner. Another independent variable is a dummy variable indicating whether or not the restaurant had a liquor license.

1. Explain how to calculate the effects of the owner's years of experience on the probability a restaurant goes bankrupt.

2. Explain how to calculate the effects of having a liquor license on the probability a restaurant goes bankrupt.

| CASE STUDY | Econometrics in the Grocery Store |

We've all been there. It's late at night, we're picking up groceries, and we have to choose between a brand-name and a store-brand product. The store brand is a bit cheaper, and we know the product in the bottle is basically the same as the brand name, so why not save a quarter? And yet, maybe the brand-name is better and the brand-name label is so pretty …

Marketing people want to know how we solve such existential dilemmas. And they have lots of data to help them, especially when they can link facts about consumers to their grocery receipts. Ching, Erdem, and Keane (2009) discuss a particular example involving purchase of ketchup in two U.S. cities. Their model is an interesting two-stage model of decision making, but for our purposes, we will focus on whether people who buy ketchup choose store-brand or name-brand versions.

Such decisions by consumers are affected by marketing choices like pricing, displays, and advertisements. Characteristics of the consumer, such as income and household size, also matter.

An LPM model of the purchase decision is

$$Pr\ (Purchase\ store\ brand_i = 1) = \beta_0 + \beta_1\ Price\ difference_i + \beta_2\ Brand\ name\ display_i$$
$$+ \beta_3\ Store\ brand\ display_i + \beta_4\ Brand\ name\ featured_i$$
$$+ \beta_5\ Store\ brand\ featured_i + \beta_6\ Income_i$$
$$+ \beta_7\ Household\ size_i + \varepsilon_i$$

where the price difference is the average price of the brand-name products (e.g., Heinz and Hunt's) minus the store-brand product, the display variables are dummy variables indicating whether brand-name and store-brand products were displayed, and the featured variables are dummy variables indicating whether brand-name and store-brand products were featured in advertisements.[7]

A probit model of the purchase decision is

$$Pr\ (Purchase\ store\ brand_i = 1) = \Phi(\beta_0 + \beta_1\ Price\ difference_i$$
$$+ \beta_2\ Brand\ name\ display_i + \beta_3\ Store\ brand\ display_i$$
$$+ \beta_4\ Brand\ name\ featured_i$$
$$+ \beta_5\ Store\ brand\ featured_i + \beta_6\ Income_i$$
$$+ \beta_7\ Household\ size_i)$$

---

[7] The income variable ranges from 1 to 14, with each value corresponding to a specified income range. This approach to measuring income is pretty common, even though it is not super precise. Sometimes people break an income variable coded this way into dummy variables; doing so does not affect our conclusions in this particular case.

	LPM	Probit	Logit
TABLE 12.3 Multiple Models of Probability of Buying Store-Brand Ketchup			
Price difference	0.134*	0.685*	1.415*
	(0.013)	(0.074)	(0.141)
	[$t = 10.31$]	[$z = 9.30$]	[$z = 10.06$]
Brand name displayed	−0.042*	−0.266*	−0.543*
	(0.006)	(0.035)	(0.071)
	[$t = 7.47$]	[$z = 7.59$]	[$z = 7.68$]
Store brand displayed	0.214*	0.683*	1.164*
	(0.014)	(0.06)	(0.101)
	[$t = 15.32$]	[$z = 11.39$]	[$z = 11.49$]
Brand name featured	−0.083*	−0.537*	−1.039*
	(0.004)	(0.027)	(0.056)
	[$t = 18.98$]	[$z = 19.52$]	[$z = 18.41$]
Store brand featured	0.304*	0.948*	1.606*
	(0.013)	(0.055)	(0.091)
	[$t = 23.31$]	[$z = 17.29$]	[$z = 17.55$]
Household income	−0.010*	−0.055*	−0.109*
	(0.001)	(0.004)	(0.008)
	[$t = 13.16$]	[$z = 12.57$]	[$z = 12.95$]
Household size	0.005*	0.030*	0.060*
	(0.002)	(0.008)	(0.016)
	[$t = 3.44$]	[$z = 3.62$]	[$z = 3.84$]
Constant	0.171*	−0.929*	−1.537*
	(0.007)	(0.037)	(0.069)
	[$t = 24.96$]	[$z = 25.13$]	[$z = 22.17$]
N	23,436	23,436	23,436
R^2	0.083		
$\log L$		−7,800.202	−7,799.8
Minimum $\hat{Y}_i$	−0.133	0.004	0.007
Maximum $\hat{Y}_i$	0.765	0.863	0.887

Standard errors in parentheses.

* indicates significance at $p < 0.05$, two-tailed.

Table 12.3 presents the results. As always, the LPM results are easy to interpret. The coefficient on price difference indicates that consumers are 13.4 percentage points more likely to purchase the store-brand ketchup if the average price of the brand-name products is $1 more expensive than the store brand, holding all else equal. (The average price difference in this data set is only $0.13, so $1 is a big difference in prices.) If the brand-name ketchup is displayed, consumers are 4.2

percentage points less likely the buy the brand-name product, while consumers are 21.4 percentage points more likely to buy the store-brand ketchup when it is displayed. These, and all the other coefficients, are statistically significant.

The fitted probabilities of buying store-brand ketchup from the LPM model range from −13 percent to +77 percent. Yeah, the negative fitted probability is weird. Probabilities below zero do not make sense, and that's one of the reasons why the LPM model makes people a little squeamish.

The second and third columns of Table 12.3 display probit and logit results. These models are, as we know, designed to avoid nonsensical fitted values and to better capture the relationship between the dependent and independent variables.

Interpreting statistical significance in probit and logit models is easy as we need simply to look at whether the z statistic is greater than 1.96. The price difference coefficients in the probit and logit models are highly statistically significant, with z statistics of 9.30 and 10.06, respectively. The coefficients on all the other variables are also statistically significant in both probit and logit models, as we can see from their z statistics.

Interpreting the coefficients in the probit and logit models is not straightforward, however. Does the fact that the coefficient on the price difference variable in the probit model is 0.685 mean that consumers are 68.5 percentage points more likely to buy store-brand ketchup when brand-name ketchup is $1 more expensive? Does the coefficient on the store brand display variable imply that consumers are 68.3 percentage points more likely to buy store-brand ketchup when it is on display?

No. No. (No!) The coefficient estimates from the probit and logit models feed into the complicated probit and logit equations on pages 412 and 413. We need extra steps to understand what they mean. Table 12.4 shows the results when we use our simulation technique to understand the substantive implications of our estimates. The estimated effect of a $1 price increase from the probit model is calculated by comparing the average fitted value for all individuals at their actual values of their independent variables to the average fitted value for all individuals when the price difference variable is increased by one for every observation (and all other variables remain at their actual values). This value is 0.191, a bit higher than the LPM estimate of 0.134 we see in Table 12.3 but still in the same ballpark.

TABLE 12.4 **Estimated Effect of Independent Variables on Probability of Buying Store-Brand Ketchup**

Variable	Simulated change	Probit	Logit
Price difference	Increase by 1, other variables at actual values	0.191	0.237
Brand name displayed	From 0 to 1, other variables at actual values	−0.049	−0.052
Store brand displayed	From 0 to 1, other variables at actual values	0.190	0.184
Brand name featured	From 0 to 1, other variables at actual values	−0.089	−0.089
Store brand featured	From 0 to 1, other variables at actual values	0.286	0.279
Household income	Increase by 1, other variables at actual values	−0.011	−0.012
Household size	Increase by 1, other variables at actual values	0.006	0.007

Our simulations are slightly different for dummy independent variables. For example, to calculate the estimated effect of displaying the brand-name ketchup from the probit model, we first calculate fitted values from the probit model assuming the value of this variable was 0 for every consumer while using the actual values of the other variables. Then, we calculate fitted values from the probit model assuming the value of the brand name displayed variable was 1 for everyone, again using the actual values of the other variables. The average difference in these fitted probabilities was −0.049, indicating our probit estimates imply that displaying the brand-name ketchup lowered the probability of buying the store brand by 4.9 percentage points, on average.

The logit-estimated effects in Table 12.4 are generated via a similar process, using the logit equation instead of the probit equation. The logit-estimated effects for each variable track the probit-estimated effects pretty closely. This pattern is not surprising because the two models are doing the same work, just with different assumptions about the error term.

Figure 12.8 on page 427 helps us visualize the results by displaying the fitted values from the LPM, probit, and logit estimates. We'll display fitted values as a function of price differences and whether the store-brand product was displayed; we could create similar graphs for other combinations of independent variables. The solid line in each panel is the fitted line for choices by consumers when the store-brand ketchup is displayed. The dashed line in each panel is the fitted line for choices by consumers when the store-brand ketchup is not displayed. We display price differences from −1.5 to 3. In the data, the lowest price difference is around −1 (for instances in which the brand-name ketchup was $1 cheaper than the store-brand ketchup), and the highest price difference is 0.75 (for instances in which the brand-name ketchup was $0.75 more expensive). We show this (perhaps unrealistic) range of price differences so that we can see a bit more of the shape of the fitted values.

In all panels we see that fitted probabilities of buying store-brand ketchup increase as the price difference between brand-name and store-brand ketchup increases. We also see that consumers are more likely to buy the store brand when it is displayed.

One of the LPM lines dips below zero. That's what LPM models do. It's screwy. On the whole, however, the LPM lines are pretty similar to the probit and logit lines. The probit and logit lines are quite similar to each other as well. In fact, the fitted values from the probit and logit models are very similar, as is common. Their correlation is 0.998. The probit and logit fitted values don't quite show the full S-shaped curve; they would, however, if we were to extend the graph to include even higher (and less realistic) price differences.

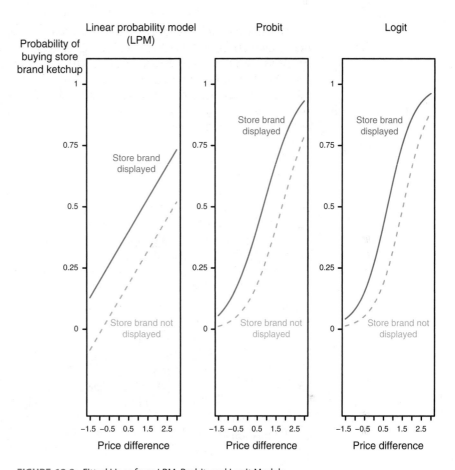

FIGURE 12.8: Fitted Lines from LPM, Probit, and Logit Models

12.6 Hypothesis Testing about Multiple Coefficients

Sometimes we are interested in hypotheses about multiple coefficients. That is, we might not want to know simply whether β_1 is different from zero, but whether is it bigger than β_2. In this section we show how to use MLE models such as probit and logit to conduct such tests.

In the OLS context we used F tests to test hypotheses involving multiple coefficients; we discussed these tests in Section 7.4 of Chapter 7. The key idea was to compare the fit of a model that imposed no restrictions to the fit of a model that imposed the restriction implicit in the null hypothesis. If the null hypothesis is true, then forcing the computer to spit back results consistent with the null will not reduce the fit very much. If the null hypothesis is false, though, forcing the computer to spit back results consistent with the null hypothesis will reduce the fit substantially.

We'll continue to use the same logic here. The difference is that we do not measure fit with R^2 as with OLS, but with the log likelihood, as described in Section 12.4. We will look at the difference in log likelihoods from the restricted and unrestricted estimates. The statistical test is called a **likelihood ratio (LR) test** and the test statistic is

▶ **likelihood ratio (LR) test** A statistical test for maximum likelihood models that is useful in testing hypotheses involving multiple coefficients.

$$LR = 2(\log L_{UR} - \log L_R) \tag{12.3}$$

If the null hypothesis is true, the log likelihood should be pretty much the same for the restricted and unrestricted versions of the model. Hence a big difference in the likelihoods indicates that the null is false. Statistical theory implies that if the null hypothesis is true, the difference in log likelihoods will follow a specific distribution and hence we can use that distribution to calculate critical values for hypothesis testing. The distribution is a χ^2, with degrees of freedom equal to the number of equal signs in the null hypothesis (recall that χ is the Greek letter chi, pronounced "ky" as in Kyle). We show in the Computing Corner how to generate critical values and p values based on this distribution. The appendix provides more information on the χ^2 distribution, starting on page 532.[8]

An example makes this process clear. It's not hard. Suppose we want to know if displaying the store-brand ketchup is more effective than featuring it in advertisements. This is the kind of thing people get big bucks for when they do marketing studies.

Using our LR test framework, we'll first want to characterize the unrestricted version of the model, which is simply the model with all the covariates in it:

$$
\begin{aligned}
Pr\,(Purchase\ store\ brand_i = 1) = \Phi(\beta_0 + \beta_1\ Price\ difference_i \\
+ \beta_2\ Brand\ name\ display_i \\
+ \beta_3\ Store\ brand\ display_i \\
+ \beta_4\ Brand\ name\ featured_i \\
+ \beta_5\ Store\ brand\ featured_i \\
+ \beta_6\ Income_i + \beta_7\ Household\ size_i)
\end{aligned}
$$

---

[8] It may seem odd that this is called a likelihood *ratio* test when the statistic is the *difference* in log likelihoods. The test can also be considered as the log of the ratio of the two likelihoods. Because $\log \frac{L_{UR}}{L_R} = \log L_{UR} - \log L_R$, however, we can use the form given. Most software reports the log likelihood, not the (unlogged) likelihood, so it's more convenient to use the difference of log likelihoods than the ratio of likelihoods. The 2 in Equation 12.3 is there to make things work; don't ask.

This is considered unrestricted because we are letting the coefficients on the store brand display and store brand featured variables be whatever best fit the data.

The null hypothesis is that the effect of displaying and featuring store-brand ketchup is the same: $H_0 : \beta_3 = \beta_5$. We impose this null hypothesis on the model by forcing the computer to give us results in which the coefficients on the display and featured variables for the store brand are equal. We do this by replacing β_5 with β_3 in the model (which we can do because under the null hypothesis they are equal), yielding a restricted model of

$$
\begin{aligned}
Pr\,(Purchase\ store\ brand_i = 1) = \Phi(&\beta_0 + \beta_1\ Price\ difference_i \\
&+ \beta_2\ Brand\ name\ display_i \\
&+ \beta_3\ Store\ brand\ display_i \\
&+ \beta_4\ Brand\ name\ featured_i \\
&+ \beta_3\ Store\ brand\ featured_i \\
&+ \beta_6\ Income_i + \beta_7\ Household\ size_i) \\
= \Phi(&\beta_0 + \beta_1\ Price\ difference_i \\
&+ \beta_2\ Brand\ name\ display_i \\
&+ \beta_3\ (Store\ brand\ display_i \\
&+ Store\ brand\ featured_i) \\
&+ \beta_4\ Brand\ name\ featured_i \\
&+ \beta_6\ Income_i + \beta_7\ Household\ size_i)
\end{aligned}
$$

Look carefully, and notice that the β_3 is multiplied by ($Store\ brand\ display_i + Store\ brand\ featured_i$) in this restricted equation.

To conduct the LR test, we need simply to estimate these two models, calculate the difference in log likelihoods, and compare this difference to a critical value from the appropriate distribution. We estimate the restricted model by creating a new variable, which is $Store\ brand\ display_i + Store\ brand\ featured_i$. Table 12.5 shows the results. The unrestricted column is the same as the probit column in Table 12.3. At the bottom is the unrestricted log likelihood that will feed into the LR test.

This is a good time to do a bit of commonsense approximating. The coefficients on the store brand display and store brand featured variables in the unrestricted model in Table 12.5 are both positive and statistically significant, but the coefficient on the store brand featured variable is quite a bit higher than the coefficient on the store brand displayed variable. Both coefficients have relatively small standard errors, so it is reasonable to expect that there's a difference, suggesting that H_0 is false.

From Table 12.5, it is easy to calculate the LR test statistic:

$$
\begin{aligned}
LR &= 2(\log L_{UR} - \log L_R) \\
&= 2(-7,800.202 + 7,804.485) \\
&= 8.56
\end{aligned}
$$

TABLE 12.5 Unrestricted and Restricted Probit Results for LR Test		
	Unrestricted model	**Restricted model for** $H_0: \beta_{\text{Store brand displayed}} = \beta_{\text{Store brand feautured}}$
Price difference	0.685*	0.678*
	(0.074)	(0.074)
	[$z = 9.30$]	[$z = 9.23$]
Brand name displayed	−0.266*	−0.267*
	(0.035)	(0.035)
	[$z = 7.59$]	[$z = 7.65$]
Store brand displayed	0.683*	
	(0.06)	
	[$z = 11.39$]	
Brand name featured	−0.537*	−0.535*
	(0.027)	(0.027)
	[$z = 19.52$]	[$z = 19.50$]
Store brand featured	0.948*	
	(0.055)	
	[$z = 17.29$]	
Household income	−0.055*	−0.055*
	(0.004)	(0.004)
	[$z = 12.57$]	[$z = 12.59$]
Household size	0.030*	0.030*
	(0.008)	(0.008)
	[$z = 3.62$]	[$z = 3.62$]
Store brand displayed + Store brand featured		0.824*
		−0.034
		[$z = 23.90$]
Constant	−0.929*	−0.928
	(0.037)	(0.037)
	[$z = 25.13$]	[$z = 25.12$]
N	23,436	23,436
$\log L$	−7,800.202	−7,804.485

Standard errors in parentheses.

* indicates significance at $p < 0.05$, two-tailed.

Using the tools described in the Computing Corner, we can calculate that the p value associated with an LR value of 8.56 is 0.003, well below a conventional significance level of 0.05.

Or, equivalently, we can reject the null hypothesis if the LR statistic is greater than the critical value for our significance level. The critical value for a significance level of 0.05 is 3.84, and our LR test statistic of 8.56 exceeds that. This means we can reject the null that the coefficients on the display and featured variables are the same. In other words, we have good evidence that consumers responded more strongly when the product was featured in ads than when it was displayed.

REMEMBER THIS

Use a likelihood ratio (LR) test to test hypotheses involving multiple coefficients for probit and logit models.

1. Estimate an unrestricted model that is the full model:

$$\text{Prob}(Y_i = 1) = \beta_0 + \beta_1 X_{1i} + \beta_2 X_{2i} + \beta_3 X_{3i} + \epsilon_i$$

2. Write down the null hypothesis.

3. Estimate a restricted model by using the conditions in the null hypothesis to restrict the full model:

- For H_0: $\beta_1 = \beta_2$, the restricted model is

$$\text{Prob}(Y_i = 1) = \beta_0 + \beta_1 X_{1i} + \beta_1 X_{2i} + \beta_3 X_{3i} + \epsilon_i$$
$$= \beta_0 + \beta_1 (X_{1i} + X_{2i}) + \beta_3 X_{3i} + \epsilon_i$$

- For H_0: $\beta_1 = \beta_2 = 0$, the restricted model is

$$\text{Prob}(Y_i = 1) = \beta_0 + 0 \times X_{1i} + 0 \times X_{2i} + \beta_3 X_{3i} + \epsilon_i$$
$$= \beta_0 + \beta_3 X_{3i} + \epsilon_i$$

4. Use the log likelihood values from the unrestricted and restricted models to calculate the LR test statistic:

$$LR = 2(\log L_{UR} - \log L_R)$$

5. The larger the difference between the log likelihoods, the more the null hypothesis is reducing fit and, therefore, the more likely we are to reject the null.

- The test statistic is distributed according to a χ^2 distribution with degrees of freedom equal to the number of equal signs in the null hypothesis.

- Code for generating critical values and p values for this distribution is in the Computing Corner on pages 437 and 439.

CASE STUDY Civil Wars

Civil wars produce horrific human misery. They are all too often accompanied by atrocities and a collapse of civilization.

What causes civil wars? Obviously the subject is complicated, but is it the case that civil wars are much more likely in countries that are divided along ethnic or religious lines? Many think so, arguing that these pre-existing divisions can explode into armed conflict. Stanford professors James Fearon and David Laitin (2003) aren't so sure. They suspect that instability stemming from poverty is more important.

In this case study we explore these possible determinants of civil war. We'll see that while omitted variable bias plays out in a broadly similar fashion across LPM and probit models, the two approaches nonetheless provide rather different pictures about what is going on.

The dependent variable is civil war onset between 1945 and 1999, coded for 161 countries that had a population of at least half a million in 1990. It is 1 for country-years in which a civil war began and 0 in all other country-years. We'll look at three independent variables, each measured within each country:

- *Ethnic fractionalization* measures ethnic divisions; it ranges from 0.001 to 0.93, with mean of 0.39 and a standard deviation of 0.29. The higher the value of this variable, the more divided a country is ethnically.

- *Religious fractionalization* measures religious divisions; it ranges from 0 to 0.78, with a mean of 0.37 and a standard deviation of 0.22. The higher the value of this variable, the more divided a country is in matters of religion.

- *GDP* is lagged GDP per capita. The GDP measure is lagged to avoid any taint from the civil war itself, which almost surely had an effect on the economy. It is measured in thousands of inflation-adjusted U.S. dollars. The variable ranges from 0.05 to 66.7, with a mean of 3.65 and a standard deviation of 4.53.

Table 12.6 shows results for LPM and probit models. For each method, we present results with and without GDP. We see a similar pattern when GDP is omitted. In the LPM (a) specification, ethnic fractionalization is statistically significant and religious fractionalization is not. The same is true for the probit (a) specification that does not have GDP.

However, Fearon and Laitin's suspicion was supported by both LPM and probit analyses. When GDP is included, the ethnic fractionalization variable becomes insignificant in both LPM and probit (although it is close to significant in the LPM model). The GDP variable is highly statistically significant in both LPM and

TABLE 12.6 **Probit Models of the Determinants of Civil Wars**

| | LPM | | Probit | |
	(a)	(b)	(a)	(b)
Ethnic	0.019*	0.012	0.451*	0.154
fractionalization	(0.006)	(0.006)	(0.141)	(0.149)
	[$t = 3.30$]	[$t = 1.84$]	[$z = 3.20$]	[$z = 1.03$]
Religious	−0.002	0.002	−0.051	0.033
fractionalization	(0.008)	(0.008)	(0.185)	(0.198)
	[$t = 0.33$]	[$t = 0.27$]	[$z = 0.28$]	[$z = 0.17$]
GDP per capita		−0.0015*		−0.108*
(in $1000 US)		(0.0004)		(0.024)
		[$t = 3.97$]		[$z = 4.58$]
Constant	0.010*	0.017*	−2.297*	−1.945*
	(0.003)	(0.004)	(0.086)	(0.108)
	[$t = 3.05$]	[$t = 4.49$]	[$z = 26.67$]	[$z = 18.01$]
N	6610	6373	6610	6373
R^2	0.002	0.004		
$\hat{\sigma}$	0.128	0.128		
$\log L$			−549.092	−508.545

Standard errors in parentheses.

* indicates significance at $p < 0.05$, two-tailed.

probit models. So the general conclusion that GDP seems to matter more than ethnic fractionalization does not depend on which model we use to estimate this dichotomous dependent variable model.

However, the two models do tell slightly different stories. Figure 12.9 shows the fitted lines from the LPM and probit models for the specifications that include the GDP variable. When calculating these lines, we held the ethnic and religious variables at their mean values. The LPM model has its characteristic brutally straight fitted line. It suggests that whatever its wealth, a country sees its probability of civil war decline as it gets even wealthier. It does this to the point of not making sense—the fitted probabilities are negative (hence meaningless) for countries with per capita GDP above about $20,000 per year.

In contrast, the probit model has a curve. We're seeing only a hint of the S curve because even the poorest countries have less than a 4 percent probability of experiencing civil war. But we do see that the effect of GDP is concentrated among the poorest countries. For them, the effect of income is relatively higher, certainly higher than the LPM model suggests. But for countries with about $10,000 per capita GDP per year, income shows basically no effect on the probability of a civil war. So even as the broad conclusion that GDP matters is similar in the LPM and probit models, the way in which GDP matters is quite different across the models.

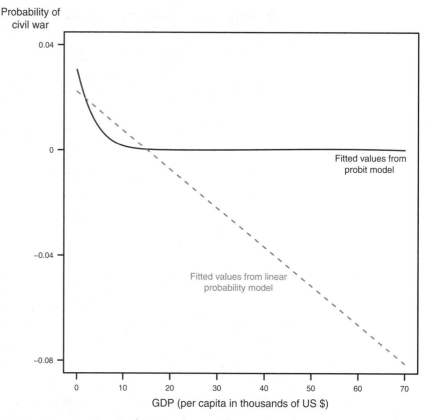

FIGURE 12.9: Fitted Lines from LPM and Probit Models for Civil War Data (Holding Ethnic and Religious Variables at Their Means)

Conclusion

Things we care about are often dichotomous. Think of unemployment, vote choice, graduation, war, or countless other phenomena. We can use OLS to analyze such data via the linear probability model (LPM), but we risk producing models that do not fully reflect the relationships in the data.

The solution is to fit an S-shaped relationship via probit or logit models. Probit and logit models are, as a practical matter, interchangeable as long as sufficient care is taken in the interpretation of coefficients. The cost of these models is that they are more complicated, especially with regard to interpreting the coefficients.

We're in good shape when we can:

- Section 12.1: Explain the LPM. How do we estimate it? How do we interpret the coefficient estimates? What are two drawbacks?

- Section 12.2: Describe what a latent variable is and how it relates to the observed dichotomous variable.

- Section 12.3: Describe the probit and logit models. What is the equation for the probability that $Y_i = 1$ for a probit model? What is the equation for the probability that $Y_i = 1$ for a logit model?

- Section 12.4: Discuss the estimation procedure used for probit and logit models and how to generate fitted values.

- Section 12.5: Explain how to interpret probit coefficients using the observed-value, discrete-differences approach.

- Section 12.6: Explain how to test hypotheses about multiple coefficients using probit or logit models.

Further Reading

There is no settled consensus on the best way to interpret probit and logit coefficients. Substantive conclusions rarely depend on the mode of presentation, so any of the methods is legitimate. Hanmer and Kalkan (2013) argue for the observed-value approach and against the average-value approach.

MLE models do not inherit all properties of OLS models. In OLS, heteroscedasticity does not bias coefficient estimates; it only makes the conventional equation for the standard error of $\hat{\beta}_1$ inappropriate. In probit and logit models, heteroscedasticity can induce bias (Alvarez and Brehm 1995), but correcting for heteroscedasticity may not always be feasible or desirable (Keele and Park 2006).

King and Zeng (2001) discuss small-sample properties of logistic models, noting in particular that small-sample bias can be large when the dependent variable is a rare event, with only a few observations falling in the less frequent category.

Probit and logit models are examples of limited dependent variable models. In these models, the dependent variable is restricted in some way. As we have seen, the dependent variable in probit models is limited to two values, 1 and 0. MLE can be used for many other types of limited dependent variable models. If the dependent variable is ordinal with more than two categories (e.g., answers to a survey question for which answers are very satisfied, satisfied, dissatisfied, and very dissatisfied), an ordered probit model is useful. It is based on MLE methods and is a modest extension of the probit model. Some dependent variables are categorical. For example, we may be analyzing the mode of transportation to work (with walking, biking, driving, and taking public transportation as options). In such a case, multinomial logit another MLE technique, is useful. Other dependent variables are counts (number of people on a bus) or lengths of time (how long between buses or how long someone survives after a disease diagnosis). Models with these dependent variables also can be estimated with MLE methods, such as count models and duration models. Long (1997) introduces maximum likelihood and covers a broad variety of MLE techniques. King (1989) explains the general approach. Box-Steffensmeier and Jones (2004) provide an excellent guide to duration models.

Key Terms

Cumulative distribution
  function (CDF) (410)
Dichotomous (401)
Latent variable (408)

Likelihood ratio (LR) test
  (428)
Linear probability model
  (LPM) (402)
Log likelihood (417)

Logit model (413)
Maximum likelihood
  estimation (MLE) (415)
Probit model (410)
z test (415)

Computing Corner

Stata

To implement the observed-value, discrete-differences approach to interpreting
estimated effects for probit in Stata, do the following.

- If X_1 is continuous:

```
** Estimate probit model
probit Y X1 X2

** Generate predicted probabilities for all observations
gen P1 = normal(_b[_cons] + _b[X1]*X1 + _b[X2]*X2) if /*
   */ e(sample)
   ** "normal" refers to normal CDF function
   ** _b[_cons] is beta0 hat,_b[X1] is beta1 hat etc
   ** "e(sample)" tells Stata to only use observations
   ** used in probit analysis

** Or, equivalently,generate predicted values via
** predict command
probit Y X1 X2
predict P1 if e(sample)

** Create variable with X1 + standard deviation of X1
** (which here equals 1)
gen X1Plus = X1 + 1

** Generate predicted probabilities for all observations
** using X1Plus
gen P2 = normal(_b[_cons] + _b[X1]*X1Plus + _b[X2]*X2) /*
   /* if e(sample)

** Calculate difference in probabilities for all
** observations
gen PDiff = P2 - P1
```

```
** Display results
sum PDiff if e(sample)
```

- If X_1 is a dummy variable:
```
** Estimate probit model
probit Y X1 X2

** Generate predicted probabilities for all observations
** with X1=0

gen P0 = normal(_b[_cons] + _b[X1]*0 + _b[X2]*X2) if /*
  /* e(sample)

** Generate predicted probabilities for all observations
** with X1=1
gen P1 = normal(_b[_cons] + _b[X1]*1 + _b[X2]*X2) if /*
  /* e(sample)

** Calculate difference in probabilities for all
** observations
gen PDiff = P1 - P0

** Display results
sum PDiff if e(sample)
```

- The `margins` command produces average marginal effects, which are the average of the slopes with respect to each independent variable evaluated at observed values of the independent variables. See page 546 for more details. These are easy to implement in Stata, with similar syntax for both probit and logit models.
```
probit Y X1 X2
margins, dydx(X1)
```

- To conduct an LR test in Stata, use the `lrtest` command. For example, to test the null hypothesis that the coefficients on both $X2$ and $X3$ are zero, we can first run the restricted model and save the results using the `estimates store` command:
```
probit Y X1
estimates store RESTRICTED
```
Then we run the unrestricted command followed by the `lrtest` command and the name of the restricted model:
```
probit Y X1 X2 X3
lrtest RESTRICTED
```
Stata will produce a value of the LR statistic and a p value. We can implement an LR test manually simply by running the restricted and unrestricted models and plugging the log likelihoods into the LR

test equation of $2(\log L_{UR} - \log L_R)$ as explained on page 421. To ascertain the critical value for LR test with one degree of freedom (d.f. = 1) and 0.95 confidence level, type `display invchi2(1, 0.95)`

To ascertain the p value for LR test with d.f. = 1 and substituting log likelihood values in for `logLunrestricted` and `logLrestricted`, type `display 1-chi2(1, 2*(logLunrestricted - logLrestricted))` Even easier, we can use Stata's `test` command to conduct a Wald test, which is asymptotically equivalent to the likelihood ratio test (which is a fancy way of saying the test statistics get really close to each other as the sample size goes to infinity). For example,

```
probit Y X1 X2 X3
test X2 = X3 =0
```

- To estimate a logit model in Stata, use logic and structure similar to those for a probit model. Here are the key differences for the continuous variable example:

```
logit Y X1 X2
gen LogitP1 = exp(_b[_cons]+_b[X1]*X1+_b[X2]*X2)/*
        */(1+exp(_b[_cons]+_b[X1]*X1+_b[X2]*X2))
gen LogitP2 = exp(_b[_cons]+_b[X1]*X1Plus+_b[X2]*X2)/*
        */(1+exp(_b[_cons]+_b[X1]*X1Plus+_b[X2]*X2))
```

- To graph fitted lines from a probit or logit model that has only one independent variable, first estimate the model and save the fitted values. Then use the following command:

```
graph twoway (scatter ProbitFit X)
```

R

To implement a probit or logit analysis in R, we use the glm function, which stands for "generalized linear model" (as opposed to the lm function, which stands for "linear model").

- If X_1 is continuous:

```
## Estimate probit model and name it Result
Result = glm(Y ~ X1 + X2, family = binomial(link =
"probit"))

## Create variable named P1 with fitted values from
## probit model
P1 = pnorm(Result$coef[1] + Result$coef[2]*X1
+ Result$coef[3]*X2)
    ## pnorm is the normal CDF function in R
    ## Result$coef[1] is beta0 hat, Result$coef[2] is
    ## beta1 hat etc
```

```
## Create variable named X1Plus which is X1 + standard
## deviation of X1 (which here equals 1)
X1Plus = X1 +1

## Create P2: fitted value using X1Plus instead of X1
P2 = pnorm(Result$coef[1] + Result$coef[2]*X1Plus
+ Result$coef[3]*X2)
## Calculate average difference in two fitted probabilities
mean(P2-P1, na.rm=TRUE)
     ## "na.rm=TRUE" tells R to ignore observations with
     ## missing data
```

- If X_1 is a dummy variable:
```
## Estimate probit model and name it Result
Result = glm(Y ~ X1 + X2, family = binomial(link =
"probit"))

## Create: P0 fitted values with X1 set to zero
P0 = pnorm(Result$coef[1] + Result$coef[2]*0
+ Result$coef[3]*X2)

## Create P1: fitted values with X1 set to one
P1 = pnorm(Result$coef[1] + Result$coef[2]*1
+ Result$coef[3]*X2)

## Calculate average difference in two fitted probabilities
mean(P1-P0, na.rm=TRUE)
```

- To produce average marginal effects (as discussed on page 546) for continuous X_1, use the following:
```
MargEffects = Result$coef[2]* dnorm(Result$coef[1]
+ Result$coef[2]*X1 + Result$coef[3]*X2)
    ## dnorm is PDF function in R
mean(MargEffects, na.rm=TRUE)
```

- To estimate an LR test of $H_0: \beta_1 = \beta_2$ in R, do the following:
```
## Unrestricted probit model
URModel = glm(Y ~ X1 + X2 + X3, family = binomial(link =
"probit"))

## Restricted probit model
X1plusX2 = X1 + X2
RModel = glm(Y ~ X1plusX2 + X3, family = binomial(link =
"probit"))

## Calculate LR test statistic using logLik function
```

```
LR = 2*(logLik(URModel)[1] - logLik(RModel)[1])


## Critical value for LR test with d.f. =1 and 0.95
## confidence level
qchisq(0.95, 1)

## p-value for likelihood ratio test with d.f. =1
1-pchisq(LR, 1)
```

> If we wanted to test $H_0: \beta_1 = \beta_2 = 0$, we would use a different restricted equation:

```
## Restricted probit model
RModel = glm(Y ~ X3, family = binomial(link =
"probit"))
```

> and proceed with the rest of the test.

- To estimate a logit model in R, use logic and structure similar to those for a probit model. Here are the key differences for the continuous variable example:

```
Result = glm(Y ~ X1+X2, family = binomial(link ="logit"))
P1 = exp(Result$coef[1]+Result$coef[2]*X1+Result$coef[3]*X2)/
     (1+exp(Result$coef[1]+Result$coef[2]*X1+Result$coef[3]*X2))
P2 = exp(Result$coef[1]+Result$coef[2]*X1Plus+Result$coef[3]*X2)/
     (1+exp(Result$coef[1]+Result$coef[2]*X1Plus+Result$coef[3]*X2))
```

- To graph fitted lines from a probit or logit model that has only one independent variable, first estimate the model and save it. In this case, we'll save a probit model as `ProbResults`. Create a new variable that spans the range of the independent variable. In this case, we create a variable called Xsequence that ranges from 1 to 7 in steps of 0.05 (the first value is 1, the next is 1.05, etc.). We then use the coefficients from the ProbResults model and this *Xsequence variable* to plot fitted lines:

```
Xsequence = seq(1, 7, 0.05)
plot(Xsequence, pnorm(ProbResults$coef[1] +
ProbResults$coef[2]*Xsequence), type = "l")
```

Exercises

1. In this question, we use the data set BushIraq.dta to explore the effect of opinion about the Iraq War on the presidential election of 2004. The variables we will focus on are listed in Table 12.7.

   (a) Estimate two probit models: one with only *ProIraqWar02* as the independent variable and the other with all the independent variables

TABLE 12.7	Variables for Iraq War Data
Variable	**Description**
Bushvote04	Dummy variable = 1 if person voted for President Bush in 2004
ProIraqWar02	Position on Iraq War, ranges from 0 (opposed war) to 3 (favored war)
Party02	Partisan affiliation, ranges from 0 for strong Democrats to 6 for strong Republicans
BushVote00	Dummy variable = 1 if person voted for President Bush in 2000
CutRichTaxes02	Views on cutting taxes for wealthy, ranges from 0 (oppose) to 2 (favor)
Abortion00	Views on abortion, ranges from 1 (strongly oppose) to 4 (strongly support)

listed in the table. Which is better? Why? Comment briefly on statistical significance.

(b) Use the model with all the independent variables and the observed-value, discrete-differences approach to calculate the effect of a one standard deviation increase in *ProIraqWar*02 on support for Bush.

(c) Use the model with all the independent variables listed in the table and the observed-value, discrete-differences approach to calculate the effect of an increase of one standard deviation in *Party*02 on support for Bush. Compare to the effect of *ProIraqWar*02.

(d) Use Stata's marginal effects command to calculate the marginal effects of all independent variables. Briefly comment on differences from calculations in parts (a) and (c).

(e) Use logit to run the same model and

  (i) Briefly comment on patterns of statistical significance compared to probit results.

  (ii) Briefly comment on coefficient values compared to probit results.

  (iii) Use Stata's `margins` commands to calculate marginal effects of variables and briefly comment on differences or similarities from probit results.

(f) Calculate the correlation of the fitted values from the probit and logit models.

(g) Run a likelihood ratio test on the null hypothesis that the coefficients on the three policy opinion variables (*ProIraqWar*02,

*CutRichTaxes*02, *Abortion*00) all equal zero. Do this work manually (showing your work) and using the Stata commands for an LR test.

2. Public attitudes toward global warming influence the policy response to the issue. The data set EnvSurvey.dta provides data from a nationally representative survey of the U.S. public that asked multiple questions about the environment and energy. Table 12.8 lists the variables.

   (a) Use a linear probability model to estimate the probability of saying that global warming is real and caused by humans (the dependent variable is *HumanCause*2). Control for sex, being white, education, income, age, and partisan identification.

      (i) Which variable has the most important influence on this opinion? Why?

      (ii) What are the minimum and maximum fitted values from this model? Discuss implications briefly.

      (iii) Add age-squared to the model. What is the effect of age? Use a simple sketch if necessary, with key point(s) identified.

   (b) Use a probit model to estimate the probability of saying that global warming is real and caused by humans (the dependent variable is *HumanCause*2). Use the independent variables from part (a), including the age-squared variable.

      (i) Compare statistical significance with LPM results.

TABLE 12.8 Variables for Global Warming Data

Variable	Description
Male	Dummy variable = 1 for men
White	Dummy variable = 1 for whites
Education	Education, ranging from 1 for no formal education to 14 for professional/doctorate degree (treat as a continuous variable)
Income	Income, ranging from 1 for household income < $5,000 to 19 for household income > $175,000 (treat as a continuous variable)
Age	Age in years
Party7	Partisan identification, ranging from 1 for strong Republican, 2 for not-so-strong Republican, 3 leans Republican, 4 undecided/independent, 5 leans Democrat, 6 not-so-strong Democrat, 7 strong Democrat

(ii) What are the minimum and maximum fitted values from this model? Discuss implications briefly.

(iii) Use the observed-value, discrete-differences approach to indicate the effect of partisan identification on the probability of saying global warming is real and caused by humans. For simplicity, simulate the effect of an increase of 1 unit on this seven-point scale (as opposed to the effect of one standard deviation, as we have done for continuous variables in other cases). Compare to LPM and Stata's "marginal-effects" interpretations.

(iv) Use the observed-value, discrete-differences approach to indicate the effect of being male on the probability of saying global warming is real and caused by humans. Compare to LPM and Stata's "marginal-effects" interpretations.

(c) The survey described in this item, also included a survey experiment in which respondents were randomly assigned to different question wordings for an additional question about global warming. The idea was to see which frames were most likely to lead people to agree that the earth is getting warmer. The variable we analyze here is called *WarmAgree*. It records whether respondents agreed that the earth's average temperature is rising. The experimental treatment consisted of four different ways to phrase the question.

- The variable *Treatment* equals 1 for people who were asked "Based on your personal experiences and observations, do you agree or disagree with the following statement: The average temperature on earth is getting warmer."

- The variable *Treatment* equals 2 for people who were given the following information before being asked if they agreed that the average temperature of the earth is getting warmer: "The following figure [Figure 12.10] shows the average global temperature compared to the average temperature from 1951–1980. The temperature analysis comes from weather data from more than 1,000 meteorological stations around the world, satellite observations of sea surface temperature, and Antarctic research station measurements."

- The variable *Treatment* equals 3 for people who were given the following information before being asked if they agreed that average temperature of the earth is getting warmer: Scientists working at the National Aeronautics and Space Administration (NASA) have concluded that the average global temperature has

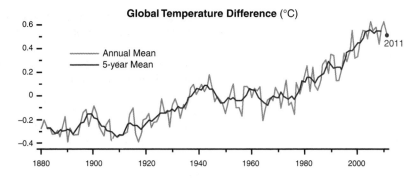

FIGURE 12.10: Figure Included for Some Respondents in Global Warming Survey Experiment

increased by about a half degree Celsius compared to the average temperature from 1951–1980. "The temperature analysis comes from weather data from more than 1,000 meteorological stations around the world, satellite observations of sea surface temperature, and Antarctic research station measurements."

- The variable *Treatment* equals 4 for people who were simply asked "Do you agree or disagree with the following statement: The average temperature on earth is getting warmer." This is the control group.

Which frame was most effective in affecting opinion about global warming?

3. What determines whether organizations fire their leaders? It's often hard for outsiders to observe performance, but in sports many facets of performance (particularly winning percentage) are easily observed. Michael Roach (2013) provides data on the performance and firing of NFL football coaches. Table 12.9 lists the variables.

TABLE 12.9 Variables for Football Coach Data

Variable name	Description
FiredCoach	A dummy variable if the football coach was fired during or after the season
WinPct	The winning percentage of the team
LagWinPct	The winning percentage of the team in the previous year
ScheduleStrength	A measure of schedule difficulty based on records of opposing teams
NewCoach	A dummy variable indicating if the coach was new
Tenure	The number of years the coach has coached the team

(a) Run a probit model explaining whether the coach was fired as a function of winning percentage. Graph fitted values from this model on same graph with fitted values results from a bivariate linear probability model (use the `lfit` command to plot LPM results). Explain the differences in the plots.

(b) Estimate LPM, probit, and logit models of coach firings by using winning percentage, lagged winning percentage, a new coach dummy, strength of schedule, and coach tenure as independent variables. Are the coefficients substantially different? How about the z statistics?

(c) Indicate the minimum, mean, and maximum of the fitted values for each model and briefly discuss.

(d) What are the correlations of the three fitted values?

(e) It's kind of odd to say that lag winning percentage affects the probability that new coaches were fired because they weren't coaching for the year associated with the lagged winning percentage. Include an interaction for the new coach dummy variable and lagged winning percentage. The effect of lagged winning percentage on probability of being fired is the sum of the coefficients on lagged winning percentage and the interaction. Test the null hypothesis that lagged winning percentage has no effect on new coaches (meaning coaches for whom *NewCoach* = 1). Use a Wald test (which is most convenient) and a likelihood ratio test.

4. Are members of Congress more likely to meet with donors than with mere constituents? To answer this question, Kalla and Broockman (2015) conducted a field experiment in which they had political activists attempt to schedule meetings with 191 congressional offices regarding efforts to ban a potentially harmful chemical. The messages the activists sent out were randomized. Some messages described the people requesting the meeting as "local constituents" and others described the people requesting the meeting as "local campaign donors." Table 12.10 describes two key variables from the experiment.

(a) Before we analyze the experimental data, let's suppose we were to conduct an observational study of access based on a sample of Americans and we ran a regression in which the dependent variable indicates having met with a member of Congress and the independent variable was whether the individual donated money to a member of Congress. Would there be concerns about endogeneity? If so, why?

TABLE 12.10 **Variables for Donor Experiment**

Variable	Description
donor_treat	Dummy variable indicating that activists seeking meeting were identified as donors
staffrank	Highest-ranking person attending the meeting: 0 no one attended meeting, 1 for non-policy staff, 2 for legislative assistant, 3 for legislative director, 4 for chief of staff, and 5 for member of Congress

(b) Use a probit model to estimate the effect of the donor treatment condition on probability of meeting with a member of Congress. Interpret the results. Table 12.10 describes the variables.

(c) What factors are missing from the model? What does this omission mean for our results?

(d) Use a linear probability model (LPM) to make your estimate. Interpret the results. Assess the correlation of the fitted values from the probit and LPM models.

(e) Use an LPM model to assess the probability of meeting with a senior staffer (defined as *staffrank* > 2).

(f) Use an LPM model to assess the probability of meeting with a low-level staffer (defined *staffrank* = 1).

(g) Table 12.11 shows results for balance tests (covered in Section 10.1) for two variables: Obama vote share in the congressional district and the overall campaign contributions received by the member of Congress contacted. Discuss the implication of these results for balance.

TABLE 12.11 **Balance Tests for Donor Experiment**

	Obama percent	Total contributions
Treated	−0.71	−104,569
	(1.85)	(153,085)
	[z = 0.38]	[z = 0.68]
Constant	65.59	1,642,801
	(1.07)	(88,615)
	[z = 61.20]	[z = 18.54]
N	191	191

Standard errors in parentheses.

PART IV

Advanced Material

Time Series: Dealing with Stickiness over Time   **13**

Global warming is a policy nightmare. Truly addressing it requires complex international cooperation that could have serious costs. Within each country, policies to address global warming require costly changes today to *possibly* prevent climate-related damage for future generations.

Empirically, global warming is no picnic either. A hot day or a major storm comes and invariably someone says global warming is accelerating. The end is near! If it gets cold or snows, someone says global warming is a fraud. Kids, put some more coal on the campfire!

The global temperature data we use to try to pin down trends and associated variables is called *time series data*; it's data for a particular unit (such as a country or planet) over time. Time series data is distinct from **cross-sectional data**, which is data for many units at a given point in time (such as data on the GDP per capita in all countries in 2012).

▶ **cross-sectional data**
Data having observations for multiple units for one time period.

Analyzing time series data is deceptively tricky because the data in one year almost certainly depends on the data in the year before. This seemingly innocuous fact creates complications. Some are relatively easy to deal with, while others are a major pain in the tuckus.

In this chapter we introduce two approaches to time series data. The first treats the year-to-year interdependence as the result of autocorrelated errors. As discussed earlier on page 69, autocorrelation doesn't cause our OLS coefficients to be biased, but it will typically cause standard OLS estimates of the variance of $\hat{\beta}_1$ to be incorrect. It's pretty easy to purge the data of this autocorrelation; our estimates will continue to be unbiased, but now our standard errors will be appropriate.

The second approach to time series data treats the dependent variable in one period as directly depending on what the value of the dependent variable was in the previous period. In this approach, the data remembers: a bump up in year 1 will affect year 2, and because the value in year 2 will affect year 3, and so on, the bump in year 1 will percolate through the entire data series. Such a *dynamic model* includes a lagged dependent variable as an independent variable. Dynamic models might seem pretty similar to other OLS models, but they actually differ in important and funky ways.

This chapter covers both approaches to dealing with time series data. Section 13.1 introduces a model for autocorrelation. Section 13.2 shows how to use this model to detect autocorrelation, and Section 13.3 shows how to purge autocorrelation from the model. Section 13.4 introduces dynamic models, and Section 13.5 discusses an important but complicated aspect of dynamic models called *stationarity*.

13.1 Modeling Autocorrelation

One reasonable approach to time series data is to think of the errors as being correlated over time. If errors are correlated, $\hat{\beta}_1$ is unbiased, but Equation 5.10, the standard equation for the variance of $\hat{\beta}_1$ (see page 147) is not accurate.[1] Often the variance estimated by OLS will be too low and will cause our confidence intervals to be too small, thus sometimes leading us to reject the null hypothesis when we shouldn't.

In this section we lay the groundwork for dealing with autocorrelation by developing a model with autoregressive errors. Autoregressive errors are one type of possibly autocorrelated errors; they are the most widely used and quite intuitive. We also provide examples of various patterns associated with autoregressive errors.

Model with autoregressive error

We start with a familiar regression model:

▶ **autoregressive model** A time series model in which the dependent variable is a function of previous values of the dependent variable. Autocorrelation is often modeled with an autoregressive model such that the error term is a function of previous error terms.

$$Y_t = \beta_0 + \beta_1 X_t + \epsilon_t \tag{13.1}$$

This model has notation slightly different from that for our earlier OLS model. Instead of using "*i*" to indicate each individual observation, we use "*t*" to indicate each time period. Y_t therefore indicates the dependent variable at time *t*; X_t indicates the independent variable at time *t*.

We'll focus on an **autoregressive model** for error terms. This is the most common model for addressing autocorrelation. Here we model the error as depending on the error in the previous period. In Section 13.4 we'll use an

---

[1] We show how the OLS equation for the variance of $\hat{\beta}_1$ depends on the errors being uncorrelated on page 487.

autoregressive model for the dependent variable—that is, not for the error, as we're doing here.[2]

The equation for error in this autoregressive model is

$$\epsilon_t = \rho \epsilon_{t-1} + v_t \tag{13.2}$$

This equation says that the error term for time period t equals ρ times the error in the previous term plus a random error, v_t. We assume that v_t is uncorrelated with the independent variable and other error terms. We call ϵ_{t-1} the *lagged error* because it is the error from the previous period. We'll lag other variables as well, which means using the value from the previous period. We indicate **lagged variables** with the subscript $t-1$ instead of t. A lagged variable is a variable with the values from the previous period.

▶ **lagged variable** A variable with the values from the previous period.

Suppose we're looking at global temperature data from 1880 to 2012 as a dependent variable and carbon emissions as an independent variable. Suppose we lack a good measure of sunspots, a solar phenomenon that may affect temperature. Because sunspots strengthen and weaken over a roughly 11-year cycle, they will be correlated from period to period. This factor could be in the error term of our global temperature model and could therefore cause the error to be correlated from year to year.

Examples of autocorrelated errors

The ρ term indicates the extent to which the errors are correlated over time. If ρ is zero, then the errors are not correlated and the autoregressive model reduces to a simple OLS model (because Equation 13.2 becomes $\epsilon_t = v_t$ when $\rho = 0$). If ρ is greater than zero, then a high value of ϵ in period $t-1$ is likely to lead to a high value of ϵ in period t. Think of the errors in this case as being a bit sticky. Instead of bouncing around like independent random values, they tend to run high for a while, then low for a while.

If ρ is less than zero, we have negative autocorrelation. With negative autocorrelation, a positive value of ϵ in period $t-1$ is more likely to lead to a negative value of ϵ in the next period. In other words, the errors bounce violently back and forth over time.

Figure 13.1 shows examples of errors with varying degrees and types of autocorrelation. Panel (a) shows an example in which ρ is 0.8. This positive autocorrelation produces a relatively smooth graph, with values tending to be above zero for a few periods, then below zero for a few periods, and so on. This graph is telling us that if we know the error in one period, we have some sense of what it will be in the following period. If the error is positive in period t, then it's likely (but not certain) to be positive in period $t+1$.

---

[2] The terms here can get a bit confusing. "Autocorrelation" refers to errors being correlated with each other. An autoregressive model is one way (the most common way) to model autocorrelation. It is possible to model correlated errors differently. In a *moving average* error process, for example, errors can be the average of errors from some number of previous periods.

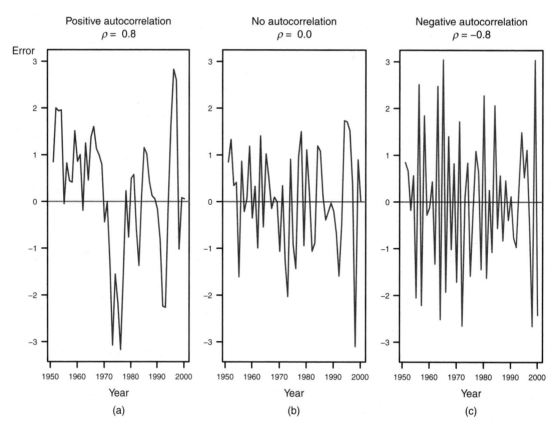

FIGURE 13.1: Examples of Autocorrelation

Panel (b) of Figure 13.1 shows a case of no autocorrelation. The error in time *t* is not a function of the error in the previous period. The telltale signature of no autocorrelation is the randomness: the plot is generally spiky, but here and there the error might linger above or below zero, without a strong pattern.

Panel (c) of Figure 13.1 shows negative serial correlation with $\rho = -0.8$. The signature of negative serial correlation is extreme spikiness because a positive error is more likely to be followed by a negative error, and vice versa.

The absolute value of ρ must be less than one in autoregressive models. If ρ were greater than one, the errors would tend to grow larger in each time period and would spiral out of control.

We often refer to autoregressive models as *AR models*. In AR models, the error is a function of error in previous periods. If the error is a function of only the error from the previous period, the model is referred to as an **AR(1) model** (pronounced A-R-1). If the error is a function of the error from two previous periods, the model is referred to as an *AR(2) model*, and so on. We'll focus on AR(1) models.

▶ **AR(1) model** A model in which the errors are assumed to depend on their value from the previous period.

> ## REMEMBER THIS
>
> 1. Autocorrelation refers to the correlation of errors with each other.
>
> 2. One type of autocorrelated error occurs when errors come from an autoregressive model in which the error term in period t is a function of the error in previous periods.
>
> 3. The equation for error in an AR(1) model is
>
> $$\epsilon_t = \rho\epsilon_{t-1} + v_t$$

Discussion Question

Discuss whether autocorrelation is likely in each of the following examples.

(a) Monthly unemployment data in Mexico from 1980 to 2014.

(b) Daily changes of stock price of Royal Dutch Shell (the largest company traded on the London stock market) from January 1, 2014, to December 31, 2014.

(c) Responses to anonymous telephone surveys about ratings of musical bands by randomly selected individuals in Germany.

(d) Responses to in-person, public questions about ratings of musical bands by a class of 14-year-olds in Germany.

(e) Monthly levels of interest rates in China from 2000 to 2015.

(f) Monthly changes of interest rates in China from 2000 to 2015.

13.2 Detecting Autocorrelation

We know what autocorrelation is. We know what it causes. But just because data is time series data does not necessarily mean the errors will be correlated. We need to assess whether autocorrelation exists in our data and model. If it does, we need to correct for it. If it does not, we can go on our merry way with OLS. In this section we show how to detect autocorrelation graphically and with auxiliary regressions.

Using graphical methods to detect autocorrelation

The first way to detect autocorrelation is simply to graph the error terms over time. Autocorrelated data has a distinctive pattern and will typically jump out pretty clearly from a graph. As is typical with graphical methods, looking at a picture doesn't yield a cut-and-dried answer. The advantage, though, is that it allows us to understand the data, perhaps helping us catch a mistake or identify an unappreciated pattern.

To detect autocorrelation graphically, we first run a standard OLS model, ignoring the autocorrelation, and generate residuals, which are calculated as $\hat{\epsilon}_t = Y_t - \hat{\beta}_0 - \hat{\beta}_1 X_t$. (If our model had more independent variables, we would include them in the calculation.) We simply graph these residuals over time and describe what we see.

If the errors move slowly, as in panel (a) of Figure 13.1, they're positively correlated. If errors bounce violently, as in panel (c) of Figure 13.1, they're negatively correlated. If we can't really tell, probably the errors are not strongly correlated.

Wait a minute! Why are we looking at residuals from an OLS equation that does not correct for autocorrelation? Isn't the whole point of this chapter that we need to account for autocorrelation? Busted, right?

Actually, no. And here's where understanding the consequences of auto-correlation is so valuable. Autocorrelation does not cause bias. The $\hat{\beta}$'s from an OLS model that ignores autocorrelation are unbiased even when there is autocorrelation. Because the residuals are a function of these $\hat{\beta}$'s, they are unbiased too. The OLS standard errors are flawed, but we're not using them to create the residuals in the graph.

Positive autocorrelation is common in time series data. Panel (a) of Figure 13.2 shows global climate data over time with a fitted line from the following model:

$$Temperature_t = \beta_0 + \beta_1 Year_t + \epsilon_t$$

The temperature hovers above the trend line for periods (such as around World War II and now) and below the line for other periods (such as 1950–1980). This hovering is a sign that the error in one period is correlated with the error in the next period. Panel (b) of Figure 13.2 shows the residuals from this regression. For each observation, the residual is the distance from the fitted line; the residual plot is essentially panel (a) tilted so that the fitted line in panel (a) is now the horizontal line in panel (b).

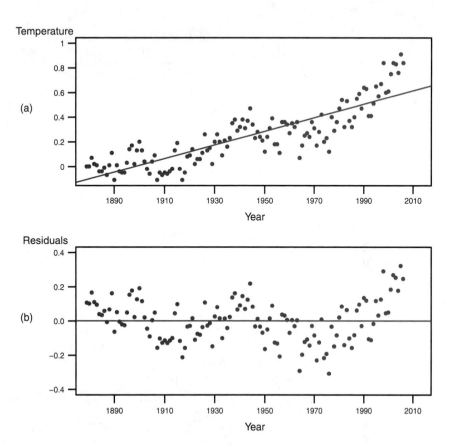

FIGURE 13.2: Global Average Temperature since 1880

Using an auxiliary regression to detect autocorrelation

A more formal way to detect autocorrelation is to use an auxiliary regression to estimate the degree of autocorrelation. We have seen auxiliary regressions before (in the multicollinearity discussion on page 149, for example); they are additional regressions that are related to, but not the same as, the regression of interest. When detecting autocorrelation, we estimate the following model:

$$\hat{\epsilon}_t = \rho\hat{\epsilon}_{t-1} + v_t \tag{13.3}$$

where $\hat{\epsilon}_t$ and $\hat{\epsilon}_{t-1}$ are simply the residuals and lagged residuals from the initial OLS estimation of $Y_t = \beta_0 + \beta_1 X_t + \epsilon_t$. Details on how to implement this model in

TABLE 13.1 Using OLS and Lagged Error Model to Detect Autocorrelation	
Lagged error	0.608*
	(0.072)
	[$t = 8.39$]
Constant	0.000
	(0.009)
	[$t = 0.04$]
N	127
R^2	0.36

Standard errors in parentheses.

* *indicates significance at $p < 0.05$, two-tailed.*

Stata and R are in the Computing Corner. If $\hat{\rho}$ is statistically significantly different from zero, we have evidence of autocorrelation.[3]

Table 13.1 shows the results of such a lagged error model for the climate data in Figure 13.2. The dependent variable in this model is the error from the model, and the independent variable is the lagged value of the error. We're using this model to estimate how closely $\hat{\epsilon}_t$ and $\hat{\epsilon}_{t-1}$ are related. The answer? They are strongly related. The coefficient on $\hat{\epsilon}_{t-1}$ is 0.608, meaning that our $\hat{\rho}$ estimate is 0.608, which is quite a strong relation. The standard error is 0.072, implying a t statistic of 8.39, which is well beyond any conventional critical value. We can therefore handily reject the null that $\rho = 0$ and conclude that errors are autocorrelated.

REMEMBER THIS

To detect autocorrelation in time series:

1. Graph the residuals from a standard OLS model over time. If the plot is relatively smooth, positive autocorrelation is likely to exist.

2. Estimate the following OLS model:

$$\hat{\epsilon}_t = \rho \hat{\epsilon}_{t-1} + v_t$$

A statistically significant estimate of ρ indicates autocorrelation.

---

[3] This approach is closely related to a so-called Durbin-Watson test for autocorrelation. This test statistic is widely reported, but it has a much more complicated distribution than a t distribution and requires use of specific tables. In general, it produces results very similar to those from the process we explained with the auxiliary regression.

Fixing Autocorrelation

The way to deal with autocorrelation is to get rid of it. That doesn't really sound like something we're supposed to do, but a few steps will take care of the problem. In this section we derive a model that purges error and explain how to estimate the model itself.

Our goal is to purge autocorrelation from the data by transforming the dependent and independent variables before we estimate our model. Once we have purged the autocorrelation, OLS will use the transformed data to produce an unbiased estimate of $\hat{\beta}_1$ *and* an appropriate estimate of $\text{var}(\hat{\beta}_1)$. In contrast, OLS on the untransformed data will produce an unbiased estimate of $\hat{\beta}_1$ with an *inappropriate* estimate of $\text{var}(\hat{\beta}_1)$.

ρ-Transforming the data

The purging process is called ρ-*transforming* ("rho transforming") the data. Because these steps are automated in many software packages, we typically will not do them manually. If we understand the steps, though, can use the computed results more confidently and effectively.

We begin by replacing the ϵ_t in the main equation (Equation 13.1) with $\rho\epsilon_{t-1} + v_t$ from Equation 13.2:

$$Y_t = \beta_0 + \beta_1 X_t + \rho\epsilon_{t-1} + v_t \tag{13.4}$$

This equation looks like a standard OLS equation except for a pesky $\rho\epsilon_{t-1}$ term. Our goal is to zap that term. Here's how.

1. Write an equation for the lagged value of Y_t that simply requires replacing the t subscripts with $t-1$ subscripts in the original model:

$$Y_{t-1} = \beta_0 + \beta_1 X_{t-1} + \epsilon_{t-1} \tag{13.5}$$

2. Multiply both sides of Equation 13.5 by ρ:

$$\rho Y_{t-1} = \rho\beta_0 + \rho\beta_1 X_{t-1} + \rho\epsilon_{t-1} \tag{13.6}$$

3. Subtract the equation for ρY_{t-1} (Equation 13.6) from Equation 13.4. That is, subtract the left side of Equation 13.6 from the left side of Equation 13.4 and subtract the right side of Equation 13.6 from the right side of Equation 13.4.

$$Y_t - \rho Y_{t-1} = \beta_0 - \rho\beta_0 + \beta_1 X_t - \rho\beta_1 X_{t-1} + \epsilon_t - \rho\epsilon_{t-1}$$

4. Notice in Equation 13.2 that $\epsilon_t - \rho\epsilon_{t-1} = v_t$ and rewrite:

$$Y_t - \rho Y_{t-1} = \beta_0 - \rho\beta_0 + \beta_1 X_t - \rho\beta_1 X_{t-1} + v_t$$

5. Rearrange things a bit:

$$Y_t - \rho Y_{t-1} = \beta_0(1-\rho) + \beta_1(X_t - \rho X_{t-1}) + v_t$$

6. Use squiggles to indicate the transformed variables,
where $\tilde{Y}_t = Y_t - \rho Y_{t-1}$, $\tilde{\beta}_0 = \beta_0(1-\rho)$, and $\tilde{X}_t = X_t - \rho X_{t-1}$:

$$\tilde{Y}_t = \tilde{\beta}_0 + \beta_1 \tilde{X}_t + v_t$$

The key thing is to look at the error term in this new equation. It is v_t, which we said at the outset is the well-behaved (not autocorrelated) part of the error term. Where is ϵ_t, the naughty autocorrelated part of the error term? Gone! That's the thing. That's what we accomplished with these equations: we end up with an equation that looks pretty similar to our OLS equation with a dependent variable ($\tilde{Y}_t$), parameters to estimate ($\tilde{\beta}_0$ and β_1), an independent variable ($\tilde{X}_t$), and an error term (v_t). The difference is that unlike our original model (based on Equations 13.1 and 13.2), this model has no autocorrelation. By using $\tilde{Y}_t$ and $\tilde{X}_t$, we have transformed the model from one that suffers from autocorrelation to one that does not.

Estimating a ρ-transformed model

What we have to do, then, is estimate a model with the $\tilde{Y}$ and $\tilde{X}$ (note the squiggles over the variable names) instead of Y and X. Table 13.2 shows the transformed variables for several observations. The columns labeled Y and X show the original data. The columns labeled $\tilde{Y}$ and $\tilde{X}$ show the transformed data. We assume for this example that $\hat{\rho} = 0.5$. In this case, the $\tilde{Y}$ observation for 2001 will be the actual value in 2001 (which is 110) minus $\hat{\rho}$ times the value of Y in 2000: $\tilde{Y}_{2001} = 110 - (0.5 \times 100) = 60$. Notice that the first observation in the ρ-transformed

TABLE 13.2 **Example of ρ-Transformed Data (for $\hat{\rho} = 0.5$)**

Year	Original data		ρ-Transformed data	
	Y	**X**	**$\tilde{Y}$** ($= Y - \hat{\rho}Y_{t-1}$)	**$\tilde{X}$** ($= X - \hat{\rho}X_{t-1}$)
2000	100	50	—	—
2001	110	70	110 − (0.5 * 100) = 60	70 − (0.5 * 50) = 45
2002	130	60	130 − (0.5 * 110) = 75	60 − (0.5 * 70) = 25

data will be missing because we don't know the lagged value for that observation.

Once we've created these transformed variables, things are easy. If we think in terms of a spreadsheet, we'll simply use the columns $\tilde{Y}$ and $\tilde{X}$ when we estimate the ρ-transformed model. Unlike the standard errors from a model with untransformed data, the standard errors produced by this ρ-transformed model will not be corrupted by autocorrelation.

The ρ-transformed model is also referred to as a *Cochrane-Orcutt model* or a *Prais-Winsten model*.[4] These names are useful to remember when we use Stata to analyze time series data.

Running the ρ-transformed model produces coefficient estimates that are unbiased and consistent (as were simple OLS coefficients) and *also* produces accurate standard errors. Usually (but not always), analysis of ρ-transformed data will produce larger standard errors than those that crop up in the simple OLS model. That means our estimates are less precise (but more honest!). Confidence intervals will be larger, and it will be harder to reject null hypotheses.

It is worth emphasizing that the $\hat{\beta}_1$ coefficient we estimate in the ρ-transformed model is an estimate of β_1. Throughout all the rigmarole of the transformation process, the value of β_1 doesn't change. The value of β_1 in the original equation is the same as the value of β_1 in the transformed equation. Hence when we get results from ρ-transformed models we still speak of them in the same terms as β_1 estimates from standard OLS. That is, a one-unit increase in X is associated with a $\hat{\beta}_1$ increase in Y.

One thing that is unintuitive is that we get different coefficient estimates than with the simple OLS model. Are ρ-transformed results "better"? No and yes, actually. No, in the sense that both OLS and ρ-transformed estimates are unbiased and consistent, which means that in expectation, the estimates equal the true value, and as we get more data they converge to the true value. These things can be true and the models can still yield different estimates. Just as it is the case that if we flip a coin 100 times, we are likely to get something different every time, we go through the process even though the expected number of heads is 50. That's pretty much what is going on here, as the two approaches are different realizations of random processes that are correct on average but still have random noise. The ρ-transformed estimates *are* better in the sense that they come with correct standard errors. The estimates from OLS do not come with correct standard errors when there is autocorrelation.[5]

---

[4] The Prais-Winsten approximates the values for the missing first observation in the ρ-transformed data.

[5] The intercept estimated in a ρ-transformed model is actually $\beta_0(1 - \hat{\rho})$. If we want to know the fitted value for $X_t = 0$ (which is the meaning of the intercept in a standard OLS model), we need to divide $\tilde{\beta}_0$ by $(1 - \hat{\rho})$. The appendix discusses an additional assumption implicit in the ρ-transformed model.

REMEMBER THIS

We correct for autocorrelation by ρ-transforming the data, a process that purges autocorrelation from the data.

1. We estimate the following model:

$$\tilde{Y}_t = \tilde{\beta}_0 + \beta_1 \tilde{X}_t + v_t$$

where $\tilde{Y}_t = Y_t - \rho Y_{t-1}$, $\tilde{\beta}_0 = \beta_0(1 - \rho)$, and $\tilde{X}_t = X_t - \rho X_{t-1}$.

2. We interpret $\hat{\beta}_1$ from a ρ-transformed model the same as we do for standard OLS.

3. This process is automated in many statistical packages.

CASE STUDY Using an AR(1) Model to Study Global Temperature Changes

Figure 13.3 shows the global average temperature data we worked with in Chapter 7 on page 216. Temperature appears to rise over time, and we want to assess whether this increase is meaningful.

We noted in our discussion of Table 7.1 that autocorrelation probably made the OLS standard errors incorrect. Here we revisit the example and use ρ-transformation to provide more accurate standard errors. We work with the quadratic model that allows the rate of temperature change to change over time:

$$Temperature_t = \beta_0 + \beta_1 Year_t + \beta_2 Year_t^2 + \epsilon_t$$

The first column of Table 13.3 shows results from a standard OLS analysis of the model. The $\hat{\beta}$ coefficients are precisely estimated, with t statistics above 5.

However, we suspect that the errors in this model are autocorrelated. If so, we cannot believe the standard errors from OLS, which in turn means the t statistics are wrong because t statistics depend on standard error estimates.

Table 13.3 reports that $\hat{\rho} = 0.514$; this result was generated by estimating an auxiliary regression with errors as the dependent variable and lagged error as the independent variable. The autocorrelation is lower than in the model that does not include squared year as an independent variable

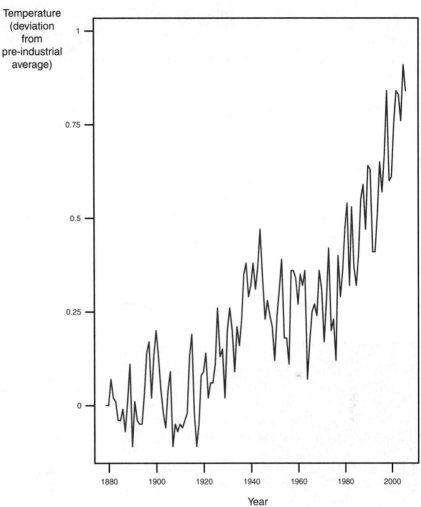

FIGURE 13.3: Global Temperature Data

(as reported on page 456). Nonetheless, autocorrelation is highly statistically significant, suggesting that to get proper standard errors, we need to correct for autocorrelation.

The second column of Table 13.3 shows results from a ρ-transformed model. $\hat{\beta}_1$ and $\hat{\beta}_2$ haven't changed much from the first column. This outcome isn't too surprising, given that both OLS and ρ-transformed models produce unbiased estimates of β_1 and β_2. The difference is in the standard errors. The standard error on each of the *Year* and *Year*^{2} variables has almost doubled, which has almost halved the t statistics for $\hat{\beta}_1$ and $\hat{\beta}_2$ to near 3. In this particular instance, the relationship between year and temperature is so strong that even with these larger standard errors, we will reject the null hypotheses of no relationship at any conventional significance level (such as $\alpha = 0.05$ or $\alpha = 0.01$). What we see,

TABLE 13.3 Global Temperature Model Estimated by Using OLS and via ρ-Transformed Data

	OLS	ρ-Transformed
Year	−0.165*	−0.174*
	(0.031)	(0.057)
	[$t = 5.31$]	[$t = 3.09$]
Year squared	0.000044*	0.000046*
	(0.000008)	0.000015)
	[$t = 5.48$]	[$t = 3.20$]
Constant	155.68*	79.97*
	(30.27)	(26.67)
	[$t = 5.14$]	[$t = 2.99$]
$\hat{\rho}$	0.514*	−0.021
(From auxiliary regression)	(0.077)	(0.090)
	[$t = 6.65$]	[$t = 0.28$]
N	128	127
R^2	0.79	0.55

Standard errors in parentheses.

* *indicates significance at $p < 0.05$, two-tailed.*

though, is the large effect on the standard errors of addressing autocorrelation. The standard errors produced by OLS were too small owing to autocorrelation. In other words, we overestimated the amount of information we had when we ignored autocorrelation.

Several aspects of the results from the ρ-transformed model are worth noting. First, the $\hat{\rho}$ from the auxiliary regression is now very small (−0.021) and statistically insignificant, indicating that we have indeed purged the model of first-order autocorrelation. Well done! Second, the R^2 is lower in the ρ-transformed model; it's reporting the traditional goodness of fit statistic for the transformed model, but it is not directly meaningful or comparable to the R^2 in the original OLS model. Third, the constant changes quite a bit, from 155.68 to 79.97. Recall, however, that the constant in the ρ-transformed model is actually $\beta_0(1 - \rho)$, where ρ is the estimate of autocorrelation in the untransformed model. This means that the estimate of β_0 is $\frac{79.97}{1-0.514} = 164.5$, which is close to the estimate of $\hat{\beta}_0$ in the OLS model.

13.4 Dynamic Models

Another way to deal with time series data is to use a *dynamic model*. In a dynamic model, the value of the dependent variable directly depends on the value of the dependent variable in the previous term. In this section we explain the dynamic model and discuss three ways in which the model differs from OLS models.

Dynamic models include the lagged dependent variable

▶ **dynamic model** A time series model that includes a lagged dependent variable as an independent variable.

In mathematical terms, a basic **dynamic model** is

$$Y_t = \gamma Y_{t-1} + \beta_0 + \beta_1 X_t + \epsilon_t \tag{13.7}$$

where the new term is γ times the value of the lagged dependent variable, Y_{t-1}. The coefficient γ indicates the extent to which the dependent variable depends on its lagged value. The higher it is, the more the dependence across time. If the data is really generated according to a dynamic process, omitting the lagged dependent variable would put us at risk for omitted variable bias, and given that the coefficient on the lagged dependent variable is often very large, that means we risk large omitted variable bias if we omit the lagged dependent variable when $\gamma \neq 0$.

As a practical matter, a dynamic model with a lagged dependent variable is super easy to implement: just add the lagged dependent variable as an independent variable.

Three ways dynamic models differ from OLS models

Be alert, though. This seemingly modest change in the model shakes up a lot of our statistical intuition. Some things that seemed simple in OLS become weird.

First, the interpretation of the coefficients changes. In non-dynamic OLS models (which simply means OLS models that do not have a lagged dependent variable as an independent variable), a one-unit increase in X is associated with a $\hat{\beta}_1$ increase in Y. In a dynamic model, it's not so simple. Suppose X increases by 1 in period 1. Y_1 will go up by β_1; we're used to seeing that kind of effect. Y_2 will also go up because Y_2 depends on Y_1. In other words, an increase in X has not only immediate effects but also long-term effects because the boost to Y will carry forward via the lagged dependent variable.

In fact, if $-1 < \gamma < 1$, a one-unit increase in X will cause a $\frac{\beta_1}{1-\gamma}$ increase in Y over the long term.[6] If γ is big (near 1), then the dependent variable has a lot of memory. A change in one period strongly affects the value of the dependent variable in the next period. In this case, the long-term effect of X will be much bigger than $\hat{\beta}_1$ because the estimated long-term effect will be $\hat{\beta}_1$ divided by a small number. If γ is near zero, on the other hand, then the dependent variable has little memory, meaning that the dependent variable depends little on its value in the previous period. In this case, the long-term effect of X will be pretty much $\hat{\beta}_1$ because the estimated long-term effect will be $\hat{\beta}_1$ divided by a number close to 1.

---

[6] The condition that the absolute value of γ is less than 1 rules out certain kinds of explosive processes where Y gets increasingly bigger or smaller every period. This condition is related to a requirement that data be "stationary" as discussed on page 465.

A second distinctive characteristic of dynamic models is that correlated errors cause a lot more trouble in dynamic models than in non-dynamic models. Recall that in OLS, correlated errors mess up the standard OLS estimates of the variance of $\hat{\beta}_1$, but they do not bias the estimates of $\hat{\beta}_1$. In dynamic models, correlated errors cause bias. It's not too hard to see why. If ϵ_t is correlated with ϵ_{t-1}, it also must to be correlated with Y_{t-1} because Y_{t-1} is obviously a function of ϵ_{t-1}. In such a situation, one of the independent variables (Y_{t-1}) is correlated with the error, which is a bias-causing no-no in OLS. The bias is worse for the estimate of the coefficient on the lagged dependent variable than for $\hat{\beta}_1$. If the autocorrelation in the errors is modest or weak, this bias is relatively small.

A third distinctive characteristic of dynamic models is that including a lagged dependent variable that is irrelevant (meaning $\gamma = 0$) can lead to biased estimates of $\hat{\beta}_1$. Recall from page 152 that in OLS, including an irrelevant variable (a variable whose true coefficient is zero) will increase standard errors but will not cause bias. In a dynamic model, though, including the lagged dependent variable when $\gamma = 0$ leads $\hat{\beta}_1$ to be biased if the error is autocorrelated, and the independent variable itself follows an autoregressive process (such that its value depends on its lagged value). When these two conditions hold, including a lagged dependent variable when $\gamma = 0$ can cause the estimated coefficient on X to be vastly understated: the lagged dependent variable will have wrongly soaked up much of the explanatory power of the independent variable.

Should we include a lagged dependent variable in our time series model? On the one hand, if we exclude the lagged dependent variable when it should be there (when $\gamma \neq 0$), we risk omitted variable bias. On the other hand, if we include it when it should be there (when $\gamma = 0$), we risk bias if the errors are autocorrelated. It's quite a conundrum.

There is no firm answer, but we're not helpless. The best place to start is with theory about the nature of the dependent variable being modeled. If we have good reasons to suspect that the process truly is dynamic, then including the lagged dependent variable is the best course. For example, many people suspect that political affiliation is a dynamic process. What party a person identifies with depends not only on external factors like the state of the economy, but also on what party he or she identified with last period. It's well known that many people interpret facts through partisan lenses. Democrats will see economic conditions in a way that is most favorable to Democrats; Republicans will see economic conditions in a way that is most favorable to Republicans. This means that party identification will be sticky in a manner implied by the dynamic model, and it is therefore sensible to include a lagged dependent variable in the model.

In addition, when we include a lagged dependent variable we should test for autocorrelated errors. If we find that the errors are autocorrelated, we should worry about possible bias in the estimate of $\hat{\beta}_1$; the higher the autocorrelation of errors, the more we should worry. We discussed how to test for autocorrelation on page 456. If we find autocorrelation, we can ρ-transform the data to purge the autocorrelation; we'll see an example in another case study on global warming on page 471.

REMEMBER THIS

1. A *dynamic* time series model includes a lagged dependent variable as a control variable. For example,

$$Y_t = \gamma Y_{t-1} + \beta_0 + \beta_1 X_t + \epsilon_t$$

2. Dynamic models differ from standard OLS models.

   (a) Independent variables have short-term effects (β_1) and long-term effects ($\frac{\beta_1}{1-\gamma}$). The long-term effects occur because a short-term effect on Y will affect subsequent values of the dependent variable through the influence of the lagged dependent variable.

   (b) Autocorrelation causes bias in models with a lagged dependent variable.

   (c) Including a lagged dependent variable when the true value of γ is zero can cause severe bias if the errors are correlated and the independent variable follows some kind of autoregressive process.

13.5 Stationarity

▶ **stationarity** A time series term indicating that a variable has the same distribution throughout the entire time series. Statistical analysis of nonstationary variables can yield spurious regression results.

We also need to think about **stationarity** when we analyze time series data. A stationary variable has the same distribution throughout the entire time series. This is a complicated topic and we'll only scratch the surface. The upshot is that stationarity is good and its opposite, nonstationarity, is a pain in the tuckus. When working with time series data, we want to make sure our data is stationary.

In this section we define nonstationarity as a so-called unit root problem and then explain how spurious regression results are a huge danger with nonstationary data. Spurious regression results are less likely with stationary data. We also show how to detect nonstationarity and what to do if we find it.

Nonstationarity as a unit root process

A variable is stationary if it has the same distribution for the entire time series. A variable is nonstationary if its distribution depends on time. A variable for which the mean is getting constantly bigger, for example, is a nonstationary variable. Nonstationary variables come in multiple flavors, but we'll focus on a case in which data is prone to display persistent trends in a way we define more precisely soon. In this case, the mean of the distribution of the variable changes over time, making the variable nonstationary.

To help us understand nonstationarity, we begin with a very simple dynamic model in which Y_t is a function of its previous value:

$$Y_t = \gamma Y_{t-1} + \epsilon_t \tag{13.8}$$

We consider three cases for γ, the coefficient on the lagged dependent variable: when it is less than one, equal to one, or greater than one.

If the absolute value of γ is less than one, life is relatively easy. The lagged dependent variable affects the dependent variable, but the effect diminishes over time. To see why, note that we can write the value of Y in the third time period as a function of the previous values of Y simply by substituting for the previous values of Y (e.g., $Y_2 = \gamma Y_1 + \epsilon_2$):

$$Y_3 = \gamma Y_2 + \epsilon_3$$
$$= \gamma(\gamma Y_1 + \epsilon_2) + \epsilon_3$$
$$= \gamma(\gamma(\gamma Y_0 + \epsilon_1) + \epsilon_2) + \epsilon_3$$
$$= \gamma^3 Y_0 + \gamma^2 \epsilon_1 + \gamma \epsilon_2 + \epsilon_3$$

When $\gamma < 1$, the effect of any given value of Y will decay over time. In this case, the effect of Y_0 on Y_3 is $\gamma^3 Y_0$; because $\gamma < 1$, γ^3 will be less than one. We could extend the foregoing logic to show that the effect of Y_0 on Y_4 will be γ^4, which is less than γ^3, when $\gamma < 1$. The effect of the error terms in a given period will also have a similar pattern.

This case presents some differences from standard OLS, but it turns out that because the effects of previous values of Y and error fade away, we will not face a fundamental problem when we estimate coefficients.

What if we have $\gamma > 1$? In this case, we'd see an explosive process because the value of Y would grow by an increasing amount. Time series analysts rule out such a possibility on theoretical grounds. Variables just don't explode like this, certainly not indefinitely, as implied by a model with $\gamma > 1$.

The tricky case occurs when $\gamma = 1$ exactly. In this case, the variable is said to have a **unit root**. In a model with a single lag of the dependent variable, a unit root simply means that the coefficient on the lagged dependent variable (γ for the model as we've written it) is equal to one. The terminology is a bit quirky: "unit" refers to the number 1 and "root" refers to the source of something, in this case the lagged dependent variable that is a source for the value of the dependent variable.

> **unit root** A variable with a unit root has a coefficient equal to one on the lagged variable in an autoregressive model.

Nonstationarity and spurious results

> **spurious regression** A regression that wrongly suggests that X has an effect on Y.

A variable with a unit root is nonstationary and causes several problems. The most serious is that **spurious regression** results are highly probable when a variable is being regressed with a unit root on another variable with a unit root. A spurious regression is one in which the regression results suggest that X affects Y when in fact X has no effect on Y; spurious results might be simply thought of as bogus results.[7]

It's reasonably easy to come up with possible spurious results in time series data. Think about the U.S. population from 1900 to 2010. It rose pretty steadily,

---

[7] Other problems are that the coefficient on the lagged dependent variable will be biased downward, preventing the coefficient divided by its standard error from following a t distribution.

right? Now think about the price of butter since 1900 to 2010. Also rose steadily. If we were to run a regression predicting the price of butter as a function of population, we would see a significant coefficient on population because low values of population went with low butter prices and high values of population went with high butter prices. Maybe that's true, but here's why we should be skeptical: it's quite possible these are just two variables that both happen to be trending up. We could replace the population of the United States with the population of Yemen (also trending up) and the price of butter with the number of deer in the United States (also trending up). We'd again have two variables trending together, and if we put them in a simple OLS model, we would observe a spurious positive relationship between the population of Yemen and deer in the United States. Silly, right?

A nonstationary variable is prone to spurious results because a variable with a unit root is trendy. Not in a fashionable sense, but in a streaky sense. A variable with a unit root might go up for while, then down for even longer, blip up, and then continue down. These unit root variables look like Zorro slashed out their pattern with his sword: a zig up, a long zag down, another zig up, and so on.[8]

Figure 13.4 shows examples of two simulated variables with unit roots. In panel (a), Y is simulated according to $Y_t = Y_{t-1} + \epsilon_t$. In this particular simulation, Y mostly goes up, but in some periods it goes down for a bit. In panel (b), X is simulated according to $X_t = X_{t-1} + v_t$. In this particular simulation, X trends mostly down, with a flat period early on and some mini-peaks later in the time series. Importantly, X and Y have absolutely nothing to do with each other with respect to the way they were generated. For example, when we generated values of Y, the values of X played no role.

Panel (c) of Figure 13.4 scatterplots X and Y and includes a fitted OLS regression line. The regression line has a negative slope that is highly statistically significant. And completely spurious. The variables are completely unrelated. We see a significant relationship simply because Y was working its way up while X was working its way down for most of the first part of the series. These movements create a pattern in which a negative OLS coefficient occurs, but it does not indicate an actual relationship. In other words, panel (c) of Figure 13.4 is a classic example of a spurious regression.

Of course, this is a single example. It is, however, quite representative because unit root variables are so prone to trends. When Y goes up, there is a pretty good chance that X will be on a trend, too: If X is going up, too, then the OLS coefficient on X would be positive. If X is trending down when Y is trending up, then the OLS coefficient on X would be negative. Hence, coefficient signs in these spurious regression results are not predictable. What is predictable is that two such variables will often exhibit spurious statistically significant relationships.[9]

---

[8] Zorro's slashes would probably go more side to side, so maybe think of unit root variables as slashed by an inebriated Zorro.

[9] The appendix has R code to simulate variables with unit roots and run regressions using those variables. Using the code makes it easy to see that the proportion of simulations with statistically significant (spurious) results is very high.

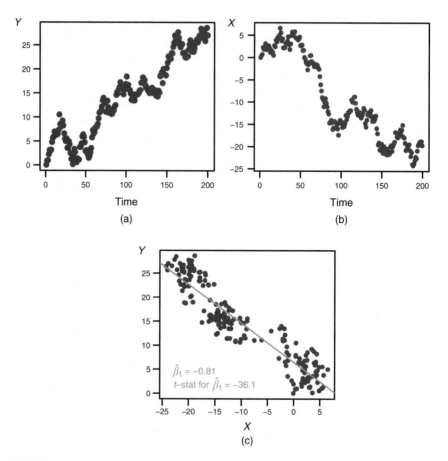

FIGURE 13.4: Data with Unit Roots and Spurious Regression

Spurious results are less likely with stationary data

Variables without unit roots behave differently. Panels (a) and (b) of Figure 13.5 show a simulation of two time series variables in which the coefficient on the lagged dependent variable is 0.5 (as opposed to 1.0 in the unit root simulations). They certainly don't look like Zorro sword slashes. They look more like Zorro sneezed them out. And OLS finds no relationship between the two variables, as is clear in panel (c), a scatterplot of X and Y. Again, this is a single simulation, but it is a highly representative one because variables without unit roots typically don't exhibit the trendiness that causes unit root variables to produce spurious regressions.

Unit roots are surprisingly common in theory and practice. Unit roots are also known as *random walks* because the series starts at Y_{t-1} and takes a random step (the error term) from there. Random walks are important in finance; the efficient-market hypothesis holds that stock market prices account for all information, and therefore there will be no systematic pattern going forward. A

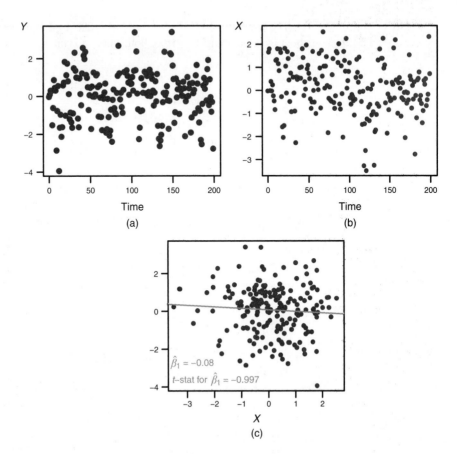

FIGURE 13.5: Data without Unit Roots

classic book about investing is *A Random Walk Down Wall Street* (Malkiel 2003); the title is not, ahem, random, but connects unit roots to finance via the random walk terminology. In practice, many variables show signs of having unit roots, including GDP, inflation, and other economic variables.

Detecting unit roots and nonstationarity

To test for a unit root (which means the variable is nonstationary), we test whether γ is equal to one for the dependent variable and the independent variables. If γ is equal to one for a variable or variables, we have nonstationarity and worry about spurious regression and other problems associated with nonstationary data.

▶ **Dickey-Fuller test** A test for unit roots, used in dynamic models.

The main test for unit roots has a cool name: the **Dickey-Fuller test**. This is a hypothesis test in which the null hypothesis is $\gamma = 1$ and the alternative hypothesis is $\gamma < 1$.

The standard way to implement the Dickey-Fuller test is to transform the model by subtracting Y_{t-1} from both sides of Equation 13.8:

$$Y_t - Y_{t-1} = \gamma Y_{t-1} - Y_{t-1} + \epsilon_t$$
$$\Delta Y_t = (\gamma - 1)Y_{t-1} + \epsilon_t$$
$$\Delta Y_t = \alpha Y_{t-1} + \epsilon_t$$

where the dependent variable ΔY_t is now the *change* in Y in period t and the independent variable is the lagged value of Y. We pronounce ΔY_t as "delta Y". Here we're using notation suggesting a unit root test for the dependent variable. We also run unit root tests with the same approach for independent variables.

This transformation allows us to reformulate the model in terms of a new coefficient we label as $\alpha = \gamma - 1$. Under the null hypothesis that $\gamma = 1$, our new parameter α equals zero. Under the alternative hypothesis that $\gamma < 1$, our new parameter $\alpha < 0$.

▶ **augmented Dickey-Fuller test** A test for unit root for time series data that includes a time trend and lagged values of the change in the variable as independent variables.

It's standard to estimate a so-called **augmented Dickey-Fuller test** that includes a time trend and a lagged value of the change of Y (ΔY_{t-1}):

$$\Delta Y_t = \alpha Y_{t-1} + \beta_0 + \beta_1 Time_t + \beta_2 \Delta Y_{t-1} + \epsilon_t \qquad (13.9)$$

where $Time_t$ is a variable indicating which time period observation t is. *Time* is equal to 1 in the first period, 2 in the second period, and so forth.

The focus of the Dickey-Fuller approach is the estimate of α. What we do with our estimate of α takes some getting used to. The null hypothesis is that Y is nonstationary. That's bad. We *want* to reject the null hypothesis. The alternative is that the Y is stationary. That's good. If we reject the null hypothesis in favor of the alternative hypothesis that $\alpha < 0$, then we are rejecting the nonstationarity of Y in favor of inferring that Y is stationary.

The catch is that if the variable actually is nonstationary, the estimated coefficient is not normally distributed, which means the coefficient divided by its standard error will not have a t distribution. Hence we have to use so-called Dickey-Fuller critical values, which are bigger than standard critical values, making it hard to reject the null hypothesis that the variable is nonstationary. We show how to implement Dickey-Fuller tests in the Computing Corner; more details are in the references indicated in the Further Reading section and the appendix.

How to handle nonstationarity

If the Dickey-Fuller test indicates that a variable data is nonstationary, the standard approach is to move to a differenced model in which all variables are converted from levels (e.g., Y_t, X_t) to differences (e.g., ΔY_t, ΔX_t, where Δ indicates the difference between the variable at time t and time $t - 1$). We'll see an example on page 474.

REMEMBER THIS

A variable is stationary if its distribution is the same for the entire data set. A common violation of stationarity occurs when data has a persistent trend.

1. Nonstationary data can lead to statistically significant regression results that are spurious when two variables have similar trends.

2. The test for stationarity is a Dickey-Fuller test. Its most widely used format is an augmented Dickey-Fuller test:

$$\Delta Y_t = \alpha Y_{t-1} + \beta_0 + \beta_1 Time_t + \beta_2 \Delta Y_{t-1} + \epsilon_t$$

If we reject the null hypothesis that $\alpha = 0$, we conclude that the data is stationary and can use untransformed data. If we fail to reject the null hypothesis that $\alpha = 0$, we conclude the data is nonstationary and we therefore should use a model with differenced data.

CASE STUDY ## Dynamic Model of Global Temperature

One of the central elements in discussions about global warming is the role of carbon dioxide. Figure 13.6 plots carbon dioxide output and global temperature from 1880 into the twenty-first century. The solid line is temperature, measured in deviation in degrees Fahrenheit from pre-industrial average temperature. The values for temperature are on the left. The dotted line is carbon dioxide emissions, measured in parts per million, with values indicated on the right. These variables certainly seem to move together. The question is: how confident we are that this relationship is in any way causal?

We'll analyze this question with a dynamic model. We begin with a model that allows for the non-linear time trend from page 460; this model has $Year$ and $Year^2$ as independent variables.[10]

We'll also include temperature from the previous time period. This is the lagged dependent variable—including it makes the model a dynamic model. The independent variable of interest here is carbon dioxide. We want to know if increases in carbon dioxide are associated with increases in global temperature.

---

[10] Including these variables is not a no-brainer; one might argue that the independent variables are causing the non-linear time trend, and we don't want the time trend in there to soak up variance. Welcome to time series analysis. Without definitively resolving the question, we'll include time trends as an analytically conservative approach in the sense that it will typically make it harder, not easier, to find statistical significance for independent variables.

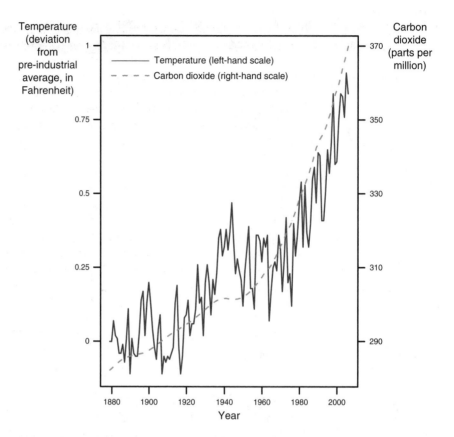

FIGURE 13.6: Global Temperature and Carbon Dioxide Data

The model is

$$Temperature_t = \gamma \, Temperature_{t-1} + \beta_0 + \beta_1 Year_t + \beta_2 Year_t^2 + \beta_3 CO2_t + \epsilon_t \quad (13.10)$$

where $CO2_t$ is a measure of the concentration of carbon dioxide in the atmosphere. This is a much (much!) simpler model than climate scientists use; our model simply gives us a broad-brush picture of whether the relationship between carbon dioxide and temperature can be ascertained in macro-level data.

Our first worry is that the data might not be stationary. If that is the case, there is a risk of spurious regression. Therefore the first two columns of Table 13.4 show Dickey-Fuller results for the substantive variables, temperature and carbon dioxide. We use an augmented Dickey-Fuller test of the following form:

$$\Delta Temperature_t = \alpha \, Temperature_{t-1} + \beta_1 Year_t + \beta_2 \Delta Temperature_{t-1} + \epsilon_t$$

Recall that the null hypothesis in a Dickey-Fuller test is that the data is nonstationary. The alternative hypothesis in a Dickey-Fuller test is that the data is stationary; we will accept this alternative only if the coefficient is sufficiently negative. (Yes, this way of thinking takes a bit of getting used to.)

To show that data is stationary (which is a good thing!), we need a sufficiently *negative t* statistic on the estimate of α. For the temperature variable, the t statistic in the Dickey-Fuller test is −4.22.[11] As we discussed earlier, the critical values for the Dickey-Fuller test are not the same as those for standard t tests. They are listed at the bottom of Table 13.4. Because the t statistic on the lagged value of temperature is more negative than the critical value, even at the 1 percent level, we can reject the null hypothesis of nonstationarity. In other words, the temperature data is stationary. We get a different answer for carbon dioxide. The t statistic is positive. That immediately dooms a Dickey-Fuller test because we need to see t statistics more negative than the critical values to be able to reject the null. In this case, we do not reject the null hypothesis and we therefore conclude that the carbon dioxide data is nonstationary. This means that we should be wary of using the carbon dioxide variable directly in a time series model.

A good way to begin to deal with nonstationarity is to use differenced data, which we generate by creating a variable that is the change of a variable in period t, as opposed to the level of the variable.

We still need to check for stationarity with the differenced data, so back we go to Table 13.4 for the Dickey-Fuller tests; this time we see that the last two columns use the changes in the temperature and carbon dioxide variables to test for stationarity. The t statistic on the lagged value of the change in temperature of −12.04 allows us to easily reject the null hypothesis of nonstationarity for temperature. For carbon dioxide, the t statistic on the lagged value of the change in carbon dioxide is −3.31, which is more negative than the critical value at the 10 percent level. We

TABLE 13.4 Dickey-Fuller Tests for Stationarity

	Temperature	Carbon dioxide	Change in temperature	Change in carbon dioxide
Lag value	−0.353	0.004	−1.669	−0.133
	(0.084)	(0.002)	(0.139)	(0.040)
	[$t = -4.22$]	[$t = 0.23$]	[$t = -12.04$]	[$t = -3.31$]
Time trend	0.002	0.000	0.000	0.002
	(0.001)	(0.001)	(0.000)	(0.001)
Lag change	−0.093	0.832	0.304	0.270
	(0.093)	(0.054)	(0.087)	(0.088)
(Intercept)	−3.943	−1.648	−0.487	−4.057
	(0.974)	(1.575)	(0.490)	(1.248)
N	126	126	125	125
R^2	0.198	0.934	0.673	0.132
Dickey-Fuller critical values		1%: −3.99 5%: −3.43 10%: −3.13		
Decision	Stationary	Nonstationary	Stationary	Stationary

Standard errors in parentheses.

---

[11] So far in this book we have been reporting the absolute value of t statistics as the sign does not typically matter. Here we focus on negative t statistics to emphasize the fact that the α coefficient needs to be negative to reject the null hypothesis of stationarity.

conclude that carbon dioxide is stationary. However, because $CO2$ is stationary only at the 10 percent level, a thorough analysis would also explore additional time series techniques, such as the error correction model discussed in the appendix.[12]

Because of the nonstationarity of the carbon dioxide variable, we'll work with a differenced model in which the variables are changes. The dependent variable is the change in temperature. The independent variables reflect change in each of the variables from Equation 13.10. Because the change in $Year$ is 1 every year, this variable disappears (a variable that doesn't vary is no variable!). The intercept will now capture this information on the rise or fall in the dependent variable each year. The other variables are simply the changes in the variables in each year.

$$\Delta Temperature_t = \gamma \Delta Temperature_{t-1} + \beta_0 + \beta_1 \Delta Year_t^2 + \beta_2 \Delta CO2_t + \epsilon_t$$

Table 13.5 displays the results. The change in carbon dioxide is, indeed, statistically significant, with a coefficient of 0.052 and a t statistic of 2.004. In this instance, then, the visual relationship between temperature and carbon dioxide holds up even after we have accounted for apparent nonstationarity in the carbon dioxide data.

TABLE 13.5 **Change in Temperature as a Function of Change in Carbon Dioxide and Other Factors**

Change of carbon dioxide	0.052*
	(0.026)
	$[t = 2.004]$
Lag temperature change	−0.308*
	(0.087)
	$[t = 3.548]$
Change year squared	−0.0003
	(0.0002)
	$[t = 1.208]$
(Intercept)	0.992
	(0.830)
	$[t = 1.202]$
N	126
R^2	0.110

Standard errors in parentheses.

* indicates significance at $p < 0.05$, two-tailed.

---

[12] Dickey-Fuller tests tend to be low powered (see, e.g., Kennedy 2008, 302). This means that these tests may fail to reject the null when the null is false. For this reason, some people are willing to use relatively high significance levels (e.g., $\alpha = 0.10$). On the other hand, the costs of failing to account for nonstationarity when it is present are high, while the costs of accounting for nonstationarity when data is stationarity are modest. In other words, consequences of failing to address nonstationarity are serious when data is nonstationary, but the consequences of addressing nonstationarity when data is stationary are not such a big deal. Thus many researchers are inclined to use differenced data when there are any hints of nonstationarity (Kennedy 2008, 309).

Conclusion

Time series data is all over: prices, jobs, elections, weather, migration, and much more. To analyze it correctly, we need to address several econometric challenges.

One is autocorrelation. Autocorrelation does not cause coefficient estimates from OLS to be biased and is therefore not as problematic as endogeneity. Autocorrelation does, however, render the standard equation for the variance of $\hat{\beta}$ (from page 147) inaccurate. Often standard OLS will produce standard errors that are too small when there is autocorrelation, giving us false confidence about how precise our understanding of the relationship is.

We can correct for autocorrelation by ρ-transforming the data. This approach produces not only unbiased estimates of β_1 (just like OLS) but also correct standard errors of $\hat{\beta}_1$ (an improvement over OLS). In the ρ-transformation approach, we model the error at time t as a function of ρ times the error in the previous period.

Another, more complicated, challenge associated with time series data is the possibility that the dependent variable is dynamic, which means that the value of the dependent variable in one period depends directly on its value in the previous period. Dynamic models include the lagged dependent variable as an independent variable.

Dynamic models exist in an alternative statistical universe. Coefficient interpretation has short-term and long-term elements. Autocorrelation creates bias. Including a lagged dependent variable when we shouldn't creates bias, too.

As a practical matter, time series analysis can be hard. Very hard. This chapter lays the foundations, but there is a much larger literature that gets funky fast. In fact, sometimes the many options can feel overwhelming. Here are some considerations to keep in mind when working with time series data:

- Deal with stationarity. It's often an advanced topic, but it can be a serious problem. If either a dependent or independent variable is stationary, one relatively easy fix is to use variables that measure changes (commonly referred to as *differenced data*) to estimate the model.

- It's probably a good idea to use a lagged dependent variable—and it's then advisable to check for autocorrelation. Autocorrelation does not cause bias in standard OLS, but when a lagged dependent variable is included, it can cause bias. If we don't check for autocorrelation ourselves, eventually someone will check it for us. We want to know the answer before someone else does.

We may reasonably end up estimating a ρ-transformed model, a model with a lagged dependent variable, and perhaps a differenced model. How do we know which model is correct? Ideally, all models provide more or less the same result.

Whew. All too often, though, they do not. Then we need to conduct diagnostics and also think carefully about the data-generating process. Is the data dynamic, such that this year's dependent variable depends directly on last year's? If so, we should probably lean toward the results from the model with the lagged dependent variable. If not, we might lean toward the ρ-transformed result. Sometimes we may simply have to report both and give our honest best sense of which one seems more consistent with theory and the data.

After reading and discussing this chapter, we should be able to describe and explain the following key points:

- Section 13.1: Define autocorrelation and describe its consequences for OLS.

- Section 13.2: Describe two ways to detect autocorrelation in time series data.

- Section 13.3: Explain the process of ρ-transforming data to address autocorrelation in time series data.

- Section 13.4: Explain what a dynamic model is and three differences between dynamic models and OLS models.

- Section 13.5: Explain stationarity and how nonstationary data can produce spurious results. Explain how to test for stationarity.

Further Reading

Researchers do not always agree on whether lagged dependent variables should be included in models. Achen (2000) discusses bias that can occur when lagged dependent variables are included. Keele and Kelly (2006) present simulation evidence that the bias that occurs when one includes a lagged dependent variable is small unless the autocorrelation of errors is quite large. Wilson and Butler (2007) discuss how the bias is worse for the coefficient on the lagged dependent variable.

De Boef and Keele (2008) provide a nice discussion of the error correction model, a model that can accommodate a broad range of time series dynamics in a single model.

Box-Steffensmeier, Freeman, Hitt, and Pevehouse (2014) provide an accessible discussion of the latest in time series modeling techniques. Wooldridge (2009, chapters 11 and 18) discusses advanced topics in time series analysis, including stationarity and cointegration. Stock and Watson (2011) provide an extensive introduction to the use of time series models to forecast economic variables.

Key Terms

AR(1) model (452)

Augmented Dickey-Fuller test (470)

Autoregressive model (450)

Cross-sectional data (449)

Dickey-Fuller test (469)

Dynamic model (463)

Lagged variable (451)

Spurious regression (466)

Stationarity (465)

Unit root (466)

Computing Corner

Stata

1. To detect autocorrelation, proceed in the following steps:

```
** Estimate basic regression model
regress Temp Year
** Save residuals using resid subcommand
predict Err, resid
** Plot residuals over time
scatter Err Year
** Tell Stata which variable indicates time
tsset year
** An equivalent way to do the auxiliary regression
reg Err L.Err
** " L." for lagged values requires tsset command
```

2. To correct for autocorrelation, proceed in two steps:

```
tsset Year
prais AvgTemp Year, corc twostep
```

The tsset command informs Stata which variable orders the data chronologically. The prais command (pronounced "price" and named after one of the originators of the technique) is the main command for estimating ρ-transformed models. The subcommands after the comma (corc twostep) tell Stata to handle the first observation as we have here. There are other options described in the Stata help which can be accessed by typing help prais.

3. Running a dynamic model is simple: just include a lagged dependent variable. If we have already told Stata which variable indicates time by using the tsset command described in item 1 we can simply run reg Y L.Y X1 X2. Or we can create a lagged dependent variable manually before running the model

```
gen LagY = Y[_n-1] /* Generate lagged Y using [_n-1] */
reg Y LagY X1 X2 X3
```

4. To implement an augmented Dickey-Fuller test, type
   `dfuller Y, trend lags(1) regress`
   In so doing, you're using Stata's dfuller command; the `trend` sub-command will include the trend variable, and the `lags(1)` subcommand will include the lagged change. The `regress` subcommand displays the regression results underlying the Dickey-Fuller test. Stata automatically displays the relevant critical values for this test.

R

1. To detect autocorrelation in R, proceed in the following steps:

```
# Estimate basic regression model
ClimateOLS = lm(Temp ~ Year)
# Save residuals
Err = resid(ClimateOLS)
# Plot residuals over time
plot (Year, Err)
# Generate lagged error variable
LagErr = c(NA, Err[1:(length(Err)-1)])
# Auxiliary regression
LagErrOLS = lm(Err ~ LagErr)
# Display results
summary(LagErrOLS)
```

2. To correct for autocorrelation, proceed in the following steps:

```
# Rho is rho-hat
Rho = summary(LagErrOLS)$coefficients[2]
# Length of Temp variable
N = length(Temp)
# Lagged temperature
LagTemp = c(NA, Temp[1:(N-1)])
# Lagged year
LagYear = c(NA, Year[1:(N-1)])
# Rho-transformed temperature
TempRho = AvgTemp - Rho*LagTemp
# Rho-transformed year
YearRho = Year- Rho*LagYear
# Rho-transformed model
ClimateRho = lm(TempRho ~ YearRho)
# Display results
summary(ClimateRho)
```

3. Running a dynamic model is simple: just include a lagged dependent variable.

```
ClimateLDV = lm(Temp ~ LagTemp + Year)
```

4. We can implement an augmented Dickey-Fuller test by creating the variables in the model and running the appropriate regression. For example,

```
ChangeTemp = Temp - LagTemp                # Create Delta Temp
LagChangeTemp = (NA, ChangeTemp[1:(N-1)])  # Create lag of Delta Temp
AugDickeyF = lm(ChangeTemp ~ LagTemp + Year + LagChangeTemp)
summary(AugDickeyF)                         # Display results
```

Exercises

1. The *Washington Post* published data on bike share ridership (measured in trips per day) over the month of January 2014. Bike share ridership is what we want to explain. The *Post* also provided data on daily low temperature (a variable we call *lowtemp*) and a dummy variable for weekends. We'll use these as our explanatory variables. The data is available in BikeShare.dta.

   (a) Use an auxiliary regression to assess whether the errors are autocorrelated.

   (b) Run a model that corrects for AR(1) autocorrelation. Are these results different from a model in which we do not correct for AR(1) autocorrelation? So that everyone is on same page, use the `, corc twostep` subcommands.

2. These questions revisit the monetary policy data we worked with in Chapter 6 (page 202).

   (a) Estimate a model of the federal funds rate, controlling for whether the president was a Democrat, the number of quarters from the last election, an interaction of the Democrat dummy variable and the number of quarters from the last election, and inflation. Use a plot and an auxiliary regression to assess whether there is first-order autocorrelation.

   (b) Estimate the model from part (a) by using the ρ-transformation approach and interpret the coefficients.

   (c) Estimate the model from part (a), but add a variable for the lagged value of the federal funds rate. Interpret the results and use a plot

TABLE 13.6 **Variables for James Bond Movie Data**

Variable name	Description
GrossRev	Gross revenue, measured in millions of U.S. dollars and adjusted for inflation
Rating	Average rating by viewers on online review sites (*IMDb* and *Rotten Tomatoes*) as of April 2013
Budget	Production budget, measured in millions of U.S. dollars and adjusted for inflation
Actor	Name of main actor
Order	A variable indicating the order of the movies; we use this variable as our "time" indicator even though movies are not evenly spaced in time

and an auxiliary regression to assess whether there is first-order autocorrelation.

(d) Estimate the dynamic model (with a lagged dependent variable); use the ρ-transformation approach and interpret the coefficients.

3. The file BondUpdate.dta contains data on James Bond films from 1962 to 2012. We want to know how budget and ratings mattered for how well the movies did at the box office. Table 13.6 describes the variables.

(a) Estimate an OLS model in which the amount each film grossed is the dependent variable and ratings and budgets are the independent variables. Assess whether there is autocorrelation.

(b) Correct for autocorrelation. Did the results change? Did the autocorrelation go away?

(c) Now estimate a dynamic model. Find the short-term and (approximate) long-term effects of a 1-point increase in rating.

(d) Assess the stationarity of the revenue, rating, and budget variables.

(e) Estimate a differenced model and explain the results.

(f) Build from the above models to assess the worth (in terms of revenue) of specific actors.

Advanced OLS **14**

In Chapters 3 through 5 we worked through the OLS model from the basic bivariate model to a variety of multivariate models. We focused on the practical and substantive issues that researchers deal with every day.

It can also be useful to look under the hood to see exactly how things work. That's what we do in this chapter. We also go into more detail about omitted variable bias by deriving the conditions for it to exist in a particular case and discussing how these results generalize.

We derive the OLS estimate of $\hat{\beta}_1$ in a simplified model and show it is unbiased in Section 14.1. Section 14.2 derives the variance of $\hat{\beta}_1$, showing that the basic equation for variance of $\hat{\beta}_1$ requires that errors be homoscedastic and not correlated with each other. Section 14.3 derives the omitted variable bias conditions explained in Chapter 5. Section 14.4 shows how to anticipate the sign of omitted variable bias, a useful tool when we're faced with an omitted variable problem. Section 14.5 extends the omitted variable bias framework to models with multiple independent variables. Things get complicated fast. However, we can see how the core intuition carries on. Section 14.6 derives the equation for attenuation bias due to measurement error.

14.1 How to Derive the OLS Estimator and Prove Unbiasedness

The best way to appreciate how the OLS assumptions come together to produce coefficient estimates that are unbiased, consistent, normally distributed, and with a specific standard error equation is to derive the equations for the $\hat{\beta}$ estimates. The good news is that the process is really quite cool. The other good news is that it's not that hard. The bad news is, well, math. Two good newses beat one bad news, so off we go.

In this section we derive the equation for $\hat{\beta}_1$ for a simplified regression model and then show how $\hat{\beta}_1$ is unbiased if X and ϵ are not correlated.

Deriving the OLS estimator

We work here with a simplified model that has a variable and coefficient, but no intercept. This model builds from King, Keohane, and Verba (1994, 98).

$$Y_i = \beta_1 X_i + \epsilon_i \qquad (14.1)$$

Not having β_0 in the model simplifies the derivation considerably while retaining the essential intuition about how the assumptions matter.[1]

Our goal is to find the value of $\hat{\beta}_1$ that minimizes the sum of the squared residuals; this value will produce a line that best fits the scatterplot. The residual for a given observation is

$$\hat{\epsilon}_i = Y_i - \hat{\beta}_1 X_i$$

The sum of squared residuals for all observations is

$$\sum \hat{\epsilon}_i^2 = \sum (Y_i - \hat{\beta}_1 X_i)^2 \qquad (14.2)$$

We want to figure out what value of $\hat{\beta}_1$ minimizes this sum. Some simple calculus does the trick. A function reaches a minimum or maximum at a point where its slope is flat—that is, where the slope is zero. The derivative is the slope, so we simply have to find the point at which the derivative is zero.[2] The process is the following:

1. Take the derivative of Equation 14.2:

$$\frac{d\sum \hat{\epsilon}_i^2}{d\hat{\beta}_1} = \sum 2(Y_i - \hat{\beta}_1 X_i)X_i$$

2. Set the derivative to 0:

$$\sum 2(Y_i - \hat{\beta}_1 X_i)X_i = 0$$

3. Divide both sides by 2:

$$\sum (Y_i - \hat{\beta}_1 X_i)X_i = 0$$

---

[1] We're actually just forcing β_0 to be zero, which means that the fitted line goes through the origin. In real life we would virtually never do this; in real life we probably would be working with a multivariate model, too.

[2] For any given "flat" spot, we have to figure out if we are at a peak or in a valley. It is very easy to do this. Simply put, if we are at a peak, our slope should get more negative as X gets bigger (we go downhill); if we are at a minimum, our slope should get bigger as X goes higher. The second derivative measures changes in the derivative, so it must be negative for a flat spot to be a maximum (and we need to be aware of things like "saddle points"—topics covered in any calculus book).

4. Separate the sum into its two additive pieces:

$$\sum Y_i X_i - \sum \hat{\beta}_1 X_i^2 = 0$$

5. Move terms to opposite sides of the equal sign:

$$\sum Y_i X_i = \sum \hat{\beta}_1 X_i^2$$

6. $\hat{\beta}_1$ is a constant, so we can pull it out of the summation:

$$\sum Y_i X_i = \hat{\beta}_1 \sum X_i^2$$

7. Divide both sides by $\sum X_i^2$:

$$\frac{\sum Y_i X_i}{\sum X_i^2} = \hat{\beta}_1 \qquad (14.3)$$

Equation 14.3, then, is the OLS estimate for $\hat{\beta}_1$ in a model with no β_0. It looks quite similar to the equation for the OLS estimate of $\hat{\beta}_1$ in the bivariate model with β_0 (which is Equation 3.4 on page 49). The only difference is that here we do not subtract $\overline{X}$ from X and $\overline{Y}$ from Y. To derive Equation 3.4, we would do steps 1 through 7 by using $\sum \hat{\epsilon}_i^2 = \sum (Y_i - \hat{\beta}_0 - \hat{\beta}_1 X_i)^2$, taking the derivative with respect to $\hat{\beta}_0$ and with respect to $\hat{\beta}_1$ to produce two equations, which we would then solve simultaneously.

Properties of OLS estimates

The estimate $\hat{\beta}_1$ is a random variable because its equation includes Y_i, which we know depends on ϵ_i, which is a random variable. Hence $\hat{\beta}_1$ will bounce around as the values of ϵ_i bounce around.

We can use Equation 14.3 to explain the relationship of $\hat{\beta}_1$ to the true value of β_1 by substituting for Y_i in the $\hat{\beta}_1$ equation.

1. Begin with the equation for $\hat{\beta}_1$:

$$\hat{\beta}_1 = \frac{\sum Y_i X_i}{\sum X_i^2}$$

2. Use Equation 14.1 (which is the simplified model we're using here, in which $\beta_0 = 0$) to substitute for Y_i:

$$\hat{\beta}_1 = \frac{\sum (\beta_1 X_i + \epsilon_i) X_i}{\sum X_i^2}$$

3. Distribute X_i in the numerator:

$$\hat{\beta}_1 = \frac{\sum \beta_1 X_i^2 + \epsilon_i X_i}{\sum X_i^2}$$

4. Separate the sum into additive pieces:

$$\hat{\beta}_1 = \frac{\sum \beta_1 X_i^2}{\sum X_i^2} + \frac{\sum \epsilon_i X_i}{\sum X_i^2}$$

5. β_1 is constant, so we can pull it out of the first sum:

$$\hat{\beta}_1 = \beta_1 \frac{\sum X_i^2}{\sum X_i^2} + \frac{\sum \epsilon_i X_i}{\sum X_i^2}$$

6. This equation characterizes the estimate in terms of the unobserved "true" values of β_1 and ϵ:

$$\hat{\beta}_1 = \beta_1 + \frac{\sum \epsilon_i X_i}{\sum X_i^2} \qquad (14.4)$$

In other words, $\hat{\beta}_1$ is β_1 (the true value) plus an ugly fraction with sums of ϵ and X in it.

From this point, we can show that $\hat{\beta}_1$ is unbiased. Here we need to show the conditions under which the expected value of $\hat{\beta}_1 = \beta_1$. In other words, the expected value of $\hat{\beta}_1$ is the value of $\hat{\beta}_1$ we would get if we repeatedly regenerated data sets from the original model and calculated the average of all the $\hat{\beta}_1$'s estimated from these multiple data sets. It's not that we would ever do this—in fact, with observational data the task is impossible. Instead, thinking of estimating $\hat{\beta}_1$ from multiple realizations from the true model is a conceptual way for us to think about whether the coefficient estimates on average skew too high, too low, or are just right.

It helps the intuition to note that we could, in principle, generate the expected value of $\hat{\beta}_1$'s for an experiment by running it over and over again and calculating the average of the $\hat{\beta}_1$'s estimated. Or, more plausibly, we could run a computer simulation in which we repeatedly regenerated data (which would involve simulating a new ϵ_i for each observation for each iteration) and calculating the average of the $\hat{\beta}_1$'s estimated.

▶ **expected value** The average value of a large number of realizations of a random variable.

To show that $\hat{\beta}_1$ is unbiased, we use the formal statistical concept of **expected value**. The expected value of a random variable is the value we expect the random variable to be, on average. (For more discussion, see page 521.)

1. Take expectations of both sides of Equation 14.4:

$$E[\hat{\beta}_1] = E[\beta_1] + E\left[\frac{\sum \epsilon_i X_i}{\sum X_i^2}\right]$$

2. The expectation of a fixed number is that number, meaning $E[\beta_1] = \beta_1$. Recall that in our model, β_1 (without the hat) is some unknown number—maybe 2, maybe 0, maybe -0.341. Hence the expectation of β_1 is simply whatever number it is. It's like asking what the expectation of the number 2 is. It's 2!

$$E[\hat{\beta}_1] = \beta_1 + E\left[\frac{\sum \epsilon_i X_i}{\sum X_i^2}\right]$$

3. Use the fact that $E[k \times g(\epsilon)] = k \times E[g(\epsilon)]$ for constant k and random function $g(\epsilon)$. Here $\frac{1}{\sum X_i^2}$ is a constant (equaling 1 over whatever the sum of X_i^2 is) and $\sum \epsilon_i X_i$ is a function of random variables (the ϵ_i's).

$$E[\hat{\beta}_1] = \beta_1 + \frac{1}{\sum X_i^2} E\left[\sum \epsilon_i X_i\right]$$

4. We can move the expectation operator inside the summation because the expectation of a sum is the sum of expectations:

$$E[\hat{\beta}_1] = \beta_1 + \frac{1}{\sum X_i^2} \sum E[\epsilon_i X_i] \qquad (14.5)$$

Equation 14.5 means that the expectation of $\hat{\beta}_1$ is the true value (β_1) plus some number $\frac{1}{\sum X_i^2}$ times the sum of $\epsilon_i X_i$'s. At this point we use our Very Important Condition, which is the exogeneity condition that ϵ_i and X_i be uncorrelated. We show next that this condition is equivalent to saying that $E[\epsilon_i X_i] = 0$, which means $\sum E[\epsilon_i X_i] = 0$, which will imply that $E[\hat{\beta}_1] = \beta_1$, which is what we're trying to show.

1. If ϵ_i and X_i are uncorrelated, then the covariance of ϵ_i and X_i is zero because correlation is simply a rescaled version of covariance:

$$\text{correlation}(X_i, \epsilon_i) = \frac{\text{cov}(X_i, \epsilon_i)}{\sqrt{\text{var}(X_i)\text{var}(\epsilon_i)}}$$

2. Using the definition of covariance and setting it to zero yields the following, where we refer to the mean of X_i as μ_X and the mean of the ϵ_i distribution as μ_ϵ (the Greek letter μ is pronounced "mew," which rhymes with dew).

$$\text{cov}(X_i, \epsilon_i) = E[(X_i - \mu_x)(\epsilon_i - \mu_\epsilon)] = 0$$

3. Multiplying out the covariance equation yields

$$E[X_i \epsilon_i - X_i \mu_\epsilon - \mu_x \epsilon_i + \mu_x \mu_\epsilon] = 0$$

4. Using the fact that the expectation of a sum is the sum of expectations, we can rewrite the equation as

$$E[X_i\epsilon_i] - E[X_i\mu_\epsilon] - E[\mu_x\epsilon_i] + E[\mu_x\mu_\epsilon] = 0$$

5. Using the fact that μ_ϵ and μ_X are fixed numbers, we can pull them out of the expectations:

$$E[X_i\epsilon_i] - \mu_\epsilon E[X_i] - \mu_x E[\epsilon_i] + \mu_x\mu_\epsilon = 0$$

6. Here we add an another assumption that is necessary, but not of great substantive interest. We assume that the mean of the error distribution is zero. In other words, we assume $\mu_\epsilon = 0$, which is another way of saying that the error term in our model is simply the random noise around whatever the constant is.[3] This assumption allows us to cancel any term with μ_ϵ or with $E[\epsilon_i]$. In other words, if the exogeneity condition is satisfied and the error is uncorrelated with the error term, then

$$E[X_i\epsilon_i] = 0$$

If $E[X_i\epsilon_i] = 0$, Equation 14.5 tells us that the expected value of $\hat{\beta}_1$ will be β_1. In other words, if the error term and the independent variable are uncorrelated, the OLS estimate $\hat{\beta}_1$ is an unbiased estimator of β_1. The same logic carries through in the bivariate model that includes β_0 and in multivariate OLS models as well.

Showing that $\hat{\beta}_1$ is unbiased does not say much about whether any given estimate will be near β_1. The estimate $\hat{\beta}_1$ is a random variable after all, and it is possible that some $\hat{\beta}_1$ will be very low and some will be very high. All that unbiasedness says is that, on average, the $\hat{\beta}_1$ will not run higher or lower than the true value.

REMEMBER THIS

1. We derive the $\hat{\beta}_1$ equation by setting the derivative of the sum of squared residuals equation to zero and solving for $\hat{\beta}_1$.

2. The key step in showing that $\hat{\beta}_1$ is unbiased depends on the condition that X and ϵ are uncorrelated.

---

[3] In a model that has a non-zero β_0, the estimated constant coefficient would absorb any non-zero mean in the error term. For example, if the mean of the error term is actually 5, the estimated constant is 5 bigger than what it would be otherwise. Because we so seldom care about the constant term, it's reasonable to think of the $\hat{\beta}_0$ estimate as including the mean value of any error term.

14.2 | How to Derive the Equation for the Variance of $\hat{\beta}_1$

In this section we show how to derive an equation for the standard error of $\hat{\beta}_1$. This, in turn, reveals how we use the conditions that errors are homoscedastic and uncorrelated with each other. Importantly, these assumptions are not necessary for unbiasedness of OLS estimates. If these assumptions do not hold, we can still use OLS, but we'll have to do something different (as discussed in Chapter 13, for example) to get the right standard error estimates.

We'll combine two assumptions and some statistical properties of the variance operator to produce a specific equation for the variance of $\hat{\beta}_1$. We assume that the X_i are fixed numbers and the ϵ's are random variables.

1. We start with the $\hat{\beta}_1$ equation (Equation 14.4) and take the variance of both sides:

$$\mathrm{var}[\hat{\beta}_1] = \mathrm{var}\left[\beta_1 + \frac{\sum \epsilon_i X_i}{\sum X_i^2}\right]$$

2. Use the fact that the variance of a sum of a constant (the true value β_1) and a function of a random variable is simply the variance of the function of the random variable (see variance fact 1 in the appendix on page 522).

$$\mathrm{var}[\hat{\beta}_1] = \mathrm{var}\left[\frac{\sum \epsilon_i X_i}{\sum X_i^2}\right]$$

3. Note that $\frac{1}{\sum X_i^2}$ is a constant (as we noted on page 485, too) and use variance fact 2 (on page 523) that variance of k times a random variable is k^2 times the variance of that random variable.

$$\mathrm{var}[\hat{\beta}_1] = \left(\frac{1}{\sum X_i^2}\right)^2 \mathrm{var}\left[\sum \epsilon_i X_i\right]$$

4. The no-autocorrelation condition (as discussed in Section 3.6 of Chapter 3) means that $\mathrm{corr}(\epsilon_i, \epsilon_j) = 0$ for all $i \neq j$. If this condition is satisfied, we can treat the variance of a sum as the sum of the variances (using variance fact 4 on page 523, which says that the variance of a sum of uncorrelated random variables equals the sum of the variances of these random variables).

$$\mathrm{var}[\hat{\beta}_1] = \left(\frac{1}{\sum X_i^2}\right)^2 \sum \mathrm{var}[X_i \epsilon_i]$$

5. Within the summation, reuse variance fact 2 (page 523).

$$\text{var}[\hat{\beta}_1] = \left(\frac{1}{\sum X_i^2}\right)^2 \sum X_i^2 \text{var}[\epsilon_i]$$

6. If we assume homoscedasticity (as discussed in Chapter 3, Section 3.6), we can make additional simplifications. If the error term is homoscedastic, the variance for each ϵ_i is σ^2, which we can pull out of the summation and cancel.

$$\text{var}[\hat{\beta}_1] = \left(\frac{1}{\sum X_i^2}\right)^2 \sum X_i^2 \sigma^2$$

$$= \sigma^2 \frac{\sum X_i^2}{(\sum X_i^2)^2}$$

$$= \frac{\sigma^2}{\sum X_i^2} \qquad (14.6)$$

7. If we don't assume homoscedasticity, we can use $\hat{\epsilon}_i^2$ as the estimate for variance of each observation, yielding a heteroscedasticity-consistent variance estimate.

$$\text{var}[\hat{\beta}_1] = \left(\frac{1}{\sum X_i^2}\right)^2 \sum X_i^2 \hat{\epsilon}_i^2 \qquad (14.7)$$

Equation 14.7 is great in that it provides an appropriate estimate for the variance of of $\hat{\beta}_1$ even when errors are heteroscedastic. However, it is quite unwieldy, making it harder for us to see the intuition about variance that we can access with the variance of $\hat{\beta}_1$ when errors are homoscedastic.

In this section we have derived the variance of $\hat{\beta}_1$ in our simplified model with no constant (for both homoscedastic and heteroscedastic cases). If we write the denominator in Equation 14.6 as $\frac{N \sum X_i^2}{N}$ instead of $\sum X_i^2$, Equation 14.6 looks similar to the equation for the var($\hat{\beta}_1$) in a bivariate model that we saw in Chapter 3 on page 62. The difference is that when β_0 is included in the model, the denominator of the variance is $N \sum (X_i - \overline{X}_N^2)$ which equals $N \text{var}(X)$ for large samples. The derivation process is essentially the same and uses the same assumptions for the same purposes.

Let's take a moment to appreciate how amazing it is that we have been able to derive an equation for the variance of $\hat{\beta}_1$. With just a few assumptions, we can characterize how precise our estimate of $\hat{\beta}_1$ will be as a function of the variance of ϵ and the X_i values.

The equation for the variance of $\hat{\beta}_1$ in the multivariate model is similar (see Equation 5.10 on page 147), and the intuition discussed here applies for that model as well.

> ## REMEMBER THIS
>
> 1. We derive the variance of a $\hat{\beta}_1$ by starting with the $\hat{\beta}_1$ equation.
>
> 2. If the errors are homoscedastic and not correlated with each other, the variance equation is in a convenient form.
>
> 3. If the errors are not homoscedastic and uncorrelated with each other, OLS estimates are still unbiased, but the easy-to-use standard OLS equation for the variance of $\hat{\beta}_1$ is no longer appropriate.

14.3 How to Derive the Omitted Variable Bias Conditions

On page 141 in Chapter 5 we discussed omitted variable bias, a concept that is absolutely central to understanding multivariate OLS. In this section we derive the conditions for omitted variable bias to occur.

Suppose the true model is

$$Y_i = \beta_0 + \beta_1 X_{1i} + \beta_2 X_{2i} + v_i \tag{14.8}$$

where Y_i is the dependent variable, there are two independent variables, X_{1i} and X_{2i}, and v_i is an error term that is not correlated with any of the independent variables. For example, suppose the dependent variable is test scores and the independent variables are class size and family wealth. We assume (for this discussion) that v_i is uncorrelated with X_{1i} and X_{2i}.

What happens if we omit X_2 and estimate the following model?

$$Y_i = \beta_0^{\text{Omit}X_2} + \beta_1^{\text{Omit}X_2} X_{1i} + \epsilon_i \tag{14.9}$$

where we will use $\beta_1^{\text{Omit}X_2}$ to indicate the estimate we get from the model that omits variable X_2. How close will $\hat{\beta}_1^{\text{Omit}X_2}$ (the coefficient on X_{1i} in in Equation 14.9) be to the true value (β_1 in Equation 14.8)? In other words, will $\hat{\beta}_1^{\text{Omit}X_2}$ be an unbiased estimator of β_1? This situation is common with observational data because we will almost always suspect that we are missing some variables that explain our dependent variable.

The equation for $\hat{\beta}_1^{\text{Omit}X_2}$ is the equation for a bivariate slope coefficient (see Equation 3.4 in Chapter 3). It is

$$\hat{\beta}_1^{\text{Omit}X_2} = \frac{\sum_{i=1}^{N}(X_{1i} - \overline{X}_1)(Y_i - \overline{Y})}{\sum_{i=1}^{N}(X_{1i} - \overline{X}_1)^2} \tag{14.10}$$

Will $\hat{\beta}_1^{\text{Omit}X_2}$ be an unbiased estimator of β_1? With a simple substitution and a bit of rearranging we can answer this question. We know from Equation 14.8 that the true value of Y_i is $\beta_0 + \beta_1 X_{1i} + \beta_2 X_{2i} + v_i$. Because the values of β are fixed, the average of each is simply its value. That is, $\overline{\beta}_0 = \beta_0$, and so forth. Therefore $\overline{Y}$ will be $\beta_0 + \beta_1 \overline{X}_{1i} + \beta_2 \overline{X}_{2i} + \overline{v}_i$. Substituting for Y_i and $\overline{Y}$ in Equation 14.10 and doing some rearranging yields

$$\hat{\beta}^{\text{OmitX}_2} = \frac{\sum (X_{1i} - \overline{X}_1)(\beta_0 + \beta_1 X_{1i} + \beta_2 X_{2i} + v_i - \beta_0 - \beta_1 \overline{X}_1 - \beta_2 \overline{X}_{2i} - \overline{v}_i)}{\sum (X_{1i} - \overline{X}_1)^2}$$

$$= \frac{\sum (X_{1i} - \overline{X}_1)(\beta_1 (X_{1i} - \overline{X}_1) + \beta_2 (X_{2i} - \overline{X}_2) + v_i - \overline{v}_i)}{\sum (X_{1i} - \overline{X}_1)^2}$$

Gathering terms and recalling that $\sum \beta_1 (X_{1i} - \overline{X}_{1i})^2 = \beta_1 \sum (X_{1i} - \overline{X}_{1i})^2$ yields

$$\hat{\beta}^{\text{OmitX}_2} = \beta_1 \frac{\sum (X_{1i} - \overline{X}_1)^2}{\sum (X_{1i} - \overline{X}_1)^2} + \beta_2 \frac{\sum (X_{1i} - \overline{X}_1)(X_{2i} - \overline{X}_2)}{\sum (X_{1i} - \overline{X}_1)^2} + \frac{\sum (X_{1i} - \overline{X}_1)(v_i - \overline{v})}{\sum (X_{1i} - \overline{X}_1)^2}$$

We then take the expected value of both sides. Our assumption that v is uncorrelated with X_1 means that the expected value of $\sum (X_{1i} - \overline{X}_1)(v_i - \overline{v})$ is zero, which causes the last term with the v's to drop from the equation.[4] This leaves us with

$$E\left[\hat{\beta}_1^{\text{OmitX}_2}\right] = \beta_1 + \beta_2 \frac{\sum (X_{1i} - \overline{X}_1)(X_{2i} - \overline{X}_2)}{\sum (X_{1i} - \overline{X}_1)^2} \tag{14.11}$$

meaning that the expected value of $\hat{\beta}_1^{\text{OmitX}_2}$ is β_1 plus β_2 times a messy fraction. In other words, the estimate $\hat{\beta}_1^{\text{OmitX}_2}$ will deviate, on average, from the true value, β_1, by $\beta_2 \frac{\sum (X_{1i} - \overline{X}_1)(X_{2i} - \overline{X}_2)}{\sum (X_{1i} - \overline{X}_1)^2}$.

Note that $\frac{\sum (X_{1i} - \overline{X}_1)(X_{2i} - \overline{X}_2)}{\sum (X_{1i} - \overline{X}_1)^2}$ is simply the equation for the estimate of $\hat{\delta}_1$ from the following model:

$$X_{2i} = \delta_0 + \delta_1 X_{1i} + \tau_i$$

See, for example, page 49, and note the use of X_2 and $\overline{X}_2$ where we had Y and $\overline{Y}$ in the standard bivariate OLS equation.

Therefore, we can conclude that our coefficient estimate $\hat{\beta}_1^{\text{OmitX}_2}$ from the model that omitted X_2 will be an unbiased estimator of β_1 if $\beta_2 \hat{\delta}_1 = 0$. This condition is most easily satisfied if $\beta_2 = 0$. In other words, if X_2 has no effect on Y (meaning $\beta_2 = 0$), then omitting X_2 does not cause our coefficient estimate to be biased. This is excellent news. If it were not true, our model would have to include variables that had nothing to do with Y. That would be a horrible way to live.

---

[4] The logic is similar to our proof on page 486 that if X and ϵ are uncorrelated, then $E\left[\sum X_i \epsilon_i\right] = 0$; in this case, $\sum (X_{1i} - \overline{X}_1)$ is analogous to X_i in the earlier proof and $(v_i - \overline{v})$ is analogous to ϵ_i in the earlier proof.

The other way for $\beta_2 \hat{\delta}_1$ to be zero is for $\hat{\delta}_1$ to be zero, which happens whenever X_1 would have a coefficient of zero in a regression in which X_2 is the dependent variable and X_1 is the independent variable. In short, if X_1 and X_2 are independent (such that regressing X_2 on X_1 yields a slope coefficient of zero), then even though we omitted X_2 from the model, $\hat{\beta}_1^{\text{Omit}X_2}$ will be an unbiased estimate of β_1, the true effect of X_1 on Y (from Equation 14.8). No harm, no foul.

The flip side of these conditions is that when we estimate a model that omits a variable that affects Y (meaning that β_2 doesn't equal zero) and is correlated with the included variable, OLS will be biased. The extent of the bias depends on how much the omitted variable explains Y (which is determined by β_2) and how much the omitted variable is related to the included variable (which is reflected in $\hat{\delta}_1$).

What is the takeaway here? Omitted variable bias is a problem if *both* of the following conditions are met: (1) the omitted variable actually matters ($\beta_2 \neq 0$) and (2) X_2 (the omitted variable) is correlated with X_1 (the included variable). This shorthand is remarkably useful in evaluating OLS models.

REMEMBER THIS

The conditions for omitted variable bias can be derived by substituting the true value of Y into the $\hat{\beta}_1$ equation for the model with X_2 omitted.

14.4   Anticipating the Sign of Omitted Variable Bias

It is fairly common that an omitted variable must remain omitted because we simply do not have a measure of it. In these situations, all is not lost. (A lot is lost, but not all.) We can use the concepts we have developed so far to work through the implication of omitting the variable in question. In this section we show how to anticipate the effects of omitting a variable.

Suppose we are interested in explaining the effect of education on wages. We estimate the model

$$Income_i = \beta_0 + \beta_1 Education_i + \epsilon_i \qquad (14.12)$$

where $Income_i$ is the monthly salary or wages of individual i and $Education_i$ is the number of years of schooling individual i completed. We are worried, as usual, that certain factors in the error term are correlated with education.

We worry, for example, that some people are more productive than others (a factor in the error term that affects income) and that productive folks are more likely to get more schooling (school may be easier for them). In other words, we fear the true equation is

$$Income_i = \beta_0 + \beta_1 Education_i + \beta_2 Productivity_i + \epsilon_i \qquad (14.13)$$

where $Productivity_i$ taps the combination of intelligence, diligence, and maturity that leads person i to add a lot of value to his or her organization. Most data sets will not have a good measure of it. What can we do?

Without the variable, we're stuck, but at least we can figure our whether omitting productivity will push our estimates of the effect of education higher or lower.[5] Our omitted variable bias results (such as Equation 14.11) indicate that the bias from omitting productivity depends on the effect of productivity on the dependent variable (β_2) and on the relationship between productivity and education, the included variable.

In our example, we believe productivity boosts income ($\beta_2 > 0$). We also believe that there is a positive relationship between education and productivity. Hence, the bias will be positive because it is $\beta_2 > 0$ times the effect of the productivity on education. A positive bias implies that omitting productivity induces a positive bias for education. In other words, the effect of education on income in a model that does not control for productivity will be overstated. The magnitude of the bias will be related to how strong these two components are. If we think productivity has a huge effect on income and is strongly related to education levels, then the size of the bias is large.

In this example, this bias would lead us to be skeptical of a result from a model like Equation 14.12 that omits productivity. In particular, if we were to find that $\hat{\beta}_1$ is greater than zero, we would worry that the omitted variable bias had inflated the estimate. On the other hand, if the results showed that education did not matter or had a negative coefficient, we would be more confident in our results because the bias would on average make the results larger than the true value, not smaller.

This line of reasoning, called "signing the bias," would lead us to treat the estimated effects based on Equation 14.12 as an upper bound on the likely effects of education on income.

Table 14.1 summarizes the relationship for the simple case of one omitted variable. If X_2, the omitted variable, has a positive effect on Y (meaning $\beta_2 > 0$) and X_2 and X_1 are correlated, then the coefficient on X_1 in a model with only X_1 will produce a coefficient that is biased upward: the estimate will be too big because some of the effect of unmeasured X_2 will be absorbed by the variable X_1.

---

[5] Another option is to use panel data that allows us to control for certain unmeasured factors as we did in Chapter 8. Or we can try to find exogenous variation in education (variation in education that is not due to differences in productivity); that's what we did in Chapter 9.

TABLE 14.1	Effect of Omitting X_2 on Coefficient Estimate for X_1		
Correlation of X_1 and X_2	β_2 Effect of omitted variable on Y		
	> 0	0	< 0
> 0	Overstate coefficient	No bias	Understate coefficient
0	No bias	No bias	No bias
< 0	Understate coefficient	No bias	Overstate coefficient

Cell entries show sign of bias for omitted variable bias problem in which a single variable (X_2) is omitted.

The true equation is Equation 14.8 and the estimated model is Equation 14.9. If $\beta_2 > 0$ and X_1 and X_2 are positively correlated, $\hat{\beta}_1^{\text{Omit}X_2}$ (the expected value of the coefficient on X_1 from a model that omits X_2) will be larger than the actual value of β_1.

REMEMBER THIS

We can use the equation for omitted variable bias to anticipate the effect of omitting a variable on the coefficient estimate for an included variable.

Discussion Questions

1. Suppose we are interested in knowing how much social media affect people's income. Suppose also that Facebook provided us data on how much time each individual spent on the site during work hours. The model is

$$Income_i = \beta_0 + \beta_1 Facebook\ hours_i + \epsilon_i$$

What is the implication of not being able to measure innate productivity for our estimate of β_1?

2. Suppose we are interested in knowing the effect of campaign spending on election outcomes.

$$Vote\ share_i = \beta_0 + \beta_1 Campaign\ spending_i + \epsilon_i$$

We believe that the personal qualities of a candidate also matter. Some are more charming and/or hardworking than others, which may lead to better election results for them. What is the implication of not being able to measure "candidate quality" (which captures how charming and hardworking candidates are) for our estimate of β_1?

14.5 Omitted Variable Bias with Multiple Variables

Our omitted variable discussion in Section 5.2 was based on a case in which the true model had two variables and a single variable was omitted. Now we show the complications that arise when there are additional variables.

Suppose the true model has three independent variables

$$Y_i = \beta_0 + \beta_1 X_{1i} + \beta_2 X_{2i} + \beta_3 X_{3i} + \nu_i \tag{14.14}$$

and that we estimate a model that omits variable X_3:

$$Y_i = \beta_0^{\text{Omit}X_3} + \beta_1^{\text{Omit}X_3} X_{1i} + \beta_2^{\text{Omit}X_3} X_{2i} + \epsilon_i \tag{14.15}$$

Assuming that the error in the true model (ν) is not correlated with any of the independent variables, the expected value for $\hat{\beta}_1^{\text{Omit}X_3}$ is

$$E\left[\hat{\beta}_1^{\text{Omit}X_3}\right] = \beta_1 + \beta_3 \frac{r_{31} - r_{21} r_{32}}{1 - r_{21}^2} \sqrt{\frac{V_3}{V_1}} \tag{14.16}$$

where r_{31} is the correlation of X_3 and X_1, r_{21} is the correlation of X_2 and X_1, r_{32} is the correlation of X_3 and X_2, and V_3 and V_1 are the variances of X_3 and X_1, respectively. Clearly, there are more moving parts in this case than in the case we discussed earlier.

Equation 14.16 contains commonalities with our simpler omitted variables bias example of Section 5.2. The effect of the omitted variable in the true model looms large. Here β_3 is the effect of the omitted variable X_3 on Y, and it plays a central role in the bias term. If β_3 is zero, there is no omitted variable bias because the crazy fraction will be multiplied by zero and thereby disappear. As with the simpler omitted variable bias case, omitting a variable causes bias only if that variable actually affects Y.

The bias term has more factors, however. The r_{31} term is the correlation of the excluded variable (X_3) and the first variable (X_1). It is the first term in the denominator of the bias term, playing a similar role to that of the correlation of the excluded and included variables in the simpler model. The complication now is that the correlations of the two included variables (r_{21}) and correlation of the omitted variable and the included variable (r_{32}) also matter.

We can take away some simple principles. If the included independent variables are not correlated (which would mean that $r_{21} = 0$), then the equation simplifies to essentially what we were dealing with in the simple case. If the excluded variable is not correlated with the other included variable $(r_{32} = 0)$, we again can go back to the intuition from the simple omitted variable bias model. If, however, both correlations are non-zero (and, to be practical, relatively large), then the simple-case intuition may not travel well and we should tread carefully. We'll still be worried about omitted variable bias, but our ability to sign the bias will be weakened.

> ## REMEMBER THIS
>
> When there are multiple variables in the true equation, the effect of omitting one of them depends in a complicated way on the interrelations of all variables.
>
> 1. As in the simpler model, if the omitted variable does not affect Y, there is no omitted variable bias.
>
> 2. The equation for omitted variable bias when the true equation has only two variables often provides a reasonable approximation of the effects for cases in which there are multiple independent variables.

14.6   Omitted Variable Bias due to Measurement Error

We discussed measurement error in Section 5.3 of Chapter 5. Here we derive the equation for attenuation bias due to measurement error in an independent variable for the case of one independent variable. We also discuss implications of measurement error when there are multiple variables.

Model with one independent variable

We start with a true model based on the actual value of the independent variable, which we denote with X_{1i}^*:

$$Y_i = \beta_0 + \beta_1 X_{1i}^* + \epsilon_i \tag{14.17}$$

The independent variable we observe has some error:

$$X_{1i} = X_{1i}^* + v_i \tag{14.18}$$

where we assume that v_i is uncorrelated with X_{1i}^*. This little equation will do a lot of work for us in helping us understand the effect of measurement error.

Substituting for X_{1i}^* in the true model yields

$$Y_i = \beta_0 + \beta_1(X_{1i} - v_i) + \epsilon_i$$
$$= \beta_0 + \beta_1 X_{1i} - \beta_1 v_i + \epsilon_i \tag{14.19}$$

Let's treat v as the omitted variable and $-\beta_1$ as the coefficient on the omitted variable. (Compare these to X_2 and β_2 in Equation 5.7.) Doing so allows us to write the omitted variable bias equation as

$$\beta_1^{\text{OmitX}_2} = \beta_1 - \beta_1 \frac{\text{cov}(X_1, v)}{\text{var}(X_1)} \tag{14.20}$$

where we use the covariance-based equation from page 60 to calculate δ_1 in the standard omitted variable equation.

Recalling that $X_{1i} = X_{1i}^* + v_i$ and using the rules for covariance in the appendix on page 523, we can show that $\text{cov}(X_1, v) = \sigma_v^2$.[6] Also, because $X_1 = X_1^* + v$, $\text{var}(X_1) = \sigma_{X^*}^2 + \sigma_v^2$.

We can therefore rewrite Equation 14.20 as

$$\beta_1^{\text{OmitX}_2} = \beta_1 \doteq \beta_1 \frac{\sigma_v^2}{\sigma_{X^*}^2 + \sigma_v^2} \tag{14.21}$$

Collecting terms yields

$$\text{plim } \hat{\beta}_1 = \beta_1 \left(1 - \frac{\sigma_v^2}{\sigma_v^2 + \sigma_{X^*}^2} \right)$$

Finally, we use the fact that $1 - \frac{\sigma_v^2}{\sigma_v^2 + \sigma_{X^*}^2} = \frac{\sigma_{X_1^*}^2}{\sigma_v^2 + \sigma_{X^*}^2}$ to produce

$$\text{plim } \hat{\beta}_1 = \beta_1 \frac{\sigma_{X_1^*}^2}{\sigma_v^2 + \sigma_{X_1^*}^2}$$

which is the equation we discussed in detail in Section 5.3.

Measurement error with multiple independent variables

We have so far dealt with a bivariate regression with a single, poorly measured independent variable for which the error is a mean-zero random variable uncorrelated with anything else. If we have multiple independent variables and a single badly measured variable, it is still the case that the coefficient on the poorly measured independent variable will suffer from attenuation bias, as defined in Chapter 5 on page 146. The other coefficients will also suffer, although in a way that is hard to anticipate. This source of measurement-related bias is seldom emphasized in real applications.

REMEMBER THIS

1. We can use omitted variable logic to derive the effect of a poorly measured independent variable.

2. A single poorly measured independent variable can cause other coefficients to be biased.

---

[6] First, note that $\text{cov}(X_1, v) = \text{cov}(X_1^* + v, v) = \text{cov}(X_1^*, v) + \text{cov}(v, v) = \text{cov}(v, v)$ because v is not correlated with X_1^*. Finally, note that $\text{cov}(v, v) = \sigma_v^2$ by standard rules of covariance.

Conclusion

OLS goes a long way with just a few assumptions about the model and the error terms. Exogeneity gets us unbiased estimates. Homoscedasticity and noncorrelated errors get us an equation for the variance of our estimates.

How important is it to be able to know exactly how these assumptions come together to provide all this good stuff? On a practical level, not very. We can go about most of our statistical business without knowing how to derive these results.

On a deeper level, though, it is useful to know how the assumptions matter. The statistical properties of OLS are not magic. They're not even that hard, once we break the derivations down step by step. The assumptions we rely on play specific roles in figuring out the properties of our estimates, as we have seen in the derivations in this chapter. We also formalized our understanding of omitted variable bias, helping us know where conditions come from, as well as if and how they apply to various circumstances.

We don't need to be able to produce all the derivations from scratch. If we can do the following, we will have a solid understanding of the statistical foundations of OLS:

- Section 14.1: Explain the steps in deriving the equation for the OLS estimate of $\hat{\beta}_1$. What assumption is crucial for $\hat{\beta}_1$ to be an unbiased estimator of β_1?

- Section 14.2: What assumptions are crucial to a derivation of the standard equation for the variance of $\hat{\beta}_1$?

- Section 14.3: Show how to derive the omitted variable bias equation.

- Section 14.4: Show how to use the omitted variable bias equation to "sign the bias."

- Section 14.5: Explain how omitted variable bias works when the true model contains multiple variables.

- Section 14.6: Show how to use omitted variable bias tools to characterize the effect of measurement error.

Further Reading

See Clarke (2005) for further details on omitted variables. Greene (2003, 148) offers a generalization that uses matrix notation.

Greene (2003, 86) discusses the implications of measurement error when the model contains multiple independent variables. Cragg (1994) provides an accessible overview of problems raised by measurement error and offers strategies for dealing with them.

Key Term

Expected value (484)

Computing Corner

Stata

1. To estimate OLS models, use the tools discussed in the Computing Corner in Chapter 5.

2. To generate a normal random variable (useful in the simulation of a variable measured with error), use gen Noise = rnormal(0,1), where the first number in parentheses is the mean of the normal random variable and the second number is the standard deviation of the normally distributed random variable. For a uniformly distributed random variable, use gen NoiseUniform = runiform().

R

1. To estimate OLS models, use the tools discussed in the Computing Corner in Chapter 5.

2. To generate a standard normal random variable (useful in the simulation of a variable measured with error), use Noise = rnorm(N), where the number in parentheses is the number of observations. A more general form adds subcommands for mean and standard deviation. For example, rnorm(500, mean = 1, sd = 2) creates a normally distributed random variable of length 500 with mean of 1 and a standard deviation of 2. For a uniformly distributed random variable, use NoiseUniform = runif(N), where N is the desired length of the variable.

Exercises

1. Apply the logic developed in this chapter to the model $Y_i = \beta_0 + \beta_1 X_i + \epsilon_i$. (There was no β_0 in the simplified model we used in Section 14.1.) Derive the OLS estimate for $\hat{\beta}_0$ and $\hat{\beta}_1$.

TABLE 14.2	Variables for Winter Olympics Data
Variable name	**Description**
ID	Unique number for each country in the data set
country	Name of country
year	Year
time	A time variable equal to 1 for first Olympics in data set (1980), 2 for second Olympics (1984), and so forth. Useful for time series analysis.
medals	Total number of combined medals won
population	Population of country (in 100,000)
GDP	Per capita gross domestic product, in $10,000 U.S. dollars
host	Dummy variable indicating if country hosted Olympics in that year
temp	Average high temperature (in Fahrenheit) in January (in July for countries in the Southern Hemisphere)
elevation	Highest peak elevation in the country

2. Show that the OLS estimate $\hat{\beta}_1$ is unbiased for the model $Y_i = \beta_0 + \beta_1 X_i + \epsilon_i$.

3. Using the data in olympics_HW.dta on medals in the Winter Olympics from 1980 to 2014 to answer the following questions. Table 14.2 describes the variables.

    (a) Run a model with medals as the dependent variable and population as the independent variable and briefly interpret the results.

    (b) The model given omits GDP (among other things). Use tools discussed in Section 14.4 to anticipate the sign of omitted variable bias for $\hat{\beta}_1$ in the results in part (a) that are due to omission of GDP from that model.

    (c) Estimate a model explaining medals with both population and GDP. Was your prediction about omitted variable bias correct?

    (d) Note that we have also omitted a variable for whether a country is the host for the Winter Olympics. Sign the bias of the coefficient on population in part (a) that is due to omission of the host country variable.

    (e) Estimate a model explaining medals with both population and host (do not include GDP at this point). Was your prediction about omitted variable bias correct?

(f) Estimate a model explaining medals with population, GDP, host country, average elevation, and average temperature. Use standardized coefficients and briefly discuss the results.

(g) Use tips in the Computing Corner to create a new GDP variable called *NoisyGDP* that is equal to the actual GDP plus a standard normally distributed random variable. Think of this as a measure of GDP that has been corrupted by a measurement error. (Of course, the actual GDP variable itself is almost certainly tainted by some measurement error already.) Estimate the model from part (f), but use *NoisyGDP* instead of *GDP*. Explain changes in the coefficient on GDP, if any.

Advanced Panel Data **15**

In Chapter 8 we used fixed effects in panel data models to control for unmeasured factors that are fixed within units. We did so by including dummy variables for the units or by rescaling the data. We can also control for many time factors by including fixed effects for time periods.

The models get more complicated when we start thinking about more elaborate dependence across time. We face a major choice of whether we want to treat serial dependence in terms of serially correlated errors or in terms of dynamic models in which the value of Y_t depends directly on the value of Y in the previous period. These two approaches lead to different modeling choices and, in some cases, different results.

In this chapter, we discuss how these approaches connect to the panel data analysis we covered in Chapter 8. Section 15.1 shows how to deal with autocorrelation in panel data models. Section 15.2 introduces dynamic models for panel data analysis. Section 15.3 presents *random effects models*, an alternative to fixed effects models. Random effects models treat unit-specific error as something that complicates standard error calculations but does not cause bias. They're not as useful as fixed effects models, but it can be helpful to understand how they work.

15.1 Panel Data Models with Serially Correlated Errors

In panel data, it makes sense to worry about autocorrelation for the same reasons it makes sense to worry about autocorrelation in time series data. Remember all the stuff in the error term? Lots of that will stick around for a while. Unmeasured factors in year 1 may linger to affect what is going on in year 2, and so on. In this section we explain how to deal with autocorrelation in panel models, first without fixed effects and then with fixed effects.

Before we get into diagnosing and addressing the problem, let's recall the stakes: Autocorrelation does not cause bias in the standard OLS framework, but it does cause OLS estimates of standard errors to be incorrect. Often, it causes the OLS estimates of standard errors to be too small because we don't really have the number of independent observations that OLS thinks we do.

Autocorrelation without fixed effects

We start with a model without fixed effects. The model is

$$Y_{it} = \beta_0 + \beta_1 X_{1it} + \beta_2 X_{2it} + \epsilon_{it}$$

$$\epsilon_{it} = \rho \epsilon_{i,t-1} + \nu_{it}$$

where ν_{it} is a mean-zero, random error term that is not correlated with the independent variables. There are N units and T time periods in the panel data set. We limit ourselves to first-order autocorrelation (where the error this period is a function of the error last period). The tools we discuss generalize pretty easily to higher orders of autocorrelation.[1]

Estimation is relatively simple. First we use standard OLS to estimate the model. We then use the residuals from the OLS model to test for evidence of autocorrelated errors. This works because OLS $\hat{\beta}$ estimates are unbiased even if errors are autocorrelated, which means that the residuals (which are functions of the data and $\hat{\beta}$) are unbiased estimates, too.

We test for autocorrelated errors in this context using something called a *Lagrange multiplier (LM) test*. The LM test is similar to our test for autocorrelation in Chapter 13 on page 455. It involves estimating the following:

$$\hat{\epsilon}_{it} = \rho \hat{\epsilon}_{i,t-1} + \gamma_1 X_{1it} + \gamma_2 X_{2it} + \eta_{it}$$

where η_{it} (η is the Greek letter eta) is a mean-zero, random error term. We use the fact that $N \times R^2$ from this auxiliary regression is distributed χ_1^2 under the null hypothesis of no autocorrelation.

If the LM test indicates autocorrelation, we will use ρ-transformation techniques we discussed in Chapter 13 (Section 13.3) to estimate an AR(1) model.

Autocorrelation with fixed effects

To test for autocorrelation in a panel data model that has fixed effects, we must deal with a slight wrinkle. The fixed effects induce correlation in the de-meaned errors even when there is no correlation in the actual errors. The error term in the de-meaned model is $(\epsilon_{it} - \bar{\epsilon}_{i\cdot})$, which means that the de-meaned error for unit

---

[1] A second-order autocorrelated process would also have the error in period t correlated with the error in period $t - 2$, and so on.

i will include the mean of the error terms for unit i ($\bar{\epsilon}_{i.}$), which in turn means that $\frac{1}{T}$ of any given error term will appear in all error terms. So, for example, ϵ_{i1} (the raw error in the first period) is in the first de-meaned error term, the second de-meaned error term, and so on via the $\bar{\epsilon}_{i.}$ term. The result will be at least a little autocorrelation because the de-meaned error term in the first and second periods, for example, will move together at least a little bit because both have some of the same terms.

Therefore, to test for AR(1) errors in a panel data model with fixed effects, we need to use robust errors that account for autocorrelation.

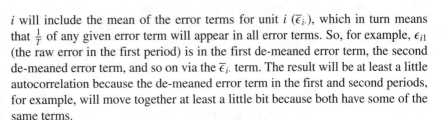

REMEMBER THIS

To estimate panel models that account for autocorrelated errors, proceed in the following steps:

1. Estimate an initial model that does not address autocorrelation. This model can be either an OLS model or a fixed effects model.

2. Use residuals from the initial model to test for autocorrelation, and apply a Lagrange multiplier (LM) test based on the R^2 from the following model:

$$\hat{\epsilon}_{it} = \rho\hat{\epsilon}_{i,t-1} + \gamma_1 X_{1it} + \gamma_2 X_{2it} + \eta_{it}$$

3. If we reject the null hypothesis of no autocorrelation (which will happen when the R^2 in the equation above is high), then we should remove the autocorrelation by ρ-transforming the data as discussed in Chapter 13.

15.2 Temporal Dependence with a Lagged Dependent Variable

We can also model temporal dependence with the dynamic models we discussed in Section 13.4. In these models the current value of Y_{it} could depend directly on $Y_{i,t-1}$, the value of Y in the previous period.

These models are sneakily complex. They seem easy because they simply require us to include a lagged dependent variable in an OLS model. They actually have many knotty aspects that differ from those in standard OLS models. In this section we discuss dynamic models for panel data, first without fixed effects and then with fixed effects.

Lagged dependent variable without fixed effects

We begin with a panel model without fixed effects. Specifically,

$$Y_{it} = \gamma Y_{i,t-1} + \beta_0 + \beta_1 X_{1it} + \beta_2 X_{2it} + \epsilon_{it} \tag{15.1}$$

where γ is the effect of the lagged dependent variable, the β's are the immediate effects of the independent variables, and ϵ_{it} is uncorrelated with the independent variables and homoscedastic.

We see how tricky this model is when we try to characterize the effect of X_{1it} on Y_{it}. Obviously, if X_{1it} increases by one unit, there will be a β_1 increase in Y_{it} that period. Notice, though, that an increase in Y_{it} in one period affects Y_{it} in future periods via the $\gamma Y_{i,t-1}$ term in the model. Hence increasing X_{1it} in the first period, for example, will affect the value of Y_{it} in the first period, which will then affect Y in the next period. In other words, if we change X_{1it} we get not only β_1 more Y_{it} but we get $\gamma \times \beta_1$ more Y in the next period, and so on—a change in X_{1it} today dribbles on to affect Y forever through the lagged dependent variable in Equation 15.1.

As a practical matter, including a lagged dependent variable is a double-edged sword. On the one hand, it is often highly significant, which is good news in that we have a control variable that soaks up variance that's unexplained by other variables. On the other hand, the lagged dependent variable can be *too* good—so highly significant that it sucks the significance out of the other independent variables. In fact, if there is serial autocorrelation and trending in the independent variable, including a lagged dependent variable causes bias. In such a case, Princeton political scientist Chris Achen (2000, 7) has noted that the lagged dependent variable

> does not conduct itself like a decent, well-behaved proxy. Instead it is a kleptomaniac, picking up the effect, not only of excluded variables, but also of the included variables if they are sufficiently trended. As a result, the impact of the included substantive variables is reduced, sometimes to insignificance.

This conclusion does not mean that lagged dependent variables are evil, but rather that we should tread carefully when we are deciding whether to include them. In particular, we should estimate models both with them and without. If results differ substantially, we should decide to place more weight on the model with or without the lagged dependent variable only after we've run all the tests and absorbed the logic described next.

The good news is that if the errors are not autocorrelated, using OLS for a model with lagged dependent variables works fine. Given that the lagged dependent variable commonly soaks up any serial dependence in the data, this approach is reasonable and widely used.[2]

If the errors are autocorrelated, however, OLS will produce biased estimates of $\hat{\beta}$ when a lagged dependent variable is included. In this case, autocorrelation does more than render conventional OLS standard error estimates inappropriate—autocorrelation in models with lagged dependent variables actually messes up the estimates. This bias is worth mulling over a bit. It happens because models with lagged dependent variables are outside the conventional

---

[2] See Beck and Katz (2011).

OLS framework. Hence even though autocorrelation does not cause bias in OLS models, autocorrelation *can* cause bias in dynamic models.

Why does autocorrelation cause bias in a model when we include a lagged dependent variable? It's pretty easy to see: $Y_{i,t-1}$ of course contains $\epsilon_{i,t-1}$. And if $\epsilon_{i,t-1}$ is correlated with ϵ_{it}—which is exactly what first-order autocorrelation implies—then one of the independent variables in Equation 15.1, $Y_{i,t-1}$, will be correlated with the error.

This problem is not particularly hard to deal with. Suppose there is no autocorrelation. In that case, OLS estimates are unbiased, meaning that the residuals from the OLS model are consistent too. We can therefore use these residuals in an LM test like the one we described earlier (on page 502). If we fail to reject the null hypothesis (which is quite commonly done, since lagged dependent variables often zap autocorrelation), then OLS it is. If we reject the null hypothesis of no autocorrelation, we can use an AR(1) model like the one discussed in Chapter 13 to rid the data of autocorrelation and thereby get us back to unbiased and consistent estimates.

Lagged dependent variable with fixed effects

The lagged dependent variable often captures the unit-specific variance that fixed effects capture. Hence it is not uncommon to see lagged dependent variables used in place of fixed effects. If we want both in our model, we move on to consider dynamic models with fixed effects.

Beware! Things get complicated when we include a lagged dependent variable and fixed effects in the same model.

Here's the model:

$$Y_{it} = \gamma Y_{i,t-1} + \beta_0 + \beta_1 X_{1it} + \beta_2 X_{2it} + \alpha_i + \epsilon_{it}$$

where ϵ_{it} is uncorrelated with the independent variables.

OLS is biased in this situation. Bummer. Recall from Section 8.2 that fixed effects models are equivalent to de-meaned estimates. That means a fixed effects model with a lagged dependent variable will include a variable $(Y_{i,t-1} - \overline{Y}_{i,t-1})$. The $\overline{Y}_{i,t-1}$ part of this variable is the average of the lagged dependent variable over all periods. This average will therefore include the value of Y_{it}, and Y_{it}, in turn, contains ϵ_{it}. Hence the de-meaned lagged dependent variable will be correlated with ϵ_{it}. The extent of this bias depends on the magnitude of this correlation, which is proportional to $\frac{1}{T}$, where T is the length of the time series for each observation (often the number of years of data). For a small panel with just two or three periods, the bias can be serious. For a panel with 20 or more periods, the problem is less serious. One piece of good news here is that the bias in a model with a lagged dependent variable and fixed effects is worse for the coefficient on the lagged dependent variable; simulation studies indicate that bias is modest for coefficients on the X_{it} variables, the variables we usually care most about.

Two ways to estimate dynamic panel data models with fixed effects

What to do? One option is to follow instrumental variable (IV) logic, covered in Chapter 9. In this context, the IV approach relies on finding some variable that is correlated with the independent variable in question and not correlated with the error. Most IV approaches rely on using lagged values of the independent variables, which are typically correlated with the independent variable in question but not correlated with the error, which happens later. The Arellano and Bond (1991) approach, for example, uses all available lags as instruments. These models are quite complicated and, like many IV models, imprecise.

Another option is to use OLS, accepting some bias in exchange for better accuracy and less complexity. While we have talked a lot about bias, we have not yet discussed the trade-off between bias and accuracy, largely because in basic models such as OLS, unbiased models are also the most accurate, so we don't have to worry about the trade-off. But in more complicated models, it is possible to have an estimator that produces coefficients that are biased but still pretty close to the true value. It is also possible to have an estimator that is unbiased, but very imprecise. IV estimators are in the latter category—they are, on average, going to get us the true value, but they have higher variance.

Here's a goofy example of the trade-off between bias and accuracy. Consider two estimators of average height in the United States. The first is the height of a single person, randomly sampled. This estimator is unbiased—after all, the average of this estimator will have to be the average of the whole population. But clearly this estimator isn't very precise because it is based on a single person.

The second estimator of average height in the United States is the average height of 500 randomly selected people, but measured with a measuring stick that is inaccurate by 0.25 inch (making every measurement a quarter-inch too big).[3] Which estimate of average height would we rather have? The second one may well make up what it loses in bias by being more precise. That's the situation here because the OLS estimate is biased, but more precise than the IV estimates.

Nathaniel Beck and Jonathan Katz (2011) have run a series of simulations of several options for estimating models with lagged dependent variables and fixed effects. They find that OLS performs better in that it's actually more likely to produce estimates close to the true value than the IV approach, even though OLS estimates are a bit biased. The performance of OLS models improves relative to the IV approach as T increases.

H. L. Mencken said that for every problem there is a solution that is simple, neat, and wrong. Usually that's a devastating critique. Here it is a compliment. OLS is simple. It is neat. And yet, it is wrong in the sense of being biased when we have a lagged dependent variable and fixed effects. But OLS is more accurate (meaning the variance of $\hat{\beta}_1$ is smaller) than the alternatives, which nets out to a pretty good approach.

---

[3] Yes, yes, we could subtract the quarter-inch from all the height measurements. Work with me here. We're trying to make a point!

> ## REMEMBER THIS

1. Researchers often include lagged dependent variables to account for serial dependence. A model with a lagged dependent variable is called a dynamic model.

   (a) Dynamic models differ from conventional OLS models in many respects.

   (b) In a dynamic model, a change in X has an immediate effect on Y, as well as an ongoing effect on future Y's, since any change in Y associated with a change in X will affect future values of Y via the lagged dependent variable.

   (c) If there are no fixed effects in the model and there is no autocorrelation, then using OLS for a model with a lagged dependent variable will produce unbiased coefficient estimates.

   (d) If there are no fixed effects in the model and there is autocorrelation, the autocorrelation must be purged from the data before unbiased estimates can be generated.

2. OLS estimates from models with both a lagged dependent variable and fixed effects are biased.

   (a) One alternative to OLS is to use an instrumental variables (IV) approach. This approach produces unbiased estimates, but it's complicated and yields imprecise estimates.

   (b) OLS is useful to estimate a model with a lagged dependent variable and fixed effects.

   - The bias is not severe and decreases as T, the number of observations for each unit, increases.

   - OLS in this context produces relatively accurate parameter estimates.

15.3 Random Effects Models

The term "fixed effects" is used to distinguish from "random effects." In this section we present an overview of random effects models and discuss when they can be used.

▶ **random effects model** Treats unit-specific error as a random variable that is uncorrelated with the independent variable.

In a **random effects model**, the unit-specific error term is itself considered a random variable. Instead of eliminating or estimating the α_i as is done in fixed effects models, random effects models leave the α_i's in the error term and account for them during the calculation of standard errors. We won't cover the calculations here other than to note that they can get tricky.

An advantage of random effects models is that they estimate coefficients on variables that do not vary within a unit (the kind of variables that get dropped in fixed effects models). Fixed effects models, on the other hand, cannot estimate coefficients on variables that do not vary within a unit (as discussed on page 262).

The disadvantage of random effects models is that the random effects estimates are unbiased only if the random effects (the α_i) are uncorrelated with the X. The core challenge in OLS (which we have discussed at length) is that the error term might be correlated with the independent variable; this problem continues with random effects models, which address correlation of errors across observations, but not correlation of errors and independent variables. Hence random effects models fail to take advantage of a major attraction of panel data, which is that we can deal with the possible correlation of the unit-specific effects that might cause spurious inferences regarding the independent variables.

The Hausman test is a statistical test that pits random against fixed effects models. Once we understand this test, we can see why the bang-for-buck payoff for random effects models is generally pretty low. In a Hausman test we use the same data to estimate both a fixed effects model and a random effects model. Under the null hypothesis that the α_i are uncorrelated with the X, the $\hat{\beta}$ estimates should be similar. Under the alternative, the estimates should be different because the random effects should be corrupted by the correlation of the α_i with the X and the fixed effects should not.

The decision rule for a Hausman test is the following:

- If fixed effects and random effects give us pretty much the same $\hat{\beta}$, we fail to reject the null hypothesis and can use random effects.

- If the two approaches provide different answers, we reject the null and should use fixed effects.

Ultimately, we believe either the fixed effects estimate (when we reject the null hypothesis of no correlation between α_i and X_i) or pretty much the fixed effects answer (when we fail to reject the null hypothesis of no correlation between α_i and X_i).[4]

If used appropriately, random effects have some advantages. When the α_i are uncorrelated with the X_i, random effects models will generally produce smaller standard errors on coefficients than fixed effects models. In addition, as T gets large, the differences between fixed and random effects decline; in practice, however, the differences can be substantial in many real-world data sets.

REMEMBER THIS

Random effects models do not estimate fixed effects for each unit but, rather, adjust standard errors and estimates to account for unit-specific elements of the error term.

1. Random effects models produce unbiased estimates of $\hat{\beta}_1$ only when the α_i's are uncorrelated with the X variables.

2. Fixed effects models are unbiased regardless of whether the α_i's are uncorrelated with the X variables, making fixed effects a more generally useful approach.

---

[4] For more details on the Hausman test, see Wooldridge (2002, 288).

Conclusion

Serial dependence in panel data models is an important and complicated challenge. There are two major approaches to dealing with it. One is to treat the serial dependence as autocorrelated errors. In this case, we can test for autocorrelation and if necessary purge it from the data by ρ-transforming the data.

The other approach is to estimate a dynamic model that includes a lagged dependent variable. Dynamic models are quite different from standard OLS models. Among other things, each independent variable has a short- and a long-term effect on Y.

Our approach to estimating a model with a lagged dependent variable depends on whether there is autocorrelation and whether we include fixed effects. If there is no autocorrelation and we do not include fixed effects, the model is easy to estimate via OLS and produces unbiased parameter estimates. If there is autocorrelation, the correlation of error needs to be purged via standard ρ-transformation techniques.

If we include fixed effects in a model with a lagged dependent variable, OLS will produce biased results. However, scholars have found that the bias is relatively small and that OLS is likely to work better than alternatives such as IV or bias-correction approaches.

We will have a good start on understanding advanced panel data analysis when we can answer the following questions:

- Section 15.1: How do we diagnose and correct for autocorrelation in panel data models?

- Section 15.2: What are consequences of including lagged dependent variables in models with and without fixed effects? Under what conditions is it reasonable to use lagged dependent variables and fixed effects, despite the bias?

- Section 15.3: What are random effects models? When are they appropriate?

Further Reading

There is a large and complicated literature on accounting for time dependence in panel data models. Beck and Katz (2011) is an excellent guide. Among other things, these authors discuss how to conduct an LM test for AR(1) errors in a model without fixed effects, the bias in models with autocorrelation and lagged dependent variables, and the bias of fixed effects models with lagged dependent variables.

There are many other excellent resources. Wooldridge (2002) is a valuable reference for more advanced issues in analysis of panel data. An important article by Achen (2000) pushes for caution in the use of lagged dependent variables. Wawro (2002) provides a nice overview of Arellano and Bond methods.

Another approach to dealing with bias in dynamic models with fixed effects is to correct for bias directly, as suggested by Kiviet (1995). This procedure works reasonably well in simulations, but it is quite complicated.

Key Term

Random effects model (507)

Computing Corner

> **Stata**

1. It can be useful to figure out which variables vary within unit, as this will determine if the variable can be included in a fixed effects model. Use
   ```
   tabulate unit, summarize(X1)
   ```
   which will show descriptive statistics for X_1 grouped by the variable called *unit*. If the standard deviation of a X_1 is zero for *all* units, there is no within-unit variation and, for the reasons discussed in Section 8.3, this variable cannot be included in a fixed effects model.

2. The Computing Corner in Chapter 8 discusses how to run one- and two-way fixed effects models in Stata. We need to indicate the unit and time variables by using the "time series set" commands (e.g., `tsset unit time`).

3. To save residuals from a fixed effects model in Stata, use
   ```
   xtreg Y X1 X2, fe i(unit)
   predict Resid, e
   ```
   The predict command here produces a variable named *Resid* (and we could choose any name we wanted). The , e subcommand in the predict command tells Stata to calculate the ϵ_{it} portion of the error term.[5]

4. The Computing Corner in Chapter 13 discusses how to estimate $\hat{\rho}$ in an AR(1) model.

---

[5] If we want to know the $\alpha_i + \epsilon_{it}$ portion of the error term, we type
```
predict ResidAE, ue
```
Note that Stata uses the letter u to refer to the fixed effect we denote with α in our notation.

5. Stata has a command called `xtregar` that estimates ρ-transformed models for panel data. There are quite a few subcommands, but the version that most closely follows the model as we have presented is
`xtregar Y X1 X2, fe rhotype(regress) twostep`

6. To estimate a panel data model with a lagged dependent variable, use
`xtreg Y L.Y X1 X2, fe i(unitcode)`
where the `L.Y` independent variable is simply the lag of Y. Note that for this command to work, we need to have invoked the `tsset` variable as described above. This approach also works for `xtregar`.

7. To estimate a random effects model, use
`xtreg Y X1 X2, re`
where the `, re` tells Stata to use a random effects model.

| R |

1. It can be useful to figure out which variables vary within unit, as this will determine if the variable can be included in a fixed effects model. Use `tapply(X1, unit, sd)` which will show the standard deviation of the variable X_1 grouped by the variable called *unit*. If the standard deviation of an X_1 is zero for *all* units, there is no within-unit variation for the reasons discussed in Section 8.3, and this variable cannot be included in a fixed effects model.

2. The Computing Corner in Chapter 8 discusses how to run one- and two-way fixed effects models in R.

3. R automatically creates a variable with the residuals for every regression object. For example, if we ran
`TwoWay = plm(Y ~ X1 + X2, data = DTA, index = c("ID",`
`"time"), effect = "twoways")`
the residuals would be in the variable `TwoWay$residuals`.

4. Estimating $\hat{\rho}$ in an AR(1) model can be a bit tricky with panel data. There are two issues. The first is that R's residual variable will contain only observations for non-missing observations, meaning that when data is missing, the variable and the original variables are of different lengths. The second issue is that when we use panel data to create lagged residuals, we need to be careful to use lagged values only within each unit. Suppose we have panel data on countries in which the United Kingdom is listed above data on the United States. If we blindly lagged variables, the lagged value of the dependent variable for the first United States observation would be the last United Kingdom observation. That's wrong. Therefore

we need to be careful to manage our missing data accurately and to have only lagged variables within unit. This can be achieved in many ways; here is one.

(a) Make sure your data is listed by stacking units—that is, the observations for unit 1 are first—and then ordered by time period. Below the lines for unit 1 are observations for unit 2, ordered by time period, and so on.[6]

(b) Create a variable with residuals, first by creating an empty variable with all missing data and then by putting R's residuals (which exist only for non-missing data) into this variable.
```
Resid = rep(NA, length(ID))
Resid[as.numeric(names(TwoWay$residuals))]
= TwoWay$residuals
```

(c) Create lag variables, one for the unit identifier and one for residuals. Then set all the lag residuals to missing for the first observation for each unit.
```
LagID = c(NA, ID[1:(length(ID)-1)])
LagResid = c(NA, Resid[1:(length(Resid)-1)])
LagResid[LagID != ID] = NA
```

(d) Use the variables from part (c) to estimate the model from Chapter 13:
```
RhoHat = lm(Resid ~ LagResid)
```

5. The Computing Corner in Chapter 13 discusses how to estimate $\hat{\rho}$ in an AR(1) model.

6. The most direct way to estimate a ρ-transformed model in R is to transform the variables manually. There are three steps.

(a) Create lag variables for dependent and independent variables, as we just did (for *LagID*, for example).

(b) Create ρ-transformed variables by first creating an empty variable and then filling it with ρ-transformed value. For example,
```
XRho = rep(NA, length(X))
XRho[LagID == ID] = (X[LagID == ID]
- RhoHat$coefficients[2]*LagX[LagID == ID])
```

---

[6] It is possible to stack data by year. The way we'd create lagged variables would be different, though.

(c) Use the `plm` command in R (described in the Computing Corner of Chapter 8) to run a fixed effects model via the transformed data. For example,

```
TwoWayRho = plm(YRho ~ X1Rho + X2Rho,
data = Rho.Frame, index = c("ID", "TIME"),
effect = "twoways")
```

7. To estimate a panel data model with a lagged dependent variable, use

```
LDV = plm(Y ~ lag(Y) + X1 + X2, data = Data,
index = c("ID", "TIME"), effect = "twoways")
```

8. To estimate a random effects model, use

```
plm(Y ~ X1 + X2, model = "random")
```

Exercises

1. Use the data in olympics_HW.dta on medals in the Winter Olympics from 1980 to 2014 to answer the following questions. Table 15.1 describes the variables.

   (a) Estimate a one-way fixed effects model explaining the number of medals with population, GDP, host country, average temperature, and maximum elevation as independent variables. Use country as the unit for fixed effects.[7] Briefly discuss the results and

TABLE 15.1 Another Set of Variables for Winter Olympics Data

Variable name	Description
ID	Unique number for each country in the data set
country	Name of country
year	Year
time	A time variable equal to 1 for first Olympics in data set (1980), 2 for second Olympics (1984) and so forth; useful for time series analysis.
medals	Total number of combined medals won
population	Population of country (in millions)
GDP	Per capita gross domestic product (GDP) (in $10,000 U.S. dollars)
host	Equals 1 if host nation and 0 otherwise
temp	Average high temperature (in Fahrenheit) in January if country is in Northern Hemisphere or July if Southern Hemisphere
elevation	Highest peak elevation in the country

[7] For simplicity, use the de-meaned approach, implemented with the `xtreg` command in Stata and the `plm` command in R.

explain what is going on with the coefficients on temperature and elevation.

(b) Estimate a two-way fixed effects model with population, GDP, and host country as independent variables. Use country and time as the fixed effects. Explain any differences from the results in part (a).

(c) Estimate $\hat{\rho}$ for the two-way fixed effects model. Is there evidence of autocorrelation? What are the implications of your finding?

(d) Estimate a two-way fixed effects model that has population, GDP, and host country as independent variables and accounts for autocorrelation. Discuss any differences from results in part (b). Which is a better statistical model? Why?

(e) Now estimate a two-way fixed effects model with a lagged dependent variable included as a control variable. Discuss differences from the two-way fixed effects model in part (b).

(f) Is there evidence of autocorrelation in the two-way fixed effects model that includes a lagged dependent variable? Compare your answer to your answer in part (c). Use concepts discussed in Section 13.4 to explain the implications of autocorrelation in a model that includes a lagged dependent variable model.

(g) Estimate a lagged dependent variable model that also controls for autocorrelation. Compare the results to your answer in parts (d) and (e).

(h) Section 15.2 discusses potential bias when a fixed effects model includes a lagged dependent variable. What is an important determinant of this bias? Assess this factor for this data set.

(i) Use the concepts presented at the end of Section 13.4 to discuss whether it is better to approach the analysis in an autocorrelation or a lagged dependent variable framework.

(j) Use the concept of model robustness from Section 2.2 to discuss which results are robust and which are not.

2. Answer the following questions using the Winter Olympics data described in Table 15.1 that can be found in olympics_HW.dta

(a) Investigate whether each of the independent variables varies within unit. Discuss how whether a variable varies within unit matters for fixed effects and random effects models.

(b) Estimate a pooled OLS model where the dependent variable is medals and the independent variables are population, GDP, host country, average temperature, and maximum elevation. Briefly comment on the results.

(c) Estimate a random effects model with the same variables as in part (b). Briefly explain the results, noting in particular what happens to variables that have no within-unit variation.

(d) What is necessary to avoid bias for a random effects model? Do you think this condition is satisfied in this case? Why or why not?

16 Conclusion: How to Be an Econometric Realist

After World War II, George Orwell (1946) famously wrote

> . . . we are all capable of believing things which we know to be untrue, and then, when we are finally proved wrong, impudently twisting the facts so as to show that we were right. Intellectually, it is possible to carry on this process for an indefinite time: the only check on it is that sooner or later a false belief bumps up against solid reality, usually on a battlefield.

The goal of econometrics is to provide a less violent empirical battlefield where theories can bump up against cold, hard data.

Unfortunately, econometric analysis is no stranger to the twisting rationalizations that allow us to distort reality to satisfy our preconceptions or interests. We therefore sometimes end up on an emotional roller coaster. We career from elation after figuring out a new double-tongue-twister econometric model to depression when multiple seemingly valid analyses support wildly disparate conclusions.

Some econometricians cope by fetishizing technical complexity. They pick the most complicated approach possible and treat the results as the truth. If others don't understand the analysis, it is because their puny brains cannot keep up with the mathematical geniuses in the computer lab. Such overconfidence is annoying and intellectually dangerous.

Others become econometric skeptics. For them, econometrics provides no answers. They avoid econometrics or, worse, they manipulate them. This nihilism, too, is annoying and intellectually dangerous.

What are we to do? It might seem that avoiding econometrics may limit harm. Econometrics are a bit like a chain saw: if used recklessly, the damage can be terrible. So it may be best to put down the laptop and back slowly away. The problem with this approach is that there really is no alternative to statistics and econometrics. As baseball analyst Bill James says, the alternative to statistics is not "no statistics." The alternative to statistics is bad statistics. Anyone who makes any empirical argument about the world is making a statistical argument. It might be based on vague data that is not systematically analyzed, but that's what people do when they judge from experience or intuition. Hence, despite the inability of statistics and econometrics to answer all questions or to be above manipulation, a serious effort to understand the world will involve some econometric reasoning.

A better approach is *realism* about econometrics. In the right hands, chain saws are awesome. If we learn how to use the tool properly, realizing what it can and can't do, we can make a lot of progress.

An econometric realist is committed to robust and thoughtful evaluation of theories. Five behaviors characterize this approach.

First, an econometric realist prioritizes. A model that explains everything is impossible. We must simplify. And if we're going to simplify the world, let's do it usefully. Statistician George Box (1976, 792) made this point wonderfully:

> Since all models are wrong the scientist must be alert to what is importantly wrong. It is inappropriate to be concerned about mice when there are tigers abroad.

The tiger abroad is almost always endogeneity. So we must prioritize fighting this tiger by using our core econometric toolkit: experiments, OLS, fixed effects models, instrumental variables, and regression discontinuity. There will be many challenges in any econometric project, but we must not let them distract us from the fight against endogeneity.

The second characteristic of an econometric realist is that he or she values robustness. Serious analysts do not believe assertions based on a single significant coefficient in a single statistical specification. Even for well-designed studies with good data, we worry that the results could depend on a very specific model specification. An econometric realist will show that the results are robust by assessing a reasonable range of specifications, perhaps with and without certain variables or with alternative measures of important concepts.

Third, an econometric realist adheres to the replication standard. Others must see our work and be able to recreate, modify, correct, and build off our analysis. Results cannot be scientifically credible otherwise. Replications can be direct: that is, others can do exactly the same procedures on the same data. Or they can be indirect, with new data or a different context used in a research design similar to one that has proved successful. We need replications of both types if our results are to be truly credible.

Fourth, an econometric realist is wary of complexity. Sometimes complex models are inevitable. However, just because one model is more complicated than another, it is not necessarily more likely to be true. It *is* more likely to have mistakes. Sometimes complexity becomes a shield behind which analysts hide, intentionally or not, moving their conclusions effectively beyond the realm of reasonable replicability and, therefore, beyond credibility.

Remember, econometric analysis is hard, but not because of the math. Economics is hard because the world is a complicated place. If anything, the math makes things easier by providing tools to simplify the world. A certain amount of jargon among specialists in the field is inevitable and helps experts communicate efficiently. If a result holds only underneath layers of impenetrable math, however, be wary. Check your wallet. Count your silverware.

Investor Peter Lynch often remarked that he wouldn't invest in any business idea that couldn't be illustrated with a crayon. If the story isn't simple, it's probably wrong. This attitude is useful for econometric analysts as well. A valid model will almost certainly entail background work that is not broadly accessible, but to be most persuasive, the results should include a figure or story that simply summarizes the basis for the finding. Perhaps we'll have to use a sharp crayon, but if we can't explain our results with a crayon, we should keep working.

Fifth, an econometric realist thinks holistically. We should step back from any given result and consider the totality of the evidence. The following indicators of causality provide a useful framework. None is necessary; none is sufficient. Taken together, though, the more these conditions are satisfied, the more confident we can be that a given causal claim is true.

- *Strength*: This is the simplest criterion. Is there a strong relationship between the independent variable and the dependent variable?

  - A strong observed relationship is less likely to be due to random chance. Even if the null hypothesis of no relationship is true, we know that random variation can lead to the occasional "significant" result. The random noise producing such a result is more likely to produce a weak connection than a strong observed relationship. A very strong relationship is highly unlikely to simply be the result of random noise.

  - A strong observed relationship is less likely to be spurious for reasons that aren't obvious. A strong relationship is not immune to endogeneity, of course, but it is more likely that a strong result due to endogeneity alone will be attributable to a relatively clear source of endogeneity. For a weak relationship, the endogeneity could be subtle, but sufficient to account for what we observe.

  - A strong observed relationship is more likely to be important. A weak relationship might not be random or spurious; it might simply be uninteresting. Life is short. Explain things that matter. Our goal is not to intone the words "statistically significant" but rather to produce useful knowledge.

- *Consistency*: Do different analysts consistently find the relationship in different contexts?

– All too often, a given theoretical claim is tested with the very data that suggested the result. That's not much to go on; a random or spurious relationship in one data set does not a full-blown theory make. Hence we should be cautious about claims until they have been observed across multiple contexts. With that requirement met, it is less likely that the result is due to chance or to an analyst's having leaned on the data to get desired a result.

– If results are not observed across multiple contexts, are there contextual differences? Perhaps the real finding would lie in explaining why a relationship exists in one context and not others.

– Or, if other results are different, can we explain why the other results are wrong? It is emphatically not the case that we should interpret two competing statistical results as a draw. One result could be based on a mistake. If that's true, explain why (nicely, of course). If we can't explain why one approach is better, though, and we are left with conflicting results, we need to be cautious about believing we have identified a real relationship.

• *Specificity*: Are the patterns in the data consistent with the specific claim? Each theory should be mined for as many specific claims as possible, not only about direct effects, but also about indirect effects and mechanisms. As important, the theory should be mined for claims about when we won't see the relationship. This line of thinking allows us to conduct placebo tests in which we *should* see null results. In other words, the relationship should be observable everywhere we expect it and nowhere we don't.

• *Plausibility*: Given what we know about the world, does the result make sense? Sometimes results are implausible on their face: if someone found that eating french fries led to weight loss, we should probably ask some probing questions before supersizing. That doesn't mean we should treat implausible results as wrong. After all, the idea that the earth revolves around the sun was pretty implausible before Copernicus. Implausible results that happen to be true just need more evidence to overcome the implausibility.

Adherence to these criteria is not as cut and dried as looking at confidence intervals or hypothesis tests. Strength, consistency, and the others are more important because they determine not "statistical significance" but what we conclude about empirical relationships. They should never be far from the mind of a an econometric realist who wants to use data to learn about how the world really works.

So we have done a lot in this book. We've covered a vast array of econometric tools. We've just now described a productive mind-set, that of a an econometric realist. There is one more element: creativity. Think of econometrics as the grammar for good analysis. It is not the story. No one reads a book and says "Great grammar!" A terrible book might have bad grammar, but a good book needs more than good grammar. The material we covered in this book provides the grammar for making convincing claims about the way the world works. The rest is up to you. Think hard, be creative, take chances. Good luck.

Further Reading

In his 80-page paean to statistical realism, Achen (1982) puts it this way: "The uninitiated are often tempted to trust every statistical study or none. It is the task of empirical social scientists to be wiser." Achen followed this publication in 2002 with an often-quoted article arguing for keeping models simple.

The criteria for evaluating research discussed here are strongly influenced by the Bradford-Hill criteria from Bradford-Hill (1965). Nevin (2013) assesses the Bradford-Hill criteria for the theory that lead in gasoline was responsible for the 1980s crime surge in the United States (and elsewhere).

APPENDICES: MATH AND PROBABILITY BACKGROUND

A. Summation

- $\sum_{i=1}^{N} X_i = X_1 + X_2 + X_3 + \cdots + X_N$

- If a variable in the summation does not have a subscript, it can be "pulled out" of the summation. For example,

$$\sum_{i=1}^{N} \beta X_i = \beta X_1 + \beta X_2 + \beta X_3 + \cdots + \beta X_N$$
$$= \beta (X_1 + X_2 + X_3 + \cdots + X_N)$$
$$= \beta \sum_{i=1}^{N} X_i$$

- If a variable in the summation has a subscript, it cannot be "pulled out" of the summation. For example, $\sum_{i=1}^{N} X_i Y_i = X_1 Y_1 + X_2 Y_2 + X_3 Y_3 + \cdots + X_N Y_N$ cannot as a general matter be simplified.

- As a general matter, a non-linear function in a sum is not the same as the non-linear function of the sum. For example, as a general matter, $\sum_{i=1}^{N} X_i^2$ will not equal $(\sum_{i=1}^{N} X_i)^2$ except for very particular circumstances (such as $X_i = 1$ for all observations).

B. Expectation

- Expectation is the value we expect a random variable to have. The expectation is basically the average of the random variable if we could sample from the variable's distribution a huge (infinite, really) number of times.

- For example, the expected value of the value of a six-sided die is 3.5. If we roll a die a huge number of times, we'd expect each side to come up an equal proportion of times, so the expected average will equal the average of 1, 2, 3, 4, 5, and 6. More formally, the expected value will be $\sum_1^6 p(X_i)X_i$, where X is 1, 2, 3, 4, 5, and 6 and $p(X_i)$ is the probability of each outcome, which in this example is $\frac{1}{6}$ for each value.

- The expectation of some number k times a function is equal to k times the expectation of the function. That is, $E[kg(X)] = kE[g(X)]$ for constant k, where $g(X)$ is some function of X. Suppose we want to know what the expectation of 10 times the number on a die is. We can say that the expectation of that is simply 10 times the expectation. Not rocket science, but useful.

C. Variance

The variance of a random variable is a measure of how spread out the distribution is. In a large sample, the variance can be estimated as

$$\text{var}(X) = \frac{1}{N} \sum_{i=1}^{N} (X_i - \overline{X})^2$$

In small samples, a degrees of freedom correction means we divide by $N - 1$ instead of N. For large N it hardly matters whether we use N or $N - 1$; as a practical matter, computer programs take care of this for us.

It is useful to deconstruct the variance equation to determine exactly what it does. The math is pretty simple:

1. Take deviation from the mean for each observation.

2. Square it to keep it positive.

3. Take the average.

Here are some useful properties of variance, the "variance facts" cited in Chapter 14.

1. The variance of a constant plus a random variable is the variance of the random variable. That is, let k be a fixed number and ϵ be a random variable with variance σ^2, then

$$\text{var}(k + \epsilon) = \text{var}(k) + \text{var}(\epsilon)$$
$$= 0 + \text{var}(\epsilon)$$
$$= \sigma^2$$

2. The variance of a random variable times a constant is the constant squared times the variance of the random variable. That is, let k be some constant and ϵ be a random variable with variance σ^2, then

$$\text{var}(k\epsilon) = k^2\text{var}(\epsilon)$$
$$= k^2\sigma^2$$

3. When random variables are correlated, the variance of a sum (or difference) of random variables depends on the variances and covariance of the variables. Let ϵ and τ be random variables:

   • $\text{var}(\epsilon + \tau) = \text{var}(\epsilon) + \text{var}(\tau) + 2\text{cov}(\epsilon,\tau)$, where $\text{cov}(\epsilon,\tau)$ refers to the covariance of ϵ and τ

   • $\text{var}(\epsilon - \tau) = \text{var}(\epsilon) + \text{var}(\tau) - 2\text{cov}(\epsilon,\tau)$, where $\text{cov}(\epsilon,\tau)$ refers to the covariance of ϵ and τ

4. When random variables are uncorrelated, the variance of a sum (or difference) of random variables equals the sum of the variances. This outcome follows directly from the previous, which we can see by noting that if two random variables are uncorrelated, their covariance equals zero and the covariance term drops out of the equations.

D. Covariance

• Covariance measures how much two random variables vary together. In large samples, the covariance of two variables is

$$\text{cov}(X_1, X_2) = \frac{\sum_{i=1}^{N}(X_{1i} - \overline{X}_1)(X_{2i} - \overline{X}_2)}{N} \qquad (\text{A.1})$$

• As with variance, several useful properties apply when we are dealing with covariance.

   1. The covariance of a random variable, ϵ, and some constant, k, is zero. Formally, $\text{cov}(\epsilon,k) = 0$.

   2. The covariance of a random variable, ϵ, with itself is the variance of that variable. Formally, $\text{cov}(\epsilon,\epsilon) = \sigma_\epsilon^2$.

   3. The covariance of $k_1\epsilon$ and $k_2\tau$, where k_1 and k_2 are constants and ϵ and τ are random variables, is $k_1 k_2 \text{cov}(\epsilon,\tau)$.

4. The covariance of a random variable with the sum of another random variable and a constant is the covariance of the two random variables. Formally, let ϵ and τ be random variables; then $\text{cov}(\epsilon, \tau + k) = \text{cov}(\epsilon, \tau)$.

E. Correlation

The equation for correlation is

$$\text{corr}(X, Y) = \frac{\text{cov}(X, Y)}{\sigma_X \sigma_Y}$$

where σ_X is the standard deviation of X and σ_Y is the standard deviation of Y. If $X = Y$ for all observations, $\text{cov}(X, Y) = \text{cov}(X, X) = \text{var}(X)$ and $\sigma_X = \sigma_Y$, implying that the denominator will be σ_X^2, which is the variance of X. These calculations therefore imply that the correlation for $X = Y$ will be $+1$, which is the upper bound for correlations.[1] For perfect negative correlation $X = -Y$ and correlation is -1.

The equation for correlation (Equation A.1) looks a bit like the equation for the slope coefficient in bivariate regression on page 49 in Chapter 3. The bivariate regression coefficient is simply a restandardized correlation:

$$\hat{\beta}_1^{\text{BivariateOLS}} = \text{corr}(X, Y) \times \frac{\sigma_Y}{\sigma_X}$$

F. Probability Density Functions

▶ **probability density function** A mathematical function that describes the relative probability for a continuous random variable to take on a given probability.

A **probability density function (PDF)** is a mathematical function that describes the relative probability for a continuous random variable to take on a given probability. Panels (c) and (d) of Figure 3.4 from Section 3.2 provides examples of two PDFs.

While the shapes of PDFs can vary considerably, they all share certain fundamental features. The values of a PDF are greater than or equal to zero for all possible values of the random variable. The total area under the curve defined by the PDF equals one.

One tricky thing about PDFs is that they are continuous functions. Thus we cannot say that the probability that a random variable equals 2.2 is equal to the value of the function evaluated at 2.2 because the value of the function is pretty much the same at 2.2000001 and 2.2000002, and pretty soon the total probability

---

[1] We also get perfect correlation if the variables are identical once normalized. That is, X and Y are perfectly correlated if $X = 10Y$ or if $X = 5 + 3Y$, and so forth. In these cases, $\frac{(X_i - \bar{X})}{\sigma_X} = \frac{(Y_i - \bar{Y})}{\sigma_Y}$ for all observations.

would exceed one because there are always more possible values very near to any given value. Instead, we need to think in terms of probabilities that the random variable is in some (possibly small) region of values. Hence we need the tools from calculus to calculate probabilities from a PDF.

Figure A.1 shows the PDF for an example of a random variable. Although we cannot use the PDF to simply calculate the probability the random variable equals, say, 1.5, it is possible to calculate the probability that the random variable is between 1.5 and any other value. The figure highlights the area under the PDF curve between 1.5 and 1.8. This area corresponds to the probability this random variable is between 1.5 and 1.8. In the next section we show example calculations of such probabilities based on PDFs from the normal distribution.[2]

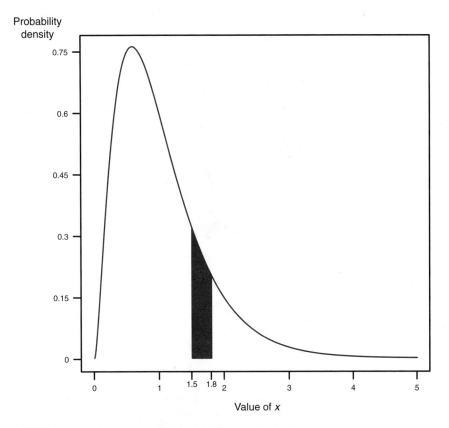

FIGURE A.1: An Example of a Probability Density Function (PDF)

---

[2] More formally, we can indicate a PDF as a function, $f(x)$, that is greater than zero for all values of x. Since the total area under the curve, we know that $\int_{-\infty}^{\infty} f(x)dx = 1$. The probability that the random variable x is between a and b is $\int_{a}^{b} f(x)dx = F(b) - F(a)$, where $F()$ is the integral of $f()$.

G. Normal Distributions

▶ standard normal distribution A normal distribution with a mean of zero and a variance (and standard error) of one.

We work a lot with the **standard normal distribution**. (Only to us stats geeks does "standard normal" not seem repetitive.) A normal distribution is a specific (and famous) type of PDF, and a standard normal distribution is a normal distribution with mean zero and a variance of one. The standard deviation of a standard normal distribution is also one, because the standard deviation is the square root of the variance.

One important use of the standard normal distribution is to calculate probabilities of observing standard normal random variables that are less than or equal to some number. We denote the function $\Phi(x) = \Pr(X < Z)$ as the probability that a standard normal random variable X is less than Z. This is known as the cumulative distribution function (CDF) because it indicates the probability of seeing a random variable less than some value. It simply expresses the area under a PDF curve to the left of some value.

Figure A.2 shows four examples of the use of the CDF for standard normal PDFs. Panel (a) shows $\Phi(0)$, which is the probability that a standard normal

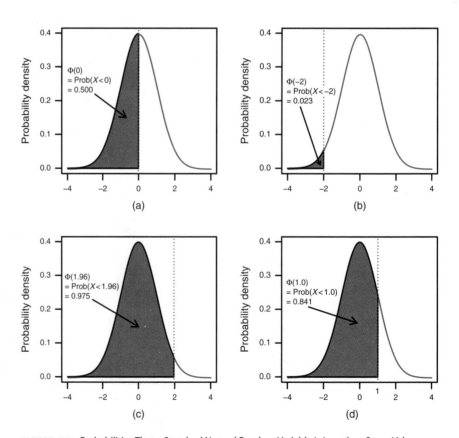

FIGURE A.2: Probabilities That a Standard Normal Random Variable Is Less than Some Value

random variable will be less than 0. It is the area under the PDF to the left of the zero. We can see that it is half the total area, meaning that the area to the left of the zero is 0.50 and, therefore, the probability of observing a value of a standard normal random variable that is less than 0 is 0.50. Panel (b) shows $\Phi(-2)$, which is the probability that a standard normal random variable will be less than -2. It is the proportion of the total area that is left of -2, which is 0.023. Panel (c) shows $\Phi(1.96)$, which is the probability that a standard normal random variable will be less than 1.96. It is 0.975. Panel (d) shows $\Phi(1)$, which is the probability that a standard normal random variable will be less than 1. It is 0.841.

We can also use our knowledge of the standard normal distribution to calculate the probability that $\hat{\beta}_1$ is greater than some value. The trick here is to recall that if the probability of something happening is P, then the probability of its not happening is $1 - P$. This property tells us that if there is a 15 percent chance of rain, then there is a 85 percent probability of no rain.

To calculate the probability that a standard normal variable is greater than some value, Z, use $1 - \Phi(Z)$. Figure A.3 shows four examples. Panel (a) shows

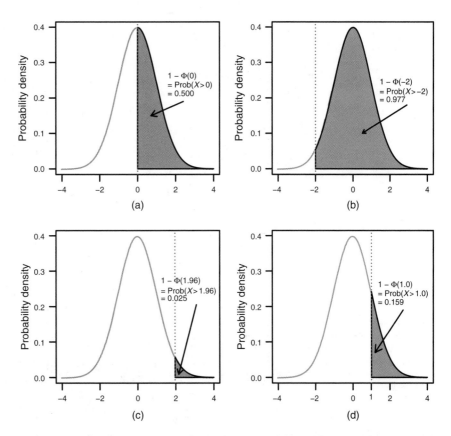

FIGURE A.3: Probabilities That a Standard Normal Random Variable Is Greater than Some Value

$1 - \Phi(0)$, which is the probability that a standard normal random variable will be greater than zero. This probability is 0.50. Panel (b) highlights $1 - \Phi(-2)$, which is the probability that a standard normal random variable will be greater than –2. It is 0.98. Panel (c) shows $\Phi(1.96)$, which is the probability that a standard normal random variable will be greater than 1.96. It is 0.025. Panel (d) shows $\Phi(1)$, which is the probability that a standard normal random variable will be greater than 1. It is 0.16.

Figure A.4 shows some key information about the standard normal distribution. In the left-hand column of the figure's table are some numbers, and in the right-hand column are the corresponding probabilities that a standard normal random variable will be less than the respective numbers. There is, for example, a 0.01 probability that a standard normal random variable will be less than –2.32.

SD = number of standard deviations above or below the mean, β_1	Probability $\hat{\beta}_1 \le SD$	
−3.00	0.0001	
−2.58	0.005	
−2.32	0.010	⇒
−2.00	0.023	
−1.96	0.025	
−1.64	0.050	
−1.28	0.100	
−1.00	0.160	
0.00	0.500	⇒
1.00	0.840	
1.28	0.900	
1.64	0.950	
1.96	0.975	⇒
2.00	0.977	
2.32	0.990	
2.58	0.995	
3.00	0.999	

Suppose $\hat{\beta}_1$ is distributed as standard normal. The values in the right-hand column are the probabilities $\hat{\beta}_1$ is less than the value in left-hand column. For example, the probability $\hat{\beta}_1 < -2.33 = 0.010$.

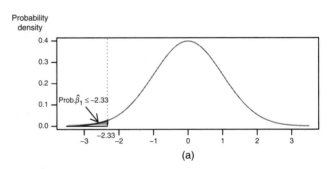

(a)

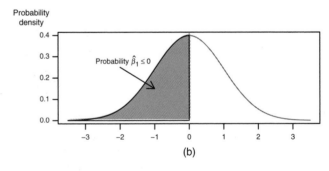

(b)

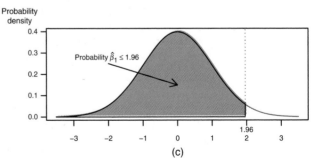

(c)

FIGURE A.4: Standard Normal Distribution

We can see this graphically in panel (a). In the top bell-shaped curve, the portion that is to the left of –2.32 is shaded. It is about 1 percent.

Because the standard deviation of a standard normal is 1, all the numbers in the left-hand column can be considered as the number of standard deviations above or below the mean. That is, the number -1 refers to a point that is a single standard deviation below the mean, and the number $+3$ refers to a point that is 3 standard deviations above the mean.

The third row of the table shows that there is a probability of 0.01 that we'll observe a value less than –2.32 standard deviations below the mean. Going down to the shaded row SD = 0.00, we see that if $\hat{\beta}_1$ is standard normally distributed, it has a 0.50 probability of being below 0. This probability is intuitive—the normal distribution is symmetric, and we have the same chance of seeing something above its mean as below it. Panel (b) shows this graphically.

In the last shaded row, where SD = 1.96, we see that there is a 0.975 probability that a standard normal random variable will be less than 1.96. Panel (c) shows this graphically, with 97.5 percent of the standard normal distribution shaded. We see this value a lot in statistics because twice the probability of being greater than 1.96 is 0.05, which is a commonly used significance level for hypothesis testing.

We can convert any normally distributed random variable to a standard normally distributed random variable. This process, known as *standardizing values*, is pretty easy. This trick is valuable because it allows us to use the intuition and content of Figure A.4 to work with any normal distribution, whatever its mean and standard deviation.

For example, suppose we have a normal random variable with a mean of 10 and a standard deviation of 1 and we want to know the probability of observing a value less than 8. From common sense, we realize that in this case 8 is 2 standard deviations below the mean. Hence we can use Figure A.4 to see that the probability of observing a value less than 8 from a normal distribution with mean 10 and standard deviation of one is 0.023; accordingly, the fourth row of the table shows that the probability a standard normal random variable is less than –2 is 0.023.

How did we get there? First, subtract the mean from the value in question to see how far it is from the mean. Then divide this quantity by the standard deviation to calculate how many standard deviations away from the mean it is. More generally, for any given number B drawn from a distribution with mean β_1 and standard deviation, $se(\hat{\beta}_1)$, we can calculate the number of standard deviations B is away from the mean via the following equation:

$$\text{Standard deviations from mean} = \frac{B - \beta_1}{se(\hat{\beta}_1)} \qquad (A.2)$$

Notice that the β_1 has no hat but $se(\hat{\beta}_1)$ does. Seems odd, doesn't it? There is a logic to it. We'll be working a lot with hypothetical values of β_1, asking, for example, what the probability $\hat{\beta}_1$ is greater than some number would be if the

TABLE A.1 **Examples of Standardized Values**

Number	Hypothetical Distribution β_1	$se(\hat{\beta}_1)$	Standardized B	Description
3	0	3	$\dfrac{3-0}{3}=1$	3 is 1 standard deviation above the mean of 0 when $se(\hat{\beta}_1)=3$
1	0	3	$\dfrac{1-0}{1}=0.33$	1 is 0.33 standard deviation above the mean of 0 when $se(\hat{\beta}_1)=3$
7	4	3	$\dfrac{7-4}{3}=1$	7 is 1 standard deviation above the mean of 4 when $se(\hat{\beta}_1)=3$
1	4	3	$\dfrac{1-4}{3}=-1$	1 is 1 standard deviation below the mean of 4 when $se(\hat{\beta}_1)=3$
6	8	2	$\dfrac{6-8}{2}=-1$	6 is 1 standard deviation below the mean of 8 when $se(\hat{\beta}_1)=2$
1	8	2	$\dfrac{1-8}{2}=-3.5$	1 is 3.5 standard deviations below the mean of 8 when $se(\hat{\beta}_1)=2$

true β_1 were zero. But since we'll want to work with the precision implied by our actual data, we'll use $se(\hat{\beta}_1)$.[3]

To get comfortable with converting the distribution of $\hat{\beta}_1$ to the standard normal distribution, consider the examples in Table A.1. In the first example (the first two rows), β_1 is 0 and the standard error of $\hat{\beta}_1$ is 3. Recall that the standard error of $\hat{\beta}_1$ measures the width of the $\hat{\beta}_1$ distribution. In this case, 3 is 1 standard deviation above the mean and 1 is 0.33 standard deviation above the mean.

In the third and fourth rows of Table A.1, $\beta_1 = 4$ and the standard deviation is 3. In this case, 7 is 1 standard deviation above the mean and 1 is 1 standard deviation below the mean. In the bottom portion of the table (the last two rows), β_1 is 8 and the standard deviation of $\hat{\beta}_1$ is 2. In this case, 6 is 1 standard deviation below the mean and 1 is 3.5 standard deviations below the mean.

To calculate $\Phi(Z)$ we use a table such as the one in Figure A.4 or, more likely, computer software as discussed in the Computing Corner of this appendix.

---

[3] Another thing that can be hard to get used to is the mixing of standard deviation and standard error. Standard deviation measures the variability of a distribution and, in the case of the distribution of $\hat{\beta}_1$, its standard deviation is the $se(\hat{\beta}_1)$. The distinction between standard deviation and standard error seems larger when calculating the mean of a variable. The standard deviation of X indicates the variability of X while the standard error of a sample mean indicates the variability of the estimate of the mean. The standard error of the mean depends on the sample size while the standard deviation of X is only a measure of the variability of X. Happily, this distinction tends not to be a problem in regression.

REMEMBER THIS

1. A standard normal distribution is a normal distribution with a mean of zero and a standard deviation of one.

   (a) Any normally distributed random variable can be converted to a variable distributed according to a standard normal distribution.

   (b) If $\hat{\beta}_1$ is distributed normally with mean β and standard deviation $\text{se}(\hat{\beta}_1)$, then $\frac{\hat{\beta}-\beta}{\text{se}(\hat{\beta}_1)}$ will be distributed as a standard normal random variable.

   (c) Converting random variables to standard normal random variables allows us to use standard normal tables to discuss any normal distribution.

2. To calculate the probability $\hat{\beta}_1 \leq B$, where B is any number of interest, do the following:

   (a) Convert B to the number of standard deviations above or below the mean using $\frac{B-\beta_1}{\text{se}(\hat{\beta}_1)}$.

   (b) Use the table in Figure A.4 or software to the calculate probability that $\hat{\beta}_1$ is less than B in standardized terms.

3. To calculate the probability that $\hat{\beta}_1 > B$, use the fact that the probability $\hat{\beta}_1$ is greater than B is 1 minus the probability that $\hat{\beta}_1$ is less than or equal to B.

Review Questions

1. What is the probability that a standard normal random variable is less than or equal to 1.64?

2. What is the probability that a standard normal random variable is less than or equal to −1.28?

3. What is the probability that a standard normal random variable is greater than 1.28?

4. What is the probability that a normal random variable with a mean of zero and a standard deviation of 2 is less than −4?

5. What is the probability that a normal random variable with a mean of zero and a variance of 9 is less than −3?

6. Approximately what is the probability that a normal random variable with a mean of 7.2 and a variance of 4 is less than 9?

H. Other Useful Distributions

The normal distribution may be the most famous distribution, but it is not the only workhorse distribution in statistical analysis. In this section we briefly discuss three other distributions that are particularly common in econometric practice, the χ^2, t, and F distributions. Each is derived from the normal distribution.

The χ^2 distribution

▶ **χ^2 distribution** A probability distribution that characterizes the distribution of squared standard normal random variables.

The **χ^2 distribution** describes the distribution of squared normal variables. The distribution of a squared standard normal random variable is a χ^2 distribution with one degree of freedom. The components of the sum of n independent squared standard normal random variables are distributed according to a χ^2 distribution with n degrees of freedom.

The χ^2 distribution arises in many different statistical contexts. We'll show that it is a component of the all-important t distribution. The χ^2 distribution also arises when we conduct likelihood ratio tests for MLE models.

The shape of the χ^2 distribution varies according to the degrees of freedom. Figure A.5 shows two examples of χ^2 distributions. Panel (a) shows a χ^2 distribution with 2 degrees of freedom. We have highlighted the most extreme 5 percent of the distribution, which demonstrates that the critical value from a $\chi^2(2)$ distribution is roughly 6. Panel (b) shows a χ^2 distribution with 4 degrees of freedom. The critical value from a $\chi^2(4)$ distribution is around 9.5.

The Computing Corner in Chapter 12 (pages 437 and 439) shows how to identify critical values from an χ^2 distribution. Software will often, but not always, provide critical values for us automatically.

The *t* distribution

The t distribution characterizes the distribution of the ratio of a normal random variable and the square root of a χ^2 random variable divided by its degrees of freedom. While such a ratio may seem to be a pretty obscure combination of things to worry about, we've seen in Section 4.2 that the t distribution is incredibly useful. We know that our OLS coefficients (among other estimators) are normally distributed. We also know (although we talk about this less) that the estimates of the standard errors are distributed according to a χ^2 distribution. Since we need to standardize our OLS coefficients by dividing by our standard error estimates, we want to know the distribution of the ratio of the coefficient divided by the standard error.

Formally, if z is a standard normal random variable and x is a χ^2 variable with n degrees of freedom, the following represents a t distribution with n degrees of freedom:

$$t(n) = \frac{z}{\sqrt{x/n}}$$

Virtually every statistical software package automatically produces t statistics for every coefficient estimated. We can also use t tests to test hypotheses about

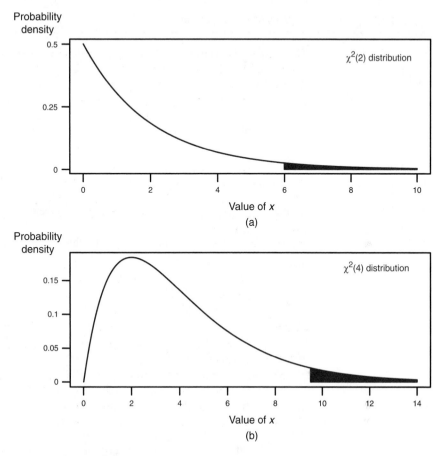

Probability density

$\chi^2(2)$ distribution

Value of x

(a)

Probability density

$\chi^2(4)$ distribution

Value of x

(b)

FIGURE A.5: Two χ^2 Distributions

multiple coefficients, although in Section 7.4 we focused on F tests for this purpose on the grounds of convenience.

The shape of the t distribution is quite similar to the normal distribution. As shown in Figure 4.3 in Chapter 4, the t distribution is a bit wider than the normal distribution. This means that extreme values are more likely to be from a t distribution than from a normal distribution. However, the difference is modest for small sample sizes and disappears as the sample size increases.

The *F* distribution

▶ **F distribution** A probability distribution that characterizes the distribution of a ratio of χ^2 random variables.

The **F distribution** characterizes the distribution of a ratio of two χ^2 random variables divided by their degrees of freedom. The distribution is named in honor of legendary statistician R. A. Fisher.

Formally, if x_1 and x_2 are independent χ^2 random variables with n_1 and n_2 degrees of freedom, respectively, the following represents an F distribution with degrees of freedom n_1 and n_2:

$$F(n_1, n_2) = \frac{x_1/n_1}{x_2/n_2}$$

Since χ^2 variables are positive, a ratio of two of them must be positive as well, meaning that random variables following F distributions are greater than or equal to zero.

An interesting feature of the F distribution is that the square of a t-distributed variable with n degrees of freedom follows an $F(1,n)$ distribution. To see this, note that a t-distributed variable is a normal random variable divided by the square root of a χ^2 random variable. Squaring the t-distributed variable gives us a squared normal in the numerator, which is χ^2, and a χ^2 in the denominator. In other words, this gives us the ratio of two χ^2 random variables, which follow an F distribution. We used this fact when noting on page 304 that in certain cases we can square a t statistic to produce an F statistic that can be compared to a rule of thumb about F statistics in the first stage of 2SLS analyses.

We use the F distribution when doing F tests which, among other things, allows us to test hypotheses involving multiple parameters. We discussed F tests in Section 7.4.

The F distribution depends on two degrees of freedom parameters. In the F test examples, the degrees of freedom for the test statistic depends on the number of restrictions on the parameters and the sample size. The order of the degrees of freedom is important and is explained in our discussion of F tests.

The F distribution does not have an easily identifiable shape like the normal and t distributions. Instead, its shape changes rather dramatically, depending on the degrees of freedom. Figure A.6 plots four examples of F distributions, each with different degrees of freedom. For each panel we highlight the extreme 5 percent of the distribution, providing a sense of the values necessary to reject the null hypotheses for each case. Panel (a) shows an F distribution with degrees of freedom equal to 3 and 2,000. This would be the distribution of an F statistic if we were testing a null hypothesis that $\beta_1 = \beta_2 = \beta_3 = 0$ based on a data set with 2,010 observations and 10 parameters to be estimated. The critical value is 2.61, meaning that an F test statistic greater than 2.61 would lead us to reject the null hypothesis. Panel (b) displays an F distribution with degrees of freedom equal to 18 and 300, and so on.

The Computing Corner in Chapter 7 on pages 237 and 238 shows how to identify critical values from an F distribution. Often, but not always, software will automatically provide critical values.

I. Sampling

Section 3.2 of Chapter 3 discussed two sources of variation in our estimates: sampling randomness and modeled randomness. This section elaborates on sampling randomness.

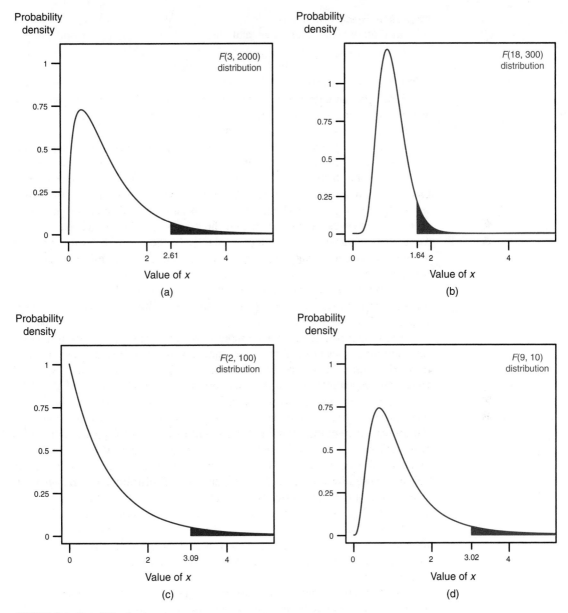

FIGURE A.6: Four *F* Distributions

Imagine that we are trying to figure out some feature of a given population. For example, suppose we are trying to ascertain the average age of everyone in the world at a given time. If we had (accurate) data from every single person, we'd be done. Obviously, that's not going to happen, so we take a random sample. Since this random sample will not contain every single person, the average age of people from it probably will not exactly match the population average. And if we were to take another random sample, it's likely that we'd get a different average because we'd have different people in our sample. Maybe the first time our sample contained more babies than usual, and the second time we got the world's oldest living person.

The genius of the sampling perspective is that we can characterize the degree of randomness we should observe in our random sample. The variation will depend on the sample size we observe and on the underlying variation in the population.

A useful exercise is to take some population, say the students in your econometrics class, and gather information about every person in the population for some variable. Then if we draw random samples from this population we will see that the mean of the variable in the sampled group will bounce around for each random sample we draw. The amazing thing about statistics is that we will be able to say certain things about the mean of the averages we get across the random samples and the variance of the averages. If the sample size is large, we will be able to approximate the distribution of these averages with a normal distribution with a variance we can calculate based on the sample size and the underlying variance in the overall population.

This logic applies to regression coefficients as well. Hence if we want to know the relationship between age and wealth in the whole world, we can draw a random sample and know that we will have variation related to the fact that we observe only a subset of the target population. And recall from Section 6.1 that OLS easily estimates means and difference of means, so even our average-age example works in an OLS context.

It may be tempting to think of statistical analysis only in terms of sampling variation, but this is not very practical. First, it is not uncommon to observe an entire population. For example, if we want to know the relationship between education and wages in European countries from 2000 to 2014, we could probably come up with data for each country and year in our target population. And yet, we would be naive to believe that there is no uncertainty in our estimates. Hence there is almost always another source of randomness, something we referred to as modeled randomness in Section 3.2.

Second, the sampling paradigm requires that the samples from the underlying target population be random. If the sampling is not random, the type of observations that make their way into our analysis may systematically differ from the people or units that we do not observe, thus causing us to run the risk of introducing endogeneity. A classic example is observing the wages of women who work, but this subsample is unlikely to be a random sample from all women. The women who work are likely more ambitious, more financially dependent on working, or both.

Even public opinion polling data, a presumed bastion of random sampling, seldom provides random samples from underlying populations. Commercial polls often have response rates of less than 20 percent, and even academic surveys struggle to get response rates near 50 percent. It is reasonable to believe that the people who respond differ in economic, social, and personality traits, and thus simply attributing variation to sampling variation may be problematic.

So even though sampling variation is incredibly useful as an idealized source of randomness in our coefficient estimates, we should not limit ourselves to thinking of variation in coefficients solely in terms of sampling variation. Instead, it is useful to step back and write down a model that includes an error term representing uncertainty. If the observations are drawn from a truly random sample of the target population (*Hint*: they never are), we can proceed with thinking of uncertainty reflecting only sampling variation. However, if there is no random sampling, either because we don't have data on the full population or because the sample is not random, we can model the selection process and assess whether the non-random sampling process induced correlation between the independent variables and the error term. The Heckman selection model referenced in Chapter 10 (page 348) provides a framework for considering such issues. Such selection is very tricky to assess, however, and researchers continue to seek the best way to address the issue.

Further Reading

Rice (2007) is an excellent guide to probability theory as used in statistical analysis.

Key Terms

F distribution (533)

Probability density function (PDF) (524)

Standard normal distribution (526)

χ^2 Distribution (532)

Computing Corner

Excel

Sometimes Excel offers the quickest way to calculate quantities of interest related to the normal distribution.

- There are several ways to find the probability a standard normal is less than some value.

  1. Use the NORM.S.DIST function, which calculates the normal distribution. To produce the cumulative probability, which is the percent of the distribution to the left of the number indicated, use a 1 after the comma: =NORM.S.DIST(2, 1).

2. Use the NORMDIST function and indicate the mean and the standard deviation, which, for a standard normal, are 0 and 1, respectively. Use a 1 after the last comma to produce the cumulative probability, which is the percent of the distribution to the left of the number indicated: =NORMDIST(2, 0, 1, 1).

- For a nonstandard normal variable, use the NORMDIST function and indicate the mean and the standard deviation. For example, if the mean is 9 and the standard deviation is 3.2, the probability that this distribution will yield a random variable less than 7 is =NORMDIST(7, 9, 3.2, 1).

Stata

- To calculate the probability that a standard normal is less than some value in Stata, use the normal command. For example, display normal(2) will return the probability that a standard normal variable is less than 2.

- To calculate probabilities related to a normally distributed random variable with any mean and standard deviation, we can also standardize the variable manually. For example, display normal((7-9)/3.2) returns the probability that a normal variable with mean 9 and standard deviation 3.2 is less than 7.

R

- To calculate the probability that a standard normal is less than some value in R, use the pnorm command. For example, pnorm(2, mean= 1, sd=1) will return the probability that a standard normal variable is less than 2.

- To calculate probabilities related to a normally distributed random variable with any mean and standard deviation, we can also standardize the variable manually. For example, pnorm((7-9)/3.2) returns the probability that a normal variable with a mean of 9 and a standard deviation of 3.2 is less than 7.

CITATIONS AND ADDITIONAL NOTES

Student preface

- Page xxvi On the illusion of explanatory depth, see http://scienceblogs.com/mixingmemory/2006/11/the_illusion_of_explanatory_de.php.

Chapter 1

- Page 3 Gary Burtless (1995, 65) provides the initial motivation for this example—he used Twinkies.

- Page 21 See Burtless (1995, 77).

Chapter 3

- Page 45 Sides and Vavreck (2013) provide a great look at how theory can help cut through some of the overly dramatic pundit-speak on elections.

- Page 57 For a discussion of the central limit theorem and its connection to the normality of OLS coefficient estimates see, for example, Lumley et al. (2002). They note that for errors that are themselves nearly normal or do not have severe outliers, 80 or so observations is usually enough.

- Page 60 See, for example, biojournalism.com/2012/08/correlation-vs-causation/.

- Page 67 Stock and Watson (2011, 674) present examples of estimators that highlight the differences between bias and inconsistency. The estimators are silly, but they make the authors' point.

  - Suppose we tried to estimate the mean of a variable with the first observation in a sample. This will be unbiased because in expectation it will be equal to the average of the population. Recall that expectation can be thought of as the average value we would get for an estimator if we ran an experiment over and over again. This estimator will not be consistent, though, because no matter how many observations we have, we're using only the first observation, which means that the variance of the estimator will not get smaller as the sample size gets very large. So, yes, no one in their right mind would use this estimator, but it is nonetheless unbiased—but also inconsistent.

- Suppose we tried to estimate the mean of a variable with the sample mean plus $\frac{1}{N}$. This will be biased because the expectation of this estimator will be the population average plus $\frac{1}{N}$. However, this estimator will be consistent because the variance of a sample mean goes down as sample size increases, and the $\frac{1}{N}$ bit will go to zero as the sample size goes to infinity. Again, this is a nutty estimator that no one would use in practice, but it shows how it is possible for an estimator that is biased to be consistent.

Chapter 4

- Page 91 For a report on the Pasteur example, see Manzi (2012, 73) and http://pyramid.spd.louisville.edu/~eri/fos/Pasteur_Pouilly-le-fort.pdf.

- Page 98 The distribution of the standard error of $\hat{\beta}_1$ follows a χ^2 distribution. A normal random variable divided by a χ^2 random variable is distributed according to a t distribution.

- Page 109 The medical example is from Wilson and Butler (2007, 105).

Chapter 5

- Page 139 In Chapter 14 we show on page 485 that the bias term in a simplified example for a model with no constant is $E\left[\frac{\sum \epsilon_i X_i}{\sum X_i^2}\right]$. For the more standard case that includes a constant in the model, the bias term is $E\left[\frac{\sum \epsilon_i (X_i - \bar{X})}{\sum (X_i - \bar{X})^2}\right]$, which is the covariance of X and ϵ divided by the variance of X. See Greene (2003, 148) for a generalization of the omitted variable bias formula for any number of included and excluded variables.

- Page 154 Harvey's analysis uses other variables, including a measure of how ethnically and linguistically divided countries are and a measure of distance from the equator (which is often used in the literature to capture a historical pattern that countries close to equator have tended to have weaker political institutions).

Chapter 6

- Page 169 To formally show that the OLS $\hat{\beta}_1$ and $\hat{\beta}_0$ estimates are functions of the means of the treated and untreated groups requires a bit of a slog through some algebra. From page 49, we know that the bivariate OLS equation for the slope is $\hat{\beta}_1 = \frac{\sum_{i=1}^{N}(T_i - \bar{T})(Y_i - \bar{Y})}{\sum_{i=1}^{N}(T_i - \bar{T})^2}$, where we use T_i to indicate that our independent variable is a dummy variable (where $T_i = 1$ indicates a treated observation). We can break the sum into two parts, one part for $T_i = 1$ observations and the other for $T_i = 0$ observations. We'll also refer to $\overline{T}$ as p, where p indicates the percent of observations that were treated, which is the average of the dummy independent variable. (This is not strictly necessary, but it helpfully highlights the intuition that the average of our independent variable is the percent who were treated.)

$$\hat{\beta}_1 = \frac{\sum_{T_i=1}(T_i - p)(Y_i - \overline{Y})}{\sum_{i=1}^{N}(T_i - p)^2} + \frac{\sum_{T_i=0}(T_i - p)(Y_i - \overline{Y})}{\sum_{i=1}^{N}(T_i - p)^2}$$

For the $T_i = 1$ observations, $(T_i - p) = (1 - p)$ because, by definition, the value of T_i in this group is 1. For the $T_i = 0$ observations, $(T_i - p) = (-p)$ because, by definition, the value of T_i in this group is 0. We can pull these terms out of the summation because they do not vary across observations within each summation.

$$\hat{\beta}_1 = \frac{(1-p)\sum_{T_i=1}(Y_i - \overline{Y})}{\sum_{i=1}^{N}(T_i - p)^2} - \frac{p\sum_{T_i=0}(Y_i - \overline{Y})}{\sum_{i=1}^{N}(T_i - p)^2}$$

We can rewrite the denominator as $N_T(1 - p)$ where N_T is the number of individuals who were treated (and therefore have $T_1 = 1$).[1] We also break the equation into three parts, producing

$$\hat{\beta}_1 = \frac{(1-p)\sum_{T_i=1}Y_i}{N_T(1-p)} - \frac{(1-p)\sum_{T_i=1}\overline{Y}}{N_T(1-p)} - \frac{p\sum_{T_i=0}(Y_i - \overline{Y})}{N_T(1-p)}$$

The $(1 - p)$ in the numerator and denominator of the first and second terms cancel out. Note also that the sum of $\overline{Y}$ for the observations where $T_i = 1$ equals $N_T\overline{Y}$, allowing us to express the OLS estimate of $\hat{\beta}_1$ as

$$\hat{\beta}_1 = \frac{\sum_{T_i=1}Y_i}{N_T} - \overline{Y} - \frac{p\sum_{T_i=0}(Y_i - \overline{Y})}{N_T(1-p)}$$

We're almost there. Now note that $\frac{p}{N_T(1-p)}$ in the third term can be written as $\frac{1}{N_C}$, where N_C is the number of observations in the control group (for whom $T_i = 0$).[2] We denote the average of the treated group $\left(\frac{\sum_{T_i=1}^{N}Y_i}{N_T}\right)$ as $\overline{Y}_T$ and the average of

---

[1] To see this, rewrite $\sum_{i=1}^{N}(T_i - p)^2$ as $\sum_{i=1}^{N}T_i^2 - 2p\sum_{i=1}^{N}T_i - \sum_{i=1}^{N}p^2$. Note that both $\sum_{i=1}^{N}T_i^2$ and $\sum_{i=1}^{N}T_i$ equal N_T because the squared value of a dummy variable is equal to itself and because the sum of a dummy variable is equal to the number of observations for which $T_i = 1$. We also use the facts that $\sum_{i=1}^{N}p^2 = Np^2$ and $p = \frac{N_T}{N}$, which allows us to write the denominator as $N_T - 2\frac{N_T^2}{N} + \frac{NN_T^2}{N^2}$. Simplifying yields $N_T(1 - p)$.

[2] To see this, substitute $\frac{N_T}{N}$ for p and simplify, noting that $N_C = N - N_T$.

the control group $\left(\frac{\sum_{T_i=0}^{N} Y_i}{N_C}\right)$ as $\overline{Y}_C$. We can rewrite our equation as

$$\hat{\beta}_1 = \overline{Y}_T - \overline{Y} - \frac{\sum_{T_i=0} Y_i}{N_C} + \frac{\sum_{T_i=0} \overline{Y}}{N_C}$$

Using fact that $\sum_{T_i=0} \overline{Y} = N_C \overline{Y}$, we can cancel some terms and (finally!) get our result:

$$\hat{\beta}_1 = \overline{Y}_T - \overline{Y}_C$$

To show that $\hat{\beta}_0$ is $\overline{Y}_C$, use Equation 3.5 from page 50, noting that $\overline{Y} = \frac{\overline{Y}_T N_T + \overline{Y}_C N_C}{N}$.

- Page 170 Discussions of non-OLS difference of means tests sometimes get bogged down into whether the variance is the same across the treatment and control groups. If the variance varies across treatment and control groups, we should adjust our analysis according to the heteroscedasticity that will be present.

- Page 182 This data is from from Persico, Postlewaite, and Silverman (2004). Results are broadly similar even when we exclude outliers with very high salaries.

- Page 193 See Kam and Franceze (2007, 48) for the derivation of the variance of estimated effects. The variance of $\hat{\beta}_1 + D_i \hat{\beta}_3$ is $\text{var}(\hat{\beta}_1) + D_i^2 \text{var}(\hat{\beta}_3) + 2D_i \text{cov}(\hat{\beta}_1, \hat{\beta}_3)$, where cov is the covariance of $\hat{\beta}_1$ and $\hat{\beta}_3$ (see variance fact 3 on page 523).

  - In Stata, we can display $\text{cov}(\hat{\beta}_1, \hat{\beta}_3)$ with the following commands:
    ```
    regress Y X1 D X1D
    matrix V = get(VCE)
    disp V[3,1]
    ```
    For more details, see Kam and Franceze (2007, 136–146).

  - In R, generate a regression result object (e.g., OLSResults = lm(Y ~ X1 D X1D)) and use the vcov(OLSResults) subcommand to display the variance-covariance matrix for the coefficient estimates. The covariance of $\hat{\beta}_1$ and $\hat{\beta}_3$ is the entry in the column labeled X1 and the row labeled X1D.

Chapter 7

- Page 210 The data on life expectancy and GDP per capita are from the World Bank's World Development Indicators database available at http://data.worldbank.org/indicator/.

- Page 215 Temperature data is from NASA (2012).

- Page 222 In log-linear models, a one-unit increase in X is associated with a β_1 percent increase in Y. The underlying model is funky; it is a multiplicative model of e's raised to the elements of the log-linear model:

$$Y = e^{\beta_0} e^{\beta_1 X} e^{\epsilon}$$

If we use the fact that $\log(e^A e^B e^C) = A + B + C$ and log both sides, we get the log-linear formulation:

$$\ln Y = \beta_0 + \beta_1 X + \epsilon$$

If we take the derivative of Y with respect to X in the original model, we get

$$\frac{dY}{dX} = e^{\beta_0} \beta_1 e^{\beta_1 X} e^{\epsilon}$$

Divide both sides by Y so that the change in Y is expressed as a percentage change in Y and then cancel, yielding

$$\frac{dY/Y}{dX} = \frac{e^{\beta_0} \beta_1 e^{\beta_1 X} e^{\epsilon}}{e^{\beta_0} e^{\beta_1 X} e^{\epsilon}}$$

$$\frac{dY/Y}{dX} = \beta_1$$

Chapter 8

- Page 255 See Bailey, Strezhnev, and Voeten (2015) for United Nations voting data.

Chapter 9

- Page 287 Endogeneity is a central concern of Medicaid literature. See, for example, Currie and Gruber (1996), Finkelstein et al. (2012), and Baicker et al. (2013).

- Page 309 The reduced form is simply the model rewritten to be only a function of the nonendogenous variables (which are the X and Z variables, not the Y variables). This equation isn't anything fancy, although it takes a bit of math to see where it comes from. Here goes:

  1. Insert Equation 9.12 into Equation 9.13:

$$Y_{2i} = \gamma_0 + \gamma_1(\beta_0 + \beta_1 Y_{2i} + \beta_2 X_{1i} + \beta_3 Z_{1i} + \epsilon_{1i}) + \gamma_2 X_{1i} + \gamma_3 Z_{2i} + \epsilon_{2i}$$

2. Rearrange by multiplying by the γ_1 term as appropriate and combining terms for X_1:

$$Y_{2i} = \gamma_0 + \gamma_1\beta_0 + \gamma_1\beta_1 Y_{2i} + (\gamma_1\beta_2 + \gamma_2)X_{1i} + \gamma_1\beta_3 Z_{1i} + \gamma_1\epsilon_{1i} + \gamma_3 Z_{2i} + \epsilon_{2i}$$

3. Rearrange some more by moving all Y_2 terms to the left side of the equation:

$$Y_{2i} - \gamma_1\beta_1 Y_{2i} = \gamma_0 + \gamma_1\beta_0 + (\gamma_1\beta_2 + \gamma_2)X_{1i} + \gamma_1\beta_3 Z_{1i} + \gamma_1\epsilon_{1i} + \gamma_3 Z_{2i} + \epsilon_{2i}$$
$$Y_{2i}(1 - \gamma_1\beta_1) = \gamma_0 + \gamma_1\beta_0 + (\gamma_1\beta_2 + \gamma_2)X_{1i} + \gamma_1\beta_3 Z_{1i} + \gamma_1\epsilon_{1i} + \gamma_3 Z_{2i} + \epsilon_{2i}$$

4. Divide both sides by $(1 - \gamma_1\beta_1)$:

$$Y_{2i} = \frac{\gamma_0 + \gamma_1\beta_0 + (\gamma_1\beta_2 + \gamma_2)X_{1i} + \gamma_1\beta_3 Z_{1i} + \gamma_1\epsilon_{1i} + \gamma_3 Z_{2i} + \epsilon_{2i}}{(1 - \gamma_1\beta_1)}$$

5. Relabel $\frac{\gamma_0 + \gamma_1\beta_0}{(1-\gamma_1\beta_1)}$ as π_0, $\frac{(\gamma_1\beta_2+\gamma_2)}{(1-\gamma_1\beta_1)}$ as π_1, $\frac{\gamma_1\beta_3}{(1-\gamma_1\beta_1)}$ as π_2, and $\frac{\gamma_3}{(1-\gamma_1\beta_1)}$ as π_3 and combine the ϵ terms into $\tilde{\epsilon}$:

$$Y_{2i} = \pi_0 + \pi_1 X_{1i} + \pi_2 Z_{1i} + \pi_3 Z_{2i} + \tilde{\epsilon}_i$$

This "reduced form" equation isn't a causal model in any way. The π coefficients are crazy mixtures of the coefficients in Equations 9.12 and 9.13, which are the equations that embody the story we are trying to evaluate. The reduced form equation is simply a useful way to write down the first-stage model.

Chapter 10

- Page 350 See Newhouse (1993) and Gerber and Green (2012, 212–214) for more on the RAND experiment.

Chapter 12

- Page 415 A good place to start a consideration of MLE is with the name. *Maximum* is, well, maximum; *likelihood* refers to the probability of observing the data we observe; and *estimation* is, well, estimation.

  For most people, the new bit is the likelihood. The concept is actually quite close to ordinary usage. Roughly 20 percent of the U.S. population is under 15. What is the likelihood that when we pick three people randomly, we get two people under 15 and one over 15? The likelihood is $L = 0.2 * 0.2 * 0.8 = 0.03$. In other words, if we pick three people at random in the United States, there is a 3 percent chance (or, "likelihood") we will observe two people under 15 and one over 15.

  We can apply this concept when we do not know the underlying probability. Suppose that we want to figure out what proportion of the population has health insurance. Let's call $p_{insured}$ the probability that someone is insured (which is simply the proportion of insured in the United States). Suppose we randomly select three people, ask them if they are insured, and find out that two are insured and one is not. The probability (or "likelihood") of observing that combination is

$$L = p_{insured} * p_{insured} * (1 - p_{insured}) = p_{insured}^2 - p_{insured}^3$$

MLE finds an estimate of $p_{insured}$ that *maximizes* the likelihood of observing the data we actually observed.

We can get a feel for what values lead to high or low likelihoods by trying out a few possibilities. If our estimate were $p_{insured} = 0$, the likelihood, L, would be 0. That's a silly guess. If our estimate were $p_{insured} = 0.5$, then $L = 0.5 * 0.5 * (1 - 0.5) = 0.125$, which is better. If we chose $p_{insured} = 0.7$, then $L = 0.7 * 0.7 * 0.3 = 0.147$, which is even better. But if we chose, $p_{insured} = 0.9$, then $L = 0.9 * 0.9 * 0.1 = 0.081$, which is not as high as some of our other guesses.

Conceivably we could keep plugging different values of $p_{insured}$ into the likelihood equation until we found the best value. Or, calculus gives us tools to quickly find maxima.[3] When we observe two people with insurance and one without, the value of $p_{insured}$ that maximizes the likelihood is $\frac{2}{3}$ which, by the way, is the common-sense estimate when we know that two of three observed people are insured.

To use MLE to estimate a probit model, we extend this logic. Instead of estimating a single probability parameter ($p_{insured}$ in our example above) we estimate the probability $Y_i = 1$ as a function of independent variables. In other words, we substitute $\Phi(\beta_0 + \beta_1 X_i)$ for $p_{insured}$ into the likelihood equation just given. In this case, the thing we are trying to learn about is no longer $p_{insured}$; it's is now the β's that the determine the probability for each individual based on their respective X_i values.

If we observe two people who are insured and one who is not, we have

$$L = \Phi(\beta_0 + \beta_1 X_1) * \Phi(\beta_0 + \beta_1 X_2) * (1 - \Phi(\beta_0 + \beta_1 X_3))$$

where $\Phi(\beta_0 + \beta_1 X_1)$ is the probability that person 1 is insured (where X_1 refers to the value of X for the first person rather than a separate variable X_1, as we typically use the notation elsewhere), $\Phi(\beta_0 + \beta_1 X_2)$ is the probability that person is 2 insured, and $(1 - \Phi(\beta_0 + \beta_1 X_3))$ is the probability that person 3 is not insured.

MLE finds the $\hat{\beta}$ that maximizes the likelihood, L. The actual estimation process is complicated; again, that's why computers are our friends.

- Page 421 To use the average-case approach, create a single "average" person for whom the value of each independent variable is the average of that independent variable. We calculate a fitted probability for this person. Then we add one to the value of X_1 for this average person and calculate how much the fitted probability goes up. The downside of the average-case approach is that in the real data the

---

[3] Here's the formal way to do this via calculus. First, calculate the derivative of the likelihood with respect to p: $\frac{\partial L}{\partial p} = 2p_{insured} - 3p_{insured}^2$. Second, set the derivative to zero and solve for $p_{insured}$; this yields $p_{insured} = \frac{2}{3}$.

variables might typically cluster together, with the result that no one is average across all variables. It's also kind of weird because dummy variables for the "average" person will between 0 and 1 even though no single observation will have any value other than 0 and 1. This means, for example, that the "average" person will be 0.52 female and 0.85 right-handed and so forth.

To interpret probit coefficients using the average-case approach, use the following guide:

- If X_1 is continuous:

    1. Calculate P_1 as the fitted probability by using $\hat{\beta}$ and assuming that all variables are at their average values. This is

    $$\Phi(\hat{\beta}_0 + \hat{\beta}_1 \overline{X}_1 + \hat{\beta}_2 \overline{X}_2 + \hat{\beta}_3 \overline{X}_3 + \cdots)$$

    2. Calculate P_2 as the fitted probability by using $\hat{\beta}$, assuming that $X_1 = \overline{X}_1 + 1$ and all other variables are at their average values. This is

    $$\Phi(\hat{\beta}_0 + \hat{\beta}_1 (\overline{X}_1 + 1) + \hat{\beta}_2 \overline{X}_2 + \hat{\beta}_3 \overline{X}_3 + \cdots)$$

    Sometimes it makes more sense to increase X_1 by a standard deviation of X_1 rather than simply by one. For example, if the scale of X_1 is in the millions of dollars, increasing it by 1 will produce the tiniest of changes in fitted probability even when the effect of X_1 is large.

    3. The difference $P_2 - P_1$ is the estimated effect of an increase of one standard deviation in X_1, all other variables constant.

- If X_1 is a dummy variable:

    1. Calculate P_1 as the fitted probability by using $\hat{\beta}$ and assuming that $X_1 = 0$ and all other variables are at their average values. This is

    $$\Phi(\hat{\beta}_0 + \hat{\beta}_1 \times 0 + \hat{\beta}_2 \overline{X}_2 + \hat{\beta}_3 \overline{X}_3 + \cdots)$$

    2. Calculate P_2 as the fitted probability by using $\hat{\beta}$ and assuming that $X_1 = 1$ and all other variables are at their average values. This is

    $$\Phi(\hat{\beta}_0 + \hat{\beta}_1 \times 1 + \hat{\beta}_2 \overline{X}_2 + \hat{\beta}_3 \overline{X}_3 + \cdots)$$

    3. The difference $P_2 - P_1$ is the estimated effect of a one-unit increase in X_1, all other variables constant.

If X_1 is a dummy variable, the command `margins, dydx(X1) atmeans` will produce an estimate by the average-case method of the effect of a change in the dummy variable. If X_1 is continuous, the command `margins, dydx(X1) atmeans` will produce an average-case-method estimate of the marginal-effect of a change in the variable.

- Page 421 The marginal-effects approach uses calculus to determine the slope of the fitted line. Obviously the slope of the probit-fitted line varies, so we have to determine a reasonable point to calculate this slope. In the observed-value approach, we find the slope at the point defined by actual values of all the independent variables. This will be $\frac{\partial \text{Prob}(Y_i=1)}{\partial X_1}$. We know that the $\text{Prob}(Y_i = 1)$ is a CDF, and one of the nice properties of a CDF is that the derivative is simply the PDF. (We can see this graphically in Figure 12.5 by noting that if we increase the number on the horizontal axis by a small amount, the CDF will increase by the value of the PDF at that point.) Applying that property plus the chain rule, we get $\frac{\partial \Phi(\hat{\beta}_0 + \hat{\beta}_1 X_{1i} + \hat{\beta}_2 X_{2i})}{\partial X_1} = \phi(\hat{\beta}_0 + \hat{\beta}_1 X_{1i} + \hat{\beta}_2 X_{2i})\hat{\beta}_1$, where $\phi()$ is the normal PDF (ϕ is the lowercase Greek phi). Hence the marginal effect of increasing X_1 at the observed value is $\phi(\hat{\beta}_0 + \hat{\beta}_1 X_{1i} + \hat{\beta}_2 X_{2i})\hat{\beta}_1$.

The discrete-differences approach is an approximation to the marginal-effects approach. If the scale of X_1 is large, such that an increase of 1 unit is small, the marginal-effects and discrete-differences approach will yield similar results. If the scale of X_1 is small, such that an increase of 1 unit is a relatively large increase, the results from the marginal-effects and discrete-differences approaches may differ noticeably.

We show how to calculate marginal effects in Stata on page 436 and in R on page 438.

Chapter 13

- Page 451 Another form of correlated errors is spatial autocorrelation, which occurs when the error for one observation is correlated with the error for another observation that is spatially close to it. If we polled two people per household, there may be spatial autocorrelation because those who live close to each other (and sleep in the same bed!) may have correlated errors. This kind of situation can arise with geography-based data, such as state- or county-level data, because certain unmeasured similarities (meaning stuff in the error term) may be common within regions. The consequences of spatial autocorrelation are similar to the consequences of serial autocorrelation. Spatial autocorrelation does *not* cause bias. Spatial autocorrelation does cause the conventional standard error equation for OLS coefficients to be incorrect. The easiest first step for dealing with this situation is simply to include a dummy variable for region. Often this step will capture any regional correlations not captured by the other independent variables. A more technically complex way of dealing with this situation is via spatial regression statistical models. The intuition underlying these models is similar to that for serial correlation, but the math is typically harder. See, for example, Tam Cho and Gimpel (2012).

- Page 455 Wooldridge (2009, 416) discusses inclusion of X variables in this test.

- Page 459 Wooldridge (2009, 424) notes that the ρ-transformed approach also requires that ϵ_t not be correlated with X_{t-1} or X_{t+1}. In a ρ-transformed model, the independent variable is $X_t - \rho X_{t-1}$ and the error is $\epsilon_t - \rho\epsilon_{t-1}$. If the lagged error term (ϵ_{t-1}) is correlated with X_t, then the independent variable in the ρ-transformed model will be correlated with the error term in the ρ-transformed model.

- Page 464 The so-called Breusch-Godfrey test is a more general test for autocorrelation. See, for example, Greene (2003, 269).

- Page 467 R code to generate multiple simulations with unit root (or other) time series variables:

```
Nsim = 200                      # Number of obs. per simulation
SimCount = 100                  # Number of simulations
S = rep(NA, SimCount)           # Stores t stats
for(s in 1:SimCount){           # Loop thru simulations
G = 1.0                         # 1 for unit root; <1 othwerise
Y = 0                           # Start value for Y
X = 0                           # Start value for X
for(i in 1:Nsim){               # Loop
Y = c(Y, G*Y[i-1] + rnorm(1))   # Generate Y
X = c(X, G*X[i-1] + rnorm(1))   # Generate X
S[s]=summary(lm(Y X))$coef[2,3] # Store t stats
}                               # End s loop
sum((abs(S)>2))/SimCount        # % simulations w/t stat > 2
```

- Page 469 For more on the Dickey-Fuller test and its critical values, see Greene (2003, 638).

Chapter 14

- Page 496 The attenuation bias result was introduced in Chapter 5. We can also derive it by using the general form of endogeneity from page 60, which is plim $\hat{\beta}_1 = \beta_1 + \text{corr}(X_1,\epsilon)\frac{\sigma_\epsilon}{\sigma_{X_1}} = \beta_1 + \frac{\text{cov}(X_1,\epsilon)}{\sigma_{X_1}}$. Note that the error term in Equation 14.19 (which is analogous to ϵ in the plim equation) actually contains $-\beta_1\nu_i + \epsilon_i$. Solving for $\text{cov}(X_1, -\beta_1\nu_i + \epsilon)$ yields $-\beta_1\sigma_\nu$.

Chapter 16

- Page 517 Professor Andrew Gelman, of Columbia University, directed me to this saying of Bill James.

GUIDE TO REVIEW QUESTIONS

Chapter 1

Review question on page 7:

1. Panel (a): $\beta_0 > 0$ (it's around 0.4) and $\beta_1 > 0$

    Panel (b): $\beta_0 > 0$ (it's around 0.8) and $\beta_1 < 0$

    Panel (c): $\beta_0 > 0$ (it's around 0.4) and $\beta_1 = 0$

    Panel (d): Note that the X-axis ranges from about -6 to $+6$. β_0 is the value of Y when X is zero and is therefore 2, which can be seen in Figure R.1. β_0 is not the value of Y at the left-most point in the figure, as it was for the other panels in Figure 1.4.

Chapter 3

Review questions on page 63:

1. Note that the variance of the independent variable is much smaller in panel (b). From the equation for the variance of $\hat{\beta}_1$ we know that higher variance of X is associated with lower variance of $\hat{\beta}_1$ meaning the variance of $\hat{\beta}_1$ in panel (a) should be lower.

2. Note that the number of observations is much larger in panel (d). From the equation for the variance of $\hat{\beta}_1$ we know that higher sample size is associated with lower variance, meaning the variance of $\hat{\beta}_1$, in panel (d) should be lower.

Chapter 4

Review questions on page 106:

1. Based on the results in Table 4.2 on page 95:

    (a) The t statistic for the coefficient on change in income is $\frac{2.29}{0.52} = 4.40$.

    (b) The degrees of freedom is sample size minus the number of parameters estimated, so it is $17 - 2 = 15$.

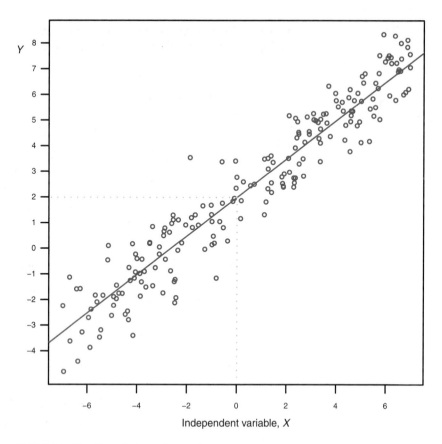

FIGURE R.1: Identifying β_0 from a Scatterplot

    (c) The critical value for a two-sided alternative hypothesis and $\alpha = 0.01$ is 2.95. We reject the null hypothesis.

    (d) The critical value for a one-sided alternative hypothesis and $\alpha = 0.05$ is 1.75. We reject the null hypothesis.

2. The critical value from a two-sided test is bigger because it indicates the point at which $\frac{\alpha}{2}$ of the distribution is larger. As Table 4.4 on page 104 shows, the two-sided critical values are larger than the one-sided critical values for all values of α.

3. The critical values from a small sample are larger because the t distribution accounts for additional uncertainty about our estimate of the standard error of $\hat{\beta}_1$. In other words, even when the null hypothesis is true, the data could work out to give us an unusually small estimate of $\mathrm{se}(\hat{\beta}_1)$, which would push up our t statistic. That is, the more uncertainty there is about $\mathrm{se}(\hat{\beta}_1)$, the more we could expect to see higher values of the t statistic even when the null hypothesis is true. As the sample size increases, uncertainty about $se(\hat{\beta}_1)$ decreases, and so this source of large t statistics even when the null hypothesis is true diminishes.

Review questions on page 115:

1. The power of a test is the probability of observing a t statistic higher than the critical value given the true value of β_1 and the $se(\hat{\beta}_1)$, α, and alternative hypothesis posited in the question. This will be

$$1 - \Phi\left(Critical\ value - \frac{\beta_1^{True}}{se(\hat{\beta}_1)}\right).$$

The critical value will be 2.32 for $\alpha = 0.01$ and a one-sided alternative hypothesis. The sketches will be normal distributions centered at $\frac{\beta_1^{True}}{se(\hat{\beta}_1)}$ with the portion of the normal distribution greater than the critical value shaded.

   (a) The power when $\beta_1^{True} = 1$ is $1 - \Phi\left(2.32 - \frac{1}{0.75}\right) = 0.162$.

   (b) The power when $\beta_1^{True} = 2$ is $1 - \Phi\left(2.32 - \frac{2}{0.75}\right) = 0.636$.

2. If the estimated $se(\hat{\beta}_1)$ doubled, the power will go down because the center of the t statistic distribution will shift toward zero (because $\frac{\beta_1^{True}}{se(\hat{\beta}_1)}$ gets smaller as the standard error increases). For this higher standard error, the power when $\beta_1^{True} = 1$ is $1 - \Phi\left(2.32 - \frac{1}{1.5}\right) = 0.049$, and the power when $\beta_1^{True} = 2$ is $1 - \Phi\left(2.32 - \frac{2}{1.5}\right) = 0.161$.

3. The probability of committing a Type II error is simply one minus the power. Hence when $se(\hat{\beta}_1) = 2.5$, the probability of committing a Type II error is 0.973 for $\beta_1^{True} = 1$ and 0.936 for $\beta_1^{True} = 2$.

Chapter 5

Review questions on page 151:

1. Not at all. R_j^2 will be approximately zero. In a random experiment, the treatment is uncorrelated with anything, including the other covariates. This buys us exogeneity, but it also buys us increased precision.

2. We'd like to have a low variance for estimates, and to get that we want the R_j^2 to be small. In other words, we want the independent variables to be uncorrelated with each other.

Chapter 6

Review questions on page 174:

1. (a) Control group: 0. Treatment group: 2. Difference is 2.

    (b) Control group: 4. Treatment group: -6. Difference is -10.

    (c) Control group: 101. Treatment group: 100. Difference is -1.

2. (a) $\hat{\beta}_0$: 0; $\hat{\beta}_1$: 2

    (b) $\hat{\beta}_0$: 4; $\hat{\beta}_1$: -10

    (c) $\hat{\beta}_0$: 101; $\hat{\beta}_1$: -1

Review questions on page 184:

1. A model in which a three-category country variable has been converted into multiple dummy variables with the United States as the excluded category looks like this:

    $$Y_i = \beta_0 + \beta_1 X_{1i} + \beta_2 Canada_i + \beta_3 Mexico_i + \epsilon_i$$

    The estimated constant ($\hat{\beta}_0$) is the average value of Y_i for units in the excluded category (in this case, U.S. citizens) after we have accounted for the effect of X_1. The coefficient on the Canada dummy variable ($\hat{\beta}_2$) estimates how much more or less Canadians feel about Y compared to Americans, the excluded reference category. The coefficient on the Mexico dummy variable ($\hat{\beta}_3$) estimates how much more or less Mexicans feel about Y compared to Americans. Using Mexico or Canada as excluded categories is equally valid and would produce substantively identical results, although the coefficients on the dummy variables will differ because they will refer to reference categories different from the ones we'd have when the United States is the excluded category.

2. (a) 25

    (b) 20

    (c) 30

    (d) 115

    (e) 5

    (f) -20

(g) 120

(h) −5

(i) −25

(j) 5

Review questions on page 194:

1. **(a)** $\beta_0 = 0, \beta_1 > 0, \beta_2 > 0, \beta_3 = 0$

(b) $\beta_0 > 0, \beta_1 < 0, \beta_2 > 0, \beta_3 = 0$

(c) $\beta_0 > 0, \beta_1 = 0, \beta_2 = 0, \beta_3 > 0$

(d) $\beta_0 > 0, \beta_1 > 0, \beta_2 = 0, \beta_3 < 0$ (actually $\beta_3 = -\beta_1$)

(e) $\beta_0 > 0, \beta_1 > 0, \beta_2 < 0, \beta_3 > 0$

(f) $\beta_0 > 0, \beta_1 > 0, \beta_2 > 0, \beta_3 < 0$

2. Bonus question: β_3 in panel (d) is $-\beta_1$.

3. False. The effect of X for the treatment group depends on $\beta_1 + \beta_3$. If β_1 is sufficiently positive, the effect of X is still positive for the treatment group even when β_3 is negative.

Chapter 7

Review questions on page 217:

1. Panel (a) looks like a quadratic model with effect accelerating as profits rise. Panel (b) looks like a quadratic model with effect accelerating as profits rise. Panel (c) is a bit of a trick question as the relationship is largely linear, but with a few unusual observations for profits around 4. A quadratic model would estimate an upside down U shape, but it would also be worth exploring if these are outliers or if these observations can perhaps be explained by other variables. Panel (d) looks like a quadratic model with rising and then falling effect of profits on investment. For all quadratic models, we would simply include a variable with the squared value of profits and let the computer program tell us the coefficient values that produce the appropriate curve.

2. The sketches would draw lines through the masses of data for panels (a), (b), and (d). The sketch for panel (c) would depend on whether we stuck with a quadratic model or treated the unusual obervations as outliers to be excluded or modeled with other variables.

3. The effects of profits on investment in each panel are roughly:

Profits go from 0 to 1 percent	**Profits go from 3 to 4 percent**
(a) Less than 1	Greater than 2
(b) Around 0	Less than –3
(c) Linear model: Around 2	Around 2
(c) Quadratic model Around 2	Very negative
(d) Around +5	Around –5

Chapter 8

Review question on page 274—see Table R.1:

TABLE R.1 Values of $\beta_0, \beta_1, \beta_2,$ and β_3 in Figure 8.6

	(a)	(b)	(c)	(d)
β_0	2	3	2	3
β_1	−1	−1	0	0
β_2	0	−2	2	−2
β_3	2	2	−1	1

Chapter 9

Review questions on page 300:

1. The first stage is the model explaining drinks per week. The second stage is the model explaining grades. The instrument is beer tax as we can infer based on its inclusion in first stage and exclusion from the second stage.

2. A good instrument needs to satisfy inclusion and exclusion conditions. In this case, beer tax does not satisfy the inclusion condition because it is not statistically significant in the first stage. As a rule of thumb, we want the variable to have a t statistic greater than 3. The exclusion condition cannot be assessed empirically. It seems reasonable that the beer tax in a state is not related to grades a student gets.

3. There is no evidence on exogeneity of the beer tax in the table because this is not something we can assess empirically.

4. We would get perfect multicollinearity and be unable to estimate a coefficient on it (or another independent variable). The fitted value of drinks per week is a linear combination of the beer tax and standardized test score variables (specifically is it 4 −0.001*test score − 2*beer tax) meaning it will be

perfectly explained by an auxiliary regression of fitted value on the test score and beer tax variables.

5. No. The first stage results do not satisfy the inclusion condition and we therefore cannot place any faith in the results in the second stage.

Chapter 10

Review questions on page 351:

1. There is a balance problem as the treatment villages have higher income, with a t statistic of 2.5 on the treatment variable. Hence we cannot be sure that the differences in the treated and untreated villages are due to the treatment or to the fact that the treated villages are wealthier. There is no difference in treated and untreated villages with regard to population.

2. There is a possible attrition problem as treated villages are more likely to report test scores. This is not surprising as teachers from treated villages have more of an incentive to report test scores. The implication of this differential attrition is not clear, however. It could be that the low performing school districts tend not to report among the control villages, but that even low performing school districts report among the treated villages. Hence the attrition is not necessarily damning of the results. Rather, it calls for further analysis.

3. The first column reports that students in treated villages had substantially higher test scores. However, we need to also control for village income as the treated villages also tended to have higher income. In addition, we should be somewhat wary of the fact that 20 villages did not report test scores. As discussed above, the direction of the bias is not clear, but it would be useful to see additional analysis of the kinds of districts that did and did not report test scores. Perhaps the data set could be trimmed and re-analyzed.

Chapter 11

Review questions on page 376:

(a) $\beta_1 = 0, \beta_2 = 0, \beta_3 < 0$

(b) $\beta_1 < 0, \beta_2 = 0, \beta_3 > 0$

(c) $\beta_1 > 0, \beta_2 < 0, \beta_3 = 0$

(d) $\beta_1 < 0, \beta_2 > 0, \beta_3 < 0$

(e) $\beta_1 > 0, \beta_2 > 0, \beta_3 < 0$ (actually $\beta_3 = -\beta_2$)

(f) $\beta_1 < 0, \beta_2 < 0, \beta_3 > 0$ (here too $\beta_3 = -\beta_2$, which means β_3 is positive because β_2 is negative)

Chapter 12

Review questions on page 418:

1. Solve for $Y_i^* = 0.0$

    Panel (a): $X = 1.5$

    Panel (b): $X = \frac{2}{3}$

    Panel (c): $X = 1.0$

    Panel (d): $X = 1.5$

2. True, false, or indeterminate, based on Table 12.2:

(a) True. The t statistic is 5, which is statistically significant for any reasonable significance level.

(b) False. The t statistic is 1, which is not statistically significant for any reasonable significance level.

(c) False! Probit coefficients cannot be directly interpreted.

(d) False. The fitted probability is $\Phi(0)$, which is 0.50.

(e) True. The fitted probability is $\Phi(3)$, which is approximately 1 because virtually all of the area under a standard normal curve is to the left of 3.

3. Fitted values based on Table 12.2:

(a) The fitted probability is $\Phi(0+0.5 \times 4 - 0.5 \times 0) = \Phi(2)$, which is 0.978.

(b) The fitted probability is $\Phi(0 + 0.5 \times 0 - 0.5 \times 4) = \Phi(-2)$, which is 0.022.

(c) The fitted probability is $\Phi(3 + 1.0 \times 0 - 3.0 \times 1) = \Phi(0)$, which is 0.5.

Review questions on page 422:

1. Use the observed-variable, discrete-differences approach to interpreting the coefficient. Calculate the fitted probability for all observations using actual

values of years of experience and the liquor license variables. Then calculate the fitted probability for all observations using years of experience equal to actual years of experience plus 1 and the actual value of the liquor license variable. The average difference in these fitted probabilities is the average estimated effect of a one unit increase in years of experience on the probability of bankruptcy.

2. Use the observed-variable, discrete-differences approach to interpreting the coefficient. Calculate the fitted probability using the actual value of the years of experience variable and setting liquor license to 0 for all observations. Then calculate the fitted probability for all observations using the actual value of years of experience and setting the liquor license variable to 1 for all obesrvations. The average difference in these fitted probabilities is the average estimated effect of having a liquor license on the probability of bankruptcy.

Appendix

Review questions on page 531:

1. The table in Figure A.4 shows that the probability a standard normal random variable is less than or equal to 1.64 is 0.95, meaning there is a 95 percent chance that a normal random variable will be less than or equal to whatever value is 1.64 standard deviations above its mean.

2. The table in Figure A.4 also shows that the probability a standard normal random variable is less than or equal to -1.28 is 0.10, meaning there is a 10 percent chance that a normal random variable will be less than or equal to whatever value is 1.28 standard deviations below its mean.

3. The table in Figure A.4 shows that the probability that a standard normal random variable is greater than 1.28 is 0.90. Because the probability of being above some value is one minus the probability of being below some value, there is a 10 percent chance that a normal random variable will be greater than or equal to whatever number is 1.28 standard deviations above its mean.

4. We need to convert the number -4 to something in terms of standard deviations from the mean. The value -4 is 2 standard deviations below the mean of 0 when the standard deviation is 2. The table in Figure A.4 shows that the probability a normal random variable with a mean of zero is less (more negative) than 2 standard deviations below its mean is 0.023. In other words, the probability of being less than $\frac{-4-0}{2} = -2$ is 0.023.

5. First, convert -3 to standard deviations above or below the mean. In this case, if the variance is 9, then the standard deviation (the square root of the variance) is 3. Therefore -3 is the same as 1 standard deviation below the mean. From

the table in Figure A.4, we see that there is a 0.16 probability a normal variable will be more than 1 standard deviation below its mean. In other words, the probability of being less than $\frac{-3-0}{\sqrt{9}} = -1$ is 0.16.

6. First, convert 9 to standard deviations above or below the mean. The standard deviation (the square root of the variance) is 2. The value 9 is $\frac{9-7.2}{2} = \frac{1.8}{2}$ standard deviation above the mean. The value 0.9 does not appear in Figure A.4, but it is close to 1 and the probability of being less than 1 is 0.84. Therefore a reasonable approximation is in the vicinity of 0.8. The actual value is 0.82 and can be calculated as discussed in the Computing Corner on page 537.

BIBLIOGRAPHY

Acemoglu, Daron, Simon Johnson, and James A. Robinson. 2001. The Colonial Origins of Comparative Development: An Empirical Investigation. *American Economic Review* 91(5): 1369–1401.

Acemoglu, Daron, Simon Johnson, James A. Robinson, and Pierre Yared. 2008. Income and Democracy. *American Economic Review* 98(3): 808–842.

Achen, Christopher H. 1982. *Interpreting and Using Regression.* Newbury Park, NJ: Sage Publications.

Achen, Christopher H. 2000. Why Lagged Dependent Variables Can Suppress the Explanatory Power of Other Independent Variables. Manuscript, University of Michigan.

Achen, Christopher H. 2002. Toward a New Political Methodology: Microfoundations and ART. *Annual Review of Political Science* 5: 423–450.

Albertson, Bethany, and Adria Lawrence. 2009. After the Credits Roll: The Long-Term Effects of Educational Television on Public Knowledge and Attitudes. *American Politics Research* 37(2): 275–300.

Alvarez, R. Michael, and John Brehm. 1995. American Ambivalence Towards Abortion Policy: Development of a Heteroskedastic Probit Model of Competing Values. *American Journal of Political Science* 39(4): 1055–1082.

Anderson, James M., John M. Macdonald, Ricky Bluthenthal, and J. Scott Ashwood. 2013. Reducing Crime by Shaping the Built Environment with Zoning: An Empirical Study of Los Angeles. *University of Pennsylvania Law Review* 161: 699–756.

Angrist, Joshua. 2006. Instrumental Variables Methods in Experimental Criminological Research: What, Why and How. *Journal of Experimental Criminology* 2(1): 23–44.

Angrist, Joshua, and Alan Krueger. 1991. Does Compulsory School Attendance Affect Schooling and Earnings? *Quarterly Journal of Economics.* 106(4): 979–1014.

Angrist, Joshua, and Jörn-Steffen Pischke. 2009. *Mostly Harmless Econometrics: An Empiricist's Companion.* Princeton, NJ: Princeton University Press.

Angrist, Joshua, and Jörn-Steffen Pischke. 2010. National Bureau of Economic Research working paper. http://www.nber.org/papers/w15794.

Angrist, Joshua, Kathryn Graddy, and Guido Imbens. 2000. The Interpretation of Instrumental Variables Estimators in Simultaneous Equations Models with an Application to the Demand for Fish. *Review of Economic Studies* 67(3): 499–527.

Anscombe, Francis J. 1973. Graphs in Statistical Analysis. *American Statistician* 27(1): 17–21.

Anzia, Sarah. 2012. The Election Timing Effect: Evidence from a Policy Intervention in Texas. *Quarterly Journal of Political Science* 7(3): 209–248.

Arellano, Manuel, and Stephen Bond. 1991. Some Tests of Specification for Panel Data. *Review of Economic Studies* 58(2): 277–297.

Aron-Dine, Aviva, Liran Einav, and Amy Finkelstein. 2013. The RAND Health Insurance Experiment, Three Decades Later. *Journal of Economic Perspectives* 27(1): 197–222.

Baicker, Katherine, Sarah Taubman, Heidi Allen, Mira Bernstein, Jonathan Gruber, Joseph P. Newhouse, Eric Schneider, Bill Wright, Alan Zaslavsky, Amy Finkelstein, and the Oregon Health Study Group. 2013. The Oregon Experiment—Medicaid's Effects on Clinical Outcomes. *New England Journal of Medicine* 368(18): 1713–1722.

Bailey, Michael A., and Elliott Fullmer. 2011. Balancing in the States, 1978–2009. *State Politics and Policy Quarterly* 11(2): 149–167.

Bailey, Michael A., Jon Mummolo, and Hans Noel. 2012. Tea Party Influence: A Story of Activists and Elites. *American Politics Research* 40(5): 769–804.

Bailey, Michael A., Jeffrey S. Rosenthal, and Albert H. Yoon. 2014. Grades and Incentives: Assessing Competing Grade Point Average Measures and Postgraduate Outcomes. *Studies in Higher Education.* Published online: December 3, 2014.

Bailey, Michael A., Daniel J. Hopkins, and Todd Rogers. 2015. Unresponsive and Unpersuaded: The Unintended Consequences of Voter Persuasion Efforts. Manuscript, Georgetown University.

Bailey, Michael A., Anton Strezhnev, and Erik Voeten. 2015. Estimating Dynamic State Preferences from United Nations Voting Data. *Journal of Conflict Resolution.*

Baiocchi, Michael, Jing Cheng, and Dylan S. Small. 2014. Tutorial in Biostatistics: Instrumental Variable Methods for Causal Inference. *Statistics in Medicine* 33(13): 2297–2340.

Baltagi, Badi H. 2005. *Econometric Analysis of Panel Data*, 3rd ed. Hoboken, NJ: Wiley.

Banerjee, Abhijit Vinayak, and Esther Duflo. 2011. *Poor Economics: A Radical Rethinking of the Way to Fight Global Poverty*. New York: Public Affairs.

Bartels, Larry M. 2008. *Unequal Democracy: The Political Economy of the New Gilded Age.* Princeton, NJ: Princeton University Press.

Beck, Nathaniel. 2010. Making Regression and Related Output More Helpful to Users. *The Political Methodologist* 18(1): 4–9.

Beck, Nathaniel, and Jonathan N. Katz. 1996. Nuisance vs. Substance: Specifying and Estimating Time-Series–Cross-Section Models. *Political Analysis* 6: 1–36.

Beck, Nathaniel, and Jonathan N. Katz. 2011. Modeling Dynamics in Time-Series–Cross-Section Political Economy Data. *Annual Review of Political Science* 14: 331–352.

Berk, Richard A., Alec Campbell, Ruth Klap, and Bruce Western. 1992. The Deterrent Effect of Arrest in Incidents of Domestic Violence: A Bayesian Analysis of Four Field Experiments. *American Sociological Review* 57(5): 698–708.

Bertrand, Marianne, and Sendhil Mullainathan. 2004. Are Emily and Greg More Employable than Lakisha and Jamal? A Field Experiment on Labor Market Discrimination. *American Economic Review* 94(4): 991–1013.

Bertrand, Marianne, Esther Duflo, and Sendhil Mullainathan. 2004. How Much Should We Trust Differences-In-Differences Estimates? *Quarterly Journal of Economics* 119(1): 249–275.

Blinder, Alan S., and Mark W. Watson. 2013. Presidents and the Economy: A Forensic Investigation. Manuscript, Princeton University.

Bloom, Howard S. 2012. Modern Regression Discontinuity Analysis. *Journal of Research on Educational Effectiveness* 5(1): 43–82.

Bound, John, David Jaeger, and Regina Baker. 1995. Problems with Instrumental Variables Estimation When the Correlation Between the Instruments and the Endogenous Explanatory Variable Is Weak. *Journal of the American Statistical Association* 90(430): 443–450.

Box, George E. P. 1976. Science and Statistics. *Journal of the American Statistical Association* 71(356): 791–799.

Box-Steffensmeier, Janet M., and Bradford S. Jones. 2004. *Event History Modeling: A Guide for Social Scientists*. Cambridge, U.K.: Cambridge University Press.

Box-Steffensmeier, Janet M., John R. Freeman, Matthew P. Hitt, and Jon C. W. Pevehouse. 2014. *Time Series Analysis for the Social Sciences.* Cambridge, U.K.: Cambridge University Press.

Bradford-Hill, Austin. 1965. The Environment and Disease: Association or Causation? *Proceedings of the Royal Society of Medicine* 58(5): 295–300.

Brambor, Thomas, William Roberts Clark, and Matt Golder. 2006. Understanding Interaction Models: Improving Empirical Analyses. *Political Analysis* 14: 63–82.

Braumoeller, Bear F. 2004. Hypothesis Testing and Multiplicative Interaction Terms. *International Organization* 58(4): 807–820.

Brown, Peter C., Henry L. Roediger III, and Mark A. McDaniel. 2014. *Making It Stick: The Science of Successful Learning.* Cambridge, MA: Harvard University Press.

Brownlee, Shannon, and Jeanne Lenzer. 2009. Does the Vaccine Matter? *The Atlantic*, November. www.theatlantic.com/doc/200911/brownlee-h1n1/2.

Brumm, Harold J., Dennis Epple, and Bennett T. McCallum. 2008. Simultaneous Equation Econometrics: Some Weak-Instrument and Time-Series Issues. Manuscript, Carnegie Mellon.

Buckles, Kasey, and Dan Hungerman. 2013. Season of Birth and Later Outcomes: Old Questions, New Answers. *The Review of Economics and Statistics* 95(3): 711–724.

Buddlemeyer, Hielke, and Emmanuel Skofias. 2003. An Evaluation on the Performance of Regression Discontinuity Design on PROGRESA. Institute for Study of Labor, Discussion Paper No. 827.

Burde, Dana, and Leigh L. Linden. 2013. Bringing Education to Afghan Girls: A Randomized Controlled Trial of Village-Based Schools. *American Economic Journal: Applied Economics* 5(3): 27–40.

Burtless, Gary, 1995. The Case for Randomized Field Trials in Economic and Policy Research. *Journal of Economic Perspectives* 9(2): 63–84.

Campbell, James E. 2011. The Economic Records of the Presidents: Party Differences and Inherited Economic Conditions. *Forum* 9(1): 1–29.

Card, David. 1990. The Impact of the Mariel Boatlift on the Miami Labor Market. *Industrial and Labor Relations Review* 43(2): 245–257.

Card, David. 1999. The Causal Effect of Education on Earnings. In *Handbook of Labor Economics*, vol. 3, O. Ashenfelter and D. Card, eds. Amsterdam: Elsevier Science.

Card, David, Carlos Dobkin, and Nicole Maestas. 2009. Does Medicare Save Lives? *Quarterly Journal of Economics* 124(2): 597–636.

Carrell, Scott E., Mark Hoekstra, and James E. West. 2010. Does Drinking Impair College Performance? Evidence from a Regression Discontinuity Approach. National Bureau of Economic Research Working Paper. http://www.nber.org/papers/w16330.

Carroll, Royce, Jeffrey B. Lewis, James Lo, Keith T. Poole, and Howard Rosenthal. 2009. Measuring Bias and Uncertainty in DW-NOMINATE Ideal Point Estimates via the Parametric Bootstrap. *Political Analysis* 17: 261–27. Updated at http://voteview.com/dwnominate.asp.

Carroll, Royce, Jeffrey B. Lewis, James Lo, Keith T. Poole, and Howard Rosenthal. 2014. DW-NOMINATE Scores with Bootstrapped Standard Errors. Updated February 17, 2013, at http://voteview.com/dwnominate.asp.

Cellini, Stephanie Riegg, Fernando Ferreira, and Jesse Rothstein. 2010. The Value of School Facility Investments: Evidence from a Dynamic Regression Discontinuity Design. *Quarterly Journal of Economics* 125(1): 215–261.

Chabris, Christopher and Daniel Simmons. Does the Ad Make Me Fat? *New York Times*, March 10, 2013.

Chakraborty, Indraneel, Hans A. Holter, and Serhiy Stepanchuk. 2012. Marriage Stability, Taxation, and Aggregate Labor Supply in the U.S. vs. Europe. Uppsala University Working Paper 2012:10.

Chen, Xiao, Philip B. Ender, Michael Mitchell, and Christine Wells. 2003. *Regression with Stata.* http://www.ats.ucla.edu/stat/stata/webbooks/reg/default.htm.

Cheng, Cheng, and Mark Hoekstra. 2013. Does Strengthening Self-Defense Law Deter Crime or Escalate Violence? Evidence from Castle Doctrine. *Journal of Human Resources* 48(3): 821–854.

Ching, Andrew, Tülin Erdem, and Michael Keane. 2009. The Price Consideration Model of Brand Choice. *Journal of Applied Econometrics* 24(3): 393–420.

Clark, William Roberts, and Arel-Bundock Vincent. 2013. Independent but Not Indifferent: Partisan Bias in Monetary Policy at the Fed. *Economics and Politics* 25(1): 1–26.

Clarke, Kevin A. 2005. The Phantom Menace: Omitted Variable Bias in Econometric Research. *Conflict Management and Peace Science* 22(4): 341–352.

Comiskey, Michael, and Lawrence C. Marsh. 2012. Presidents, Parties, and the Business Cycle, 1949–2009. *Presidential Studies Quarterly* 42(1): 40–59.

Cook, Thomas. 2008. Waiting for Life to Arrive: A History of the Regression Discontinuity Design in Psychology, Statistics and Economics. *Journal of Econometrics* 142(2): 636–654.

Currie, Janet, and Jonathan Gruber. 1996. Saving Babies: The Efficacy and Cost of Recent Changes in the Medicaid Eligibility of Pregnant Women. *Journal of Political Economy* 104(6): 1263–1296.

Cragg, John G. 1994. Making Good Inferences from Bad Data. *Canadian Journal of Economics* 27(4): 776–800.

Das, Mitali, Whitney K. Newey, and Francis Vella. 2003. Nonparametric Estimation of Sample Selection Models. *The Review of Economic Studies* 70(1): 33–58.

De Boef, Suzanna, and Luke Keele. 2008. Taking Time Seriously. *American Journal of Political Science* 52(1): 184–200.

DiazGranados, Carlos A., Martine Denis, and Stanley Plotkin. 2012. Seasonal Influenza Vaccine Efficacy and Its Determinants in Children and Non-elderly Adults: A Systematic Review with Meta-analyses of Controlled Trials. *Vaccine* 31(1): 49–57.

Duflo, Esther, Rachel Glennerster, and Michael Kremer. 2008. Using Randomization in Development Economics Research: A Toolkit. In *Handbook of Development Economics*, vol. 4, T. Schultz and John Strauss, eds. Amsterdam and New York: North Holland.

Dunning, Thad. 2012. *Natural Experiments in the Social Sciences: A Design-Based Approach.* Cambridge, U.K.: Cambridge University Press.

Drum, Kevin. 2013a. America's Real Criminal Element: Lead—New Research Finds Pb Is the Hidden Villain Behind Violent Crime, Lower IQs, and Even the ADHD Epidemic. *Mother Jones* January/February.

Drum, Kevin. 2013b. Crime Is at Its Lowest Level in 50 Years. A Simple Molecule May Be the Reason Why. *Mother Jones.* http://www.motherjones.com/kevin-drum/2013/01/lead-crime-connection.

Drum, Kevin. 2013c. Lead and Crime: A Response to Jim Manzi. *Mother Jones.* http://www.motherjones.com/kevin-drum/2013/01/lead-and-crime-response-jim-manzi.

Dynarski, Susan. 2000. Hope for Whom? Financial Aid for the Middle Class and Its Impact on College Attendance. *National Tax Journal* 53(3, part 2): 629–662.

Elwert, Felix, and Christopher Winship. 2014. Endogenous Selection Bias: The Problem of Conditioning on a Collider Variable. *Annual Review of Sociology* 40(1): 31–53.

Epple, Dennis, and Bennett T. McCallum. 2006. Simultaneous Equation Econometrics: The Missing Example. *Economic Inquiry* 44(2): 374–384.

Erikson, Robert S., and Thomas R. Palfrey. 2000. Equilibrium in Campaign Spending Games: Theory and Data. *American Political Science Review* 94(3): 595–610.

Fearon, James D., and David D. Laitin. 2003. Ethnicity, Insurgency, and Civil War. *American Political Science Review* 97(1): 75–90.

Finkelstein, Amy, Sarah Taubman, Bill Wright, Mira Bernstein, Jonathan Gruber, Joseph P. Newhouse, Heidi Allen, Katherine Baicker, and the Oregon Health Study Group. 2012. The Oregon Health Insurance Experiment: Evidence from the First Year. *Quarterly Journal of Economics* 127(3): 1057–1106.

Gaubatz, Kurt Taylor. 2015. *A Survivor's Guide to R: An Introduction for the Uninitiated and the Unnerved.* Los Angeles: Sage.

Gerber, Alan S., and Donald P. Green. 2012. *Field Experiments: Design, Analysis, and Interpretation.* New York: Norton.

Gerber, Alan S., and Donald P. Green. 2000. The Effects of Canvassing, Telephone Calls and Direct Mail on Voter Turnout: A Field Experiment. *American Political Science Review* 94(3): 653–663.

Gerber, Alan S., and Donald P. Green. 2005. Correction to Gerber and Green (2000), Replication of Disputed Findings, and Reply to Imai (2005). *American Political Science Review* 99(2): 301–313.

Gertler, Paul. 2004. Do Conditional Cash Transfers Improve Child Health? Evidence from PROGRESA's Control Randomized Experiment. *American Economic Review* 94(2): 336–341.

Goldberger, Arthur S. 1991. *A Course in Econometrics*. Cambridge, MA: Harvard University Press.

Gormley, William T., Jr., Deborah Phillips, and Ted Gayer. 2008. Preschool Programs Can Boost School Readiness. *Science* 320(5884): 1723–1724.

Green, Donald P., Soo Yeon Kim, and David H. Yoon. 2001. Dirty Pool. *International Organization* 55(2): 441–468.

Green, Joshua. 2012. The Science Behind Those Obama Campaign E-Mails. *Business Week*. (November 29). Accessed from http://www.businessweek.com/articles/2012–11-29/the-science-behind-those-obama-campaign-e-mails.

Greene, William. 2003. *Econometric Analysis*, 6th ed. Upper Saddle River, NJ: Prentice Hall.

Greene, William. 2008. *Econometric Analysis*, 7th ed. Upper Saddle River, NJ: Prentice Hall.

Grimmer, Justin, Eitan Hersh, Brian Feinstein, and Daniel Carpenter. 2010. Are Close Elections Randomly Determined? Manuscript, Stanford University.

Hanmer, Michael J., and Kerem Ozan Kalkan. 2013. Behind the Curve: Clarifying the Best Approach to Calculating Predicted Probabilities and Marginal Effects from Limited Dependent Variable Models. *American Journal of Political Science* 57(1): 263–277.

Hanushek, Eric and Ludger Woessmann. 2012. Do Better Schools Lead to More Growth? Cognitive Skills, Economic Outcomes, and Causation. *Journal of Economic Growth* 17(4): 267–321.

Harvey, Anna. 2011. What's So Great About Independent Courts? Rethinking Crossnational Studies of Judicial Independence. Manuscript, New York University. Manuscript, New York University.

Hausman, Jerry A., and William E. Taylor. 1981. Panel Data and Unobservable Individual Effects. *Econometrica* 49(6): 1377–1398.

Heckman, James J. 1979. Sample Selection Bias as a Specification Error. *Econometrica* 47(1): 153–161.

Herndon, Thomas, Michael Ash, and Robert Pollin. 2014. Does High Public Debt Consistently Stifle Economic Growth? A Critique of Reinhart and Rogoff. *Cambridge Journal of Economics* 38(2): 257–279.

Howell, William G., and Paul E. Peterson. 2004. The Use of Theory in Randomized Field Trials: Lessons from School Voucher Research on Disaggregation, Missing Data, and the Generalization of Findings. *American Behavioral Scientist* 47(5): 634–657.

Imai, Kosuke. 2005. Do Get-Out-The-Vote Calls Reduce Turnout? The Importance of Statistical Methods for Field Experiments. *American Political Science Review* 99(2): 283–300.

Imai, Kosuke, Gary King, and Elizabeth A. Stuart. 2008. Misunderstandings among Experimentalists and Observationalists about Causal Inference. *Journal of the Royal Statistical Society, Series A (Statistics in Society)* 171(2): 481–502.

Imbens, Guido W. 2014. Instrumental Variables: An Econometrician's Perspective. IZA Discussion Paper 8048. Bonn: Forschungsinstitut zur Zukunft der Arbeit (IZA).

Imbens, Guido W., and Thomas Lemieux. 2008. Regression Discontinuity Designs: A Guide to Practice. *Journal of Econometrics* 142(2): 615–635.

Iqbal, Zaryab, and Christopher Zorn. 2008. The Political Consequences of Assassination, *Journal of Conflict Resolution* 52(3): 385–400.

Jackman, Simon. 2009. *Bayesian Analysis for the Social Sciences*. Hoboken, NJ: Wiley.

Jacobsmeier, Matthew L., and Daniel G. Lewis. 2013. Barking up the Wrong Tree: Why Bo Didn't Fetch Many Votes for Barack Obama in 2012. *PS: Political Science and Politics* 46(1): 49–59.

Jacobson, Gary C. 1978. Effects of Campaign Spending in Congressional Elections. *American Political Science Review* 72(2): 469–491.

Kalla, Joshua L., and David E. Broockman. 2015. Congressional Officials Grant Access due to Campaign Contributions: A Randomized Field Experiment. *American Journal of Political Science*.

Kam, Cindy D., and Robert J. Franceze Jr. 2007. *Modeling and Interpreting Interactive Hypotheses in Regression Analysis*. Ann Arbor: University of Michigan Press.

Kastellec, Jonathan P., and Eduardo L. Leoni. 2007. Using Graphs Instead of Tables in Political Science. *Perspectives on Politics* 5(4): 755–771.

Keele, Luke, and Nathan J. Kelly. 2006. Dynamic Models for Dynamic Theories: The Ins and Outs of Lagged Dependent Variables. *Political Analysis* 14: 186–205.

Keele, Luke, and David Park. 2006. Difficult Choices: An Evaluation of Heterogenous Choice Models. Manuscript, Ohio State University.

Kennedy, Peter. 2008. *A Guide to Econometrics*, 6th ed. Malden, MA: Blackwell Publishing.

Khimm, Suzy. 2010. Who Is Alvin Greene? *Mother Jones.* http://motherjones.com/mojo/2010/06/alvin-greene-south-carolina.

King, Gary. 1989. *Unifying Political Methodology: The Likelihood Theory of Statistical Inference.* Cambridge: Cambridge University Press.

King, Gary. 1991. Truth Is Stranger than Prediction, More Questionable than Causal Inference. *American Journal of Political Science* 35(4): 1047–1053.

King, Gary. 1995. Replication, Replication. *PS: Political Science and Politics* 28(3): 444–452.

King, Gary, and Langche Zeng. 2001. Logistic Regression in Rare Events Data. *Political Analysis* 9: 137–163.

King, Gary, Robert Keohane, and Sidney Verba. 1994. *Designing Social Inquiry: Scientific Inference in Qualitative Research.* Princeton, NJ: Princeton University Press.

Kiviet, Jan F. 1995. On Bias, Inconsistency, and Efficiency of Various Estimators in Dynamic Panel Data Models. *Journal of Econometrics* 68(1): 53–78.

Klick, Jonathan, and Alexander Tabarrok. 2005. Using Terror Alert Levels to Estimate the Effect of Police on Crime. *Journal of Law and Economics* 48(1): 267–279.

Koppell, Jonathan G. S., and Jennifer A. Steen. 2004. The Effects of Ballot Position on Election Outcomes. *Journal of Politics* 66(1): 267–281.

La Porta, Rafael, F. Lopez-de-Silanes, C. Pop-Eleches, and A. Schliefer. 2004. Judicial Checks and Balances. *Journal of Political Economy* 112(2): 445–470.

Lee, David S. 2008. Randomized Experiments from Non-random Selection in U.S. House Elections. *Journal of Econometrics* 142(2): 675–697.

Lee, David S. 2009. Training, Wages, and Sample Selection: Estimating Sharp Bounds on Treatment Effects. *Review of Economic Studies* 76(3): 1071–1102.

Lee, David S., and Thomas Lemieux. 2010. Regression Discontinuity Designs in Economics. *Journal of Economic Literature* 48(2): 281–355.

Lerman, Amy E. 2009. The People Prisons Make: Effects of Incarceration on Criminal Psychology. In *Do Prisons Make Us Safer?* Steve Raphael and Michael Stoll, eds. New York: Russell Sage Foundation.

Levitt, Steven D. 1997. Using Electoral Cycles in Police Hiring to Estimate the Effect of Police on Crime. *American Economic Review* 87(3): 270–290.

Levitt, Steven D. 2002. Using Electoral Cycles in Police Hiring to Estimate the Effect of Police on Crime: A Reply. *American Economic Review* 92(4): 1244–1250.

Lochner, Lance, and Enrico Moretti. 2004. The Effect of Education on Crime: Evidence from Prison Inmates, Arrests, and Self-Reports. *American Economic Review* 94(1): 155–189.

Long, J. Scott. 1997. *Regression Models for Categorical and Limited Dependent Variables.* London: Sage Publications.

Lorch, Scott A., Michael Baiocchi, Corinne S. Ahlberg, and Dylan E. Small. 2012. The Differential Impact of Delivery Hospital on the Outcomes of Premature Infants. *Pediatrics* 130(2): 270–278.

Ludwig, Jens, and Douglass L. Miller. 2007. Does Head Start Improve Children's Life Chances? Evidence from a Regression Discontinuity Design. *Quarterly Journal of Economics* 122(1): 159–208.

Lumley, Thomas, Paula Diehr, Scott Emerson, and Lu Chen. 2002. The Importance of the Normality Assumption in Large Public Health Data Sets. *Annual Review of Public Health* 23: 151–169.

Madestam, Andreas, Daniel Shoag, Stan Veuger, and David Yanagizawa-Drott. 2013. Do Political

Protests Matter? Evidence from the Tea Party Movement. *Quarterly Journal of Economics* 128(4): 1633–1685.

Makowsky, Michael, and Thomas Stratmann. 2009. Political Economy at Any Speed: What Determines Traffic Citations? *American Economic Review* 99(1): 509–527.

Malkiel, Burton G. 2003. *A Random Walk Down Wall Street: The Time-Tested Strategy for Successful Investing*. New York: W.W. Norton.

Manning, Willard G., Joseph P. Newhouse, Naihua Duan, Emmett B. Keeler, and Arleen Leibowitz. 1987. Health Insurance and the Demand for Medical Care: Evidence from a Randomized Experiment. *American Economic Review* 77(3): 251–277.

Manzi, Jim. 2012. *Uncontrolled: The Surprising Payoff of Trial-and-Error for Business, Politics and Society*. New York: Basic Books.

Marvell, Thomas B., and Carlisle E. Moody. 1996. Specification Problems, Police Levels and Crime Rates. *Criminology* 34(4): 609–646.

McClellan, Chandler B., and Erdal Tekin. 2012. Stand Your Ground Laws and Homicides. National Bureau of Economic Research Working Paper No. 18187.

McCrary, Justin. 2002. Using Electoral Cycles in Police Hiring to Estimate the Effect of Police on Crime: Comment. *American Economic Review* 92(4): 1236–1243.

McCrary, Justin. 2008. Manipulation of the Running Variable in the Regression Discontinuity Design: A Density Test. *Journal of Econometrics* 142(2): 698–714.

Miguel, Edward, and Michael Kremer. 2004. Worms: Identifying Impacts on Education and Health in the Presence of Treatment Externalities. *Econometrica* 72(1): 159–217.

Miguel, Edward, Shanker Satyanath, and Ernest Sergenti. 2004. Economic Shocks and Civil Conflict: An Instrumental Variables Approach. *Journal of Political Economy* 112(4): 725–753.

Morgan, Stephen L., and Christopher Winship. 2014. *Counterfactuals and Causal Inference: Methods and Principals for Social Research*, 2nd ed. Cambridge, U.K.: Cambridge University Press.

Murnane, Richard J., and John B. Willett. 2011. *Methods Matter: Improving Causal Inference in Educational and Social Science Research*. Oxford, U.K.: Oxford University Press.

Murray, Michael P. 2006a. Avoiding Invalid Instruments and Coping with Weak Instruments. *Journal of Economic Perspectives* 20(4): 111–132.

Murray, Michael P. 2006b. *Econometrics: A Modern Introduction*. Boston: Pearson Addison Wesley.

Mutz, Diana C. 2010. The Dog That Didn't Bark: The Role of Canines in the 2008 Campaign. *PS: Political Science and Politics* 43(4): 707–712.

NASA. 2012. Combined Land-Surface Air and Sea-Surface Water Temperature Anomalies (Land-Ocean Temperature Index, LOTI) Global-mean monthly, seasonal, and annual means, 1880–present, updated through most recent month.

National Center for Addiction and Substance Abuse at Columbia University. 2011. *National Survey of American Attitudes on Substance Abuse XVI: Teens and Parents* (August). Accessed November 10, 2011, at www.casacolumbia.org/download.aspx?path= /UploadedFiles/ooc3hqnl.pdf.

Newhouse, Joseph. 1993. *Free for All? Lessons from the RAND Health Insurance Experiment*. Cambridge, MA: Harvard University Press.

Nevin, Rick. 2013. Lead and Crime: Why This Correlation Does Mean Causation. January 26. http://ricknevin.com/uploads/Lead_and_Crime_-_Why_This_Correlation_Does_Mean_Causation.pdf.

Noel, Hans. 2010. Ten Things Political Scientists Know That You Don't. *The Forum* 8(3): article 12.

Orwell, George. 1946. In Front of Your Nose. *Tribune*. London (March 22).

Osterholm, Michael T., Nicholas S. Kelley, Alfred Sommer, and Edward A. Belongia. 2012. Efficacy and Effectiveness of Influenza Vaccines: A Systematic Review and Meta-analysis. *Lancet: Infectious Diseases* 12(1): 36–44.

Palmer, Brian. 2013. I Wish I Was a Little Bit Shorter. *Slate*. July 30. http://www.slate.com/articles/health_and_science/science/2013/07/height_and_longevity_the_research_is_clear_being_tall_is_hazardous_to_your.html.

Parker, Jonathan A., Nicholas S. Souleles, David S. Johnson, and Robert McClelland. 2013. Consumer Spending and the Economic Stimulus Payments of 2008. *American Economic Review* 103(6): 2530–53

Persico, Nicola, Andrew Postlewaite, and Dan Silverman. 2004. The Effect of Adolescent Experience on Labor Market Outcomes: The Case of Height. *Journal of Political Economy* 112(5): 1019–1053.

Pierskalla, Jan H., and Florian M. Hollenbach. 2013. Technology and Collective Action: The Effect of Cell Phone Coverage on Political Violence in Africa. *American Political Science Review* 107(2): 207–224.

Reinhart, Carmen M., and Kenneth S. Rogoff. 2010. Growth in a Time of Debt. *American Economic Review: Papers & Proceedings* 100(2): 573–578.

Rice, John A. 2007. *Mathematical Statistics and Data Analysis*, 3rd ed. Belmont, CA: Thomson.

Roach, Michael A. 2013. Mean Reversion or a Breath of Fresh Air? The Effect of NFL Coaching Changes on Team Performance in the Salary Cap Era. *Applied Economics Letters* 20(17): 1553–1556.

Romer, Christina D. 2011. What Do We Know about the Effects of Fiscal Policy? Separating Evidence from Ideology. Talk at Hamilton College, November 7.

Rossin-Slater, Maya, Christopher J. Ruhm, and Jane Waldfogel. 2014. The Effects of California's Paid Family Leave Program on Mothers' Leave-Taking and Subsequent Labor Market Outcomes. *Journal of Policy Analysis and Management* 32(2): 224–245.

Scheve, Kenneth and David Stasavage. 2012. Democracy, War, and Wealth: Lessons from Two Centuries of Inheritance Taxation. *American Political Science Review* 106(1): 81–102.

Schrodt, Phil. 2014. Seven Deadly Sins of Contemporary Quantitative Political Science. *Journal of Peace Research* 51: 287–300

Schwabish, Jonathan A. 2004. An Economist's Guide to Visualizing Data. *Journal of Economic Perspectives* 28(1): 209–234.

Shiner, Meredith 2010. Alvin Greene: Born to Be President. *Politico*, November 17.

Sides, John, and Lynn Vavreck. 2013. *The Gamble: Choice and Chance in the 2012 Presidential Election*. Princeton, NJ: Princeton University Press.

Snipes, Jeffrey B., and Edward R. Maguire. 1995. Country Music, Suicide, and Spuriousness. *Social Forces* 74(1): 327–329.

Solnick, Sara J., and David Hemenway. 2011. The 'Twinkie Defense': The Relationship between Carbonated Non-diet Soft Drinks and Violence Perpetration among Boston High School Students. *Injury Prevention*. doi: 10.1136/Injuryprev-2011–040117.

Sovey, Allison J., and Donald P. Green. 2011. Instrumental Variables Estimation in Political Science: A Reader's Guide. *American Journal of Political Science* 55(1): 188–200.

Stack, Steven, and Jim Gundlach. 1992. The Effect of Country Music on Suicide. *Social Forces* 71(1): 211–218.

Staiger, Douglas, and James H. Stock. 1997. Instrumental Variables Regressions with Weak Instruments. *Econometrica* 65(3): 557–586.

Stock, James H, and Mark W. Watson. 2011. *Introduction to Econometrics*, 3rd ed. Boston: Addison-Wesley.

Swirl. 2014. Swirl: statistics with interactive R learning. [computer software package] http://swirlstats.com/index.html.

Tam Cho, Wendy K., and James G. Gimpel. 2012. Geographic Information Systems and the Spatial Dimensions of American Politics. *Annual Review of Political Science* 15: 443–460.

Tufte, Edward R. 2001. *The Visual Display of Quantitative Information*, 2nd ed. Cheshire, CT: Graphics Press.

University of Michigan. Center for Political Studies. National Election Studies. American National Election Studies, 2000, 2002, and 2004: Full Panel Study. ICPSR21500-v1. Ann Arbor: Inter-university Consortium for Political and

Social Research [distributor], 2009–01-30. http://doi.org/10.3886/ICPSR21500.v1.

Venables, W. N., and B.D. Ripley. 2002. *Modern Applied Statistics with S*, 4th ed. New York: Springer.

Verzani, John. 2004. *Using R for Introductory Statistics*. London: Chapman and Hall.

Wawro, Greg. 2002. Estimating Dynamic Models in Political Science. *Political Analysis* 10: 25–48.

Wilson, Sven E., and Daniel M. Butler. 2007. A Lot More to Do: The Sensitivity of Time-Series Cross Section Analyses to Simple Alternative Specifications. *Political Analysis* 15: 101–123.

Wooldridge, Jeffrey M. 2002. *Econometric Analysis of Cross Section and Panel Data*. Cambridge, MA: MIT Press.

Wooldridge, Jeffrey M. 2009. *Introductory Econometrics*, 4th ed. Mason, OH: South-Western Cengage Learning.

World Values Survey. 2008. Integrated EVS/WVS 1981–2008 Data File. http://www.worldvaluessurvey.org/.

Yau, Nathan. 2011. *Visualize This: The Flowing Data Guide to Design, Visualization, and Statistics*. Hoboken, NJ: Wiley.

Zakir Hossain, Mohammad. 2011. The Use of Box-Cox Transformation Technique in Economic and Statistical Analyses. *Journal of Emerging Trends in Economics and Management Sciences* 2(1): 32–39.

Ziliak, Stephen, and Deirdre N. McCloskey. 2008. *The Cult of Statistical Significance: How the Standard Error Costs Us Jobs, Justice, and Lives*. Ann Arbor: University of Michigan Press.

PHOTO CREDITS

Page 1, Chapter 1 Opening Photo: (© Shutterstock/NigelSpiers); **13,** Case Study 1.1: (© Shutterstock/antoniodiaz); **15,** Case Study 1.2: (© istockphoto/clickhere); **24,** Chapter 2 Opening Photo: (© istockphoto/EdStock); **30,** Case Study 2.1: (© Shutterstock/Alan C. Heison); **45,** Chapter 3 Opening Photo: (© Shutterstock/Frontpage); **73,** Case Study 3.1: (© Shutterstock/Gemenacom); **91,** Chapter 4 Opening Photo: (© Shutterstock/Torsten Lorenz); **128,** Chapter 5 Opening Photo: (© Shutterstock/Ritu Manoj Jethani); **141,** Case Study 5.1: (© Shutterstock/bibiphoto); **153,** Case Study 5.2: (© Shutterstock/pcruciatti); **156,** Case Study 5.3: (© Shutterstock/PrakapenkaAlena); **167,** Chapter 6 Opening Photo: (© Shutterstock/katatonia82); **175,** Case Study 6.1: (© Getty Images/Clarissa Leahy); **185,** Case Study 6.2: (© Shutterstock/Everett Historical); **207,** Chapter 7 Opening Photo: (© Shutterstock/gulserinak1955); **214,** Case Study 7.1: (© Shutterstock/lexaarts); **232,** Case Study 7.2: (© Shutterstock/Monkey Business Images); **247,** Chapter 8 Opening Photo: (© Shutterstock/bikeriderlondon); **266,** Case Study 8.1: (© Getty Images/Anadolu Agency); **287,** Chapter 9 Opening Photo: (© Shutterstock/Monkey Business Images); **297,** Case Study 9.1: (© istockphoto/RapidEye); **311,** Case Study 9.2: (© Shutterstock/Ivonne Wierink) **325,** Chapter 10 Opening Photo: (© Getty Images/Joe Raedle); **330,** Case Study 10.1: (© Shutterstock/De Visu); **342,** Case Study 10.2: (© istockphoto/lisafx); **349,** Case Study 10.3: (© Getty Images/Chicago Tribune); **354,** Case Study 10.4: (© istockphoto/Krakozawr); **365,** Chapter 11 Opening Photo: (© istockphoto/LauriPatterson), **381,** Case Study 11.1: (© istockphoto/CEFutcher); **387,** Case Study 11.2: (© Shutterstock/Goodluz); **401,** Chapter 12 Opening Photo: (© Getty Images/BSIP); **423,** Case Study 12.1:(© Shutterstock/06photo) **430,** Case Study 12.2: (© Shutterstock/servickuz); **449,** Chapter 13 Opening Photo: (© Shutterstock/FloridaStock); **460,** Case Study 13.1: (© Getty Images/Chris Hondros) ; **471,** Case Study 13.2: (© Shutterstock/worradirek); **481,** Chapter 14 Opening Photo: (© Getty Images/Michael Gottschalk); **501,** Chapter 15 Opening Photo: (© Getty Images/J. R. Eyerman); **516,** Chapter 16 Opening Photo: (© Shutterstock/Everett Historical)

GLOSSARY

χ^2 **distribution** A probability distribution that characterizes the distribution of squared standard normal random variables. Standard errors are distributed according to this distribution, which means that the χ^2 plays a role in the t distribution. Also relevant for many statistical tests, including likelihood ratio tests for MLE. 532

ABC issues Three issues that every experiment needs to address: attrition, balance, and compliance. 326

adjusted R^2 The R^2 with a penalty for the number of variables included in the model. Widely reported, but rarely useful. 151

alternative hypothesis An alternative hypothesis is what we accept if we reject the null. It's not something that we are proving (given inherent statistical uncertainty) but it is the idea we hang onto if we reject the null. 93

AR(1) model A model in which the errors are assumed to depend on their value from the previous period. 452

assignment variable An assignment variable determines whether someone receives some treatment. People with values of the assignment variable above some cutoff receive the treatment; people with values of the assignment variable below the cutoff do not receive the treatment. 367

attenuation bias A form of bias in which the estimated coefficient is closer to zero than it should be. Measurement error in the independent variable causes attenuation bias. 146

attrition Occurs when people drop out of an experiment altogether such that we do not observe the dependent variable for them. 346

augmented Dickey-Fuller test A test for unit root for time series data that includes a time trend and lagged values of the change in the variable as independent variables. 470

autocorrelation Errors are autocorrelated if the error in one time period is correlated with the error in the previous time period. One of the assumptions necessary to use the standard equation for variance of OLS estimates is that errors are not autocorrelated. Autocorrelation is common in time series data. 69

autoregressive model A time series model in which the dependent variable is a function of previous values of the dependent variable. Autocorrelation is often modeled with an autoregressive model such that the error term is a function of previous error terms. Dynamic models are also autoregressive models in that the dependent variable depends on lagged values of the dependent variable. 450

auxiliary regression A regression that is not directly the one of interest but is related to and yields information helpful in analyzing the equation we really care about. 139

balance Treatment and control groups are balanced if the distributions of control variables are the same for the treatment and control groups. 328

bias A biased coefficient estimate will systematically be higher or lower than the true value. 58

binned graphs Used in regression discontinuity analysis. The assignment variable is divided into bins, and the average value of the dependent variable is plotted for each bin. The plots allow us to visualize a discontinuity at the treatment cutoff. Binned graphs also are useful to help us identify possible non-linearities in the relationship between the assignment variable and the dependent variable. 378

blocking Picking treatment and control groups so that they are equal in covariates. 327

categorical variable A variable that has two or more categories but does not have an intrinsic ordering. Also known as a *nominal variable*. 181

central limit theorem The mean of a sufficiently large number of independent draws from any distribution will be normally distributed. Because OLS estimates are weighted averages, the central limit theorem implies that $\hat{\beta}_1$ will be normally distributed. 56

ceteris paribus All else being equal. A phrase used to describe multivariate regression results as a coefficient is said to, account for change in the dependent variable with all other independent variables held constant. 132

codebook A file that describes sources for variables and any adjustments made. A codebook is a necessary element of a replication file. 28

compliance The condition of subjects receiving the experimental treatment to which they were assigned. A compliance problem occurs when subjects assigned to an experimental treatment do not actually experience the treatment, often because they opt out in some way. 332

confidence interval Defines the range of true values that are consistent with the observed coefficient estimate. Confidence intervals depend on the point estimate, $\hat{\beta}_1$, and the measure of uncertainty, $se(\hat{\beta}_1)$. 117

confidence levels Term referring to confidence intervals and based on $1 - \alpha$. 117

consistency A consistent estimator is one for which the distribution of the estimate gets closer and closer to the true value as the sample size increases. For example, the bivariate OLS estimate $\hat{\beta}_1$ consistently estimates β_1 if X is uncorrelated with ϵ. 65

constant The parameter β_0 in a regression model. It is the point at which a regression line crosses the Y-axis. It is the expected value of the dependent variable when all independent variables equal zero. Also referred to as the *intercept*. 4

continuous variable A variable that takes on any possible value over some range. Continuous variables are distinct from discrete variables, which can take on only a limited number of possible values. 54

control group In an experiment, the group that does not receive the treatment of interest. 19

control variable An independent variable included in a statistical model to control for some factor that is not the primary factor of interest. 135

correlation Measures the extent to which two variables are linearly related to each other. A correlation of 1 indicates the variables move together in a straight line. A correlation of 0 indicates the variables are not linearly related to each other. A correlation of -1 indicates the variables move in opposite directions. 9

critical value In hypothesis testing, a value above which a $\hat{\beta}_1$ would be so unlikely that we reject the null. 101

cross-sectional data Data having observations for multiple units for one time period. Each observation indicates the value of a variable for a given unit for the same point in time. Cross-sectional data is typically contrasted to panel and time series data. 449

cumulative distribution function (CDF) Indicates how much of normal distribution is to the left of any given point. 410

de-meaned approach An approach to estimating fixed effects models for panel data involving subtracting average values within units from all variables. This approach saves us from having to include dummy variables for every unit and highlights the ability of fixed effects models to estimate parameters based on variation within units, not between them. 255

degrees of freedom (d.f.) The sample size minus the number of parameters. It refers to the amount of information we have available to use in the estimation process. As a practical matter, degrees of freedom corrections produce more uncertainty for smaller sample sizes. The shape of a t distribution depends on the degrees of freedom. The higher the degrees of freedom, the more a t distribution looks like a normal distribution. 63

dependent variable The outcome of interest, usually denoted as Y. It is called the *dependent variable* because its value depends on the values of the independent variables, parameters, and error term. 3

dichotomous Divided into two parts. A dummy variable is an example of a dichotomous variable. 401

dichotomous variable A dichotomous variable takes on one of two values, almost always zero or one, for all observations. Also known as a *dummy variable*. 169

Dickey-Fuller test A test for unit roots, used in dynamic models. 469

difference of means test A test that involves comparing the mean of Y for one group (e.g., the treatment group) against the mean of Y for another group (e.g., the control group). These tests can be conducted with bivariate and multivariate OLS and other statistical procedures. 169

difference-in-difference model A model that looks at differences in changes in treated units compared to untreated units. These models are particularly useful in policy evaluation. 268

discontinuity Occurs when the graph of a line makes a sudden jump up or down. 365

distribution The range of possible values for a random variable and the associated relative probabilities for each value. Examples of four distributions are displayed in Figure 3.4. 54

dummy variable A dummy variable equals either zero or one for all observations. Dummy variables are sometimes referred to as *dichotomous variables*. 169

dyad An entity that consists of two elements. For the trade data set, a dyad indicates a pair of countries and the data indicates how much trade flows between the members of the dyad. 266

dynamic model A time series model that includes a lagged dependent variable as an independent variable. Among other differences, the interpretation of coefficients differs in dynamic models from that in standard OLS models. Sometimes referred to as an *autoregressive model*. 463

elasticity The percent change in Y associated with a percent change in X. Elasticity is estimated with log-log models. 219

endogenous An independent variable is endogenous if changes in it are related to other factors that influence the dependent variable. 8

error term The term associated with unmeasured factors in a regression model, typically denoted as ϵ. 5

excluded category When a model includes dummy variables indicating the multiple categories of a nominal variable, we need to exclude a dummy variable for one of the groups, which we refer to as the excluded category. The coefficients on all the included dummy variables indicate how much higher or lower the dependent variable is for each group

relative to the excluded category. Also referred to as the *reference category*. 182

exclusion condition For two-stage least squares 2SLS, a condition that the instrument exert no direct effect in the second-stage equation. This condition cannot be tested empirically. 292

exogenous An independent variable is exogenous if changes in it are unrelated to other factors that influence the dependent variable. 9

expected value The average value of a large number of realizations of a random variable. 484

external validity A research finding is externally valid when it applies beyond the context in which the analysis was conducted. 21

F distribution A probability distribution that characterizes the distribution of a ratio of χ^2 random variables. Used in tests involving multiple parameters, among other applications. 533

F statistic The test statistic used in conducting an F test. Used in testing hypotheses about multiple coefficients, among other applications. 227

F test A type of hypothesis test commonly used to test hypotheses involving multiple coefficients. 226

fitted value A fitted value, $\hat{Y}_i$, is the value of Y predicted by our estimated equation. For a bivariate OLS model, it is $\hat{Y}_i = \hat{\beta}_0 + \hat{\beta}_1 X_i$. Also called *predicted value*. 48

fixed effect A parameter associated with a specific unit in a panel data model. For a model $Y_{it} = \beta_0 + \beta_1 X_{1it} + \alpha_i + \nu_{it}$, the α_i parameter is the fixed effect for unit i. 253

fixed effects model A model that controls for unit- and/or period-specific effects. These fixed effects capture differences in the dependent variable associated with each unit and/or period. Fixed effects models are used to analyze panel data and can control for both measurable and unmeasurable elements of the error term that are stable within unit. 253

fuzzy RD models Regression discontinuity models in which the assignment variable imperfectly predicts treatment. 384

generalizable A statistical result is generalizable if it applies to populations beyond the sample in the analysis. 21

goodness of fit How well a model fits the data. 70

heteroscedastic A random variable is heteroscedastic if the variance differs for some observations. Heteroscedasticity does not cause bias in OLS models, but violates one of the assumptions necessary to use the standard equation for variance of OLS estimates. 67

heteroscedasticity-consistent standard errors Standard errors for the coefficients in OLS that are appropriate even when errors are heteroscedastic. 68

homoscedastic Describing a random variable having the same variance for all observations. To use the standard equation for variance of OLS estimates. 67

hypothesis testing A process assessing whether the observed data is or is not consistent with a claim of interest. The most widely used tools in hypothesis testing are t tests and F tests. 91

identified A statistical model is identified on the basis of assumptions that allow us to estimate the model. 310

inclusion condition For 2SLS, a condition that the instrument exert a meaningful effect in the first-stage equation in which the endogenous variable is the dependent variable. 292

independent variable A variable that possibly influences the value of the dependent variable. It is usually denoted as X. It is called *independent* because its value is typically treated as independent of the value of the dependent variable. 3

instrumental variable Explains the endogenous independent variable of interest but does not directly explain the dependent variable. Two-stage least squares uses instrumental variables to produce unbiased estimates. 289

intention-to-treat (ITT) analysis ITT analysis addresses potential endogeneity that arises in experiments owing to non-compliance. We compare the means of those assigned treatment and those not assigned treatment, irrespective of whether the subjects did or did not actually receive the treatment. 335

intercept The parameter β_0 in a regression model. It is the point at which a regression line crosses the Y-axis. It is the expected value of the dependent variable when all independent variables equal zero. Also referred to as the *constant*. 4

internal validity A research finding is internally valid when it is based on a process that is free from systematic error. Experimental results are often considered internally valid, but their external validity may be debatable. 21

irrelevant variable A variable in a regression model that should not be in the model, meaning that its coefficient is zero. Including an irrelevant variable does not cause bias, but it does increase the variance of the estimates. 151

jitter A process used in scatterplotting data. A small random number is added to each observation for purposes of plotting only. This procedure produces cloudlike images, which overlap less than the unjittered data, and therefore providing a better sense of the data. 172

lagged variable A variable with the values from the previous period. 451

latent variable For a probit or logit model, an unobserved continuous variable reflecting the propensity of an individual observation of Y_i to equal one. 408

least squares dummy variable (LSDV) approach An approach to estimating fixed effects models in the analysis of panel data. 254

likelihood ratio (LR) test A statistical test for maximum likelihood models that is useful in testing hypotheses involving multiple coefficients. 428

linear probability model (LPM) Used when the dependent variable is dichotomous. This is an OLS model in which the coefficients are interpreted as the change in probability of observing $Y_i = 1$ for a one-unit change in X. 402

linear-log model A model in which the independent variable is not logged, but the independent variable is. In such a model, a one percent increase in X is associated with a $\frac{\beta_1}{100}$ change in Y. 219

local average treatment effect (LATE) The causal effect for those people affected by the instrument only. Relevant if the effect of X on Y varies within the population. 316

log likelihood The log of the probability of observing the Y outcomes we report, given the X data and the $\hat{\beta}$'s. It is a by-product of the MLE estimation process. 417

log-linear model A model in which the dependent variable is transformed by taking its natural log.

A one-unit change in X in a log-linear model is associated with a β_1 percent change in Y (on a 0-to-1 scale). 219

log-log model A model in which the dependent variable and the independent variables are logged. 219

logit model A way to analyze data with a dichotomous dependent variable. The error term in a logit model is logistically distributed, pronounced "low–jit". 413

maximum likelihood estimation (MLE) The estimation process used to generate coefficient estimates for probit and logit models, among others. 415

measurement error Measurement error occurs when a variable is measured inaccurately. If the dependent variable has measurement error, OLS coefficient estimates are unbiased, but less precise. If an independent variable has measurement error, OLS coefficient estimates suffer from attenuation bias, with the magnitude of the attenuation depending on how large the measurement error variance is relative to the variance of the variable. 144

model fishing Occurs when researchers add and subtract variables until they get just the answers they were looking for. 156

model specification The process of deciding which variables should go in a statistical model. 156

modeled randomness Variation attributable to inherent variation in the data-generation process. This source of randomness exists even when we observe data for an entire population. 54

monotonicity A condition invoked in discussions of instrumental variables models. Monotonicity requires that the effect of the instrument on the endogenous variable go in the same direction for everyone in a population. 316

multicollinearity Variables are multicollinear if they are correlated. The consequence of multicollinearity is that the variance of $\hat{\beta}_1$ will be higher than it would have been in the absence of multicollinearity. Multicollinearity does not cause bias. 149

multivariate OLS OLS with multiple independent variables. 128

natural experiment Occurs when a researcher identifies a situation in which the values of the independent variable have been determined by a random, or at least exogenous, process. 352

nominal variable Has two or more categories but does not have an intrinsic ordering. Also known as a nominal variable. Typical examples include region (North, South, East, West) and religion (Catholic, Protestant, Jewish, Muslim, Other, Secular). Also known as a *categorical variable*. 181

normal distribution A bell-shaped probability density that characterizes the probability of observing outcomes for normally distributed random variables. Because of the central limit theorem, many statistical quantities are distributed normally. 55

null hypothesis A hypothesis of no effect. Statistical tests will reject or fail to reject such hypotheses. The most common null hypothesis is $\beta_1 = 0$, written as $H_0 : \beta_1 = 0.$ 92

null result A finding in which the null hypothesis is not rejected. 114

observational studies Use data generated in an environment not controlled by a researcher. They are distinguished from experimental studies and are sometimes referred to as *non-experimental studies*. 21

omitted variable bias Bias that results from leaving out a variable that affects the dependent variable and is correlated with the independent variable. 139

one-sided alternative hypothesis An alternative to the null hypothesis that indicates whether the coefficient (or function of coefficients) is higher or lower than the value indicated in the null hypothesis. Typically written as $H_A : \beta_1 > 0$ or $H_A : \beta_1 < 0.$ 94

one-way fixed effects model A panel data model that allows for fixed effects at the unit level. 263

ordinal variable A variable that expresses rank but not necessarily relative size. An ordinal variable, for example, is one indicating answers to a survey question that is coded 1 = strongly disagree, 2 = disagree, 3 = agree, 4 = strongly agree. 181

outlier An observation that is extremely different from those in the rest of sample. 76

overidentification test A test used for two-stage least squares models having more than one instrument. The logic of the test is that the estimated coefficient on the endogenous variable in the second-stage equation should be roughly the same when each individual instrument is used alone. 301

p **value** The probability of observing a coefficient as high as we actually observed if the null hypothesis were true. 106

panel data Has observations for multiple units over time. Each observation indicates the value of a variable for a given unit at a given point in time. Panel data is typically contrasted to cross-sectional and time series data. 247

perfect multicollinearity Occurs when an independent variable is completely explained by a linear combination of the other independent variables. 150

plim A widely used abbreviation for probability limit, the value to which an estimator converges as the sample size gets very, very large. 66

point estimates Point estimates describe our best guess as to what the true value is. 117

polynomial model A model that includes values of X raised to powers greater than one. A polynomial model is an example of a non-linear model in which the effect of X on Y varies depending on the value of X. The fitted values will be defined by a curve. A quadratic model is an example of a polynomial model. 209

pooled model Treats all observations as independent observations. Pooled models contrast with fixed effects models that control for unit-specific or time-specific fixed effects. 249

power The ability of our data to reject the null. A high-powered statistical test will reject the null with a very high probability when the null is false; a low-powered statistical test will reject the null with a low probability when the null is false. 111

power curve Characterizes the probability of rejecting the null for each possible value of the parameter. 112

predicted values The value of Y predicted by our estimated equation. For a bivariate OLS model, it is $\hat{Y}_i = \hat{\beta}_0 + \hat{\beta}_1 X_i$. Also called *fitted values*. 48

probability density A graph or formula that describes the relative probability that a random variable is near a specified value. 55

probability density function (PDF) A mathematical function that describes the relative probability for a continuous random variable to take on a given probability. 524

probability distribution A graph or formula that gives the probability across the possible values of a random variable. 54

probability limit The value to which a distribution converges as the sample size gets very large. When the error is uncorrelated with the independent variables, the probability limit of $\hat{\beta}_1$ is β_1 for OLS models. The probability limit of a consistent estimator is the true value of the parameter. 65

probit model A way to analyze data with a dichotomous dependent variable. The key assumption is that the error term is normally distributed. 410

quadratic model A model that includes X and X^2 as independent variables. The fitted values will be defined by a curve. A quadratic model is an example of a polynomial model. 210

quasi-instrument An instrumental variable that is not strictly exogenous. Two-stage least squares with a quasi-instrument may produce a better estimate than OLS if the correlation of the quasi-instrument and the error in the main equation is small relative to the correlation of the quasi-instrument and the endogenous variable. 303

random effects model Treats unit-specific error as a random variable that is uncorrelated with the independent variable. 507

random variable Takes on values in a range and with the probabilities defined by a distribution. 54

randomization The process of determining the experimental value of the key independent variable based on a random process. If successful, randomization will produce as independent variable that is uncorrelated with all other potential independent variables, including factors in the error term. 19

reduced form equation In a reduced form equation Y_1 is only a function of the nonendogenous variables (which are the X and Z variables, not the Y variables). Used in simultaneous equation models. 309

reference category When a model includes dummy variables indicating the multiple categories of a nominal variable, we need to exclude a dummy variable for one of the groups, which we refer to as the *reference category*. The coefficients on all the included dummy variables indicate how much higher or lower the dependent variable is for each group relative to the reference category. Also referred to as the *excluded category*. 182

regression discontinuity (RD) Regression discontinuity techniques use regression analysis to identify possible discontinuities at the point at which some treatment applies. 366

regression line The fitted line from a regression. 48

replication Research that meets a replication standard can be duplicated based on the information provided at the time of publication. 28

replication files Files that document how exactly data is gathered and organized. When properly compiled, these files allow others to reproduce our results exactly. 28

residual The difference between the fitted value and the observed value. Graphically, it is the distance between an estimated line and an observation. Mathematically, a residual for a bivariate OLS model is $\hat{\epsilon}_i = Y_i - \hat{\beta}_0 - \hat{\beta}_1 X_i$. An equivalent way to calculate a residual is $\hat{\epsilon}_i = Y_i - \hat{Y}_i$. 48

restricted model The model in an F test that imposes the restriction that the null hypothesis is true. If the fit of the restricted model is much worse than the fit of the unrestricted model, we infer that that the null hypothesis is not true. 227

robust Statistical results are robust if they do not change when the model changes. 30

rolling cross section data Repeated cross sections of data from different individuals at different points in time: for example, an annual survey of U.S. citizens in which different citizens are chosen each year. 271

sampling randomness Variation in estimates that is seen in a subset of an entire population. If a given sample had a different selection of people, we would observe a different estimated coefficient. 53

scatterplot A plot of data in which each observation is located at the coordinates defined by the independent and dependent variables. 3

selection model Simultaneously accounts for whether we observe the dependent variable and what the dependent variable is. Often used to deal with attrition problems in experiments. The most famous selection model is the Heckman selection model. 348

significance level For each hypothesis test, we set a significance level that determines how unlikely a result has to be under the null hypothesis for us to reject the null hypothesis. The significance level is the probability of committing a Type I error for a hypothesis test. 96

simultaneous equation model A model in which two variables simultaneously cause each other. 307

slope coefficient The coefficient on an independent variable. It reflects how much the dependent variable increases when the independent variable increases by one. In a plot of fitted values, the slope coefficient characterizes the slope of the fitted line. 4

spurious regression A regression that wrongly suggests that X has an effect on Y. Can be caused by, for example, omitted variable bias and nonstationary data. 466

stable unit treatment value assumption (SUTVA) The condition that an instrument has no spillover effect. This condition rules out the possibility that the value of an instrument going up by one unit will cause a neighbor to become more likely to change X as well. 316

standard deviation (sd) The standard deviation describes the spread of the data. For large samples, it is calculated as $\frac{\sum (X_i - \bar{X})^2}{N}$. For probability distributions, the standard deviation refers to the width of the distribution. For example, we often refer to the standard deviation of the ϵ distribution as σ; it is the square root of the variance (which is σ^2). To convert a normally distributed random variable into a standard normal variable, we subtract the mean and divide by the standard deviation of the distribution of the random variable. 26

standard error (se) Refers to the accuracy of a parameter estimate, which is determined by the width of the distribution of the parameter estimate. For example, the standard error of $\hat{\beta}_1$ from a bivariate OLS model is the square root of the variance of the estimate. It is $\sqrt{\frac{\hat{\sigma}^2}{N \times var(X)}}$. Sometimes the standard error and standard deviation do similar work. For example, the standard deviation of the distribution of $\hat{\beta}_1$ distribution is estimated by the standard error of $\hat{\beta}_1$. A good rule of thumb is to associate standard errors with parameter estimates and standard deviations with the spread of a variable or distribution, which may or may not be a distribution associated with a parameter estimate. 61

standard error of the regression A measure of how well the model fits the data. It is the square root of the variance of the regression. 70

standard normal distribution A normal distribution with a mean of zero and a variance (and standard error) of one. 526

standardize Standardizing a variable converts it to a measure of standard deviations from its mean. This is done by subtracting the mean of the variable from each observation and dividing the result by the standard deviation of the variable. 224

standardized coefficient The coefficient on an independent variable that has been standardized according to $X_1^{Standardized} = \frac{X_1 - \bar{X}_1}{\text{sd}(X_1)}$. A one-unit change in a standardized variable is a one-standard-deviation change no matter what the unit of X is (e.g., inches, dollars, years). Therefore effects across variables can be compared because each $\hat{\beta}$ represents the effect of a one-standard-deviation change in X on Y. 225

stationarity A time series term indicating that a variable has the same distribution throughout the entire time series. Statistical analysis of nonstationary variables can yield spurious regression results. 465

statistically significant A coefficient is statistically significant when we reject the null hypothesis that it is zero. In this case, the observed value of the coefficient is a sufficient number of standard deviations from the value posited in the null hypothesis to allow us to reject the null hypothesis. 93

substantive significance If a reasonable change in the independent variable is associated with a meaningful change in the dependent variable, the effect is substantively significant. Some statistically significant effects are not substantively significant, especially for large data sets. 116

t distribution A distribution that looks like a normal distribution, but with fatter tails. The exact shape of the distribution depends on the degrees of freedom. This distribution converges to a normal distribution for large sample sizes. 99

t statistic The test statistic used in a t test. It is equal to $\frac{\hat{\beta}_1 - \beta^{Null}}{\text{se}(\hat{\beta}_1)}$. If the t statistic is greater than our critical value, we reject the null hypothesis. 103

t test A test for hypotheses about a normal random variable with an estimated standard error. We compare $|\frac{\hat{\beta}_1}{\text{se}(\hat{\beta}_1)}|$ to a critical value from a t distribution determined by the chosen significance level (α). For large sample sizes, a t test is closely approximated by a z test. 98

time series data Consists of observations for a single unit over time. Each observation indicates the value of a variable at a given point in time. The data proceed in order, indicating, for example, annual, monthly, or daily data. Time series data is typically contrasted to cross-sectional and panel data. 69

treatment group In an experiment, the group that receives the treatment of interest. 19

trimmed data set A trimmed data set is one for which observations are removed in a way that offsets potential bias due to attrition. 347

two-sided alternative hypothesis An alternative to the null hypothesis that indicates the coefficient is not equal to 0 (or some other specified value). Typically written as $H_A : \beta_1 \neq 0$. 94

two-stage least squares (2SLS) Uses exogenous variation in X to estimate the effect of X on Y. In the first-stage, we estimate a model in which the endogenous independent variable is the dependent variable and the instrument, Z, is an independent variable. In the second-stage, we estimate a model in which we use the fitted values from the first-stage, $\hat{X}_{1i}$, as an independent variable. 287

two-way fixed effects model A panel data model that allows for fixed effects at the unit and time levels. 263

Type I error A hypothesis-testing error that occurs when we reject a null hypothesis that is in fact true. 93

Type II error A hypothesis-testing error that occurs when we fail to reject a null hypothesis that is in fact false. 93

unbiased estimator An unbiased coefficient estimate will on average equal the true value of the parameter. An unbiased estimator can produce individual estimates that are quite incorrect; on average, though, the too-low estimates are probabilistically balanced by too-high estimates for unbiased estimators. OLS produces unbiased parameter estimates if the independent variables are uncorrelated with the error term. 58

unit root A variable with a unit root has a coefficient equal to one on the lagged variable in an autoregressive model. A variable with a unit root is nonstationary and must be modeled differently than a stationary variable. 466

unrestricted model An unrestricted model is the model in an F test that imposes no restrictions on the coefficients. If the fit of the restricted model is much worse than the fit of the unrestricted model, we infer that that the null hypothesis is not true. 227

variance A measure of how much a random variable varies. In graphical terms, the variance of a random variable characterizes how wide the distribution is. 61

variance inflation factor A measure of how much variance is inflated owing to multicollinearity. It can be estimated for each variable and is equal to $\frac{1}{1-R_j^2}$, where R_j^2 is from an auxiliary regression in which X_j is the dependent variable and all other independent variables from the main equation are included as independent variables. 149

variance of the regression The variance of the regression measures how well the model explains variation in the dependent variable. For large samples, it is estimated as $\hat{\sigma}^2 = \frac{\sum_{i=1}^{N}(Y_i - \hat{Y}_i)^2}{N}$. 62

weak instrument An instrumental variable that adds little explanatory power to the first-stage regression in a two-stage least squares analysis. 304

window The range of observations we analyze in a regression discontinuity analysis. The smaller the window, the less we need to worry about non-linear functional forms. 378

z test A hypothesis test involving comparison of a test statistic and a critical value based on a normal distribution. 415

INDEX

Entries with page numbers followed by *t* will be found in Tables, by an *f* in Figures and by an *n* in footnotes.